D0203621

THE BEAST REAWAKENS

MARTIN A. LEE

ROUTLEDGE

NEW YORK LONDON

Published in 2000 by
Routledge
29 West 35th Street
New York, NY 10001

Originally published in 1997 in hardcover by Little, Brown and Company

Printed in the United States of America on acid-free paper.

A portion of chapter 7 originally appeared in *Progressive*.

Photo Credits: Skorzeny: Hoover Institution, H. Keith Thompson Collection; young Remer: Hoover Institution, H. Keith Thompson Collection; Thompson: Hoover Institution, H. Keith Thompson Collection; Rudel: Hoover Institution, H. Keith Thompson Collection; Peróns: National Archives; SRP leadership: Hoover Institution, H. Keith Thompson Collection; Yockey: AP/Wide World Photo; de Benoist: courtesy of Alain de Benoist; Rostock: Bettman Archives; Lyons: Jennifer Warburg; Beam: Paul Strang/*Southwest Times*; Trochmann: Jennifer Warburg; Fini: AP/Wide World Photo; Buchanan: Jennifer Warburg

Library of Congress Cataloging-in-Publication Data
Lee, Martin A.
The beast reawakens : fascism's resurgence from Hitler's spymasters to today's neo-Nazi groups and right-wing extremists / Martin A. Lee.
p. cm.
Originally published: Boston : Little, Brown, 1997.
Includes bibliographical references and index.
ISBN 0-415-92546-0
1. Neo-Nazism. 2. Right-wing extremists. I. Title.
JC481.L43 1999 99-32969
320.53'3'09045–dc21 CIP

10 9 8 7 6 5 4 3 2 1

For the spirit of Uncle Max

All men dream: but not equally.
Those who dream by night
in the dusky recesses of their minds,
wake in the day to find that it was vanity:
but the dreamers of the day
are dangerous men,
for they may act their dream
with open eyes, to make it possible.

T. E. LAWRENCE
Seven Pillars of Wisdom

CONTENTS

PART TWO: POLITICAL SOLDIERS

PART THREE: POST-COLD WAR FASCISM

ACKNOWLEDGMENTS

While researching and writing this book, I relied on the help of many people. I especially wish to thank Jaye Muller and Jack Rieley for their inspiring friendship, their passion, and their remarkable music. I also wish to thank Graeme Atkinson and Gerry Gable of *Searchlight* for their diligent watchdog efforts. Carl Ogelsby and Kevin Coogan deserve special thanks for introducing me to several ideas and insights, without which this book would never have taken shape.

I am particularly grateful to David Sobel for guiding me through the Freedom of Information Act process, to Eben Forbes for his research assistance, to Jeff Cohen and the staff at FAIR, and to Chip Berlet of Political Research Associates. In addition, many thanks to Antifa Infoblatt in Berlin, Henrik Kruger, Richard Herding of Informationdienst, Xavier Vinader, Al Ross, Lorenzo Ruggero, Paola Ortenzi, Edgardo Pelligrini, Wolfgang Purtscheller, Loise Bernstein, REFLEX, Christopher Simpson, John Goetz, Leonard Zeskind, Margitta Fahr, and Petko Azmanov.

For translating foreign-language source material, I thank my aunt Bertha Jellinek and Ariel Zevon. Others who provided translation help include Sabine Freizer, Claudia Plass-Fiedler, Rommy Arndt, Jennifer Heilman, Miriam Lanskoy, Deanna Rodriguez, Eric Olsen, Ulricke Bode, Val Tekavec, and Ghislaine Vautier.

For their financial support and encouragement, I am indebted to the Pope Foundation, the Fund for Constitutional Government, and the Institute for Social Justice. Very special appreciation to Pia Gallegos.

Thanks also to John Taylor, who navigated me through the National Archives, and to Ruven Navat, Allison Glass, Lawrence Pruski, Bruce Murray, John Eskow, Analleyse Arch, Gottfried Wagner, Paul Hoch, Dan Levy, Bill Smith, Hewitt Pratt, and Stuart Sender.

Jim Silberman, Jordan Pavlin, and Geoff Kloske provided editorial input at various stages of this project. Stephen H. Lamont massaged the manuscript with his copyediting. And Geri Thoma of the Elaine Markson Literary Agency did more for this book than a literary agent should ever have to do.

Last, but far from least, thanks to Silva and Goodwin Lee, Michael Lardner and my sister Alana, Zak and Colby, and Tom and Ronnie Devitt.

And my wife, Tiffany, who gave birth to two remarkable children while this book was being written, I thank most of all.

PREFACE

Late one night in June 1997, a disabled black man named James Byrd was chained to the back of a pickup truck in Jasper, Texas, and dragged by his ankles on a rough rural road for several miles until his head ripped off his body. This gruesome attack stunned the nation both for its cruelty and its echoes of an earlier era when racist lynchings were common in the Deep South. Twenty-four-year-old white supremacist John King and two of his friends were charged with the murder. While incarcerated for a prior burglary conviction, King had joined an Aryan prison gang. Nazi and Ku Klux Klan symbols—including a black man hanging from a tree—were tattooed across his arms and upper body, and the words "White Pride" were scribbled on the door of King's jail cell.

After he was convicted, King showed no emotion when the death sentence was handed down. He responded in court by issuing a terse statement through his lawyer that ended with haughty words from American fascist ideologue Francis Parker Yockey, who committed suicide nearly four decades earlier: "The promise of success is with the man who is determined to die proudly when it is no longer possible to live proudly." That Yockey's name should have surfaced in connection with the horrific racial slaying in Jasper attests to his enduring reputation as a cult figure within neofascist circles. It also highlights the link between those who promote extremist ideology and the fanatical disciples who carry it out.

A man with many aliases, Yockey was a fierce and influential anti-Semite whose book *Imperium* has become a modern-day bible of neo-Nazism. This self-styled racist philosopher and part-time gigolo traveled around the world, weaving a web of mysterious contacts. Most curious of all were Yockey's exploits behind the Iron Curtain, where he collaborated with Soviet bloc intelligence. When the FBI finally caught up with him in 1960, Yockey was carrying seven birth certificates and three passports, all bearing his photo but each with a different name. Shortly thereafter, Yockey took his own life in a San Francisco jail by swallowing a cyanide capsule.

The last person to visit Yockey before his suicide was Willis Carto, founder and godfather of the Liberty Lobby, a virulently anti-Semitic organization based in Washington, DC. An inveterate Nazi apologist, Carto has done more than anyone else to promote Yockey's writings and his posthumous reputation among fascists as an "American visionary." Thanks largely to Carto's efforts, Yockey emerged as an intellectual patron saint of neo-Nazis worldwide.

In addition to reiterating Yockey's contention that the Nazi Holocaust never happened, the Liberty Lobby's weekly newspaper, *The Spotlight,* publishes articles by unabashed fascists and white supremacists. Excerpts of Yockey's pungent prose—including an essay addressed to America's youth—have been featured in this far Right tabloid.[1]

Today the Liberty Lobby and the conspiracy-obsessed *Spotlight* are closely linked to the American militia movement and neofascist groups around the world. Oklahoma City bombers Timothy McVeigh and Terry Nichols were *Spotlight* readers. McVeigh actually placed a classified ad in the paper when he wanted to sell some weapons and ammunition. And it was from the *Spotlight* that McVeigh obtained the telephone calling card that he used to make long-distance calls in the months leading up the Oklahoma City massacre. Federal prosecutors used this important piece of evidence to trace and convict McVeigh and Nichols, whose range of associates included American and German white supremacists.

Like the hate crime in Jasper, Texas, the Oklahoma City bombing was not a random occurrence, but a deliberate act that flowed from a specific set of beliefs and ideas that are germane to an ongoing political movement. Fascism and ethnic cleansing have a heritage and history in the United States of America that are explored from a particular vantage point in this book. *The Beast Reawakens* tells the story of a committed cadre of American extremists, including the mysterious Francis Parker Yockey, who teamed up with Adolf Hitler's bodyguard and other key German Nazis to carry on the struggle in the aftermath of World War II. This malignant nucleus of old guard fascists kept the ideological flame alive and mentored a new generation of "political soldiers" that is making dramatic headlines around the world today.

Since *The Beast Reawakens* was first published, fascist and right-wing extremist movements have continued their numerous activities around the world. This edition provides an update on these groups, and I have also added new material in the last two chapters and the conclusion, including the section on the Oklahoma City bombing.

While McVeigh waited on death row, there was little indication that the carnage in Oklahoma City had a deterrent effect on America's homegrown rabid Right. If anything, it appears that global economic convulsions and the approach of the turn of the Millennium combined to fire up Christian patriot passions and apocalyptic paranoia even more than usual. The number of terrorist attacks on U.S. soil rose sharply, as federal officials uncovered a multitude of plots to bomb government buildings and abortion clinics, derail trains, assassinate public figures, and violently secede from the United States. Hell-bent on raising a guerrilla army to create a religious nation for whites only, groups like the Montana Freemen, which engaged in an eighty-one-day stand-off with federal agents, were gearing up for the coming racial Armageddon.[2]

Just how crazed these true believers could get became evident when the FBI tried to interview the brother of fugitive Eric Robert Rudolf, the chief suspect in a fatal abortion clinic bombing in Birmingham, Alabama, in 1998. Instead of cooperating with law enforcement, Eric's brother videotaped himself amputating his hand with an electric saw, and he sent the tape to the FBI as a way of telling the feds to back off. This grisly act of self-mutilation epitomized the fanatical alienation that has engulfed America's right-wing extremist fringe.

The elusive Eric Rudolf, a Holocaust-denier and militant back-woods survivalist, would also be charged in connection with three bomb blasts in the Atlanta area, including the 1996 Olympic Park explosion that killed one woman and injured 111 people. A gay bar was among the targets of his demented wrath—one of a litany of homophobic assaults that has become an ugly fact of life across America. The torture-killing of Matthew Shephard in Laramie, Wyoming, in October 1998 was followed by the brutal murders of gay men in Buffalo and Richmond. In rural Alabama, a gay textile worker was kidnapped, castrated, beaten to death, and his body burned by an assailant who often wore a Ku Klux Klan T-shirt and taunted black people.

Hate crimes are imbued with odious political, racial, cultural, and ideological implications that amplify their impact upon individual victims and the communities in which they occur. They are offenses directed against an entire group of people—which is why hate crimes warrant special legislation. Despite the increasing frequency and viciousness of such attacks, many are not reported to the police and only rarely do hate crimes provoke significant news coverage.[3]

The three-day white supremacist shooting spree in Illinois and Indiana over Fourth of July weekend in 1999, which left two people dead and nine wounded, was exceptional in terms of the international publicity it received. Blacks, Asians, and orthodox Jews were gunned down by twenty-one-year-old Benjamin Smith, a denizen of the World Church of the Creator, whose credo is "Rahowa"—racial holy war. The rampage reached a morbid climax when Smith took his own life after a police chase on Independence Day. Several other members of this neo-Nazi church, which maintains that the U.S. government favors ethnic minorities over whites, have been linked to violent attacks in recent years. The church's web site has featured animated pictures of people firing at "Jew pigs" and the Pope.

Fueled by racial, ethnic, and religious intolerance, the hate crime epidemic is a global malady. The Fourth of July bloodbath occurred the same week that neo-Nazi car bombs severely injured a Swedish journalist, his young son, and two policemen in Stockholm. Two months earlier, a bomb blast ripped through a parking lot near the main Jewish synagogue in Moscow, not far from the Kremlin, and a second bomb detonated moments later next to another synagogue in the Russian capital. These incidents coincided with a wave of neo-Nazi nail-bomb attacks that terrorized ethnic minority neighborhoods and gay pubs in London, England, killing two people and wounding more than one hundred.

The bombings in Moscow and London were overshadowed by what happened at Columbine High School in Littleton, Colorado, on April 20, 1999, when two deranged teenagers killed themselves after shooting to death twelve students and a teacher and injuring twenty-three others. Shouting racial slurs as they opened fire, the young gunmen targeted African-American and Latino students, among others. Influenced by white supremacist rhetoric and Nazi literature, they timed their slaughter to coincide with the anniversary of Adolf Hitler's birthday.

While experts debate whether the Columbine tragedy, strictly speaking, qualifies as a hate crime, it is important to emphasize that dramatic incidents of extremist violence may actually serve to distract attention from a more insidious and far-reaching danger. Radical right-wing populist movements with openly fascist roots have made significant inroads into mainstream politics and are now a serious force to be reckoned with in several countries around the world.

For evidence of extreme Right encroachment on the American political landscape, consider the ties that bind the Council of Conservative Citizens (CCC) to powerful U.S. elected officials as well as neofascist groups at home and abroad. Dubbed the "uptown" or "white collar Klan," this churlish gaggle of white supremacists was endorsed by no less a figure than U.S. Senate Majority leader Trent Lott, the highest-ranking Republican in the country. Sporting suits and ties rather than sheets and hoods, several of Lott's uncles and cousins served as local officers of the council, which equates race-mixing with genocide. "White Americans have never been in greater danger of destroying themselves through intermarriage and assimilation," warns CCC executive director Gordon Lee Baum.[4]

Known more for his antihomosexual invective than gutter racism, Lott appeared at several CCC functions and hosted its leaders at his Washington office. A photo of Lott delivering a keynote address to the council in 1992 was published in the group's newsletter. During his speech, Lott lavished praise on council members, describing them as good folk who "stand for the right principles and the right philosophy."

The "right philosophy" was driven home by CCC board member Sam Francis, who lamented in a syndicated column: "One thing you can't get at an American university is a course on Southern history that has anything good to say about slavery or slave holders." Ardent defenders of Confederate lore, the CCC described Abraham Lincoln as "surely the most evil American in history" and called Martin Luther King, Jr., a "depraved miscreant." But a CCC delegation had much kinder words for French neofascist führer Jean-Marie Le Pen when it presented him with a Confederate flag as a gift in 1998. "I certainly recognize that flag," Le Pen told his American admirers. "We are sympathetic to the Confederate cause."[5]

A few months after the love-fest with Le Pen, a flurry of U.S. news accounts brought unflattering attention to Lott's association with the council. This belated media exposure provoked shifting explanations and Clintonesque verbal contortions from the senator, who first denied speaking to the CCC, then backpedaled and pled memory lapse, insisting all the while that he had "no firsthand knowledge" of the council's ideas. Lott's response was as deceitful as President Clinton's claim that he never had sex with a White House intern. But unlike Clinton who was impeached for lying under oath, Lott escaped with his reputation largely intact as Congress failed to muster enough support to condemn the CCC for promoting racism.[6]

When all was said and done, Lott issued a tepid denunciation of prejudice in general. But the senator never explicitly rebuked the council, which remains an influential bipartisan presence among state lawmakers in Mississippi and other southern bastions. It continues to lobby for the elimination of the King Holiday, civil rights legislation, the Voting Rights Act, affirmative action, and nonwhite immigration—policies that are turning American society into a "slimy brown mass of glop," according to a CCC spokesperson.[7]

Lott's spin-controlled dalliance with the CCC underscores the extent to which American right-wing extremists have gained access to mainstream political power. It also shows why it's necessary for groups like the council to mask their racist ideology. Seeking to project a kinder, gentler face of hatred for public consumption, white power advocates often couch their arguments in coded language that recasts bigotry as racial pride. They claim to be *for* white

Americans rather than *against* people of color. They talk about preserving white identity and protecting white rights, which are allegedly under assault. Mouthing what has become the standard GOP line on "giveaway programs" and "special preferences" for minorities, white supremacists maintain that their deteriorating status in society is primarily a consequence of "reverse discrimination" aimed at white people—not the result of global economic trends and social processes that are having a negative effect on almost everyone.[8]

Veteran white power proponent DeWest Hooker summed up the challenge during a CCC gathering in December 1998: "Be a Nazi, just don't use the word." By dispensing such advice, Hooker was in effect throwing down the gauntlet to unabashed Hitlerites such as Reverend Richard Butler, the aging chief of the Aryan Nations in Idaho, whose followers still eagerly wear the swastika on their sleeves. For several years, this armed neo-Nazi enclave was "the hub of the wheel of racist revolution" in North America; by the late 1990s, however, Butler's health had declined and so had his group's status within America's violent racialist underground. Benefiting from a sizable injection of cash by two Silicon Valley millionaires, the Aryan Nations continued to invite supporters to its annual "summer conference and nigger shoot." But attendance sagged as an increasing number of white power stalwarts gravitated to other organizations.[9]

It was not by mere happenstance that David Duke, the former Grand Wizard of the Ku Klux Klan, announced his decision to run for Congress in 1999 at a forum sponsored by the neo-Nazi National Alliance. Duke was then chairman of a GOP executive committee in a Louisiana parish; he was also a featured speaker at CCC meetings where books by National Alliance supremo William Pierce (who wrote *The Turner Diaries*, the hate novel that inspired Timothy McVeigh) were on sale along with copies of Duke's autobiography. Picking up the slack when the Aryan Nations began to falter, Pierce's West Virginia–based group set up thirty-five branches across the United States and developed extensive contacts with European fascist leaders. These cross-border relationships are emblematic of a radical right-wing Euro-American subculture that links white supremacist movements on both sides of the Atlantic.[10]

Rooted in a shared set of symbols, myths, and beliefs, this violent racialist subculture has its own conspiratorial lingua franca. "ZOG," or the Zionist Occupation Government, a missive coined by neo-Nazis in the United States, traversed the ocean as easily as email messages on the Internet; it is now common parlance among white nationalists in Europe, where a large influx of refugees and migrants has forced many countries to grapple with multiculturalism and questions of identity. Scapegoating ethnic minorities and asylum-seekers, ultra-right-wing demagogues have touched a raw nerve in a tumultuous post–Cold War world that is still reeling from the demise of Soviet bloc Communism, the reunification of Germany, major technological change, and economic globalization.[11]

Nobody could predict the lethal wave of neo-Nazi brutality that swept across Germany after the Berlin Wall crumbled in November 1989. Following an initial surge of post-unification violence, the frequency of hate crimes abated somewhat, partly in response to the government's decision to change the German constitution and ditch its liberal asylum policy in 1993—a move applauded by neofascists and other right-wing extremists. Several neo-Nazi organizations were banned the following year and some key rabble-rousers were jailed. By 1997, however, most of the ringleaders had been released from prison, and felonious cruelty was again sharply on the rise. Police found a neo-Nazi bomb factory in Jena and confiscated sizable amounts of dynamite, machine guns, ammunition, and military gear. The local prosecutor said the arsenal reflected "a new quality in weaponry and violent preparations" of German neo-Nazi groups.[12]

The neo-Nazi scene grew by leaps and bounds in eastern Germany, where skinhead gangs attacked visitors—including tourists from the western part of the country—with baseball bats and bullets. Embittered by staggering unemployment and lack of economic opportunity, a lost generation of ex–East German youth turned large parts of the formerly Communist German Democratic Republic into virtual no-go areas for foreigners. The situation had deteriorated to the point where several Third World diplomats posted in Bonn voiced concern about their personal safety in anticipation of the German capital moving to Berlin in 1999. In a particularly ugly incident that year, an Algerian asylum-seeker bled to death after smashing through the glass entrance door of a building while fleeing from a band of neo-Nazi youth in Brandenburg, which has the highest rate of anti-foreigner crime in reunified Deutschland.[13]

By this time, overt sympathy for fascist views, especially among those under thirty, had become the norm in many east German villages, towns, and urban districts, where antipathy toward the new capitalist order was imbued with a brown odor. Easterners were increasingly apt to view the fall of the Berlin Wall not as a moment of liberation but as the prelude to a different kind of exploitation in which West Germans replaced the Soviets as their oppressors. "To say that one third of east German youth is now prone to the extreme right is an understatement," warned east Berlin criminologist Berndt Wagner. "The point of no return has already been reached for many. It's very depressing. It's growing. It's getting worse."[14]

While racist violence is often perpetrated by bald-shaven, leather-clad thugs, right-wing extremist tendencies are not restricted to down-and-out adolescents. "The problem here is not so much with right-wing youth, but with the center of society which thinks in a very nationalistic way," explained Günter Piening, the official responsible for foreigners' affairs in the economically depressed eastern state of Saxony-Anhalt.[15]

It was in Saxony-Anhalt that the neo-Nazi Deutsche Volksunion (DVU) scored a major breakthrough in regional elections in April 1998. Grabbing 13 percent of the vote, the DVU registered the strongest performance by an ultra-right-wing party in Germany's postwar history. Its success, along with significant grassroots penetration by the neo-Nazi National Democratic Party in other eastern states, hinged on stirring up anti-foreigner sentiment by accusing immigrants of stealing German jobs. This strategy proved efficacious even though foreigners comprised barely 1 percent of the population in the desolate east, while unemployment officially hovered around 25 percent and was actually twice that in many areas.[16]

Reacting to the neo-Nazi groundswell in the east, mainstream politicians hastened to ratchet up the nationalist rhetoric. Desperate to reverse his withering popularity, Chancellor Helmut Kohl started beating the jingoist drum during the run-up to his country's general elections in September 1998. This, perhaps, is the most benign interpretation of chauvinist rumblings from Kohl's party, which made it increasingly difficult to discern where political expediency ended and right-wing extremism began.

After years of championing European integration as "a matter of life and death" for the twenty-first century and the only way to avoid another war, Kohl suddenly found it expedient to echo some of the arguments of neofascist organizations that derided economic globalization and a single European currency. Engaging in the time-honored tactic of politicians who run against their own record, Kohl bemoaned the bureaucratic clout of the European Union (EU). He complained that Germany was footing too much of the bill for the EU, when, in fact, the EU system favored Germany and enhanced its wealth and power relative to rest of Europe. (Germany was the chief beneficiary of "free trade" among large EU members.) Kohl's belated pot-shots at the EU coincided with growing popular opposition to European economic integration among Germans who, by a large majority, were reluctant to give up their beloved deutsche mark for an uncertain euro.[17]

Instead of focusing on the creation of a Europe in which nationality would matter far less than before, German politicians trawled the sewers of racial prejudice for votes and fretted over how to keep their country as ethnically homogenous as possible. Shrill denunciations of "criminal foreigners" became the obligatory mantra of Kohl's Christian Democratic Union and its conservative coalition partner, the Christian Social Union, which likened immigrants to rabble and disparaged refugees as if they were carriers of some incurable disease. Eager to distract attention from their own policy failures, German officials proposed cutting off foreign aid to impoverished countries that were slow to take back their deported citizens. Bavaria's right-wing state government announced plans to expel entire non-German families if their children were caught shoplifting. A fourteen-year-old Turkish juvenile delinquent, who had been born in Germany and lived there all his life, was the first to be deported by Bavarian officials under the new rules; they also sought to deport the boy's parents, who were charged with endangering public safety by failing to raise their son properly.[18]

Contrary to all the overheated rhetoric, there was no statistical difference in crime rates among native Germans and foreigners. But mainstream politicians, aware that 15 percent of the German electorate held extreme Right views, frantically sought to outbid each other on anti-immigration and law-and-order issues. Leaders of the ostensibly left-of-center Social Democratic opposition party jumped on the bandwagon and called for the swift deportation of foreigners who abused German hospitality. This incessant pandering to xenophobic bigotry reached a crescendo when joblessness throughout Germany was officially stuck at 12 percent. For the first time since the Hitler era, unemployment had risen above four million.

The Social Democrats were able to parlay widespread economic anxiety into a national election victory. But the new ruling coalition, led by Chancellor Gerhard Schröder, quickly stumbled into a political minefield when it tried to alter Germany's blood-line citizenship requirements. Confronted by fierce grassroots opposition, the Schröder government scaled back its plans and pushed through a watered-down measure that made it easier for immigrants and their children to obtain German citizenship. At the same time, German cabinet officials emphasized that additional newcomers were not welcome in their country. "We have reached the limits, the point where we cannot bear any more," asserted Interior Minister Otto Schilly, a Social Democrat. "The majority of Germans agree with me: Zero immigration for now."[19]

Born in 1944, Schröder was the first modern German head-of-state without direct experience of World War II. After his election, he declared that he wanted to lead a nation that looked to the future, not one encumbered by the past. But some felt that Schröder was pushing too fast to disclaim Germany's legacy of guilt and historical debt to its victims. The chancellor's critics cited a recent survey by the Cologne Institute for Mass Communications, which indicated that almost 20 percent of Germans between the ages of fourteen and seventeen have no idea what Auschwitz was, and 18 percent of those who had heard of the concentration camp thought reports about what happened there were exaggerated.[20]

Despite these sobering figures, Schröder opposed the construction of a national Holocaust memorial—which had been discussed, planned, revised, and debated for more than a decade—in the center of Berlin. The row over the long-delayed Holocaust memorial did not necessarily signify a reluctance to confront the crimes of the Third Reich, which many Germans readily acknowledged. Rather, this controversy, along with the highly charged dispute over citizenship criteria, shows that Germany's struggle to come to terms with its Nazi history continues to define its identity as a nation.

It has often been said that no country had done as much as Germany to make amends for its past. Since World War II, the German government paid more than $100 billion in reparations to Jews and other victims, according to calculations by the German finance ministry. When he became chancellor, Schröder announced that he wanted to resolve all outstanding financial claims against German industry related to Nazi-era injustice by the year 2000. His government moved swiftly to broker an agreement with Germany's twelve largest banks and businesses to create a fund for compensating those who were used as slave labor by private companies during the Third Reich. Schröder hoped that by settling accounts with the past, his country would inaugurate a new era of confidence and normality after a half century of postwar contrition.

The decision to join the war in the Balkans was hailed as a major milestone for Germany, which celebrated its fiftieth anniversary as a democratic republic in May 1999 while NATO jets pounded Yugoslavia. No other NATO member had been so constrained by the sheer weight of historical memory as Germany. An important threshold was crossed when German military forces were sent into combat for the first time since Hitler. Chancellor Schröder defended Germany's participation in NATO air-strikes as a "historic responsibility" to redeem the Nazi legacy by fighting against the repression and ethnic cleansing in Kosovo promulgated by Serbian strongman Slobodan Milošević. Germany was a normal nation, Schröder insisted, and it would show the world what it learned from Nazism by fighting for human rights in Kosovo. Nazi atrocities during the Second World War were once considered reason enough for Germany never again to deploy military power outside its borders, particularly in an area that had been savaged by Hitler; now these same atrocities were being invoked to justify Germany's role in the NATO campaign.

Although German intervention in the Balkans was widely depicted in humanitarian terms, news reports in 1997 indicated that the German secret service had infiltrated the European Union's monitoring mission in former Yugoslavia and used it as a cover to illegally run arms and cash to Croatian and Bosnian forces. This disclosure received far less attention than a videotape that aired on German television, which showed German military officers and conscripts—some of whom had been slated for peacekeeping duties in the Balkans—acting out rapes, killings, torture sessions, and neo-Nazi skits. A senior officer was recalled from Bosnia after he and another German soldier on peacekeeping detail hurled racial epithets at Albanian troops, telling them, "Adolf Hitler would have stuck you in the gas chamber."[21]

While the German government expressed noble intentions regarding its latest foray into the Balkan war zone, there was something rather hypocritical about NATO launching a military operation to counter xenophobic violence, while it supported a Kosovo Albanian militia commanded by a ruthless Croatian mercenary who played a major role a few years earlier in the vicious expulsion of a quarter-million Serbian civilians from enclaves in Croatia. What's more, the U.S.-led NATO campaign against Yugoslavia relied on "Apache" helicopters and "Tomahawk" missiles—an Orwellian twist that prompted a reporter for *Le Monde Diplomatique* to ask: "Is it cynicism? Amnesia? Or have the Americans just not stopped to reflect that the arms they [used] to attack the Serb regime with its odious ethnic cleansing are named after the Indians exterminated last century?"[22]

Loath to confront their own demons from the past, U.S. officials have yet to own up to one of the dirtiest secrets of the Cold War: CIA and NATO use of an extensive Nazi spy network to wage a shadow war against the Soviet Union. The decision to recruit thousands of Third Reich veterans—including many war criminals—shortly after World War II had a negative impact on U.S.-Soviet relations and set the stage for Washington's tolerance of human rights abuses and other criminal acts in the name of anti-Communism. With that fateful sub rosa embrace, the die was cast for a litany of antidemocratic CIA interventions.[23]

As far as U.S. policy-makers were concerned, western integration and economic reconstruction took precedence over aggressive de-Nazification in Germany. The survival of fascism was guaranteed by the crude demands of the East-West face-off, which provided a kind of life-raft for tens of thousands of Nazi culprits who escaped punishment by serving as anti-Communist assets. In the murky world of Cold War espionage, some of Hitler's highest fliers flourished and passed on their deadly message. Ironically, several "ex-Nazis" employed by the CIA would go on to play leading roles in neofascist organizations that despised the United States. One of the unintended consequences of the CIA's ghoulish postwar alliance with Nazi spy veterans is evident today in a resurgent right-wing extremist movement in Europe that traces its ideological lineage back to the Third Reich through fascist collaborators who worked for U.S. intelligence.

"Neofascism and neo-Nazism are gaining ground in many countries—especially in Europe," warns Maurice Glele-Ahanhanzo, special rapporteur of the United Nations Commission on Human Rights. Of particular concern, Glele-Ahanhanzo noted in a ten-page report to the U.N. General Assembly in 1998, is the "increase in the power of the extreme right-wing parties," which are thriving in "an economic and social climate characterized by fear and despair" due to "the combined effects of globalization, identity crises, and social exclusion."[24]

In Western Europe today, there are 50 million poor, 18 million unemployed, and 3 million homeless—and post-Communist Eastern Europe is faring much worse. Such conditions are ripe for exploitation by extreme Right organizations, which range from tiny splinter groups and underground terrorist cells to sizeable political parties. While easily recognizable skinhead gangs may function as shock troops of the far Right's march through Europe, the more successful mass-based neofascist organizations have, according to Glele-Ahanhanzo, "made changes designed to make them look like radical right-wing democratic parties, softening their image while enabling them to conceal an unchanged preference for racism and xenophobia."

The post–Cold War resurgence of fascism in Europe is not orchestrated by a sieg-heiling dictator flanked by men in brown shirts and swastika armbands. Rather, a slick new breed of right-wing extremists, epitomized by Austrian Freedom Party führer Jorg Haider, have tailored their message and manner to suit the moment. Haider—who maintains that all soldiers in World War II, regardless of which side they were on, had fought for peace and freedom—topped all contestants with 42 percent of the vote in a March 1999 state election, putting him a strong position to contend for Austria's chancellorship. Jewish groups decried the election result, calling it "a genuine disaster for Austria."

In an effort to stymie Haider's inexorable rise to power, Austrian mainstream parties have increasingly embraced the slogans and policies of the far Right. "Gradually ruling politicians are fulfilling what Haider is saying and even sometimes before he says it," observed Nikolaus Kumrath, head of a Vienna-based immigrant advocacy group. "Everybody is looking like a rabbit to the snake. It is as though they fear his opinion and feel that they have to enact it before he can."[25]

Short of actually seizing control at the national level, the significance of Haider and his European counterparts lay in the extent to which they have been able to take their mainstream rivals hostage on key policy issues. Even when they lose elections, neofascists are like a toxic chemical in the water supply of the political landscape, polluting public discourse and pressuring establishment parties to adopt heretofore extremist positions to fend off challenges from the far Right.

French political scientist Pierre-André Taguieff calls this process the "Le Pen-ization of the political debate"—an acknowledgement of the considerable influence wielded by Jean-Marie Le Pen, leader of the neofascist Front National, which has steadily expanded its base of support in France since it bounced out of obscurity in the early 1980s. Attracting a broad spectrum of voters, Le Pen's organization developed into a potent political force. By the mid-1990s, it had become the first choice among the French working class, second among new voters, and the third largest party nationwide. In municipalities governed by the Front National, local officials censored library books and removed the names of antifascists and left-wingers—such as South African president Nelson Mandela—from street signs. The Front National's strength at the ballot box would cause all manner of havoc within the mainstream Right, which was bitterly divided over whether to form an alliance with Le Pen's party.

The Front National has also been hampered by serious infighting that recently split the organization in two. It would be premature, however, to write off the party given that its xenophobic populism continues to resonate with disillusioned voters. The far Right is a rooted presence in the French political psyche, as evidenced by recent surveys that show significant support for Le Pen's ideas. In a 1998 opinion poll by the French National Commission, 38 percent of all French men and women admitted they were racist, 27 percent said there were too many black people in France, and 56 percent said there were too many Arabs.[26]

Right-wing extremist parties have made considerable headway in several countries in Western Europe, polling more than 15 percent or more nationwide in France, Italy, and Norway. While this percentage may seem inconsequential in terms of America's two-party system, it can carry great weight in parliamentary balloting and determine the political make-up of the government.[27]

The neofascist Vlaams Blok has established itself as major player in Belgian politics, outpolling all rivals as it gained more than 30 percent of the vote in Antwerp, Belgium's second largest city. And in Turkey, the ultra-right-wing Nationalist Action Party captured 18 percent of the electorate in 1999, emerging as the second largest party in parliament. ("The Turkish race above all others" was the Nazi-like credo of the Nationalist Action Party founders, who were enthusiastic wartime supporters of Hitler.) The Nationalist Action Party sponsored a neo-Nazi youth group, the Grey Wolves, which has terrorized Turkish society since the 1960s. Today this party is a coalition partner in the national government.

Right-wing extremists and anti-Semitic hate-mongers stalk mainstream politicians and their parliamentary system in every nation in Eastern Europe, where high hopes and noble dreams evoked by the end of the Cold War were soon eclipsed by "the post-Communist nightmare," as Vaclav Havel put it. According to a 1998 World Bank study, Eastern European states suffered a dramatic decline in economic output and living standards since the disintegration of the Soviet bloc. "The total estimated number of poor in the 18 countries has risen twelvefold from nearly 14 million, or about four percent of the population, to 168 million, or approximately 45 percent," World Bank economist Brank Milanovic reported.[28]

The ongoing economic crisis—comparable in scope to the Great Depression in the United States and Germany in the 1930s—is fodder for demagogic forces that fan simmering ethnic tensions between people who had lived together, however restively, for many years in Soviet-dominated Eastern Europe without resorting to communal acts of violence. Whether instilled or remembered, hatred of the other has become a salient feature of Eastern European politics in the post–Cold War era. Much of the region is beset by "a mood of absolute demands and righteous wrath," in the words of Czech writer Ezraim Kohak, "a mood of frustration and anger, of deep and bitter anger seeking an excuse to vent itself."[29]

In Hungary the radical nationalist Life and Justice Party, led by Istvan Csurka, won parliamentary seats for the first time in 1998 after an election campaign marred by violence. An abrasive extremist who denigrates Roma (gypsies) and espouses lurid anti-Jewish conspiracy theories, Csurka exerts a pernicious influence on Hungarian politics. Prime Minister Viktor Orban once prided himself on his refusal to brandish the language of ethnocentric populism, but he has lurched rightward to accommodate Csurka's hard-core constituency.[30]

Half of all Romanians believe life was better under Communist rule and three-quarters want a strong figure to lead the country, according to a poll released by the Open Society Institute in November 1998. The same poll showed big gains in popular support for the extreme nationalist and anti-Semitic Greater Romania Party led by Corneliu Vadim Tudor, who accused the Romanian government of selling out to "a Jewish-led conspiracy." A reborn legionnaire movement, which venerates the Iron Guard (as the Nazis in Romania were known during the Hitler period), has been successfully recruiting disillusioned youth. Romanian fascists recently constructed a 40-foot-by-20-foot monument to the Iron Guard on a Black Sea beach resort. "From a civic point of view, I am delighted by their activity," said Ion Vasile, deputy mayor of Eforie Sud. "It is a tourist attraction because it arouses curiosity."[31]

Ethnic hatreds surfaced at a Waffen SS reunion in Riga, Latvia's capital, in the spring of 1998. Latvia's army commander and its chief of police were sacked after they paraded in full uniform with veterans of the pro-Nazi Latvian Legion. A few weeks later, bomb blasts in Riga damaged a Jewish synagogue, a Soviet war memorial, and the Russian mission.[32]

In Zagreb, the capital of Croatia, a museum that documented the atrocities of the wartime Ustaše regime is closed, and throughout the country some 3,000 monuments to the antifascist resistance struggle have been destroyed by Ustaše sympathizers. Meanwhile, Ustaše-booster Franco Tudjman has parlayed his status as Croatia's political strongman into hefty personal financial gain. In 1997, an Austrian newspaper pegged him as "the richest man in Central Europe." Amid widespread poverty in Croatia, Tudjman's family controlled the lucrative duty-free enterprises and the state intelligence apparatus. Most state-owned companies and public utilities were run by officials of Tudjman's corrupt, extremist-dominated political organization, the Croatian Democratic Union, which formed a governing coalition with a small neo-Nazi party. Brooking little dissent, Tudjman refused to authorize the clear-cut victory of the Croatian opposition in a local election in Zagreb, and his chief political rival was bludgeoned unconscious by uniformed thugs during a campaign rally.[33]

As in Croatia and other Eastern European states, so too in post-Soviet Russia, where the much ballyhooed privatization process was used as a smokescreen by a small klatch of tycoons in cahoots with government bureaucrats who plundered existing national resources and enriched themselves in what amounted to a highway robbery of unprecedented proportions. Abetted by economic aid programs that greased the theft of state enterprises, Russia's so-called seven oligarchs quickly amassed huge fortunes alongside destitution unparalleled elsewhere in Europe.

In pursuit of a snake-oil free market miracle, Russia jettisoned Communism and plunged helter skelter into "savage capitalism," as Aleksandr Solzhenitsyn aptly described it. No industrialized country had ever suffered such severe and prolonged economic deterioration during the twentieth century. The statistics are truly staggering: 150 million people pushed into poverty in the former Soviet Union; 70 to 80 percent of Russians living below or scarcely above the subsistence level; two million Russian children homeless;

a life expectancy of fifty-eight years that ranks with the poorest Third World nations.

The decrepit health of Russian President Boris Yeltsin could be construed as a metaphor for the overall debilitation of his country, where wages were not paid, taxes went uncollected, and old age pensioners died of starvation. Moscow and other Russian cities had the highest murder rates in the Western world. The police acted like gangsters and the judicial system was moribund. For all practical purposes, the central state apparatus had ceased to function. Russian military forces were reduced to a beggar's army with tales of conscripts eating dog food. Imagine Weimar Germany, then add thousands of nuclear weapons guarded by people earning less than five dollars a month. Demoralized post-Soviet Russia had become fertile turf for a very dangerous brand of Slavic fascism.[34]

The stage was set for the emergence of someone like Vladimir Zhirinovsky, the bombastic ultranationalist who captured the mania of the moment in Russia and led his neofascist party to victory in 1993 parliamentary elections. "Vlad the Mad" proceeded to invite members of the Duma, Russia's parliament, to drink a jar of his own urine. And he threatened to fan radioactive waste toward any uppity Baltic state that discriminated against ethnic Russians. But Zhirinovsky's role as a lightning rod for popular discontent would soon fade as he proved himself adept at converting his political capital into cash.

As the only party besides the Communists that could field candidates nationwide, Zhirinovsky's organization was wooed by a slurring Yeltsin, who often relied on Vlad's support in parliamentary balloting. Although he condemned Yeltsin's policies to gain publicity, Zhirinovsky delivered the vote for the Russian president on several occasions. After Zhirinovsky threw his weight behind Yeltsin's nomination for prime minister in April 1998, Yeltsin sent him an effusive thank-you message. "Your party has played a significant part in the establishment of political pluralism and a truly multiparty system in Russia," said Yeltsin, who also praised Zhirinovsky for protecting "the civil rights of our compatriots abroad." A few days earlier, in widely publicized press accounts, Zhirinovsky had blamed the Jews for starting World War II.[35]

A climate of terror intensified in Moscow that spring. Reveling in violence and intimidation, some 4,000 skinheads prowled subway stations, markets, and public squares in search of non-Russian prey. These racist youth gangs were responsible for an escalating number of hate crimes in the Russian capital, including the savage beating of an African-American Marine who worked at the U.S. embassy. This came on the heels of a more shocking incident in which twenty skinheads set upon two Asian women and pummeled them in broad daylight at a major thoroughfare in central Moscow. During this period, ambassadors from South Africa, Zaire, and Sudan complained to the Russian foreign ministry about a spate of attacks on their nationals. Fifteen hundred Azerbaijanis protested in the streets of Moscow after an Azeri trader was stabbed to death by skinheads, a killing witnessed by police who did not intervene. Darker-skinned peoples were systematically abused by Russian police officers, according to Human Rights Watch, which documented rampant police brutality that involved electric shock torture, sexual assault, and murder.[36]

When in need of a multibillion-dollar fix from the International Monetary Fund (IMF), Yeltsin found it expedient to warn that fascism posed "a big danger for society." But his government consistently failed to act against more than eighty neofascist groups that operated with virtual impunity in Russia, despite a criminal code that punished terrorism and a constitutional ban on ethnic and religious incitement.

The chaotic free-for-all that ensued after the collapse of the USSR strengthened the hand of Alexander Barkashov, the ponytailed karate expert who commanded the Russian National Union (RNU), Russia's leading national socialist organization. By 1998, the RNU had expanded its network of affiliates into sixty-four of Russia's eighty-nine component regions. Wearing black uniforms and swastika-like symbols at public rallies, many of Barkashov's followers were drawn from the police, the security services, and the Russian army. RNU acolytes attended annual weapons training camps near the southern city of Stavropol, where military veterans prepared youth for combat and indoctrinated them with fascist ideology. The *barkashovtsi* were often looked upon favorably by local and regional authorities in the Russian hinterlands that operated beyond the Kremlin's control. RNU paramilitary units mounted joint patrols with the city police in Kstovo in the Nizhny Novgorod region. And city officials in Borovichi, also in Novgorod, turned a deaf ear when the small Jewish community, which had been brutalized by Barkashov's thugs, requested police protection. "They can go around and beat someone up and no one will touch them," a Moscow-based RNU youth leader boasted of his neo-Nazi colleagues.[37]

In some ways even more disturbing than the proliferation of neofascist groups in Russia is the ultranationalist wing of the Communist Party, headed by General Albert Makashov, one of the most vitriolic anti-Semites in the Duma. In the wake of Russia's devastating financial meltdown in the summer of 1998, Makashov vowed to take revenge against the "Jewish entourage" inside Yeltsin's government that had allegedly caused his country's economic woes. "Round up all the Yids and send them to the next world," he ranted to enthusiastic crowds while barnstorming in several Russian provinces.[38]

Other members of the Communist hierarchy, including party boss Gennadi Zyuganov, expressed or hinted at similar views. Zyuganov said he had nothing against Jews per se, but he maintained that "Zionists"—long a target of Soviet propaganda—were secretly plotting to take over the world. Periodic surges of official anti-Semitism had deep roots in Russian history, harkening back to the bloody pogroms of the czarist era in which thousands of Jews were slaughtered. A prescient Lenin understood the abiding influence of noxious ethnic nationalism when he wrote disparagingly in 1919: "Scratch some Communists and you'll find Russian chauvinists."[39]

Fearful of political extremism in post-Soviet Russia, Jews once again began to flee the country in droves. Russia's chief rabbi Adolf Shayevich expressed concern about "the limp reaction of society and the inaction of the authorities" in the face of shrill anti-Semitic rhetoric and violent eruptions. "If there was a desire, they would have been able to rein in those people," he asserted. Instead, the Russian parliament resoundingly defeated a measure to censure General Makashov after the hard-line Communist deputy publicly called for the extermination of the Jews.[40]

Russia was already chafing under the humiliation of an expanded NATO stretching right up to the borders of the former Soviet

Union; then came NATO's decision to unleash the sustained bombing of Yugoslavia, a traditional Russian ally, in the spring of 1999. The U.S.-led air assault, combined with the abject failure of U.S.-crafted economic reforms, produced a strong anti-American backlash among Russians and helped swell the ranks of extreme nationalist groups. On the heels of an attempted rocket grenade attack on the U.S. embassy in Moscow, TV reports showed pictures of Russian shop workers mopping filthy floors with the Stars and Stripes. Hostility toward the United States was fast becoming an overarching national idea, a unifying theme hitherto sorely absent in a country bereft of a coherent sense of identity since the collapse of the USSR.

Russian nationalists also take umbrage at the slurry of American cultural artifacts—music, films, fast food restaurants—that have cropped up in large cities. Today a stroll along Moscow's main drag, the "Tverskaya," is much like taking a walk through a mall in Anytown, USA. The signs all have Cyrillic letters, but the corporate logos are uninspiringly familiar: McDonald's, Pizza Hut, a Marriott hotel, ubiquitous ATMs, and a Kentucky Fried Chicken outlet where young Muscovites wearing NFL insignia consume hormone-inflated meat.

President Bill Clinton has spoken about "the inexorable logic of globalization" from which no country presumably can escape. While economically driven, this seemingly unstoppable phenomenon has far-reaching cultural and social consequences. Profoundly antithetical to *savoir verve* and regional distinctiveness, global commerce acts as the great homogenizer, blurring indigenous differences and smothering unique ethnic traits. People are fearful of losing not only their jobs (if they are employed), but their cultural and national identity. Where local traditions are rendered impotent, individuals tend to become atomized and uprooted psychologically. This makes them more susceptible to the lure of ultranationalists who rail against what Benjamin R. Barber fittingly describes as "the numbing and neutering uniformities" of McWorld. And globalization, let's face it, is indistinguishable in so many ways from Americanization. Global monoculture has Mickey Mouse ears, it drinks Coke and Pepsi, eats Big Macs, watches endless reruns of *Dallas* and

Melrose Place, and computes on IBM laptops with the latest version of Microsoft Windows.

The new information technologies, which paradoxically enhance communication while also deepening alienation, have created an environment especially conducive to financial speculation and the rapid growth of global commerce. Increasingly the key players in the global economy are multinational corporations, transnational lobbies, and elite trade associations—rather than popularly conscripted officials. These global forces have usurped many of the usual prerogatives of the nation-state, while also calling into question democratic notions of political power and representation. The capacity of national governments to regulate their own economies has been significantly curtailed by the globalization of financial markets.

Although free markets are supposed to guarantee maximum efficiency, instead they have magnified severe inequalities and hastened the breakdown of social structures, leading to widespread instability, impoverishment, mass migration, and ethnic strife. On the cusp of the twenty-first century, the world appears mired in a postmodern form of feudalism, where big business runs its digitized fiefdoms in feeble states, while central authority lies with the new popes—the IMF and the central bankers. At the same time, the waning power of the nation-state has triggered a harsh ultranationalist reaction, particularly in areas hard hit by economic turmoil.

In April 1999, during a difficult economic recession, Japanese voters elected Shintaro Ishihara, a fiery right-wing nationalist, as mayor of Tokyo. Whereas Japanese rightists once looked to the United States as a close ally against their sworn enemy, the USSR, Ishihara loudly castigated a handful of influential American Jews for bullying Asia and he urged Japanese leaders to take a tougher stand against Washington. Ishihara also denounced as "a lie" the Rape of Nanking, in which 300,000 Chinese civilians were massacred by the Japanese imperial army in 1937.[41]

Traumatic aftershocks from the Asian economic implosion in the summer of 1997 were felt far and wide, including in Indonesia where a currency crash sparked food riots and ethnic violence. Scapegoat-hungry mobs attacked and killed Chinese shop owners throughout the archipelago, while gangs armed with muskets, spears, and swords roamed villages in Borneo eager to hunt down migrant workers who were also blamed for the crisis. Perceived as a threat to jobs for locals, migrants were vilified and assaulted with frightful regularity from Seoul to South Africa to Saxony and beyond.

Riding the crest of a populist backlash against globalization, far Right demagogues in Europe coupled their anti-immigrant tirades with pointed criticisms of the Maastricht Treaty and its provisions for a single continental currency. They have gotten a lot of mileage out of exploiting justifiable qualms about the European Monetary Union, which, in essence, is an attempt on the part of big business in Europe to adapt to the needs of the new global order. Full participation in the EU required painful budgetary retrenchment by member states that relinquished authority on key fiscal matters to unelected central bankers in Frankfurt. The adoption of the euro precluded the possibility for national governments to redress high unemployment and widening income disparities by adjusting their currencies and tweaking their own interest rates.[42]

Not surprisingly, voter turn-out among Europeans dropped precipitously, along with public confidence in elected representatives who apparently have little intention or means to make good on their most important promises. Disenchantment with the conventional political spectrum was reinforced by the failure of erstwhile left-of-center social democratic parties to offer an alternative agenda to rigid EU policy nostrums, which are "leading to a concentration of wealth and power that is undermining democracy," as Nicholas Hilyard, formerly of *The Ecologist,* has warned.

EU supporters have argued that economic integration is a crucial step in Europe's march toward political union, which they hope will end forever the scourge of pitiless nationalism that has ravaged the continent. But just the opposite seems to be happening. As economic globalization has accelerated in the post–Cold War era, producing definite categories of winners and losers, so too has the momentum of neofascist and right-wing extremist organizations. If anything, the process of European integration is likely to foster the continued growth of radical right-wing parties, which have successfully tapped into popular resentment against remote and unresponsive state governments. Burgeoning ultranationalist movements are collateral damage inflicted by unfettered globalization, which breeds the very monstrosities that it purports to oppose. And the extreme Right provides an alibi for globalization while revolting against it. In effect, the big corporations and the little draculas feed off of each other; they are two sides of the same coin.[43]

A product of democratic decay, radical right-wing populism and its contemporary fascist manifestations, which vary from one country to the next, can thrive only in situations where social injustice is prevalent. Buffeted by the unforgiving winds of economic and social change, most forlorn souls who gravitate toward right-wing extremist groups are driven not by personal pathologies, but by anger, desperation, and confusion. In the United States, according to Chip Berlet of Political Research Associates, a Christian patriot subculture has coalesced, involving some five million Americans who believe the U.S. government is manipulated by secret forces and conspiratorial cliques that have supposedly been running the show for centuries. Fearing the loss of national sovereignty, which they associate with a spurious United Nations plot to tyrannize America, these self-styled patriots and their armed wing, the militias, mistake the omnipresence of global monoculture for the phantasm of one-world government. This type of delusional thinking can be dangerous as it opens the door for neofascist recruiters who advocate quick and drastic measures to right deep-seated wrongs.[44]

No one can predict with certainty those sudden, circuit-breaking moments when the free-floating anxieties and hatreds of acutely disenfranchised individuals will intensify and transmute into crazed outbursts of terror and bloodletting. But converging social, economic, and political trends suggest that increasing numbers of people in the Western democracies and elsewhere will become vulnerable to the appeals of neofascists posing as national populists, who offer simple solutions to complex problems. And simple solutions, as we know, run the risk of turning into final solutions.

Under the circumstances, it behooves us to pay heed to the late George Mosse and other scholars who argue persuasively that fascism, far from being a historical aberration, was constructed on the basis of popular consensus in Europe and arose out of deeply ingrained values and traditions that were hardly inconsistent with the dominant currents of mainstream culture and society. But the successes and failures of interwar European fascist movements were not preordained; nor were they without key accomplices. Mussolini and Hitler might never have seized power if not for decisions by conservative and big business elites, which at a crucial juncture opted to back the Italian Fascist and the German Nazi parties as a hedge against the Left.[45]

Could a similar alliance be forged anew, even though today's opportunistic far Right leaders frequently unleash verbal volleys against globalization? Will the managers of the new global economy—like Europe's politically beleaguered businessmen in the 1930s—be tempted to support right-wing authoritarian movements in order to divert mounting social rancor away from themselves and toward scapegoats?

"It is becoming frighteningly evident that unspeakable evil can take the stage again," Swedish prime minister Goran Persson declared at a recent conference on resurgent racism and neofascism in Europe. The ghastly miscarriage of free market restructuring in much of Eastern Europe and the Third World, the abdication of the socialist Left as a vehicle for discontent in Western Europe, and the homogenizing juggernaut of soul-less transnational capitalism across the globe—all are elements of a potent witches brew that feeds the poisoned ground where flowers of evil bloom and propels mainstream governance further and further into the politics of resentment.[46]

Shortly before he died in 1987, Primo Levi, a Holocaust survivor who had been imprisoned at Auschwitz, warned of the advent of "a new fascism . . . walking on tiptoe and calling itself by other names." This new fascism is a decidedly contemporary phenomenon that looks different in many ways from its antecedents. When Hitler came to power he took the world by surprise. Those who remain fixated on images of the fascist past, and neglect the growing dangers of the present, may be taken by surprise again.[47]

Martin A. Lee
August 10, 1999

NOTES FOR PREFACE

1. Francis Parker Yockey in *The Spotlight,* p. 22, September 7, 1998. "Is American youth to wait supinely . . . for the butchers to start their bloodbath here?" Yockey wrote. "Youth of America—awake. It's your problem and your task." See, in general, the forthcoming biography of Yockey by Kevin Coogan.

2. As of December 1997, the FBI was involved in more than 900 investigations into right-wing extremist activity, compared to one hundred such cases prior to the April 1995 Oklahoma City attack. Among the incidents that surfaced in the news: a Michigan militia scheme to bomb expressways, federal property, and a TV station; a plot by seven West Virginia Mountaineer Militia members to collect and transport explosive materials weapons with the aim of destroying a federal fingerprint center; plans by four snipers involved with the heavily armed Southern California Minuteman Association, led by reserve officer of the Los Angeles Police Department, to murder illegal immigrants trying to cross the border; a plot by three members of a white supremacist group called The New Order to contaminate a large water supply with cyanide as a diversionary tactic while they embarked on an antigovernment bombing spree; three self-described "ambassadors from Yahweh" who were convicted on murder, kidnapping, and conspiracy charges stemming from plans to overthrow the federal government and create an "Aryan People's Republic," which they intended to populate energetically through polygamy; and the taking of hostages by members of the renegade Republic of Texas, which declared independence from the United States after flooding the Texas courts and banking system with bogus property claims, bad checks, liens, and petty lawsuits.

3. The Southern Poverty Law Center reported that there were 537 hate groups in the U.S. in 1998, 63 more than in 1997. At the same time, there was an almost 60 percent increase in the number of racist websites, to 254.

4. Fairness & Accuracy In Reporting, "The CCC in Its Own Words," *Extra!,* March–April 1999.

5. Michael Powell, "White Wash," *Washington Post,* January 17, 1999; Sam Francis, "Cultural Bolshevism on Campus," *The Spotlight,* December 21, 1998; Francis's weekly syndicated column is featured in the Liberty Lobby's *Spotlight,* as well as on the Council of Conservative Citizens website.

6. In March 1999, GOP congressional leaders—with Senator Trent Lott's help—killed a strongly worded resolution that reprimanded the Council of Conservative Citizens for its mean-spirited bigotry. The Republican officials said they nixed the resolution on the grounds that it was inappropriate to single out one particular organization while many other hate groups were active. Yet no such reasoning applied when Congress unanimously condemned the vicious anti-Semitic remarks of Black Muslim leader Khalid Muhammad, one of Louis Farrakhan's right-hand men.

7. Thomas B. Edsall, "GOP Chairman Denounces 'Racist' Group," *Washington Post,* January 20, 1999. Several influential GOP officials schmoozed with the Council of Conservative Citizens and spoke at its events, including Congressman Bob Barr from Georgia, a leading crusader for Clinton's impeachment; Kirk Fordice when he was governor of Mississippi; North Carolina Senator Jesse Helms; and South Carolina GOP National Committeeman Buddy Witherspoon, who remains an unrepentant member of the council.

8. For a powerful rebuttal to those who oppose affirmative action and alleged "reverse discrimination," see William G. Bowen and Derek Bok, *The Shape of the River* (Princeton, N.J.: Princeton University Press, 1999).

9. The Southern Poverty Law Center, "Sharks in the Mainstream," *Intelligence Report,* Winter 1999; Kim Murphy, "Last Stand of an Aging Aryan," *Los Angeles Times,* January 10, 1999. In an effort to finance their activities, some "Christian patriots" turned to drug trafficking. Profits from methamphetamine labs boosted the efforts of white supremacist groups and organized militias; one consequence of this was the rapid spread in usage of highly addictive crystal meth from cities to rural communities in the late 1990s. During this period, there was a rise in the number of right-wing extremists

nabbed for dealing drugs to bankroll the revolution. Randy Graham, a member of the northern Michigan militia, was convicted of growing marijuana to bankroll a plot to assassinate state officials, blow up the federal building in Battle Creek, and bomb an IRS building in another city.

10. The Southern Poverty Law Center, "The Alliance and Its Allies," *Intelligence Report,* Winter 1999. Duke's 1998 autobiography, *My Awakening,* is rife with conspiracy theories and derision of blacks, Jews, and gays.

11. In general, see Jeffrey Kaplan and Leonard Weinberg, *The Emergence of a Euro-American Radical Right* (New Brunswick, N.J.: Rutgers University Press, 1998); and Jeffrey Kaplan and Tore Bjorgo, *Race and Nation* (Boston: Northeastern University Press, 1998).

12. Erik Kirschbaum, "Germany says far-right crime surges in 1997," Reuters, May 6, 1998; "Bomb Factory Linked to neo-Nazis," AP Online, February 13, 1998; "German Police Confiscate Arms," AP Online, March 25, 1998. According to the German Federal Office for the Protection of the Constitution, the number of criminal acts with a right-wing extremist orientation in Germany surged to 11,719 in 1997 from 8,730 in 1996. Figures released by the German army indicate that neo-Nazi episodes within the German military jumped fourfold during this period. The groundswell of neo-Nazi activity paralleled an increase in acts of anti-Semitic violence, which jumped by 27 percent to 790, including 13 cases of attempted manslaughter and 677 assaults. A disproportionate number of these attacks occurred in the formerly Communist eastern states, where six people were killed and more than one thousand injured in neo-Nazi assaults in 1997.

13. Amnesty International expressed concern about the abusive treatment of Aamir Ageeb, a thirty-year-old Sudanese asylum-seeker, who died in custody on May 28, 1999, as the German police were trying to forcibly deport him from the Frankfurt airport. Earlier, a Kurdish refugee about to be deported to Turkey doused himself with gasoline and burned to death. Immigration attorneys rebuked the German government for its maltreatment of ethnic Albanian

refugees from Kosovo in the months leading up to the NATO bombing campaign—a campaign that was waged, with German backing, allegedly to protect human rights in the Balkans.

14. Ray Moseley, "Specter of 'ethnic cleansing' haunts Germany," *San Francisco Examiner,* April 5, 1998; Ian Traynor, "German neo-Nazi tide creates no-go zones for foreigners," *The Guardian,* January 21, 1998; Martin A. Lee, "Germany Goosesteps to the Right," *Moment,* June 1998.

15. Roger Boyles, "Neo-Nazi poll blitz wins jobless voters," *The Times* (London), April 23, 1998.

16. The National Democratic Party (NPD) became a haven for hard-core neo-Nazis who needed a legal umbrella for their political activities. Because the NPD was recognized as a political party, its marches were rarely prohibited, thereby enabling neo-Nazis to stage public demonstrations. Three thousand neo-Nazis gathered in Leipzig on May Day 1998 for an NPD rally, which ended in rioting, looting, and burning barricades, as right-wing extremists clashed with antifascist groups. That year, according to the Verfassungsschutz (German internal security service), the number of active right-wing extremists in Germany increased to 53,600, compared with 48,400 the previous year. The number of violent fascists also grew—from around 7,600 to 8,200 in 1998.

17. Andrei S. Markovits and Simon Reich, *The German Predicament* (Ithaca: Cornell University Press, 1997), pp. 150–182. Ironically, it was the European Union that upheld the right of member citizens to buy property and settle anywhere within its domain. Many Poles and Czechs feared that joining the European Union would make their countries vulnerable to wealthy, land-grabbing Germans who had their sights set on regaining former homes and property in contested border zones. Although the German government publicly swore off designs on Polish territory as a precondition for reunification, it still considered private land claims open. This emotive topic bubbled to the surface once again during the 1998 election campaign when the German parliament passed a resolution condemning the post–World War Two expulsion of over five million ethnic Germans from Poland as an unjust violation of

international law. Renewed calls to compensate German expellees prompted an angry rebuke from legislators in Warsaw, who decried what they saw as "dangerous tendencies, which can rightly be worrying not just for Poland." For several years the German government has been sending mixed messages about border issues. A 1973 ruling by the Constitutional Court in Karlsruhe affirmed that Germany's 1937 borders were still legitimate—and this decision has never been formally overturned. In effect, this meant that one of Germany's most respected government institutions maintains, at least theoretically, that a large chunk of Poland actually belongs to Germany.

18. Ullrich Fichtner, "Germany's Energetic Taboo-Breakers," *Frankfurter Rundschau* (English online version), April 23, 1998.

19. A number of factors, including strong anti-immigration policies advocated by the Social Democrats and their main rival, the Christian Democrats, undercut the appeal of several neofascist and extreme right-wing parties, which tallied a combined vote of 2,280,219 (or 4.6 percent of the total) in Germany's national elections in September 1998.

20. Roger Boyles, "Postwar generation seeks release from shackles of Nazi guilt," *The Times* (London), November 9, 1998.

21. Tim Judah, "German spies accused of arming Bosnian Muslims," *Daily Telegraph,* April 20, 1997; "Neo-Nazi Incident Reported in Bosnia," AP Online, February 18, 1998.

22. "Apaches and Tomahawks," *Le Monde Diplomatique,* May 1999.

23. Martin A. Lee, "The CIA's original sin," *Miami Herald,* September 21, 1997.

24. Thalif Deen, "U.N. Worried Over Alarming Rise in Xenophobia," Interpress Service, September 20, 1998.

25. Andrew Gimson and Peter Hoffer, "Austrian urged to quit over insults," *Daily Telegraph,* July 3, 1997; Tracy Wilkinson, "Rising Star of Austrian Nationalism," *Los Angeles Times,* December 11, 1997; Michael Leidig, "Hitler fan is voted back in power in Austria,"

Daily Telegraph, April 9, 1999. *Searchlight,* the London-based antifascist magazine, reports that Haider's Freedom Party is home to some of the most virulent fascists and anti-Semites in Austria, including Reinhard Gaugg, deputy mayor of Klagenfurt, who said "Nazi" stood for "New, Attractive, Zealous, Ideas-Rich," and Marcus Ertl, Freedom Party counselor in Spittal an der Drau, who claimed that those who perished at Auschwitz were killed by Anglo-American air raids.

26. Ignacio Ramonet, "Neo-fascism," *Le Monde Diplomatique,* April 1998; Thalif Deen, "U.N. Worried Over Alarming Rise in Xenophobia," Interpress Service, September 20, 1998.

27. The Progress Party, headed by Carl Hager, emerged as the second biggest political force in Norway when it won 15 percent nationwide and twenty-five parliamentary seats in 1997 elections. Norway's immigration and asylum policies were already so tight that even Hager found it difficult to propose new and more restrictive laws. But the right-wing extremist Progress Party still found it expedient to vilify Samis (native Laplanders) and other ethnic minorities, even though they comprise only a tiny portion of the Norwegian population. Elsewhere in Scandinavia, the ultranationalist Danish People's Party garnered 14 parliamentary seats in a March 1998 general election. And in Italy, the National Alliance, led by self-proclaimed "post-fascist" Gianfranco Fini, got 15.7 percent of the vote and fifty-three parliamentary representatives in national elections. The up-and-coming Fini has been angling to replace billionaire media tycoon Silvio Berlusconi, who was convicted of multiple bribery and corruption charges, as the preeminent leader of the Italian Right.

28. World Bank report cited in "Ex-communist states' plight like Great Depression," Reuters, May 22, 1998.

29. Ezraim Kohak quoted in Laszlo Kurti, "The Emergence of Postcommunist Youth Identities," in Kaplan and Tore, *Race and Nation,* p. 194.

30. "Hungary's right plays nationalist card in election," *Independent* (London), May 11, 1998.

31. "Communism was better, Romanians say in poll," Reuters, November 26, 1998; "Followers of Fascist Iron Guard Build Monument on Romanian Beach," Associated Press, August 1, 1997.

32. Roger C. Paddock, "Old Ethnic Rifts Run Deep in Latvia," *Los Angeles Times,* April 6, 1998; "Bomb damages Russian mission in Latvia," UPI, April 6, 1998; "Blast damages Latvian Soviet war memorial," Reuters, May 4, 1998.

33. Tom Walker, "Hard-faced men of Balkans still doing well out of the war," *The Times* (London), May 28, 1997; Tracy Wilkinson, "Prognosis Uncertain for Croatia, Leader," *Los Angeles Times,* June 22, 1997; "Croatia's Dangerous Extremism," *New York Times,* April 28, 1997; Marinko Culic, "Croatia and Serbia—Two Sides of a Bent Penny," Interpress Service, January 25, 1998; Chris Hedges, "Rival of Croatian President Is Attacked at Rally," *New York Times,* June 7, 1997.

34. Moshe Lewin, "A Country Falling Apart," *Le Monde Diplomatique,* November 1998; Stephen F. Cohen and Katrina vanden Heuvel, "Help Russia," *The Nation,* January 11/18, 1999.

35. Mark Franchetti, "Method lurks behind Zhirinovsky's madness," *Sunday Times* (London), April 12, 1998; "Yeltsin in message of support to neo-fascist Zhirinovsky's party," *Irish Times,* April 27, 1998.

36. Nick Wadhams, "Moscow Skinhead Violence Growing," Associated Press, May 14, 1998; Mark Franchetti, "Nazi race attacks sweep Moscow," *Sunday Times* (London), May 10, 1998; "Neo-Nazis carrying out threats?" *Orange County Register,* May 8, 1998; Phil Reeves, "Russia's racist skinheads terrorize foreigners," *Independent,* May 8, 1998.

37. ITAR/TASS, Russian national press review, June 8–9, 1998; Robin Lodge, "Synagogue bomb marks sinister rise of Russia's neo-Nazis," *Daily Telegraph,* May 17, 1998; James Meek, "They wear the swastika and hate Jews but no-one dares to call them fascists," *The Observer* (London), July 5, 1998; Celestine Bohlen, "Russia's Stubborn Strains of anti-Semitism," *New York Times,* March 2, 1999; "Trial exposes Russian nazis' official links," *Searchlight,* April 1998.

38. James Meek, "Russian left descends into dark well of anti-Semitism, *Guardian,* November 5, 1998; Richard Beeston, "Russia's Jews in plea to the West," *The Times* (London), December 9, 1998.

39. Lenin quoted in Maura Reynolds, "Economic Ills Give Rise to Anti-Semitism in Russia," *Los Angeles Times,* November 22, 1998. See, in general, Yitzhak M. Brudny, *Reinventing Russia: Russian Nationalism and the Soviet State* (Cambridge, Mass.: Harvard University Press, 1998).

40. "Rabbi pans indifference to anti-Semitism in Russia," Reuters, March 9, 1999; "More Jews leave Russia amid crisis, anti-Semitism," Reuters, March 15, 1999.

41. Japanese authorities are still reluctant to admit the atrocities committed by Unit 731 of the Japanese Army, which conducted gruesome chemical and biological warfare experiments on live Chinese and Korean prisoners who were deliberately infected with anthrax, cholera, plague, and other pathogens before and during World War II. The Japanese government continues to maintain a virtual blockade against telling the truth about the torture chambers of Unit 731 and other aspects of Japanese history to its younger generations. Japan's neighbors, particularly China and Korea, worry that Japanese denials of wartime atrocities make it more likely that the country will rip up its "peace" constitution in the coming years and resume its militaristic and belligerent ways.

42. As Stephen Castle reported in *The Independent* (June 22, 1999): "Confirming the suspicions of Euroskeptics that life inside the single currency could be like being stuck in a burning house with no fire escape, Brussels insisted yesterday that Italy cannot legally pull of the euro."

43. "Bioregionalism Versus Fascism," Peter Berg and Martin A. Lee, *Raise The Stakes: Planet Drum Review,* no. 28, Spring 1998. Also see, in general, Benjamin R. Barber, *Jihad vs. McWorld* (New York: Times Books, 1995).

44. Chip Berlet, "Dances with Devils: How Apocalyptic and Millennialist Themes Influence Right-Wing Scapegoating and Conspiracism," *The Public Eye,* Fall 1998.

45. See, in general, George Mosse, *The Fascist Revolution* (New York: Fertig, 1999). Arguing along similar lines, Mark Mazower asserts in *Dark Continent* (New York: Knopf, 1999) that National Socialism "fits into the mainstream not only of German but also of European history far more comfortably than most people like to admit." Moreover, says Mazower, "As we now know, Sweden, Switzerland and several other European countries continued to employ sterilization and other coercive measures in social policy until relatively recently. Such practices make Hitler's Germany look less exceptional and closer to the mainstream of European thought than once seemed possible."

46. Goran Persson quoted in "International effort to raise Holocaust awareness," Reuters, May 7, 1998.

47. Primo Levi cited in Roger Griffin, ed., *Fascism* (New York: Oxford University Press, 1995), p. 392.

THE BEAST REAWAKENS

INTRODUCTION

Adolf Hitler and his top military advisors had gathered at the Wolf's Lair, the Führer's headquarters in East Prussia, for an early-afternoon strategy session on July 20, 1944. They were listening to Lieutenant General Adolf Heusinger, chief of operations of the Wehrmacht (German army), deliver a bleak report about Germany's latest misfortunes on the eastern front. Suddenly a violent explosion hurled everyone onto the floor. Writhing and coughing amid thick smoke and dust, several German officers could hear Field Marshal Wilhelm Keitel shout, *"Wo ist der Führer?"* ("Where is the Führer?")

Somehow unharmed, Keitel made his way through a tangle of dead and injured men until he found a groggy Hitler, his uniform shredded and bloodstained. Helped to his feet, the Führer stared at Keitel with a dazed expression before collapsing in the field marshal's arms. Hitler was carried to a hospital bed, where a doctor dressed his wounds. He had a punctured eardrum and a lacerated back, his legs were burned, his face and hair were charred, and his right arm was temporarily paralyzed. A badly shaken Hitler had barely survived the only serious assassination attempt on him.

Meanwhile, confusion reigned in Berlin, where a handful of German officers who had organized the bomb plot sought to gain control of the city. But their efforts would soon be thwarted by the fateful intervention of Major Otto Ernst Remer, a relatively obscure, thirty-two-year-old leader of the Grossdeutschland guard battalion, which was responsible for protecting government offices in the capital.

As rumors of Hitler's death swept through the barracks, Remer was told by his commanding officer to arrest Joseph Goebbels, the top Nazi official in Berlin that day. With pistols drawn, Remer led a twenty-man contingent into the Propaganda Ministry, where Goebbels held sway. At that moment, Remer was probably the single most important military officer in Germany.

Encircled by gun-pointing soldiers, a quick-thinking Goebbels told Remer that the conspiracy had failed: Hitler was still alive. To prove his point, he picked up the phone, called the Wolf's Lair, and handed the receiver to Remer. The tall, strapping young officer breathed a sigh of relief when he heard the Führer's voice. Hitler put Remer in charge of all troops in Berlin and ordered him to crush the putsch. Anyone who resisted was to be shot immediately.

It was a heady assignment for Remer, who immediately took control and instructed his troops to establish roadblocks and patrols. They sealed off the city command center and surrounded the army buildings where some of the coup ringleaders were ensconced. Remer was posted at the entrance of the War Office when SS Colonel Otto Skorzeny, a fierce Hitler loyalist, arrived on the scene with a band of armed men.

Remer introduced himself to Skorzeny and apprised him of the crisis situation. They agreed that no one, regardless of how high in rank, would be allowed to enter or leave until they finished searching the premises. Skorzeny and his SS squadron encountered a mayhem of murder and suicide inside the building. The can-do colonel quickly put a halt to a wave of executions so that suspects could be tortured into naming others and exposing the extent of the plot before they were sent to the gallows.

With Skorzeny in charge of the War Ministry, it didn't take long before the revolt was smashed and the affairs of the High Command were once again in smooth working order. During the weeks that followed, he helped track down the remaining suspects in one of history's most gruesome manhunts. It was an occasion to settle old scores, as two thousand people, including dozens of high-ranking German officers, were killed in a paroxysm of military fratricide.

Some of the leading plotters were garroted with piano wire and impaled on meathooks, while Nazi cameramen recorded the victims' death throes so that Hitler could view the film in his personal cinema.[1]

For the colonel's invaluable support during the aftermath of the coup attempt, the Führer gratefully declared, "You, Skorzeny, saved the Third Reich." But it was Remer who stole the limelight. His decisive actions were crucial in restoring order in Berlin. Hitler showed his appreciation by promoting Remer to the rank of major general, a distinction that instantly propelled him into Nazi superstardom. Henceforth, Remer would serve as Hitler's bodyguard.

The Twentieth of July would prove to be more than just the date when an ill-prepared coup attempt, led by the one-armed Count Claus von Stauffenberg, failed to topple a mad dictator. The events that transpired that afternoon were destined to become a hot-button issue that deeply divided the German people in the years ahead. Nazi diehards and their sympathizers saw the putsch as yet another stab in the back that deprived Germany of its rightful empire. They embraced Otto Ernst Remer as the epitome of the loyal soldier, a symbol of unflinching resistance to "the traitors" who betrayed the Fatherland from within and caused Germany's defeat. For many others, the Twentieth of July became a legend of exoneration and redemption, offering a moral basis for expunging the sins of the Nazi past and beginning anew. After the war, West Germany's leaders would seize upon the anti-Hitler insurrectionists as a source of historical legitimacy. The coup plotters were touted as a shining example of the "other Germany" that had valiantly opposed the Third Reich.

Far from being a national reaction against Hitler, the July 20 conspiracy was actually the work of a relatively small number of individuals who were not necessarily inspired by lofty ideals. Evidence produced during the International Military Tribunal at Nuremberg showed that one of the army officers involved in the coup plot had been the commander of an *Einsatzgruppen* mobile killing squad, which perpetrated some of the first large-scale murders of Jews on the eastern front.[2]

Some of those who belatedly turned against Hitler were motivated not by moral outrage but by fears that they were losing the war. Theirs was a desperate attempt to restore an authoritarian order stripped of Nazi trappings, rather than a first step toward political liberalism and democracy. The complete disintegration of Germany could be prevented only, they surmised, if Hitler were overthrown. Toward this end, the conspirators were encouraged by American spymaster Allen Dulles, who intimated from his intelligence headquarters in Switzerland that a non-Nazi government might be spared the harsh terms of an unconditional surrender. Ignoring the Nuremberg data, Dulles later offered unequivocal praise for the coup plotters' efforts "to rid Germany of Hitler and his gang and establish a decent regime."[3]

The myth of the "other Germany" that was fostered by the Twentieth of July provided a convenient alibi not only for the West German government but also for various Western espionage agencies that recruited Third Reich veterans en masse during the early years of the Cold War. As far as America's intelligence chiefs were concerned, it didn't really matter where these men stood with respect to the July 20 debacle as long as they were steadfastly anti-Communist. Among those who later worked with the Central Intelligence Agency, under the directorship of Allen Dulles, was Colonel Otto Skorzeny.

The Americans also tried to recruit Skorzeny's partner from the July 20 affair, Major General Otto Ernst Remer. But Remer spurned their offers, opting instead to collaborate with the Soviets during the Cold War. Those who looked to the East after the Third Reich fell took their historical cue from Bismarck, the Prussian realpolitiker who unified Germany "by blood and iron" in 1871. Bismarck insisted that Germany must align with Russia, its proximate and mineral-rich neighbor. This was also Remer's wholehearted belief.

Yet, even as they gravitated toward rival superpowers, Skorzeny and Remer remained friends and stayed in contact over the years. Both men continued to move in the same neo-Nazi circles while trafficking in military hardware and expertise. Their shady business ventures embroiled them in high-stakes, international intrigue. Having crossed paths for the first time on the Twentieth of July, their overlapping stories embody the dual-pronged nature of postwar Nazi subterfuge. Together, they helped lay the groundwork for a multifaceted neofascist revival that gained alarming momentum in the post–Cold War era.

The speed and ferocity with which the extreme Right asserted itself after the Berlin Wall crumbled — not only in Germany but across Europe and North America — caught nearly everyone by surprise. The growing clout of far Right political parties in Europe; the emergence of a "Red-Brown alliance" in Russia; the rise of the U.S. militia movement; the mounting pattern of violence against refugees, immigrants, guest workers, asylum seekers, and racial minorities throughout much of the Northern Hemisphere — all are manifestations of a widespread neofascist resurgence. Accentuated by the reunification of Germany, the collapse of Soviet bloc Communism, and major changes in the global economy, the sharp escalation of neofascist activity constitutes one of the most dangerous trends in international politics.

Focusing primarily on Germany, and to a lesser extent on the United States, Russia, and other countries, this book examines how and why fascism — utterly vanquished and discredited fifty years ago — has once again become a force to be reckoned with. In the ensuing pages, I attempt several extended treatments of major personalities in the postwar fascist scene. These political malefactors have demonstrated remarkable tenacity and resourcefulness as they grappled to fashion an effective strategy in an era when fascism seemed defunct as a legitimate political alternative.

During the immediate aftermath of World War II, fascists had no choice but to maintain a low profile. This was the "catacombs" period for Third Reich veterans. They were placed on the defensive by the unique scope of the Nazi horror, now indelibly associated with state terror, genocide, and mass destruction on an unprecedented scale in human history. Between 50 million and 60 million died as a direct result of World War II, which Hitler started. Many millions more suffered unfathomable cruelty and hardship. The face of global politics was irretrievably altered. With the Axis armies smashed, the Western European Allies exhausted, and their colonies on the verge of rebellion, a huge vacuum appeared in the world power structure. The United States and the Soviet Union were the only countries with sufficient military strength and political resolve to fill this lacuna.

The onset of the Cold War was triggered in part by the superpowers' struggle over how to integrate Germany into the new world order. Although it had been conquered on the battlefield and stripped of its political sovereignty, Germany remained a potentially important player in Europe. Even when divided between East and West, the two Germanys were not merely client states under someone else's thumb. "The theory of the Cold War as a Soviet-American duopoly is sometimes defended on the grounds that, after all, the United States and the Soviet Union were in full command of their respective alliances," Arthur Schlesinger notes. "But nationalism, the most potent political emotion of the age, challenged the reign of the superpowers almost from the start." De Gaulle's quarrel with NATO, Tito's break from Moscow, and the bitter Sino-Soviet conflict were among the examples cited by Schlesinger, who concludes: "The impact of clients on principals is another part of the unwritten history of the Cold War."[4]

In a different way, German nationalists also brought their influence to bear on the U.S.-Soviet conflict. A coterie of Third Reich veterans quickly reconstituted a covert network of neofascist groups, which tried to exploit the deepening rift between the two superpowers. The Cold War became a walking stick for Nazi spies who sought to parlay their overwhelming military defeat into a partial but significant victory once the guns had been silenced. Nazi espionage agents skillfully plied their trade on both sides of the East-West divide, playing one superpower off the other, proffering services to both American and Soviet intelligence. Instead of truly denazifying the German menace, the United States and Soviet Union plunged into the deep freeze of the Cold War, thereby allowing the fascist beast to acquire a new lease on life.

Many Nazi operatives, including Otto Skorzeny, curried the favor of Western secret-service agencies by touting themselves as rock-solid anti-Communists. At the same time, other Third Reich veterans, such as Otto Ernst Remer, were careful not to burn bridges to the Soviet Union in accordance with the centuries-old geopolitical imperative that beckoned for a German-Russian alliance. Whether opting for expedient relations with East or West, they never ceased dreaming of a fascist comeback. The clandestine milieu they inhabited was awash in intrigue, shifting alliances, internecine disputes, and unexpected linkages that defied standard interpretations. It was a strange world in which the political categories of "Right" and "Left" at times seemed to blur beyond recognition.

While the Cold War raged, several scholars who wrote about fascism provided intellectual fodder for the East-West propaganda contest. But mass-based fascist organizations were never just pawns of big business, as Marxist historians have asserted; nor were they simply the totalitarian soul mates of Stalinism, as anti-Communist polemicists have argued. In addition to avoiding awkward truths about the indigenous appeal of fascism, neither theory could account for the recrudescence of fascism in the 1990s.

Over the years, academics have engaged in much debate and semantic hairsplitting without arriving at a universally accepted definition of fascism. The lack of agreement as to what constitutes the "fascist minimum" (the lowest common denominator of features found in all examples of fascism) stems in part from the protean nature of the fascist experience. Fascism during the 1920s and 1930s was an ideologically ambiguous movement that metamorphosed through several phases or sequences. Fascist parties initially attracted support among the hoi polloi by campaigning as social revolutionaries against the inequities of the free market; later, as serious contenders for power, they won over conservative elites in Italy and Germany by promising to thwart the Red Menace. In places where fascists governed, they inevitably violated their early platforms, especially their anticapitalist pretensions. Ultimately, their main political enemy was the worker Left, which placed fascism in the right-wing extremist camp.[5]

Several fascist leaders, including Benito Mussolini, started out as socialists but eventually lost faith in the revolutionary capacity of the working class. In order to mobilize an inert proletariat, they embraced nationalism. The mythos of national rebirth was germane to fascism, which assumed widely diverging forms based on a constellation of historical and social factors that differed from one country to the next.

The National Socialist German Workers' Party (NSDAP), led by Hitler, emphasized Nordic mysticism, biological racialism, anti-Semitic conspiracy theories, and aggressive militarism. In its formative period, the NSDAP shared the ultranationalist stage with several non-Nazi variants of fascism that flourished in Germany during the so-called Conservative Revolution of the 1920s. A plethora of German fascisms embraced *Volk*-ish and anti-Semitic assumptions — unlike Italian Fascism (sometimes referred to as "corporatism"), which was not inherently racialist. Mussolini's followers may have been racist in the general sense of viewing nonwhites or non-Europeans as culturally inferior, but they did not inflate their racism into an obsessive, all-encompassing ideology. Nor did Franco's hyperauthoritarian Catholics in Spain, who had little sympathy for the pagan and anti-Christian motifs that Nazis often espoused.[6]

Unfortunately, the blanket usage of the terms *fascist* and *neofascist* belies the diverse and sometimes conflicting tendencies that these labels encompass. Umberto Eco describes fascism as "a *fuzzy* totalitarianism, a collage of different philosophical and political ideas," which "had no quintessence." The word itself derives from *fasces*, a cluster of sticks with protruding axheads that symbolize the power and the glory of ancient Rome. In Latin, *fasces* is related to *fascinum*, "to fascinate or charm."[7]

The abracadabra of fascism casts a spell over people by diverting economic and social resentments toward national and racial preoccupations. Proclaiming the need for a new spirit and a new man, fascist demagogues have extolled action for its own sake and romanticized violence as regenerative and therapeutic. Although many of their ideas are a by-product of the Enlightenment, they vehemently reject egalitarian social theories that formed the basis of the French Revolution in 1789. The "anti" dimensions of fascism are manifold and well known: antidemocratic, anti-Marxist, anticapitalist, antimaterialist, anticosmopolitan, antibourgeois, antiliberal, antifeminist, and so on.

But fascism was always more than just a negative crusade. Its eclectic style incorporated elements of competing ideologies that fascist rhetoric ostensibly repudiated. Herein lay the essential paradox of fascism: its ability to embody social and political opposites, to be at once elitist and populist, traditionalist and avant-garde. ("I am a reactionary and a revolutionary," Mussolini boasted.) Within the fascist milieu, there has always been a nostalgia for preindustrial societies and an attraction to advanced technology, a pathos for uncontrolled brutality and a fetish for obedience and order. Promising to remedy the malaise and anomie of modern life, fascist leaders manipulated deep-seated longings for a better society. The skewed utopian impulse of fascism was the basis for part of its magnetism as a political movement, which appealed to all social strata — urban and rural, young and old, poor and wealthy, the intelligentsia and the uneducated.

The massive defeat they suffered during World War II did not refute the innermost convictions of many fascists, who kept pining for the day when they might again inflict their twisted dream of a new order on much of the world. Within the neofascist scene, there has always been a residual subculture of nostalgics who clung to the heritage of the Third Reich and the Mussolini regime. Holocaust-denial literature and other racialist screeds have circulated like political pornography among the deeply devoted who cluster in small marginalized groups and clandestine cells. Others showed more resiliency as they tried to adapt to the changing realities of the postwar era. But the East-West conflict, which initially afforded a means of survival for these ideological miscreants, also stranded many of them on the farther shores of politics. They realized that sooner or later the binary logjam of the Cold War would have to be broken for revisionist forms of fascism to take hold.

The more sophisticated tacticians understood that the fascist game could be played in many ways. Some deemed it best not to advertise their allegiance to the creed. Discarding the fascist appellation was an initial step toward articulating a political discourse more in tune with modern times, one that spoke of preserving identity and cultural uniqueness instead of white supremacy. Of necessity, a second coming of fascism would look quite different from the first. Pragmatic and opportunistic, neofascist leaders reinvented themselves and crafted euphemisms into electoral platforms that concealed an abiding hatred of the democratic process. Campaigning as national populists, they managed to rack up significant vote totals in several countries and redefine the post–Cold War political landscape.

This is the saga of an underground political movement that has reawakened after nearly half a century of hibernation. It is the history of something long hidden reappearing in a new form, a thing once forbidden that is gradually gaining influence and respectability. Most of all, it is a story about a cadre of old-guard fascists who kept the torch burning and bequeathed it to a younger generation of extremists who are carrying on the struggle today.

PART ONE

A SURFEIT OF SPIES

CHAPTER ONE

SHIFTING ALLIANCES

Scarface

Otto Skorzeny was a towering, 220-pound hulk with broad shoulders, slate gray eyes, and dark, springy hair atop a six-foot-five-inch frame. Born in Vienna in 1908, he had endured hard economic times as a youth, tasting butter for the first time when he was fifteen. He studied engineering at the University of Vienna, earning his degree in able fashion while frequenting the local fencing fraternities that attracted a tough, freewheeling crowd. Intense and fearless, he loved to fight duels with a schläger, a sharp-edged sword with a blunt tip. His lean, muscular body boasted fifteen scars, including a melodramatic sword slash that cut across the left side of his face from forehead to chin. Stitched on the spot without anesthesia, this disfiguring wound earned him the nickname "Scarface."

The swashbuckling Skorzeny was among the first to join the Austrian Nazi Party in the early 1930s. Restless and quick-tempered, he thrived in the political fast lane, winning a gold medal in Nazi-sponsored auto races. He became a prominent figure in the Vienna Gymnastics Club, a Nazi front organization that actively supported the *Anschluss,* whereby Austria merged with Germany. In hindsight, this union was a decisive step toward World War II. By 1938, Skorzeny was a member of both the Schutzstaffel (SS) and the Gestapo. That year, according to subsequent legal testimony, he participated in the infamous Kristallnacht pogrom in Vienna. It was a night of sheer terror throughout Hitler's Reich, as Jewish synagogues, shops, and homes burned to the ground; one hundred Jews were killed; and another thirty thousand were herded into concentration camps.[1]

With the onset of World War II, Skorzeny quit his engineering job and enlisted in the Waffen SS, the most ruthless of all the Nazi forces. Drawn from a cesspool of political fanaticism and honed into military athletes, the crack troops of the Waffen SS exterminated, plundered, and enslaved their way through Eastern Europe. Their unmatched sadism was the main reason why the Nuremberg tribunal condemned the SS in toto as a criminal organization after the war.

Functioning as the military arm of the black-shirted Schutzstaffel, most Waffen SS divisions consisted of volunteers from various ethnic groups in Europe. Other units, such as the one Skorzeny joined, were composed entirely of German conscripts. Trained as a munitions expert, Scarface soon got into trouble with his superiors because of insubordination and undisciplined conduct. He smoked cigarettes constantly and tended to be drunken and unruly, but his sheer physical prowess was such that higher-ups were inclined to overlook his erratic behavior. During the early part of the war, he saw duty in France, Holland, and Yugoslavia. "It was seldom that a friendly smile greeted us," Skorzeny remarked with disarming candor while posted in Belgrade.[2]

After the Germans invaded the Soviet Union, Skorzeny was sent to the eastern front, carrying among his supplies a copy of *The Seven Pillars of Wisdom* by T. E. Lawrence and plenty of schnapps. The Waffen SS and other Nazi units left a moonscape of massive devastation as they careened toward Moscow and Leningrad. For a while it seemed that the whole continent lay under Hitler's jackboot. But the Führer had erred in thinking he could destroy the USSR by using the same blitzkrieg tactics that subdued his enemies in the west. As the supply lines stretched thin and the Nazi armies stalled in subzero temperatures deep inside Russia, the Soviet Union's greater troop strength and industrial resources bore down heavily on Hitler's soldiers.

Toward the end of December 1942, as the Germans blasted away relentlessly at Stalingrad, Skorzeny was nearly killed by a fragment of a Russian artillery shell that hit the back of his head and knocked him unconscious. Although it was a serious injury, he refused any medication other than an aspirin and a shot of whiskey. A few days later, he was sent back to Germany with gallstones and an excruciating headache that would torment him intermittently in the years ahead.

After convalescing for a few months at an army hospital, Skorzeny craved a new assignment. He eagerly responded when Walter Schellenberg, head of the Sicherheitsdienst, or SD (the SS foreign intelligence service), summoned him to Berlin. Schellenberg ordered Skorzeny to organize a school where special agents would be taught sabotage, espionage, and paramilitary skills. One hundred and fifty candidates were put through a grueling series of physical and mental exercises until they were deemed fit to serve in an elite special commando unit called Jagdverbände (Hunting Group) 502, led by Skorzeny, who henceforth was nominally under Schellenberg's control. But Scarface often circumvented his boss and went directly to Hitler, who took a personal interest in Skorzeny's projects.

The Führer was particularly fond of Skorzeny, in part because both men were from Austria. Scarface recalled their first encounter at the Wolf's Lair in July 1943: "I lived through an unforgettable moment. Here was the man who, more than any other chief of state, had taken so decisive a hand in the destiny of Germany. Here was my master whom I had been following loyally for years. Here was my leader in whom I had absolute confidence."[3]

It was during this meeting that Hitler placed Skorzeny in charge of a mission-impossible operation to rescue Italian dictator Benito Mussolini, who had recently been deposed and arrested by the Italian government. The first challenge was to figure out where the Duce was being held. SS chief Heinrich Himmler's eccentric beliefs in the occult prompted him to seek Mussolini's whereabouts with the aid of black magic. Skorzeny tapped into more mundane channels, drawing upon a network of informants who determined that Mussolini was holed up at a remote ski resort in the Abruzzi mountains of central Italy, a bastion that was almost inaccessible.

Skorzeny wasn't supposed to accompany the gliderborne rescue team, because his large size could have put the entire mission at risk. But he insisted on being part of the action. On September 12, 1943, they swooped down upon the mountain stronghold, stormed the Hotel Camp Imperatore, where the Duce was incarcerated, and plucked him from captivity. With little time to spare, Mussolini and Skorzeny piled into a light reconnaissance plane. The pilot used the sudden, thousand-foot drop off the side of the mountain to gather speed. When it pulled out of the dive, the plane had barely cleared the trees below. An unshaven Mussolini turned white from vertigo. With tears streaming down his cheeks, the Duce proclaimed en route to a reunion with the Führer, "I knew my friend Adolf Hitler would not leave me in the lurch."[4]

Skorzeny would pull off other kidnapping missions, but none as spectacular as this one. A delighted Hitler festooned him with honors, including the prestigious Knight's Cross, for his role in the raid, which some say was greatly exaggerated. This did not matter to Propaganda Minister Joseph Goebbels, who was quick to exploit a truly amazing operation that outdid any fictional thriller. Goebbels realized that it had all the ingredients of a much-needed, morale-boosting legend to perk up the spirits of the increasingly demoralized German people. Catapulted instantly into the hagiography of the Third Reich, Skorzeny acquired an almost mythical reputation. He was revered as a Teutonic superman by those who pined for some secret-service miracle that might somehow alter the course of the war, which was not going well for Germany. A sympathetic biographer would later describe Skorzeny as "a buccaneer, a military highwayman — a spectacular trapeze artist upon whose lone brilliance Hitler had counted to pull the show together."[5]

Endgames

Adolf Hitler had hoped that the rescue of Mussolini would reinvigorate fascist military energy and galvanize his combat-weary soldiers. But realists in the Führer's inner circle knew the war effort was doomed ever since Germany's monumental setback at the Battle of Stalingrad in January 1943. The avowed purpose of Operation Barbarossa, as the drive to the east was called, had been to gain more lebensraum for Hitler's master race. But as the military tide turned against Germany, Nazi officials began to talk less about living space and more about defending Western civilization against "the Asiatic-Mongol peril." Saving Europe from the Bolshevik horde became the focus of a new disinformation campaign emanating from Joseph Goebbels's indefatigable Propaganda Ministry.

While Hitler still ranted of a thousand-year Reich, top-level Nazis quietly began preparing for their impending defeat. They devised a strategy based on the premise that relations between the Allies were politically tenuous and the antifascist coalition — an unlikely combination linking Communist East and capitalist West — would not hold together for long. Nazi operatives sought to exploit this weakness by sowing distrust between the Soviet Union and the United States.

With German infantrymen hopelessly mired in the mud and snow of the Russian steppes, high-ranking Nazi officials began sending peace feelers to the Office of Strategic Services (OSS), the CIA's wartime predecessor. Most of these efforts were launched by Skorzeny's boss, Walter Schellenberg, in consultation with SS chief Himmler. At various times the Vatican helped to facilitate a secret dialogue between the Germans and the Americans. The Iberian dictators — Franco in Spain and Salazar in Portugal — also offered to serve as intermediaries. While these initiatives took place behind Hitler's back, it is by no means clear that they all took place against his wishes.

The main contact for disillusioned Axis officials who wanted to communicate discreetely with the West was Allen Dulles, the tweedy, pipe-smoking, corporate-attorney-turned-spook who ran the OSS station in neutral Switzerland, the most important U.S. intelligence outpost in Europe during the war.[6] Dulles brought his knowledge of international finance and his prior experience as a diplomat with him when he set up his spy nest in Bern. The first signal from Schellenberg (who also happened to be a director of ITT's German subsidiary) came in December 1942, just when German troops were faltering on the Russian front. Schellenberg dispatched Prince Max von Hohenlohe, a Prussian aristocrat and businessman, to Bern to see whether a rapprochement with the United States was possible. Such a reconciliation, Schellenberg suggested through his envoy, would enable Germany to concentrate its undivided attention on pulverizing the Soviets. In subsequent cables to OSS headquarters in Washington, Dulles weighed in strongly on behalf of Schellenberg's proposal, warning that if the United States dropped the ball, there were "powerful elements" among the Nazis who "are prepared to cast their lot with Russia."[7]

Schellenberg later acknowledged in his memoirs that he had been playing a double game with the United States and the Soviet Union in an attempt to exacerbate antagonism between East and West to the point where the anti-Nazi alliance would collapse. "It was important therefore," he wrote, "to make contact with Russia at the same time we initiated our negotiations with the West. An increasing rivalry between the Allied Powers would strengthen our position."[8]

Thus, while Prince Hohenlohe and other furtive emissaries parried with Dulles, Nazi spies also reached out to their Soviet counterparts and alerted them to secret deals brewing behind their back. Schellenberg's objective was to play on Joseph Stalin's doubts about the fidelity of his Western allies and convince him that the Americans were conniving with Germany.

The Soviets responded to Schellenberg's overtures by establishing a clandestine channel with the Nazis in Stockholm. Hinting that a second wartime reconciliation with Berlin was not out of the question, Stalin also gave his blessing to a free-Germany committee in Moscow led by German commander Friedrich von Paulus, who had been taken captive after he surrendered the Sixth Army at Stalingrad.[9]

The Nazis' covert strategy was summed up in a March 15, 1944, directive issued by Admiral Wilhelm Canaris, chief of the Abwehr (German military intelligence):

> *We must do our utmost to create a state of confusion and distrust among our enemies. . . . Such a state of disunity would enable us to sue for a quick separate peace with either side. . . . [N]o effort should be spared to stir up, through carefully directed propaganda, political animosity inside the Anglo-Saxon countries which would enrage the Soviets to such a degree that, as a consequence, they would welcome a chance to conclude a separate peace with Germany. . . . Right*

> *now, the chances for a separate peace with the West are a little better, especially if we succeed, through our propaganda campaign and our "confidential" channels, to convince the enemy that Roosevelt's policy of "unconditional surrender" drives the German people towards Communism. . . . We must point to the danger that Germany may be forced to cooperate with Russia.*

Canaris concluded by urging that the "greatest caution had to be observed in all talks and negotiations by those who, as 'anti-Nazis,' maintain contact with the enemy."[10]

In an effort to bail out of Hitler's war, various segments of the German military, the SS, and the business elite were working along similar lines. They often found themselves using the same murky pathways, the same go-betweens, the same Allied agents; and they always got the same ultimatum: Hitler must go. Although Himmler had flirted with the idea, he couldn't muster the courage to strike against the Führer. But others tried. After the generals' plot of July 1944 fizzled, the SS moved swiftly against its rivals. In the purge that followed, the SS seized all power, Admiral Canaris was executed, and the Nazi hierarchy was restructured — with Schellenberg emerging as the supreme head of the Third Reich's intelligence apparatus. Henceforth, Skorzeny would work for Amt VI (Department 6) of the SS Reich Security Office, which was responsible for foreign intelligence, sabotage, paramilitary operations, and propaganda. It was, in effect, the CIA of Nazi Germany.

On August 10, 1944, twenty days after the abortive coup attempt, sixty-seven prominent German industrialists — including leaders of Messerschmitt, Krupp, Volkswagenwerk, and other major companies — gathered at the Hotel Maison Rouge in Strasbourg. During this top-secret conclave, they made preparations "for the economic campaign which will follow the end of the war," according to the minutes of the meeting, which were subsequently discovered by the U.S. Army Counterintelligence Corps. Conference records indicate that the participants had agreed to shift a prodigious amount of Nazi loot to neutral countries. Some Nazi firms would be relicensed outside Germany in order to dodge reparations claims, the minutes noted, "so that after the defeat a strong, new Reich can be built."[11]

A pivotal figure in the expatriation scheme was the illustrious SS fix-it man, Scarface Skorzeny, who organized the physical transfer of Nazi loot to hiding places abroad. During the waning days of the war, a group of masked SS brigands, led by SS Brigadier General Josef Spacil, held up the Reichsbank in Berlin, removing at gunpoint jewels, securities, and foreign-exchange assets valued at a total of 23 million marks. It was at that time the biggest robbery in history. Spacil passed the booty to Karl Radl, Skorzeny's adjutant. Assisted by a handful of SS officers, Skorzeny is said to have buried the Reichsbank treasure in the Austrian Alps. Most of this money has never been accounted for, giving rise to speculation that Skorzeny may have recovered some of the hidden wealth and used it to finance his postwar Nazi activities.[12]

With the Third Reich on the verge of collapse, Skorzeny found himself serenaded by a number of financiers and top SS officers who wanted to hide personal fortunes they had accumulated. Doing favors for Germany's richest men was just the kind of assignment relished by Skorzeny, who cut himself in for a share of whatever he moved. In an effort to camouflage the contraband operation, Skorzeny used Red Cross ambulances to transport gold, jewelry, and cash through southern Germany.

By September 1944, there were several confirmed reports that German submarines were taking both people and plundered capital from Spain to South America. Self-confessed Nazi spy Angel Alcazar de Velasco later acknowledged that several hundred million pounds of gold and other assets had passed through ports on the southern coast of Spain en route to Argentina. Additional gold shipments were disseminated through the German Foreign Office to its embassies in Lisbon, Madrid, Stockholm, Ankara, and Bern.[13]

During this period, Skorzeny was perpetually in motion, an all-purpose marauder commandeering special operations in Denmark, Belgium, and Hungary. He also conducted several clandestine missions behind enemy lines on the Russian front. In this capacity he worked closely with another Nazi espionage whiz, General Reinhard Gehlen.

As chief of the Foreign Armies East, Gehlen was responsible for all of Germany's military-intelligence capabilities throughout Eastern Europe and the Soviet Union. He was, in effect, Hitler's top anti-Soviet spy. Hailing from a family of Prussian aristocrats, the thin, bespectacled espionage prodigy had a hand in the details of virtually every Wehrmacht campaign in the East, despite his doubts about the wisdom of invading the Soviet Union. Highly professional and respectful of rank, he did whatever he was asked to do, often signing his wartime memoranda, "Your obedient servant, Gehlen."[14]

Although enmity between the officers of the German General Staff and the SS ran strong and deep, Skorzeny respected the superior quality of Gehlen's intelligence work. They were an odd combo, to be sure. Skorzeny, the insatiable publicity hound with massive shoulders and a barking voice, epitomized raw physical power as he towered over the smaller Gehlen, who eschewed the spotlight at all costs. A stiff, unassuming man of five foot seven, he had sparse blond hair, a toothbrush mustache, and huge ears that flared from his head like radar dishes. There was, one historian has remarked, "a rodent-like scurry and quickness to everything Gehlen attempted, accentuated by crimped, sharp features and an all-seeing personality." This mousy, little Junker would figure prominently in Skorzeny's postwar Nazi machinations.[15]

Scarface Skorzeny first appeared at General Gehlen's side late in 1944, when both were involved in planning resistance operations in the Soviet rear. Some of these raids were designed to sabotage key roadways and cut off Russian communications, others sought to rescue German soldiers who had been abandoned deep inside the Soviet Union when the Nazi armies retreated. Skorzeny's special-service troops were also instructed to link up with anti-Communist partisans identified by Gehlen, who had amassed a formidable array of contacts among Eastern European fascist groups. The Romanian Iron Guard, the Vanagis of Latvia, the Croatian Ustaše, the Organization of Ukrainian Nationalists, Polish quislings, and an army of Russian defectors led by General Andrei Vlasov — all were pieces of a giant intelligence jigsaw puzzle that Gehlen played with incessantly in his head. This network of Nazi collaborators formed the basis of an anti-Communist espionage apparatus that Gehlen would carry into the postwar era.

With the military situation rapidly deteriorating, the existence of clandestine guerrilla squads operating in enemy territory gave rise to the idea of forming similar units that would make a last-ditch stand inside Germany itself. Composed primarily of Hitler Youth and die-hard Nazi fanatics, these "stay behind" teams were supposed to fight on indefinitely, harassing, sabotaging, and snooping on the Fatherland's invaders. Skorzeny and Gehlen were ordered to train and equip what became known as the Werewolves. The name itself was a product of Goebbels's macabre imagination, which drew upon medieval lore about a person who became a ferocious man-eating wolf at night and reverted to human form at sunrise. That's how the Nazi "stay behind" fighters were supposed to operate — as normal citizens by day, but meting out death and destruction to their enemies under the cover of darkness. Organized in five-man cells, Werewolf units had access to buried depots of food, radio equipment, weapons, explosives, and other liquidation devices. They were expected to lie low for a year or two before launching into action.

Evidence of a postwar Nazi underground's taking shape was picked up by various U.S. intelligence sources. The U.S. Army Counterintelligence Corps prepared a detailed report, based largely on OSS fieldwork, that forecast what American troops could expect in the closing phase of the war: "The enemy secret intelligence services, security and secret police, and paramilitary organizations are believed to have made elaborate plans for progressively going underground as our forces advance. It is believed that the basic policy of the organized underground is of long-range character. In the later stages, guerrilla warfare and sporadic resistance . . . will probably be forthcoming to a much greater degree from resistance groups and fanatical individuals."[16]

Reports filtered in that Otto Skorzeny was broadcasting urgent appeals to the German people to join the resistance against the Allied presence. This only served to underscore concerns on the part of U.S. military strategists, who were anticipating a bitter-end stand by the Nazis in a well-fortified hideaway in the heart of the Austrian Alps. It was thought that there, behind snowy mountain walls, in near-impenetrable caverns, ravines, and tunnels, Hitler's faithful might hold out for years. An April 1945 OSS memo pegged Scarface as the key figure in this operation: "Otto Skorzeny, with the special units he trained, appears to be the most likely head of sabotage and subversive activities planned for the Alpine Redoubt."[17]

But the much-feared climactic showdown in the Alps was never to be. Skorzeny, it seems, did not intend to go out in a blaze of Wagnerian glory on some forsaken mountaintop. He had other plans in mind when he selected the "stay behind" teams. Under his tutelage, they formed the nucleus of a committed, postwar Nazi underground. Werewolf personnel would be instrumental in facilitating travel along "ratlines" and escape routes that enabled tens of thousands of SS officers and other Nazis to flee to safe locations after the Third Reich bit the dust.[18]

Allen Dulles, meanwhile, continued to entertain a procession of Nazi raconteurs bearing misleading gifts. One of those who primed his pump was the wily SS Lieutenant Colonel Wilhelm ("Willi") Höttl, who later acknowledged that he had hyped rumors of an impending bitter-end battle in the icy highlands. "Phony blueprints were drawn up and intelligence was leaked to the Americans, who seemed to be most prepared to believe such a romantic military plot," Höttl recounted. The SS disinformation specialist spiced his offerings with "intelligence information, not about Germany . . . but about what we had found out about the Russians."[19] Passing along anti-Soviet scuttlebutt to the OSS was a gesture calculated to smooth the way for a larger understanding between the Western Allies and the Axis, one that harkened of a combined effort against the Communists in the years ahead.[20]

Not surprisingly, Stalin was livid when he learned through his espionage contacts that Dulles was trying to cut a last-minute deal with certain high-level Nazis. He accused the Americans of acting in bad faith. President Roosevelt quickly protested the Soviet dictator's "vile misrepresentation," but as British prime minister Winston Churchill admitted privately, Stalin's complaint was not entirely off the mark. The acrimonious exchange between Stalin and FDR occurred shortly before Roosevelt died of a stroke on April 12, 1945. Although both men had wanted East-West cooperation to continue during peacetime, Nazi double-dealing succeeded in fomenting discord between the emerging superpowers and hastening the split in their ranks.[21]

SS General Karl Wolff, one of Dulles's secret negotiating partners, confirmed this was the Nazis' intention all along. Detained briefly at the end of the war, Wolff shared his vision of the future with two SS subordinates: "We'll get our Reich back again. The others will begin to fight amongst themselves eventually and then we'll be in the middle and can play one against the other." [22]

Otto Skorzeny had similar thoughts as he pondered his long-range opportunities. Going into hiding under an assumed name wasn't a viable option, given his notoriety. He figured it would be wiser to surrender to the Americans and offer himself as someone who could make a vital contribution in the forthcoming struggle against the Communists. On May 16, 1945, he emerged from the woods with a small group of German soldiers and strutted into the command post of the U.S. Thirtieth Infantry Regiment near Salzburg, Austria. Standing head and shoulders above the rest, Skorzeny presented himself to a startled American lieutenant. The scarfaced giant wore a paratrooper's uniform, sidearms, and numerous decorations, including the Knight's Cross, one of the highest Nazi military awards. Speaking in German, he made a perfunctory declaration: "SS *Obersturmbannführer* Otto Skorzeny constituting himself as a prisoner of war."

Skorzeny's well-informed colleague, General Reinhard Gehlen, was also convinced that the United States and the Soviet Union would soon be at loggerheads. Realizing that none of the Western Allies had a viable intelligence network functioning in Eastern Europe, the Prussian spymaster crafted a plan to keep his experienced staff together and to maintain as much as possible the clandestine cells, radio posts, and guerrilla groups that he and Skorzeny had nurtured in the East. While serving under Hitler, Gehlen had accumulated a vast archive on the Soviet Union, its army, its espionage organizations, its industrial and human resources. He microfilmed as much data as he could, making triplicate copies of the most important material. Shortly before he turned himself in, Skorzeny helped bury Gehlen's top-secret files at three different locations in the Bavarian mountains, not far from where Hitler's ace commando had stashed gold and other documents. All this material would enhance Gehlen's bargaining power with the Americans, who lacked precisely the espionage capacity that he could provide.

During the final days of the war, Gehlen retreated to a scenic hideaway called Misery Meadow in the Bavarian Alps. His attitude at the time was summed up by the motto above his bed: Never give up. Soon he was apprehended by an American search party and interned at a POW camp in Wiesbaden, where he had a chance encounter with Grand Admiral Karl Doenitz, Hitler's formally designated successor as head of the German state. A stickler for protocol, Gehlen wanted to clear his plans with the highest authority. He told Doenitz of his idea to strike a deal with the United States. Doenitz gave his blessing to Gehlen, even though the Grand Admiral had recently encouraged other Nazis to cooperate with the Russians. "What is important," Doenitz stated in his farewell address to the Nazi Officer Corps, "is that we maintain at the highest level the comradeship amongst us. Only through this unity will it be possible for us to master the coming difficult times. . . . Let us use all our strength for Germany!"[23]

A Critical Hiatus

In February 1945, the leaders of the Big Three — the United States, Great Britain, and the Soviet Union — met at Yalta, a pleasant Black Sea resort town. Broad spheres of influence were agreed upon, as they redrew the map of Europe in anticipation of the defeat of Germany. According to legend, it was here that Winston Churchill decided the fate of postwar Poland with three matchsticks, using them to show Stalin how the border would be shifted when the fighting ceased. The eastern boundary of Germany would move westward to the Oder and Neisse Rivers, and part of eastern Poland would become Russia. But Churchill also warned, "One day the Germans would want their territory back, and the Poles would not be able to stop them."[24]

This simple trick with matches sent millions of refugees fleeing to new lands after the war. Large numbers of ethnic Germans would be thrown out of their homes and forcibly deported from Poland, Czechoslovakia, and other parts of Europe; many were mistreated or murdered in the process. What remained of Germany was divided into four zones of occupation, which would be administered by a council of military governors from the Big Three plus France. One of the Allied Control Council's first directives was an edict banning the Nazi Party. But the Allies could agree on little else between 1945 and 1949, during which time there was no longer a legal German state and not yet two.

At the beginning of this critical hiatus, Germany was a country unraveled, a bombed-out disaster area enveloped by a dazed silence and the stench of death. Into this surreal landscape marched the triumphant Allied armies. The U.S. military immediately dispatched teams of specialists to sweep across Germany, searching for any scrap of industrial material and scientific data that could be garnered from the smoking carcass of the Third Reich. The Soviet Union, France, and Britain were also eager to profit from German technical know-how, and a mad scramble ensued among the Allies to exploit the talents of German scientists.[25]

While the victors feasted on the spoils of war, the majority of Germans withdrew into a cocoon of sullen compliance. They became a nation of bowed heads, begrudgingly submitting to their conquerors. Although they had no choice but to admit defeat, most showed little remorse for the crimes of the Third Reich. The deleterious impact of thirteen years of Hitlerism on Germany's moral conscience would not be easily undone.[26]

The discovery of the concentration camps toward the end of the war strengthened the case of those who argued that little mercy should be shown the Germans. The scope of Nazi cruelty was so enormous, its technical refinements so obscene and systematic, that the Allies came to realize, in the words of the United Nations War Crimes Commission, that "many of the criminal acts perpetrated by the enemy . . . were of an altogether novel nature." Accordingly, the Big Three vowed to break up the German industrial cartels, decapitate the General Staff, and bring the war criminals to justice even if it meant tracking them "to the uttermost ends of the earth."[27]

Of course, not every Nazi was a true believer. Some had been forced to join the Nazi Party lest they risk losing their jobs, while others, the so-called small Nazis, had voted for Hitler during an economic crunch, hoping to improve their lot; they did not envision the impending tragedy that they helped set in motion. But there was also a significant number of hard-core Nazis on the loose after the war. They were the prime targets of the U.S. Army Counterintelligence Corps (CIC) units that fanned out across the American zone of occupation in southern Germany. The most pressing concern at the outset was rounding up the ideologically committed Nazis who had been marked for automatic detention. The CIC apprehended a total of 120,000 individuals who fell into this category — mainly SS and Gestapo members, high-ranking military officers, and some government officials. Those considered to be dangerous were kept in confinement and interrogated by U.S. specialists.

Such was the case with SS Colonel Otto Skorzeny, who created quite a stir when he gave himself up to the Americans. Scarface was immediately handcuffed and driven to Salzburg for questioning by two CIC officers. Confident and loquacious, he emphasized how eager he was to carry on the fight against the USSR, boasting that he knew a great deal about Soviet industrial sites in the Urals. Skorzeny also spoke of his contacts with Ukrainian anti-Communists itching for an insurrection inside the Soviet Union. A preliminary CIC report sized up Scarface as follows: "Despite the short time allotted for the interrogation of Skorzeny, these Agents believe that he is sincere in his desire to give all possible information. . . . Skorzeny seriously considers the eventuality of a Western bloc against communism. This consideration certainly was primordial in his voluntary surrender in the hope that he might be given an active part in this undertaking. Due to his Austrian ancestry, he is clear-minded and pliable but politically short-sighted to the point of naïveté."[28]

Events would later prove that the two CIC rookies were politically naive, not the man they debriefed. As soon as the initial interrogation had concluded, Skorzeny was besieged by journalists who rushed to Salzburg upon hearing that Hitler's legendary commando had been captured. An impromptu press conference generated international publicity. The *New York Times* described Skorzeny as "handsome despite the scar that stretched from ear to chin." To the *Christian Science Monitor*, he had "an aggressive personality to go with his physical equipment and a mind adapted to subversive activity." The *Daily News* declared: "He was a true Nazi throughout. He walked with his head high — and with a flock of American soldiers wishing he would make just one dash for freedom."[29]

A few days later, Skorzeny was driven by jeep to the Twelfth

Army Group Interrogation Center in Augsburg for another lengthy question-and-answer session. He maintained an upbeat demeanor while chatting about paramilitary training, the latest sabotage techniques, and other areas of expertise. But he never said a word about any of the gold and stolen loot he had stashed away. Overall, a CIC document noted, Skorzeny tried "to paint himself as a military rather than a political figure." Various U.S. Army intelligence reports fleshed out his profile: "oval round face," "large mouth with thin lips," "clean shaven," "Herculean build," "large, strong hands," "musical voice," "energetic." Another CIC memo characterized him as an "arrogant type" who "walks as if he is fully conscious of his own importance and drinks enough for four men."[30]

In September 1945, Skorzeny was escorted to Nuremberg, where the war crimes trials were about to begin. There he was reunited with several members of Hitler's cabinet. Some felt that Skorzeny should have walked the scaffold along with the upper echelon of the Nazi regime, but he merely watched from the sidelines as twelve of the top leaders of the Third Reich were condemned to death; seven other defendants received prison sentences, and three were acquitted. The Nuremberg verdicts reinforced what most Americans believed — that World War II was a good fight for a noble cause, and those who had committed heinous acts would get the punishment they deserved. Intrinsic to America's sense of national identity was the comforting myth that the United States wholeheartedly opposed everything the Nazis stood for.

But even before the Nuremberg proceedings began, U.S. officials had already begun to waver on their commitment to denazify. The determination to mince up the conglomerates and punish the German industrialists quickly faded as American attention shifted to the imagined Red Menace, within and without. As Christopher Simpson and others have documented, U.S. policy toward Germany was heavily influenced by investment bankers who had close ties to Hitler's Reich prior to the war. By the summer of 1945, these financial interests concluded that a full-fledged denazification and decartelization of the German economy would not be attempted, despite what was said for public consumption.[31]

The Allies had originally planned to hold a second tribunal at Nuremberg that would have focused on crimes by German industrialists, but the United States abruptly canceled the proceedings. According to U.S. War Department chief Robert Patterson, American officials were not going to let the Russians cross-examine bankers and industrialists "in view of the many connections between the German and American economies before the war." Rather than participating in potentially embarrassing international prosecutions, the United States opted to try German business leaders and other accused war criminals separately in the American zone of occupation. Before long, however, these legal proceedings also came to an abrupt halt.[32]

American backpedaling on denazification ensured that the captains of German industry, many of whom had personally profited from the horrific exploitation of concentration camp prisoners, would survive the fall of the Third Reich without losing much of their status or prestige. Soon the United States launched the Marshall Plan in an effort to pump up the economies of Western Europe. The idea that a strong and prosperous Germany would serve as a bulwark against Communism was a major reason why it initially obtained more Marshall Plan funds than any other country. Helping to steer the cash flow was the deeply compromised Deutsche Bank director Hermann Abs, who had been marked for prosecution as a war criminal by the Allies until round two of Nuremberg was nixed.[33]

Germany's much ballyhooed postwar "economic miracle" was largely the result of American largesse. But the rehab program also had a distinct downside: by concentrating wealth among the few, it accentuated antidemocratic and inegalitarian trends in German society that favored ex-Nazis with chummy connections to Wall Street. The real miracle would have been a truly denazified Germany, but that wasn't about to happen while numerous Third Reich veterans got away with lenient treatment from U.S. officials and their Western allies.

Among those who stood trial in the American zone of occupation was Otto Skorzeny. Hitler's favorite commando faced war crimes charges for his activities during the Battle of the Bulge in December 1944, when Germany launched a last, desperate counterattack in the Ardennes on the western front. The Führer had chosen Skorzeny to lead a special mission involving German saboteurs attired in U.S. Army uniforms who infiltrated behind enemy lines and wreaked all sorts of havoc. (Some of Skorzeny's agents posed as American military police and misdirected Allied traffic.) Amid the confusion, on a cold winter night the SS summarily executed seventy-one captured American soldiers in what became known as the Malmédy massacre.

The activities of Skorzeny's deception units triggered rampant speculation and amplified the uncertainty of the moment just when U.S. forces were suffering heavy losses as a result of the surprise German offensive. Skorzeny's reputation was such that Allied military brass thought him capable of nearly any undertaking, no matter how outrageous. At one point, U.S. intelligence got wind of rumors that Skorzeny's men were on their way to Paris to assassinate General Dwight D. Eisenhower, the Supreme Allied Commander. Eisenhower was not amused when he had to spend his 1944 Christmas isolated for security reasons to prevent a kidnapping attempt, while a look-alike served as a decoy double just in case the plot was for real.

Eisenhower retaliated by ordering a no-holds-barred manhunt to capture the Nazi paladin who was allegedly menacing him. "Wanted" posters, like those used by the FBI, were distributed throughout the western-front combat zone, featuring a photograph of Skorzeny with a detailed physical description and a warning: "This man is extremely clever and very dangerous. He may be in American or British uniform or civilian clothes. . . . Any information concerning this man should be furnished to the nearest G-2 [army intelligence] office right away."

"Wanted" poster of Otto Skorzeny distributed throughout Europe by the Allies

At Skorzeny's arraignment before a U.S. military court at Dachau, the chief prosecutor called him "the most dangerous man in Europe." Nevertheless, in September 1947 he was acquitted of illegal actions during the Battle of the Bulge after a British officer testified that Skorzeny had done nothing that his Allied counterparts had not themselves considered or attempted. Despite the Dachau verdict, Hitler's ace commando made a lasting impression on Eisenhower, who, as president of the United States, kept a photo of Skorzeny in his White House office.

Gehlen's Gambit

While Skorzeny stewed in internment camps for more than three years, his once and future collaborator, General Reinhard Gehlen, made the Americans an offer they couldn't refuse. Gehlen told his U.S. debriefers about the vast espionage archive on the USSR that lay buried in the mountains. Not only did he know where the spy treasure was hidden, he assured his interlocutors, but if necessary he could activate an underground network of battle-hardened anti-Communists who were well placed to make mischief throughout much of Eastern Europe and the Soviet Union.[34]

The ink had barely dried on the Yalta agreements (which required the United States to give the Soviets any captured German officers who had been involved in "eastern area activities") when Gehlen and three of his top assistants were at Fort Hunt, Virginia, wining and dining with U.S. officials, whose appetite for Cold War gossip had fast become gluttonous. The flop-eared Prussian general played their psyches like piano keys, with a pitch so seductively anti-Soviet that competing elements in the U.S. espionage establishment fought over who would get to work with him.

Among his chief negotiating partners in the United States was the ubiquitous Allen Dulles, who maintained that it was incumbent upon the United States to counter Soviet aggression in Europe. But American intelligence, by and large a wartime improvisation, was ill-prepared to wage a clandestine campaign against the USSR. Hence the need for Gehlen, who promised to fill a gaping hole in

America's espionage apparatus — a hole that had gotten even wider when the OSS was disbanded, ironically enough, on September 20, 1945, the same day the Prussian spy chief arrived in the United States.

Throughout his ten-month stay at Fort Hunt, Gehlen cultivated a fastidious professional image, passing himself off as the pure technician who liked nothing better than to immerse himself in maps, flowcharts, and statistics. The persona he projected was in crucial respects false; it was, to use a bit of espionage parlance, a "legend" — one that hinged on Gehlen's claim that he was dedicated above all to fighting Communism.

Gehlen's defenders in the United States noted that his bleak intelligence reports from the eastern front had made Hitler so angry that he dismissed his chief anti-Soviet spy during the final weeks of the war. To some, this showed that Gehlen was neither an ardent Nazi nor a war criminal. But Gehlen, like most German army officers, had welcomed the Nazi seizure of power. During the war, he oversaw a brutal interrogation program of Soviet prisoners and maintained close relations with the German General Staff. Significantly, Gehlen was not targeted for retribution by SS fanatics after the July 20 putsch failed. Upon examining Gehlen's wartime record, British historian Hugh Trevor-Roper has concluded that Gehlen was "certainly a Nazi in his mental structure and it is clear from his memoirs that his only objection to Hitler was that he lost the war."[35]

Gehlen's side may have taken a beating on the battlefield, but it appears that he did quite well at Fort Hunt. American negotiators agreed to virtually all his conditions for a German espionage organization that would operate under his leadership while receiving directives and assignments from U.S. officials. The purpose of this American-financed spy network was to continue information-gathering in the East just as Gehlen had been doing before. Having promised not to enlist unrepentant Nazis, Gehlen was free to select his own agents, who would be released from POW and internment camps, if necessary, to work for him.

The arrangement brokered at Fort Hunt had major implications for the future of U.S.-Soviet relations. "From that moment on," wrote historian Carl Oglesby, "from the summer of 1945 when the Army brought [Gehlen] into the United States and made a secret deal with him, the Cold War was locked in." Also at stake was the fate of tens of thousands of Third Reich veterans who puffed their anti-Communist credentials in order to please the Americans. Instead of destroying the Nazi infrastructure as promised, U.S. policy makers opted to retain a crucial part of it for use against the Soviet Union. Functioning as America's secret eyes and ears in central Europe, Gehlen's spies would work initially for army intelligence and then for the CIA, which was founded in 1947. In this capacity, and later as head of the West German secret service, Gehlen was able to exert considerable influence on U.S. policy toward the Soviet bloc.[36]

With Germany looming as a pivotal battleground of the Cold War, Gehlen had a mandate from the Americans to revive his old Foreign Armies East department — or what was left of it — as quickly as possible. Upon returning to Germany in July 1946, he immediately pulled together the makings of a sophisticated espionage apparatus known as "the Org." Supported by regular subsidies from U.S. taxpayers and wealthy German industrialists, he set up his base of operations inside a mysterious, high-walled compound near Munich that had once housed the staff of Rudolf Hess and Martin Bormann, Hitler's deputies. Gehlen's most urgent task was to gather up-to-date information from the East. His American sponsors were particularly hungry for details on troop movements and other military matters in the Soviet zone of occupation in Germany.

Although Gehlen was ostensibly under U.S. Army supervision, the Org quickly threw its doors wide open to Gestapo, Wehrmacht, and SS veterans, despite his solemn promise to U.S. officials that he would not employ hard-core Nazis. Even the vilest of the vile — the senior bureaucrats who ran the central administrative apparatus of the Holocaust — were welcome in the Org. "It seems," the *Frankfurter Rundschau* editorialized, "that in the Gehlen headquarters one SS man paved the way for the next and Himmler's elite were having happy reunion ceremonies."[37]

While Gehlen busily enlisted unrepentant Nazis, some U.S. Army Counterintelligence Corps agents were still trying to bust as many Hitlerites as they could get their hands on. Under the auspices of Operation Nursery, the CIC infiltrated an array of subversive groups that clung to the National Socialist creed. The schizoid quality of the U.S. occupation policy became evident to Nikolaus J.

Ryschkowsky, a Nazi hunter from CIC Unit 7970, when he tried to apprehend a circle of black marketeers in Munich, only to learn they had immunity. "I wasn't able to arrest them because they were working for Herr Gehlen," Ryschkowsky recounted. "It was hard to feel good about this."[38]

By 1947, there had officially been "a change in emphasis," according to a once-classified CIC report, "from the denazification mission to the collection of positive intelligence" — which meant that anti-Communism rather than Nazi hunting was now the guiding principle of CIC policy. To the extent that CIC operatives continued to chase after Nazis, it was usually not to capture them but to recruit them. American officials knew that many of the people they were hiring had committed horrible crimes against humanity, but atrocities were overlooked as the anti-Communist crusade acquired its own momentum. Ironically, some of the Nazis who worked for American intelligence would later play significant roles in neofascist organizations that agitated vociferously against the United States.[39]

At least half a dozen U.S. Army programs — with colorful code names such as Pajamas, Dwindle, Birchwood, and Apple Pie — were devoted to exploiting the nefarious skills of former SS and Gestapo members. Klaus Barbie, the infamous "Butcher of Lyon," did double duty as a CIC informant while also snooping for the Gehlen Org. So did many of Barbie's comrades.[40]

The growing dependence on Gehlen's network for data about Soviet forces and armament turned American spy agencies into sitting ducks for disinformation. Much of what Gehlen passed along was tailored to whip up fears about Russian military intentions. At one point, he succeeded in convincing General Lucius Clay, the military governor of the U.S. zone of occupation, that a major Soviet war mobilization was in progress in Eastern Europe. This prompted Clay to dash off a top-secret telegram to Washington in March 1948, warning that war "may come with dramatic suddenness."[41]

Although it proved to be a false alarm, Gehlen continued to dispense tainted information to his avid American patrons, who needed little prodding to think the worst of Russian ambitions. By consistently exaggerating the Soviet threat, the Nazi spymaster played a significant role in exacerbating tensions between the superpowers and fostering paranoia in the West about a world Communist conspiracy. "The Agency loved Gehlen because he fed us what we wanted to hear," a former CIA officer admitted. "We used his stuff constantly, and we fed it to everybody else — the Pentagon, the White House, the newspapers. They loved it, too. But it was hyped up Russian bogeyman junk, and it did a lot of damage to this country."[42]

Was Gehlen merely improvising as he fabricated dire reports about Red Army machinations? Or was this part of a conscious effort to bind U.S. foreign policy to the Cold War for his own purposes? Gehlen's strategy was based on a rudimentary equation — the colder the Cold War got, the more political space for Hitler's heirs to maneuver. He realized that the Org could flourish only under Cold War conditions; as an institution it was therefore committed to perpetuating the Soviet-American conflict. As Hugh Trevor-Roper has said of Gehlen: "He lived on the primacy of the Cold War and on the favor of those American and German governments which believed in the primacy of the Cold War."[43]

There were plenty of true believers in the CIA, which was given the green light to engage in political action, propaganda, and paramilitary operations that relied heavily on the services of Gehlen and his "spooky Nazi outfit," as one U.S. agent described it.[44] The Org already employed four thousand Germans when it was bolted lock, stock, and barrel into the CIA in 1949. This was during the peak of the "Chicken Little" era of American espionage, when the sky was always on the verge of falling, or so it seemed. The Agency began shelling out what amounted to $200 million (some of it siphoned from the Marshall Plan kitty) to satisfy the Org's voracious, covert appetite. At times, Gehlen's skewed reports were simply retyped onto CIA stationery with little alteration and integrated directly into President Harry Truman's morning intelligence briefing.[45]

Gehlen's biggest booster at the CIA was Allen Dulles, who started running off-the-shelf intelligence activities in Eastern Europe from the office of his Wall Street law firm before he formally joined the Agency in 1950. Three years later he became CIA director, a position he held until shortly after the disastrous Bay of Pigs invasion in 1961. Throughout this period, Dulles played godfather to Gehlen, protecting him from detractors who suspected that something was amiss at the Org, which served as a kind of subcontracting syndicate for harebrained CIA rollback schemes, guerrilla airdrops, and other ill-fated covert attempts to topple Communist regimes in Eastern Europe. In addition to providing plausible deniability, Gehlen had access to former leaders of virtually every Nazi puppet government from the Baltics to the Black Sea, as well as an assortment of Waffen SS fanatics who joined the American-led campaign to "liberate" their native lands. "It was a visceral business of using any bastard as long as he was anti-Communist," explained Harry Rositzke, ex-head of CIA operations in the Soviet Union. "The eagerness to enlist collaborators meant that you didn't look at their credentials too closely."[46]

In the wake of successive paramilitary fiascos in Eastern Europe, some CIA officers wondered if Soviet agents had infiltrated the Org. Clearly Gehlen was a political hot potato. A conflict raged within U.S. intelligence as to what advantages the United States had in fact accrued by supporting a shadowy spy network run by a moody ex-Nazi officer. The CIA's James Critchfield, who worked with Gehlen on a daily basis for nearly eight years, recalled that "hundreds of flaps . . . kept breaking out between the [Org] and elements of the occupation." Suspicions were such that the CIA and the army both began spying on the Org. Born of concern that U.S. intelligence lacked effective control over its surrogate, Operation Campus became the designated code name for a secret army investigation into Gehlen's activities.[47]

American army sleuths discovered that Gehlen's agents had employed various stratagems to undercut U.S. intelligence. During interrogations at displaced-persons camps, for example, his men would warn inmates not to talk with the Americans on the grounds that the United States was secretly still in cahoots with the Soviets. The Agency also learned of a rabidly nationalist newsletter, *Orientierung,* that circulated among Gehlen staffers, giving rise to "the uneasy feeling that we, namely U.S. intelligence, were being misused for German nationalist purposes," as one CIA operative put it. But as long as Allen Dulles ruled the roost, Gehlen continued to live a charmed existence. "He's on our side and that's all that matters,"

Dulles said of his German counterpart. "Besides, one needn't ask him to one's club."[48]

Was Gehlen really on America's side, as Dulles glibly asserted? "What we had, essentially, was an agreement to exploit each other, each in his own national interest," said Critchfield, who considered Gehlen "a consummate political operator."[49] It seemed to work as long as Gehlen's objectives coincided with the CIA's, but being on the U.S. payroll did not guarantee abiding loyalty. While Gehlen sought to satisfy his sponsor's craving for details on their mutual enemy, he also pursued another agenda, which entailed running interference for the legions of war criminals who flocked to the Org for cover. By coopting the CIA's anti-Communist bias, Gehlen was able to neutralize the immediate threat posed by U.S. intelligence, which otherwise might have pursued a more rigorous denazification program.

The CIA eventually found out that the Nazi old-boy network nesting inside the Org had a dangerous and unexpected twist to it. By bankrolling Gehlen, the Agency had unknowingly laid itself open to manipulation by a foreign intelligence service that was riddled with Soviet spies. Although far more Nazis gravitated to the West, some went over to the Soviets, who took advantage of every opportunity to infiltrate the Gehlen network. Certain Third Reich veterans collaborated with the Russians while also pawning secrets to the Americans, the British, and the French, depending who offered more money. Willi Höttl, the SS disinformation adept who later worked for U.S. Army intelligence and the Gehlen Org, described the free-for-all that ensued at war's end: "The German Secret Service is broken and scattered both to East and West. Some serve the Americans and some the Russians. Others lie low and watch which way the wind blows. Some play with fire on both sides of the Iron Curtain. . . ."[50]

The U.S. Army's ODESSA File

As early as 1947, the U.S. Army Counterintelligence Corps began tracking the activities of an underground pro-Soviet network called

Theo, which recruited ex-Nazis and spread rumors "prejudicial to U.S. interests" in the American zone of occupation. The Theo organization was allegedly composed of former SS members interned in Russian POW camps who were secretly working for Soviet intelligence. Many of these men had previously served under Colonel Otto Skorzeny, the CIC determined, and "their mission [was] to assist in a parachute invasion by the Soviets in the event that such an action should take place."[51]

Skorzeny was also wooed by the Russians during his postwar incarceration. The Teutonic swashbuckler told American interrogators that he had "openly and overtly been offered the opportunity of collaborating with communist and Soviet circles." These overtures were supposedly tendered by both German and Soviet parties. "Skorzeny believes that the Soviets want him both because he is an educated engineer and because his name would be an attraction to young former members of the SS to jump on the Soviet bandwagon," a CIC analyst concluded.[52]

Scarface resisted blandishments from the East, choosing instead to hitch a ride with his old friend Gehlen. But first there were important matters that required his attention at the American internment center where he was being held. Skorzeny's legal problems didn't end in September 1947, when he was acquitted of charges stemming from his behind-the-lines shenanigans during the Battle of the Bulge. He was still wanted by the Danish and Czech governments for war crimes.

The chain-smoking Austrian giant raised more than a few eyebrows when his captors discovered that even while imprisoned, he exerted considerable influence over other Nazis. In an effort to learn more about Skorzeny's activities, the CIC planted an informant in his midst. The informant soon learned of "an SS underground movement to aid internees in escaping and securing false identity papers. This group was alleged to be under the leadership of Otto Skorzeny and known as the 'Skorzeny Gruppe.' " According to the CIC report: "It was established that this 'Skorzeny Gruppe' was actually part of a larger organization known as ODESSA [Organisation der Ehemaligen SS-Angehörigen] or Organization of Former SS Members." Although the precise number of ODESSA members was not known, the CIC believed "that many former SS men were aware of its activities and were in communication and contact with them." The tentacles of ODESSA were said to stretch throughout Germany; some members were reportedly armed, and its couriers were rumored to be "transporting currency from the Russian to the American zone."[53]

ODESSA — the fabled postwar Nazi network whose alleged exploits have generated profuse literary and cinematic embellishments: CIC documents confirm that a Nazi "Brown aid" network actually existed and that Skorzeny was immersed in this web of intrigue. Many names have alluded to this shadowy Nazi underground — die Spinne (the Spider), Kamradenwerk (Comradeship), der Bruderschaft (the Brotherhood). Operation Brandy, a CIC probe of ODESSA, discerned signs of a "well organized illegal mail service" among German POWs. People living in the vicinity of internment camps were said to be "particularly anxious to aid [war prisoners] in escaping, in procuring money, in disposing of and storing stolen property, and in giving rooms to visitors at the camps."[54]

Curious as to where the ratlines led, a CIC mole arranged the escape of himself and two inmates from Dachau. The experience of this informant provided additional corroboration of "an underground movement, bearing the codename of ODESSA." The CIC explicitly identified "Otto Skorzeny, who is directing this movement out of Dachau," as a leader of ODESSA. One of Skorzeny's activities involved stage-managing sudden departures from the camp. "This is being done with the help of the Polish guards," the CIC disclosed. "The Polish guards are helping the men that receive orders from Skorzeny to escape."[55]

The Polish prison guards at Dachau, hired by the U.S. Army because of their presumed anti-Communist reliability, were small cogs in a far-flung escape mechanism that delivered tens of thousands of Nazis to expatriate communities in Latin America and the Middle East after the war. Some ODESSA operatives secured jobs driving U.S. Army trucks on the Munich–Salzburg autobahn and hid people in the backs of these vehicles. Aided by men of the cloth, the well-traveled southern escape route consisted of a chain of monasteries throughout Austria and Italy. A Vatican-run way station in Rome dispensed false papers to fascist fugitives, who were farmed out to distant pastures. A top-secret May 1947 State

Department report described the Vatican as "the largest single organization involved in the illegal movement of emigrants," including many Nazis.[56]

Another major ratline — "ODESSA North" — stretched through Denmark, Sweden, and Norway, where an underground network of SS veterans and Werewolves smuggled Nazi renegades over land and sea until they were picked up by ships heading to Spain and Argentina. According to Danish journalist Henrik Kruger, Scandinavian police officials and Argentine diplomats were instrumental in facilitating traffic along this route. The key legmen on the ground were personnel who had undergone Werewolf training toward the end of World War II. Skorzeny was instrumental in selecting and schooling the Werewolves, some of whom later resurfaced as ODESSA operatives in Scandinavia while Scarface orchestrated the escape of Nazis from detention camps. A large number of fascist collaborators also ended up in the United States, Canada, Great Britain, Australia, and South Africa.[57]

Of course, the wholesale emigration of fascist collaborators would not have been possible without the tacit approval of the U.S. government, whose efforts to bring war criminals to book waned as the Cold War intensified. Skorzeny was still in U.S. custody in June 1948, when the Soviet Union imposed a land blockade of Berlin in response to American steps to consolidate the three Western zones of occupation under a single administration. A few months earlier, the USSR had backed a coup in Czechoslovakia. And the Communist parties in Italy and France appeared to be gaining strength. With the Berlin airlift in full gear, denazification was no longer a priority for U.S. policy makers.

By this time, both the CIA and army intelligence had revised their assessment of Skorzeny. "The most dangerous man in Europe" was now viewed as a potential asset in the Cold War struggle. The CIA in particular was interested in his services. Warned by American officials that the Czech government might succeed in its request to extradite him, Skorzeny decided it was time for a change of scenery. On the evening of July 27, 1948, a car with American military license plates carrying three former SS officers arrived at the Darmstadt internment camp, where Skorzeny was then being held. The German SS veterans, who had donned the khaki uniforms of U.S. Army police, entered the detention center and announced they had come to take Skorzeny to Nuremberg for a legal hearing scheduled for the next day. A few minutes later, Skorzeny walked out of the camp and disappeared.

When asked about his vanishing act, Skorzeny subsequently maintained that the American authorities helped him escape. What about the U.S. military uniforms worn by the SS men who retrieved him? "They weren't stolen," Skorzeny insisted. "They were provided by the Americans."[58]

Given his celebrity status, Skorzeny thought it best to lie low for a while. He hid at a farm in Bavaria rented by Countess Ilse Lüthje, whose uncle, Hjalmar Schacht, had served as Hitler's finance minister. It was love at first sight when Skorzeny met Schacht's beautiful niece, even though both were already married. He and Ilse frolicked and romanced in the woods, a happy respite after three years of confinement. "Otto was a fabulous-looking animal," she confided. "He had everything you could want in a man, lots of charm, charisma, a good sense of humor."[59]

While Skorzeny indulged in amorous pursuits, his fearsome reputation stalked far and wide. In September 1948, German police reported that a "Skorzeny movement" had sprung up in the U.S. zone of occupation. "This movement is alleged to be spreading all over Germany," a U.S. Army document stated. Its chief purpose was supposedly to "fight against communism." Another army intelligence report noted that a "group of former German SS and paratroopers have attached themselves to an underground movement which is under Skorzeny's direction." This movement was said to be linked to underground organizations in Austria as well as in the Soviet zone in Germany. British officials concluded that Skorzeny was "working for U.S. Intelligence" during this period, "building a sabotage organization."[60]

Once-classified CIA and army documents indicate that American intelligence officials seriously entertained the possibility of enlisting the infamous Nazi commando. Army Major Sidney U. Barnes proposed that "the U.S. Government sponsor Skorzeny," but another army officer, George T. Nakamura, stated, "In view of . . . the notoriety received by Skorzeny in the press during the past years, it is felt that any *open* sponsorship or support of Skorzeny by the U.S.

Government, or any influence exerted by the U.S. Government on behalf of Skorzeny, would probably expose the U.S. Government to extreme international embarrassment. Furthermore, the possibility exists that Skorzeny has been and is being utilized by U.S. intelligence [emphasis added]." Of course, "open sponsorship" was not necessary when the CIA could use the Gehlen Org as a cutout for sticky situations.[61]

Countess Ilse recalled that Skorzeny was in contact with the chief of the Org while hiding at her Bavarian farm. "Gehlen was marvelous," she asserted. "He and Otto respected each other very much." At one point, according to Ilse, Gehlen warned that the Russians were going to try to kidnap Skorzeny: "One of Gehlen's men brought a machine gun to the house and told Otto to be careful. But Otto was fearless. He had nerves of steel."

Occasionally Skorzeny strayed from the farm into Munich, where he and Hermann Lauterbacher, former deputy leader of the Hitler Youth, scouted potential recruits for the Org. Whenever Skorzeny traveled, he would round up Nazis and draw them into Gehlen's orbit. His effusive personality rekindled the esprit de corps of Third Reich veterans, who joined the Org in droves.[62]

Skorzeny's ongoing association with Gehlen was emblematic of the pivotal alliance between ODESSA and the Org — and, by implication, the CIA as well. For many of those unsavory characters who constituted the ODESSA underground, Gehlen was the life raft; he was the one who commandeered the vehicle to rescue the comradeship. In the end, the most important service performed by the Org had little to do with gathering information for the CIA. "Gehlen's organization was designed to protect the ODESSA Nazis. It amounts to an exceptionally well-orchestrated diversion," maintains historian William Corson, a retired U.S. intelligence officer.[63]

Seen from this perspective, Gehlen's primary accomplishment was to neutralize American intelligence so that a sizable contingent of former SS officers represented by ODESSA could carry on their struggle. Instead of ostentatious mountaintop heroics, the objective of their subtly conceived efforts was the survival, and ultimately the revival, of the Nazi movement. The ghoulish espionage tryst they formed with Gehlen and the CIA enabled many unrepentant fascists, Skorzeny among them, to catch their breath, reestablish themselves, and mount a response to the daunting challenges of a new political era. In the Gehlen Org, U.S. officials thought they had found a consistent means of access to events in the Communist world. But Gehlen always had his own agenda, a German nationalist agenda, that dovetailed with the machinations of Skorzeny and ODESSA.

Skorzeny's undercover activities were briefly interrupted when a photographer snapped his picture at a café on the Champs-Elysées in Paris on February 13, 1950. The next day his scarfaced visage appeared on the front pages of the French press. It was time to beat another quick retreat — this time to Salzburg, where Skorzeny met with German war veterans. Skorzeny also had a personal motive for visiting Austria; he retained an attorney to file for a divorce so he could marry Ilse. Afterward he made his way to Madrid, where Ilse had already found a posh apartment in the best part of town. Spain became their base of operations, but they always kept abreast of developments in Germany.

CHAPTER TWO

THE SEESAW STRATEGY

Hitler's Bodyguard

Major General Otto Ernst Remer stared petulantly at a British occupation officer, ignoring orders to remove his hands from his pockets at a legal hearing. Although hardly a serious infraction, it was yet another sign of disrespect from the tall, slender, dark-haired prisoner of war. Herr Remer, it seems, had a bad attitude, which he flaunted in the presence of his Anglo overlords. He was often in a surly mood during twenty months of confinement in various internment camps. A testy encounter now and then with the Allied authorities was sometimes all he could muster to defy the monotony of incarceration. That was the worst part — the sheer boredom. It nearly drove him mad.

Born in 1912 in the German province of Mecklenburg, Ernst Remer had plenty of spare time to brood over his hapless circumstance. This was not what he expected when he graduated from a cadet academy and embarked on a career as a professional soldier. Wounded nine times during the war, his company officer described him as "the prototype of a respectable and brave swordsman." But after five years in the service, he had risen only to the rank of major in charge of a guard battalion in Berlin. As fate would have it, Remer happened to be on duty during that seminal episode on July 20, 1944, when his nick-of-time intervention saved the day for Adolf Hitler.[1]

Rewarded for his efforts, Remer became the Führer's chief bodyguard. "I was responsible for Hitler's personal security. I saw him frequently and spoke with him many times," Remer recalled years later. "I never met a man with his qualities. What he said was reasonable and made sense. Hitler was a totally normal man who knew what he wanted."[2]

Although Remer had never officially joined the National Socialist German Workers' Party, his intimate relationship with the Führer clinched him a spot on a "watch list" of German generals in the British and U.S. zones of occupation. Issued in April 1946, this elite roster included the names of top German officers who were viewed as serious security risks and who were therefore deemed priority surveillance targets by Allied military intelligence. The entry on Remer — by far the longest and most detailed of all the names on the watch list — described him as "a very dangerous man and potential Werewolf leader. The youngest General in the German Army. . . . A fanatical Nazi."[3]

To break up the stultifying routine of prison life and, as he put it, "to set the German record straight," Remer agreed to write an account of the Battle of the Bulge for the U.S. Army. Remer knew a lot about the Ardennes offensive from firsthand experience. It was yet another instance in which his wartime activities brought him into contact with Otto Skorzeny, who was technically under Remer's command when the Ardennes assault began in December 1944.

Remer worked on this war history from December 1946 to February 1948. After his release from the Allendorf internment center, he began apprenticing as a bricklayer with Menkens, a construction firm near his home in Oldenburg. *Der Spiegel* ran a "where is he now?" story on Remer the mason that featured a picture of his handsome, smiling mug, with sunken cheeks and prominent, pointed ears, on the cover. But Hitler's former bodyguard soon found cement mixing almost as distasteful as race mixing. He decided to throw in the trowel and try his hand at politics, which he took up with a vengeance in 1949.[4]

It was a pivotal year for postwar Germany. In May, the British, French, and American zones of occupation congealed into a single unit, forming the Federal Republic of Germany, with Bonn as its capital. A number of political parties licensed by the Allied authorities were permitted to compete in state and national elections. In August, seventy-three-year-old Konrad Adenauer of the Christian Democratic Union was elected the first chancellor of West Germany. Two months later, Adenauer installed his cabinet, which included several prominent ex-Nazis. Shortly thereafter, the Soviets countered by inaugurating the German Democratic Republic in the East. The Cold War division of Germany was now firmly in place.

Nineteen forty-nine was also the year that National Socialists and other right-wing extremists began flexing their political muscle after laying low during the immediate postwar years. This was an important incubation period in which the seeds of a reborn radical nationalism quietly germinated. Some Nazis had gone into hiding, living with assumed names and ersatz identities. Many others went through the motions of denazification, knowing they had to proceed cautiously if they were to ever mount a political comeback.

It happened in phases. The first wave of far Right rehabs surfaced in 1946 after the United States, finding the denazification program too cumbersome to manage, turned over administrative responsibilities to the Germans themselves. As a result, any possibility of salvaging the Allied pledge to eradicate all remnants of Nazism was lost. Millions of Third Reich veterans received a blanket amnesty and never faced charges for their wartime deeds. In successive stages, they were granted democratic privileges, including the right to vote and compete for political office. John J. McCloy, U.S. high commissioner of the Federal Republic of Germany, acknowledged in an August 1949 radio address that "some thirty percent" of the positions in government and industry were already occupied by ex-Nazis. By this time, only a few hundred war criminals remained in prison.[5]

As millions of former Hitlerites quietly filtered back into the mainstream, details of their Nazi past were swept under the rug and repressed. There was no revolutionary self-purging or liberating catharsis among the German people after the war. Nor had an earnest effort been made to educate the German public about the realities of World War II. The absence of a profound confrontation with the horrors of the Third Reich "was to have serious and adverse effects on the political climate of the postwar years," scholar Kurt Tauber observes in his encyclopedic study *Beyond Eagle and Swas-*

tika. "It provided the preconditions of the rebirth of radical antidemocratic nationalistic attitudes and organizations."[6]

In light of the significant shortcomings of the denazification process, U.S. officials were concerned about Germany's political reliability. Public-opinion polls showed that in spite of dreadful revelations about Auschwitz and proddings in the direction of democracy, anti-Semitic prejudice remained deeply entrenched in German society. A study conducted in the U.S. zone of occupation during the years 1945 through 1949 concluded that 15 to 18 percent of German adults were unreconstructed Nazis.[7]

Shortly before McCloy assumed the role of high commissioner, U.S. intelligence analysts accurately predicted that there would soon be a nationalist revival in West Germany. Leading the way was Otto Ernst Remer, the first of Hitler's generals to enter the political arena. In October 1949, Remer became the deputy director of the Sozialistische Reichs-Partei (SRP), one of several neo-Nazi groups that had mushroomed throughout the Fatherland. The SRP quickly outflanked the rest of the ultranationalist pack, emerging as West Germany's leading far Right organization. It immediately claimed representation in the West German Bundestag when two parliamentary deputies from other parties jumped over to the more overtly extreme SRP.

Many other incorrigibles joined the Socialist Reich Party, thanks in large part to the energetic campaigning of Major General Remer, the "big name" in the organization, who kicked off a noisy recruitment effort with a brazen appeal to former Nazis: "We want them, we need them!" A major drawing card whenever he barnstormed around the country, Remer railed against the "shit democracy" that American occupiers had imposed on Germany. "The Nazis achieved more than all the parties today put together! . . . I am and will remain a [N]ational [S]ocialist!" he cried, to thunderous applause. As a U.S. State Department observer remarked, "This is the first party in which the Old Nazis can really feel at home."[8]

Party meetings typically opened with bands performing martial music amid flags and banners that displayed the SRP insignia of a black eagle set against a red background within a white border. The symbolism and color motif were purposely chosen to evoke the Nazi era. Flanked by a strong-arm squad of young toughs in jackboots,

Remer preached a gospel of national resentment, flavoring his speeches with shrill Nazi rhetoric. "National Socialism cannot be eradicated. The idea marches on. After all, Christendom did not end with the death of Christ, either!" Remer declared, as if he were the Saint Paul of the neo-Nazi movement.[9]

During the SRP's heyday in the early 1950s, Remer was constantly on the move, inciting crowds against Bonn's accommodation with the United States. He continually attacked Adenauer for being a U.S. puppet who had shamefully acquiesced to the division of the Fatherland. And he repeatedly referred to Admiral Karl Doenitz, Hitler's chosen successor, as the last legitimate sovereign of an all-German Reich. Dismissing stories about Nazi atrocities as Allied propaganda, Remer charged that Dachau's crematory ovens were built after the war, on American orders, in an effort to discredit Germany. Films of concentration camps were faked, he insisted.[10]

Remer's oratorical excess triggered a series of wild club-room brawls in which chairs and tables were hurled during SRP rallies. Such outbursts prompted local officials to prohibit him from speaking publicly in Schleswig-Holstein and North Rhine–Westphalia, two West German *Länder* (states) where the SRP had wide grassroots support among old Nazis, alienated youth, German refugees, and other down-and-out constituencies. It was the first of Remer's many brushes with the law in West Germany.

Not surprisingly, U.S. intelligence experts were keeping close tabs on Remer, who frequently thumbed his nose at Washington and its *Kaugummi* (chewing gum) soldiers. State Department officials began compiling weekly reports on the SRP, noting that it rejected any form of cooperation with the Western powers. Instead, the SRP endorsed the idea of Europe as an independent third force, opposed to capitalism as well as Communism, led by a strong, reunified German Reich. Remer's "nationalist-neutralist" line struck a responsive chord among a large minority of Germans who shared his belief that Chancellor Adenauer often put American priorities ahead of the interests of the German people.

American occupation authorities watched with dismay as the SRP gained momentum, attracting about ten thousand members. It established a number of auxiliary organizations, including a women's league, a youth group, and an anti-Marxist labor union. Remer also set up the Reichsfront, an elite paramilitary formation whose members were drawn largely from employees of the British-run German Service Organization. According to British press accounts cited by the U.S. State Department, most of Remer's "Brownshirt army" were housed in British military installations. "Remer pictures, Remer posters and Remer slogans cover the walls of the barracks provided by the British," one report stated.[11]

Remer's Reichsfront was a short-lived, if overblown, initiative, dissolved by an edict from Bonn. In September 1950, after the SRP scored well in several local electoral contests, the West German government denounced the party as an enemy of the state. Federal civil employees were told that they risked dismissal from their jobs if they joined the SRP. This get-tough policy was backed by U.S. intelligence officials, who considered Remer's organization "the most successful as well as the most dangerous" of all the radical rightist parties. "If unchecked," a State Department analyst cautioned, "such a party as the SRP might eventually come to power legally, as in the case of the pre-war Nazis, by gaining control of the Bundestag."[12]

A significant threshold was crossed in May 1951, when the SRP tallied 11 percent of the vote in state elections in Lower Saxony, outpolling Adenauer's Christian Democratic Union in several districts.* The results were dramatic proof that shameless appeals to the memory of the Third Reich could mobilize large masses of people, underscoring what Bertolt Brecht, the German playwright, once said: "The womb that brought forth this unclean thing is fruitful still."

In the wake of the SRP's electoral breakthrough, Western observers commented on the widespread apathy among the German populace over neo-Nazi advances. A public-opinion survey showed that only 20 percent of the population would do "everything in their power" to stop a group like the SRP from taking over. This was

* While 11 percent may not seem like much by U.S. voting standards, it is very significant for an electoral system in which proportional representation is allotted. Under such a system, vote tallies of little more than 5 percent could sometimes tip the balance and determine the political complexion of the governing coalition.

worrisome to State Department officials, who warned that "any recrudescence of German nationalism must inevitably arouse concern and necessitate caution. . . . The huge refugee mass, the veterans, the ex-Nazis, groups conscious of economic grievances . . . and most of all, disillusioned youth who have not found an outlet for their energies and ambitions in a war-damaged country — these elements are far from happy with the Bonn system and may be tempted to espouse a nationalistic short-cut to the political millennium."[13]

Restoration

Chancellor Konrad Adenauer had never been a Nazi, but he could hardly afford to ignore the enduring sympathy for extreme right-wing ideas among the German electorate. A creaky old geezer who "walked as if his legs were hinged by rusty joints," he strutted his nationalist stuff during speeches and campaign appearances in a way that reminded journalists of "a wrinkled mummy breaking into voice." Adenauer had squeaked by in a close vote — with an ex-Nazi casting the deciding ballot in his favor in the Bundestag. Following a round of consultations with High Commissioner McCloy, the chancellor stitched together a precarious governing coalition led by the Christian Democratic Union.[14]

Although he was not a National Socialist, Adenauer often displayed "dictatorial tendencies," according to a State Department analyst based in Bonn. A savvy politician, he realized that it would be very difficult to govern the country without the support of some former Nazis. As Remer's party gained in the polls, Adenauer sharpened his nationalist pitch, prompting an American consular officer to observe that "middle-of-the-road political figures are now repeating SRP lines because they realize it is politically profitable."[15]

With mainstream rhetoric becoming ever more strident, McCloy released a report in December 1951 with a grim assessment: "Unhappily, most of the established political parties have also been stockpiling the merchandise of nationalism. . . . They seek to draw the followers of the extreme rightist forces or to prevent losses of their own, by attempting to appear as nationalistic as the extremists. . . . The use of the extreme nationalist narcotic creates the need for larger doses. . . . The consequences of such a course, if long continued, must be general disaster."[16]

Adenauer sought to bolster his fragile governing coalition by courting the All-German Bloc, a fanatical revanchist organization that purported to represent some 11 million Germans who had been expelled after the war from neighboring countries. With one out of four people in West Germany a recent refugee, this constituency elicited profuse sympathy from Bonn. Adenauer repeatedly asserted that he did not accept the Oder–Neisse line (named after the two rivers separating Poland and East Germany) as a valid international boundary. "This frontier we shall never recognize!" he insisted.[17]

Led by an assortment of former SS officers who dreamed of reclaiming the so-called eastern territories, the All-German Bloc accepted a cabinet position in Bonn. Theodor Oberländer, a veteran of the SS Nightingale Battalion, became Adenauer's minister for refugees, despite his well-known wartime role in terrorizing thousands of Polish Jews. Another cabinet member, Interior Minister Gerhard Schröder, had cut his teeth as a Hitler storm trooper; he was now in charge of the West German police apparatus, which employed numerous former SS and Gestapo officers, who, for obvious reasons, were not eager to pursue German war criminals. Bonn's justice minister Fritz Schäffer had once praised Hitler as the "savior of the Reich," but this did not dissuade Adenauer from picking him to lead the West German government's fight against anti-Semitism and neo-Nazism.[18]

Even more controversial was Adenauer's choice for state secretary of the West German chancellory. Hans Globke, a man with a notorious Nazi past, controlled key personnel appointments in every governmental department and supervised authority over the Press and Public Information Office, Bonn's main propaganda organ. As Adenauer's chief aide and close personal friend, Globke was arguably the most powerful official in Bonn — with the single exception of the chancellor himself. *Die Welt* described him as the "only man who has access to Adenauer at all times or who can call the Chancellor at any hour."[19]

Just who was Globke? As the Reich's commissioner for the protection of German blood and German honor, Globke played a key role in drawing up the racialist Nuremberg Laws in 1935, which served as the "legal" basis for the persecution of Jews. While directing the Office of Jewish Affairs in Hitler's Interior Ministry, he worked closely with SS Colonel Adolf Eichmann in the deportation and liquidation of Macedonian Jews. Globke also provided the guidelines for the "Germanization" of conquered peoples in occupied countries. His wartime boss, Interior Minister Wilhelm Frick, praised Globke as "the most capable and efficient official in my ministry." But Adenauer subsequently chose to believe Globke's claim that he had tried to mitigate the legal measures demanded by Hitler.[20]

Perhaps more than anyone else, it was Globke who facilitated the return to power of numerous ex-Nazis in West German society. He was responsible for engineering a law, approved by the Bundestag in May 1951, whereby civil servants who had been fired during the occupation were to be reinstated at their respective jobs. Although the top elite of the Nazi regime had been eliminated by suicide, flight, or the hangman's noose at Nuremberg, many senior officials took advantage of the new law and crept back into positions of power. Invariably they staffed their departments with scores of Third Reich collaborators, proving once again the old German saying *"Regierung vergeht, Verwaltung gesteht"* ("Governments come and go, bureaucracy remains"). Adenauer admitted during an October 1951 parliamentary floor debate that his Foreign Office was loaded with ex-Nazis and diplomatic protégés of Joachim von Ribbentrop, Hitler's foreign minister. Nearly half the new Foreign Service Corps once belonged to the Nazi Party; many were instrumental in preparing and executing the Führer's policies in occupied areas where Nazi atrocities were legion.[21]

Dubbed "the gray eminence," Globke secured his Richelieu-like grip on postwar Bonn through his jurisdiction over West Germany's prodigious secret-service outfit, the Gehlen Org. Gehlen himself described working with Globke as "pleasant and stimulating." Together with Adenauer — who referred appreciatively to Gehlen as "my dear general" — they formed a high-powered troika that dominated West German politics until 1962, when the eighty-five-year-old chancellor finally stepped aside.[22]

At a time when Adenauer was virtually unknown in Germany, Gehlen leaned on his influential U.S. contacts to support him for chancellor. Adenauer also had the backing of the financial and industrial oligarchs of the Rhine–Ruhr area, who, like Gehlen, favored his Atlantic-oriented approach to international affairs. Adenauer's political longevity was enhanced by the meddling of the Org, which spied on the chancellor's domestic opponents. The list of targets included nearly everyone who did not readily fall into step with Adenauer's march toward economic and political integration with the West.

The Bund Deutscher Jugend (BDJ) — an elite, CIA-trained paramilitary cadre composed largely of former Hitler Youth, Wehrmacht, and SS personnel — also set its sights on Adenauer's domestic political opponents. Among the members of this ultranationalist youth group were future movers and shakers within West Germany's hard-core neo-Nazi scene, such as Friedhelm Busse, who went on to direct several violent ultra-right-wing organizations during and after the Cold War. Back in the early 1950s, Busse and his fellow Bundists were supposed to remain underground and engage in acts of sabotage and resistance in the event of a Soviet invasion, much like Skorzeny's Werewolves. But instead of focusing on foreign enemies, the leaders of Busse's "stay behind" unit proceeded to draw up a death list that included future chancellor Willi Brandt and several other leading Social Democrats (West Germany's main opposition party) who were marked for liquidation in case of an ill-defined national security emergency.[23]

The BDJ's cover was blown in October 1952 when the West German press got wind of the fact that the United States was backing a neo-Nazi death squad. Embarrassed State Department officials, who tried to cover up the full extent of American involvement with the youth group, admitted privately that the scandal had resulted in "a serious loss of U.S. prestige." After a brief media storm, West German "stay behind" forces regrouped with a helping hand from the Gehlen Org, which organized several Werewolf-type "sleeper" nets throughout the Federal Republic on the CIA's behalf.* Extraconstitutional forays of this sort were common under Adenauer, who rewarded Gehlen by appointing him chief of the Bundesnachtrichtendienst (BND), West Germany's first officially independent federal intelligence service, in 1955.[24]

By this time, many former Hitlerites had found comfortable lodging in the Christian Democratic Union (CDU). Adenauer's conservative party provided a convenient facade for those who wished to regain the leading status they enjoyed during the Third Reich. High Commissioner McCloy was aware that Nazis and anti-Semites had deluged the civil service, including the educational and legal systems. But their presence in the government was tolerated as long as they officially recanted their Nazi views and swore allegiance to the Western alliance.

The CDU's role as a Trojan horse for large numbers of ex-Nazis called into question pronouncements by Adenauer and his American patrons that the Bonn Republic represented an authentic new beginning. It also guaranteed that heavy doses of denial would be a staple of West German politics. "Something approaching a national amnesia gripped the country," scholar Henry Ashby Turner, Jr., bluntly observes in his history of postwar Germany. Deep-rooted nationalist complexes were never ventilated or challenged in a serious way. Instead, the wholesale Nazi restoration during the Adenauer era induced a standard of double morality that has since persisted as an indelible feature of German public life. American government policies — which included the massive covert recruit-

* The Bund Deutscher Jugend was the West German component of a CIA-backed guerrilla army that covered all of non-Communist Europe like a spiderweb. Neo-Nazis and neofascists also served as "stay behind" foot soldiers in several other countries. The French section, for example, included notorious collaborators such as René Bousquet, top cop of the Vichy regime, who approved the deportation of French Jews to death camps during World War II. Italian "stay behind" personnel included former members of Mussolini's secret police. In Greece, members of the so-called resistance units played a major role in the 1967 coup that brought a far Right military junta to power. The Turkish arm worked in tandem with the Grey Wolves, a violent neo-Nazi youth group. "Stay behind" divisions also existed in Portugal, Holland, Belgium, Denmark, Luxembourg, and England, as well as ostensibly neutral countries such as Sweden and Austria.

ment of fascists for espionage purposes — doubtless contributed to Germany's national amnesia about Nazi atrocities and the criminals who perpetrated them.[25]

It was perhaps wishful thinking to assume that a democratic system could effectively take root if superimposed from on high — particularly when "democracy" was associated with military defeat, national humiliation, and foreign occupation troops on German soil. While Globke's ghoulish bureaucrats may have put away their swastikas and whips, most of them brought little genuine commitment to the new political order. Friedrich von der Heydte, one of the founders of Adenauer's CDU, spoke frankly on this matter: "Today it is fashionable in Germany to be a democrat. Every German is a good democrat as a matter of course — if you want to 'belong' you have to be. But basically the Germans do not cherish democracy. They submit to it as perhaps people submit to a fashion, although deep inside they resent their uncomfortable plight."[26]

The smart ones realized that their postwar success depended largely on jettisoning the image of radicalism and projecting a sober, constitutional demeanor. Consequently, anti-Semitism was officially frowned upon, as Bonn commenced financial reparations to the state of Israel. For some West Germans, the decision to provide restitution for Jewish suffering was a genuine expression of remorse. But many government officials embraced this policy as an expedient, high-profile reputation cleanser. At the same time, the leaders of the Federal Republic systematically withheld indemnification payments to widows of antifascist resistance fighters and numerous victims of Nazi persecution (including Gypsies, homosexuals, and leftists), while former Hitlerites and their families were rewarded with generous pensions. Ex-Nazi yes-men now back in power understood it was beneficial to adapt to democratic routines. That meant keeping their distance from the Third Reich nostalgics and Remer-led incorrigibles, who continued to be an acute source of embarrassment to Bonn.

Remaining true to the Nazi creed, Remer sneered at his erstwhile comrades who professed a swift conversion to democracy after the war. Like so many other Nazis, he had been approached by U.S. intelligence in the late 1940s, but Remer rebuffed attempts to woo him. "I said that as long we were an occupied country, I would not help them," he recounted. Instead, Remer and a growing number of SRP activists opted to agitate from the outside, relentlessly attacking the United States and "Adenauer's American satellite policy" for splitting their beloved Fatherland in two. After monitoring a well-attended SRP campaign meeting, a State Department sleuth reported back to Washington: "If nations could bring suit for slander and character assassination, we would have an air-tight case against the SRP."[27]

Remer's party continued to score well in local elections, gaining nearly as many votes as Adenauer's CDU in Bremen, even though SRP candidates had been prohibited from campaigning publicly prior to the vote. Shortly thereafter, West German police raided SRP offices in Hamburg and other cities, breaking up meetings with tear gas and billy-club attacks. Bonn also banned the *Reichszeitung*, a newspaper touting the views of the SRP, and initiated legal proceedings to outlaw the entire organization.

All this was grist for Remer's mill; he threatened that the SRP would answer terror with terror. Notching up the radical rhetoric, he vigorously denounced the Western alliance, while avoiding criticism of the Soviet Union and East Germany. "With regard to foreign affairs," a State Department document noted, "the SRP is extremely anti-American and anti-British. It is professedly anti-Communist but does not criticize the Soviet Union or the East Zone government. . . . The party is suspected of willingness to effect a large compromise with Russia in order to unify Germany."

For U.S. officials, any thought of cutting a deal with the East was akin to political heresy. Referring to Remer and other neo-Nazi demagogues as "rat-catchers," a State Department informant recommended that "for the good of the country the SRP should be stepped on like a poisonous snake."[28]

Exile in Madrid

Otto Skorzeny was in good cheer, feasting and drinking at Horcher's, one of Madrid's swankiest restaurants and the favorite watering hole of the high-powered German exile community in Spain. He often entertained there with Countess Ilse on his arm and an ever present cigarette dangling from his lips. Tonight they would raise and clink their glasses in honor of Hjalmar Schacht, who occasionally visited Madrid to discuss business matters with his niece and her famous husband. (As Hitler's finance minister and later as president of the Reichsbank, Schacht had favored the expropriation of Jewish property in an effort to promote Germany's economic Aryanization drive.) Otto Horcher, the transplanted German proprietor, prepared a sumptuous spread whenever Schacht appeared at Skorzeny's table.[29]

Once Göring's pet restaurateur in Berlin, Horcher had moved his business to Madrid in 1944, when German agents were pouring into the Spanish capital, prompting a *New York Times* correspondent to report: "In Madrid, spies swarm in the big hotels in such numbers that even casual visitors cannot help noticing them." The U.S. Army Counterintelligence Corps soon discovered that Horcher's restaurant was serving as a letter drop for German spooks. "It appears that Horcher went to Madrid to establish a center of German subversive and espionage activities," a CIC memo noted. "The restaurant, after the war, became the collecting and distributing point for Germans who fled to Spain."[30]

The CIC sleuths in occupied Germany picked up the trail of "a large escape organization" that enabled high-ranking SS officers, business executives, technicians, and "cogs in Germany's vast diplomatic, consular, and propaganda machinery" to settle in Spain "with falsified papers and passports." Spain also served as a way station for Nazis en route to South America. The mass migration of Nazi personnel and flight capital was part of a plan launched late in the war by SS chief Heinrich Himmler and his top aides in an effort to reestablish German influence in various countries after the Third Reich crumbled.[31]

A colony of sixteen thousand Nazi expatriates was already thriving in Madrid when Skorzeny arrived on the scene in February 1950. Welcomed with open arms by Spanish authorities, he and Ilse took up residence in a large villa on Lopez de Hoyos and were married shortly thereafter. A Bavarian house servant cooked meals for friends and associates who frequently turned up at the Skorzeny abode. "It seemed that the entire Spanish army came to our home,"

Ilse recalled. "It was one party after another. We met all the important military officers and government ministers, including General Franco. Otto liked Franco a lot."

Apparently the feeling was mutual. Treated like a celebrity, Skorzeny got lots of help from the Franco regime, which previously had close ties to Nazi Germany. Franco also provided a safe haven for Nazi financial assets that were shifted to neutral countries as the war drew to a conclusion. These hidden Nazi funds, according to a U.S. Treasury Department probe, were secretly used to acquire controlling interest in 750 business enterprises spread across different continents (including 112 Spanish firms). Hjalmar Schacht played a key role in orchestrating the transfer of large sums through a complex web of camouflaged front companies and bank accounts. Fearing that Nazi survivors would utilize the hidden wealth for nefarious purposes, U.S. investigators tried to follow the money trail but were frustrated by Schacht's intricate financial maneuvers.[32]

After the war, Skorzeny's uncle-in-law resumed his activities as a financial mover and shaker. He opened a bank in Düsseldorf that specialized in international trade and he served as a consultant to various governments. During a trip to Madrid in May 1952, Schacht delivered a speech to an audience of Spanish and German businessmen. Sporting a white high-collared tunic and pince-nez glasses, he pulled no punches when it came to disparaging U.S. economic policy in Germany. Noting that Schacht's remarks "were particularly acid," a confidential State Department memo indicated that his "comments critical of the United States were well-received, and were applauded at some points."[33]

Schacht's snide attitude toward the U.S. government resonated favorably with Major General Otto Ernst Remer and the Socialist Reich Party, whose economic platform was "almost exactly patterned on the formula of Schacht under the Third Reich," according to a State Department analyst. On the campaign stump, Remer often stated that Germany "needs a Dr. Schacht" to overcome its postwar economic difficulties. Remer also endorsed Schacht's prediction that National Socialism would one day conquer the world without having to wage another war.[34]

From his comfortable vantage point in Madrid, Skorzeny closely followed the progress of Remer's neo-Nazi party. Countess Ilse recalled that her husband respected what Remer was trying to do. "Otto thought Remer was a good man. He thought [the SRP] was a great effort, but it was impossible for Remer to succeed," said Ilse. Skorzeny felt that Remer was in too much of a hurry; if the SRP did not proceed more cautiously, it might end up causing a lot of trouble for the entire neo-Nazi movement.

While Remer blazed the electoral trail back in Germany, Skorzeny was busy cavorting with fascist fugitives who had sought refuge across the Pyrenees. He struck up a close relationship with Horia Sima, commander of the bloodthirsty Romanian Iron Guard, which had opened a headquarters in Spain. Sima was joined by other Eastern European collaborators, including members of the Hungarian Arrow Cross and the Croatian Ustaše.[35]

Skorzeny's closest comrade in Spain was General Léon Degrelle, the most decorated non-German member of the Nazi military. Leading the Walloon [French-speaking Belgian] Division of the Waffen SS, Degrelle had immersed himself in that "cataract of horrors," as Churchill referred to the eastern front. A close confidant of the Führer, Degrelle had his proudest moment when Hitler told him, "If I had a son, I would want him to be just like you." Degrelle fled to the Iberian Peninsula while the Third Reich was on its last legs. Sentenced to death in absentia by the Belgian government for war crimes, he kept in close contact with many Nazi veterans, including Skorzeny. "We had lunch together every week," Degrelle reminisced. "He was a great friend of mine."[36]

When he first met Degrelle in Spain, Skorzeny confided to him that the Americans had helped him escape from an internment camp in Germany. "The Americans were convinced there would be a war against the Soviet Union, and they wanted Skorzeny's assistance," Degrelle recalled. "He was a specialist with unique skills, a very strong man with a strong will." Degrelle described Skorzeny as "a soldier, not a philosopher, who had a very simple view of the world — that Europe had to be anti-Communist and unified."

During the early 1950s, Hitler's all-star commando contacted a U.S. military attaché in Madrid to explore the possibility of training

German soldiers in Spain for combat against the Soviet Union. An American air force officer who befriended him during this period reported that a customary greeting from Skorzeny was "not unlike being welcomed by a huge bear or engulfed by a huge Saint Bernard dog. Skorzeny loves to talk about the war [and] has a rather high opinion of his prowess. . . . He likes good scotch whiskey and mixes only a little plain water with it."[37]

Speaking English with a heavy British accent, Skorzeny elaborated upon his plan to organize anti-Communist guerrilla units, which would be dispatched behind enemy lines if the Soviets invaded Western Europe. He made a similar pitch to a Madrid-based FBI informant, who recommended that American officials support his proposal: "Personally I am convinced that Skorzeny means well and will help us if it is within his power, and I frankly feel his price in one form or another will not be too high." But the CIA had already set in motion secret plans for a European-wide "stay behind" network, and it didn't need Skorzeny's help on this project. American intelligence operatives had other plans for Skorzeny, as he would soon find out.[38]

Skorzeny, meanwhile, was aggressively pursuing various business ventures, thanks in large part to Uncle Schacht, who taught him the proper protocol and opened lucrative doors. Adopting the alias Rolf Steinbauer, Skorzeny set up an engineering office and an import-export firm in two rooms overlooking the Gran Via, Madrid's main boulevard — a stone's throw from the CIA headquarters in the Spanish capital. He proceeded to parlay his wide range of Spanish and German contacts into hefty monetary gain. The beautiful Ilse, an astute businesswoman in her own right, was instrumental in facilitating a number of major commercial transactions. "We represented a big consortium of German companies, which were contracted to build the Spanish national railroad in 1952," she explained. Netting a sizable commission for brokering the deal, Skorzeny and his talented wife went on to amass a personal fortune estimated at $15 million.[39]

One of Skorzeny's business associates, Willi Messerschmitt, had previously supplied Hitler's air force with state-of-the-art fighter planes. Seized by the advancing Red Army in 1945 at the Peenemünde rocket installation, Messerschmitt's aeronautical blueprints were transferred to the Soviet Union, as were hundreds of German scientists who used the Messerschmitt design to develop a prototype of the high-speed MiG jet. Since he was unable to work in West Germany in the early 1950s because of restrictions imposed by the Allies, Messerschmitt sought to bring fifty technicians with him to Madrid to develop a Spanish aircraft industry. Drawing on reports from other U.S. intelligence agencies, the FBI noted that Skorzeny was allied with Messerschmitt "in the physical transplanting of German industry to Spain." While ostensibly they were working on this project for the Spanish government, "it seems entirely logical we will be having the German air industry re-created under our very noses," an FBI agent cautioned.[40]

Playing the Eastern Card

From time to time, Skorzeny would slip back into Germany to confer with Hjalmar Schacht and other business leaders. During the summer of 1951, according to U.S. intelligence reports, he traveled "the length and breadth of Germany as fast as a car would take him." Skorzeny's peregrinations caused a ripple among American spymasters, prompting an exchange of memos between FBI chief J. Edgar Hoover and CIA director Walter Bedell Smith. Although technically a fugitive, Skorzeny "appears to travel freely in the Western zone of Germany and has high level contacts among the former German military," Hoover noted. In addition to commercial pursuits, Skorzeny spent much of his time "seeing friends and contacts" and keeping his hand in German affairs. "Rumors of Skorzeny's presence in Germany or of his influence being felt in Nazi circles are intermittently heard," McCloy wrote in a cable to Secretary of State Dean Acheson.[41]

Other U.S. intelligence reports indicated that Skorzeny was active behind the scenes "pulling all wires available" in a number of German veterans associations. The most prominent of these, the Hilfsgemeinschaft auf Gegenseitigkeit (Mutual Aid Society), or

HIAG, was a hard-nosed lobbying group for former Waffen SS personnel in the Bonn Republic. Founded in October 1951, the HIAG campaigned for legal and economic measures that would benefit Waffen SS vets who had been denied government pensions and other privileges in light of the Nuremberg decision that deemed the entire SS a criminal organization.[42]

Picking up where Goebbels had left off, HIAG spokesmen portrayed the Waffen SS — including the Death's Head division that ran the concentration camps — as idealists who defended European civilization against the Asiatic Bolshevik swarm. German soldiers were similarly glorified in hundreds of cheap, popular war-adventure novels, replete with sex and sadism, that inundated West Germany during the early 1950s. Nationalistic publishing houses also churned out memoirs of numerous Third Reich warriors, including several books by Colonel Otto Skorzeny, who exonerated the Hitler regime by blaming death-camp atrocities on a handful of wayward fanatics. "It is a malevolent twisting of the facts to pretend that the Waffen SS had anything to do with the concentration camps' horrors," Skorzeny wrote in *We Fought — We Lost.* Commenting on another autobiographical treatise, *Skorzeny's Secret Missions,* a *New York Times* reviewer concluded: "If a new Hitler appeared in Germany tomorrow, one feels after reading this book, Skorzeny would be by his side."[43]

Skorzeny was a real-life hero to many Waffen SS men who attended annual HIAG meetings, where old soldiers dressed in military drag (with illegal SS insignia) drank an abundance of beer, sang war songs, and listened to their leaders exhort them to work for the resurrection "of our holy German Reich." Such intemperate displays were particularly problematic for Chancellor Adenauer, who sought to generate support among veterans for his number one policy initiative — the American-backed plan to remilitarize the Federal Republic so that it could contribute to the defense of Western Europe.[44]

At the outset, there was considerable grassroots opposition to rearmament, particularly among ex-soldiers who composed a large and potentially disruptive element in West Germany. Resentful of the way they had been treated after the war, many former military men identified with the defiant slogan *"Ohne mich!"* ("Count me out!") that Major General Otto Ernst Remer had popularized. *"Ohne mich!"* became the SRP rallying cry against the Bonn-Washington rearmament axis. "First we were told that guns and ammunition were poison and now this poison has changed to sweets which we should eat," sneered SRP Bundestag deputy Fritz Rössler (under the assumed name Franz Richter). "But we are not Negroes or idiots to whom they can do whatever they want. It is either they or us who should be admitted to the insane asylum."[45]

Dead set against any accommodation with the West, Remer declared that he "would only consider German rearmament when it was possible to assure that all of Germany was to be defended." He insisted that Germans should not fight to cover an American retreat if the Russians got the upper hand in a war. Taunting U.S. officials, he announced that if an armed conflict erupted, he would "show the Russians the way to the Rhine." Remer promised that his SRP comrades would "post themselves as traffic policemen, spreading their arms so that the Russians can find their way through Germany as quickly as possible."[46]

Seeking to take the wind out of the SRP's sails and to boost his lagging popularity, Chancellor Adenauer became an outspoken advocate for the HIAG and other soldiers associations. During his first year in office, he reassured a delegation of Wehrmacht retirees that his government "energetically opposed all attempts to defame the former members of the military." As for the Waffen SS, they "were soldiers like all the rest," Adenauer insisted. His courtship of this fickle constituency, which had mixed feelings about rapid remilitarization on U.S. terms, led to generous government subsidies of ultranationalistic publications. One Bonn-financed magazine, the HIAG-affiliated *Deutsche Soldaten Zeitung,* was banned in Austria because of its "openly pan-German and neo-Nazistic" content.[47]

Many veterans felt vindicated by Adenauer's solicitude, which only served to harden widespread illusions that Hitler had been right in his assessment of the Soviet menace and that the Allies had been wrong. Cold War U.S. realpolitik fostered revisionist mythologies that reinforced the propensity among Germans not to face up to their past.* Whitewashed in the process was the deep complicity of the German General Staff and the army in supporting Hitler's rise to power and in carrying out his genocidal schemes. Instead of being punished for their crimes, numerous senior officers from the Hitler era were eagerly sought after by Adenauer and his military planners.[48]

The rearmament debate took place in an atmosphere of heightened urgency stemming from the Korean War, in which U.S. soldiers were pitted directly against Communist firepower for the first time. The implications of the Korean conflict reverberated all along the East-West fault line, particularly in Germany, where American soldiers also stood eyeball to eyeball with the Russians. As far as American policy makers were concerned, this was no time for Bonn to waver in its commitment to the West. In the wake of Red Chinese intervention in Korea and the first Soviet A-bomb explosion, U.S. military strategists flatly declared that German rearmament was essential to save Western Europe from Communism.

Once again, American paranoia was stoked by General Reinhard Gehlen, who sought to convince his U.S. partners that Korea was merely a dress rehearsal for a Soviet invasion of Western Europe. Ironically, the CIA came to fear just the opposite — that the Russians might decide to abruptly withdraw their troops from East Germany in order to prevent an American military buildup in the West and undermine the fledgling North Atlantic Treaty Organization (NATO). Despite Gehlen's increasingly dubious track record, his espionage organization would go on to play a major role in NATO, supplying two-thirds of its raw intelligence on the Warsaw Pact countries.[49]

Even before the Korean War, Gehlen had developed plans to revive the German army. Instrumental in this effort was Adolf Heusinger, formerly a high-ranking Wehrmacht officer and a survivor of

* An opinion poll in 1953 found that more than half the population (55 percent) rejected criticism of how German soldiers behaved in Nazi-occupied territories, while only 6 percent considered the criticism justified. The following year, the *New York Times* reported: "A large proportion, and possibly a majority of the German people, and members of the Bundestag, do not accept the doctrine of German war guilt."

the July 20 bomb blast (for which he was later awarded a Silver Medal by Hitler). Together with Gehlen, Heusinger laid the groundwork for what was tantamount to a new General Staff. He emerged as Adenauer's principal advisor on military affairs and would later serve as chairman of NATO's Permanent Military Committee in Washington. In September 1950, the chancellor proposed that West Germany create a quasi-military "protective police force" of 150,000 men — a move that was envisioned as the first step toward a fully reconstituted West German army.[50]

The same month Adenauer floated this idea, a group of German strategists in Madrid issued a confidential report analyzing the world situation in light of the Korean conflict. Known informally as the German Geopolitical Center, this think tank was staffed by a klatch of Third Reich carryovers, mostly from von Ribbentrop's Foreign Office, who had been sheep-dipped into Spain in the mid-1940s. Acknowledging that the Korean War could "bring great opportunities to Germany if she follows a prudent foreign policy," they laid out a calculated plan designed to transform Germany's pivotal geographic position — smack-dab in the middle of Europe — into political negotiating power.

In the past, Germany's status as a bridge between East and West had caused a lot of trouble and contributed in no small way to that country's perpetual identity crisis. But the Madrid-based think tankers believed that this historical liability could be turned into a tactical asset by deftly maneuvering between rival superpowers, wresting concessions from one by threatening to embrace the other. SS General Walter Schellenberg and other Nazi spies had employed a similar modus operandi with some success in the waning days of World War II.

There's a word for it in German — *Schaukelpolitik* — which means "seesaw politics," shifting back and forth, playing two sides off each other. The Madrid circular was explicit about this: "Germany has exploited the tension between East and West to the utmost and she must continue her effort in that direction. . . . The Yankees are willing to pay a high price for our help. This is clear from all the confidential reports which we have obtained from circles close to the American High Commissioner." Driven by their anti-Soviet zealotry, the Americans had begun "seeking the advice of our generals whom they formerly called criminals," but the German people would not be "inclined to defend Europe, so long as Germany is treated as a defeated nation." With this in mind, the circular recommended a course of action that entailed "squeezing concessions out of the victors" in order to regain German sovereignty. "The fact that the Americans would now like us to join them in the defense of Europe and become their ally will thereby enhance our bargaining position with the Russians," the circular added.[51]

The seesaw strategy, as outlined in this lengthy memo, called for German nationalists to "be on guard against both sides to avoid being swallowed up by one of the two colossi. The dollar imperialism is certainly in no way less aggressive or reckless than communism. . . . We must not let ourselves become befogged by Washington's stupid and meaningless slogans about the 'Struggle of Democracy versus Communism.' The so-called American democracy does not deserve the sacrifice of the bones of a single German soldier." The circular also provided a blueprint for a nonaligned foreign policy in what would later be described as the Third World, by which emerging nations could also reap advantages by playing the East off the West. Predicting the "coming revolt of the Arab world," the think tank concluded that Germany should concentrate on building "a new political bloc" in Asia, Africa, and Latin America.

Skorzeny's Madrid-based colleagues distributed this circular among influential Germans in Bonn and other parts of the world. Meanwhile, the von Ribbentrop clique in Spain stayed in close contact with their former Nazi colleagues, also from the von Ribbentrop school, who were running Adenauer's Foreign Office. They were like a brotherhood who continued to collaborate after World War II, even though some of them officially worked for the West German government and others lived in exile. General Gehlen also served as an intermediary between Bonn and the neo-Nazi network in Spain, where Skorzeny occasionally took on special assignments at his request. Scarface would later play a role in behind-the-scenes negotiations between Spain and West Germany regarding the establishment of a joint arms industry on the Iberian Peninsula. There were even feelers about setting up West German military bases in Spain outside of NATO's purview.[52]

Acting upon the advice of his Foreign Office, Adenauer played hardball with High Commissioner McCloy, insisting on major concessions in matters of sovereignty in exchange for cooperation with the United States and the Western alliance. The chancellor was determined to bring about the end of the occupation as such. He hoped to accelerate this process as much as possible by using rearmament as a bargaining chip. Some called him "the real McCloy," for it seemed that Adenauer was manipulating the high commissioner, who grew increasingly frustrated by the chancellor's habit of linking every issue to West Germany's defense contribution. Demands included the "complete restoration of German sovereignty in the administration of justice," permission to open up consular and commercial relations with whomever the government saw fit, and an end to restrictions on scientific and industrial research.[53]

The chancellor also pressed for the release of the few hundred war criminals who were still imprisoned in West Germany, warning that support for rearmament would be seriously compromised if leniency were not displayed. Hanging in the balance was the future of some of the most egregious criminals of the Hitler era, including people like SS officers Sepp Dietrich and Jochen Peiper, who had been convicted by a U.S. military tribunal for their principal role in the Malmédy massacre at the outset of the Ardennes offensive, when seventy-one unarmed American POWs were lined up in a snow-covered field and machine-gunned to death by Waffen SS killers.

Adenauer dispatched his top military aide, Lieutenant General Adolf Heusinger, who put it country simple to McCloy: freeing the soldiers was a prerequisite to West Germany's joining the Western defense mission. Otto Skorzeny chimed in with a similar message from Madrid. "If Peiper dies it is all over," he threatened. "In good faith, even with a certain amount of enthusiasm, we have put ourselves at the disposal of the Americans. Yet, I repeat in the name of all German officers who are working for the future victory of the West, if Peiper dies we will no longer lift a finger to help but will yield to the opposing point of view."[54]

Back in Washington, Senator Joseph McCarthy had launched a high-profile lobbying effort in an attempt to overturn the Malmédy convictions. McCarthy claimed that crucial evidence related to the massacre had been extracted through the torture of German prisoners, some of whom allegedly had their testicles crushed by U.S. interrogators. The ensuing furor resulted in an early publicity windfall for McCarthy, who would soon initiate his infamous anti-Communist witch-hunts. Ironically, McCarthy based his false charges regarding the Malmédy affair on information provided by Dr. Rudolf Aschenauer, a German attorney with close ties to Remer's SRP and the postwar Nazi underground, who had previously represented a number of Nuremberg defendants.[55]

Buffeted by demands from the entire spectrum of German nationalist groups, the high commissioner mulled over requests to declare a full amnesty for the remaining prisoners, even the mass murderers on death row. McCloy was not one to shy away from controversial decisions. During World War II, he had argued in favor of the internment of Japanese Americans, yet opposed all but a trickle of Jewish immigration into the United States. He also successfully sought to forestall Allied military action against railways servicing the Nazi death camps on the grounds that doing so would divert resources from "decisive operations elsewhere." Now he had to wrestle with the problem of what to do about the condemned Nazis in light of the U.S. government's resolve to build up the West German military.

In January 1951, McCloy announced that verdicts would be reduced in 74 out of 104 cases. All but five death sentences were commuted. Sepp Dietrich and Jochen Peiper had their prison terms cut; a few years later, both men were paroled. Other SS war criminals, such as Dr. Franz Six (leader of a mobile killing unit on the eastern front), immediately joined the Gehlen Org when their sentences were overturned. Thanks to McCloy, high-ranking Nazi judges who had dispensed Gestapo justice during the Third Reich also walked free and resumed their careers as legal arbiters in West Germany; some of these former People's Tribunal judges had imposed the death penalty on persons convicted of telling an anti-Hitler joke or having sexual relations with a Jew. Imprisoned doctors who had conducted ghastly experiments on concentration camp inmates were also released from West German penitentiaries.[56]

Outside Germany, McCloy's mass clemency provoked a mixture of shock and indignation that Nazi criminals of such magnitude were back in circulation little more than five years since the war. Perhaps no decision provoked greater outrage than the release of

Alfried Krupp, whose mammoth steel company had helped finance Hitler's path to power. Known as a "super-Nazi" among German industrialists, Krupp had been convicted of plundering occupied territories and utilizing slave labor to boost company profits during the war. In addition to pardoning the steel magnate, McCloy rescinded a property-confiscation order, thereby restoring Krupp's vast holdings as well as his status as one of the world's wealthiest men. A beaming Krupp strode out of Landsberg prison and celebrated at a champagne brunch with his supporters. Ilse and Otto Skorzeny quickly picked up Krupp Steel as one of their most prestigious clients, representing the firm in Spain and South America. Soon the Krupp company began assembling jet fighters and other necessities for America's Cold War military buildup.[57]

The Spook Who Never Returned

Joseph Stalin's recurring nightmare of an Anglo-German strategic alliance haunted him once again as the Soviet dictator watched West Germany rev up its military-industrial engines at the behest of the United States and NATO. The Kremlin condemned "plans for resurrecting the fascist Wehrmacht under American control," but verbal attacks did little to deter Adenauer and McCloy in their efforts to integrate the Federal Republic into an anti-Communist military bloc. To that end, the Western powers had already begun "contractual negotiations" on matters of sovereignty with the Bonn government.

Alarmed by the rapidly developing course of events, Soviet leaders decided to play their ace in the hole. In March 1952, they threw down the gauntlet in the form of a "peace bombshell" that was designed to upset NATO's applecart and derail the rearmament express. Stalin endorsed German reunification in free elections up to the Oder–Neisse line. The offer was made in a diplomatic note, which stipulated that Germany would be allowed to maintain its own military and its own armament industry; that there would be no limits on German trade and economic development; and that all foreign troops would be withdrawn within a year after an agreement was reached. The note also called for the full restoration of civil and political rights to "all former members of the German army, including officers and generals, [and] all former Nazis, excluding those who are serving court sentences for the commission of crimes." The only proviso the Soviets insisted upon was that a reunited Germany could not enter into a military pact with any of its former enemies or join "any kind of coalition or military alliance directed against any power which took part with its armed forces in the war against Germany." Neutrality was a nonnegotiable cornerstone of the Soviet plan.[58]

Stalin had correctly surmised that such a dramatic proposal would sway fence-sitters and galvanize neutralist feeling in West Germany. The prospect of a united Germany had immense appeal. Polls conducted by the U.S. high commissioner's office indicated that a majority favored putting the contractual negotiations on hold while the Soviet offer was seriously explored. According to some surveys, reunification was preferred to "westintegration" by a two-to-one margin. Even a few members of Adenauer's Christian Democratic Union were warm to the Soviet note. It was, after all, a rather alluring package: reunification and self-determination without war, a German army not subject to foreign command, and a huge potential market for German industrial products in the USSR and Eastern Europe. This seemed a lot more attractive than the American plan for permanently dividing the country, with a West German army under U.S. control and no chance in the foreseeable future for regaining any land lost during the war.[59]

Stalin repeated the same proposal on two more occasions that year, but in each case Adenauer and McCloy dismissed the Soviet offer as a public-relations gesture calculated to disrupt the Western alliance. Privately, however, frantic State Department officials conceded that the Soviet note "has the ring of considered policy rather than propaganda." In one fell swoop, the Soviet gambit had succeeded in putting the onus for the partition of Germany on the United States. American policy makers were suddenly backed into a diplomatic corner. They tried to wriggle out by asserting that only a democratically elected German government could decide whether or not to align itself with either superpower. Fearing that German neutrality was "more favorable to Soviet plans than to our own . . .

and readily lends itself to Eastern manipulation," the State Department refused to accede to Russian demands on this crucial point. American distrust of Germany was too strong to permit such a deal — and a chance to end the Cold War was aborted.[60]

The resurgence of neutralist sentiment in the wake of the Soviet note was a boon for Major General Otto Ernst Remer and the Socialist Reich Party. They viewed the Russian offer as the basis for genuine negotiations and vilified Adenauer for his stubborn intransigence. For once the SRP found itself in good company, as opposition to U.S. plans for rearming the country ran the gamut of the West German political spectrum — from sincere, war-weary pacifists to Social Democrats, Communists, and bitter-end Nazis. This crazy quilt of groups and factions that composed the neutralist scene made for strange political bedfellows, as the SRP began to work in tandem with the West German Communist Party (KPD).

In May 1951, SRP chairman Fritz Dorls met with KPD leaders in an effort to cement their anti-Adenauer ties. Both organizations had campaigned against U.S. intervention in Korea. But the KPD, an obedient tool of Soviet foreign policy, wielded little influence in West German politics. The SRP, by contrast, was a growing mass-based party that espoused neutralism for far different reasons than the Communists. Remer and his colleagues pursued a strategic relationship with the Soviet Union because they hoped to achieve a reunited Fatherland, armed to the teeth, that would be able to use its pivotal position between East and West to dominate Europe. "The only danger to our plans," said Dorls, "is an understanding between the United States and Russia. If that happens, of course, we are lost — but then that cannot happen."[61]

Dorls and other SRP operatives occasionally traveled across the great superpower divide for clandestine encounters with the East German National Front, which had been set up by the Soviets as a sop for ex-Nazis, army officers, and others tainted by their association with the Hitler regime. Closely supervised by Communist officials, the Front was one of several nationalist formations that sprang up in the Soviet zone after the Russians abruptly announced the end of denazification in 1948.[62]

Certainly the Soviet Union, which had suffered more losses on the battlefield and in the POW and concentration camps during

World War II than any other country, did a much better job than its Western counterparts in purging Third Reich veterans from public institutions and bringing Nazi war criminals to trial. Over half a million former Nazi Party members were expelled from their posts and thirteen thousand war criminals were given lengthy sentences in East German prisons. But Soviet policy shifted as the Cold War hardened and the United States began taking steps to rearm West Germany.[63]

Soon East Germany embarked upon a new "nationalist course," and former Hitlerites who had "atoned by honest labor" were officially welcomed back into the fold. By professing a swift conversion to Communism, ex-Nazis became eligible for immediate rehabilitation. Many with a tainted past were absorbed into the ranks of the East German police and the Staatssicherheitsdienst (state security service). Although smaller in scope than the wholesale restoration that occurred in West Germany, the return to power of numerous Gestapo, SS, and Wehrmacht veterans under Soviet auspices prompted a State Department analyst to remark, "[T]he USSR has decided to take a risk on the former Nazis in the expectation that they will be salvageable for pro-Communist, or at least, police and paramilitary work. [This] may well be a 'Pandora's Box' which produces unforeseen consequences to the carefully laid Soviet plans." That a Pandora's box may already have been opened in Bonn went unmentioned.[64]

In addition to conferring with erstwhile Nazis, SRP representatives took their case directly to the Russian authorities in East Germany. "I sent my people there," Remer admitted years later. "They were all received at the Soviet headquarters in Pankow." At the time, however, SRP leaders were not inclined to publicly acknowledge these contacts — contacts that led to Soviet financial support for Remer's party. In this instance, ideological differences were deemed less important than tactical considerations for both sides. Apparently Soviet intelligence saw the neo-Nazi SRP as a better investment than the ineffectual KPD. And the SRP, needing funds, was willing to tango with the Russians. "It's one of those funny parts of German history after the war," a close associate of Remer's explained. "For a while in the early 1950s, the Socialist Reich Party was funded by Russia, the KPD was not."[65]

The State Department suspected that the SRP was consciously in cahoots with the Soviets. It is "the first sizable party that shows clear signs of playing with the Communists," a State Department official warned in December 1950. A few months later, another State Department document indicated that the SRP "has gained something of a reputation for having ties to the East." Their suspicions were confirmed by a number of local SRP officials who quit the party after they learned of links to the Soviet bloc. A Berlin-based State Department officer concluded that the SRP, although "committed to right radicalism," was "receiving assistance from the East German authorities, in return for which it parrots the communist line on such subjects as neutrality. The communists also appear to be exploiting the SRP's value as a disruptive element in West Berlin."[66]

As it turned out, the SRP was but one of several radical nationalist organizations that obtained support from the East. Chancellor Adenauer would have had to look no further than the German Party, which participated in the original national governing coalition in the West German Bundestag, to find right-wing extremists who danced to the Soviet tune. Former SS Major Fritz Brehm, a major figure in the Bavarian section of the German Party, played a leading role in a number of East-financed newspapers that promoted a nationalist-neutralist line.[67]

Needless to say, not all neo-Nazis who adopted an anti-American stance were paid Soviet agents. As Kurt Tauber explains, "Some radical nationalists, for one reason or another, wanted essentially what the Russian strategists had stipulated as their first objective. Since they were doing for their own purposes what the Soviets would have wanted them to do, there was no need for special solicitude or bribery on the Communists' part. In other cases, it was the nationalist radicals who — again for a variety of reasons — sought contact with the East Zonal or Soviet authorities, rather than being sought out by them."[68]

While the Eastern turn was central to Remer's vision of an independent postwar Germany, many former Nazis firmly believed that hitching a ride with the Western powers would open up the greatest possibilities for reasserting national strength. These conflicting perspectives resulted in a curious and somewhat ironic lineup of forces: on one side, there were men (like Gehlen and Globke) who pulled official strings and worked with Western intelligence agencies that subsidized rabid authoritarians and antidemocrats; on the other side stood the SRP and like-minded fanatics who were often in collusion with the Communists. And some ex-Nazis moved back and forth between both camps, depending on what seemed most expeditious at the moment.

The internecine maneuvering within the radical nationalist milieu was epitomized by the bizarre saga of the Bruderschaft, a half political, half mystical secret society composed of former Hitler Youth, Wehrmacht, and SS officers. Founded in July 1949 as a paramilitary cadre organization, the 2,500-strong Bruderschaft developed a close working relationship with the SRP and cultivated ties with neo-Nazi groups in South America, the Middle East, and elsewhere in Europe. It was instrumental in the underground railroad that enabled war criminals and other Third Reich fugitives to establish themselves abroad. "Because of the relatively small number of members," the State Department discerned, "the [Bruderschaft] does not entertain the hope of ever being able to achieve its aims through democratic processes."[69]

Alfred Franke-Gricksch, a former SS officer and the Bruderschaft's chief ideologist, was an avid proponent of the "Europe as a third force" concept. On much the same wavelength as the SRP, he agitated for a nonaggression pact with the Soviet Union. In response to an invitation by Lieutenant General Vincent Müller, vice-chairman of the Communist-led National Democratic Party in East Germany, Franke-Gricksch traveled to the Soviet zone for a series of meetings designed to coordinate a common struggle for reunification. He quickly opened lines of communication with the Soviet Military Administration and east zone authorities. An American consular officer in Bremen noted in his weekly intelligence assessment that Franke-Gricksch was also in contact with Otto Skorzeny, a Bruderschaft bigwig, regarding these forays into the east zone.[70]

Meanwhile, Bruderschaft founder and co-leader Helmut Beck-Broichsitter had also been visiting the east zone, but this was only part of a dangerous, double-faced game that he was playing. A mercurial figure, Beck negotiated behind the scenes with the East while simultaneously offering his services to the Americans. On several occasions, he engaged in lengthy discussions with State Department officials, trying to interest them in a proposal for a paramilitary vigilante network, hand-picked by the Bruderschaft, that would combat "Red terror" throughout West Germany. His father confessor at the American consulate in Hamburg soon learned that Beck and Franke-Gricksch, unable to agree on which way to tilt in the East-West conflict, had gotten embroiled in a major dispute that split the Bruderschaft into competing factions and eventually destroyed the organization. Their feud, both personal and political, was emblematic of the continual splintering and reuniting of radical grouplets within the ultranationalist matrix.[71]

According to various State Department accounts, Beck often complained that his rival had more money than he did because of the largesse of his Eastern patrons. Beck also accused Franke-Gricksch of extorting cash from West German industrialists, who sought to buy protection in the event of a Soviet invasion. At another meeting, Beck disclosed that he, too, "had offers of Soviet financial support," but an astute U.S. official discerned that he was only trying to use this as a lever to obtain money from the Americans. Beck "appears to drive for his objective in a somewhat devious manner," the State Department concluded.[72]

Such shenanigans did not bode well for Franke-Gricksch, as word of Beck's association with U.S. intelligence quickly got back to the Russians. Suspecting that the Bruderschaft was honeycombed with American agents, Soviet authorities henceforth cast a wary eye on Franke-Gricksch. In October 1951, he disappeared in East Berlin and was never heard from again. His wife also vanished while searching for him. After a few years, she returned to West Germany with the news that Franke-Gricksch had been condemned to death by a Russian military court. Decades later, Franke-Gricksch's son would emerge as a figure of some repute in neo-Nazi circles.[73]

Golden Handcuffs

The mysterious demise of Franke-Gricksch underscored the high stakes inherent in the Cold War spy drama that was unfolding on German soil, as Third Reich veterans plied their cloak-and-dagger skills on both sides of the superpower divide. Furtive Nazi overtures to the USSR after the fall of the Third Reich constituted yet another strange chapter in an ongoing historical drama involving Germany and Russia.

Prussia, the kernel of the German nation-state, perennially looked eastward in keeping with the long military tradition of its General Staff, which had viewed Russia as a natural ally ever since Frederick the Great was enthroned in the mid-eighteenth century. Several royal weddings united the Prussian monarchy with its Russian counterpart. The importance of this geopolitical alliance was driven home again when czarist forces helped Prussia defeat Napoleon in the early 1800s. With mineral-rich Russia needing German manufactured goods and Germany coveting raw materials from Russia, the two countries carried on a brisk trade from Bismarck's time until World War I.

Humiliated and embittered by the terms of the Versailles Treaty, Germany struck a secret deal with beleaguered Soviet Russia, which also had been ostracized by the victorious Western powers. In an effort to circumvent Versailles-imposed military restrictions, the Prussian-dominated Reichswehr (as the German army was called) began to collaborate with the fledgling Red Army shortly after the Russian Revolution. The conservative Prussian military elite steadfastly maintained that the national interests of Germany and Russia were compatible in spite of their ideological differences. Of mutual benefit to both countries, the German-Russian partnership was codified in the April 1922 Rapallo pact.*

* Confronted with a Versailles-imposed limitation of one hundred thousand soldiers for the German army, General Hans von Seeckt, chief of the German army High Command during the Weimar years, succeeded in carrying out a massive deception operation that duped the Western powers, which mistakenly assumed that conflicting ideologies would preclude any chance of serious cooperation between capitalist Germany and Communist Russia. As historian Edward Hallett Carr notes, von Seeckt negotiated a deal whereby German military officers traveled to the Soviet Union to test new weapons and instruct German troops while also sharing their expertise with the Red Army. In exchange for military assistance and help in rebuilding the war-shattered Soviet economy, von Seeckt was able to take advantage of the wide-open spaces of the Russian

At the time it was enacted, the tie-up with Russia drew support from all shades of political opinion in post-Versailles Germany, including some radical nationalists who began to think of themselves as "Bolsheviks of the right" or "National Bolsheviks." Fearing that the German soul would be corrupted by "Americanization," these ideological dissidents viewed parliamentary democracy as an alien import to be resisted at all costs. This was obvious to D. H. Lawrence when he visited Germany in 1924. "The great leaning of the Germanic spirit is once again more Eastwards, toward Russia," Lawrence observed.[74]

Several varieties of non-Nazi fascism percolated in Germany during the crucial decade before Hitler seized power. Nourished by a deep-rooted culture of despair, Oswald Spengler, Arthur Moeller van den Bruck, Ernst Jünger, and other widely read critics associated with the so-called Conservative Revolution lamented the loss of community and *Volk*-rootedness. Insisting that the Weimar Republic be replaced by a dictatorship, these brooding prophets "attacked, often incisively and justly, the deficiencies of German culture and the German spirit," says historian Fritz Stern. They were instrumental in shaping the mental and psychological climate that set the stage for

---

steppes, which were well suited to accommodate aviation and tank training, joint German-Soviet war games, and other conspicuous, large-scale exercises. Eager to do business with the Soviets, major German industrialists and bankers threw their weight behind von Seeckt's plan. Hjalmar Schacht was in the thick of it, conducting sensitive negotiations that provided credit for the Bolshevik government as German firms established factories on Russian soil that produced poison gas, tanks, airplanes, heavy weapons, and explosives proscribed by the Versailles Treaty. Krupp Steel was particularly adept at disguising its illegal preparations for rearmament; it owned several munitions plants and an oil concession in the Caucasus. At the same time, Germany also began to put out feelers for a gradual rapprochement with the Western powers. With one of its directors serving as Germany's ambassador to Washington, the Krupp company sought to cultivate better relations with the United States. British and American loans soon exceeded the amount of German reparations required by Versailles. But even as U.S. banks and corporations pumped up the German economy with investments, two powerful institutional forces — the Prussian-dominated General Staff and a rejuvenated military-industrial complex — remained committed to a geopolitical alliance with the Soviet Union.

the Nazi movement, which "gathered together the millions of malcontents, of whose existence the conservative revolutionaries had for so long spoken, and for whose relief they had designed such dangerous and elusive ideals."[75]

Many leading thinkers of the Conservative Revolution favored a geopolitical tryst with Bolshevik Russia — a passion shared by Joseph Goebbels, the young rabble-rouser who emerged as a mainstay of the Eastern-oriented wing of the Nazi Party. Goebbels praised the Soviet Union as "an ally which nature has given us against the devilish temptation and corruption of the West." But the Hitler-Stalin pact of August 1939, which was greeted with enthusiasm in Prussian officer circles, proved to be only a temporary reprieve.[76]

Despite warnings from his military advisors, Hitler initiated battle on two fronts simultaneously. Ironically, many of the weapons that pounded Russian cities during World War II had been produced in Soviet factories under the auspices of the Rapallo agreement. The ensuing catastrophe at Stalingrad underscored to many Third Reich veterans the validity of Bismarck's injunction that Germany must never allow its interests to conflict with Russia's. That was certainly how Major General Otto Ernst Remer and the leaders of the Socialist Reich Party felt.

Invoking the memory of Rapallo — which remains a potent symbol and slogan in German-Russian diplomacy — Remer insisted that German national interests required an agreement with the East, this time on the basis of the Soviet proposals of March 1952. Paradoxically, Remer's hard-core, pro-Soviet posturing may have played to the advantage of those German nationalists who favored cooperation with the West as long as they could keep extracting political concessions from the United States.

With the threat of a new Rapallo casting a shadow over American plans to rearm West Germany, Adenauer pressured High Commissioner McCloy for additional compromises as they haggled over an overarching treaty that would grant independence to the Federal Republic. "Time is on our side," the chancellor told a group of his close collaborators in Bonn. "American insistence on a German army will eventually force the Western powers to accede to our demands."[77]

Driven by an almost pathological fear that West Germany would drift into a neutral orbit if he turned down Adenauer's requests, McCloy yielded on nearly every point. Signed on May 1952, the so-called Contractual Agreement stipulated that Bonn would exercise authority over both its internal and external affairs; for his part, Adenauer consented to pitch in twelve divisions to a European defense force. West German sovereignty, although still somewhat limited by old Allied prerogatives and new obligations to NATO, officially went into effect three years later.

With its newfound freedom, Bonn soon passed a law allowing former SS members to join the West German army with the same rank as they held during World War II. Kurt "Panzer" Meyer, the head of HIAG, greeted this belated recognition with enthusiasm. "Yes, my comrades," he proclaimed at an SS reunion, "this Federal Republic is really our State." The Bundeswehr, as the new army was called, was commanded in large part by the same generals who had earned their stripes in Hitler's Wehrmacht. War veterans and ex-Nazis were given generous government pensions, and industrialists (including Skorzeny's business associate, Willi Messerschmitt) received lucrative contracts to produce weapons for NATO and the West German military. The very existence of a West German weapons industry was a closely guarded secret during the 1950s and 1960s.[78]

But what assurance did the U.S. government have that a revived West German army would function as an effective bulwark against the Soviet Union? Would a strong West Germany necessarily be a dependable ally? McCloy questioned the political reliability of the Germans, but this made him all the more intent on staying the course with Adenauer. The high commissioner deemed it preferable to live with the risks of the Cold War than to tangle with a neutral, unified Germany — even if it meant that much of the country had to toil under Communism. He was not willing to hazard the uncertainties of an unfettered, nonaligned Germany that might, once again, be tempted to engage in *Schaukelpolitik,* to play the East off the West and vice versa, in an effort to dominate the Continent. Therefore, U.S. officials pursued a dual containment policy aimed at putting golden handcuffs on West Germany while keeping the Soviets at bay. "Overtly, NATO was a Western alliance to contain the Soviet Union," explained Walter Russell Mead. "Tacitly, it was also expected to contain Germany." Historians Joyce and Gabriel Kolko argue that protecting "the West against Germany rather than Russia was the ultimate basis of this calculus."[79]

American officials believed that anchoring Bonn within the Atlantic system would provide the best defense against a possible resurgence of nationalist and irredentist sentiment, a development that McCloy anticipated. "The all-prevailing power of the National Socialist regime has left many former officials with a longing for power," the high commissioner wrote in his report for the last quarter of 1952, adding that "the undercurrent of extreme nationalism might form a combination willing again to set Germany off on another dangerous adventure." But he was willing to gamble that over time, if the economic recovery continued and living standards kept rising, the Germans could be weaned of their *Volk*-ish obsessions.[80]

Incipient signs of West German prosperity made the golden handcuffs seem much more attractive than Soviet-backed repression in East Germany, where a workers' rebellion was swiftly crushed in June 1953. Neo-Nazis who favored neutralism were further weakened by splits that bedeviled the radical nationalist scene. In the end, the debate over rearmament proved so divisive that it seriously undermined the anti-Communist opposition to Adenauer, who won over prominent right-wing leaders by offering them ministerial posts and other blandishments. While dangling these carrots, the chancellor also wielded a mighty stick when dealing with incorrigibles like Otto Ernst Remer and the SRP.

Kept under close surveillance by Western intelligence agencies, several leading SRP members were convicted on various charges, ranging from slandering the Federal Republic to tearing down the West German flag. Remer himself was sentenced to a four-month prison term in 1951 because he had publicly insulted Adenauer and other Bonn officials. Noting the "rather strange reaction" to the verdict, an American vice-consul in Bremen reported that every political figure surveyed by his office "criticized the decision in private, even though they all said they were against Remer. . . . The feeling is that Remer will now become a martyr and his party will benefit from it."[81]

Quick to make hay out of the difficulties put in his way, Remer compared his own persecution to that of Jesus Christ. He referred to High Commissioner McCloy as "the Pontius Pilate who had caused Herod [to] crucify the SRP." Remer felt that McCloy was out to get him because of "the SRP's strong line against remilitarization and adherence to the Atlantic Pact." Remer's Christ complex was further in evidence when he declared, "If we should be banned, we shall descend into the catacombs like the early Christians."[82]

While serving time in prison for offending the chancellor, Remer was tried and convicted for making defamatory remarks about the Twentieth of July conspirators. A number of books devoted to the anti-Hitler coup attempt had already achieved wide distribution in ultranationalist circles. Among the most popular was *July 20th, 1944,* by Remer, whose landmark defamation case established the principle that the Nazi state was illegal and that Germans who conspired to overthrow Hitler were not guilty of treason. This verdict set an important precedent for subsequent legal measures against neo-Nazi propagandists in West Germany.[83]

While incarcerated, a defiant Remer made noises about staging a general strike. "We agree to any means of overthrowing the state," he proclaimed. But the other SRP leaders, bickering increasingly among themselves, saw the writing on the wall. Their days as a party were numbered.[84]

Under intense government pressure, the SRP began to fracture. Key members bolted to form new groups. Other SRP stalwarts vowed to carry on the struggle underground, if necessary. Anticipating that the party would soon be proscribed, some drew up elaborate plans for salvaging as much as possible of the SRP apparatus. There was talk of infiltrating other parties, taking them over, and delivering the SRP vote in the 1953 national elections. Dr. Rudolf Aschenauer — the pro-Nazi attorney who represented some of the Nuremberg defendants — consented to head a new nationalist party that would function as a camouflaged SRP successor organization. Aschenauer's close ties to the pro-Soviet SRP were particularly ironic given that he also collaborated with Senator Joseph McCarthy, the rabid anti-Communist, in an effort to overturn the Malmédy verdicts.[85]

But Aschenauer's scheme to continue the SRP under a new name was doomed, as U.S. intelligence quickly got wind of his intentions.

After October 23, 1952, the SRP faithful would have to fend for themselves. On that day, Remer's party was outlawed by the West German Constitutional Court, which branded the SRP as the direct successor of the Nazi Party. Agreeing with Bonn's charge that Remer was "engrossed in national socialistic ideology" and had "objectively abused the basic right of freedom of expression," the court stripped him of his right to vote and hold public office.[86]

Facing a second prison term — this time for three months — stemming from the July 20 libel conviction, Remer scampered for cover. He hid for a while in the Bavarian Alps at a hunting chalet owned by the wealthy Faber-Castell family, the pencil manufacturers, who were SRP supporters. There Remer considered his dwindling options. With political engagement on the home front ruled out for the moment, he could hide in the mountains, go to jail, or flee the country. It was a tough decision, but help was on the way from some unlikely places.

CHAPTER THREE

NEO-NAZI DIASPORA

Wotan at the Funny Farm

Harold Keith Thompson, a New Jersey-born businessman and public-relations specialist, spent much of his time in the late 1940s and early 1950s carrying on behind the scenes as the principal U.S. point man for die Spinne (the Spider), the postwar Nazi support network. Although not yet thirty years old, this strapping, dark-haired, six-foot bachelor had become, in his own words, "the chief and almost exclusive representative in North America for the interests of the surviving National Socialist German Workers' Party (NSDAP) and the SS."[1]

Descended from a line of Prussian field marshals and Scottish noblemen, Thompson got his first taste of Nazi ideology as a teenager when he joined the German-American Bund and the isolationist America First movement, both of which were secretly financed by Hitler's Reich. Boasting fifteen thousand U.S. members and one hundred thousand supporters in its heyday, the Bund held uniformed rallies and celebrations, including Hitler birthday dances, where pictures of George Washington were framed with swastikas. The Bund also sponsored summer camps for German-American children that featured paramilitary drills and exercises in addition to sports and social activities. "The leadership was not the best," Thompson acknowledged, "but the spirit was there, and I liked it."[2]

Thompson's political sympathies and his penchant for covert activity made him a natural ally of German intelligence during World War II. "I did some very sensitive work," he admitted somewhat elliptically. "A high school student carrying around a bundle of books could get into things, you know." Thompson hinted that he was involved in sabotage operations, referring to "a steamship that sank, things like that." But he wouldn't elaborate further. "That was a long time ago. No sense in bringing it out now."

This much, however, can be confirmed: on July 27, 1941, Thompson became a special agent of the Nazi SD/Overseas Intelligence Unit. A document to this effect, signed by Hitler himself, was captured by a U.S. Army team that moved into Munich. "It was not a misrepresentation," Thompson acknowledged. "The document came from Interpol, which had it in their files."

When it became obvious that Germany was going to lose the war, Thompson and his colleagues started "to set things up quietly," as he put it, in preparation for the post-Hitler era. Thompson resumed his studies at Yale and graduated in 1946. ("It was a good place to learn how to drink," he quipped.) Shortly thereafter, he went on an expedition to Antarctica, where he reflected upon the fall of the Third Reich. "It was a great shame. The infernal meddling of the United States in two world wars was quite unnecessary," he later remarked.

Upon returning to the United States, Thompson redoubled his efforts to assist the flotsam and jetsam of the Axis that drifted precariously in the postwar mix. "The real National Socialists were on the lam if they could get out of Germany at all," he stated. "That worked in a number of ways. Several organizations maintained a service to get individuals out, using false passports and the like. People were available to help at various stages of the process." South America, the Iberian Peninsula, and the Middle East were favored havens for fascist fugitives.

Through his political activities, Thompson befriended several important personalities in the international neofascist scene, including Otto "Scarface" Skorzeny, the premier web-spinner. "Skorzeny was not an intellectual. He was a get-it-done type, a soldier. Very daring. He would take on anything," said Thompson. "He played a significant role after the war in the escape routes."

The versatile Thompson made himself available when Skorzeny

and other ODESSA wire-pullers needed a favor done in the United States. "Those were difficult years," Thompson confided. "Sure, some money was put away. But, by and large, the people who fled Germany had to depend on the generosity of those who had already settled in the area." Thompson had signature control of an ODESSA bank account at the Royal Trust in Kitchener, Ontario, a small city west of Toronto. "Funds were always limited, as the costs of ODESSA were enormous," he explained. "There were officials to be bribed (in the good old American way), lawyers to be engaged, identity papers to be procured and/or forged from scratch."[3]

It didn't matter to Thompson that Skorzeny tilted expediently toward the West while other Third Reich veterans played the Eastern card during the Cold War. He was willing to assist any committed Nazi who required a helping hand, including the leaders of the Socialist Reich Party in the Federal Republic of Germany.

During the early 1950s, Thompson was one of the SRP's busiest boosters. In an effort to drum up American support for the controversial West German political party, he registered with the Justice Department as the U.S. representative of the SRP. In this capacity, he lobbied American officials and press outlets for more favorable treatment of the SRP and raised funds for those individuals who were being harassed by Bonn. A smooth, mild-mannered operator, Thompson contacted hundreds of German-American groups and alerted them to the plight of his idol, Otto Ernst Remer.

"Remer was the only man in postwar Germany that I thought had a chance of achieving some political power and whose views represented basically my own," Thompson explained years later. "There were very few people of his stature. In my opinion, he was a great man."

While his hero was in jail in 1952, Thompson set up the Committee for the Freedom of Major General Remer and began bombarding anyone who would listen with announcements and press releases. He filed legal briefs on Remer's behalf, hoping to spring him from prison. "I established the committee as a means of publicizing the SRP, the battles in which it was engaged, and the attempt to suppress it," said Thompson. "I produced some money for them."

Threatening to petition the United Nations, Thompson argued in a letter to Secretary of State Dean Acheson that the incarceration of

Remer was "an international civil liberties case of primary importance." He wrote to Chancellor Adenauer and members of the West German Bundestag, calling for an end to "the persecution of General Remer and minority rightist political parties." In an unpublished letter to the editors of *Time* magazine, Thompson described Remer as "a young, vigorous, far-seeing political leader of the New Germany." His final statement to the Justice Department paid tribute to "the courageous leadership of General Remer," whom he called "the hope of Germany and the Free World."[4]

After the SRP was banned, Thompson terminated the Committee for the Freedom of Major General Remer. But he did not cut his ties with key people who were involved in the party. "Please inform General Remer of my loyalty to him and my continuing desire to be of service in any way possible," Thompson assured the SRP leadership. An appreciative Remer thanked his American friend in a letter that concluded with an aphorism from Nietzsche: "What doesn't kill you makes you stronger."[5]

Thompson's devotion to Remer was not sullied when he learned that the SRP had received funds from the USSR. "Take money where you can get it," Thompson explained, shrugging. "I always said that if the Soviets wanted to give me money to support my activities, I'd rush to the bank with the check and hope it was good." Defending Remer's tactics, he maintained that several neo-Nazi organizations in West Germany were happy to take Communist funds, "provided they didn't have to compromise their political principles."[6]

While representing the SRP, H. Keith Thompson also served as a registered U.S. agent for *Die Andere Seite (The Other Side)*, a Munich-based periodical published by Dr. Rudolf Aschenauer, West Germany's big-wheel ultranationalist attorney who worked closely with Remer's party as well as with Senator Joseph McCarthy. Aschenauer and Thompson were both involved in waging a public-relations campaign to free Nazi war criminals from West German jails.[7]

Grand Admiral Karl Doenitz, Hitler's chosen successor, thanked Thompson for his support after Doenitz was released from prison in 1957, somewhat later than most convicted Nazis. The West German government subsequently restored full pension rights to Doenitz, thanks in part to an international campaign mounted by Thompson, who carried on a lively correspondence with fascist sympathizers throughout the world. "My principal contacts," Thompson acknowledged, "were within nationalist parties and organizations, not only in the United States and Germany but in Canada, England, South Africa, Argentina, Brazil, Spain, Portugal, Italy, Sweden, and the Middle East."

The tentacles of die Spinne reached into the Soviet bloc as well. "There were a number of people in power in East Germany who were very friendly to our circles," Thompson recalled. "I suddenly began to receive a lot of East German press releases and publications of a historical institute that they had. They were seeking an exchange of information. In East Germany we had contact with people who had worked for the SD [the SS foreign intelligence service]. . . . It made sense for the East Germans to hire ex-Nazis. They knew what was what."

Thompson also got involved with a bizarre neo-Nazi sect called the National Renaissance Party (NRP). Based in New York City, the NRP took its name from Hitler's "Last Political Testament," written just before the Führer committed suicide: "I die with a happy heart aware [that there] will spring up . . . the seed of a radiant renaissance of the National Socialist movement." In an attempt to generate publicity for the party, Thompson agreed to appear as the featured speaker at several NRP meetings. Gathering in hotels and private homes, a handful of nomadic NRP members listened to Thompson carry on about alleged injustices perpetrated by the U.S. government against convicted Nazi war criminals and other German kinfolk.[8]

James Madole, the nominal chief of the NRP, was a balding shipping clerk in his mid-forties who lived with his mother, a raving anti-Semite. Defining the goal of the NRP as a "racial nationalist state," Madole vowed to defend the Aryan people against "contamination" by deporting all nonwhites. And he promised to put an end to Communism by eliminating the Jews. "Although Adolf Hitler is dead," Madole wrote in the NRP's monthly mimeograph bulletin, "his philosophy lives again in the growing strength of fascist forces in America, Europe and the Middle East. What Hitler accomplished in Europe, the National Renaissance Party shall yet accomplish in America."[9]

In seasonable weather, Madole could be seen haranguing some two dozen followers in the Yorkville section of Manhattan, where many German immigrants lived. Dressed in Hitler storm-trooper uniforms, a bevy of NRP oddballs passed out pamphlets that featured inflammatory messages, such as "You are being brainwashed by a pro-Communist, Jew-controlled press. . . ." These rowdy displays invariably attracted hecklers, who jeered while Madole praised Hitler and Mussolini and berated racial minorities.[10]

Such gatherings, which often ended in fisticuffs, prompted the House Un-American Activities Committee (HUAC) to depart momentarily from its Red-hunting activities in order to investigate Madole's goons. Characterizing the NRP as an "avowed neofascist organization," a HUAC preliminary report recommended that the Justice Department ascertain "whether prosecution of its leaders under the provisions of the Smith Act was possible." But no action was ever taken.[11]

The HUAC probe identified Frederick C. F. Weiss, a hawk-nosed, heavyset German World War I veteran, as the main force behind the NRP (although he held no official position in the organization). The ruddy-complected Weiss was H. Keith Thompson's most visible political ally during the period when he represented the Socialist Reich Party. Both men were part of a small circle of Nazi intellectuals in the New York City area, which became an important relay point for the postwar international fascist network. Through Weiss, the NRP maintained ties to a panoply of white racialist groups in the United States and abroad. He was in contact with the Viking Youth, an SRP spin-off organization, which often sent layouts of material to be printed by the NRP. LeBlanc Publications, run by Weiss and Thompson, handled many requests from overseas. This propaganda support role by neo-Nazis in the United States would continue throughout the Cold War and later.[12]

Every so often, Weiss hosted a racialist conclave at his run-down farmhouse outside Middletown, New York. "I was never very comfortable there," Thompson confessed. "His wife was positively nuts. She maintained such a filthy house that I didn't want to eat anything they served. She was constantly talking about visits from [the German god] Wotan and her father's rising from the grave, or some such damned thing." Yet, Frau Weiss, for all her idiosyncrasies, hardly stood out among the weird assortment of cranks, fanatics, social misfits, closeted homosexuals, and undercover informants who turned up regularly at the farm.

Among those who frequented the Weiss household was Eustace Mullins, the NRP's self-proclaimed expert on the U.S. Federal Reserve System. Described by H. Keith Thompson as a "veteran crackpot propagandist of the radical Right," Mullins wrote an article for the *National Renaissance Bulletin* entitled "Adolf Hitler: An Appreciation." He also organized the Free Ezra Pound Committee while the fascist poet was sequestered in a psychiatric hospital in Washington, D.C.[13]

Mullins occasionally joined NRP members at street-corner demonstrations, where he ranted about how the Jews had killed Eisenhower and replaced him with a double whom they controlled. He peppered his speeches with snide remarks about President "Rosenfeld" (an anti-Semitic put-down of FDR) and the "Jew Deal" (instead of "New Deal"). Mullins's roommate and intimate friend, Matt Koehl, was in charge of the NRP's Security Echelon Guard, whose members wore surplus army fatigue caps, black ties, and khaki shirts with lightning-flash armbands. Koehl would become the head of the American Nazi Party in the late 1960s. Another NRP security guard, the deeply troubled Dan Burros, concealed from his colleagues the fact that he was Jewish.

The Man with Many Aliases

Of all the strange characters associated with America's homegrown neo-Nazi scene after the war, none was more enigmatic than Francis Parker Yockey, a shadowy intellectual who made his presence felt whenever he turned up in New York, which was usually on short notice. Yockey wandered perpetually from place to place, visiting prominent fascists in North America and Europe. A mystery man with many aliases, he emerged as one of the leading philosophers within the postwar fascist milieu. "He didn't like to sit still anywhere. It was against his nature," said H. Keith Thompson, who was one of Yockey's few friends.

Thompson first met Yockey at an expensive Jewish luncheonette — where else? — in midtown Manhattan. They were introduced by Frederick Weiss, who was always trying to grub a free meal off Thompson. "Weiss was quite drunk, as usual, on that Greek wine he drank so much of, made of shellac or something like that," Thompson recalled. Dining Yiddish was somewhat like conducting a reconnaissance mission in enemy territory; H. Keith, who had a business office nearby, invariably picked up the tab.[14]

Looking back on their initial encounter, Thompson confided, "I was delighted to find that Yockey was as anti-American as I was. I couldn't say that he was more anti-American than me, because I don't think that would have been possible. We got along very well."

Yockey's saga is partially chronicled in more than a thousand pages of once-classified FBI documents describing him as a loner and a "secretive individual who did not tolerate anyone who would not wholeheartedly agree with his solution to world problems." A brilliant mind with an IQ of 170, Yockey was "nervous, high-strung, erratic, unpredictable and dictatorial," according to his FBI profile. He was also "extremely outspoken," "very well read," and "a veritable storehouse of information." But his air of superiority often rubbed others the wrong way. He had "an amazing capacity for alienating people," the FBI concluded.[15]

A slim, wiry figure of five foot eight, Yockey was somewhat bohemian in appearance, with brown hair, a protruding lower jaw, sallow complexion, and dark, deep-set eyes. He dressed "one notch above Bowery bum," said Thompson. Walking with his shoulders hunched over and his hands in his pockets, Yockey at times wore a Hitler-like mustache.

Born and raised in the Chicago area, Yockey was trained as a classical pianist. He could play the works of Chopin and Liszt concert-hall-style. A gifted speaker, Yockey addressed a meeting of the Silver Shirts, a pro-Nazi group, in Chicago in 1939, when he was twenty-two years old. He was also in contact with the German-American Bund and the America First movement. Despite his high degree of intelligence, he was said to be extremely immature and prone to temper tantrums.[16]

Yockey received a B.A. from Georgetown University and a law degree cum laude from Notre Dame. The FBI reported that he outraged officials at Michigan State University, where he also studied, by playing the "Internationale," a communist anthem, on the piano during a faculty party. This spoof belied his fascist beliefs, which were evident to some of his fellow students. An FBI informant stated that Yockey "was completely opposed to people of the Hebrew faith and followed the philosophy of the German Nazis wholeheartedly." He expressed nothing but contempt for "Negroes, Jews and Communists," claiming that he "would not sit at the same table with them in the dining hall."[17]

Although Yockey was opposed to America's entering World War II, he enlisted in the army and was assigned to a G-2 intelligence unit in Georgia. After disappearing for two months in the fall of 1942 (the FBI suspected he was on a spy mission for the Nazis in Mexico City), Yockey returned to his base camp and suffered a nervous breakdown. In July 1943, he received an honorable discharge "by reason of disability due to dementia praecox, paranoid type, cause undetermined."[18]

Yockey subsequently applied for employment with the Office of Strategic Services but was turned down because his name had appeared on a list of Americans with suspected Nazi sympathies. This, however, did not prevent him from getting a job as assistant prosecuting attorney for Wayne County, Michigan. H. Keith Thompson recalled his shock when Yockey told him a few years later how he had deliberately lost the cases of several legal clients "just to prove that he could do it."[19]

Despite his dubious track record, Yockey somehow managed to secure a position with the U.S. Army in Germany after the war — this time as a civilian member of the prosecution at the trials of second-string war criminals held in Wiesbaden. "Undoubtedly his motive was to help out some of the people on trial," asserted Thompson. American officials came to believe that Yockey was actually a mole for the Nazi defendants, seeking to subvert the Allies' case against them. Relations between Yockey and other members of the U.S. legal team were already strained when he began tickling those eighty-eights and playing provocative tunes at the U.S. Army officers club. In one impromptu piano set, Yockey did a buoyant rendition of "Deutschland über Alles."

Shortly thereafter, Yockey was fired. From then on, he considered himself a marked man. The U.S. Army Counterintelligence Corps raided his home in Germany in 1947, but Yockey managed to stay one step ahead of his pursuers. Abandoning his wife and two small children, he fled to Brittas Bay, Ireland. There, in a quiet inn by the seashore, Yockey decided to put his thoughts down on paper. Working without notes or access to a library, he composed his intellectual magnum opus, a six-hundred-page, two-volume tome called *Imperium*.[20]

Conceived as a kind of extended philosophical pep talk for brainier right-wing radicals, *Imperium* was nothing if not grandiose in scope. In his introduction, Yockey called the book "the first blow in the gigantic war for the liberation of Europe." He pitched an upbeat message to beleaguered Nazis, summoning them to engage in a "world-historical struggle" at a time when things looked rather bleak for them. Yockey insisted that the destruction of National Socialist Germany was merely a temporary setback that paved the way for a future triumph: "Widened and chastened by tragedy, defeat, and catastrophe the Western soul is emerging from the ruins, unbroken in its will, and purer in its spiritual unity than ever before. . . . [I]t must look ahead, it must believe when there is apparently no hope, it must obey even if it means death, it must fight to the end rather than submit. Fortifying it is the knowledge that against the Spirit of Heroism no materialistic force can prevail."[21]

The political upshot of Yockey's clarion call could be gleaned from the pseudonym he affixed to the book — Ulick Varange, which symbolized the full spread of a united Europe — with *Ulick,* Irish for "reward of the mind," indicating the western boundary, while *Varange,* a Norse tribe that civilized Russia in the ninth century, staked out the eastern fringes. But his conception of Europe as a single, integrated entity contrasted sharply with what he described as "the miserable plans of retarded souls to 'unite' Europe as an economic area for purposes of exploitation by and defense of the Imperialism of extra-European forces" — that is to say, the United

States and the Soviet Union, which, in Yockey's view, had conquered the Continent and turned it into a spiritual swamp.[22]

Convinced that it would be impossible for Germany, Italy, and other countries to regain their sovereignty unless they acted in concert, Yockey denounced nationalism as a bankrupt notion and decried the "petty-stateism" of European politicians who felt they could achieve independence on their own. Instead of individual nation-states, he promoted the notion of Europe in toto as a third force that could challenge the supremacy of the Cold War superpowers: "Politics is destined to move into a new realm: the Western nations are gone, and the Western nation is coming."[23]

Yockey borrowed many ideas from Oswald Spengler, author of the monumental *Decline of the West* and one of the leading voices of the Conservative Revolution in Germany during the 1920s. Like Spengler, Yockey was a severe critic of parliamentary democracy and other nineteenth-century political forms traceable to the French Revolution. Popular elections entailed "the lowering of everything human to the level of the least valuable human beings," said Yockey, who dismissed the "idea of basing political power on the masses of the population [as] a mere cover for unhampered looting by the financier." He equated liberalism with weakness, calling it "an escape from hardness into softness, from masculinity into femininity, from History to herd-grazing, from reality to herbivorous dreams, from Destiny into Happiness."[24]

Whereas Hitler's eternal schematics posited an indestructible thousand-year Reich, Spengler maintained that all cultures are governed by an organic life cycle, blossoming and wilting through various phases until they eventually die. Very much under Spengler's spell, Yockey glorified the West and bemoaned its decay in a sweeping historical tour de force. But unlike his philosophical mentor, Yockey felt it was possible to defy the laws of cultural gravity, so to speak, and rejuvenate society by embracing fascism. This was the basic premise underlying Yockey's philosophy of "cultural vitalism," which he expounded upon at length in *Imperium*. He believed that a heroic sense of purpose emanating from an elite "culture-bearing stratum" would trickle down and spread among the masses, thereby ushering in a quasi-religious "Age of Authority," which Yockey contrasted to the decadent "Rule of Money." This epochal transformation would destroy the Jewish "culture-retarders" and save the white race.

Yockey also differed from Spengler in that the latter did not stress anti-Semitism. *Imperium* reeked of Judophobia and Jew-hatred. Yockey acknowledged that Jews had suffered at the hands of Christians. As a result, he argued, unforgiving Jews had embarked on a mission of revenge that assumed sci-fi proportions in Yockey's fertile imagination. He obsessed over Jewish parasites who had burrowed into the Western host culture and riddled it with disease. Describing the Ku Klux Klan as a "reaction of the American organism to the presence of the foreign matter," Yockey stated, "Anti-semitism is precisely analogous in Culture pathology to the formation of anti-bodies in the bloodstream in human pathology. In both cases, the organism is resisting the alien life."[25]

Yockey saw World War II as the outcome of a Jewish plot in America and Western Europe to build up a counterforce to thwart the "European Revolution of 1933," which he characterized as "a ray of hope." This is how Yockey referred to the Nazi takeover that culminated in "the glorious days of 1941 and 1942," when Hitler's armies controlled much of the Continent. Although he never mentioned Hitler or the Nazis by name in *Imperium,* he defended their legacy by denying the Holocaust. Yockey was one of the first to promote the idea that the Final Solution was a myth: " 'Gas-chambers' that did not exist were photographed, and a 'gasmobile' was invented to titillate the mechanically-minded." Yet, in private conversations, Yockey praised how the Germans exterminated the Jews during World War II.[26]

Yockey diverged from the party line of Hitler's Reich in at least one crucial respect. He criticized racial concepts based purely on biology as crude and provisional. Instead of materialist, genetic-based theories, Yockey held that race was primarily a spiritual matter — an assertion contested by other fascists after the war. Race, according to Yockey, had less to do with a physical type than the psychic ethos or innate character of a society. He maintained that it was perfectly conceivable that an authentic European like himself could be born and raised in the United States.[27]

Other than that, Yockey had little to say that was in any way complimentary about America. As he saw it, the United States was a much-bastardized derivative of Europe, debased by alien minorities and their perverse manifestations — Hollywood, jazz, modern art, boogie-woogie dancing, and the like. Yockey urged all true Europeans not to collaborate with America's Cold War crusade against the Soviet Union, a crusade that split the Continent in two. Denouncing the insidious impact of American culture, Yockey concluded that the Soviet Union's heavy-handed military repression of Eastern Europe was "less harmful" in the long run because it did not distort and corrupt the Western soul as American capitalism did. Branding the United States as Europe's main enemy was another point of contention that put him at odds with many postwar fascists.[28]

European Liberation Front

Having written *Imperium* in less than six months, Yockey took his unpublished manuscript to London, where he sought out Oswald Mosley, who was at one time Hitler's top British disciple. After spending much of World War II in an English prison, Mosley had returned to active politics as head of the Union Movement. Like Yockey, he maintained that Europeanism was the only viable postwar political creed. "The nations of Europe are too small to survive when they are caught between two giants like the United States and Russia," Mosley argued. "That's why they must forget their old nationalist animosities and form a united Europe as soon as they can."[29]

When he first met Moseley in 1947, Yockey tried to solicit aid for certain German officers who had been condemned to death for war crimes. But Mosley, not wanting to run afoul of the authorities once again, was careful to project a more respectable image, which entailed toning down his prewar anti-Semitism. He was a bit wary of Yockey, "a young man of some ability" who had an indiscreet "obsession with the Jewish Question," as Mosley put it. Nevertheless, Yockey ended up working for a brief period as an organizer for the Union Movement's European Contact Section, enabling him to cultivate ties to an underground neofascist network throughout the

Continent. He was in communication with, among others, Alfred Franke-Gricksch before the leader of the neo-Nazi Bruderschaft mysteriously disappeared while on an undercover mission in East Berlin.[30]

Yockey soon became a disruptive influence. He left the Union Movement when Mosley punched him in the nose during a dispute at Hyde Park. Shortly thereafter, Yockey fell in with a group of British extremists who embraced him as a fascist guru. Their first task was to raise enough funds so that *Imperium* could be circulated among a wider audience. One thousand copies of the first volume of *Imperium* and two hundred copies of the second volume were initially published by Westropa Press in London in 1948, thanks to the generosity of Baroness Alice von Pflugel, a wealthy mistress Yockey had taken up with.

It was at the baroness's home that Yockey and a handful of others decided to form the European Liberation Front (ELF) in 1949. According to Anthony Gannon, a former Mosleyite who joined Yockey's circle, theirs was the first organization to use the words *liberation front* in its title. They announced their arrival on the postwar fascist scene by publishing *The Proclamation of London,* which was basically a boiled-down, popularized version of the Nazi-Spenglerian synthesis that Yockey had penned in *Imperium.*

As Gannon explained, Yockey "long had the idea that, to coincide with the centenary of the publication of the Communist Manifesto of 1848, we should issue a European manifesto setting out the situation for the 'masses,' and calling for action to liberate Europe from its occupation by the extra-European forces of the USA and USSR." Written by Yockey, the ELF twelve-point program demanded the "immediate expulsion of all Jews and other parasitic aliens from the Soil of Europe," "the abolition of unearned income," and "the cleansing of the Soul of Europe from the ethical syphilis of Hollywood." The ELF also produced a monthly bulletin called *Frontfighter,* which featured Yockey's political analysis.[31]

"Yockey could be a charming companion, with an unsuspecting sense of humor and a great gift for mimicking others," said Gannon, who recalled how Yockey used to imitate W. C. Fields. But Gannon readily conceded there was another side to his compelling American comrade. Yockey could "become quite insulting and contemptuous to those he believed were being unduly obstinate or slow in conceding a point in dispute. Of course, this kind of behavior is fatal if one is seeking to make converts and obtain their support."

Perhaps the most controversial aspect of Yockey's political thinking was his insistence that the corrupting influence of American culture was ultimately more damaging to Europe than Communist military intervention. Instead of collaborating with U.S. intelligence, as many postwar fascists were inclined to do, Yockey and the ELF advocated a flexible neutralism and a pan-European approach to geopolitics — much like Major General Otto Ernst Remer and the Socialist Reich Party were touting in West Germany. According to *Frontfighter* editor Peter Huxley-Blythe, Yockey "praised Soviet policy in Germany" and urged his comrades "to help him organize secret partisan bands of neo-Nazis in West Germany, bands which would collaborate with the Soviet Military Authorities against the Western occupation powers." Yockey promised all who helped in this effort "would be initiated into a vast worldwide secret organization working to establish an Authoritarian State" in Europe.[32]

Their adrenal glands working overtime, Yockey and his small circle of British associates were immersed in international plots. But the abrasive and condescending personality of their American leader proved too much for the others to bear. Unable to repair his personal or political relations in England, Yockey slipped back into West Germany with false papers in hand. Army documents — which call him "Jockey" instead of Yockey — state that he was involved in "promoting a National Bolshevist movement" and contacting ex-Nazi and ex-Wehrmacht officers. As he traveled around the Continent, Yockey distributed copies of *Imperium* to key figures in the international neofascist scene.

During his sojourns, according to FBI reports, the itinerant American fascist also made contact with representatives of the Socialist Reich Party, whose political platform dovetailed largely with Yockey's own views. He arranged to have a German translation of what was essentially a condensed version of the second part of *Imperium* published under the title *Der Fiend Europas (The Enemy of Europe)*. With missives like "Prussia-Germany is the custodian of the Destiny of all Europe," Yockey's geopolitical musings were a big hit among the nationalist-neutralist set in Germany. Otto Ernst

Remer, in particular, thought highly of Yockey's exegesis, which he recommended to several of his associates.[33]

Praise for *Imperium* came from far and wide. The National Renaissance Party in New York called it "the greatest book on racial nationalism since *Mein Kampf.*" A review from South America described it as the blueprint for the next European revolution. Maurice Bardèche, a leading French fascist, was also a big fan of Yockey's book. And Julius Evola, the Italian Dadaist painter-turned-pagan fascist, extolled *Imperium* even though he disagreed with the thesis that Soviet Communism constituted a lesser evil than Western capitalism.[34]

In October 1950, Yockey traveled to Italy to attend a conference hosted by the Movimento Sociale Italiano (MSI), Europe's first neofascist party. Founded shortly after the war by veterans of Mussolini's last-gasp Saló Republic, the vociferously anti-Communist MSI managed to secure a foothold on the Italian political landscape despite a constitutional ban on reviving Fascism. As in Germany, official determination to punish Fascist collaborators faded as U.S. intelligence focused on neutralizing Italy's powerful Communist party.* This afforded some wiggle room for MSI leaders, who

* The Western Allies never implemented a coordinated postwar plan to root out and punish collaborators in Italy. The situation paralleled similar developments in West Germany: the vast majority of imprisoned Italian Fascists were quickly released under the provisions of a general amnesty that freed even torturers. There was no attempt to punish the captains of Italian industry who had profited greatly from their close relationship with the Fascist regime. A serious purge never occurred, thereby allowing much of the old Fascist bureaucracy to survive. With implicit U.S. support, many Fascist government administrators were retained in positions of power. Most Italian judges from the Fascist era, for example, kept their posts, and the Fascist penal code remained largely intact. As a result, Fascist tendencies persisted in Italian society and government, particularly in the armed forces and the secret service. Some Italian officials were plucked straight from the Duce's final holdout and incorporated into an Atlantic-oriented espionage structure, although nothing like on the scale of what transpired in West Germany with the Gehlen Org. Guido Leto, ex–police chief of the Saló Republic, became the director of Italy's postwar police academies, while postwar Interior Minister Mario Scelba enlisted veterans of OVRA, Mussolini's secret police. Specializing in hit-and-run tactics, Scelba's infamous *celere* (flying squads) targeted Italy's powerful, Communist-

placed a great deal of emphasis on cross-border networking. The emphasis on international linkage was in part a pragmatic response to the realization that no single European country was strong enough on its own to challenge the postwar economic and political might of the two superpowers.

Hoping to forge a united international front with other neofascists, MSI chieftains invited representatives from numerous countries to a four-day congress in Naples. Yockey participated in several strategy sessions, but there was little that all delegates could agree upon. Boorish biological bigots who were into blood myths and far-flung Jewish conspiracies argued with those who suggested it would be wise to soft-pedal their anti-Semitic views, if only for tactical reasons.

Although postwar fascists paid a great deal of lip service to European unity, they were unable to reconcile the national egotism that often flared at such gatherings. A major sore point, for example, was the status of South Tyrol, the predominantly German-speaking region of northern Italy. Coveting this territory, Austrian neo-Nazis were at loggerheads with Italian Fascists, who took umbrage, not surprisingly, when several targets in South Tyrol were bombed. Neo-Nazi terror attacks continued intermittently in this area over the next few decades.

In addition to feuding with neofascists from other countries, the MSI was also vexed by internal strife, which nearly destroyed the organization. Its members struggled in vain to reach a consensus on whether to embrace a "third force" approach or align themselves with NATO and the Western powers. This key axis of division was indicative of the Janus-faced nature of postwar European fascism, which encompassed two major geopolitical perspectives: one Atlantic-oriented, the other pan-European. Those who opted for the latter strongly identified with the slogan "Against the gold of

---

dominated labor movement during the early years of the Cold War. According to historian Paul Ginsborg, "In 1960 it was calculated that sixty-two out of sixty-four prefects (the central government's principal representatives in the provinces) had been functionaries under Fascism. So too had all 135 police chiefs and their 139 deputies. Only five of these last had in any way contributed to the Resistance."

America and the iron of the USSR, the blood of Europe." As well as being staunchly anti-Communist, they were vehemently opposed to the cultural, political, and economic domination of Western Europe by the United States.[35]

Third-position fascists sought to ride the crest of popular enthusiasm for a European economic union — a trend that paralleled and abetted their own deceptive efforts to create an independent geopolitical force strong enough to negotiate on even terms with East and West. In that sense, emphasizing a united Europe was a clever way to camouflage a neofascist agenda.* But pan-European fascists also argued among themselves. It was not clear, for example, exactly how Russia's "Eurasian" land mass fit into the picture. People like Yockey, Remer, and Thompson advocated a strategic linkup with the Soviet Union, but other pan-European fascists, such as Julius Evola, remained unconvinced.

By the early 1950s, MSI leaders who favored an opportunistic anti-Communist alliance with NATO and its principal backer, the United States, had gained the upper hand over their pan-European rivals in Italy. This set the stage for future meetings between MSI bigwigs and members of the U.S. National Security Council as well as for covert American support for Italian secret-service officials who were closely associated with their country's neofascist

* First promoted in the early 1920s by Count Richard Coudenhove-Kalergi of Austria, pan-Europeanism embodied popular aspirations for a continent-wide confederation, an objective endorsed by a range of thinkers, including Miguel de Unamuno of Spain and Hermann Keyserling of Germany. To many ultranationalists, however, the pan-European ideal smacked of cosmopolitanism and was therefore highly suspicious. Thus, it was somewhat ironic that the slogan of a united Europe proved to be one of the Nazis' most successful propaganda weapons in the wake of their defeat at Stalingrad. Henceforth, Joseph Goebbels trumpeted a kind of Eurofascism, whereby the Nazi cause had become that of all racially superior whites fighting for their continental homeland. Accordingly, he downplayed the subhuman Slav theme and placed greater emphasis on saving "Europe" from the Asiatic swarm. Postwar pan-European fascists thus had ample precedent for including the concept of a "united Europe" in their revisionist arsenal.

party.* As in West Germany, those who continued to identify with the "third force" concept were officially shoved to the margins while their Atlantic-leaning counterparts ingratiated themselves with the governing powers.

Rumblings from Prague

After the MSI conference, Francis Parker Yockey hit the road again, lugging around a large steamer trunk full of books and papers as he zigzagged across mainland Europe and North America. Suspecting that U.S. intelligence agents were on his trail, he adopted a series of disguises that would change with every hasty departure. "Yockey was always concerned about being spied upon. That's why he trusted so few people and never stayed very long in one place," said H. Keith Thompson. "He was very secretive in his movements. He engaged in countless conspiracies to mislead those who were searching for him."

When Yockey telephoned his political associates, he never used his real name. Occasionally he signed his letters "Torquemada," the Spanish Grand Inquisitor of the Middle Ages. "I always had to wait for him to contact me," Thompson recounted. "He would identify

* American ambassador Graham Martin passed $800,000 to Vito Miceli, head of Italian military intelligence, to disburse during the 1972 election campaign in an effort to keep the Italian Communist Party out of power. At the time, Miceli was "clearly linked to anti-democratic elements of the right," according to a congressional report on CIA activities. A few years later, Miceli ran successfully for parliament as a candidate of the neofascist MSI. General Giovanni de Lorenzo, another former Italian intelligence chief, also became an MSI deputy in the mid-1970s, when the neofascist party was led by Giorgio Almirante, an ex–cabinet minister in Mussolini's Saló Republic. Although Almirante had disparaged democracy as "an infection of the mind," he met with representatives of the U.S. National Security Council in Washington in September 1975. The cordial reception given to Almirante, who touted the MSI as Italy's toughest anti-Communist bastion, was widely reported in the European press, prompting criticism of U.S. government contacts with avowed neofascists.

himself as 'Oswald Spengler' or someone else. But I knew who it was."

A relentless womanizer, Yockey had plenty of bed partners when he came to New York, including Hazel Guggenheim (sister of Peggy, the famous art collector and philanthropist). An oft-married Jewish woman of rather large proportions, Hazel dyed her hair blond, wore heavy purple eyeliner, and smoked cigarettes in a long cigarette holder. Apparently she liked young men and found the idea of sleeping with a fascist particularly appealing. "I am sure he received some financial remuneration for any services rendered to her," alleged Thompson.

When he wasn't squiring some female, Yockey would drop by Thompson's public-relations office on Fifty-second Street near Madison Avenue in Manhattan. During the early 1950s, H. Keith was busy with various projects, including the Committee for the Freedom of Major General Remer and another short-lived effort called the American Committee for the Survival of Western Culture. Volunteering to assist Thompson in his political work, Yockey helped prepare press releases, letters to the State Department, and other correspondence. Yockey's rhetorical flourishes were evident in an October 1952 communiqué to Secretary of State Dean Acheson, which quoted passages from *Imperium* and strongly endorsed the efforts of Ernst Remer and the recently banned Socialist Reich Party.[36]

Since he was required by law to mention anyone who assisted his work as a registered foreign agent, Thompson dutifully indicated in his annual statement to the Justice Department that he had been aided by Frank Healy, the alias Yockey was then using in New York. Yockey later regretted that "Healy" had been cited in official documents. His association with Thompson resulted in some unwelcome publicity in 1954 when Drew Pearson, the nationally syndicated columnist, drew attention to a sensational exposé in *The Reporter* that described Yockey as "fairly prominent in the political demimonde of international fascism" and discussed his ties to the SRP in Germany and the National Renaissance Party in New York.[37]

Realizing that his mercurial comrade had little visible means of support, Thompson donated a wad of cash on several occasions to cover printing costs for articles that Yockey had written under different pen names. He also invited Yockey to some lively, late-evening soirees hosted by George Sylvester Vierick at Manhattan's swanky Hotel Belleclaire. Dubbed "Hitler's prostitute" because of his role as Nazi Germany's highest paid publicist in the United States, Vierick was a defendant in a famous wartime sedition trial. He served time in a U.S. prison after flooding millions of American mailboxes and bookstores with pro-German material. Shortly before he was indicted by U.S. officials, Vierick entrusted his "little black book" to his future literary agent, H. Keith Thompson. This book, according to Thompson, contained handwritten records of all the payoffs that Vierick had made to U.S. congressmen and senators right up to Pearl Harbor, and the services he got back. "Vierick didn't want it to fall into the wrong hands while any of these people were still alive," said Thompson, who ended up burning the book just to be on the safe side.[38]

A poet of some repute who sang the praises of "pan-sexuality," Vierick threw plenty of parties at his large, circular suite at the Belleclaire after he got out of prison. For the most part, these were jocular, high-spirited gatherings that attracted an unusual assortment of intellectuals, artists, Nazi sympathizers, and offbeat lifestyle experimentalists. Mingling among the guests one could often find Dr. Alfred Kinsey, the famous sexologist, and Dr. Harry Benjamin, the sex-change-operation pioneer (who counted Christine Jorgenson among his well-publicized clients). Yockey proceeded to have an affair with Benjamin's attractive receptionist, Virginia Allen, who was also sleeping with her boss. The licentious atmosphere that prevailed at Vierick's weekly get-togethers, where bisexuality was encouraged, enhanced the sense of living on the edge that many postwar fascists shared.[39]

Vierick took an immediate liking to Yockey when Thompson first brought him over to the Belleclaire. With H. Keith tending bar, discussions broke off into a few small groups. Yockey was a capable conversationalist, and he genuinely enjoyed talking with Lawrence Dennis and Harry Elmer Barnes, two pro-German "revisionist" historians who frequented Vierick's suite.

For the most, however, such interludes were atypical of Yockey's complex and, in many ways, tormented relationship with other right-wing extremists in the United States. He had a very low opinion of knee-jerk, anti-Communist flag-wavers who obsessed over little else than Russia and the Red Menace. Impatient with America's dyspeptic radical Right and profoundly ill at ease on this side of the Atlantic, Yockey confessed to one of his mistresses, "America always did fill me with a terrible feeling that I didn't know where I was, a feeling of being on the edge of the world, of being isolated. . . ."[40]

So Yockey darted off to Europe again, carrying messages from Thompson to his comrades in the Socialist Reich Party and other West German neo-Nazis. Yockey's strange trajectory had already taken him way beyond the typical right-wing orbit. Just how far he was willing to push the political envelope became evident when the American fascist turned up in Prague, a center of Soviet espionage activity, to witness the infamous anti-Semitic show trials that were staged in late 1952.

Fourteen Czech leaders had been accused of espionage, high treason, sabotage, and assorted crimes against the state. Of these, eleven were Jews, including Rudolf Slánský, the general secretary of the Czech Communist Party. Slánský and the others faced charges of plotting with "Zionists" to assassinate key leaders, overthrow the government, and restore capitalism. The indictment lumped together all of Stalin's current bogeymen — "Trotskyists," "Titoists," "Western imperialists," "Zionist adventurers," "rootless cosmopolitans," "valets of the bourgeoisie," etc. — in a huge conspiracy against the Soviet bloc. It was particularly ironic that Slánský should be slandered by the government he served so faithfully, given that he had been shunned by Israeli diplomats as the most anti-Zionist of all the Czech Communist leaders.[41]

As Yockey watched with rapt attention in the visitors gallery, Slánský went on automatic pilot and confessed to everything. He and the other Jewish defendants were put to death by hanging. For Yockey, the spectacle of Slánský's choreographed performance signified nothing less than a historic watershed, "an unmistakable turning point" that heralded "the beginning of the end of American hegemony in Europe." Noting his enthusiasm for developments in the Soviet bloc, an FBI memo quoted an article written by Yockey, who said that the Prague show trial "foretold a Russian break with Jewry which is becoming deeper and more complete every day. This development, arising as it did from the absolute identity of American and Jewish policy, is favorable to our fight for the liberation of Europe."[42]

Yockey went so far as to characterize the anti-Semitic purges that occurred in several Soviet bloc countries during the 1950s as "a war-declaration by Russia on the American-Jewish leadership." He denounced "the satanic project of constructing a German army to fight Russia on behalf of the occupying Jewish-American enemy," while repeating his belief that the inability of the Soviet Union to impose itself culturally upon its conquests made it a lesser danger to Europe than the United States. "[T]he Russian leadership is killing Jews for treason to Russia, for service to the Jewish entity. Nothing can gainsay or reverse this fact," Yockey asserted.[43]

Yockey argued that under the circumstances, it would be tactically advantageous to forge an alliance with the USSR in an effort to free Europe from American domination. His eagerness to play the Eastern card prompted him to collaborate with Soviet bloc espionage agencies. During the 1950s, Yockey became a paid courier for the Czech secret service, which functioned as a cat's-paw for the Soviet KGB. "Yockey got behind the Iron Curtain. He ran some papers for the Czech secret service. I heard this directly from him," H. Keith Thompson disclosed. "The Czechs were operating a courier service on behalf of Soviet intelligence."[44]

After the Prague trials, Yockey made his way back to New York, where he briefed Thompson and the man who had originally introduced them, Frederick Weiss, about what had transpired in the Czech capital. They enthusiastically endorsed Yockey's analysis, which he summarized in an essay entitled "What is Behind the Hanging of the Eleven Jews in Prague?" Weiss gave a copy of Yockey's article to James Madole, leader of the National Renaissance Party. Until then, Madole, like many Nazis, believed that Bolshevism was part of a Jewish conspiracy to take over the world. But the two-bit NRP führer was turned around by Yockey's commentary. He published Yockey's Prague ruminations — without attribution — in the *National Renaissance Bulletin.* The distribution, foreign and domestic, of Yockey's Prague piece was considerable, thanks to Thompson and Weiss, who paid Madole for an extra-large print run.[45]

Endorsing the frenzied campaign against "Zionism" and "rootless cosmopolitans" in the USSR, Madole told NRP members that Communist ideology had served as a mask for Russian nationalism ever since "the fat peasant Stalin" (Yockey's description) prevailed in a power struggle over his archrival, Leon Trotsky, the leader of the Jewish internationalist faction. Thanks to Stalin, Jewish Bolshevism had been transformed into National Bolshevism, which should be supported, according to Yockeyan logic, in its struggle against the Jewish-controlled United States of America.

Apparently this explanation managed to win over a few ex-Commies, who began hanging around the NRP's New York City headquarters. The change in the NRP's office decor reflected the new political line — a picture frame hanging on the wall featured interchangeable portraits of Hitler and Stalin, depending upon who was visiting at the time. An undercover operative who infiltrated the NRP described the office as a veritable madhouse. "All day long," he stated, "there was a constant procession of Communists, uniformed Nazis, motorcycle gang hoodlums, some ballet dancers . . . and a Jamaican medical student from Columbia University who kept parts of cadavers in the icebox."[46]

Frederick Weiss, the ostensible brains behind the NRP, proceeded to publish a series of articles that praised the Soviet Union. Like Remer and his cohorts in the Socialist Reich Party, Weiss called for a renewed German-Russian alliance. "We Germans must find out whether we can get more out of the East or the West," Weiss stated. "I've come to the conclusion — and this is disclosing my innermost thought — that we can work out a better deal in going along with the East rather than the West. With our know-how and with our experience, we can get ahead faster with the USSR. . . . True, the West gives lip-service to a united Germany, but it really fears a united powerful Germany."[47]

In addition to Thompson, Weiss, and the wacky NRP clique, a number of other American right-wing extremists began to reappraise the Soviet Union after they were exposed to Yockey's analysis of Russia as "the lesser danger."[48] But Yockey's views did not sit well with those postwar fascists who steadfastly maintained that any attempt to cast the Soviets in a positive light was wrongheaded and outrageous. Disillusioned by the mixed response his ideas received in far Right circles, "Torquemada" sank into a deep depression. He saw himself as a hero in unheroic times, a misunderstood prophet moving toward a climactic rendezvous with destiny.

Like the archetypal wandering Jew he so despised, Yockey meandered from one country to the next. At one point, he told NRP leader James Madole of his intention to travel to East Germany. The FBI suspected that Yockey was also "in touch with Soviet authorities" and may have visited the USSR. In an effort to gather additional information on his activities, FBI chief J. Edgar Hoover contacted CIA director Allen Dulles and the head of the Office of Naval Intelligence. Twenty-nine FBI field offices were told to be on the lookout for Yockey, while Hoover's G-men queried his relatives in the Midwest, hoping for clues to his whereabouts. The feds briefly picked up his scent in Los Angeles, where he was reportedly living as a gigolo with some wealthy women. While drifting around the United States, Yockey also earned some money by playing piano in honky-tonk bars and gambling casinos. But the enigmatic fascist continued to elude the domestic and international gumshoes who were chasing him.[49]

The Flying Ace

While Yockey was wrestling with his own private demons, Colonel Otto Skorzeny continued to amass a considerable fortune through various business deals. Representing the Krupp Company, he ventured to Argentina, where he met with President Juan Perón on several occasions during the early 1950s. Skorzeny encouraged Perón to hire German firms to construct highways, airports, military installations, schools, and other public works projects. With his preference for dashing capes and white military uniforms, Perón managed to charm Ilse Skorzeny. But she was even more impressed by his wife, Evita, the charismatic former actress and grand dame of Buenos Aires, who held the Argentine masses in thrall.[50]

During Perón's nine-year tenure (1946–55) as his country's popularly elected leader, Argentina became the preferred haven for tens of thousands of Nazi war criminals and fellow travelers, as well as a repository for a large amount of stolen Nazi funds. Much of the cash was deposited in Argentine bank accounts controlled by Evita Perón. While rolling out the red carpet for war criminals, El Presidente occasionally crossed swords with U.S. officials, who took him to task for welcoming fugitive fascists — a criticism not without cynicism, given how U.S. intelligence agencies had secretly assisted the large-scale emigration of Nazis to the Americas, both North and South.[51]

The U.S. officials were peeved by Perón's repeated denunciations of Yankee imperialism and by his willingness to embrace dissident left-wing intellectuals who were drawn toward "justicialism," the ambiguous political doctrine he espoused. Akin in many respects to Italian Fascism, Perón's third-position ideology was stridently nationalistic, blatantly authoritarian, and contemptuous of both capitalism and Communism. Appealing to much of the Argentine working class, it also resonated favorably among the boatloads of refugees from the Third Reich, who inundated Buenos Aires in the late 1940s and early 1950s.[52]

The most celebrated figure in the German exile community was Colonel Hans-Ulrich Rudel, the ace fighter pilot of Hitler's air force. The young Silesian reportedly flew more than twenty-five hundred sorties against the Allies, destroying more than eight hundred combat vehicles, five hundred tanks, and three battleships. In the process, Rudel was shot down thirty times and wounded on five occasions. Toward the end of the war, his right leg was amputated because of a battle injury he suffered. Yet, Rudel continued to fly missions for the Luftwaffe (German air force). His martial feats were so extraordinary that Hitler created a special award just for him. Rudel was the only German soldier to receive the Golden Oak Leaves with Diamonds and Swords to the Knight's Cross of the Iron Cross — a military mouthful that constituted Germany's highest decoration for valor during World War II.[53]

Rudel's dark gray eyes overflowed with tears when he learned of Hitler's suicide. But the Führer's demise did not dampen Rudel's enthusiasm for the Nazi creed. Released after a year in an internment camp, the flying whiz became a leading operator of the Nazi escape routes. Rudel founded the Kamradenwerk organization to aid imprisoned comrades. He also directed traffic along ratlines stretching north and south. These covert machinations brought him in contact with Skorzeny's ODESSA network, and the two heroes of the Third Reich became close, lifelong friends. They hung out together when Skorzeny visited Argentina. And Rudel was a guest at Skorzeny's summer hideaway on the island of Majorca during several trips to Spain. "He came to our house, carrying an assortment of wooden legs with him," Ilse remembered fondly. "He was a marvelous man."[54]

Rudel appreciated the assistance rendered by sympathetic figures within the Vatican, who helped Nazi renegades find their way to safe pastures during the early years of the Cold War. "One may otherwise view Catholicism as one wishes," Rudel acknowledged. "But what the Church, especially certain towering personalities within the Church, undertook in those years to save the best of our nation, often from certain death, must never be forgotten! In Rome itself, the transit point of the escape routes, a vast amount was done. With its own immense resources, the Church helped many of us to go overseas. In this manner, in quiet and secrecy, the demented victors' mad craving for revenge and retribution could be effectively counteracted."[55]

Although he had not been charged with war crimes, the fair-haired Rudel decided to join many of his compatriots in Argentina, where he was greeted with open arms by Juan and Evita Perón. Serving as a paid advisor to the Argentine government, he became a fixture at diplomatic receptions and state dinners. The glamour boy of South America's postwar Nazi scene, Rudel also functioned as a roving ambassador for Siemens, the German electronics giant.

Rudel used his personal relationship with Peŕon to secure jobs for more than a hundred former Luftwaffe staffers in Argentina's fledgling air force. For a while he worked as a test pilot at an all-German engineering firm in Buenos Aires run by Dr. Willi Tank, who was previously the construction chief of the Focke-Wulf aircraft factory, which produced warplanes for Hitler's Reich. Entertaining offers from the Soviets and the British at war's end, Tank opted to set up shop in the Argentine capital, where Perón was keen on enlisting German talent to beef up his nation's industrial and military capabilities.

Dr. Carl Vaernet, a physician who had been a member of the

Danish Nazi Party, also found a congenial niche in Perón's Argentina. During the war, Vaernet conducted surgical experiments on homosexual prisoners in the Buchenwald concentration camp. Having embarked on a crusade to straighten out so-called deviants, Vaernet implanted metal sex glands in gay men after they had been castrated. Several of his artificially sexed-up subjects suffered agonizing deaths, but Vaernet kept assuring SS chief Heinrich Himmler that he had discovered a "cure" for homosexuality. A delighted Himmler ordered concentration camp officials to provide Vaernet with as many homosexuals as possible. (Gay men interned in camps were forced to wear a pink triangle on their clothes to indicate their sexual orientation, while lesbians were given a chance to avoid imprisonment if they consented to serve as breeding machines for the master race.) Dr. Vaernet subsequently became chief of the city health department in Buenos Aires, where he resided until his death in 1968.[56]

Another Nazi medical maniac who lived in Argentina for a while was the notorious Josef Mengele. As the SS doctor at Auschwitz, he sent an estimated four hundred thousand prisoners to the gas chambers and killed thousands more with his deranged genetic quackery. Twins, dwarfs, giants, hunchbacks, and cripples were his favorite specimens. The "Angel of Death" injected serum into eyeballs to change their color, amputated limbs at random, and rearranged the organs of hapless victims to suit his mad whims. He also aborted pregnant women by stomping on their stomachs and wired inmates for electroshock to ascertain their pain threshold. Mengele was briefly detained by U.S. Army officers in Vienna in 1947, but they released him, according to a U.S. Justice Department report, without realizing who he was. He made his way to Buenos Aires, where Rudel looked after him. When Mengele deemed it necessary to leave Argentina, Rudel convinced General Alfredo Stroessner, Paraguay's pro-Nazi dictator, to provide citizenship papers for the Auschwitz doctor. Using his friendship with Rudel as a calling card, Mengele visited Otto Skorzeny at his home in Madrid in 1965.[57]

Rudel helped hundreds of newly arrived Nazi emigrés establish themselves with homes and jobs in various Latin American countries, where they swelled the ranks of extremist organizations. Some would later become advisors to dictators in Chile, Bolivia, Peru, and, of course, Argentina, which swarmed with war criminals from Germany and Eastern Europe while Perón ruled the roost. Adolf Eichmann, the main administrative director of the Holocaust, lived in Buenos Aires until he was captured by Israeli spies in 1960. At least ten former concentration camp commanders also took advantage of Perón's hospitality.[58]

Some war criminals preferred the anonymity of the Argentine outback, but not Ante Pavelić, the fascist dictator of wartime Croatia, who set up a high-profile government-in-exile in Buenos Aires. Under Pavelić's command, the Croatian Ustaše had perpetrated crimes that surpassed even the Nazis in their savagery. (After murdering Serbs, Gypsies, and Jews in droves, some Ustaše fanatics reportedly gave their leader a large basket filled with forty pounds of human eyeballs.) Roman Catholic priests from Croatia subsequently played a pivotal role in the Vatican-assisted escape routes that enabled Pavelić to get to Buenos Aires, where he and a handful of Ustaše associates shared their expertise on consensus-building techniques with the Argentine secret police.[59]

For the most part, however, Perón's authoritarian reign was benign compared with the repressive measures utilized by Nazi Germany and its wartime client states. Although he instigated and tolerated more than a few excesses, Perón never transformed his prisons into slaughterhouses. At times he even cautioned his followers not to vent their wrath against the sizable Jewish community in Buenos Aires. But Perón did provide an important sanctuary for those who committed horrible crimes against humanity, thereby enabling them to regroup and launch new political initiatives in the postwar era.[60]

Convinced that it was just a matter of time before National Socialism would flourish again in Europe, Rudel and his comrades sought appropriate outlets to spread the gospel. The principal mouthpiece for the Nazi colony in Argentina was a monthly periodical called *Der Weg (The Way),* which glorified Prussian militarism and praised Nazi eugenics experts for trying to improve "the health of the German people." *Der Weg* also ridiculed "Grand Rabbi Adenauer" and his U.S. patrons. Several German-owned firms in Argentina purchased advertisements in the journal, which received additional financial support from wealthy Nazis in South Africa, where *Der Weg* had many subscribers. The publication was banned in Germany by U.S. occupation officials, but copies circulated at events organized by the Socialist Reich Party. The SRP's main contact in Argentina was Hans-Ulrich Rudel.[61]

Der Weg ran several articles by Rudel, accompanied by photos that showed the former flying ace in a variety of macho poses — high diving, mountain climbing, skiing — despite his physical handicap. Rudel's one-legged will-to-power shtick was geared toward evoking the lost spirit of German heroism that *Der Weg* continually tried to conjure up in its pages. As well as reprinting pieces from neo-Nazi hate sheets in Europe, *Der Weg* featured contributions by prominent Third Reich veterans such as Otto Skorzeny, who was described in an editorial as "one who continues to fight the enemy even after the war." Otto Ernst Remer also wrote for *Der Weg,* which emerged as the most significant neo-Nazi journal to appear outside Germany during the 1950s.[62]

Der Weg was one of several products issued by Dürer Verlag, an Argentina-based company that published new editions of Hitler's *Mein Kampf* in German and Spanish, along with the memoirs of leading Nazis, including *Trotzdem* (*Despite All*) and other titles by Hans-Ulrich Rudel. When he needed a literary agent to secure a U.S. publisher for his books, Rudel contacted the New York office of H. Keith Thompson, who represented an array of notables, including Cuban dictator Fulgencio Batista, the exiled Romanian monarch King Carol II, and a handful of American generals and admirals. Thompson, it turns out, was also registered as the United Nations correspondent of *Der Weg*'s parent company, Dürer Verlag. "I got credentials and could wander around and buttonhole people at the U.N. delegates' lounge," he explained. Thompson dispatched news items concerning Jewish activities and other political scuttlebutt to Rudel's circle in Buenos Aires. His contributions included a derogatory piece about Eleanor Roosevelt that ran in *Der Weg.*[63]

In his letters to Thompson, Rudel sent fraternal greetings to Frederick Weiss, who distributed bulk copies of *Der Weg* to sympathizers in the United States. Weiss, in turn, delivered a German translation of Francis Parker Yockey's controversial article on the Prague show trials, which *Der Weg* reprinted despite a lack of consensus among its editors regarding Yockey's political line. Rudel, for one, was a fan of *Imperium*. He thought that an arrangement with the Soviet Union would best serve the interests of the Fatherland. His outspoken attitude prompted U.S. embassy officials in Buenos Aires to express concern about "Rudel's highly suspicious pro-Communist activities."[64]

The State Department's worries were misdirected. Rudel was not a Communist; if anything, he despised the theories of Karl Marx. But he had no compunction about pursuing a deal with the Soviets if it might further the neo-Nazi cause. Rudel and his colleagues dreamed of the big Cold War crack-up that would loosen the superpowers' grip on Europe. Until that happened, the neo-Nazis would continue their geopolitical maneuvers, seeking to gain some advantage by playing East off West and vice versa. This is what Rudel had in mind when he returned to Germany in the early 1950s, ostensibly to obtain a new false leg. During successive visits, he conferred with Otto Ernst Remer and other radical nationalist leaders, trying to weld together the disparate political and ideological factions associated with the extreme right-wing fringe in Germany.[65]

Rudel considered the SRP to be a "milestone on the way to national regeneration," but he felt that some of the party's tactics were misguided and counterproductive. He picked up where the SRP had left off after it was outlawed and Remer dropped from sight to avoid another prison term. Many SRP faithful subsequently threw their support behind the Deutsche Reichs-Partei (DRP), which Rudel promoted when touring West Germany. With Rudel plunking for the DRP, it inherited the mantle as the SRP's successor party in the early 1950s.[66]

Worshiped as the patron saint of the neo-Nazi scene, Rudel was an inflammatory orator who insisted that all German soldiers reject Bonn's Western-oriented rearmament plans, lest they become "traitors and dishonored human beings." "What good would it do Germany if the Americans won the last battle?" he asked. "No one would be left to see a 'nigger division' marching in Germany over the atom-bombed graves of the German people." Alarmed by his anti-American vitriol, U.S. Army intelligence described Rudel as a "phrase-monger" and "a warped and vicious fanatic" who "obviously has a great deal of personal magnetism."[67]

After a particularly abrasive diatribe, Rudel was banned from speaking at political events in Bavaria. Unruffled by attempts to muzzle him, the gimpy Nazi concocted a fantastic plot to free more than a hundred German war criminals who were still incarcerated in Spandau prison in the British zone of occupation. The jailbreak was supposed to involve a daring helicopter raid almost as audacious as Skorzeny's rescue of Mussolini during the war. Fearing that Rudel's plan might undermine Bonn's more low-key approach to securing the release of convicted Nazis, a Bundestag deputy blew the whistle on the impending helicopter mission.[68]

The Deutsche Reichs-Partei, meanwhile, got trounced in the August 1953 national elections, which returned Chancellor Konrad Adenauer to a second term in office. The Christian Democratic Union (CDU) prevailed at the polls by a wide margin, thanks in large part to West Germany's brisk economic recovery. This, combined with Adenauer's staunch anti-Communist stance, managed to win over the lion's share of radical right-wing voters, who could not help but notice that the CDU-led government was filled to the brim with ex-Nazis.

The 1953 election results were sobering for Nazi incorrigibles who had deluded themselves into thinking that they could effectively challenge the Adenauer government by playing the democratic game. In a sense, they had reached a dead end. The fact that so many Third Reich veterans found it increasingly profitable to work within the new system and to share its benefits made the extremist parties much less attractive. Old-style Hitlerism was not about to rise again as long as German industrialists, reaping huge rewards from the economic upturn, continued to support the Adenauer coalition.

Bolstered by substantial U.S. economic aid, Adenauer had no intention of wavering on his commitment to NATO and the Atlantic system. As a result, radical nationalists in West Germany had essentially two choices: accept Bonn's integration into the Western alliance, which entailed remilitarization along anti-Communist lines, or languish on the political periphery. Confronted with this implicit Cold War ultimatum, neo-Nazi diehards who opposed Adenauer's Western-oriented policies struggled to devise an effective response that would prevent them from fading into irrelevance.

For those whose faith in fascism remained undimmed, the bipolar realities of the new political order had to be taken into account. Some trimmed their sails to suit the times, eschewing racist and anti-Semitic rhetoric without abandoning the quest to revive fascism in a much-altered postwar form. They set their sights on the long haul, sharing a common objective of political power but lacking consensus on how to achieve it. Given the factionalism that bedeviled the neo-Nazi scene, some felt the best they could do was to nurture a loose-knit, extraparliamentary underground movement in an effort to keep the ideological flame burning until circumstances were more conducive to a full-fledged fascist resurgence.

Frustrated in their drive for political power, neo-Nazi diehards devoted much of their energy to preparing a body of myths, symbols, and social images that might sustain the next generation of activists through a lengthy political dry season. They worked hard, in the words of Kurt Tauber, "to salvage from the past still usable parts of the conservative revolution, folkish and national socialist ideology and to shape them into a new ideological springboard from which they might once again reach their goal." Intrinsic to their revisionist methodology were various ploys designed to improve the Nazi image. A standard element in their repertory, for example, involved the claim that there was a crucial difference between an early, beneficent form of fascism and a subsequent, tainted form.[69]

By invoking such arguments, ultra-right-wing organizations, such as Rudel's Deutsche Reichs-Partei, were able to retain a small base of support throughout the middle and late 1950s, particularly among those who questioned the wisdom of Adenauer's total embrace of NATO. Smoldering resentments were sufficient to sustain several neo-Nazi groups that continued to promote a nationalist-neutralist line. East-financed newspapers and East-oriented associations were encouraged by repeated overtures from Stalin's successors, who kept raising the possibility of a nonaligned, united Germany.[70]

As a way of demonstrating their sincerity, the Soviets offered to withdraw their troops from occupied Austria if the Western powers would as well. In 1955, once U.S. policy makers overcame their misgivings, the Soviet proposal was enacted and a "neutral" (though distinctly West-leaning) Austria came into being. But wary U.S. officials balked when the Soviets pressed for an analogous solution to the German problem. American intransigence contributed to an eventual shift in Soviet tactics. In 1961, the Berlin Wall — the quintessential symbol of the Cold War — was constructed on orders from the Kremlin to stem the flow of refugees from the East to the West. With both superpowers opting for "peaceful coexistence," neo-Nazis who favored neutrality found themselves left out in the cold.

There were occasional eruptions, as when a Jewish synagogue in Cologne was desecrated with swastikas on Christmas eve, 1959, by young followers of Hans-Ulrich Rudel. This triggered a spate of anti-Semitic incidents in Western Europe. For the most part, however, hard-core neofascist activity was confined to the fringes of society. French fascist Maurice Bardèche bemoaned their plight as perennial outcasts, acknowledging that "these bands of lost soldiers" were beset by an acute identity crisis. "On the political stage, we always seem to be merely extras," Bardèche complained. "An army of nobodies has encamped all over the territory of the Right."[71]

PART TWO

POLITICAL SOLDIERS

CHAPTER FOUR

THE SWASTIKA AND THE CRESCENT

Coup d'Etat in Cairo

January 1953. A brigade of goose-stepping Arab soldiers marched along a wide boulevard in Cairo. They saluted as they passed the grandstand reserved for special dignitaries. Sitting among the honored guests, conspicuous in his dark glasses, was Otto Skorzeny. The Nazi war hero had been invited to inspect the sun-drenched military parade in celebration of the "Free Officers" coup that toppled the corrupt Egyptian monarchy six months earlier.

A key advisor to the new regime's secret service, Skorzeny was held in high regard by Egypt's young revolutionary leaders, including the up-and-coming Colonel Gamal Abdel Nasser, considered by many to be the real power behind the secular throne. Ilse Skorzeny, who often accompanied her husband during his travels to the Middle East, acknowledged that Otto and Nasser were on very friendly terms. "When we were in Cairo, they were together a lot," she recalled.[1]

While visiting Egypt, Skorzeny also kept up his contacts with the burgeoning German exile community that had taken root shortly after World War II. Cairo, like Madrid and Buenos Aires, had become a safe haven for thousands of Nazi expatriates. Many Third Reich veterans found employment with the Egyptian government.

Close ties between Germany and the Arab world had been forged initially during the Hitler years, as the Führer's geopolitical experts gave top priority to building up Nazi influence in the Middle East. Even though he loathed Arabs (he once described them as "lacquered half-apes who ought to be whipped"), Hitler was nonetheless the idol of the paramilitary Green Shirts, Egypt's indigenous protofascist movement, which referred to him as Abu Ali, the "good fighter." King Farouk, who ruled Egypt during the Hitler era, was also a Nazi sympathizer. The king's palace became a rendezvous point for Axis spies and couriers. Members of the royal family were involved in espionage for Fascist Italy, and many of the king's mistresses did double duty as Nazi agents.[2]

With Rommel's army aiming to wrest Egypt from British colonial rule, German military intelligence stepped up its activities in the land of the Sphinx. Admiral Wilhelm Canaris, chief of the Abwehr, counted among his confidential agents two young Egyptian lieutenants, Abdel Nasser and Anwar Sadat, both of whom belonged to a secret officers association known as the Ring of Iron. "We made contact with the German headquarters in Libya," Sadat said of his wartime activities, "and we acted in complete harmony with them." Imprisoned for three years by the British because of his subversive efforts, Sadat would later succeed Nasser as president of Egypt.[3]

The most influential Arab leader to seek an alliance with Nazi Germany was Haj Amin al-Husayni, the notorious Grand Mufti of Jerusalem. A scion of a prominent Muslim family in British-controlled Palestine, the Mufti fled his native land two years before the outbreak of World War II. Lean and intense, this worldly man of letters with a scraggly red beard remained the preeminent religious leader of Palestinian Muslims despite his refugee status.

In November 1941, the Mufti had a meeting with Adolf Hitler in Berlin, which became his residence-in-exile for the duration of the war. Haj Amin al-Husayni managed to impress the Führer, who spoke highly of his "exceptional cleverness," which made him "almost equal to the Japanese." Heinrich Himmler also respected the Mufti and often complimented his blue eyes, which the SS chief described as "appropriately Nordic." A so-called racial expert at the Abwehr concluded in an intelligence report that the Mufti was not really much of an Arab after all: "Pure Arab blood . . . could not have been so consistent and systematic in the struggle against the English and the Jews; he would certainly have been bought off.

What is more, that Caucasian or Aryan blood enables us to expect from the Mufti in the future that faithfulness in an ally of which pure Arab blood would be incapable."[4]

While Arabs in Germany suffered discriminatory treatment consistent with Nazi racial theories, the Mufti was chauffeured around by an SS guard in a black Mercedes. Referring in effusive terms to his friendship with Hitler, he sought promises of assistance for the anti-British and anti-Zionist struggle in Palestine. But the Mufti's demands — which included explicit Axis endorsement of Arab self-determination and unity — conflicted with the colonial interests of Fascist Italy and Vichy France, Germany's wartime allies. Consequently, Hitler refrained from giving his full-fledged support to Arab cries for independence, even though Third Reich officials spouted "anti-imperialist" rhetoric when talking about the Islamic world.

Undaunted, the Mufti was convinced that the immediate objectives of Arab nationalism and Nazi strategy coincided, given their common enemies — Brits, Jews, and Communists. Powerful radio transmitters were put at the Mufti's disposal so that his inflammatory pro-Axis propaganda could be heard throughout the Arab world. He was also instrumental in organizing a special Muslim division of the Waffen SS, which consisted of young recruits from the Balkans — primarily Bosnians — and elsewhere. The Mufti visited these troops regularly, leading them in prayer and exhorting them to fight for Allah. He also blessed Nazi-trained sabotage teams before they were dispatched to Palestine, Iraq, and Transjordan. As it became increasingly obvious that the military tide was turning against the Axis, Haj Amin al-Husayni urged Germany and its puppet regimes in Eastern Europe to send thousands of Jews to concentration camps rather than allow them to emigrate to Palestine. It does not appear, however, that the Mufti decisively influenced the Nazis, who needed little encouragement to exterminate more Jews.[5]

After the war, the Mufti made his way to Egypt. He settled into a luxurious villa in Alexandria, courtesy of King Farouk. The Mufti's arrival in 1946 was a prelude to a steady stream of Third Reich veterans, including several badly compromised Nazis, who chose Cairo as a hideout. One of King Farouk's ministers suggested that former Nazis should be hired as advisors in an effort to upgrade the Egyptian armed forces. Although the king showed little enthusiasm for the proposal, some of his military officers went ahead anyway and secured the services of several German technicians and industrial experts.[6]

During the early 1950s, a forty-man contingent of German paratroopers, artillery and demolition experts, frogmen, and tank veterans of Rommel's Afrika Korps began sharing their skills with students at Egyptian military academies. Their contribution was recognized by Colonel Gamal Abdel Nasser and the other leaders of the Free Officers Society, who asked them to continue working in Egypt after the overthrow of the monarchy on July 23, 1952. "The most intriguing aspect [of] the revolt against King Farouk," *Newsweek* reported, "was the role played in the coup by the large group of German advisers serving with the Egyptian army." While there was no evidence that former Nazis initiated the coup, according to *Newsweek,* "the young officers who did the actual planning consulted the German advisers as to 'tactics.' " This would account for the "the smoothness of the operation," the magazine suggested.[7]

Nasser emerged as Egypt's uncontested leader in 1954 after shoving aside the avuncular Muhammad Naguib, who had served as titular chief of the country immediately following the Free Officers coup. This power grab was endorsed by CIA officials, who viewed Nasser as a valuable anti-Communist ally. One of Nasser's first measures was to crack down hard on the Egyptian Communist Party and imprison its leaders. His henchmen also rounded up several left-wing trade unionists, and after a summary trial, they were hanged.[8]

The CIA gladly assented to Nasser's request for assistance in overhauling the mothballed Egyptian espionage apparatus. Such a sensitive assignment, however, required that American advisors not get their hands dirty. An off-the-shelf style of nation-tampering was deemed preferable, so the CIA turned to the readily available Gehlen Org.

Miles Copeland, the CIA's man on the spot in Cairo throughout the 1950s, recalled that U.S. intelligence "had on its hands a number of Germans who were not — or in some cases not *quite* — war criminals." He and his CIA cohorts "combed the files of these Germans in a search for talent which could be put to use, in some cases in the United States [but] mostly in other countries. This effort was well on the way to being completed when, in 1953, it became apparent that Nasser needed outside help for his intelligence and security services and our Government found it highly impolitic to help him directly."[9]

After conferring with Dulles, Gehlen decided that the best man for the job was Otto Skorzeny. The CIA chief concurred, confident in the presumption that Skorzeny, an ardent anti-Communist, would help solidify Nasser's power base within the Egyptian military. Skorzeny was "a particular favorite of American Counter-Intelligence, having made friends with several of his captors before escaping from them, and was believed to be especially suited, in temperament and personality, for getting along with Nasser," remarked Copeland. It was a decision that U.S. policy makers would come to regret.[10]

At first, Skorzeny played hard to get. He was approached "in a routine manner," wrote Copeland, "then at a higher level, then through a personal visit from a certain well-known Major General of the American Army." In the end, it took some diligent persuasion by Hjalmar Schacht to convince his nephew-in-law that it would be in everyone's best interests if he swaggered off to the Pyramids on a mission for Gehlen and the Americans. Scarface accepted the assignment after he was assured that his stay in Egypt would be limited and that the CIA would supplement the salary offered by Nasser.[11]

Over the next year and a half, Skorzeny used CIA funds to recruit a slew of SS veterans and other Third Reich luminaries, who jumped at the chance "to inject new life and expertise into the Egyptian secret service," as Gehlen put it. More than one hundred additional German advisors were pressed into service under Skorzeny's auspices; some were drawn from the ranks of neo-Nazi organizations and remnants of the ODESSA escape networks that crisscrossed through Madrid. Skorzeny's team included fugitives like SS Major Leopold Gleim, who had been sentenced to death for wartime atrocities committed while he was the Gestapo chief of Poland, and Franz Bünsche, a Goebbels propagandist best known for his pornographic book *The Sexual Habits of Jews*. Miles Copeland of the CIA took it all in stride: "Perhaps someone will one day devise a means for inducing gentlemen of finer sensibilities to become security officers, but certainly no such means were known, either by Nasser or his American advisers."[12]

The fact that Egypt was technically at war with Israel made many of the Gehlenites, with their anti-Semitic proclivities, all the more enthusiastic about helping the Free Officers once they were in power. And the Arab countries, for their part, were "eager to embrace Germans with an ostensibly 'Nazi' past," Gehlen notes in his memoirs. Nasser, in particular, had a great deal of respect for Skorzeny. To the leaders of the Egyptian military, he was the scarfaced master of ambush, the Third Reich's fearless cloak-and-dagger man who could out–James Bond the best of them. British officials, peeved at their diminishing status in the Middle East, were less sanguine about Skorzeny's presence in Cairo. In a speech before the House of Commons, Prime Minister Winston Churchill warned that the Egyptian army was "being aided and trained by Nazi instructors and staff officers in unusual numbers." But an Egyptian government spokesperson, wondering what all the fuss was about, replied swiftly, "Britain herself is using more than 4,000 German experts, the United States is employing several thousand, and many other countries are doing the same."[13]

A Mecca for Fascists

Having checked into a room at the Luna Park Hotel, Francis Parker Yockey stood by a window and gazed upon the city that Arabs call the "Mother of the World." From the right vantage point, he could see the massive bastion of Saladin's Citadel, the dominant landmark of Cairo, and the three slender minarets of Al-Azhar that towered over a sweeping panorama of mosques and huddled rooftops. Beyond the boundaries of the old city, a few skyscrapers were under construction. And off in the distance, the Pyramids loomed like silent sentinels guarding the mysteries of an ancient era.

A revolutionary in search of a revolution, Yockey had come to Egypt in the summer of 1953, the same year Skorzeny arrived on the scene with a passel of German advisors. During a stint in Cairo that lasted only a few months, the American fascist spent much of his time writing anti-Semitic propaganda for the Egyptian Information Ministry. Although he considered Nasser to be "a great and vigorous man," Yockey could not handle the scorching heat of the Nile Valley. "The climate here is so torrid that it takes everything out of a man. There are 20,000 Germans here, and they're all slowly growing oblivious. They are all going black. If I stay here, I will, too," he wrote to an associate. "I'm rather sensitive . . . I hate the sun, always have." Short on cash, Yockey tried to sell one of his U.S. passports before he resumed his wandering ways.[14]

As more Nazis inundated the Egyptian capital, the posh bars and elite social clubs of Cairo attracted a rogues' gallery of SS renegades, Gestapo "interrogation" specialists, and German rocket scientists, all mingling freely with fervent Arab radicals, shadowy arms merchants, and Israeli spies. It was a world that Major General Otto Ernst Remer found irresistible. Fleeing from West Germany to avoid a second prison term, Remer also made his way to Egypt in 1953. Unlike Yockey, he did not wilt under the desert sun. The Middle East — initially Cairo and later Damascus — would become Remer's principal theater of operations for the better part of three decades. He, too, would be employed by the Egyptian government, serving, in his own words, as a "political advisor to Nasser."[15]

Joining Remer in Egypt were several of his associates from the outlawed Socialist Reich Party, including Ernst-Wilhelm Springer, who would later be implicated in various gunrunning schemes to an Arab clientele. According to West German press reports cited by U.S. Army intelligence, Remer and Springer offered to set up a new system for policing Egypt. But this wasn't necessary, as the Nasser government already had several Nazi experts assisting with police work.[16]

While living in Egypt, Remer wrote an article for *Der Weg,* the Nazi monthly published in Buenos Aires. Alleging that both Germans and Arabs were being oppressed by "international Jewry," he denounced as "a national disgrace" the recent decision by Bonn to provide reparations to the state of Israel. (East Germany, by contrast, did not contribute a single pfennig as restitution for Jewish suffering under the Nazis.) Worried that making these payments would "disrupt the traditional friendship between the Arab world and the Germans," Remer went on to declare that "the creation of a strong Arab army is the immediate and direct concern to Germany's patriotic forces, which are prepared to offer the services of their best men."[17]

Remer's presence in Cairo was particularly embarrassing to the West German government, which wanted him behind bars. While both men were in Egypt, Skorzeny adroitly steered clear of any direct association with the former SRP leader, who had a propensity for getting into trouble. Shortly after he absconded from the Fatherland, Hitler's illustrious bodyguard was arrested for disturbing the peace — an infraction that might have prompted local authorities to throw him in jail if not for his amicable relations with the influential Grand Mufti, who took a liking to Remer.[18]

During the post-Farouk era, the Grand Mufti held court at a closely guarded villa on Sharia Assuit Street in Heliopolis, a suburb of Cairo. There he entertained delegations from throughout the Arab world while maintaining close contact with radical nationalists from Germany and other countries. Among those who gathered at the Mufti's home during the mid-1950s was his distant cousin, Yasser Arafat, then an engineering student at the University of Cairo. Remer, who would collaborate with Arafat in the years ahead, also visited the esteemed *Grossmufti* on several occasions. Over cups of strong Arabian coffee, they shared fond recollections of Adolf Hitler and indulged in the usual talk of driving the Jews into the sea.[19]

The Grand Mufti's network of sympathizers extended far and wide. "I did a couple of jobs for him, getting some documents from files that were otherwise unavailable," recalled H. Keith Thompson. Otto Skorzeny also collaborated with the Muslim religious leader. According to A. F. X. Baron, a prominent British fascist, Skorzeny was instrumental in funneling more than a million dollars, which the Mufti had raised for anti-Zionist and anti-Jewish propaganda, to various neo-Nazi groups around the world.[20]

Several German propaganda experts adopted Arabic names when they emigrated to Egypt. Johann von Leers, one of the Third Reich's most prolific Jew-baiters, converted to Islam and became Omar Amin. He got a job with the Egyptian Information Ministry, thanks to the good offices of the *Grossmufti.* With von Leers in charge, Cairo's anti-Israeli propaganda machine churned out hate literature and inflammatory broadcasts on a regular basis. Assisting von Leers were dozens of European Nazis who welcomed a fresh opportunity to continue their vendetta against the Jews. They had regular access to Radio Cairo, which utilized a powerful CIA-constructed transmitter to spread the message throughout much of the Arab world.[21]

Taking a cue from von Leers, Hans Appler, another Goebbels protégé, changed his name to Salah Shafar when he started preparing anti-Semitic material for the Nasser regime. And Louis Heiden, alias Louis Al-Hadj, a wartime employee of the German Press Agency, pitched in by translating Hitler's *Mein Kampf* into Arabic. The Egyptian government also published an Arabic version of *The Protocols of the Elders of Zion* (the infamous forgery concocted by the czarist secret police), which Nasser recommended to a visiting Indian journalist in 1958. "It is very important that you should read it," the Egyptian president explained. "I will give you a copy. It proves beyond the shadow of a doubt that three hundred Zionists, each of whom knows all the others, govern the fate of the European continent."[22]

Prior to World War II, vicious European-style anti-Semitism, as typified by the *Protocols,* was uncommon in the Arab world; while Jews were often discriminated against, they were rarely persecuted. But this began to change when Nazi propagandists assumed key positions inside the ten-story building that housed the Information Ministry in Cairo. Inevitably, the racialist views of these German expatriates rubbed off on Egypt's leaders, who launched a repressive campaign against members of the local Jewish community, many of whom were expelled from the country after their property and possessions had been confiscated. Such measures were applauded by von Leers and the other European fascists who found favor with Nasser in the mid-1950s.[23]

The Nazis on the Egyptian government payroll were engaged in more than just a war of words. According to *The Times* (London), in addition to serving as advisors to the Egyptian army, German war veterans were also instructing Arab volunteers in guerrilla tactics for possible action against British troops in the Suez Canal zone. The *Frankfurter Allgemeine Zeitung* subsequently reported that Otto Skorzeny had met with Colonel Nasser to discuss the training of commando troops.[24]

Several young Palestinian refugees, including Yasser Arafat, joined the Egyptian soldiers who were learning the ways and means of unconventional warfare. Although initially the intended target was the British, the future PLO chief realized that rigorous commando exercises would help prepare the Palestinian militants who were eager to renew the battle for their lost homeland. A grateful Arafat recognized Skorzeny's abundant skills in this area, and the two men struck up a relationship that lasted for many years. Apparently the Palestinian leader was quite fond of the scarfaced paladin. "Arafat would have done anything for Otto!" remarked Ilse Skorzeny.[25]

With Skorzeny commuting between Cairo and Madrid, the hands-on schooling of commando units was conducted by a team of German specialists that included former SS General Oskar von Dirlewanger, who was wanted in Poland for war crimes. Dirlewanger also tutored the Egyptian guards responsible for the personal security of Nasser and his important guests — a task shared by Eugen Eichberger, one of Dirlewanger's wartime assistants, who had participated in the extermination of Jews in the Ukraine.[26]

In the early and mid-1950s, Arab "irregulars" conducted dozens of commando operations against Israel that turned large stretches of land bordering the Gaza Strip and the West Bank into de facto combat zones. About three hundred Israelis were killed by infiltrators during this period, prompting reprisal raids against Egypt by Israeli soldiers. These "counterterrorist" attacks usually hit targets that were unrelated to the source of the border transgressions, resulting in civilian casualties much greater than those suffered by Israel.[27]

Seeking to avenge continued Arab commando operations, in February 1955 the Israeli military launched a massive assault that destroyed the Egyptian military headquarters in Gaza. Nasser countered by throwing his full weight behind the Palestinian cause. He authorized Egyptian military officers to oversee a German-trained strike force of seven hundred Palestinian guerrillas, who were given a new name. They were called the *Fedayeen,* an ancient and honorable Islamic phrase that means "men of sacrifice." After a number of successful forays into Israel, the *Fedayeen* quickly became legends throughout the Arab world.

Nasser realized that hit-and-run attacks were of limited value in the long run unless they were backed up by substantial military hardware. Skorzeny had already been dabbling in the international arms trade, and he was willing to help his friends in Cairo. Alert to new business opportunities, he persuaded General Franco of Spain to sell $3.5 million of military equipment (including mortars, shells, and machine guns) to Egypt. Effected through an intermediary company in Switzerland, this secret arms transaction was one of several deals involving military, industrial, and consumer products that Skorzeny arranged on behalf of the Egyptian government.[28]

But Nasser was convinced that his army needed much greater firepower than Skorzeny could deliver. So the Egyptian president asked the United States for assistance. The Americans wanted Egypt to join an anti-Soviet military alliance, which would have allowed U.S. bases in Egypt. But Nasser balked, insisting that this would violate his country's national integrity. Moreover, he had no axe to grind with the USSR. "The Soviet Union never occupied our country," Nasser told Secretary of State John Foster Dulles. "It has no imperial past in the Middle East. I don't see why I should turn my country into a base to threaten the Soviet Union with nuclear warheads when they have never threatened us."[29]

Dulles refused to believe that Nasser was acting solely out of nationalistic motives. By linking arms sales to conditions that Nasser regarded as an infringement on Egyptian sovereignty, U.S. policy makers left him little choice but to seek help from the Soviet bloc. If the Americans objected, they could try to woo him back. Prodded by his German advisors, Nasser decided that Egypt's future lay in not committing wholeheartedly to either side in the Cold War. He would pursue his own version of the seesaw strategy, pitting one superpower against the other in order to collect from both. Or so he hoped.

Double-Agent Intrigue

In April 1955, Gamal Abdel Nasser ventured to Indonesia to attend the first conference of nonaligned nations in the city of Bandung. This seminal gathering drew delegates from twenty-nine Asian and

African countries, most of which had only recently cast off the shackles of colonialism or were still fighting for independence. They discussed mutual problems and reaffirmed the importance of not taking sides in the East-West conflict. The Grand Mufti of Jerusalem surfaced at the Bandung parley somewhat incongruously as the representative of Yemen, a place he had never visited. But he was upstaged by Nasser, who introduced a resolution in support of the Palestinian struggle, which the assembly overwhelmingly endorsed.[30]

Nasser emerged as a major figure at the nonaligned conference, which was hosted by Sukarno, Indonesia's new revolutionary leader. During this historic conclave, Nasser met Chou En-lai, the foreign minister of the People's Republic of China, for the first time. The Egyptian president discreetly asked Chou En-lai about the possibility of obtaining weapons from the Soviet Union. A few months later, the Kremlin gave Czechoslovakia the green light to sell a large consignment of military equipment to Egypt. Shortly before the deal was publicly disclosed, Nasser met with Skorzeny and asked him to convey a message "to whom it may concern." Alerting his American contacts to the impending arms transaction and other Soviet aid proposals, Skorzeny suggested that they try to sway Nasser with a better offer. Kermit Roosevelt of the CIA proceeded to discuss the matter directly with the Egyptian president, but they made little headway at their secret meeting.[31]

Strategically situated as a bridge between Africa and Asia, Egypt was coveted by the Soviets as a gateway to the rest of the Arab world. The Kremlin had long been trying to gain a foothold in the Western-dominated Middle East, but a lack of suitable personnel undermined the best efforts of Soviet intelligence to infiltrate the region. Muslim recruits from the USSR's southern republics were not very reliable as agents, and Russian espionage stiffs made little headway on their own. The first breakthrough came in 1945, when Fritz Grobba, Hitler's top cloak-and-dagger operative in the Middle East, turned himself and his entire spy net over to the Soviet Union. Formerly Nazi Germany's ambassador to Saudi Arabia and Iraq, Grobba became the director of Arab affairs at the Soviet Foreign Ministry in Moscow after the war. He later helped to facilitate the sensational arms deal between Nasser and the Czechs.[32]

One of the more curious aspects of the $80-million Czech-Egyptian weapons transaction was the pivotal, behind-the-scenes role of Dr. Wilhelm Voss, a key German advisor to the War Ministry in Cairo. During World War II, Voss supervised Skoda Works, the huge armament firm in Nazi-occupied Czechoslovakia. Three of Skoda's top engineers were later recruited by Voss for a stint in Egypt. According to *Der Spiegel,* these three engineers were actually "communist agents [who] operated under the facade of being refugees" from Sudetenland, the heavily Germanic area of Czechoslovakia that Hitler grabbed at the outset of the war. The Czech operatives helped Voss seal the deal with Skoda Works, which furnished most of the weapons that were delivered to Egypt in 1955.[33]

Dr. Voss's wheeling and dealing raised eyebrows at the State Department. Jefferson Caffery, the U.S. ambassador in Cairo, was convinced that Voss had aided Ernst Remer's escape to Egypt. The SRP chief's flirtation with the Soviets did not faze Voss, who saw advantages in cultivating contacts in the East as well as in the West.[34]

The double game that Voss was playing did not escape the attention of Ernst Wollweber, a leading East German security official who convinced his Soviet masters that several former SS officers with Arab connections could be useful to Moscow. In particular, Wollweber had his eye on Bernhardt Bender, a Middle East expert who once held the rank of lieutenant colonel on Himmler's personal staff. After the war, Bender resurfaced in Cairo, where he served as chief of the political department of Nasser's secret police. In this capacity, Bender (aka Colonel Ben Salem) dispensed funds to a whole gang of SS émigrés that two-timed for the Soviets. Meanwhile, the British secret service and the CIA, seeing red in the wrong places, kept snooping among Egyptian locals who were thought to harbor Communist sympathies.[35]

Apparently American intelligence experts never anticipated that ex-Nazis would serve as vehicles for Communist penetration of the Arab world. Yet, there were several clues that Skorzeny, among others, may have been working both sides of the Cold War street. In February 1953, while Scarface was hobnobbing with Nasser, a Waffen SS veteran — identified only by the code name Kluf in a State Department report — approached the American consulate in Marseilles, France, and disclosed "the existence of a secret international organization composed of former SS officers and partially funded by the Soviets [and who were] supposed to work with the Russians against the Western orbit." Kluf pegged Skorzeny as an important figure in this underground operation. The State Department stool pigeon said he had remained in contact with Skorzeny ever since they served together during the war. He even gave J. Roland Jacobs, the U.S. consular official in Marseilles, Skorzeny's private telephone number, indicating that they had recently met in Spain, where Kluf learned of "couriers from the Russian zone [in Germany], carrying either money or pouches . . . weekly or biweekly to Madrid."

In addition, Kluf explained, this international neo-Nazi network "received funds from German industry." He specifically identified Countess Faber-Castell of the large German pencil manufacturing firm as an important financial backer. (An SRP supporter during the party's brief heyday, Countess Faber-Castell hid Otto Ernst Remer in her Bavarian chalet before he fled to Egypt.) Kluf told the State Department officer that Remer had "also been cooperating with the Russians." He proceeded to spin what sounded like a fantastic yarn about a group of SS fanatics who were preparing to instigate an armed insurrection against Western oil companies in Iran. Although Kluf was right on target about Remer, Jacobs concluded that his informant's story "did not quite ring true," and no official follow-up inquiries were made.[36]

More evidence linking Skorzeny to the East surfaced after British military police arrested seven former high-ranking Nazi officials in January 1953 for conspiring to overthrow the Bonn Republic. Figuring prominently in this strange affair was the H. S. Lucht Company, an import-export firm that provided cover for the coup plotters. Owned by Frau Lea Lucht (a cousin of exiled Waffen SS General Léon Degrelle), this shadowy corporation employed Otto Skorzeny as its Madrid representative. What's more, the H. S. Lucht Company was deeply involved in illegal trade with the Soviet bloc. It had an office in the East German city of Leipzig, which Skorzeny used to recruit technicians and military experts for special projects in the Middle East.[37]

Reassured by General Gehlen, U.S. intelligence strategists naively believed that their hired Nazi guns would prevent Egypt from straying into the Soviet camp. But that's where Nasser appeared to be heading in the mid-1950s. His abrupt volte-face toward Moscow was encouraged by Skorzeny, who favored the seesaw policy that the Egyptian president had recently begun to implement. Of course, Nasser was nobody's flunky; he may have needed little coaching on the best way to comport himself with respect to the great superpower rivalry. Nevertheless, the influence exerted by the likes of Skorzeny and Voss cannot be dismissed. It is yet another example of how Nazi operatives played the East off the West while pursuing their own agenda in support of Arab nationalists and other nonaligned forces in the Third World.[38]

Miles Copeland, the Cairo-based CIA spook, completely misread the situation when he opines that Skorzeny's big mistake was not to recruit "unrepentant Nazis" for duty in Egypt. This was "unfortunate," Copeland argues, "because as mere survivalists rather than men of principle, even wrong principle, they find no difficulty in adjusting to Leftish influences in Nasser's Government." As if Skorzeny and Voss were merely adjusting to unforeseen events, rather than helping to bring them about! The operative CIA premise was that an unrepentant Nazi must, of necessity, be a rock-solid anti-Communist. This was true to a degree, but ideological considerations in this instance accounted for much less than CIA professionals were inclined to assume.[39]

The CIA's ill-fated Nazi caper in Egypt was emblematic of a series of colossal blunders that characterized U.S. intervention in the Middle East. In the wake of the Czech arms deal and Nasser's decision to recognize Communist China, the United States reneged on its commitment to finance the construction of the Aswan Dam. Unwilling to accommodate Nasser's assertions of independence, American officials left Egypt little choice but to seek additional aid from Moscow, which promptly offered to pick up the tab for the Aswan Dam and much more. The Kremlin's generosity seemed to show the efficacy of playing one superpower off the other. At least that's how it appeared to Nasser, who proceeded to nationalize the Suez Canal in July 1956, brazenly declaring that if "the imperialist powers" didn't like it, they could "choke on their rage."

Three months later, British and French warplanes bombed Egyptian airfields and military targets, and Israeli ground troops rolled across the Sinai Peninsula. Unable to accept the end of the colonial era, the two Western European powers were intent on toppling the Nasser regime in order to regain control of the strategic waterway. Israel, for its part, wanted to eliminate the *Fedayeen* bases in the Gaza Strip. In the days leading up to the October 1956 Suez Crisis, Israeli politicians and journalists frequently raised the specter of Nazi advisors in Egypt. A leading Israeli newspaper, *Ma'ariv,* ran a full-page article headlined SWASTIKA IN THE LAND OF THE NILE that described former SS officer Otto Skorzeny as "the man behind Nasser."[40]

Worried that the Soviet Union would gain additional prestige in the Arab world as a result of the tripartite attack against Egypt, President Eisenhower denounced the invasion. Israel, under American pressure, agreed to withdraw from the Sinai in March 1957 in exchange for a pledge by Nasser to halt the border incursions by Palestinian guerrillas. Although Nasser's military had been badly defeated, his anti-Western defiance endeared him to the Arab masses, who viewed the Egyptian president as their liberator, a kind of Simón Bolívar of the Middle East.

The success of Nasser's seesaw strategy underscored that a nonaligned approach to international affairs could produce credible results. The Russians, for their part, placed a high priority on cultivating good relations with Egypt, which set a precedent for Soviet involvement with nonaligned movements throughout the emerging Third World. The Dulles brothers were apoplectic. John Foster denounced neutralism as "an immoral and shortsighted conception," while Allen scolded Miles Copeland. "If that colonel of yours pushes us too far, we will break him in half."[41]

The CIA quickly drew up plans to knock the pesky Nasser off his pedestal. One scheme called for slipping the Egyptian president a surreptitious dose of LSD to induce bizarre public behavior that would tarnish his heroic image and discredit him in front of his followers. When this ploy proved unfeasible, the CIA sent three assassination teams to Egypt, but Nasser managed to elude his stalkers.[42]

With Nasser thumbing his nose at the West, the CIA forged a closer alliance with its Israeli counterpart, the Mossad, in an effort to curb what was perceived as increasing Soviet encroachment into the Middle East. Although the United States had been the first country to recognize the Jewish state, the American superpower was only lukewarm toward Israel at the outset so as not to sully relations with the Arabs. A strong Arabist faction within the State Department and the CIA — which included Kermit Roosevelt and Miles Copeland — had the upper hand in the early 1950s. But their stock plunged when the CIA's Nazi caper boomeranged in Egypt. "Later on," Roosevelt admitted, "we came to the conclusion that it was not a smart thing to be training the Egyptian secret service."[43]

The espionage debacle in Cairo provided a decisive opening for Mossad chief Isser Harel and Israeli prime minister David Ben-Gurion, who were determined to forge closer relations with the Western alliance. For a number of years, Israeli intelligence had provided the Americans with a steady stream of information gleaned from Jewish immigrants of Eastern European origin — who had a lot to say about life under the Soviet boot. After the Suez Crisis, contacts between the Mossad and the CIA expanded dramatically. One bittersweet consequence of this for the Israelis entailed newly forged links with the Gehlen Org, which officially became the BND (the West German version of the CIA) in 1955. These intelligence ties were a prelude to high-level military contacts and eventual diplomatic recognition, despite strong reservations in both countries.

"I have always regarded it as something of a tragedy," Gehlen confessed in his memoirs, "that West Germany was inevitably dragged into an alliance with the state of Israel against the Arab countries." But he recognized "the political debt that Germany owed to the Jews," and thus, according to Gehlen, "[w]e began to take a more professional interest in the Israelis. We gave them expert advice on the development of their small but powerful secret service; we made facilities available to them and aided them in placing key agents in the Arab countries, especially since Nasser was becoming increasingly involved with Moscow." Harel remembered it differently. "We had only limited contact with West German intelligence," he asserted. "Gehlen wanted more."[44]

A coolheaded pragmatist, Harel understood that the Gehlen organization occupied a special position in NATO and the Atlantic system. Some kind of rapprochement between Bonn and Tel Aviv was therefore necessary, even if it meant dealing with the BND's Nazi-infested spy apparatus. "We had to do it," Harel shrugged, "because Gehlen was important to the United States." The Israeli spy chief was painfully aware that the Gehlen-Org-cum-BND employed and protected heinous war criminals who belonged behind bars. But he knew the same was true for many other West German institutions, which were also staffed with former Nazis. Even as Bonn doled out reparation payments to Jews and the State of Israel, the Mossad collected damning information on the past Nazi activities of top West German politicians.[45]

West German relations with Egypt took an official turn for the worse following the Suez war, but a number of important ex-Nazi advisors, some with close connections to Bonn, persisted in helping Nasser. Dr. Wilhelm Voss, for example, continued to advise the Helwan arms factory outside Cairo, and the Ruhr steel magnate, Alfried Krupp, was commissioned to develop iron ore resources in the region where the Aswan Dam was being built. And Siemens, the huge German firm that utilized slave labor during World War II, volunteered to undertake the electrification of the entire Nile Delta area. Gehlen, meanwhile, still ran a network of agents in Cairo even though he had ostensibly washed his hands of the Egyptian secret service.[46]

During this period, the BND set up shop in several Arab countries where pro-Nasser sentiment was rising. Gehlen counseled Saudi Arabian intelligence, among others, and expanded the BND's operation in Damascus. The BND station chief in the Syrian capital in the mid-1950s was Alois Brunner, the former SS captain who had served as deputy and personal secretary to Adolf Eichmann, the chief administrator of the Final Solution. Described during the Nuremberg trials as "the most cold-blooded killer in Eichmann's retinue," Brunner was given to boasting about how he directed the slaughters at the Drancy concentration camp north of Paris in 1943. He also bragged of rounding up prisoners for Auschwitz. Eichmann relied heavily on this roving mass murderer, who traveled from one country to the next, personally supervising the deportation of more than 120,000 people, nearly all of whom were killed.[47]

Condemned to death in absentia by two French military courts in 1954, Brunner escaped to Cairo, where he became part of the CIA-financed program to train the Egyptian security forces (his forte was interrogation techniques). When Gehlen downsized the

BND team in Egypt, Brunner moved to Syria and resumed his intelligence work. He was a relative latecomer to the neo-Nazi scene in Damascus. Since 1951, the Syrian armed forces had been receiving instruction from a team of German military advisors led by General Rainer Kriebel.[48]

Whereas many Germans came and went, Brunner remained in Syria for the next three decades. He lived under an assumed name (Dr. George Fischer) in a heavily guarded flat on George Haddad Street in the Abu Rumaneh district of Damascus. Brunner knew how to ingratiate himself with a succession of Syrian strongmen. In 1960, he helped to arrange the purchase of two thousand electronic bugging devices from East Germany — a peculiar arrangement, to say the least, given Brunner's ostensible affiliation with the West German intelligence apparatus commanded by Gehlen.[49]

Two years later, Major General Otto Ernst Remer settled in for a long-term stay in Damascus. He and Brunner would become business partners, brokering deals for various Arab governments. Remer had already proved his worth as a versatile middleman when he aided the Algerian rebels in their war against the French.

The Wrath of the Red Hand

One of the most brutal episodes of colonial rule in Africa occurred in 1830 when French troops occupying Algeria chopped off the limbs of Arab women to collect the silver leg and arm bracelets they wore. This was not an isolated instance of the white man's burden gone berserk — it typified the colonial authorities who ruthlessly subdued the native population. Tribal lands were confiscated and settled by French *colons,* also known as the *pied noirs.* By 1954, the year the war for Algerian independence began in earnest, some 25 percent of all farmland was owned by only 2 percent of the agricultural population. Over a million Arabs were totally or partially unemployed, and another 2 million were seriously underemployed.[50]

Such bleak conditions fueled the anger and resolve of the Algerian National Liberation Front (FLN), which vowed to free the country. Indicative of the old Arab adage "The enemy of my enemy is my friend," some top FLN personnel had previously sided with the Nazis, hoping that an alliance with Hitler would dislodge the French and inaugurate a brighter era. Such was the case with Mohammed Said, who always wore his Wehrmacht steel helmet when commanding FLN guerrilla operations near the Tunisian border. During World War II, Said had joined the Muslim SS legion formed by the Grand Mufti of Jerusalem. Parachuted into North Africa as an Abwehr agent in 1943, he was caught by the French and sentenced to life imprisonment. Paroled after a few years, Said joined the nascent FLN underground. He would later serve as a minister in Algeria's first postcolonial government led by President Ahmed Ben Bella.

While Said had previously collaborated with the Nazis, Ben Bella's wartime contribution to the Allied cause earned him the *medaille militaire,* which was pinned to his chest personally by General Charles de Gaulle, leader of the anti-Nazi Free French forces. Of course, de Gaulle, the future French president, had not the slightest inkling that he was decorating the man who would become one of the initiators of the revolt against France.[51]

Ben Bella's anticolonial agitation landed him in Blinda prison after the war, but he managed to escape (in best Hollywood fashion) by sawing through the bars of his Algerian cell with a blade hidden inside a loaf of bread. By 1953, Ben Bella had made his way to Cairo, where he was joined by other FLN leaders. They opened an office in the Egyptian capital that recruited Arab volunteers for combat duty in Algeria. Cairo became a nerve center of the Algerian rebellion and the seat of the provisional government set up by the FLN. This was one of the main reasons why the French instigated the Suez Crisis in 1956 — to deliver what they hoped would be a knockout blow against the Algerian rebel leaders.

But the French portrayal of Nasser as the guiding hand behind the Arab revolt in Algeria was vastly exaggerated. Much to the dismay of Ben Bella and the other exiled FLN leaders, the Egyptian president was long on rhetoric and short on crucial material assistance. Although the FLN pressured him for additional aid, Nasser sent very little in the way of arms or money to bolster the Algerian cause. For the most part, only vocal support was forthcoming, as when Nasser introduced a motion affirming Algeria's right to independence at the nonaligned conference in Bandung. The FLN delegation appreciated the gesture, but what they needed most was weapons to fight the French.

All signs pointed toward a bitter, protracted conflict. The French military, which had recently suffered a humiliating defeat at Dien Bien Phu in Vietnam, was determined to stay the course in North Africa. But it was impossible for French forces to thoroughly patrol a desert terrain the size of Algeria (then the tenth-largest country in the world), particularly when the FLN enjoyed wide support among indigenous Arabs. The rebels, however, were woefully deficient in training and armament. With few alternative sources available, the FLN leaders were receptive to offers from several Cairo-based Third Reich veterans who had revamped Egypt's military capabilities. Otto Ernst Remer and a handful of other German advisors were eager to do the same thing for the Algerian rebels.

While in Cairo as a fugitive from West German justice, Remer developed many contacts that would serve him well when he returned to the Fatherland in 1954 after a legal amnesty nullified the slander sentence pending against him. As the Algerian conflict escalated into a full-fledged civil war, Remer became the front man for a group of German-based arms traffickers who supplied the FLN and other Arab nationalists. "I'll never forget one order," Remer recalled. "The Algerians wanted five tons of black pepper. They needed the spice to mask the smell of explosives. It was a difficult request, but I got it for them."[52]

Remer was traveling frequently, spending months at a time hawking his wares in different Arab states. He set up a base of operations in Rabat, Morocco, where he occasionally entertained Ben Bella and other FLN leaders. Remer's cozy ties to the Algerian rebels put him at odds with the French secret service, which dispatched death squads and saboteurs to disrupt the FLN's European support network. Several neo-Nazi gunrunners were murdered by the Red Hand, an unofficial arm of the French secret service that claimed dozens of victims during the Algerian war. A nervous Remer asked the state government in Lower Saxony to provide him with special police protection because he felt his life was in danger, but the German authorities turned him down. "I couldn't travel through France because of my connections to the FLN," he asserted.[53]

High on the Red Hand's list of targets was Dr. Wilhelm Beisner, a former Gestapo officer who lived in Cairo during the mid-1950s but also maintained an office in Munich. Beisner, a postwar Gehlen operative, figured in a number of neo-Nazi gunrunning networks. He served as the chief contact in Egypt for a group of arms dealers in northern Germany who were associated with Remer. At the same time, Beisner worked for the Cairo affiliate of the Madrid-based Alfa Company, which was run by Otto Skorzeny. A U.S. Army intelligence document described Beisner as "Skorzeny's representative in Egypt."[54]

Linked to both Skorzeny and Remer by the black-market arms trade, Beisner miraculously survived a shrapnel-laden bomb that blew him through the roof of his car. Rushed to a hospital in critical condition, Beisner was severely crippled for life by the blast. Once again, the Red Hand had left its mark.[55]

The French made it very clear that anyone who smuggled weapons to the FLN had better be prepared to pay with his life. The message was not lost upon Skorzeny, who secretly supplied arms to the Algerian rebels while pursuing a variety of other business ventures. On several occasions, he traveled to areas of sub-Saharan Africa where uranium deposits were suspected to be. He did a lot of business in South Africa, the adopted home of a sizable number of German Nazis who favored the white supremacist policies of the apartheid state. During his African journeys, Skorzeny also managed to befriend anticolonial tribal chiefs in Kenya and other countries, some of whom later turned up on his doorstep in Madrid. At times it got to be too much even for the feisty Countess Ilse, who complained of being inundated by a constant stream of guests. "One weekend we had the king of the Mau Maus at our house!" she huffed.[56]

Otto Ernst Remer was among the visitors who breezed in and out of Madrid during the eight-year Algerian war. He and Skorzeny met at the engineering office of "Rolf Steinbauer" to coordinate the delivery of locomotives to Egypt, a shipment that both men were involved in arranging. The fact that Skorzeny had lined his pockets with a CIA stipend while Remer accepted funds from the Soviet bloc was never a point of contention between the two men. "Skorzeny was a good friend. I knew him very well," said Remer. "We saw each other over the years." Ever since their initial encounter on July 20, 1944, they viewed themselves as comrades in the same struggle. The superpower rivalry was important to them only insofar as it impinged upon or facilitated their postwar political strategies.

With Arab and Third World nationalism gaining worldwide momentum, some neo-Nazi propagandists began envisioning a German-Islamic neutralist belt stretching from the heart of Europe to the South China Sea. They urged the creation of a third-power bloc, an intercontinental alliance of all "uncommitted nations" and non-aligned elements that opposed the Yalta system. Such was the upshot of a myriad of German-Arab and Eurafrican societies that sprang up in the mid-1950s on both sides of the Iron Curtain, which was proving to be rather porous when it came to neo-Nazi machinations. For the likes of Otto Skorzeny and Uncle Schacht, the third-force strategy conveniently dovetailed with their own efforts to recapture traditional markets for German industry.[57]

Under the guise of anti-imperialism, some German neo-Nazis sang the praises of nonaligned movements in the Third World. Typical was this spiel by Erwin Schönborn, founder of the German-Arab community in Heidelberg and editor of *Nation Europa,* the leading West German neo-Nazi publication:

> *We see in the struggle of the Arab peoples against colonialism and imperialism of both West and East a fateful parallel to our own struggle for freedom from occupation by the enemy and for the reunification of Germany. . . . If we lived in the East we would be primarily fighters against Bolshevism. . . . As we live, however, in the West we are consciously directing our attack primarily against the other, equally dangerous, enemy of all peoples, liberal-capitalist colonialism. . . . We herewith call upon the German people to join our ranks to work and fight alongside us until the common goal of all oppressed peoples is achieved; namely, liberation from the foreign yoke.*[58]

A highfalutin declaration of this sort did not, in and of itself, detract from the legitimacy of Third World independence struggles. But it underscored the vulnerability of nonaligned movements as they sought to extricate themselves from the bipolar gridlock of the Cold War. The neo-Nazis, for their part, would support anything "to destroy the Democratic-Communist world tyranny forced upon us in 1945," as Goebbels's protégé Johann von Leers put it. Von Leers accordingly commended "the heroic Algerians" in their struggle against French colonialism. In this particular case, he and other neo-Nazi propagandists may have been backing the right side for the wrong reasons — or perhaps it was the Left side for rightist reasons. Their third-position pitch was calculated to obfuscate political differences. "We stand neither 'right' nor 'left'. . . . We consider those conceptions inappropriate," Schönborn asserted.[59]

In addition to smuggling arms to the Algerian rebels, German advisors provided military instruction at remote camps in North Africa. Fresh FLN recruits attended a training school in an old castle two miles outside Tétouan, Spanish Morocco, which was directed by a former SS officer, Ritter Franz von Scholl, whose left arm had been amputated because of a war injury. Another SS veteran, Graf Zimmerman, organized the so-called flying columns of the Algerian rebels in the mid-1950s. During this period, Zimmerman is said to have acted as a kind of executive officer under Otto Skorzeny. Several non-German FLN support networks sprang into being as well; some were coordinated by left-wing Catholics in France. Whatever the political coloration, they all provoked the wrath of the Red Hand, which was hell-bent on stopping arms traffic to Algeria, by fair means or foul.[60]

Conceived in the hotbed of North African violence, the Red Hand was the bastard offspring of a sub-rosa alliance between French colonial extremists and French intelligence. While officials in Paris vehemently denied its existence, the Red Hand reached out to murder and maim in a dozen countries, wreaking much of its havoc in West Germany and Belgium. The Red Hand blew up ships with weapons bound for the FLN in several European ports. North African diplomats, trade union leaders, students, lawyers, and arms merchants were rubbed out by Red Hand hitmen, who occasionally dug into their bag of 007 tricks to pull off an operation. One of the more exotic weapons wielded by the Red Hand was a long South American blowpipe equipped with a poison dart, which killed Marcel Leopold, a German arms trafficker, in Geneva.[61]

Ahmed Ben Bella, one of the directors of the FLN provisional government, was also targeted by the Red Hand. Following several death threats, a bomb exploded outside his Cairo headquarters in early 1956. On October 22 of that year, French secret-service operatives pulled off their most audacious mission yet — they diverted an airplane carrying Ben Bella and forced it to land in Algiers. He and four other FLN leaders were en route to Tunis from Rabat, where they had recently met with Otto Ernst Remer, as their flight was interrupted by the world's first airplane hijacking. The captured Algerians were hauled off the plane by French gendarmes waving tommy guns.[62]

The following year, France won what appeared to be a decisive victory in the famous Battle of Algiers, but this was possible only because of the colonists' overwhelming military force and the frequent use of torture, which French officers acknowledged. It was a particularly dirty war, which claimed the lives of 10 percent of the Algerian population (over a million people) and displaced another 30 percent. But the rebellion refused to die, triggering a crisis of confidence in metropolitan France that set the stage for General Charles de Gaulle's return to power in 1958.[63]

Expectations on the part of French *colons* that de Gaulle would bring the Algerian war to a swift and decisive conclusion in their favor were dashed when he endorsed the concept of Algerian self-determination. About the same time, de Gaulle began making noises about a phased withdrawal of French forces from NATO's integrated military command structure. The anti-NATO rhetoric emanating from Paris perked up Kremlin officials, who turned a deaf ear to FLN pleas for military aid as long as de Gaulle flirted with détente.

De Gaulle's change of policy regarding NATO and Algerian self-rule knocked the French colonists for a loop and generated a lot of anger among right-wing military officers stationed in North Africa. When the president commenced negotiations with the FLN, the barricades went up throughout the *pied noir* districts. Resisting the winds of change, implacable elements in the French army, the Foreign Legion, the police, and right-wing ultras in Algeria banded together with remnants of the Red Hand and other secret-service factions. The result was a Frankenstein monster called the Secret Army Organization (OAS), which lurched into being in 1961.

After four wayward French generals defied de Gaulle and seized power in Algiers, the OAS vowed to topple the government of France and replace it with an authoritarian regime that would be committed to the defense of all colonial possessions. A series of spectacular bank robberies swelled the OAS treasury, and members of the secret underground army perpetrated random outrages against the Muslim population. They indulged in "a festival of *plastique*," detonating bombs in Algeria and the mother country while drawing up lists of prominent Frenchmen who were marked for elimination along with target number one, Charles de Gaulle. The president survived several OAS murder attempts, some by a whisker.[64]

Among the ringleaders of the OAS were several unabashed French fascists who viewed the Algerian war as white Christian civilization's last stand against the heathens of North Africa. Militant anti-Semitism was vogue in OAS circles, which attracted a large number of former Vichy collaborators and French Waffen SS veterans. Khaki-shirted OAS shock troops sported the insignia of the Celtic cross, with its explicit racialist connotation.[65]

Needless to say, the anti-Gaullist ultras did not take kindly to a significant number of German neo-Nazis' supporting the FLN. In effect, the Algerian war had split the extreme Right in Europe into two camps, one of which backed the OAS while clamoring for a common front of white Europeans against the rising masses of the colored world; the other group, faithful to Nazi Germany's wartime alliance with Arab nationalists and enthusiastic about the emerging nonaligned movement, supported the Algerian rebels.

Otto Skorzeny was hooked into both sides of the Algerian struggle. That he had sold weapons to the Algerian guerrillas did not stop him from conferring with a handful of OAS ringleaders who sought his counsel in Madrid. Hedging his bets made sense to Skorzeny, as France appeared to be teetering on the brink of civil war. For a while it seemed that the OAS might actually succeed in ousting de Gaulle. But a multitude of terrorist attacks on French soil turned public opinion strongly against the ultras and weakened their cause.

Algeria finally celebrated its independence on July 1, 1962. Shortly thereafter, disgruntled French military officers who had rebelled against de Gaulle were put on trial. Some served time in prison, and a few OAS leaders were convicted of treason and executed. But full-fledged retribution was not forthcoming, as French officials feared that revelations regarding the Red Hand and the French secret service prior to the anti-Gaullist rebellion might embarrass the government.[66]

Secret Army Organization members who eluded the authorities dispersed into armed gangs and melded in with a bewildering array of groups and factions that composed Europe's increasingly fragmented neofascist underground. Some returned to their gangster roots by robbing banks; the most famous heist was the 1976 "sewer coup" in Nice, in which former OAS commandos stole more than $10 million in cash and jewelry. Other OAS fascists got involved in smuggling heroin and running protection rackets. With more anticolonial upheaval brewing in Africa, they would make their presence felt in the years ahead.[67]

Trials and Tribulations

One month before Algeria gained its independence, Adolf Eichmann looked at the world for the last time as a noose was placed around his neck in an Israeli prison. The principal architect of the Final Solution knew he was doomed ever since a team of Israelis snatched him from his neighborhood on the outskirts of Buenos Aires. The Mossad's spectacular move against Eichmann in April 1961 generated considerable fear among Nazi war criminals hiding in various locales around the world.[68]

Mossad chief Isser Harel first learned of Eichmann's whereabouts in Argentina from Dr. Fritz Bauer, a West German public prosecutor who decided to give Israel the information because he feared that his own government would sabotage efforts to bring Eichmann to justice. More than any other Nazi war criminal then still alive, Eichmann epitomized the cold bureaucratic horror of Hitler's genocidal policies. It was he who had commissioned the design of the first gas chambers. He oversaw on a daily basis the diabolical plan to exterminate European Jewry.

Israeli officials felt strongly that Eichmann should stand trial not simply for the sake of justice but as a moral lesson and as a reminder to Jews and non-Jews alike. His execution on June 1, 1962, was the culmination of an emotional legal ordeal that garnered international attention. Soviet and East German officials, hoping to score propaganda points while the trial was in progress, asserted that West Germany had been lax about arresting Nazi war criminals. In particular, they cited the flourishing career of Hans Globke, Chancellor Adenauer's right-hand man, who had favored the deportation of German Jews and the expropriation of their property during the Third Reich. Globke's name was also invoked by the defense team, which charged that he was responsible for increasing the power and authority of Eichmann's Gestapo bureau. Moreover, the CIA had financed and protected several senior officers of Eichmann's SS section after the war. Israeli prime minister Ben-Gurion, however, had little interest in ruffling feathers in Washington or Bonn. Instead, he preferred to emphasize the continuing ties between Nazis and some Arab rulers. In an effort to discredit the Palestinians, Eichmann's prosecutors tried to link him with the Grand Mufti, but the connection was threadbare.[69]

The propaganda sideshow proved irresistible to die-hard Nazis as well. Johann von Leers, then in charge of the Department for Jewish Questions in the Egyptian Information Ministry, traveled to Spain to discuss the Eichmann situation with General Léon Degrelle. The main item on their agenda was how to counter the trial's impact on world opinion. There followed the predictable gush of vitriol in neo-Nazi publications around the world. For example, *Thunderbolt*, the mouthpiece of the National States' Rights Party (the political arm of the Ku Klux Klan) in the United States, waged a "Help Free Eichmann!" campaign, alleging that his trial was a "giant propaganda hoax" designed to prop up the myth that the Nazis murdered 6 million Jews. Back in West Germany, Dr. Rudolf Aschenauer, the former SRP-linked attorney who had collaborated with Senator Joseph McCarthy, arranged for the publication of an apologetic book, *Ich, Adolf Eichmann*, which argued that the Nazis did not intend to murder the Jews but merely sought to bring about their emigration and that Eichmann failed to do so because the Western democracies refused to admit them.[70]

The Eichmann trial doubtless gave a jolt to the conscience of decent-minded people around the world. It was obvious that those who shielded him had also been protecting many other Nazi criminals, including some of the death-camp doctors who were guilty of mutilating thousands of men, women, and children. The Mossad had considered going after a few of the worst offenders, such as Dr. Josef Mengele and Gestapo chief Heinrich Müller. But the Israelis felt the onus should be on the Germans to make amends for their shameful lassitude in this area. In West Germany, incredibly lenient sentences had been meted out to some of the cruelest Nazi criminals, many of whom benefited from early pardons.[71]

In the wake of the Eichmann affair, a West German district court issued an order for the arrest of Alois Brunner. Praised by Eichmann as "my best man," Brunner was also sought by the Austrian government, which demanded his extradition from Syria, only to be told that the infamous Nazi did not reside in that country. It was a flagrant lie. Brunner not only lived there, he served as an advisor to the Syrian police, training special personnel in interrogation techniques. He had developed an ingenious device for extracting information from recalcitrant subjects. Reporting for the British *Independent,* Robert Fisk described Brunner's torture contraption as "a wheel upon which prisoners could be strapped and beaten with electric cable. Every few minutes an electronic pump would spray water through the wheel to open the prisoner's wounds. Then the whippings would start again."[72]

Although Syria fended off repeated extradition requests, Brunner did not go unscathed. Parcel bombs mailed by the Israeli secret service cost him his left eye and four fingers on his left hand. He always kept a suicide pill with him, vowing to swallow it if the Israelis caught him. "I will not become a second Eichmann," Brunner declared.[73]

Letter bombs were also sent to several German and Austrian rocket technicians working in Egypt during the early 1960s. It was the Mossad's way of signaling that they had better abandon Nasser's pet project — the development of missiles capable of striking Israel.

The effort to create an Egyptian munitions industry with the help of German scientists was originally the bailiwick of Dr. Wilhelm Voss, who mediated the groundbreaking 1955 Czech arms deal. Voss recruited several missile experts who had previously worked at Nazi Germany's top secret research station known as Peenemünde, which produced the V-2 rockets that terrorized London during the war. Some of these men were employed at the Helwan aircraft factory near Cairo, an advanced facility Voss had established.[74]

Many German technicians were replaced by Soviet advisors when collaboration between Egypt and the USSR peaked in the late 1950s. But Nasser's relationship with the Russians proved to be testy. (At one point, Soviet premier Nikita Khrushchev described the Egyptian president as "a rather hot-headed young man [who] took upon himself more than his stature permits." Nasser responded by calling Khrushchev "a meddler.") When the Soviet Union failed to supply spare parts for MiG fighter jets, the Egyptian president resolved anew to create his own aircraft industry. "Help Wanted" ads began appearing in German publications: "Aeronautical industry in Northern Africa requires specialists . . ." Another wave of German scientists checked into Cairo, prompting kudos from ultra-right-wing newspapers, such as Gerhard Frey's *Deutsche National-Zeitung,* which complimented Nasser: "He knows how to play with several balls."[75]

By the early 1960s, five hundred Europeans were working on aircraft and guided-missile projects in Egypt. Included among the Germans were a number of scientists who would later render assistance to Libyan and Iraqi chemical-warfare projects. Walter Busse, for example, designed ballistic missiles and military jet engines for Nasser in the late 1950s and 1960s; he subsequently turned up as an advisor to Saddam Hussein's military R&D program prior to the 1991 Gulf War.[76]

German scientists often were not able to pursue their chosen professions because of research-and-manufacturing restrictions imposed by the Allies that were still operative in the Bonn Republic. This is one of the main reasons why so many went abroad for employment — a process discreetly encouraged by the West German government, which had a perennial interest in securing access to rocket and air bases in Africa. The financial rewards were high for qualified experts. Those who opted for Egypt typically lived in air-conditioned luxury apartments with swimming pools and drove their sports cars to exclusive restaurants and clubs. It was a social scene that Wolfgang Lotz, an Israeli spy disguised as an adventurous German aristocrat, came to know quite well.

Lotz showed up in Egypt in early 1961 and pretended to be a former captain in Rommel's Afrika Korps. Through hints and innuendo, this blond, Aryan-looking specimen encouraged rumors that he had actually served in the SS during the war. This brought him in contact with a secretive Nazi clique that included the aging Dr. Johann von Leers, who often hosted parties at his house, where guests smoked hashish and imbibed generous quantities of liquor. Lotz was less interested in "the never-ceasing recital of reminiscences from the Third Reich" and the "belching and bawling of Nazi songs" than in the notables he encountered at these gatherings. Whenever he visited von Leers, the Israeli spook sucked up news from an assortment of Hitler fanatics, Egyptian officials, and key personnel involved in the rocket program. Lotz communicated to the Mossad what he learned by a hidden radio transmitter.[77]

Otto Ernst Remer called upon von Leers whenever he visited Cairo on business in the early 1960s — which was fairly often. "I knew him very well," Remer acknowledged. "I also had good contact with the people who constructed the rockets." Remer's home base at this time was Damascus, where he had recently gone into business with Eichmann's personal favorite, Alois Brunner. A number of Peenemünde graduates were also working on an aeronautics project in Syria.[78]

But the main action for German scientists during this period was in the Nile Delta, not far from where Lotz owned a large stud farm, where he bred racehorses and watched for clues regarding rocket-and-aircraft production, as well as other military-related data. Lotz was eventually caught by the Egyptian secret service, but not before the information he supplied to the Mossad was splashed all over the international press. After U.S. intelligence confirmed that the Egyptian missile program was making progress, Israeli officials demanded that Nasser expel the rocket scientists pronto. At the same time, the Israelis lodged a formal protest with Bonn for its role in condoning the presence of German technicians in Egypt.

Mossad chief Isser Harel was sure that West German officials were being disingenuous when they claimed that the scientists had been contracted by private companies, not by a foreign government. Technically, no West German law had been broken; thus, Bonn did not try to convince the German scientists to return home. Nor did the West German government seek to restrict the export of strategic materials to Egypt. "It was a criminal operation by the West German government," Harel insisted.[79]

Rebuffed by Bonn officials, Harel decided to lower the boom with Operation Damocles, a lethal campaign directed at German rocket experts and other top Nazis in the Middle East. At least two scientists were kidnapped; others were injured when they opened booby-trapped parcels that arrived in the mail. Several of Willi Messerschmitt's men were targets of letter-bomb attacks, which resulted in a number of deaths.[80]

A curious wrinkle in the Damocles affair occurred when Harel dispatched a team of Mossad operatives to Madrid to chat with Otto Skorzeny, who remained on friendly terms with many of the German technicians in Cairo. It's not clear whether Skorzeny knew he was dealing with Israeli agents, who masqueraded as NATO officials when they visited the infamous former SS officer. Given that most of the scientists working in Egypt were ex-Nazis, the Mossad assumed that some of them would be susceptible to the influence of one of their former commanders. After an all-night dinner at Skorzeny's sumptuous villa in Madrid, the Israeli spies persuaded Skorzeny to help convince the German technicians to leave Egypt.

Dr. Willi Tank immediately got the message. He had built aircraft in Argentina in the early 1950s before he came to Egypt to oversee construction of the He-300 supersonic fighter plane. Now it was time for Tank to pull up stakes again; he accepted an offer from the government of India, which sought assistance for its fledgling aeronautics program. Dr. Wolfgang Pilz, another German rocket scientist, departed from Cairo and went to work in the People's Republic of China, where he played an important role in developing guided nuclear missiles. Threatened by the Mossad, several other German scientists quickly returned to Europe.[81]

Where did Skorzeny actually stand amid all the espionage maneuvering? Was he a really hard-core anti-Communist, as the CIA assumed? Of course — and not at all. Of course, in that his entire background and personal history viscerally predisposed him against Marxism. Not at all, insofar as ideological factors were tempered by the vagaries of postwar Nazi realpolitik. Thus, Skorzeny had no compunction about double-dealing when it suited his objectives. His recruitment of East German technicians through the H. S. Lucht Company to serve in Egypt pointed up Skorzeny's willingness to play both ends off the middle as far as the superpowers were concerned.

Skorzeny was hardly unique in this respect. Several Third Reich veterans, including Dr. Wilhelm Voss, parried alternately with East and West during the Cold War. So did Remer's business partner, Alois Brunner, who helped Syria acquire bugging devices from the East German secret service even though he served as the BND's chief representative in Damascus. Shortly thereafter, Brunner was cut loose by Reinhard Gehlen, whose professional reputation had nose-dived as a result of a huge spy scandal that rocked West Germany in the early 1960s.

Given the BND's pivotal status within the Atlantic alliance, it came as quite a shock to CIA officials when Heinz Felfe, one of Gehlen's most powerful and trusted operatives, was exposed as a Soviet mole. A former SS officer, Felfe had run amok with Nazi gangs during the Kristallnacht looting-and-burning spree, but this obviously did not deter Gehlen from hiring him after the war. In addition to functioning as Gehlen's liaison with the CIA and other Western intelligence agencies, Felfe was responsible for ferreting out East bloc spies inside the Org and the BND. For nearly a decade, he supplied the Soviets with copies of the same weekly digests Gehlen shared with the CIA. It was heady stuff for Felfe, who likened his activity as a double agent to "dancing at two weddings, with the Russians and with Gehlen."[82]

Felfe's sensational trial began on July 8, 1963, the same day that Hans Globke, Adenauer's closest aide, was tried in absentia in East Berlin. Both legal proceedings generated adverse publicity for Washington and Bonn. Most troubling to the CIA was that it had no way of knowing how many other moles remained inside the Gehlen organization after Felfe received a fourteen-year prison sentence. He was subsequently freed in a high-level spy swap. Explaining his motives, Felfe said he felt compelled to defend true German values against the "cultural barbarism of Coca-Cola, gum, narcotics and sex" imposed by the United States.[83]

Gehlen's habit of employing ex-Nazis — and the CIA's willingness to sanction this practice — enabled the Soviet Union to penetrate West Germany's secret service from the get-go. In effect, the United States had hired Gehlen to keep the Soviets out, but he ended up letting them in! The Org was particularly susceptible to Russian infiltration given that many former Nazis found themselves in agreement with Soviet policy on the all-important question of German unification. West Germans with an unsavory Nazi past who worked for Gehlen were also susceptible to blackmail by the East Germans and the Soviets.

The notion that Gehlen's intelligence apparatus had been pierced by Soviet bloc spies was accurate to an extent. But the Felfe affair obscured a more perplexing aspect of the double-agent imbroglio. Whereas Felfe had faithfully served his masters in Moscow, for Skorzeny and many of his postwar colleagues, it was never ultimately a matter of choosing between Uncle Sam or the great Russian bear. Skorzeny's links to the H. S. Lucht Company's branch in Leipzig, East Germany, in the early 1950s — which could not have escaped Gehlen's attention — did not make him a Soviet loyalist any more than he was a CIA or a Mossad loyalist. He was, rather, a radical German nationalist, a third-positionist, and a seesaw opportunist who used his high-powered business connections and paramilitary skills to advance his personal and political agenda during the Cold War.

Slow to recognize that some neo-Nazis would feign an allegiance to the Western alliance as along as they deemed it tactically advantageous, CIA officials invested far too much in the Gehlen network. "One of the biggest mistakes the United States ever made in intelligence was taking on Gehlen," a U.S. army espionage specialist later admitted. When Miles Copeland finally caught on, he felt betrayed by Gehlen, whom he called a "slimy little intriguer." Gehlen retired in 1968. By then, however, the damage had been done.[84]

CHAPTER FIVE

NOSTALGICS AND REVISIONISTS

Cult of the Inquisitor

Francis Parker Yockey had outfoxed the U.S. authorities for more than a decade as he traversed North America and Europe, with occasional forays behind the Iron Curtain and into the Middle East. Moving around incessantly, "Torquemada" spent a few weeks in Havana, Cuba, after Batista, the Mafia-backed dictator, was overthrown by Fidel Castro's rebels.[1]

Yockey's luck finally ran out not long after he returned to the United States in early 1960. After years of playing cat and mouse with J. Edgar Hoover's agents, the wandering anti-Semite was spotted by an FBI informant at a private party in San Francisco. During the evening, the FBI snitch reported, a photo of a nude woman was removed from the wall, revealing a swastika, which prompted a salute by Yockey and several others, who shouted, "Heil Hitler!"[2] Yockey subsequently misplaced his suitcase during a plane flight to the Bay Area. An American Airlines employee at the Dallas–Fort Worth airport opened his baggage and found seven birth certificates and three passports, all bearing the same photo but each with a different name.

The FBI traced the luggage to a residence in Oakland, California, where Yockey occasionally visited. When he came to pick up his suitcase, he was arrested by two G-men and taken to the San Francisco County jail. The forty-seven-year-old American fascist was subjected to a thorough strip search by police officers. If that wasn't humiliating enough, Yockey had to fend off reporters after a legal hearing in which his bail was set at $50,000, ten times the usual amount for cases of passport fraud. Asked by a local TV journalist if he had ever been to Russia, Yockey screamed, "You dirty swine, get out of here!" A government source told the *San Francisco Examiner,* "This is not a small fish. This is a man that we are very, very interested in."[3]

While incarcerated, Yockey expressed regret to a jailmate over the recent capture of Adolf Eichmann by the Israelis. Whispering throughout the night because he thought his cell was bugged, he talked at length about fascism and praised Hitler as one of history's great heroes. Then, in the early-morning hours of June 17, 1960, after spending eleven days in jail, Yockey munched on a cyanide capsule. His body was found lying on a bunk bed, dressed only in underwear and a pair of black SS-type boots.[4]

Yockey died as mysteriously as he had lived, leaving others to ponder how he managed to get his hands on a poison pill despite frequent police searches during his incarceration. (It was the same method used by Hermann Göring to cheat the gallows at Nuremberg.) According to H. Keith Thompson, "Yockey took his own life in a prison cell, rather than run the risk of being, 'through torture,' forced to reveal his operations with the European Liberation Front, a group doing a job for Moscow among European rightists."[5]

Within a few years, Yockey would become a cult figure among the fascist fringe in the United States, thanks largely to the efforts of Willis Allison Carto, a former bill collector and an indefatigable promoter of extreme right-wing causes. More than any other person, it was Carto who kept alive — and distorted — Yockey's legacy. A dapper man who often sported a bow tie, Carto was the last person from the outside to visit Yockey in jail (aside from his lawyer) before he committed suicide. Carto was at the time the director of Liberty and Property, a San Francisco–based letter-box organization that put out a monthly newsletter called *Right.* He eulogized Yockey in his publication, describing him as "a great creative genius" and "a martyr" who had been "hounded and persecuted like a wild beast."[6]

Drawing upon white supremacist literature and anti-Semitic conspiracy theories, *Right* championed a variety of political projects that ranged from staunchly conservative to neofascist. In addition to commending the American Nazi Party and the National States' Rights Party in the late 1950s, Carto's newsletter welcomed the advent of the *National Review* and praised its young editor, William F. Buckley, as a brilliant writer. Years later, however, the *National Review* would run a scathing indictment of Carto, excoriating him for giving conservatives a bad name because of his pro-Nazi sympathies. (Carto sued Buckley for libel, but the court ruled in favor of the *National Review.*) Employed briefly by the John Birch Society, Carto also had a falling-out with its leader, Robert Welch, who did not share his anti-Jewish obsession. "The Jew is an alien in our midst and will remain so until he is driven out or conquered," Carto declared in *Right.*[7]

With the nativist Right reawakening in reaction to the civil rights movement, Carto began to develop an extensive network of front groups and journals that he marketed through mail order. In 1957, he established the Liberty Lobby, which became the institutional pivot of his growing political empire. After Yockey died, the Liberty Lobby and several of its spin-offs began to tout *Imperium* as the *Mein Kampf* of the postwar American Nazi scene. Noontide Press, which Carto acquired in the early 1960s, published a mass-market edition of *Imperium,* along with *The Protocols of the Elders of Zion* and other neo-Nazi favorites. The Institute for Historical Review, yet another tentacle of the Carto complex, would devote itself in subsequent years to elaborating upon Yockey's contention that the Holocaust was a hoax.

The Noontide Press version of *Imperium* — which went through numerous printings — includes a lengthy introduction signed by Carto, who describes Yockey's treatise as "prophetic, the work of an intuitive seer." The Liberty Lobby founder waxed poetic as he recounted his fateful encounter with Yockey in jail a few days before he killed himself: "I knew that I was in the presence of a great force. . . . I could feel History standing beside me." As for the significance of *Imperium*? "Simply this," said Carto. "That now, for the first time, those soldiers who enlist in the service of the West have a profound theory to inspire and guide them." Alluding to the Third Reich, he predicted that Yockey's tome would "live a thousand years."[8]

Although Yockey had many posthumous extreme right-wing admirers, it seems that some of his fans did not understand or did not agree with his racial theories. As Carto privately admitted, Yockey was "not a scientific racist." The author of *Imperium* did not view genetics as the be-all and end-all of politics; committed to a kind of spiritual fascism, he considered race fundamentally a matter of the soul rather than skin color or skull shape. Carto, by contrast, maintained that "the genetic interpretation of race is a necessary, useful and valid one if we are to see all of our problem clearly and accurately."[9]

Carto, for his part, assumed the guise of a super-American patriot, wrapping himself in Old Glory at every opportunity. This undoubtedly would have sickened Yockey, whose philosophical ruminations did not square with Carto's thinking on other key points, either. Carto soft-pedaled Yockey's idea that Russia constituted a lesser evil than the United States. H. Keith Thompson, who knew both men quite well, asserted that "Yockey had Soviet connections [but] the current bunch who exploit him don't want to hear about that angle." Indeed, it would have been embarrassing and politically disastrous for Carto if it were known that he revered a man who engaged in espionage missions for Czech Communists.[10]

During the early 1960s, the Liberty Lobby set up an office in Washington, D.C., and began to cultivate contacts on Capitol Hill. Projecting himself as a red-white-and-blue conservative rather than a racial nationalist, Carto made a favorable impression on several members of Congress, who received financial contributions as well as research and speechwriting favors from Liberty Lobby staffers. Most of his congressional supporters, such as Senator Strom Thurmond, were boll weevils from the Deep South who adamantly opposed civil rights legislation.

Warning of the dangers of "mongrelization" in America's schools, Carto advocated a repatriation scheme for sending blacks back to Africa. "Negro equality is easier to believe if there are no Negroes around to destroy the concept," he quipped. Musings of this sort elicited praise from James Eastland, chairman of the Senate

Internal Security Subcommittee, who stated, "Carto is a great patriot doing a great service to all Americans." The super-anti-Communist Liberty Lobby also attracted the support of some retired generals and admirals, as well as a handful of wealthy businessmen.[11]

Carto's operation got a big boost when Barry Goldwater ran for president in 1964. Although he lost by a landslide, the Liberty Lobby drew a large bloc of Goldwater followers into its orbit by distributing over 20 million pieces of pro-Republican literature. Carto's strategy was to use the names culled from the Goldwater campaign to gain leverage within the GOP. Hiding behind a conservative veneer, he sought to build "a party within a party" so that eventually the racialist Right might seize power by stealth. If that approach failed, a third-party bid remained an option in the future. Carto was willing to try different tactics.

Assisted by his German wife, Elisabeth Waltrud (dubbed "Eva Braun" by some Liberty Lobby employees), Carto compiled a huge mailing list to further his political objectives. Some U.S. congressmen lent their signatures to fund-raising letters that the Liberty Lobby rolled out en masse to gullible rightists. By the late 1960s, Carto's intricate web of political fronts was milking funds from an estimated one-quarter million people. Most donors thought they were giving to legitimate conservative groups. Carto, meanwhile, continued to cultivate ties to neo-Nazi and racialist factions. With links to Congress and paramilitary groups like the whites-only Minutemen, the Liberty Lobby served as a bridge between various sectors of the American far Right.[12]

In the late 1960s, a disgruntled Liberty Lobby staffer stumbled upon a file that included private correspondence between Carto and some of his political collaborators. The Liberty Lobby whistleblower found the contents eye-opening, and he leaked copies to columnist Drew Pearson. In one letter Carto wrote: "Hitler's defeat was the defeat of Europe. And of America. How could we have been so blind? The blame, it seems, must be laid at the door of the international Jews. It was their propaganda, lies and demands which blinded the West as to what Germany was doing."[13]

On various occasions, according to former Liberty Lobby employee Robert Bartel, Carto asserted to his colleagues that the

United States needed a right-wing dictatorship. But the Liberty Lobby wire-puller wouldn't say so publicly. After supporting Alabama governor George Wallace's third-party presidential bid in 1968, Carto tried to seize control of Youth for Wallace, which was renamed the National Youth Alliance. Former directors of the Wallace youth group grew chagrined when they discovered that the real movers and shakers behind Carto's political apparatus were part of a subterranean neo-Nazi cult known as the Francis Parker Yockey Society. "They belong to secret cells," Drew Pearson reported, "where they are known only by code names. . . . They sing the old Nazi songs, hoard Nazi war relics and display the swastika at their meetings. . . . They seek the overthrow of democracy in the United States."[14]

The Wallace youth group soon fell apart amid heated internecine strife, and the lechers of the Francis Parker Yockey cult went searching elsewhere for suitable prey. In the coming years, Willis Carto would establish himself as one of the most enduring — and shadowy — figures in the postwar American far Right. Under his command, the Liberty Lobby grew into the largest and best-organized anti-Semitic group in the United States. Functioning as the white racialist movement's leading umbrella organization, it developed close ties to the U.S. militia movement and forged extensive links with right-wing extremists around the world.

White Power Politics

Negative fallout from a number of unflattering articles in the mainstream press convinced the leaders of the Liberty Lobby of the importance of keeping their extremist proclivities in the closet, lest they end up as marginalized as George Lincoln Rockwell, the self-styled führer of the American Nazi Party. An obnoxious exhibitionist, Rockwell believed that the only way to really be a Nazi was to be entirely open about it. He had little patience for camouflaged Nazis who were reluctant to wear their swastikas on their sleeves.

Originally a devotee of Senator Joseph McCarthy, Rockwell decided that the anti-Communist witch-hunts were too namby-pamby for his tastes. He formed the American Nazi Party in 1958, attracting a pathetic band of followers who used shock tactics to gain attention for their decidedly unpopular cause. Based in Arlington, Virginia, Rockwell and some two dozen storm troopers clad in Nazi regalia lived together in a suburban house that featured an altar with a bust of Adolf Hitler in the center. A picture of George Washington and a self-portrait of Rockwell hung on the wall; a printing press spewed forth anti-Semitic propaganda.

Roy Frankhauser, a veteran of the ultra-right-wing scene in the United States, had a memorable encounter with Rockwell during his first visit to "Hatemonger Hill," as the American Nazi Party headquarters was known. The obese, chain-smoking Frankhauser telephoned to secure an appointment for himself and a few friends, but Rockwell, heavily bandaged from recent oral surgery, had trouble pronouncing his words. As a result, Frankhauser and company, dressed in Nazi outfits and armed to the teeth, went to the wrong address, only to be chased away by an old woman brandishing a broomstick. When they finally arrived at Rockwell's domicile, Frankhauser and the others were ushered into a waiting room with a very low ceiling, their rifles in hand. Surprised by these motley interlopers, one of Rockwell's bodyguards reached for his gun and accidentally squeezed the trigger, shooting a hole through his pants and scalding his thigh. Moments later, Rockwell barged in to see what all the ruckus was about. Frankhauser and company immediately snapped to attention and hoisted their bayonets straight into the ceiling, while the injured bodyguard hopped around on one leg cursing.

"Who the fuck are you?" Rockwell screamed.

"We're Nazi soldiers," Frankhauser responded earnestly.

"The hell you are," said Rockwell. "You're nothing but a bunch of Hollywood Nazis!"[15]

It was quite a comment coming from a comic-book character like Rockwell, whose political vaudeville act included regular forays into the nation's capital to picket the White House and harass bystanders. Frankhauser joined Rockwell for a heckling session at the Washington Monument, where they were pelted with bagels and lox by

Jewish tourists from New York. After another incident, Rockwell complained ruefully that one of his men "had his ear almost bitten off by a Jew."[16]

In 1963, the American führer and several of his heel-clicking stalwarts embarked upon a pilgrimage to Senator Joe McCarthy's grave in Wisconsin, where they held a memorial service on Hitler's birthday. Rockwell subsequently traveled to Chicago to speak before Elijah Muhammad's Black Muslim organization. Although the American Nazi Party produced hate literature that belittled "Negroes," Rockwell was favorably received by the Black Muslims, who advocated similar ideas regarding racial separation. Contact between white supremacists and Black Muslims — particularly Louis Farrakhan's organization — would continue sporadically over the years.

Rockwell also visited England, where he cemented ties with the British National Socialist Movement directed by Colin Jordan. Like his American counterpart, Jordan was an incurable Nazi nostalgic who disagreed with the idea that Soviet Communism constituted a lesser danger to Europe than did Western capitalism. Together they launched the World Union of National Socialists, which was viewed by its founders as the crucial dike that held back the waters of the great Jewish-Bolshevik conspiracy. They sent heaps of racialist literature to West Germany and cultivated links to sympathizers in South America and the Middle East. In the early 1960s, Jordan was in contact with an Egyptian military attaché in London who would emerge as one of the extremist plotters behind the 1981 murder of Egyptian president Anwar Sadat after he made peace with Israel.[17]

Rockwell communicated regularly with neofascists around the world, but his main focus was on stirring up trouble in the United States. "He used the Nazi swastika the way *Playboy* used a naked woman on its cover," said Roy Frankhauser. Not surprisingly, Rockwell's organization became a magnet for kooks, criminals, juvenile delinquents, psychopathic misfits, and other mentally unbalanced individuals who joined the American Nazi Party to gain a sense of self-worth and belonging that was otherwise lacking in their alienated existence. Often these losers drifted from one extremist group to another, their frequent departures having less to do with political tiffs than personality conflicts that were endemic to the neo-Nazi scene.

Such was the case with Frankhauser's friend, Dan Burros, who once edited *Stormtrooper,* the American Nazi Party's newsletter. Burros quit the group because he felt that Rockwell was too moderate. A former Nazi Party associate claimed that Burros enjoyed torturing dogs, including his own pet, Gas Chambers. Curiously, Burros's name and address (along with Rockwell's) were subsequently discovered in the notebook of Lee Harvey Oswald, the man accused of assassinating President John F. Kennedy. After JFK was murdered, Burros wore a button with the words "Lee Harvey Oswald Fan Club."[18]

In addition to admiring Oswald, Burros was a great fan of Yockey's *Imperium,* which he called "the Bible of the American right-wing." He read the book over and over, talking about it with his friends. Burros subsequently joined the National Renaissance Party (NRP), whose chief, James Madole, had published several essays by Yockey. Madole appreciated Burros's dedication and put him in charge of the NRP's elite Security Echelon. Before long, however, he had a falling-out with Madole. Burros apparently wanted to drop the H-bomb on Communist China, a country that Madole had grown increasingly fond of. Madole was strongly pro-Nasser and spoke well of anti-imperialist leaders such as Castro, Ben Bella, Sukarno, and Chairman Mao.[19]

While Madole professed admiration for left-wing revolutionaries, Burros cottoned to the Ku Klux Klan. He also became a practitioner of Odinism, the putative sun-worshipping religion of pre-Christian Nordics. A short, pudgy man who wore thick glasses, Burros had a disconcerting habit of cocking his head to one side and walking at an angle. He also giggled uncontrollably when nervous or excited, in a way that tended to strike others as a bit weird.

Roy Frankhauser liked Burros in spite of his eccentricities. The young Nazi was visiting Frankhauser's home in Reading, Pennsylvania, on October 31, 1965, when the *New York Times* ran a story about Burros that revealed he was Jewish and had been bar mitzvahed. Devastated by the article, a hysterical Burros ran upstairs raving "like a madman," according to Frankhauser, who was then the Grand Dragon of the United Klans of Pennsylvania. Burros destroyed Frankhauser's bed with several karate kicks, grabbed a gun, and blew his own brains out.[20]

Burros died from three gunshot wounds, unusual for a suicide, which led the FBI to suspect that Frankhauser may have finished the job. Bloodstains and bullet holes from the incident were still splattered on the walls and ceiling of Frankhauser's house nearly thirty years later. That he never bothered to clean up the gory mess is a testament to Frankhauser's peculiar mind-set. Those who dropped by could not help but notice the photos of lynchings and concentration camp atrocities on the walls, along with an abundance of Nazi memorabilia and racialist ornaments. "It was like a scene straight out of *Silence of the Lambs,*" said one visitor.[21]

A Klansman who wore many different hats, Frankhauser was, to put it mildly, a complicated chap. In addition to the American Nazi Party and the KKK, he joined some thirty different far Right groups over the years while also serving as an undercover informant for the FBI and the Alcohol, Tobacco and Firearms (ATF) unit of the Treasury Department. On one occasion, he carried out a covert mission at the behest of President Nixon's National Security Council.[22]

Described by his ATF handler as "an excellent infiltrator and confidential informant," the rotund, five-foot-six-inch Frankhauser took to wearing a bulletproof vest after several incidents when unidentified gunmen tried to kill him. He lost one eye while engaged in unspecified Aryan maneuvers — which gave a new twist to the appellation Exalted Cyclops, as Klan members traditionally referred to their leader. An emotionally unstable personality that reveled in spookery, Frankhauser later claimed he was actually a double agent who used his role as government spy to gain access to information that the FBI and the ATF held in their files about his ultra-right-wing colleagues. This must have sounded credible to his neo-Nazi buddies, for they continued to treat Frankhauser as one of their own, despite widely publicized reports that he was working for the Feds.[23]

Frankhauser's bizarre career epitomizes the murky clandestine milieu where intelligence operations overlap with neo-Nazi activity and the ultimate loyalty of undercover snitches is difficult to discern. Although they floundered on the political fringes while condemning the race-traitors who purportedly controlled the U.S. government, the white supremacist organizations haunted by Frankhauser were at times willing to engage in undercover operations for American spy agencies when their objectives coincided. Herein lay an essential paradox of the ultra-Right in the United States: it agitated against the U.S. government while simultaneously supporting covert activities mounted by American intelligence.

During the 1960s, for example, U.S. Army intelligence came to regard the Reverend Martin Luther King as a threat to national security because he denounced U.S. involvement in the Vietnam War. In a no-holds-barred effort to monitor King and his associates, the army utilized infiltrators, electronic wiretaps, and aerial photographs by U-2 spy planes. Headquartered in Birmingham, Alabama, the U.S. Army's Twentieth Special Forces Group sought out members of the Ku Klux Klan and instructed them to gather information on civil rights demonstrators. "In return for paramilitary training at a farm in Cullman, Alabama, Klansmen soon became the 20th's intelligence network, whose information was passed to the Pentagon," the Memphis *Commercial Appeal* reported years later.[24]

Had George Lincoln Rockwell been alive, he would have rejoiced over King's slaying in April 1968. But Rockwell was killed eight months earlier by a disgruntled recruit who had been booted out of the American Nazi Party. The führer's body was cremated in a pagan ceremony, and his ashes were kept by Matt Koehl, who claimed to be the authentic heir to the American Nazi throne. As the executor of Rockwell's estate, Koehl assumed command of his organization, which was renamed the National Socialist White People's Party.

A former contributor to Willis Carto's *Right,* Koehl had passed through several ultra-right-wing sects — including the National Renaissance Party — before teaming up with Rockwell. But Koehl lacked the perverse charisma of his mentor and had a difficult time keeping the group together. To shore up his authority, he traveled to West Germany and had his photo taken with several Third Reich veterans who had known Hitler. Koehl proceeded to publish pictures of himself shaking hands with Skorzeny's friend, Hans-Ulrich Rudel, who was shown in an adjacent photo pressing the flesh of Adolf himself. This ploy was repeated with photographs of several other old Nazis who had shaken Hitler's hand — as if to demonstrate a direct lineage between Hitler and Matt Koehl.

But Koehl's efforts to make it appear as though he had the endorsement of the old guard in Germany did little to enhance his standing among younger Nazis in the United States. Fending off accusations that he was a homosexual, Koehl tried unsuccessfully to prevent his party from splintering into several entities, each purporting to be the rightful successor to Rockwell's group.[25]

In an effort to boost his sagging reputation within America's homegrown Nazi scene, Koehl sought to expand his network of international contacts. Most notable in this regard was his alliance with Povl Riis-Knudsen, a youthful and energetic neo-Nazi leader from Denmark. Forlorn about the prospects for a genuine Nazi comeback in Europe, Riis-Knudsen surmised that the United States, less encumbered by historical baggage, was a more likely setting for a revival of National Socialism. He was pleased when Koehl appointed him general-secretary of the World Union of National Socialists, the cross-border umbrella organization that Rockwell had cofounded in the early 1960s.

Before long, however, Riis-Knudsen grew disenchanted with Koehl and his tawdry operation. The Danish neo-Nazi was particularly dismayed by Koehl's decision to invent a new religion — Hitlerism. With this in mind, Koehl and a handful of true believers sought refuge on a neo-Nazi commune in New Berlin, Wisconsin, where they worshipped Adolf as an infallible avatar whose every utterance was gospel. They called themselves the New Order, but there was nothing novel about their reactionary creed, which only appealed to those who were somewhat touched in the head. "What struck me as I moved around these circles is that normal people were few and far between," a disillusioned Riis-Knudsen admitted years later.[26]

Hoping to shake up the dead-end Hitler nostalgics and challenge them to rethink their ideas, Riis-Knudsen wrote a provocative essay called "National Socialism: A Left-Wing Movement" in which he criticized right-wing conservatives who favored the status quo. Riis-Knudsen argued that National Socialism was essentially "a left-wing movement," for it opposed NATO and U.S. domination of Western Europe and, like left-wing revolutionaries, it did not want "to preserve the present system or any part thereof." Jumbling the political vocabulary in such a manner was for Riis-Knudsen a kind of marketing strategy that reflected both the strength of left-wing progressive movements, which had blossomed in the 1960s, and the need for neo-Nazis to move beyond their perennial role as bit players languishing on the edges of society. "We must leave all half-cocked right-wing attitudes behind us and realize that we are left-wingers," he urged his neo-Nazi cohorts.[27]

In this essay, Riis-Knudsen also praised Russia, which he visited in 1978, as a Caucasian bastion. He had no trouble obtaining a visa from Soviet officials, who were well aware of Riis-Knudsen's Nazi affiliations, given the media controversy that erupted when Danish journalists learned that he was planning to travel to Moscow. After his sojourn, Riis-Knudsen concluded: "[T]he racial consciousness of the Russians, who are the dominant nation in the Soviet Union, definitely promises a better prospect for the survival of the Aryan race than the visions of liberal and conservative American politicians. . . . It is true, of course, that Communism does not support racial principles in theory — but with Communism theory and practice are two very different things."[28]

Several other Western neo-Nazis were impressed by evidence of a growing race consciousness in Russia during the Brezhnev years. A new wave of state-sponsored anti-Semitism — under the guise of anti-Zionism — attested to the fact that top Soviet officials felt they had to invoke a traditional Russian bogeyman, the Jew, to galvanize support for an ailing regime. A key turning point was the 1967 Six-Day War, in which Israel humiliated the Soviet Union's Arab allies. Soviet propaganda organs responded by launching a sustained anti-Zionist campaign that dredged up old Black Hundred myths of a worldwide Jewish conspiracy whose main goal was to destroy Mother Russia. The political directorate of the Soviet armed forces was one of the principal supporters of the anti-Zionist crusade.[29]

In widely circulated books published by official Soviet press outlets, anti-Zionist proselytizers quoted freely from *The Protocols of the Elders of Zion,* the notorious anti-Jewish forgery that had been concocted by the czar's secret police. Soviet writers engaged in almost talmudic debates as to whether Zionism was an instrument of American imperialism — or vice versa. Addressing this question,

Komsomolskaya Pravda, the newspaper of the Communist Youth League, lifted anti-Semitic passages from a neo-Nazi pamphlet entitled *America — A Zionist Colony* (published in Cairo), which was coauthored by Goebbels's protégé Johann von Leers. Appalled by such flagrant displays of bigotry, a leading Italian Communist, Senator Umberto Terracini, denounced anti-Semitic press accounts in the USSR as "a heap of idiocies built on rotting quotations."[30]

As the Brezhnev years wore on, Soviet propagandists weighed in with greater doses of racism, chauvinism, militarism, and anti-Semitism. Aping their Nazi forebears, some Soviet authors added Freemasons to the list of conspirators who were allegedly in cahoots with international Jewry. Others promoted a kind of gnostic racism, depicting the Russian folk as the original Aryans, a master race that once ruled a glorious pagan civilization.[31]

Infused with Nazi overtones, the Soviet Union's anti-Zionist campaign resonated favorably with ultra-right-wing zealots in Europe and the United States, who felt a racial kinship with their Russian brethren that outweighed theoretical concerns about Communism. Povl Riis-Knudsen and other neo-Nazi revisionists realized that a pure, universal, all-embracing form of Communism was an abstraction that existed only in the minds of Marxist thinkers. In the real world, Communism assumed a variety of guises that differed from one country to the next. The Soviet Union implemented its brand of Communism, while China and Cuba enacted distinct versions — each according to its own national interests. And because national interests ultimately superseded ideology, some neofascist strategists believed that it would be worthwhile to seek allies in the Communist world.

The China Option

Jean-François Thiriart, a native of Brussels, had never met Francis Parker Yockey nor had he read *Imperium,* but he shared many of the same ideas. Like Yockey, he considered the American occupation of Europe to be more dangerous than the threat of the Soviet Union, if only because U.S. domination was less heavy-handed and more difficult to recognize. Both men were obsessed with the idea of a united Europe as a third force capable of challenging the hegemony of the Cold War superpowers.

Although their political thinking may have been similar in many respects, Thiriart and Yockey had very different personalities. Compared with the latter's bohemian habits, Thiriart was the quintessential bourgeois, a stable family man who ran a prosperous business — but he, too, had his quirks. In addition to his wife and children, Thiriart lived with up to twenty cats at a time, which imparted a distinct feline odor to his household. This eccentric cat lover was one of the more unusual theoreticians to emerge from the bowels of Western Europe's neofascist underground in the 1960s. His career as a militant political activist points up just how far some right-wing extremists were willing to go to overcome their postwar isolation and achieve their goals.

Thiriart didn't start out as a fascist. A dark-haired, medium-sized, physically fit specimen who was not averse to punching it out with his enemies, he began his political journey in high school when he enlisted in the Young Socialist Guards, a left-wing student organization. His subsequent ideological zigzag had a lot to do with his mother's decision to divorce his father and marry a German Jew, who taught his stepson Jean to speak Yiddish. Filled with anger and spite at the new family arrangement, Thiriart rebelled against his upbringing and joined the extreme right-wing National Legion in 1939 at age seventeen. He also became a member of a pro-Nazi Walloon organization known as the Association of the Friends of the German Reich. His favorite hobby was skydiving — a thrill he first experienced while training with one of Otto Skorzeny's special commando units during the war.[32]

After the Third Reich collapsed, Thiriart spent three years in prison for collaborating with the Nazis. Upon his release, he established a chain of optometry stores in several countries. His professional standing was such that he became the chairman of the European Federation of Optometrists. While traveling on business, he conferred with leading figures in the neofascist scene, including Skorzeny, whom he often visited in Spain.

Thiriart generally kept a low political profile until the early 1960s, when Belgium granted independence to the Congo. This decision generated considerable anger among Belgian settlers, who felt betrayed by their government, much as the French *pied noirs* did in Algeria. Appealing to those who bemoaned the loss of the Congo, Thiriart sought to galvanize a movement that would force Brussels to reclaim its African colony. At the same time, he formed a Belgian support group for the French Secret Army Organization, which was engaged in a bitter struggle against the Arab rebels in Algeria and the Gaullist regime in Paris.

When the tide turned against the French ultras, Thiriart tried to convince the leaders of the Secret Army Organization to embrace the idea of a united Europe. "It was very difficult," he recounted. "The majority of them were blocked by their old French nationalist concepts." As far as Thiriart was concerned, the loss of the Congo was more than merely a Belgian affair and the loss of Algeria was more than just a French issue; they were both European problems that required Continent-wide solutions. But right-wing extremists who opposed decolonization often did not think in pan-European terms. This, Thiriart insisted, was a fatal flaw that inhibited their ability to mount a successful political and military initiative.[33]

In the wake of the Algerian war, Thiriart decided to create an organization called Jeune Europe (Young Europe) that would reach out to the entire continent. (Perhaps by coincidence, an SS university students magazine with the same name had been published in Berlin during World War II.) Thiriart inaugurated his new group with the "Manifesto to the European Nation," which began with the slogan "Neither Moscow nor Washington." Calling for a united European homeland with its own nuclear arsenal, he vowed to replace "chattering and corrupt parliamentarism" with a dynamic governing elite that would sanction free enterprise only if it was "civic, disciplined and controlled by the nation." Promising to reverse the "betrayal at Yalta," he denounced the Common Market and the legalist Europe of Strasbourg.[34]

Jeune Europe branches quickly sprang up in thirteen countries (the main chapters were in Belgium, Spain, Italy, and France), thanks to Thiriart's indefatigable organizing efforts. His stump speech during the early 1960s was full of bombast:

> *The U.S.A. and Soviet Russia tolerate an embryonic, weak Europe. We want a genuine Europe, and a strong one. . . . We are calling the men who are ready to die for Europe. . . . The Europe of the beautiful conceptions, the Europe of salons, will emerge from the Europe of guns, from the Europe of will power. . . . Europe needs a hundred times more soldiers than lawyers, a hundred times more leaders than reformers. . . . The Fourth Reich will be Europe, the Reich of the people from Brest to Bucharest. . . . We are for Europe the party of the last chance!*[35]

In 1964, Thiriart published his penultimate political statement, *Europe — An Empire of 400 Million Men.* Translated into several languages at his own expense, this book aimed its sharpest barbs at some familiar neofascist targets. President Franklin Delano Roosevelt was denounced as a senile and perverted megalomaniac, "windbag democracy" was depicted as a front for plutocrats, and Americans were described as "young presumptuous barbarians" and "impostors of culture" who had turned Western Europe into a colony. While purporting to be antagonists, the United States and the Soviet Union were actually involved in a "game of crossed alibis" to keep Europe divided and oppressed, said Thiriart. Thus, Washington used the excuse of the Soviet threat to keep NATO together, while Moscow asserted that it had to shield the East bloc from American imperialism.[36]

In passages that reeked of condescension, Thiriart referred to Europe's "monopoly of creative power," its cultural supremacy, and its unique mission to bring "morality" to the rest of the world. "On the train of history," Thiriart asserted, "Europe represents the energy that moves the locomotive and the black races represent the carriages." Those who intermarry were denigrated as "the trash of both nations," black and white.[37]

At the same time, however, Thiriart indignantly repudiated charges that he was a fascist. An astute strategist, he realized that he had to discard the nostalgic trappings of the pre–World War II era and adapt to the political and social realities of the 1960s, a decade in which the New Left and Third World revolutionaries were

ascendant. Dismissing National Socialism as "obsolete," he derided those who pranced around with swastikas on their arms as "past-dwellers" and "ridiculous caricatures." Instead, Thiriart purported to stake out a position beyond the ordinary political spectrum: "[W]e consider ourselves to be at the forefront of the Center, the avant-garde center. . . . The linear division of the political world, passing from extreme right to extreme left, is totally outdated."[38]

But Thiriart's attempts to distance himself from the legacy of fascism were only partially successful. Jeune Europe had emerged from the far Right, and this association persisted, even though Thiriart was advocating a new-sounding political philosophy — "communitarianism" — that supposedly transcended Left/Right distinctions. Friendly contacts with well-known Nazis, such as the former flying ace Hans-Ulrich Rudel, were publicized in Jeune Europe's weekly magazine. The Celtic cross, a symbol with fascist connotations, was featured on its masthead. Consequently, young militants of the ultra-Right were drawn toward Thiriart's movement. Many of these were emotionally warped individuals in desperate need of a father figure, prompting Thiriart to complain at one point: "Jeune Europe is a political organization, not a psychiatric clinic."[39]

Eschewing the role of substitute parent, Thiriart delineated a far-reaching geopolitical strategy that was unconventional in many respects. The leader of Jeune Europe thought in terms of big spaces: "Between nations, there is no other language than strength. . . . Power resides most notably in size, dimension." Maintaining that countries "are guided by interests and facts rather than ideologies," he characterized Communism as an agent of pan-Russian politics that masked the Kremlin's traditional imperialist appetite. "Since 1935," he asserted, "Moscow has been infinitely more Russian than Communist." Thiriart was confident that "the instinct of self-preservation will in time outweigh ideology and that one day Russia will have need of Europeans to help them stem the yellow flood." In light of the Sino-Soviet split, Thiriart felt that a rapprochement between Europe and Russia was inevitable. "Europe will renew the Bismarckian policies of relations between Berlin and Petrograd," he predicted, and when it happens, "the racial frontiers of Europe will coincide with its geopolitical frontiers."[40]

Thiriart dreamed of a massive white-power bloc stretching all the way from Brest to Vladivostok. "The Soviet Union is an intrinsic part of our territorial concept," he maintained. "It's a Eurasian Europe, a Very Great Europe, the New Rome. . . ." But before such a vision could be realized, the Soviet Union would have to change its imperialist ways and stop dominating Eastern Europe. With this in mind, Thiriart urged European revolutionaries to "exploit the internal contradictions within the communist world, i.e., by treating differently, the different varieties of communism." Specifically, he called for a tactical linkup with Red China so that the Soviet Union would be forced to divert more attention to its southern flank and loosen its grip on Eastern Europe. "In the short term," Thiriart reasoned, "we must hope for an anti-Russian thrust by the Chinese, and in the long term we must do everything to help the Russians contain the Asian flood. We must weaken Russia but not conquer it." In the future, he added, Russia would be absorbed "into an immensely vast Europe."[41]

Thiriart also had a plan for expelling the Yankees from Western Europe: support Latin American revolutionaries and Black Power proponents in the United States in order to keep Washington preoccupied with troubles close to home. "Latin America, like Europe, must fight against American imperialism. . . . We have common enemies, and this leads us to seek an alliance," he argued.[42]

Such prescriptions were not standard fascist fare by any means. His apparent shift to the Left alienated several members of Jeune Europe. To dispel confusion in the ranks, Thiriart set up a series of training camps in Western Europe for "political soldiers." After an internal shake-up, his organization was restructured along Leninist lines as a vanguard party dedicated to leading the European revolution. Around this time, the Celtic cross disappeared from the masthead of Jeune Europe's magazine. Acknowledging that it was wrong to have opposed independence for Algeria and the Congo, Thiriart started a new monthly, *La Nation Européenne,* that reflected both his radical anti-Americanism and his steady drift toward a more explicit "National Communist" perspective.[43]

Thiriart was particularly intrigued by developments in Romania, which since Nicolae Ceauşescu ascended to power in 1965, seemed like one of the few bright spots on an an otherwise dreary Eastern

European landscape. In contrast to the stodgy, bureaucratic style of his predecessor, Ceauşescu showed signs of a fresh approach to governance as he loosened domestic controls and guided his country toward an independent foreign policy. During the height of Sino-Soviet tensions, he made friendly gestures toward China. But certain unpleasant features of Romania's fascist past continued to cast a shadow over that country's political culture. This became evident when Ceauşescu began to promote an extreme form of Romanian chauvinism that harkened back to the 1920s and 1930s. In all likelihood, the large-scale postwar recruitment of fascist Iron Guard veterans by Romania's secret police influenced the development of National Communism during the Ceauşescu era.[44]

Jean Thiriart traveled to Romania in the summer of 1966 and introduced himself to Ceauşescu. They recognized each other as kindred spirits, and Ceauşescu agreed to contribute an article to *La Nation Européenne.* Ceauşescu also arranged a meeting between Thiriart and Chou En-lai, the Chinese foreign minister, in Bucharest.

"In its initial phase," Thiriart recounted, "my conversation with Chou En Lai was but an exchange of anecdotes and memories. At this stage all went well. Chou En Lai was interested in my studies in Chinese writing and I in his stay in France, which represented for him an enjoyable time of his youth. The conversation then moved to popular armies — a subject that interested both of us. Things started to go downhill when we got to concrete issues. I had to sit through a true Marxist-Leninist catechism class. Chou followed with an inventory of the serious psychological errors committed by the Soviet Union."

Thiriart tried to persuade Chou En-lai that Europe could be an important partner in a united struggle waged by all the world's anti-American forces, but he made little headway. He then asked the Chinese foreign minister for financial assistance so that he could establish a revolutionary army to carry out anti-American attacks in Europe. An elite military apparatus of this sort also needed a base outside Europe, and Thiriart hoped that China would provide sanctuary for his guerrilla brigades. A skeptical Chou referred Thiriart to contacts in the Chinese secret service, but these never bore fruit.[45]

For Thiriart, Maoist China was at best a tactical ally rather than a political or ideological model to be emulated. In this context, his overtures to Beijing made sense to several West German neo-Nazis, including the editors of *Nation Europa,* which recommended a pro-Chinese foreign policy in 1967: "We Germans see no reason why we should adopt an anti-Chinese line. True, from the biological point of view the old slogan of the Yellow Peril may indicate a possible threat to Europe. But for the present we have more pressing worries. As yet we are separated from China by the gigantic Soviet Empire, and we have no reason to oblige the Soviets, who deny us self-determination, by opposing Mao."[46]

Curiously, even General Reinhard Gehlen, the retired superspy, agreed with the gist of Thiriart's proposal. "In my view," Gehlen wrote in his memoirs, "it was of utmost importance to put out feelers to Beijing with the aim of securing a détente in Russia's rear. If we were to strengthen our hand in dealing with the Russians, then we had to come to terms with our potential enemies."[47]

One of Thiriart's closest allies in West Germany was Adolf von Thadden, a veteran right-wing extremist who also dreamed of a nonaligned European bloc. Nicknamed "Bubi" because of his youthful appearance, von Thadden had chaired the Deutsche Reichs-Partei (DRP) in the 1950s and early 1960s when it functioned as the de facto successor to Ernst Remer's banned Socialist Reich Party. These were lean years for hard-core Nazis in the Fatherland. With few exceptions, they remained largely mute and incognito, preferring to cluster in secretive societies and nostalgic reunions with their collections of kitsch regalia, their unwholesome memories, and their never-ending internal quarrels. West German law explicitly prohibited any attempt to revive the Nazi program, leaving little room for them to maneuver. This was one of the main reasons why a firebrand like Remer opted to live abroad during much of the postwar period.

The extreme Right remained at a low ebb in West Germany until von Thadden launched the Nationaldemokratische Partei Deutschlands (NPD) during an economic recession in the mid-1960s. The National Democrats provided an electoral outlet for neo-Nazi incorrigibles and disgruntled conservatives who shared Bubi's vehement opposition to NATO, foreign guest workers, the creeping Americanization of German culture, and the burgeoning New Left student movement.[48]

Rebelling against a society that had allowed so many ex-Nazis to secure influential positions in business and government, many West German students took the older generation to task for its voluntary silence and its unwillingness to confront the truth about the Hitler era.* Radical left-wing youth were particularly loathed by NPD leaders, who caused a stir by placing wreaths on the graves of Nazi war criminals. With Bubi at the helm, this cryptofascist party demanded the immediate withdrawal of all foreign troops from "holy German soil," the return of the lost eastern territories, and an end to the "lie" that Hitler started World War II. Echoing Thiriart's call for a Sino-European alliance, von Thadden urged that the best German ambassador be sent to Beijing.[49]

The NPD managed to win seats in a majority of state legislatures in the mid-1960s. But its fortune declined as the economy picked up, and Bubi's party failed to gain the necessary 5 percent of the vote in the 1969 national elections, preventing it from securing representation in the Bundestag. Following this setback, the National Democrats ran out of steam and sputtered along at the political margins.

Flirting with the Left

While Bubi von Thadden was making waves in West Germany, Jean Thiriart continued to pursue his radical geopolitical agenda. Several fascist notables responded favorably to his ideas, including General Juan Perón, who left Argentina posthaste after a military coup in September 1955. Skorzeny arranged for the fallen president to live comfortably in exile in Madrid. After they were introduced by

* Among others, the newly elected chancellor, Christian Democrat Kurt Georg Kiesinger, had a murky Nazi past. Kiesinger had worked in the Nazi Propaganda Ministry during the war. Heinrich Lübke, the West German president during the mid- and late 1960s, was an ex-Nazi engineer who had designed and supervised the construction of a concentration camp. "Whether these and other men were personally guilty is not the point," remarked historian Eberhardt Jäckel. "It was bad for German democracy, and it set a bad example to the younger generation, that people with *any* kind of Nazi record should have been given such posts."

Scarface, Perón and Thiriart became close collaborators; Perón granted several interviews to *La Nation Européenne,* in which he endorsed Thiriart's political tactics and goals.[50]

An advocate of Third World unity and nonalignment, Perón viewed the struggle to liberate Latin America from the yoke of Yankee imperialism as inextricably related to Thiriart's quest to expel the United States from Europe. Thiriart predicted that a united Europe would one day be a sister state to a united Latin America — a sentiment Perón also verbalized. Both men expressed high regard for Fidel Castro and the Cuban revolution, and they lionized Che Guevera, the Argentine-born guerrilla legend.[51]

In his autobiography, *Perón As He Is,* the Argentine general asserted that Latin America's biggest problem was not the Soviet Union but economic, political, and cultural domination by the Yankee colossus. If the North Americans did not modify their imperialist conduct, Perón warned, soon Latin Americans would be multiplying by a hundredfold the drama of Cuba's confrontation with the United States. Aiming his message at radical left-wing Argentine youth who were enamored of the revolutionary mystique, Perón described the turbulent 1960s as "the Hour of the Peoples" and quoted Mao Tse-tung in a filmed interview.[52]

Encouraged by Thiriart, Perón explicitly urged his followers to undertake armed action to topple the military regime that ruled Argentina. While they prepared to fight on Perón's behalf, many of them may not have known that the exiled Argentine general was busy cavorting with European neo-Nazis. Perón's inner circle in Madrid included several hard-core fascists, such as Mila Bogetich, a Croatian Ustaše veteran who was in charge of security at Perón's residence.[53]

The peculiar conjunction of far Right and far Left within Perónist circles was exemplified by the political circumlocutions of a neofascist paramilitary sect called the Tacuara (Spear), which had longstanding ties to the Argentine secret service. When Adolf Eichmann was seized by Israeli agents in 1960, Tacuara members went on a rampage, bombing Jewish synagogues, machine-gunning Jewish homes and businesses, and defacing buildings in Buenos Aires with "Jews to the gas chambers!" and other vile graffiti. Two years later, after Eichmann's execution, they sprang into action again, abducting

Jewish students and carving swastikas on their tortured flesh. But the Argentine police consistently dragged their feet when it came to bringing these racialist gangsters to heel.[54]

Joe ("José") Baxter, a mysterious Yugoslav-born Argentine, emerged as the Tacuara's new commander in the mid-1960s. Influenced by Fidel Castro's revolutionary mixture of nationalism and Communism, Baxter steered his neofascist organization sharply to the Left. His political shift paralleled that of Jean Thiriart, who also appeared to lurch leftward during this period. They had other things in common as well — most notably, both were in contact with Juan Perón in Spain.[55]

With the exiled general's personal endorsement, Baxter proceeded to reorganize the Tacuara into Argentina's first urban guerrilla warfare organization. Several Tacuaristas, including Baxter, visited Havana, where they were schooled in guerrilla maneuvers. According to FBI and State Department reports, Baxter also visited Communist China in 1965. After he returned to Latin America, the core of the Tacuara merged with various revolutionary fragments to form the Montoneros, a left-wing nationalist youth group that engaged in armed struggle and set the stage for Perón's remarkable return home on June 20, 1973.[56]

The irreconcilable contradictions within Perón's populist coalition — which encompassed left-wing and right-wing militants — came surging to the surface when Argentina's would-be national savior stepped off his jet at Ezeiza Airport in Buenos Aires. All hell broke loose as neofascist goon squads, organized by one of Perón's chief advisors, sprayed machine-gun fire at a throng of Montoneros who were there to greet their hero. Thinking they were on the threshold of a social revolution, the Montoneros had come to claim what they felt was their rightful place adjacent to the platform where Perón was slated to address the largest public rally in Argentine history. After all, Perón himself had hailed "the glorious youth" who did his bidding while he was in exile. Their illusions were shattered by the ensuing bloodbath that claimed more than two hundred lives in a matter of minutes.[57]

After using the Montoneros as shock troops to pave the way for his political comeback, Perón abruptly renounced all talk of a "socialist fatherland." Another military coup would soon follow, plunging Argentina into seven years of horror. Invoking the spurious threat of a left-wing guerrilla movement that had already been effectively destroyed, Argentine military leaders waged a dirty war that targeted unarmed men, women, and children. Between ten thousand and thirty thousand people disappeared during this period, as several European neofascists specializing in torture and murder assisted the Argentine military regime.[58]

Jean Thiriart emphasized wooing the Left as part of an overall geopolitical plan aimed at weakening the United States. As American forces got bogged down in Southeast Asia, the Belgian extremist applauded the efforts of Ho Chi Minh and dreamed of starting a Vietnam-style conflict against U.S.-allied governments in Western Europe. As far as Thiriart was concerned, Europe was the key battlefield. If the United States were defeated in Vietnam or in another Third World country, it would not have that great an impact, but if the North Americans were trounced in Europe, the consequences would be enormous, he argued.[59]

In 1968, Thiriart visited several Arab countries in an effort to win support for his idea of a "European brigade," which he envisioned as the embryo of a future guerrilla army that would engage in armed struggle against the American "occupation forces" on the Continent. He sought to convince his Arab hosts that it would be to their advantage if the United States became embroiled in a "blind war" in Europe against "a terrorist enemy both invisible and ever-present."[60]

With this in mind, Thiriart traveled to Iraq, where officials of the ruling Ba'ath Party received him warmly. After denouncing "Zionist-American collusion in the Middle East" at a Baghdad press conference, he conferred with an up-and-coming Iraqi colonel named Saddam Hussein. Iraqi leaders were all ears when Thiriart spelled out his plan for a European military force to assist the Arabs in their fight against Israel. In addition to helping the Arab cause, Thiriart's young recruits would gain valuable combat experience that would presumably serve them well when they returned to Europe to take on the Americans. According to Thiriart, the Iraqis were enthusiastic, but the Soviet Union nixed the proposal. Iraq had no choice but to comply, given that it was largely dependent on the USSR for military aid.[61]

After Israel's victory in the 1967 Six-Day War, a mood of desperate militancy engulfed the miserable Palestinian refugee camps. Deprived of a homeland and faced with an implacable enemy, Palestinian leaders apparently felt they couldn't afford to turn down offers of help, no matter how unsavory the donors. Arab revolutionaries were continually approached by neo-Nazi suitors. Dismissing the distinction between Jews and Zionists as "a subtlety for intellectuals," Thiriart forged a close relationship with George Habbash, head of the Popular Front for the Liberation of Palestine, which hijacked several commercial jets and engaged in other international acts of terror and sabotage.* According to Luc Michel, Thiriart's secretary: "Habbash gave money to *La Nation Européenne,* and Thiriart supported Habbash in this magazine."[62]†

* In addition to his ties with Thiriart, Dr. Habbash collaborated with François Genoud, a shadowy Swiss banker with extensive neo-Nazi connections. Described by Otto Ernst Remer as "a very important person," Genoud became an early member of the Swiss Nazi Party and worked for German military intelligence during World War II. Somehow Genoud was able to secure the posthumous rights to all the writings of Hitler, Goebbels, and Martin Bormann. "He knew everybody," said Remer, who considered Genoud one of his best friends. Both men were involved in arranging arms shipments to the FLN at the height of the Algerian war. Genoud also managed the FLN war chest through the Geneva-based Arab Commercial Bank, a fiduciary outlet he created. Dr. Hjalmar Schacht was a consultant to this bank and a business associate of Genoud's. In the late 1960s, Genoud began selling weapons to various Palestinian groups, but his closest relations were with Dr. Habbash's Popular Front for the Liberation of Palestine. After three members of the Popular Front were captured during an attack on an El Al airplane in Zurich in February 1969, Genoud helped foot their legal bill. The Swiss Nazi also supported the efforts of ultra-left-wing anti-Israeli terrorists from Western Europe who were linked to the Carlos network during the 1970s. According to *Le Monde* correspondent Jean-Claude Buhrer, Genoud visited Carlos at his house in Damascus. Genoud committed suicide in 1996.

† Pro-Arab and anti-Jewish themes were explicit in Thiriart's publication, *La Nation Européenne,* which included ads for *The International Jew,* the infamous anti-Semitic screed by Henry Ford. *La Nation Européenne* also eulogized Roger Courdroy, a Belgian Waffen SS veteran who was killed fighting for the Palestinians in June 1968. Courdroy, a close collaborator with Thiriart, was not the first European volunteer to die during a guerrilla attack against Israel. West German neo-Nazi Karl von Kyna fell in a commando raid on the Suez front in September 1967. A handful of his countrymen subsequently joined the

While based in Damascus, Otto Ernst Remer was in contact with Yasser Arafat, chief of the Palestine Liberation Organization. "I know Mr. Arafat quite well, *natürlich,*" he asserted. "I saw him many times. He invited me to eat at his headquarters. I knew all his people. They wanted many things from us." For Remer, anyone who was an enemy of Israel was his friend, particularly when a profit could be turned. He claimed to have brokered several business deals between West German companies and the PLO. But Remer denied that he also arranged arms shipments for the PLO. "I couldn't have done so," he maintained. "Arafat gets all he wants from Russia. A German arms dealer can't get into business there."[63]

Thiriart continued to view the Palestinian struggle as a springboard to pursue his dream of a pan-European revolution. But after seeking financial and material support from the Chinese and several Arabs states, he had little to show for his efforts. Otto Skorzeny told a dejected Thiriart that his plan for a guerrilla army, however admirable, would never work. Having no wish to be a grand theorist to whom no one of significance paid attention, Thiriart decided to take an extended leave from political activism. Throughout the 1970s, he stayed out of the limelight, giving only a few interviews, in which he pounded home his anti-American message. "The whole of Europe, from Stockholm to Naples, must know about each American who is killed within 48 hours of the event," Thiriart told a French reporter. "European unity will only come about when 200 or 300 American occupiers are killed in every corner of Europe just to prove our point. Then there will be no going back."[64]

Some of Thiriart's disciples took his words to heart. Renato Curcio, a member of Giovane Europa, the Italian section of Jeune Europe, went on to become a leader of the Red Brigades, the left-wing terrorist group that kidnapped and murdered selected targets in Italy throughout the 1970s and early 1980s. Another Thiriart protégé,

---

Hilfskorp Arabien (Auxiliary Corps Arabia), which had been advertised in Gerhard Frey's *Deutsche National-Zeitung* in 1968. Two years later, West German police arrested Udo Albrecht, founder and leader of the Freikorps Adolf Hitler, who was found carrying an identification card linking him to El Fatah, the largest PLO faction, led by Yasser Arafat. Albrecht and twelve other German neo-Nazi militants had recently fought alongside the Palestinians against Jordan's King Hussein during the Battle of Black September.

Claudio Mutti, formed the Italian-Libyan Friendship Society after Colonel Muammar Qaddafi seized power in Tripoli. In addition to publishing an Italian translation of *The Protocols of the Elders of Zion* and Qaddafi's *Green Book,* Mutti founded an organization called Lotta di Popolo (Struggle of the People), whose Italian initials spelled "PLO," an indication of its pro-Palestinian sympathies. The name was chosen because it did not carry an obvious rightist or fascist connotation; this would make it easier to woo left-wing students. Mutti subsequently collaborated with a pro-Chinese student group, which set the stage for a bizarre political mutation in Italy known as Nazi-Maoism. Influenced by Thiriart's political analysis, a small band of Italian militants adopted a seemingly incongruous set of heroes — Hitler, Mao, Qaddafi, and Perón — and touted slogans such as "Long live the fascist dictatorship of the proletariat!" and "Hitler and Mao united in struggle!"[65]

But any possibility of creating a strategic alliance with China was dashed when Chairman Mao rolled out the red carpet for President Richard Nixon. The Sino-American rapprochement, which occurred shortly after Thiriart went into semiretirement, reinforced his belief that Europe and the Soviet Union were destined to become equal geopolitical partners. Thiriart was especially pleased when Soviet officials took an interest in his writings, which were translated into Russian by a Red Army officer. After the USSR unraveled, his ideas would generate considerable interest among a new breed of "National Bolsheviks" that emerged in a very volatile Russia.

Twilight of the Idols

Otto Skorzeny had many irons in the fire during the 1960s. He pursued a wide range of business opportunities, including a scheme to harness wind power for profit. But his main bailiwick continued to be the arms trade. A major weapons broker for the Salazar regime in Portugal, Skorzeny worked with several lucrative firms, including the Virginia-based Interarms Company, which was run by a former CIA operative named Sam Cummings. Skorzeny also helped found the Bonn-based Merex Company, which was closely linked to the

West German BND spy organization that Gehlen directed until 1968. Through Merex, the BND peddled surplus arms to Middle Eastern countries and other Third World hot spots, even though transactions of this sort were prohibited according to international agreements signed by the West German government.[66]

Skorzeny's partner in launching Merex was Gerhard Mertens, a former Wehrmacht officer. Mertens had served as a military advisor in Nasser's Egypt in the early 1950s before he became head of the Merex Company. From his office in Bonn he managed a worldwide network of agents and arms dealers. Merten's principal contact in Bolivia was Klaus Barbie, the notoriously brutal ex-Gestapo captain. Known as the "Butcher of Lyon" because of his wartime exploits, Barbie had been condemned to death in absentia by a French court for war crimes — a fact well known to the Gehlen Org and the U.S. Army Counterintelligence Corps when they recruited him as an anti-Communist spy. After trumping extradition requests from France, U.S. officials winked as Barbie made his way to South America in 1951 via the Vatican ratline. He soon became a familiar figure in La Paz, the Bolivian capital, where he served as a security advisor to a succession of military regimes. During this period, Barbie continued to provide confidential information to the CIA.[67]

Barbie's postwar career epitomizes how Nazi methods and ideology were exported to Latin America with the help of U.S. intelligence. He spread the fascist creed among leading figures in the Bolivian military who were also members of Thule, a secret neo-Nazi lodge. The Butcher lectured by candlelight at lodge meetings, expounding on National Socialist principles underneath a large swastika. But he was not merely "an old nostalgic of the Third Reich," said Ernesto Mila Rodriguez, a Spanish neofascist who crossed paths with Barbie in Bolivia. "He was a very realistic person, aware that the Reich had lost the war, which inevitably resulted in the demise of those types of ideas. He was trying to redefine and update these ideas so they could survive."[68]

Barbie's involvement in the arms trade inevitably brought him into contact with Otto Skorzeny, whom he visited during several business trips to Spain. Using an assumed name, the Butcher also traveled to the United States for commercial purposes at least half a dozen times in the late 1960s and early 1970s. Occasionally he granted interviews to journalists at his safe haven in La Paz. The exiled war criminal told a French reporter that he had worked for General Gehlen; he also named Otto Skorzeny as the chief of die Spinne, the international neo-Nazi support network.[69]

In addition to selling weapons, Skorzeny taught people ingenious and treacherous ways to use them. Toward this end, he set up the Paladin Group, which Scarface envisioned as an "international directorship of strategic assault personnel [that would] straddle the watershed between paramilitary operations carried out by troops in uniforms and the political warfare which is conducted by civilian agents." Headquartered on the Mediterranean near Alicante, Spain, the Paladin Group specialized in paramilitary instruction for men who earned their keep by killing people.[70]

TASS, the Soviet press agency, charged that the Paladin enterprise was involved in training American Green Berets for commando missions in Vietnam during the 1960s. But this seems unlikely, given that Skorzeny's methods were already somewhat antiquated. At least, that's what an American mercenary named Anthony Herbert found when he journeyed to a Paladin base camp in the mountainous region of Basque country. According to Herbert, Skorzeny "and a small group of former German troopers had formed a corporation whose service was the arming and training of groups of guerrillas." However, after several visits to Skorzeny's school for commandos, Herbert concluded that the techniques "were good, but they were dated." The only thing Herbert learned that he didn't already know was "the fine art of arson. It is no simple thing, for instance, to burn down a large factory."[71]

The hands-on manager of the Paladin Group was Dr. Gerhard Harmut von Schubert, a veteran of Goebbels's Propaganda Ministry who tutored security personnel in Argentina and Egypt after the war. Under his command, Paladin provided logistical support to a Palestinian splinter group led by Waddi Haddad, the mastermind behind several anti-Israeli terrorist attacks. Paladin's other clients included Colonel Muammar Qaddafi of Libya and the South African secret service. In addition, Paladin did odd jobs for the Greek colonels who seized power in 1967 and imposed a seven-year military dictatorship in the cradle of democracy. Paladin operatives were also recruited by the Spanish Interior Ministry to wage a clandestine war against Basque separatists, who had resorted to armed struggle against the Franco regime.[72]

In many ways, these were Skorzeny's salad days. He had bought a 170-acre farm in Ireland, where he bred horses and spent the summer months relaxing with Ilse. Dabbling in journalism, he contributed articles to the *Deutsche Wochen-Zeitung*, an ultranationalist newspaper that functioned as a mouthpiece for Bubi von Thadden's far Right National Democratic Party in West Germany.[73]

Skorzeny also counseled the leaders of a Spanish neo-Nazi group called Circulo Español de Amigos de Europa (CEDADE). Established in 1966 as a Richard Wagner fan club, the Spanish Circle of Friends of Europe counted Skorzeny among its founding fathers. Within a few years, this quasi-cultural association developed into an important neo-Nazi hub with connections to like-minded groups in Portugal, France, Austria, Great Britain, Belgium, and several Latin American countries. The CEDADE was also allied with the Liberty Lobby in the United States. After American Nazi Party leader George Lincoln Rockwell was assassinated, the CEDADE sent a telegram to the U.S. embassy in Madrid: "Deeply moved . . . we earnestly ask you to convey our sincerest regrets for this deep loss to [Rockwell's] family, comrades and the American people."[74]

Calling for a Europe "purged of inferior races," CEDADE's youthful members idolized Hitler to such a degree that vegetarianism (the Führer's alleged dietary preference) became de rigueur for this neo-Nazi sect. Its publishing house, Ediciones Wotan, brought out the Spanish edition of *Imperium* by Francis Parker Yockey, along with several books by Skorzeny's close friend General Léon Degrelle. Years later, Major General Otto Ernst Remer would avail himself of CEDADE hospitality in Spain in order to evade another prison term in Germany.[75]

Skorzeny slowed down considerably after undergoing an operation to remove a spinal tumor in 1971. He also suffered from other ailments that were exacerbated by a three-packs-a-day cigarette habit. Despite his declining physical stamina, Scarface kept up a busy social schedule. He and his wife continued to entertain a steady stream of visitors. Hans-Ulrich Rudel was a frequent houseguest, and Bubi von Thadden dropped by when he vacationed in Spain.

Several other neofascist notables availed themselves of Skorzeny's hospitality, including an old friend from Italy, Count Junio Valerio Borghese, who fled to Madrid after leading an abortive coup attempt in Rome in December 1970. Welcomed with open arms by Otto and Ilse, Borghese mixed easily with the upper crust of the expatriate scene, meeting regularly with the likes of Juan Perón and Léon Degrelle, who held the Italian admiral in high regard. "He was a very impressive man," Degrelle asserted, "the most important man of post-Fascist Italy."[76]

Known as the "Black Prince," Admiral Borghese was a descendant of an aristocratic family that gave popes and princes to Italy over the centuries. He developed a fearsome reputation as the World War II commander of the "Tenth Flotilla," Italy's tenacious frogman unit, which pulled off a series of daring, Skorzeny-like raids against Allied ships and harbors. Commandante Borghese worked with Skorzeny on several projects, including an explosives-packed speedboat that ejected its pilot just before hitting a target. Brainstorming on various occasions during the war, the two unconventional warriors struck up a close personal relationship that persisted long after the defeat of the Axis powers.[77]

Captured by vengeful partisans at the end of the war, the Black Prince survived because of the last-minute intervention of James Jesus Angleton, the OSS station chief in Rome, who rushed up to Milan when he heard that Borghese had fallen into Communist hands. At Angleton's insistence, Borghese's life was spared, even though this die-hard Fascist military officer had waged a bloody crusade against the Italian resistance in northern Italy, where Mussolini held sway as the titular head of the Saló Republic following the infamous Skorzeny glider raid. Borghese was subsequently convicted of war crimes but served only an abbreviated prison term in the late 1940s, thanks to a far-reaching amnesty declared by the Italian government. The charismatic commandante would go on to play a significant role in Italy's postwar fascist movement. By the early 1950s, Admiral Borghese had become the honorary president of the Movimento Sociale Italiano (MSI), Europe's largest neofascist political party.[78]

Accompanying Prince Borghese when he scampered into Madrid in December 1970 was a thirty-six-year-old Italian, Stefano delle Chiaie, who also participated in the botched putsch. A compact, wiry figure, delle Chiaie was nicknamed "Caccola" ("Shorty") because of his truncated physical stature. But his organizing talents and his fierce political commitment earned him the respect of several old-guard Nazis, including Otto Skorzeny and Léon Degrelle. Borghese often spoke highly of the five-foot fascist phenom, referring to delle Chiaie as "one of the few men capable of putting things in order in Italy."[79]

A Roman street gang leader, delle Chiaie glorified violence as a hygienic outburst capable of cutting through the postwar bourgeois morass. During the 1960s, his organization, Avanguardia Nazionale (National Vanguard), came to be regarded as the cudgel of Italian right-wing extremism. For guidance and inspiration, delle Chiaie looked to Julius Evola, the reactionary intellectual who emerged as the gray eminence of postwar Italian fascism. Evola's nihilistic ravings were evident in several books he wrote, including *Gli uomini e le rovine (Man among the ruins),* which bore a preface by Commandante Valerio Borghese. "It is not a question of contesting and polemicizing, but of blowing up everything," Evola proclaimed. Such words made a deep impression on delle Chiaie and his cohorts. Implicated in a series of bomb attacks in the Italian capital, they were known for meting out punishment to left-wing students and other foes. "We are for man-to-man engagements," proclaimed one of Avanguardia Nazionale's leaflets. "Before setting out our men are morally prepared, so that they learn to break the bones even of somebody who kneels down and cries."[80]

Shortly after Caccola fled to Spain with Borghese, the well-connected count took him to see Skorzeny. They had met before, but it wasn't until the Italian renegade made Spain his base of operations in the early 1970s that Skorzeny recognized delle Chiaie's leadership qualities and their relationship blossomed. With Skorzeny tendering introductions, all doors opened for delle Chiaie. Shorty hit the big-league fascist circuit, meeting with an aging but famous cast of characters — Degrelle, Perón, and General Francisco Franco himself, whose regime had entered its twilight years.[81]

In April 1974, delle Chiaie and Commandante Borghese journeyed to Santiago, Chile, for a meeting with General Augusto Pinochet, head of the CIA-backed military junta that overthrew the democratically elected government of President Salvador Allende.

During the next few years, delle Chiaie cut a swath of terror through Latin America, plying his lethal skills for a host of repressive right-wing regimes. In addition to carrying out special assignments for DINA, Chile's dreaded secret police, he worked with Argentine military intelligence as it was busy transforming that country into the killing fields of South America.[82]

Stefano delle Chiaie's activities as depicted in the Spanish press after Franco died

Caccola's expertise was greatly appreciated by Roberto d'Aubuisson, the éminence grise of the Salvadoran death squads, who asked Shorty for pointers on how to conduct a counterinsurgency campaign against left-wing guerrillas. Based in Latin America in the early 1980s, delle Chiaie also proffered his services to the fledgling Nicaraguan Contras in their war against the Sandinistas. At times he coordinated his efforts with the World Anti-Communist League, a neofascist umbrella organization that assisted U.S. intelligence operations in Latin America during the Reagan years. A CIA report during this period described the fugitive Italian as "the most prominent rightist terrorist . . . still at large."[83]

Stefano delle Chiaie's greatest triumph occurred in July 1980, when he helped plan and execute the "cocaine coup" that succeeded in putting Bolivia under the control of a profascist military junta for two years. The aftershocks of this brutal putsch, which triggered the cocaine boom of the 1980s and catalyzed the emergence of the Latin drug cartels, would be felt for a long time to come. Working closely with Nazi veteran Klaus Barbie, delle Chiaie oversaw a team of European mercenaries who taught Bolivian soldiers torture techniques and protected the flourishing cocaine trade that provided the main source of revenue for the ruling junta.[84]

But Otto Skorzeny would not be around to applaud the exploits of his Italian protégé. Stricken with a high fever on Easter Sunday, 1975, he was diagnosed with advanced lung and bronchial cancer. He passed away on July 7. Ilse was grateful for a quick death. Her husband's body was cremated at a ceremony in Madrid. Afterward, Skorzeny's ashes were flown to Vienna and buried near his birthplace in the suburban cemetery of Döbling. A memorial service attracted more than five hundred Nazi diehards from all over the world. They came to pay homage to one of their heroes. Many wore uniforms and military medallions, including Skorzeny's close friend and comrade in arms, Hans-Ulrich Rudel, who delivered the eulogy.

A *New York Times* obituary depicted Skorzeny as unrepentant to the end. "I am proud to have faithfully served my country and the Führer who was elected by the German people with an overwhelming majority," he declared shortly before his death. "The only thing I lament is that all Europe — and not only Germany — is divided and torn by those powers that I had the honor of fighting." The *Times* obituary did not mention that Skorzeny escaped from an internment camp after the war with the help of American military officers; nor was there any indication of his subsequent relationship with the Gehlen Org and the CIA.[85]

The fascist faithful had occasion to gather again a few months later when Skorzeny's long-time protector, Generalissimo Franco, finally gave up the ghost. Commandante Borghese and Juan Perón had died the previous year. The departure of these ignominious titans marked the end of an era. The torch was passed to a new generation of zealots eager to carry on the fight.

CHAPTER SIX

A GATHERING STORM

Breaking a Taboo

Every summer tens of thousands of people from all over the world flock to Dixmude, Belgium, for a weekend filled with colorful pageants and marching bands. Hundreds of yellow flags emblazoned with the Black Lion of Flanders flutter in the breeze, as a goose-stepping parade of uniformed men leads the way to a memorial service at a nearby cemetery where SS soldiers are buried. Speakers in various languages pay homage to Adolf Hitler and the glories of white supremacy, and a cheering audience responds with enthusiastic stiff-armed salutes.

Back in town, local residents sing Flemish folk songs and dance in the street. They seem oblivious to the youthful bands of right-wing extremists who roam from one café to the next, hawking Nazi trinkets and passing out brochures that claim the Holocaust never happened. Third Reich memorabilia are traded in a hobbylike way by skinheads wearing leather jackets with phrases such as "Soldiers of Hell" and "National Revolution" encrusted on their backs. Prodigious quantities of beer are consumed, invariably leading to drunken brawls. Figuring that it's best to let the ruffians blow off steam, Belgian authorities usually do not intervene unless the violence threatens to get out of hand.[1]

"The scene at Dixmude is absolutely incredible," said one first-hand observer who had infiltrated the neo-Nazi underground in the early 1980s. "It's party time, a fascist Disneyland. It's not the real world."[2]

Originally a celebration of Flemish nationalism and a forum for airing grievances against French-speaking Belgians, this annual pilgrimage became a magnet for right-wing extremists in the late 1960s when the Vlaamse Militanten Orde (VMO), a Flemish paramilitary organization, invited neofascist groups from around the globe to send delegations. Dixmude soon acquired a reputation as a place where hard-core Nazis could openly proclaim their racist ideology and recharge their batteries in a carnival-like atmosphere.

Major General Otto Ernst Remer was among those who attended the Dixmude jamboree in 1983, a year after the VMO was officially declared a terrorist organization by the Belgian government and banned. Several VMO members were arrested and some served brief prison terms, but the Flemish fascists continued to organize an alternative event alongside the mainstream assemblage at Dixmude. They treated the seventy-one-year-old Remer like royalty when he arrived for the festivities. Hitler's illustrious bodyguard had recently pulled up stakes from Syria and resettled in West Germany. After two decades in the Middle East, he was eager to renew and expand his contacts among European neo-Nazis. The Dixmude gathering was well suited for this purpose.[3]

While inebriated youth swaggered about shouting *"Sieg Heil!"* and *"Il Duce!"* representatives from various neofascist organizations, including the illegal VMO, slipped away for a series of private brainstorming sessions at a dingy bar just outside Dixmude. Each person began by reporting on the state of the neofascist game in his particular neck of the woods. The overall picture that emerged was not a bright one for these malefactors, who seemed destined to languish on the political periphery for a long time.

With little hope that their prospects would improve in the near future, several neo-Nazi groupuscles represented at Dixmude turned to terrorism during the early 1980s. Their leaders pledged to continue cross-border cooperation regarding paramilitary training and harboring fugitives. When it came to specifics, however, the discussion often degenerated into acrimonious squabbles between ultranationalist cliques. British neo-Nazis, for example, were peeved at their Flemish hosts because the breakaway-minded VMO had a separatist soft spot for the Irish Republican Army. Internecine conflict of this sort — an inevitable feature of the ultra-right-wing milieu — undermined efforts to forge a viable pan-European strategy.

Remer had his own ideas about the best way for the neo-Nazi movement to proceed. He wanted to make a personal presentation at the Dixmude strategy retreat, but his visit to Flanders was cut short by Belgian police, who arrested and deported him. Undaunted, Remer continued to make the rounds in Western Europe, meeting with neo-Nazi activists from various countries. Word began to circulate within far Right circles that Remer had returned from the Middle East loaded with money to support a new anti-Zionist political project that would strive for an alliance between Germany and the USSR. The funds allegedly came from Syria, the Soviet Union's staunchest Arab ally.[4]

Wherever he traveled, Remer promoted his formula for a German-Russian geopolitical linkup, much as he had when he campaigned for the Socialist Reich Party in the early 1950s. Only such a combination, Remer maintained, could defeat the Americans and liberate Western Europe. "There is a problem concerning who holds the real power in the United States," said Remer. "Without a doubt, the Zionists control Wall Street. That's where the evil originates, because Israel has a pro-war foreign policy. Israel is the instrument of Wall Street, and as a result, the Middle East foments war. . . ."[5]

In an effort to realize his geopolitical vision, Remer advocated total European collaboration, from Iberia to the Urals. Of necessity, this included Russia, which was worried about the threat from China (so Remer argued) and would therefore welcome a reunited Germany to hold the Western powers in check. According to this racialist scenario, Russia would become the outer shield, the bulwark of the white race in Europe against the Asiatic hordes.[6]

From his home in the Bavarian town of Kaufbeuren, Remer launched the Deutschen Freiheitsbewegung (German Freedom Movement) in 1983. Dedicated to the concept of a new Rapallo, this initiative published a rambling, thirty-page declaration entitled *The Bismarck-German Manifesto,* which embodied Remer's nationalist-neutralist politics. "The American way of life is for us synonymous with the destruction of European culture," the manifesto asserts. Vowing that Germany would not "be used as the tip of the NATO spear," it states: "We are no NATO-American legionnaires. . . . We will not participate in a NATO war against Russia."

Der

Bismarck-Deutsche

Manifest 1983

der

DEUTSCHEN FREIHEITSBEWEGUNG

für eine

DEUTSCH-RUSSISCHE ALLIANZ
RAPALLO 1983/90

The most pressing order of business for Remer and other German ultranationalists was reunifying the Fatherland. To bring this about, Remer counseled his countrymen to emulate the example of Bismarck, "the greatest German politician of recent centuries . . . who preserved the interests of the German people against East and West." Said Remer, "We have to realize and act accordingly, like Bismarck did, that Russia is the superpower in this gigantic Eurasian continent, to which we belong geographically, geopolitically and economically, even culturally. . . . We are, like Bismarck, for a close collaboration with Russia in politics, economy, culture, science, technology, and research." That the Soviet Union was officially Communist should not be an impediment for Germany to ally with the USSR, Remer insisted: "Whoever deals with Moscow does not have to be a Communist and need not become one."[7]

This was the same rationale that Remer trumpeted during the halcyon days of the SRP. Back on the lecture circuit three decades later, Hitler's former bodyguard addressed more than three hundred political meetings in a year and a half. Although his Eastern-oriented formula evoked a mixed reaction from German rightists, U.S. Army intelligence, which continued to monitor Remer's activities, feared that he was making headway among neo-Nazi youth. Noting a "trend towards neutralism" and "a rise in anti-Americanism" within the extreme Right in Germany, a May 1985 Defense Intelligence Agency report cited Remer's busy speaking schedule and his unabashed sympathy for the USSR. "It is becoming chic among many neo-Nazis to be anti-Western and anti-capitalist," a West German secret-service official concurred. "At the same time, the Soviet Union is seen as a potential friend and, in some cases, even an ally."[8]

At every opportunity, Remer defended the legacy of the Third Reich, proudly proclaiming that he still believed in National Socialism. For a new generation of far Right adolescents, he was a living symbol of the Hitler era. As such, Remer provided a sense of continuity between past and present. He instructed his young followers in Nazi ideology and geopolitics, always stressing the importance of German-Russian relations in the grand scheme of things.

Through his indefatigable proselytizing, Remer influenced a fresh crop of neo-Nazis who came of age in the late 1970s and early 1980s. Of these, the most important was Michael Kühnen, the baby-faced führer of the Action Front of National Socialists (ANS). Like Remer, Kühnen was often in trouble with the law, spending several years in prison as a result of his political endeavors. Army intelligence pegged Kühnen as "one of the key figures of [West Germany's] right-wing extremist/terrorist scene." A skillful orator with closely cropped dark hair and steel-blue eyes, he shared a platform with Remer at several meetings.[9]

Born in 1955 into a middle-class family and raised a Catholic, Kühnen became politically active at the age of fifteen when the New Left was flexing its muscles in West Germany. For a brief period, he considered himself a Maoist, which he viewed as "a sort of Chinese [N]ational [S]ocialism." While working in Hamburg's shipyards, Kühnen gravitated toward the far Right youth group associated with the National Democratic Party (NPD), then led by Bubi von Thadden. The NPD had chalked up electoral victories in a majority of West German states during the late 1960s, but its success was short-lived. However, elections were not the only way of measuring support for neo-Nazi ideas in West Germany. Skimpy vote totals of far Right candidates since the banning of Remer's Socialist Reich Party (with the brief exception of the NPD) disguised the fact that extremist attitudes remained solidly entrenched among a significant minority of the West German population.* [10]

After joining the NPD's youth group, Kühnen quickly grew disenchanted with the party's plodding, circumspect approach to politics and its insistence on working within the democratic system. He felt that a change in tactics was long overdue. Denouncing the NPD as a "bourgeois crowd of swines," Kühnen deserted the party and began to vocalize his neo-Nazi sentiments more openly.[11]

Kühnen's decision to embark upon a more militant course coincided with a bona fide "Hitler fad" that swept across West Germany during the mid-1970s. The entire country was inundated by a flood of books, films, recordings, and magazine articles that cast a retrospective — and not entirely critical — eye upon the Third Reich, which had hitherto been downplayed or routinely treated as a historical accident by West German schoolteachers. The fact that many educators were trained as civil servants under the auspices of the Nazi Party contributed to a profound ignorance about the Hitler era among West German youth. This was disclosed by several surveys that attested to both major gaps in students' knowledge and abiding notions that World War II interrupted what had otherwise been a positive government under the Nazis. Soul-searching inquiry into the German past was for the most part not encouraged.[12]

The Hitler wave crested in 1977, the year Kühnen was dishonorably discharged from the German army for pro-Nazi agitation in the barracks. Shortly thereafter, he founded the ANS, which flaunted its admiration for the Third Reich. At that time, neo-Nazi organizing was strictly verboten, and most radical nationalists took pains to distance themselves from Hitler's legacy. But not Kühnen. In calculated defiance of a long-standing taboo, he used hoary Nazi symbols and slogans to shock and antagonize. "We are a revolutionary party

* The Sinus demographic study of 1979–80 found that about 5 million West Germans (or 13 percent of the country) wished for a return of a leader like Hitler; 13 percent were committed right-wing extremists; and another 37 percent had strong right-wing views.

dedicated to restoring the values of the Third Reich, to a Greater Germany for all Germans and to unite against the threat that is now emerging from Communism and the colored races," he brazenly declared. As for the 6 million Jews: "This is a lie deliberately perpetrated by the victors of the last war."[13]

The thinly disguised swastika-like symbol of Michael Kühnen's Aktionsfront Nationaler Sozialisten

Kühnen knew that coming on strong as a neo-Nazi would generate media coverage and followers. He created a ragtag band of angry teenagers who pranced around in boots, brown shirts, and flak jackets adorned with illegal swastikas. Described by the Hamburg Interior Ministry as "a conglomerate of right extremist political rockers and rowdies," Kühnen's followers were not merely nostalgic for Hitler's "new order" — they were prepared to die for it.

Although the ANS initially consisted of no more than a few dozen Hamburg-based juveniles, Kühnen's clique quickly pushed itself into the headlines. Thanks to publicity-garnering antics, people throughout the Bonn Republic suddenly became aware that a new breed of brash neo-Nazi belligerents had emerged. It didn't matter to Kühnen if the press portrayed them as gangsters and delinquents, as long as they were able to attract attention and recruits. Before long, the ANS had evolved into a nationwide network divided into thirty-two sections or "combat groups." Kühnen structured the ANS "as a paramilitary organization whose essential rules were strict discipline and subordination," according to U.S. Army intelligence, which closely followed developments on the far Right in

Germany. Weapons training was compulsory for all ANS members.[14]

With a few hundred enlistees on board, Kühnen began to cultivate international contacts, particularly among Waffen SS veterans, by sending an ANS delegation to the annual neofascist soiree at Dixmude. Kühnen also forged ties with other neo-Nazi groups in West Germany, including the Viking Youth, which sponsored summer camps where starry-eyed *Kinder* were taught pagan lore and fighting techniques. At night, they huddled around campfires, singing nationalist hymns and chanting refrains such as "Blood must flow as thick as a stick, we shit on the freedom of the Federal Republic."[15]

Kühnen's organization and the Viking Youth proceeded to carry out a series of joint actions, including bank robberies and arms thefts. In February 1978, one of their combined units (dubbed the Werewolf Northland Cell) attacked a NATO sentry stationed in West Germany, killing two Dutch soldiers, and stole several machine guns. This successful guerrilla foray reflected their anti-NATO and anti-American political orientation, as well as their commitment to up the ante and undertake armed assaults. Later that year, West German police uncovered a cache of several hundred firearms, explosives, and bombs that was tied to the neo-Nazi underground.[16]

Suspected of masterminding the attack on the Dutch NATO patrol, Kühnen was arrested and charged with inciting violence and racial hatred. In September 1979, he stood trial along with five other neo-Nazi militants. The court disclosed that in addition to planning an attempt to free Rudolf Hess, Hitler's former deputy, from Spandau prison, Kühnen intended to mount an attack on the Berlin Wall. The ANS chief drew a three-and-one-half-year sentence and remained in prison until December 1982.

While Kühnen was ensconced behind bars, several of his acolytes participated in ultra-right-wing paramilitary camps held annually in Spain, Austria, Belgium, and England. Neo-Nazis were subsequently involved in a spate of terrorist attacks against U.S. military installations and NATO bases in West Germany. In 1980, a young neo-Nazi accidentally blew himself up while planting a bomb at Munich's crowded Oktoberfest celebration; the final toll of thirteen dead and more than three hundred wounded made it the worst terrorist incident in postwar Germany.[17]

Many had hoped that Nazism would wither away naturally as Hitler's minions advanced in age and died off. But Kühnen and his retinue of youthful followers proved them wrong. Though small in number and politically ostracized, they clawed at the German conscience. Were they merely a reminder of a past that refused to die, or a portent of something looming on the horizon?

Armies of the Right

Deeply immersed in postwar Nazi intrigue with his close friend Otto Skorzeny, Hans-Ulrich Rudel was never content to rest on his laurels. The unrepentant flying ace spoke at neo-Nazi gatherings and visited SS shrines right up until his death in December 1982. Two thousand people attended Rudel's funeral, many of whom paid their respects by stretching out a single arm and in unison bellowing the banned, pro-Nazi verses of "Deutschland über Alles." The most controversial moment came when two Luftwaffe jets swooped low during the service, dipping their wings in salute to the Third Reich's most decorated officer. But the West German defense minister, Manfred Wörner, refused to investigate the unauthorized flight. "I do not know Rudel's political opinion," Wörner, the future secretary-general of NATO, disingenuously asserted, "but even if I had to reject it, I have high respect for the man for his achievements as a soldier."[18]

Within days of Rudel's funeral, Michael Kühnen was released from prison. After serving a full three-and-half-year sentence, he immediately picked up where he had left off. A couple of hundred young stalwarts rallied to his call, prompting U.S. Army intelligence to describe the Action Front of National Socialists as "the most dangerous of all the existing [German] radical-right organizations due to its well-organized, nation-wide command and control structure." West German officials banned the ANS in December 1983, but affiliates continued to function in neighboring countries, including the Netherlands, where the Aktionsfront Nationaler Socialisten was led by SS veteran Et Wolsink. A wartime member of one of Otto Skorzeny's special sabotage units, Wolsink also ran the Dutch section of the Viking Youth.[19]

On the home front, Kühnen established a new organizational foothold by encouraging his supporters to infiltrate and take over the Freiheitliche Arbeiterpartei (Free German Worker's Party, or FAP), a small and hitherto insignificant right-wing entity. Seeking to accelerate the growth of the neo-Nazi movement, he devised a plan that entailed stirring up resentment against guest workers and asylum-seekers. By scapegoating immigrants, Kühnen hoped to win over alienated working-class youth, who had been thrown on the social and economic scrap heap. Clearly he touched a raw nerve among a majority of the population. A poll taken in the early 1980s showed that 79 percent of West Germans agreed with the neo-Nazi contention that there were too many foreigners in the country. This issue would become a major factor in German politics in the years ahead.[20]

But Kühnen's attempts to increase the FAP's membership ran into a major roadblock—the negative image of Nazism. Seeking to shed some of the cumbersome historical baggage associated with the Third Reich, several neo-Nazis began to criticize Hitler, embracing figures linked to dissident tendencies within the original Nazi movement, such as Gregor and Otto Strasser. Before Gregor Strasser was murdered in 1934 by Hitler's henchmen during the bloody Night of Long Knives, the Strasser brothers led a quasi-left-wing faction that emphasized the socialist and anticapitalist dimensions of the original Nazi project—or so it was claimed—whereas Hitler had sold out to big business and the bourgeoisie. This was the gist of a pamphlet, *Farewell to Hitlerism,* written by two young neo-Nazi militants in 1982.[21]

Like the born-again Strasserites, Kühnen was trying to develop a different ultranationalist style that would perhaps be more palatable to a wider audience. With this goal in mind, he latched onto the ghost of SA captain Ernst Röhm, whose Brownshirts had terrorized Germany during the Nazi Party's rise to power. Hitler's loyal confidant and second-in-command since the beginning, Röhm was also betrayed and slaughtered during the Long Knives purge. Kühnen felt that Hitler made a fatal mistake when he smashed the SA, given that Röhm's support for the Fuhrer had never wavered—unlike Gregor Strasser, who bolted from the Nazi Party to form his own organization. This was one reason why Kühnen identified more closely with Röhm than with Strasser. Kühnen had another, more personal motive for touting the Brownshirt bully. Like Röhm, he was a homosexual.

When Kühnen came out of the closet in the mid-1980s, he caused a scandal among his followers. The young neo-Nazi leader defended himself by pointing out that several important figures in German history, including Emperor Frederick the Great, were homosexuals. For Kühnen, there was something supermacho about being a Nazi as well as a homosexual, both of which reinforced his sense of living on the edge, of belonging to an elite that was destined to make an impact. He told a West German journalist that homosexuals were "especially well-suited for our task of winning our struggle because they do not want ties to wife, children and family." That thousands of homosexual men and women were tortured and murdered in Nazi death camps did not appear to faze Kühnen, who refused to acknowledge Hitler's genocide.[22]

When Kühnen disclosed his sexual orientation, the FAP split into two feuding sections. Major General Otto Ernst Remer appeared as a guest speaker at several FAP events, but he quarreled with Kühnen over the sexual issue. They eventually reconciled, then argued again—a pattern of bickering and making up that typified West Germany's dysfunctional neo-Nazi family.[23]

Despite the controversy surrounding his private life, Kühnen remained the most influential ultra-right-wing leader in West Germany. His notoriety was a mixed blessing, the downside being the unwelcome attention of West German and U.S. intelligence agencies. Fearing that he would be arrested and jailed for subversive activities, Kühnen fled to Paris in March 1984. While in exile, he was sheltered by Marc Friederiksen, head of an illegal French neoNazi group called Fédération d'action nationale européenne (FANE). According to French officials, at one time 20 percent of Friederiksen's two-hundred-member organization were police officers.[24]

A key nodal point within Europe's murky neo-Nazi netherworld,

FANE maintained an array of international contacts. In addition to ties with CEDADE in Spain, the VMO in Flanders, and Stefano delle Chiaie's network in Italy, it functioned as an affiliate of the World Union of National Socialists coordinated by Danish neo-Nazi Povl Riis-Knudsen. FANE also collaborated with the Turkish Grey Wolves, a neo-Nazi terrorist group whose most famous member, Mehmet Ali Agca, shot Pope John Paul II in May 1981.*

* Abdullah Catli, the high-ranking Grey Wolves member who gave Ali Agca the gun that was used to shoot the pontiff, later stated under the oath in a Roman court that he had been approached by the West German BND spy organization, which allegedly promised him a large sum of money if he implicated the Bulgarians and the Soviets in the papal plot. Ex-CIA analyst Melvin A. Goodman later disclosed that his colleagues, under pressure from CIA higher-ups, skewed their reports to make it seem that the Soviets were involved. "The CIA had no evidence linking the KGB to the plot," Goodman told the Senate Intelligence Committee on September 25, 1991.

The CIA station chief in Rome at the time of the papal shooting was Duane Dewey Clarridge, who had served with the Agency in Turkey in the early and mid-1970s when armed bands of Grey Wolves unleashed a wave of bombings and political assassinations that culminated in a military coup at the turn of the decade. Disclosures by Turkish human-rights groups indicate that during this period, the Grey Wolves worked in tandem with the Turkish army's Counter-Guerrilla Organization, which functioned as the Turkish branch of the CIA's multinational "stay behind" program.

At the same time, members of the Grey Wolves were immersed in the international drug trade. Serving as couriers for the Turkish Mafia, they crisscrossed the infamous smugglers' route passing through Bulgaria, which served as a transit point for sizable shipments of arms and heroin. An inquiry by Italian magistrates disclosed that large quantities of sophisticated NATO weaponry — including machine guns, Leopard tanks, and U.S.-built Cobra assault helicopters — were smuggled from Western Europe to countries in the Middle East during the 1970s and early 1980s; deliveries were often made in exchange for consignments of heroin that filtered back, courtesy of the Grey Wolves and other smugglers, to northern Italy, where the drugs were received by Mafia middlemen and transported to North America. Turkish morphine formed the basis of the infamous "pizza connection," which flooded the United States with high-grade heroin for many years.

The bristling contraband operation that traversed Bulgaria was a magnet for secret-service agents on both sides of the Cold War divide. Crucial, in this regard, was the role of Kintex, a Sophia-based, state-controlled import-export

In exile, Kühnen consolidated his ties with prominent European fascists. He traveled to Spain, where he met with Skorzeny's old friend General Léon Degrelle, whose seaside suite in Málaga was an essential port of call for young neo-Nazis from all over the world. Adorned with original Roman statues, Flemish oil paintings, and other priceless works of art, Degrelle's sumptuous residence seemed more like a museum than a bolt-hole for a fugitive war criminal. He gave Kühnen the grand tour, showing off many of his fascist mementos, including the Iron Cross that Hitler had personally draped around Degrelle's neck.

Immensely energetic for a man of seventy-eight, the well-attired Degrelle had receding, combed-back hair and a large shlong of a nose. An ample paunch prevented his five-foot-six inch frame from fitting into his Waffen SS uniform, which hung in the closet as if in a shrine. Awed as much by Degrelle's robust personality as by what he actually said, Kühnen listened attentively while the old Walloon regaled him with tales of his wartime heroics. Degrelle likened the Waffen SS to a holy order with its own set of rules and loyalties, an aristocratic minority that had been entrusted with a sacred mission. He extolled the fascist ideal in literary panegyrics aimed at arousing a new generation of zealots. "True elites are formed at the front," Degrelle effused, "a chivalry is created there, young leaders are born. . . . [W]hen we see a young revolutionary, from Germany or elsewhere, we feel that he is one of ours, for we are one with revolution and youth. We are political soldiers . . . we prepare the political

---

firm that played a pivotal role in the arms trade. Kintex was riddled with Bulgarian and Soviet spies — a fact that encouraged speculation that the KGB and its Bulgarian proxies were behind the 1981 papal shooting. But Western intelligence also had its hooks into the Bulgarian smuggling scene, as evidenced by the CIA's use of Kintex to channel weapons to the Nicaraguan Contras in the early 1980s. Although the CIA's link to the arms-for-drugs trade in Bulgaria was widely known in intelligence circles, Congress preferred to emphasize the testimony of former CIA agents and right-wing conspiracy theorists, who alleged that the Bulgarian secret service and the Soviet KGB had plotted to kill the pope. It proved to be one of the more efficacious disinformation schemes hatched during the Reagan era, reinforcing the notion that the USSR was an "Evil Empire" while deflecting attention from extensive — and potentially embarrassing — ties between U.S. intelligence and Turkish neo-Nazis.

cadres of the postwar world. Tomorrow, Europe will have elites such as it has never known. An army of young apostles, of young mystics, carried by a faith that nothing can check. . . ."[25]

Such perverse eloquence made a vivid impression on Kühnen, who thought of himself as one of the "political soldiers" that Degrelle swooned over. For Kühnen, it was a great honor to strategize with the man whom Hitler had wished was his own son. The young German and the exiled Waffen SS general became fast friends. They began making arrangements to celebrate the centennial of the Führer's birthday in April 1989. Although it was still five years away, they hoped that this special occasion would galvanize the international neo-Nazi movement. Degrelle agreed to serve as the honorary president of the Hitler birthday planning committee; with the general's approval, Kühnen would handle the leg work.[26]

Whenever possible, younger fascists looked to the dwindling coterie of old-guard Nazis for counsel and inspiration. Kühnen's host in Paris, FANE chief Marc Friederiksen, was proud of his special relationship with Major General Otto Ernst Remer. He often spoke in glowing terms about the Führer's bodyguard. That's how Ray Hill, a British neo-Nazi leader, first heard about Remer's so-called Bismarck Initiative during the early 1980s. At the time, none of his neo-Nazi cohorts knew that Hill was actually a spy posing as a dedicated fascist. The stocky, balding White Power advocate had recently switched sides, becoming a mole for *Searchlight*, a London-based antifascist magazine.[27]

After navigating a precarious double life for several years, Hill appeared as a witness before the European Parliament's Commission on Racism and Xenophobia. He described his harrowing journey into the heart of Europe's darkness, providing sordid details of a violent, neo-Nazi netherworld composed of interlocking groups and psychotic individuals. Among other revelations, Hill disclosed the existence of an extensive "Brown aid" network for neofascist fugitives and "political prisoners" that operated on both sides of the Iron Curtain.[28]

Some of Hill's former comrades in England played a major role in this furtive effort by safehousing neo-Nazis on the run from West Germany and other countries. Among those who availed themselves

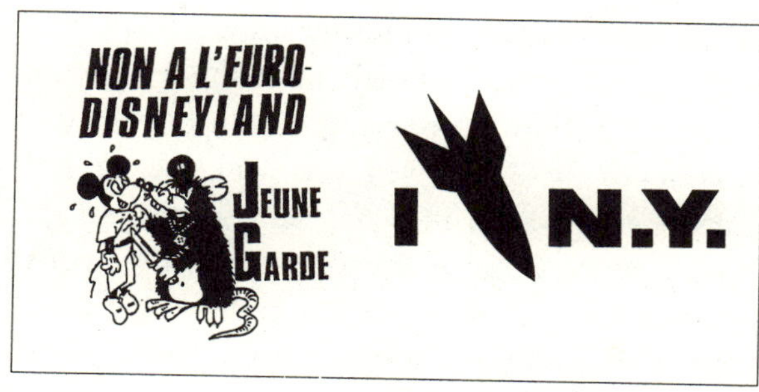

Postcards and stickers from a neofascist bookstore in Paris

of British hospitality in the early 1980s was Odfried Hepp, a young neo-Nazi renegade who had recently unleashed a wave of bombings that damaged property and injured military personnel at four U.S. Army bases in West Germany. After a brief stay in England, Hepp earned $500 a month working for the Palestine Liberation Front (PLF), led by Mohammed Abu Abass. Hepp's terrorist odyssey came to an abrupt end in April 1985 when he was arrested entering the apartment of a PLF member in Paris. Later that year, an Italian cruise ship, the *Achille Lauro,* was hijacked by the PLF; included on the PLF's list of prisoners to be exchanged for the *Achille Lauro* hostages was the name of Odfried Hepp.[29]

British Nazis also safehoused several Italian neofascists, including Luciano Petrone, who was wanted for murdering two Italian policemen and for his involvement in a massive bank robbery in Marbella, Spain, that netted $10 million of valuables. Petrone belonged to an ultra-right-wing terrorist cell that had been implicated in the August 1980 Bologna train station bombing, which killed eighty-five people and injured more than two hundred.* While in

* The Bologna bombing was the culmination of a wave of more than a decade of violent political attacks in Italy, the most terror-ridden country in postwar Europe. According to statistics cited in a CIA study, neofascists were responsible for 68 percent of the 4,298 terrorist incidents (and 87 percent of those incidents involving multiple deaths) that occurred in Italy during a twelve-year

hiding, Petrone cavorted with another Italian terrorist, Roberto Fiore, who had fled to London shortly after the Bologna massacre.

Ray Hill noticed an influx of young Italian fascists into England at this time. Many of these fugitives were sent back to Italy, but not Fiore. Although he had been indicted as a suspect in the Bologna bombing and convicted in absentia for joining a terrorist gang, repeated efforts by Italian authorities to extradite him failed on procedural grounds. The ho-hum response to Italy's request may have had something to do with Fiore's services as an informant for the British spy organization MI-6.[30]

---

period beginning in 1968. Italian magistrates believe that much of the neofascist violence that convulsed their country during this period was part of a "strategy of tension," coordinated in part by Italian secret-service operatives, in an effort to engender fear and confusion among the populace so that they would clamor for a strong government to protect them — if necessary, by imposing an authoritarian solution. Evidence linking Gladio, the CIA-sponsored "stay behind" project, to neofascist terrorist attacks in Italy was disclosed by parliamentary investigators, who found that "stay behind" personnel had access to arms depots hidden in 139 secret locales, including NATO bases and on church property. General Gerardo Serravalle, commander of Gladio during the 1970s, asserted that the CIA was concerned mostly with "internal control, that is, our level of readiness to counter street demonstrations, handling nation-wide strikes and any internal uprising." The Italian gladiators were primed to "fill the streets, creating a situation of such tension as to require military intervention," explained "stay behind" operative Roberto Cavallaro, who added, "I chose to work in — and therefore to infiltrate — neofascist movements because I have a rightist background. But other of my colleagues worked in left-wing groups, using the same techniques and pursuing the same objectives." When Italian parliamentary investigators asked Cavallero about the Red Brigades, he stated, "I had specific knowledge that many of the terrorists — both red and black — were acting on the basis of directives or suggestions from the secret services." All were entangled in a clandestine thicket that magistrates and parliamentary investigators sought to unravel. With the Italian secret service running interference, they had a difficult time sorting out who was ultimately behind the 1980 Bologna bombing and other deadly attacks. Several members of the Armed Revolutionary Nuclei were among fifty-seven right-wing extremists indicted on charges linked to the Bologna massacre. In keeping with a long-standing judicial pattern, convictions were later reversed, suspects went free, and a few Italian espionage officers had their wrists slapped for muddying the waters and deceiving investigators. Officially the bombing remains an enigma.

With Fiore as its newfound mentor, a hard-line faction within the British National Front began to transform itself into an elite paramilitary cadre. These fanatics were cheered on by neo-Nazi veteran Colin Jordan. Vowing "total war . . . to prod people out of the coma of their enslavement," Jordan called for the formation of an elite "task force" that would operate "on the lines comparable to the special units of Otto Skorzeny." In addition to weapons training, young recruits were given copies of *Rising,* a neofascist journal for "political soldiers," which harkened back to a mythic, preindustrial golden age when broad-boned, blond-haired warriors rode off to slay the infidels — a vision that contrasted sharply with the motley array of skinheads who composed the bulk of the National Front's new membership.[31]

The growing skinhead contingent was an index of the depths to which the British National Front had sunk since 1977, when it polled nearly a quarter million votes nationwide (and 10 percent in Greater London). Its swift decline was precipitated by Margaret Thatcher's Tory party, which appropriated the Front's main policy, opposition to foreign immigration. With their electoral base dwindling, neofascist organizers began to recruit skinhead youth as cannon fodder for racist attacks and other street actions. Rooted in the alternative rock scene, the skinheads became England's main contribution to the international fascist movement. By the early 1980s, this subcultural export had spread from London, the bonehead capital, to the United States and continental Europe.

Described by one observer as "a proletarian caricature of a dumb joke," the typical bonehead conjured up images of a chemotherapy patient or a concentration camp inmate — a sick, unintentional parody in light of the crude anti-Semitism they espoused. "It is a lad culture without mystery, so deadened that it uses violence to wake itself up," wrote Bill Buford, who likened their rampages to a mind-altering experience: "Violence is their antisocial kick . . . an adrenalin-induced euphoria that might be all the more powerful because it is generated by the body itself." Or as one skinhead remarked, "Violence is better than sex."[32]

Although he kept a full head of hair, Michael Kühnen saw plenty of opportunities among deviant baldies. The German neo-Nazi leader valued skinhead music as a great way to spread the word among young people. While exiled in Paris, he continued to exert his influence back home through groups like the Borussia Front, a skinhead gang that wreaked havoc at soccer matches, much like their British counterparts. Kühnen was also in touch with another shaved-head formation, the Hamburg-based Savage Army (SA), which attacked Turkish guest workers and other foreigners. "Skinheads and football fans are the people who support us," Kühnen explained, "even if they politically may not be one hundred percent on our side."[33]

In October 1984, after a few months on the lam, Kühnen was snatched by French law-enforcement authorities and deported to West Germany, where he was wanted on three different arrest warrants. At his trial in Frankfurt, the twenty-nine-year-old militant defended his campaign for "a National Socialist revolution" against the "Americanization" of Germany. An unimpressed judge sentenced Kühnen to four more years in prison for publishing forbidden insignia, advocating that a ban on the Nazi Party be lifted, and encouraging large numbers of young people to engage in proscribed political activities. "He knows very well there is no legal way to strive for Nazi aims," said the judge, who described Kühnen as "the symbol of neo-Nazism in West Germany."

When the verdict was read, Kühnen stood up and shouted, "Resistance!" to a courtroom packed with young neo-Nazi supporters wearing black leather jackets. He was quickly subdued by police and escorted off to prison. But his career as a political agitator was far from over.

New Right with an Old Twist

Alain de Benoist confounded friend and foe alike when he announced his intention to cast his ballot for the French Communist Party in the 1984 European parliamentary elections. A formidable intellectual with roots in the French neofascist scene, de Benoist was cynical, to say the least, about the electoral process as practiced in his country. Although he held Marxism in contempt, he opted to pull the lever for the Communists to emphasize his opposition to all forms of liberal democracy. Every other major party, including the up-and-coming Front National on the far Right, was loyal to the Atlantic alliance and the market system, which de Benoist despised.

De Benoist's decision to vote Communist was a symbolic gesture that dramatized the extent to which his political thought had developed since his teenage years when he joined the neofascist Jeune Nation movement, which took up the cause of French Algeria in the late 1950s. After the French government banned Jeune Nation, de Benoist served as secretary of the editorial board of its successor organization, Europe-Action. Exulting in "the violence which makes us realize our true selves," Europe-Action operated a publishing business in Paris that specialized in profascist and pro-Nazi books. Its list of titles included the French translation of Otto Skorzeny's memoirs. Like many other neofascists, de Benoist was obsessed with "defending the West" against Communist and nonwhite incursions. In the sixties, he supported American intervention in Vietnam. He also coauthored a pro-apartheid pamphlet, *Verité pour l'Africa du Sud,* which reflected his racialist views.[34]

Before long, however, de Benoist grew disenchanted with the stale, ineffectual, and wholly predictable methods of the French ultra-Right, which had failed to shake the pillars of the Gaullist state. Right-wing thinking had become, to quote a phrase of Anthony Wakeford, a thing of "cobwebs and corpses." Realizing that a new approach was necessary, de Benoist dispensed with the rhetoric of biological determinism, which he and his colleagues had previously emphasized to refute the egalitarian premises of Communism and liberal democracy. This ideological shift marked "the beginning of a 'long march,' an intellectual evolution," as de Benoist put it, that went through several phases. His thinking would reverberate most profoundly within the neofascist milieu in West Germany and elsewhere, providing a means for right-wing extremists to finally break out of the political ghetto where they had been confined since the end of World War II.[35]

Eschewing far Right conspiracy theories, de Benoist sought to fashion a systemic analysis of contemporary social problems. With this in mind, the twenty-five-year-old Frenchman founded a think tank called GRECE, the acronym for Groupement pour Recherche et d'Etudes par la Civilisation Européenne (Research and Study

Group for a European Civilization), in 1968. *Grece* was the French word for *Greece,* indicating de Benoist's affinity for Europe's ancient, pagan heritage. A handful of other militants from Europe-Action participated in this project, which became the institutional pivot of the *Nouvelle Droite* (New Right), the name bestowed upon de Benoist's Paris-based circle by the French media.

The New Right, explained French scholar Henry Rousso, "not only let its hair grow long and hid its tire irons in the attic, it also attempted to rehabilitate the very term 'right' by giving it intellectual luster and by denying [that] the word carried shameful connotations." Drawing upon the work of Italian leftist Antonio Gramsci, de Benoist and his colleagues stressed the importance of waging a war of ideas on the cultural battlefield, which they saw as a prerequisite to genuine political change. Accordingly, they devoted considerable effort to resurrecting Europe's conservative intellectual patrimony, which had been discredited by the fascist experience.

In a plethora of books and articles, de Benoist and his colleagues in GRECE reappraised right-wing (some would say "non-Nazi fascist") authors such as Oswald Spengler, Arthur Moeller van den Bruck, Ernst Jünger, Ernst Niekisch, Vilfredo Pareto, Carl Schmitt (the crown jurist of the Third Reich), and other thinkers who faded into oblivion after 1945. GRECE argued that the Conservative Revolution, which flourished in Germany between the two world wars, was more a seismograph that registered the depths of social discontent than a key factor that contributed to the demise of the Weimar Republic. Even if the Conservative Revolution was (as Armin Mohler put it) the "treasure trove from which national socialism [drew] its ideological weapon," GRECE maintained that revolutionary conservative precepts were never actually put into practice by Hitler's regime.[36]

Such logic failed to impress detractors, who charged that the French New Right was basically the same Old Right dressed up in more sophisticated finery. This was true, to some extent, given that many of the themes championed by GRECE, including its emphasis on paganism, had long been of interest to European rightists.

For de Benoist, nothing was more important than the task of rekindling Europe's sacred, polytheistic spirit that flourished before Christianity had "colonized" the Continent. His hostile diatribes against Christianity resembled those of Italian Nazi philosopher Julius Evola. Despite his status as the guru of neofascist terrorism in postwar Italy, Evola's work was embraced by members of GRECE as they began searching for an authentic European identity shorn of its Christian heritage.[37]

By rejecting Christianity as an alien ideology that was forced upon the Indo-European peoples two millennia ago, French New Rightists distinguished themselves from the so-called New Right that emerged in the United States during the 1970s. Ideologically, GRECE had little in common with the American New Right, which de Benoist dismissed as a puritanical, moralistic crusade that clung pathetically to Christianity as the be-all and end-all of Western civilization. The leader of the French New Right began to thrust his sharpest barbs at "the American way of life," with its inane TV serials; chronic mobility; ubiquitous fast food; adoration of the almighty dollar; and its quiescent, depoliticized populace held in thrall by hidden persuaders, Bible-thumpers, and other mass media tricks.

Vehemently opposed to the capitalist free market, de Benoist denounced liberalism as the ideology of an all-encompassing consumer society that was innately totalitarian by virtue of its compulsion to reduce every aspect of existence to the realm of economic utility. His thinking had evolved to the point where he identified U.S. economic and cultural imperialism as more of a threat than Soviet Communism. "Better to wear the helmet of a Red Army soldier," de Benoist wrote in 1982, "than to live on a diet of hamburgers in Brooklyn."[38]

Continuing on an anti-American trajectory, the leader of GRECE excoriated mass consumer society as a kind of "soft totalitarianism" that " 'air-conditions' hell and kills the soul." He condemned NATO and adopted a pro–Third World stance, calling for an alliance between Europe and the Islamic world on the grounds that both were threatened by the homogenizing juggernaut of American capitalism. "Europe, Third World — the same struggle," de Benoist proclaimed.[39]

His opposition to U.S. global intervention and his advocacy of a bloc-free Europe appeared to dovetail with certain ideas of the New Left, which had peaked during the student-worker Sorbonne uprising of May 1968, just when de Benoist was establishing his think tank. This belated ideological convergence was proof to some of de Benoist's erstwhile allies on the far Right that he had become a turncoat. At the same time, his neofascist pedigree made it impossible for him to find a home among left-wing radicals. The leader of GRECE, a physically unimposing man with thick eyeglasses and a vanishing hairline, was sporting a new philosophical look, they surmised, in order to further a deceptive political agenda and sow confusion among his adversaries.[40]

Relishing his role as a gadfly, de Benoist spurned attempts to pigeonhole him on the Left–Right spectrum. "Already on the international level," he stated in 1986, "the major contradiction is no longer between Right and Left, liberalism and socialism, fascism and communism, 'totalitarianism' and 'democracy.' It is between those who want the world to be one-dimensional and those who support a plural world grounded in the diversity of cultures."[41]

The celebration of "ethnopluralism" and cultural diversity signaled an important turn in de Benoist's intellectual progression. The former white supremacist had now become an ardent defender of threatened or minority cultures, of "different ways of life" that were "disappearing in a world where money is the only sign of distinction." Imagining a "Europe of a hundred flags" in the future, de Benoist rallied to the cause of cultures without countries, nations without states — the Basques, Catalans, Bretons, Lombards, Welsh, Scots, Flemish, Sami, Transylvanians, Chechens, etc. His emphasis on regionalism put him at loggerheads with Jean Thiriart, the eccentric Belgian optician who would soon come out of retirement to resume his political work. Although they shared an abiding antipathy toward the United States and American culture, de Benoist rejected Thiriart's call for a super-European nation-state stretching from Ireland all the way to the far end of Siberia. This seemed like the most grandiose form of nationalism to de Benoist, whose thinking was moving in the opposite direction.[42]

For de Benoist, the focus on preserving specific cultural and ethnic identities at all costs was viewed as a way of challenging the corrosive "single model" propagated by economic forces that sought to transform the world into one big global market. "Will the earth be reduced to something homogenous because of the deculturalizing and depersonalizing trends for which American imperialism is now the most arrogant vector?" he asked. "Or will people find the means for the necessary resistance in their beliefs, traditions, and ways of seeing the world? This is really the decisive question that has been raised at the beginning of the next millennium."[43]

Although advocating racial superiority may not have been his intention, there was little in de Benoist's analysis of enthnopluralism and the dangers of global monoculture that would prevent neofascist demagogues from using the New Right's ideas to justify racist and xenophobic campaigns. This was certainly the case with respect to Jean-Marie Le Pen, leader of the Front National, which appropriated and vulgarized de Benoist's concepts of ethnic specificity and the right to difference. "We not only have the right but the duty to defend our national character as well as our right to difference," declared Le Pen, who urged the French to defend the integrity of their culture against the "invasion" of Third World immigrants, the alleged source of France's problems.[44]

By lifting some of the New Right's rhetoric, Le Pen and like-minded national populists throughout Western Europe found a novel and highly effective way to legitimize their hateful prejudices, which would have been considered beyond the pale had they mouthed master-race rhetoric. The seductive vocabulary of ethnopluralism allowed them to feign concern about the best interests of the very people who bore the brunt of their racist tirades. "I love North Africans, but their place is in North Africa," said Le Pen.

Invoked in such a manner, "the right to difference" seemed to vindicate race-mixing phobias and demands for exclusion. It also underscored the complexity of contemporary racism, which, paradoxically, could be expressed in terms of both denying and affirming the identity of another group or person. Scholar Pierre-André Taguieff, an expert on the French New Right, detected within neofascist circles the appearance of a softer, more euphemistic form of racism that praised diversity while focusing on cultural rather than racial differences. Describing this phenomenon as "neo-racism," Taguieff noted that it was far more serviceable, and therefore more pernicious, than tarnished biological ideologies that touted the superiority of one race over another.[45]

A handful of de Benoist's former New Right colleagues jumped on the Front National bandwagon when it started to roll in the mid-1980s. But the leader of GRECE was not among them. In no uncertain terms, he condemned Le Pen's anti-immigrant scapegoating. This discord was not without irony, given that de Benoist had helped to create a climate in which certain extreme right-wing ideas could be expressed without opprobrium. For it was only after de Benoist began to articulate his thoughts on ethnopluralism and the right to difference that mass-based, neofascistic parties such as the French Front National discovered a workable, theoretical framework to promote their ugly views. While several factors contributed to the rise of radical right-wing populism in non-Communist Europe during the mid- and late 1980s, de Benoist and his intellectual cadre were instrumental in bequeathing the ideological trappings that made racism and xenophobia appear respectable. This would have a profound impact in West Germany, where right-wing extremists were beginning to mount a comeback.

Browns and Greens

Alain de Benoist occasionally traveled to the Federal Republic of Germany to speak at meetings and discuss his views. At a public forum held in Lüneberg in April 1985, he urged his German listeners to reclaim their authentic identity by working for the "abolition of neocolonialist structures." This entailed dissociating themselves from the United States as well as from the Soviet Union — although de Benoist believed that a German-Russian rapprochement would in the long run provide the basis for a collective security system in Europe. His forthright endorsement of regionalism also struck a responsive chord, given the deep-rooted federalist tradition that existed in Germany.[46]

But it was precisely the strength of this regionalist impulse that complicated the issue of German identity, which was always highly problematic. *Deutschland* as a nation did not exist until 1872, when Bismarck succeeded in Prussianizing a multiplicity of Germanic dukedoms. (The Prussians, incidentally, were a Baltic people.) Long divided between Catholics and Protestants, "Germany" derived from the medieval Holy Roman Empire, which was expansionist by nature, with fluid and insecure boundaries — much like the nation-state that Bismarck forged. By virtue of their central geographical position and the constant movement of population groups, the Germans were always a mixed breed. The mystical concept of the German *Volk* — a people bound together by common blood, language, territory, and customs — that arose in the nineteenth century was largely a form of compensation, a way of propping up a flimsy ethnic-nationalist identity.[47]

"The Germans have never been able to feel themselves comfortably settled within their borders untroubled in their belief in themselves," William Pfaff has observed. "Nationhood is a matter of anxiety for the Germans." This angst was compounded in 1945 by the partition of Germany into two countries with very different social and political systems, each integrated into hostile military blocs. After the reconfiguration of national frontiers and additional large-scale migrations, those of Germanic stock included Austrians, Dutch, Swiss, French, Czechs, Poles, Russians, and Italians. All these factors — topped by the enormous crimes of the Third Reich — contributed to a full-blown identity crisis, which became a burning issue in West Germany in the 1980s.[48]

During this period, identity politics was central to the discourse of the German extreme Right, which took many of its rhetorical cues from Alain de Benoist. "Every people has a right to its own identity. Whoever violates this right is playing with fire," asserted *Nation Europa,* a pan-European neofascist journal. Founded in 1950 by an ex-SS officer, it was one of several German publications that later adopted the jargon of *Volk*-ish or ethnopluralism. The influence of New Right and conservative revolutionary fascism was also evident in various journals (*Wir Selbst, Criticon, Mut,* and later, *Junge Freiheit*) that maintained the Germans had a right — nay, an obligation — to defend their unique cultural identity, which was threatened by immigrants, "multinational alienation," and other foreign influences.[49]

As in France, such notions were compatible with the hatred of refugees, asylum seekers, and ethnic minorities. But this animosity was obscured somewhat by the German New Right's strong endorsement of national liberation movements and "revolutionary struggles" around the world, ranging from the Basques in Spain and the IRA in Northern Ireland to the peoples of Eastern Europe, the Ukraine, the Afghan mujahideen, and the Sandinistas of Nicaragua. In short, any mortal enemy of a superpower was deemed a de facto ally by various inchoate New Right formations that sprang up in West Germany during the early 1980s.[50]

This period also saw the emergence of the Greens, the left-of-center peace-and-ecology party, as a mass-based opposition movement in West Germany. Galvanized by NATO's decision to station a new generation of medium-range nuclear missiles in Europe, the Greens adopted a neutralist stance toward the East-West conflict. Their attempts to forge a third way beyond capitalism and Communism bore certain similarities to themes stressed by New Right intellectuals and neo-Nazi militants, who tried to outflank their left-wing contemporaries by enunciating radical positions on ecology, nuclear weapons, U.S. imperialism, and "national liberation." Some right-wing extremists went so far as to call for "revolution from below" in Germany modeled after Third World independence struggles. They often employed leftist-sounding rhetoric that appealed to the Greens' supporters, who also obsessed over questions of personal and collective identity. Many Greens were receptive to arguments that German unification was an indispensable precondition to a durable peace in Europe. Such matters were debated in New Right publications that interspersed articles by left-wing authors and neo-fascistic "national revolutionaries."[51]

The political cross-fertilization that ensued in West Germany around this time provided new opportunities for far Right strategists, who were continually searching for ways to transcend their marginalized status. Toward this end, they sought to piggyback on the success of the Greens, which polled enough votes to enter the West German Bundestag — a feat that had not been accomplished by a radical right-wing party since 1949. Although most Greens were indisputably antifascist, some of them lacked the political savvy to realize that neo-Nazis and other far Right miscreants had infiltrated their ranks from the outset.[52]*

In 1980, the West Berlin chapter of the Greens, known as the Alternative List, expelled a contingent of "national revolutionaries" that had employed stealth tactics in an effort to take over the group. This was merely one skirmish in a battle for control of the Greens, as leftists feuded with Brown elements inside the party. Left-wing forces ultimately prevailed, prompting ecofascists and their fellow travelers to form a rival organization, the Democratic Ecology Party headed by Herbert Gruhl, in 1982.[53]

While German neo-Nazis and New Right intellectuals expressed concern for Green issues, their interest in ecology was often little more than a pretext for promoting a cutthroat social Darwinist ideology and a disguised form of racism. Gruhl, for example, trumpeted the "laws of nature" to justify a hierarchical social order. "All strivings of a people . . . for organized social justice are simply hopeless," he asserted. A guest speaker at Holocaust-denial confabs and other neo-Nazi functions, Gruhl was subsequently awarded the Bundesverdienstkreuz (Federal Service Cross), the country's highest official honor, by the Bonn government.[54]

Gruhl is best known for advancing dubious ecological arguments

* The first organization to call itself "the Greens" in 1977 was led by August Haussleiter, a bullnecked, red-faced veteran of Hitler's beer hall putsch, who had a long history of involvement in extreme right-wing causes after World War II. During the early 1950s, August Haussleiter's Deutsche Gemeinschaft (German Community) collaborated with the neo-Nazi Bruderschaft, which counted Otto Skorzeny among its key personnel. Shortly after the Socialist Reich Party was banned by the West German government, Haussleiter engaged in secret talks with Ernst Remer's colleagues in an effort to preserve the political punch of the SRP faithful. The SRP-linked attorney Rudolf Aschenauer was an executive board member of the Deutsche Gemeinschaft. By the late 1960s, however, Haussleiter had swung toward the Left in an effort to attract student radicals. His group, Action Community of Independent Germans, began to focus on ecology and antinuclear issues. Haussleiter subsequently became a father figure for the fledgling Greens, whose initial supporters included dissident conservatives as well as left-wing activists. In 1980, he was elected chairman of the Greens, but Haussleiter was forced to step down after a few months because of his checkered past.

for keeping foreigners out of Germany. He claimed that every *Volk* requires its own particular environment in order to flourish; as is the case with a fragile ecosystem, any outside interference will disrupt the "natural ecology of a *Volk*." According to the perverse logic of ecofascism, "[o]nly when a *Volk* maintains its characteristics can we preserve the ethnic variety to which humanity owes its adaptability." Protecting the environment was therefore tantamount to preserving the biological substance as well as the collective identity of the German people. This type of thinking would enable mainstream politicians to avoid racist terminology while advocating xenophobic views. "We have to think of the ecological consequences of unlimited immigration," declared Otto Zeitler, Bavaria's land development minister, after German unification.[55]

Rudolf Bahro, a former East German dissident who became a leader of the West German Greens, saw the ecological crisis in apocalyptic terms. He shocked many of his erstwhile allies by urging them to rediscover the "positive" side of the Nazi movement so as to "liberate" the suppressed "brown parts" of the German character. After leaving the Greens Party in the mid-1980s, he echoed the sentiments of many New Rightists by calling for authoritarian measures to rescue the biosphere. Present-day environmental problems were so serious, he asserted, that they could only be resolved through an "eco-dictatorship." Said Bahro, "There is a call in the depths of the *Volk* for a Green Adolf." People should not fear the advent of such a charismatic "prince," Bahro insisted, for he could lift Germans out of their spiritual oblivion and lead them to the promised land of ecological salvation.[56]

Pronouncements of this sort were vigorously rejected by the Greens, whose differences with the extreme Right far outweighed any similarities. The Greens were strongly committed to egalitarian principles — unlike the Brown intelligentsia, which harbored a bitter animosity toward American culture that went way beyond the anti-U.S. sentiment expressed by sectors of the West German Left. Although the Greens favored reunification on the basis of disarmament and neutrality, they deplored the concept of a Greater Germany that incorporated Austria, Silesia, Sudetenland, and other so-called eastern territories. Nor did the Greens subscribe to the right-wing argument that the division of Germany was merely a consequence of the imperialist policies of the occupation forces. Such a notion, the Greens maintained, "belittled both Hitlerism and German nationalism." Furthermore, they did not accept the proposition that decriminalizing German history was a first step toward recovering a true German identity, an idea that became fashionable among conservatives in the Fatherland in the mid-1980s. And, finally, the Greens did not see reunification coming about through an arrangement with the Soviet Union — a strategy favored by an increasing number of right-wing extremists.[57]

This, of course, had long been the view of Major General Otto Ernst Remer, the most pointedly pro-Soviet neo-Nazi in West Germany. Remer felt it was important to put out feelers to the Russians to see what price they would expect for supporting German unification. He recognized that Moscow was Germany's enemy as long as it refused to take its boot off the neck of Eastern Europe, East Germany included, but this situation could conceivably change if the Soviet bloc, burdened by economic woes, showed signs of fraying at the edges. Perhaps the USSR would be willing to permit the reunification of Germany in exchange for security guarantees and long-term economic assistance. With this in mind, Remer met with Valentin Falin, the former Soviet ambassador to West Germany who served as one of President Gorbachev's chief advisors on foreign policy. "I spoke with Falin on several occasions," said Hitler's former bodyguard. Invariably, the conversation turned to the possibility of a new Rapallo agreement and a revitalized German-Russian alliance.[58]

Remer went so far as to advocate a dialogue with all German neutralists, including the Greens and other left-wing peace activists, to put pressure on Chancellor Helmut Kohl and the Christian Democratic Union, which had returned to power in 1982 after thirteen years of Social Democratic rule. Although the West German constitution explicitly required the government to work for reunification, it did not appear that Kohl was serious about taking concrete steps to make this happen. On the contrary, his endorsement of NATO's plan to install Pershing and Cruise missiles in Europe underscored Bonn's support for the Western alliance, which entailed ipso facto the continued existence of two Germanys. A significant portion of the West German electorate did not favor the NATO missile caper.

According to a 1983 Gallop poll, 43 percent of West Germans distrusted the United States and the Soviet Union equally. Another survey a year later showed that 53 percent supported the idea of a united, neutral Germany.[59]

Anxious about rising neutralist sentiment, the West German chancellor decided that, at the very least, a symbolic gesture was necessary to placate his right-wing critics. Kohl's riposte came when President Reagan ventured to West Germany to participate in a solemn wreath-laying ceremony on May 5, 1985, at a military cemetery in Bitburg, where forty-seven SS men were buried along with two thousand Wehrmacht soldiers. Its ostensible purpose was to commemorate the fortieth anniversary of the end of World War II, but Reagan used the occasion to get in his digs at the Evil Empire — not the Third Reich, of course, but the Soviet Union. German war veterans who insisted that Hitler should not be judged too harshly, because he fought the Red Menace, felt vindicated when Reagan restricted his comments on human rights abuses to only those occurring in Communist countries. The president's one-eyed view of history transformed Nazi culprits into victims. He depicted the Third Reich not as a system of mass terror but as the work of a single maniacal despot. The fallen SS fighters were Hitler's victims "just as surely as the victims in the concentration camps," Reagan asserted. Absolving Germany of its wartime sins was the president's way of thanking Kohl for backing the unpopular nuclear missile buildup in Europe.

Not surprisingly, Jewish organizations were outraged. So, too, were U.S. veterans groups. The American Legion, usually a staunch supporter of the president, reminded Reagan that the Waffen SS had murdered more than seventy unarmed American prisoners at Malmédy, just thirty miles from Bitburg. "Are these the same SS troops buried beneath the stones of Bitburg?" a Legion spokesperson asked. Other veterans recalled that the city of Bitburg was a staging area for German soldiers — including Otto Skorzeny's notorious SS units — who fought against the Allies in the Battle of the Bulge. Bitburg also contained the graves of men from the Second SS Panzer Division, which massacred 642 French civilians in Oradour-sur-Glane in June 1942.[60]

For German Nazis and neo-Nazis, the rehabilitation of the SS at Bitburg was an event worthy of celebration. The HIAG, the SS veterans club, toasted Reagan at its annual reunion in the spring of 1985. "The Zionists will stop at nothing. But the President is an honest man," exulted one member of HIAG, which had recently been removed from the official watch list of extremist groups monitored by the Verfassungsschutz, the West German equivalent of the FBI. Even Major General Remer offered words of praise for Reagan. "It was high time," said Remer, who told reporters that he intended to send telegrams to Reagan and Kohl congratulating them for their gesture of goodwill toward the SS.[61]

The vast majority of West Germans (up to 70 percent, according to some polls) approved of Reagan's visit, underscoring the extent to which the Bitburg ritual was politically expedient for Kohl. Soon after he bid *aufwiedersehen* to the American president, Kohl publicly endorsed the German state boundaries of 1937 at a meeting of ethnic German expellees from Silesia (which became part of Poland after the war). As the chancellor spoke, revanchist banners were unfurled declaring "Silesia remains ours!" and neo-Nazis in the audience, emboldened by the Bitburg spectacle, raised their arms in Hitler-like salutes.[62]

Bitburg was a vivid reminder of how closely the Nazi era lay beneath the surface of German politics. By lifting the scab on Germany's darkest period, it brought to the fore many unresolved issues of guilt and denial, justice and forgiveness, morality and power politics. The renowned German aptitude for cultivating a protective amnesia with respect to the Third Reich had long been encouraged by American Cold War policies, which continually sought to scale down the scope of the Nazi problem and shrink the number of those who were deemed responsible for Nazi atrocities — culminating in Reagan's absurd contention that one man with a queer moustache was responsible for all the horrors that ensued. Ignoring the truth about the Nazi dictatorship doubtless took its toll on the German psyche. As West German historian Hagen Schulze warned: "[W]hat is not worked through in memory will reemerge as neurosis or hysteria." His words would prove prophetic in a few years when the Berlin Wall came down and Germany was reunified.[63]

The Politics of Denial

No matter how fervently Kohl and other German rightists tried to foster a positive German identity and an unashamed patriotism, they ran into an obstacle that defied integration — Auschwitz. The magnitude of Nazi criminality, as epitomized by the death camps, called into question whether it was psychologically possible for Germans to "emerge from the shadow of the Third Reich" and "become a normal nation again" (as Bavarian prime minister Franz-Josef Strauss put it), particularly if this entailed harkening back to an imperial tradition that reached a crescendo with Hitler. Overcoming this significant hurdle to "normalization" was the task pursued by a handful of professional historians — most notably, Ernst Nolte — who felt that Germany's wartime behavior could be put into proper perspective only when compared with other twentieth-century cases of dictatorship and mass murder. Nolte's convoluted attempts to relativize Nazi atrocities ignited a public firestorm known as the *Historikerstreit* (Historians' Dispute) in West Germany in 1986.[64]

Departing from the usual strategy of German conservatives who sought to downplay the Hitler era as a historical aberration, Nolte argued that National Socialism was an excessive but nonetheless justified response to the greater danger of Soviet Communism. He sought to deny the singularity of the Holocaust by equating it with Stalin's terror, the massacre of Armenians by Turks, Pol Pot's killing fields in Cambodia, the Allied carpet bombing of Dresden toward the end of World War II, and the expulsion of ethnic Germans from Poland and Czechoslovakia shortly thereafter. Although all of these were awful calamities, Nolte refused to acknowledge what made the Nazi genocide unique. Unlike the other examples he cited, the Holocaust was the result of a systematic campaign by the state to use every means at its disposal to exterminate an entire people, as defined by racial or religious criteria. Moreover, the Nazis did not just kill millions of people, but literally "harvested" their remains for the benefit of Germany's industrial machine.[65]

Most academic historians dismissed Nolte's conjectures; yet, if nothing else, he managed to show that the process of reckoning with the past often turns out to be just the opposite — an attempt to manipulate the historical record and twist it to suit a political agenda. For if Auschwitz was merely one among many modern-day horrors, then why continue to stigmatize Germany? The extreme Right appreciated the utility of Nolte's argument, which in one fell swoop appeared to nullify the crux of long-standing objections to German unification.

Treading on a slippery historical slope, Nolte came dangerously close to validating the bizarre worldview of those who claimed that the Holocaust never actually happened, that Auschwitz was a fabrication concocted by Jews for their own purposes. The existence of the gas chambers, Nolte asserted, "has been contested by a number of authors," and "this literature has in no way originated exclusively with Germans or neo-Fascists." This point showed that their intentions were "often honorable," said Nolte, who concluded that their work should be taken seriously. He even repeated some of the bogus allegations put forward by Holocaust-deniers, including the idea that the Jews — specifically, the World Zionist Organization — had declared war on Nazi Germany shortly after the Wehrmacht invaded Poland in September 1939 and, therefore, it was not unreasonable for Hitler to launch an anti-Jewish campaign.[66]

While Holocaust-denial had always been part of the postwar fascist scene, it was not until the founding of the California-based Institute for Historical Review (IHR) in 1978 that the "assassins of memory," as French literary historian Pierre Vidal-Naquet has called them, acquired an organizational base that facilitated their international networking efforts. A spin-off of Willis Carto's Liberty Lobby, the IHR published the *Journal of Historical Review*, which tried to impress its readers with footnotes and other scholarly trappings. As well as distributing a glut of books, pamphlets, and audio- and videotapes, the IHR arranged expeditions to the annual neofascist festival at Dixmude.[67]

The Holo-hoaxers call themselves "revisionists," but a more appropriate term would be "negationists," for their modus operandi has less to do with critical thinking than with advancing a rancid ideological agenda. They realized that the biggest barrier to a revival of National Socialism was the truth about the past — hence, their need to convince the public that Auschwitz was a lie. Toward this end, they employed arguments that were inherently contradictory — some admitted that the gas chambers existed but only to kill lice; others maintained that the gas chambers were built by the Allies after the war to discredit the Germans. They ignored evidence such as Auschwitz commander Rudolf Hoess's Nuremberg testimony in which he described how gas chambers were used to exterminate camp inmates. By picking away at specific details, the negationists hoped to plant seeds of doubt among young people that would persist after those who had survived the concentration camps were no longer alive to bear witness to the truth.[68]

IHR activities were vigorously promoted in the Liberty Lobby's weekly newspaper, the *Spotlight,* whose circulation exceeded three hundred thousand in 1981 but has since leveled off to about half that. Aptly described as "the *National Enquirer* of the American far Right," it has usually avoided the crude racialist language that typifies Klan and neo-Nazi literature. Coding its bigotry in anti–big government rhetoric, this conspiracy-obsessed tabloid purports to expose the powerful hidden forces that are supposedly responsible for all of the world's complex ills. In addition to "international banksters," its favorite whipping boys have been the Council on Foreign Relations, the Bilderberg group, Trilateral Commission, United Nations, and the Federal Reserve System. Over the years, *Spotlight* subscribers have been treated to headlines such as THE DIARY OF ANNE FRANK IS A FRAUD and SKINHEADS: THEY'RE YOUNG, THEY'RE WILD AND THEY'RE STANDING UP FOR AMERICA.[69]

In the weird world of the *Spotlight,* history is turned upside down. The exploits of the Waffen SS are glorified and convicted Nazi war criminals, such as General Léon Degrelle, are described as war heroes. In 1979, the *Spotlight* reported that Degrelle had written "An Open Letter to the Pope Concerning Auschwitz," in which he beseeched newly annointed John Paul II not to lend credence to the "myth" of the gas chambers. The following year, the *Spotlight* ran a lengthy interview with Senator-elect Dan Quayle, who thanked the Liberty Lobby for supporting his successful political campaign. Other conservatives kept their distance from the Liberty Lobby. R. Emmett Tyrell, editor of the *American Spectator,* ridiculed Carto's group as a "colorful collection of bigots and simpletons." The *Wall Street Journal* cut to the chase and called Carto and the Liberty

Lobby anti-Semitic, which prompted a lawsuit. But the court ruled against Carto, saying that it would be hard-pressed to find a case in which the evidence of anti-Semitism was "more compelling."[70]

Among those who occasionally wrote for the *Spotlight* and the *Journal of Historical Review* was Yockey's old friend H. Keith Thompson. He had been invited to join the Liberty Lobby's board of policy, but Thompson balked when he received a letter from Carto's organization asking him to sign a loyalty oath. "I took one oath of loyalty in my life and that is all I shall take," he huffed. (Thompson was referring to his pledge of allegiance to Nazi Germany when he secretly joined the SS foreign intelligence service during the war).[71]

Thompson made his feelings perfectly clear when he spoke at an IHR gathering in California in September 1983. Held in secluded locations, these annual confabs were open only to invited guests, who paid a nifty sum to listen to a lineup of Nazis, neofascists, and other negationists expound upon the latest developments in Holo-hoaxology and the gargantuan Zionist conspiracy that had tricked the masses into believing that 6 million Jews were killed. During his lecture, Thompson attacked the Nuremberg trials and recounted his postwar effort to help rehabilitate Hitler's appointed successor, Grand Admiral Karl Doenitz. At the end of his speech, he urged his audience to "stand by the Third Reich." That comment elicited a standing ovation, whereupon Thompson added, "If, in the end, the Holocaust did take place, then so much the better!" At least Thompson was more candid than the typical IHR windbag.[72]*

* On rare occasions, the IHR managed to entice mainstream historians, such as Pulitzer Prize–winner John Toland, to present papers at its conferences. Ex-CIA agent Victor Marchetti also lectured at an IHR gathering. "I've known Carto for years," said Marchetti, who was one of several former spooks who thrived in this kooky, racialist subculture. According to an IHR insider, Marchetti got financial support from the Carto empire to launch a newsletter called *Zionist Watch,* which was dedicated to exposing the nefarious influence of the pro-Israel lobby on Capitol Hill. Another favorite IHR speaker and collaborator was Issah Nakleh of the World Muslim Congress (WMC). Based in Pakistan, the WMC was initially headed by the Grand Mufti of Jerusalem, who, like his friend H. Keith Thompson, stood by the Third Reich until his death in

David McCalden, a British neo-Nazi, served as the first executive director of the Institute for Historical Review. Before long, however, he had a falling-out with Carto, as did many people who tried to work with the Liberty Lobby's godfather. Upon quitting the IHR in 1984, McCalden started to air the organization's dirty laundry. Rumors began to circulate about a "gay Nazi cult" inside the IHR that allegedly included Keith Stimely, the young editor of the *Journal of Historical Review*. An ardent Yockeyite and a protégé of H. Keith Thompson, Stimely died of AIDS after the usual parting of the ways with Carto. McCalden himself would succumb to the same disease a few years later.[73]

Backdoor links connecting the Institute for Historical Review and the Republican Party quietly persisted throughout the Reagan administration. Austin App, an IHR stalwart who wrote *The Six*

1974. A few years later, the WMC, then headed by Pakistani Dr. Inamullah Kahn, mailed Holocaust-denial literature to every member of the U.S. Congress and the British Parliament. The WMC's official mouthpiece, *Muslim World*, carried ads for *The Protocols of the Elders of Zion* and Henry Ford's *The International Jew*. Dr. Khan's congress also published *Freemasonry*, a book warning that Jews were using lodge members to extend secret control over religion and society — a paranoid theory that has long been popular among Liberty Lobby supporters and neo-Nazi groups around the world. Acknowledging their political kinship, WMC secretary-general Khan sent a letter to the *Spotlight* praising its "superb in-depth analysis" and stating that the paper deserved "the thanks of all right-minded people." Dr. Khan also served as an advisor to the Saudi Arabian royal family, which lavished funds on the WMC. In addition, the Saudi Arabian government retained the services of American neo-Nazi William Grimstead as a Washington lobbyist. Like many European neofascist groups, the WMC adopted a third-position stance toward the superpowers, as demonstrated by this headline from *Muslim World:* U.S. AND USSR — BOTH SERVE ZIONIST INTERESTS. But Khan tempered his anti-American tirades when the Soviet Union invaded Afghanistan in 1979. Soon the World Muslim Congress began working closely with U.S. intelligence and Pakistani military officials, who were covertly supporting the Afghan mujahideen in their fight against the Soviet-installed regime in Kabul. This effort was strongly endorsed by Dr. Khan, who served for many years as the Pakistani representative of the Nazi-infested World Anti-Communist League, which played an important role in the Reagan administration's "secret war" in the Golden Crescent.

Million Swindle, was a spear-carrier for the German-American National Congress, one of several far Right affiliates linked to the National Confederation of American Ethnic Groups. Cofounded by App and dominated by Nazi apologists, this confederation played an important role in the GOP's ethnic-outreach division during election campaigns.[74]

For the most part, ties between fascist old-timers and the Republican Party remained a fairly well-kept secret until near the end of the Reagan presidency, when a flurry of news reports exposed that the GOP's ethnic-outreach arm had recruited some of its key members from a fascist Eastern European émigré network. Many of these dubious characters settled in the United States with the help of the CIA, the military, and the State Department, which sponsored Nazi intelligence assets during the Cold War. Using loopholes in immigration laws, they were able to facilitate the transfer of an estimated ten thousand fascist collaborators to the United States.[75]

According to historian Christopher Simpson, these far Right émigrés did not arrive as isolated individuals but as part of "experienced, highly organized groups with distinct political agendas that differed little from the fascist programs they had promoted in their homelands." Boosted by generous CIA subsidies, several militant exile organizations gained a foothold in ethnic communities in the United States and proceeded to carve out a power base on the far Right of the American political landscape. Teaming up with homespun American Red-bashers, they gravitated toward the conservative wing of the Republican Party and assumed prominent roles in the GOP's ethnic-outreach committees.[76]

The Liberty Lobby and the Republican Party's ethnic-outreach division shared an outspoken antipathy toward the Justice Department's Office of Special Investigations (OSI), which had been established during the Carter presidency to track down and prosecute Nazi collaborators who had entered the United States illegally. After the OSI succeeded in deporting several suspected war criminals, its efforts were assailed by former White House communications director Patrick Buchanan. An admirer of Franco, Pinochet, the Argentine military junta, and South Africa's apartheid regime, Buchanan equated Allied treatment of German civilians after the war to Nazi treatment of the Jews. It was Buchanan who reportedly scripted

Reagan's chilling remarks about how SS soldiers buried at Bitburg "were victims, just as surely as the victims in the concentration camps."[77]

Buchanan described Hitler as "an individual of great courage, a soldier's soldier," and referred to Holocaust survivors' memories as "group fantasies of martyrdom." Such missives made him a favorite among readers of the *Spotlight* and the IHR journal. The negationists had occasion to gloat when a nationwide Holocaust history program for schools was denied federal funding during the Reagan administration. The Department of Education rejected the proposed Holocaust curriculum because "the Nazi point of view, however unpopular, [was] not presented, nor [was] that of the Ku Klux Klan."[78]

The following year, the IHR, represented by attorney Mark Lane, suffered a legal setback when a superior court judge in Los Angeles ruled that the Holocaust was an established fact and that the institute therefore had to pay $50,000 to a concentration camp survivor, Mel Mermelstein, who had responded to the IHR's offer to give this sum to anyone who could prove that Jews were gassed at Auschwitz.[79]

Still licking their wounds, IHR staffers sought to put the Mermelstein affair behind them as they looked forward to hosting the Eighth International Revisionist Conference, which was scheduled to begin on October 9, 1987, at the Holiday Inn in Irvine, California. Several speakers were slated to appear, including a much ballyhooed "special mystery guest" who was hyped but not identified in IHR promotional literature.

Roughly one hundred people from several different countries turned up at the conference, which was dedicated to the memory of Austin App, the Holocaust-denier and GOP ethnic mover and shaker who had recently passed away. When it was his turn to address the nearly all-male gathering, August Klapprott, a German-American Bund leader from the 1930s, tried to lighten things up a bit. Claiming FDR's prisons were worse than Hitler's, Klapprott spoke of his confinement during the war in a Michigan jail, which was overrun by cockroaches. He facetiously described how he and some of the other prisoners "pushed them together in one spot and then we exterminated them — all six million!" Guffaws emanated from the audience, then a big round of applause.

Finally, it came time to introduce the eagerly awaited "surprise mystery guest." A hush swept through the crowd when his name was announced. It was none other than Major General Otto Ernst Remer! H. Keith Thompson had arranged for the seventy-five-year-old Nazi to visit the United States so that he could deliver the keynote address at the IHR confab. For Thompson, it was a crowning moment. While serving as the registered U.S. agent for Remer's Socialist Reich Party in the early 1950s, he had sent messages to SRP leaders through Francis Parker Yockey, who often traveled to West Germany. Three and a half decades later, Thompson came full circle by bringing Remer to the Holocaust-denial convention sponsored by the IHR, which had been founded by one of Yockey's biggest fans and posthumous promoters.

Somehow Thompson was able to pull strings for Remer to enter the country that he had so often and so vociferously criticized. Despite his unrepentant Nazi views and his forthright advocacy of a German-Russian alliance during the Cold War, Remer managed to get in and out of California without any hassles — a feat all the more curious given that a West German court had just sentenced him to a six-month prison term for making a crude, anti-Semitic remark that prompted gales of laughter at an SS reunion in Bavaria. A reporter from *Stern* recalled the incident: "From the right-hand pocket of his suit, [Remer] removed with a grand gesture a gas-filled cigarette lighter. He held it under his nose, pressed carefully on the release so that the gas escaped slowly. 'What is that?' he asked, sniffing it, and then he gave the reply: 'A Jew nostalgic for Auschwitz.' "[80]

Such humor would have gone over well at the IHR conference, but Remer was decidedly more sober at this forum. During his lecture, the former commander of the crack Grossdeutschland guard battalion gave a blow-by-blow account of the events that unfolded on July 20, 1944, when he and Skorzeny saved the Third Reich from coup plotters. Translated by IHR editor Mark Weber, Remer's comments were warmly received by the audience, which applauded whenever National Socialism or Hitler was mentioned and groaned at every reference to Roosevelt or Churchill.

After his speech — which the *Spotlight* summarized in an glowing article and the *Journal of Historical Review* reprinted in full —

a klatch of youthful admirers gravitated toward Remer. Awestruck, they hung on every word as one of the last living legends of the Third Reich casually smoked a cigarette and elaborated upon the need for a European cultural revival. When asked to explain his country's foreign policy, Remer tipped his ashes and replied, "There is no policy now since it is a false state. There is no Germany . . . only two occupied populations."[81]

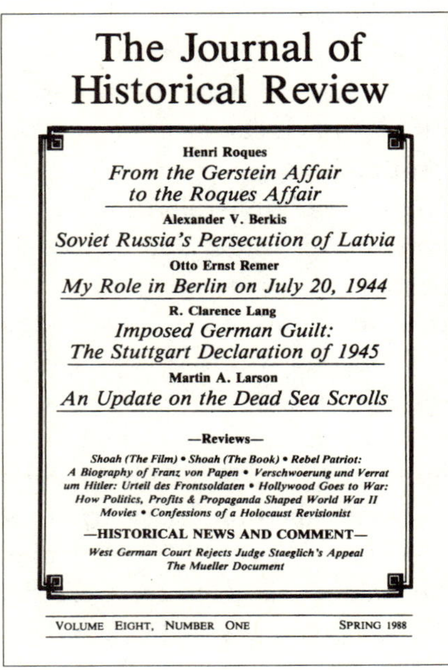
The Journal of Historical Review

Henri Roques
From the Gerstein Affair to the Roques Affair

Alexander V. Berkis
Soviet Russia's Persecution of Latvia

Otto Ernst Remer
My Role in Berlin on July 20, 1944

R. Clarence Lang
Imposed German Guilt: The Stuttgart Declaration of 1945

Martin A. Larson
An Update on the Dead Sea Scrolls

—Reviews—

Shoah (The Film) • Shoah (The Book) • Rebel Patriot: A Biography of Franz von Papen • Verschwoerung und Verrat um Hitler: Urteil des Frontsoldaten • Hollywood Goes to War: How Politics, Profits & Propaganda Shaped World War II Movies • Confessions of a Holocaust Revisionist

—HISTORICAL NEWS AND COMMENT—

West German Court Rejects Judge Staeglich's Appeal
The Mueller Document

VOLUME EIGHT, NUMBER ONE SPRING 1988

But in the future, Remer promised, a newly awakened Europe would pave the way for the unification of the entire continent under the dynamic leadership of Germany in tandem with Russia. Although he acknowledged that the two countries shared a tempestuous history, Remer commended the Russians for their moral fortitude guided by "Slavic authoritarianism." By contrast, America, with its abrasive rock music and "negroid cultural degradations" sold to the masses by "Jewish polluters," was said to be a more devious and powerful enemy. An undisciplined giant weighed down by race mixing, America bred rampant mediocrity that dulled the sensibilities of contemporary Germans and others under its sway.

Only a neo-Nazi resurgence could remedy this situation, Remer contended; and until such time it was incumbent upon all National Socialists to be cultural torch-bearers for the hidden glories of "traditional Europe." Those who huddled around him listened with rapt attention and resonated to his dream.

Before the Deluge

A few months after Ernst Remer's visit to the United States, Michael Kühnen finished serving his second prison term. Upon his release in March 1988, he immediately began a tour of West Germany, visiting old comrades and recruiting new followers. Monitoring his movements, U.S. Army intelligence made what turned out to be an accurate prediction: "Kühnen's actions and the power of his magnetism will have a deciding influence on the future of neo-Nazism. He will very likely try to gather his former associates around him with the goal to again attack the liberal democratic fundamental order."[82]

Never one to pull his rhetorical punches, Kühnen stated during a radio interview that a Nazi dictatorship should be set up in West Germany. "Our dream is a race of European Brownshirts, active political soldiers of national socialism who will fight in the streets," he told *Der Spiegel*. Remarks of this sort prompted the authorities to ban yet another group led by Kühnen, the Nationale Sammlung, in February 1989.[83]

By this time, Kühnen was busy preparing for Hitler's centennial birthday celebration, which he had planned while visiting General Léon Degrelle in Spain five years earlier. The much anticipated event turned out to be a relatively low-key affair attended by neo-Nazis from Spain, France, Denmark, Belgium, Norway, and West Germany. As they raised glasses of champagne in honor of the Führer, Kühnen and his colleagues had reason to be pleased. The upstart Republikaner Party had recently scored a breakthrough by capturing 7.5 percent of the vote in West Berlin. Not since the fleeting victories of Bubi von Thadden's National Democrats in the mid-1960s had a radical right-wing party done so well at the polls. "Nationalist thinking stands before a renaissance here," Kühnen proclaimed. "The Republikaner's success in the Berlin election has been a great encouragement to us and all nationalist forces."[84]

Founded in 1983, the fast-rising Republikaner were led by a former Bavarian talk-show host, Franz Schönhuber, who often boasted of his wartime service with the Waffen SS. His party called for the abolition of trade unions and the state welfare system, the expulsion of all foreigners, and the restoration of a united Germany within its 1937 borders. Schönhuber also played down the evils of the Nazi era, equating German misery at the end of the war with the terror it had inflicted on everyone else. But in this regard Schönhuber was hardly different from many mainstream West German politicians — just a bit more brazen and outspoken perhaps.[85]

Schönhuber eschewed terminology that could be pegged as neo-Nazi, fashioning the Republikaner into a radical, right-wing populist party that purported to advocate for the interests of the little guy. Escalating unemployment and social bifurcation had given rise to a "two-thirds society," and those who ended up on the short end of West Germany's economic miracle felt increasingly buffeted by market forces beyond their control. Rather than illuminating the structural factors that bred social inequities, Schönhuber blamed immigrants, guest workers, and asylum seekers for nearly every one of West Germany's problems. Peddling a politics ready-made for the economically disenchanted, he touted emotive slogans and simplistic solutions such as "Our own people first!" and "Germany for the Germans!" The efficacy of this strategy became evident once again when the Republikaner polled 7.1 percent nationally in the June 1989 elections for the European Parliament. After these results, few doubted that the Republikaner had become a serious force in West German politics.

Given the racially charged message promoted by the Republikaner, it's not surprising that the party attracted some people who were more extreme or more militant than the image Schönhuber sought to project. Hard-core neo-Nazis loyal to Michael Kühnen had infiltrated the Republikaner since its inception. For tactical reasons, Schönhuber sought to distance himself from Kühnen and his fellow travelers. Noting that he had friends inside Schönhuber's party, Kühnen remarked, "The Republikaner say what many people think, I say what many Republikaner think."[86]

In an effort to portray the Republikaner as a patriotic group without neo-Nazi leanings, Schönhuber followed the same formula that seemed to be working for other far-Right populist parties in Western Europe: he cloaked his racism in the language of "ethno-pluralism" and stressed the importance of safeguarding a separate national identity as a precondition to preserving the unique attributes of different cultures. The Republikaner chief also adopted a "national-neutralist" position that smacked of Ernst Remer's politics. "Russia is nearer to us than America, not merely geographically," Schönhuber maintained. "Here I am a follower of Bismarck, who believed that the key to the fruitful development of our Fatherland lay in a positive relationship with Russia."[87]

While they both embraced Bismarck as a key touchstone, Schönhuber differed from Remer in at least one crucial respect — the Republikaner leader publicly referred to Hitler as a "criminal." This may have been a pragmatic concession on the part of Schönhuber, who understood that Third Reich nostalgia was not a formula for political success in contemporary West Germany. "The likelihood that the Federal Republic will be defeated by a totalitarian enemy who grows an easily recognizable mustache and prefers brown shirts is exceptionally slight," said Schönhuber. "There will be no second Hitler to test the Bonn state, no imitation bringing people under its spell. It'll be an unmistakable original whose appearance is trimmed to its time and corresponds to its needs. At best the enciphered similarities will be evident to the experts."[88]

According to a report by the European Parliament's Committee of Inquiry on Racism and Xenophobia, the emergence of the Republikaner was "only the tip of a very large extreme-right iceberg in West Germany." Schönhuber's populist offensive, along with rumblings among *Volk*-ish New Right intellectuals and the growth of Kühnen's underground army — all were part of an expanding political force field on the extreme Right that exerted an unmistakable pull on Chancellor Kohl and the ruling Christian Democratic Union. Of foremost concern to Kohl was the possibility that many of his erstwhile supporters might stray into the Republikaner camp.[89]

The principal impact of the Republikaner, in the words of the European Parliament's report, was "to push the axis of political discussion in West Germany to the right." The Committee of Inquiry cited several disturbing examples, including an August 1989 rally in Hanover addressed by three federal government ministers, who endorsed the revanchist demands of German nationalist exiles from Silesia. There was also the claim by official government spokesman Hans Klein that the Waffen SS was merely "a group of fighting soldiers who defended the Fatherland." Such pronouncements by mainstream West German politicians did not lessen the appeal of the Republikaner Party but rather "served to legitimize many of its ideas in the public mind," the committee concluded. The European Parliament also noted with alarm the annual survey by West Germany's constitutional watchdog, the Verfassungsschutz, which charted an increase in the number of hard-core fascists in the Bonn Republic from twenty-two thousand in 1988 to more than thirty thousand in 1989.[90]

Michael Kühnen sensed the political winds were shifting in a favorable direction. But neither he nor any of his neo-Nazi colleagues could have anticipated the upheaval that would soon shake the entire continent. In November 1989, the Berlin Wall was breached. The two Germanys quickly merged, and the Soviet Union cascaded toward a monumental crack-up. "For many years, little was possible," a delighted Otto Ernst Remer remarked. "Then everything changed overnight, and a perspective whose end we can't yet determine suddenly opened up."[91]

PART THREE

POST–COLD WAR FASCISM

CHAPTER SEVEN

GERMANY REUNITED

Catharsis

A spontaneous *Volkfest* erupted on the night of November 9, 1989, as young Germans from East and West Berlin climbed atop the thirteen-and-one-half-foot slab of concrete that separated their city. Clearing away coils of barbed wire, jubilant strangers extended hands and pulled one another up onto the hated edifice. They hugged and kissed, popped champagne, and danced until dawn. Cars honked and giddy throngs surged toward the Brandenburg Gate. Among the celebrants were Chancellor Helmut Kohl and his close friend Günter Strassmeir, the leader of the Christian Democratic Union in West Berlin.

While much of the world watched the festivities on TV, a group of West German skinheads with swastika armbands scaled the Wall and headed eastward unhindered by the enthusiastic crowd. It was a hint of what lay in store for the post–Cold War era, which commenced symbolically on that fateful evening when Berlin once again became an undivided municipality. Soon a wave of neo-Nazi violence would engulf the Fatherland in a manner frighteningly reminiscent of a past that many thought had been left behind. Laden with historical significance, the date of the de facto dissolution of the Wall coincided with the anniversary of the 1938 Kristallnacht pogrom. Exactly fifteen years before that, on November 9, 1923, Hitler had been arrested for staging his abortive beer hall putsch.

Something irrevocable transpired with the opening of the 105-mile-long Berlin Wall. Erected in 1961, this booby-trapped death strip inspired spy novelists and graffiti artists, who decorated it with poetry and colorful murals. At least 255 people had been killed trying to cross the Wall. East German Communist boss Erich Honecker claimed it was an antifascist barrier designed to protect against Western imperialism. In January 1989, he confidently proclaimed that the Berlin Wall would remain in place for "the next hundred years." That same month, an opinion poll indicated that while a majority of West Germans supported unification in theory, only 3 percent believed it would happen anytime soon.

By year's end, however, the geopolitical tectonic plates started to rattle, and the Berlin Wall crumbled. Aftershocks from this pivotal, epoch-making moment would be felt across the globe long after the Wall had been sold off piece by piece to tourists and trinket collectors. In the process, the Wall's graffiti also disappeared, including a prescient Aldous Huxley quote, which warned against bigotry and narrow-mindedness: "There's no single cure for what could never have a single cause."[1]

Given the magnitude of what had occurred, it's ironic that the fall of the Wall was due to flukish bungling by tentative East German authorities. Two days earlier, the geriatric leadership of the German Democratic Republic (GDR) had resigned, affording little chance for the new Communist government to settle in. The changing of the guard came in the midst of a tremendous outpouring of popular discontent. Nearly 350,000 people (2 percent of East Germany's population) fled the GDR in the autumn of 1989. Concurrent with this massive exodus, grassroots protest inside East Germany picked up remarkable momentum. Within a few weeks, outdoor demonstrations drew more than a hundred thousand people. Originating in Leipzig and spreading throughout the country, this nonviolent citizens movement coincided with analogous upheaval in other Eastern European states. Catalyzed by Mikhail Gorbachev's reforms in the Soviet Union, bold displays of civic courage were on the verge of transforming the political landscape of the entire region.

The fledgling East German opposition — led by artists, ecologists, Protestant clergy, feminists, peace and human rights activists — never expected to topple the Communist ruling elite and precipitate a rush of events leading inexorably toward unification. The two-German predicament had come to seem like an immutable part of their existence. It was not their intention to bring about a national merger. Eager to escape from the Communist frying pan, most of them did not want to jump straight into the capitalist fire. Instead, they favored a socialist renewal in the GDR, a kind of "third way" that would combine the best of both systems. But this utopian prospect was trampled underfoot when the border opened and legions of East Germans lined up at West German banks for a promised allotment of deutsche marks and loaded up on stereos, VCRs, and big-screen TVs.

As it turned out, the emotional catharsis that accompanied the breach of the Berlin Wall drained the revolutionary project of much of its energy. Caught off guard by the sudden rupture, dissident GDR intellectuals were left gasping at the edge of the abyss. Having created the civic space for an expression of chronically pent-up feelings, the protest leaders were overwhelmed when the unsilenced majority of East Germans began to clamor for unification soon after the Wall was rendered obsolete. Emblematic of this shift in sensibility, the original chant of "*Wir sind das Volk!*" ("We are the people!") gave way at mass rallies to the rousing refrain "*Wir sind ein Volk!*" ("We are *one* people!") It did not take long before the uglier side of German nationalism began to assert itself. In Leipzig and other East German cities, skinhead youth hoisting flags of the 1937 German Reich marched alongside those demanding unification. Soon proponents of unity, including neo-Nazi militants, started to clash openly with those who still cherished the possibility of an independent East German state.

Sensing a unique opportunity to accomplish what had until then seemed like an impossible fantasy, Chancellor Helmut Kohl weighed in swiftly with a unilateral plan to unite the GDR and the Bonn Republic. Once the Wall was punctured, the embattled West German leader had the perfect issue to steal the patriotic thunder — at least, momentarily — from the insurgent Republikaner Party on the far Right.

Stoking the fires of German nationalism, Kohl drove the process of unification forward at breakneck speed. He told a double lie, promising East Germans that no one would be materially worse off (and that many would prosper) because of unification and assuring West Germans that higher taxes and cuts in social services would not be necessary to underwrite the merger. In March 1990, the Christian Democratic Union was rewarded at the polls, as GDR voters, eager for an economic uplift, sought refuge in a larger national identity. The fusion of the two German states was virtually a done deal a few months later when Gorbachev acquiesced to plans for German unification without insisting that membership in NATO be abandoned. Given the great disparity of economic strength and political legitimacy between the Federal Republic and the GDR, unification was destined to take place on West German terms. It would be more like a shotgun annexation than a marriage of equal partners.

In addition to helping Kohl recoup his popularity, the dash toward national unity played to the advantage of Michael Kühnen and his pumped-up fascist cohorts. Described by U.S. Army intelligence as "the most essential representatives of neo-Nazism" in the Federal Republic, Kühnen and his inner circle were ready to move as soon as the Berlin Wall tumbled. They viewed post-Communist East Germany as fertile turf for recruiting more people to *die Bewegung* (the Movement), as Kühnen referred to his semiclandestine network. Henceforth, he would focus on developing contacts and spreading propaganda in the waning GDR.[2]

The thirty-three-year-old Kühnen frequently traveled back and forth between the two German states. He claimed he was "simply swamped" by admirers during a January 1990 visit to the East German city of Thuringia. That month, Kühnen and his right-hand men drew up a blueprint called *Arbeitsplan Ost* (Working Plan East), which divided the GDR into several organizing zones and assigned key personnel from the West to liaise within each region. Published in an internal neo-Nazi newsletter, *Die Neue Front (The New Front),* this plan described the stealth maneuvers necessary to launch several organizations that would not appear to be related to one another, including a legal political party designed to function as a front for National Socialists. "Behind all legal activity must stand a steel-hard, ideologically sound cadre unit" that would remain invisible to the uninitiated. "The outside should be told as little as possible about the cadre and its ideological stance," the document explained. "The cadre shall remain underground."[3]

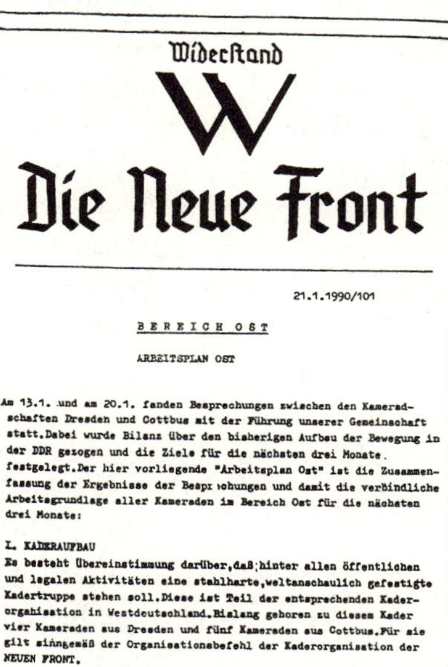

Widerstand

W

Die Neue Front

21.1.1990/101

B E R E I C H   O S T

ARBEITSPLAN OST

Am 13.1. und am 20.1. fanden Besprechungen zwischen den Kameradschaften Dresden und Cottbus mit der Führung unserer Gemeinschaft statt.Dabei wurde Bilanz über den bisherigen Aufbau der Bewegung in der DDR gezogen und die Ziele für die nächsten drei Monate festgelegt.Der hier vorliegende "Arbeitsplan Ost" ist die Zusammenfassung der Ergebnisse der Bespr›chungen und damit die verbindliche Arbeitsgrundlage aller Kameraden im Bereich Ost für die nächsten drei Monate:

I. KADERAUFBAU
Es besteht Übereinstimmung darüber,daß hinter allen öffentlichen und legalen Aktivitäten eine stahlharte,weltanschaulich gefestigte Kadertruppe stehen soll.Diese ist Teil der entsprechenden Kaderorgahisation in Westdeutschland.Bislang gehoren zu diesem Kader vier Kameraden aus Dresden und fünf Kameraden aus Cottbus.Für sie gilt sinngemäß der Organisationsbefehl der Kaderorganisation der NEUEN FRONT.

The Neue Front *newsletter that describes the "Working Plan East" of West German neo-Nazis*

Kühnen's allies established a squatters' house in the Lichtenberg section of East Berlin that became a makeshift residence for three hundred neo-Nazi skinheads, who often strayed into other parts of the city to beat up *Fidschis* (a generic term derived from *Fiji* that refers to anyone from the Third World). Armed with iron bars and baseball bats, they also engaged in fierce battles with antifascist youth, resulting in numerous injuries on both sides. Many of these attacks were instigated by members of the Nationale Alternative, which used the dingy Lichtenberg crash pad as its base of operations during the spring of 1990. Masterminded by Kühnen, the Nationale Alternative was one of several neo-Nazi groups that sprang up in East German cities and towns shortly after the Wall came down.[4]

Dressed in a bomber jacket and heavy black boots, Nationale Alternative chairman Ingo Hasselbach made fiery speeches in which he denounced immigrants, Jews, and other alleged enemies of the Fatherland. With his requisite blue eyes and chiseled features, the tall young German carried on as if he had gotten a call from central casting to be the local leader of the extreme Right. An East Berlin native, Hasselbach had rebelled against the Communist government as a teenager, becoming a hippie of sorts, then a spiky blond punk, before he gravitated toward the GDR's indigenous skinhead scene that had taken root over the previous decade. In early 1987, after butting heads with the authorities on various occasions, Hasselbach was sentenced to six months in prison for screaming, "The Wall must go!" at a public festival.[5]

After he was released from prison, Hasselbach joined the Lichtenberg Front, an East Berlin bonehead gang that dreamed of overthrowing the Communist regime and uniting the Fatherland. On the night of October 17, 1987, several chain-slinging members of this ultranationalist clique stormed a rock concert at the Zions Church, a popular meeting place for pacifists, anarchists, and other dissident youth who still identified with the socialist ideal. "We cleaned the church out," Hasselbach boasted. "We hauled the punks out and beat them up." Police units observed the bloody melee but did not intervene until the skinheads had fled. The delayed reaction of nearby law-enforcement personnel fueled speculation that the Stasi (East Germany's secret service) may have used the Lichtenberg Front to harass progressive groups. Bernd Wagner, the former head of an East Berlin police section that monitored extremist activity, subsequently confirmed that skinhead gangs had occasionally served as an instrument for attacking the nascent reform movement.[6]

GDR officials cynically attributed the violence that flared at the Zions Church to West-inspired hooliganism. Pointing the finger at Bonn was in keeping with a long history of denial by East German authorities, who dogmatically insisted that the GDR was not heir to the fascist side of German history. Nazism was supposedly a Western product — the most savage form of monopoly capitalism. And since the GDR was by definition anticapitalist, its population did not have to accept any blame for what had happened during the war. With the stroke of a rhetorical wand, millions of East Germans who had previously supported Hitler were alchemized into upstanding socialists. As a result, crucial psychological and political issues were never really confronted, much less worked through, in the GDR, whose leaders distorted and instrumentalized the past in an effort to legitimize the Communist system. Ignoring the primacy of Nazi racial policies, they claimed that those who died in concentration camps were mostly Communist resistance fighters; Jews, Gypsies, and homosexuals got short shrift. Viewed strictly in class terms, the Holocaust became one of many crimes committed by the capitalist Nazis. This is what Ingo Hasselbach and other East German youth learned by rote in school. Like their West German peers, students in the GDR were not encouraged to undertake a critical probe of the Hitler era.[7]

Contrary to its intended effect, East Germany's ritualized antifascism made reactionary ideas seem attractive to Hasselbach and his hoodlum buddies, who assumed that Nazi crimes were fabricated for Communist propaganda purposes. For these alienated youth, embracing the swastika was the most outlandish way to express their anger at an oppressive system. The fascist style they flaunted had less to do with hardened ideological convictions than a gut-level rebellion against the Communist authorities. For the most part, the skinhead underground in the GDR — which by the late 1980s had grown to include about fifteen hundred adherents — did not become politicized until the Berlin Wall crumbled and neo-Nazis from the West started to "educate" their East German counterparts. Hasselbach was approached by Michael Kühnen and his emissaries, who supplied combat boots, switchblades, imperial German war flags, racialist literature, and other neo-Nazi accoutrements. In the chaos that followed the fall of the Wall, the extreme Right began to thrive.[8]

Guided by the more experienced West German neo-Nazi leaders, disaffected juveniles in the GDR provided the muscle for an escalating series of street actions. After a soccer match in East Berlin on April 20, 1990 (the 101st anniversary of Adolf's birthday), six hundred boneheads went on a rampage, yelling, "Reds out!" and "Heil Hitler!" as they smashed shopwindows and attacked bystanders, who were shocked by the ferocious display of violence. A month later, a large group of skinheads gathered around the Marx-Engels memorial in Alexanderplatz, a prominent East Berlin landmark, where they formed a human swastika and pranced about ostentatiously while police watched warily from the sidelines. Similar demonstrations were staged in other cities, as marauding gangs of neo-Nazis ran amok throughout much of the GDR. Hateful outbursts of this sort coincided with an increasing number of skinhead attacks in West Germany during the run-up to unification, which was scheduled for October 3, 1990.[9]

Not all Germans were thrilled by the hasty merger. Fearing the growth of the radical Right, Günter Grass, Germany's preeminent postwar writer, reminded his countrymen "how convulsively they had succumbed to nationalism before." In the wake of Auschwitz, he argued, Germany was not — and could never be — worthy of the gift of reunification. Whereas some felt that Germany's past would serve as an inoculation against the spread of the neo-Nazi virus, Grass was less confident.[10]

The failure of many ordinary Germans to deal honestly with the Nazi era was a major theme of Grass's work. In his most famous novel, *The Tin Drum,* he describes a fictional nightclub where people needed onion-cutting rituals to help them cry a few tears. This inability to mourn and atone suggested that the Germany of yore, radical in its fantasies, was still festering under the thin cover of democracy and affluence in the West, where the acknowledgment of guilt for many people had been "reduced to irrelevant, belated, ritual expressions," said Grass. Those who did not work through the psychological impact of the past bequeathed it, consciously or not, to succeeding generations in the Bonn Republic as well as in the Stalinist GDR. Consider, for example, the results of a survey in the summer of 1990, which showed that more than a third of both East and West Germans felt they "need not be ashamed of the legacy of German fascism."[11]

Mounting racist violence since the Berlin Wall crumbled was a telling indication that Germany had yet to come to terms with its history. The incipient neo-Nazi revival in the Fatherland also served as a stimulus to ultra-right-wing movements in other European countries, where neofascists who used to whisper on the sidelines were starting to shout in public again. This development, however, was less of an immediate concern to Germany's neighbors than was the prospect of being dominated by an arrogant, economic bully in the middle of the Continent with reawakened dreams of great power status. No European government was particularly enthusiastic about German unification.

Qualms about Germany's intentions were exacerbated when Chancellor Kohl, playing to a domestic audience of right-wing expellees, dithered and dragged his feet before formally recognizing the Oder–Neisse line as Poland's western border. This was a sore point among neo-Nazis and other German revanchists, who maintained that unification would not be complete until Austria and the eastern territories were absorbed into the Fatherland. To make this point loud and clear, supporters of Michael Kühnen staged several noisy demonstrations near the Polish border.

When unification day finally arrived, it marked a watershed in the history of Europe. The bipolar order of the Yalta system was over, demagnetizing everybody's compass and providing fresh opportunities for neofascists in Germany and elsewhere. Across the globe, old certitudes had disappeared and new dangers were emerging.

Paramilitaries and Poison Gas

"We are here in Berlin, we are in the capital of the Reich," thundered Gottfried Küssel, his formidable, thirty-two-year-old jowls wobbling as he waved a fist and expounded upon the heroic struggle of the "political soldier." There he stood, a huge mass of flesh, preaching to a room full of young Nazis. "If our German racial soul would boil for once! It's still just lukewarm, it's got to get hot, it's got to boil! It must burn with love. . . . Let us hunger for victory and never be satisfied with less! Let us remain faithful, rock hard: you in the East, we in the West . . . and before you can blink, we will move on to Breslau, we will move on to Königsberg," he raved, referring to cities that were part of Germany during the Hitler period.[12]

A violent, menacing presence, Küssel was one of Michael Kühnen's top henchmen. Appointed as regional head of "the Eastern Borderlands," which is how neo-Nazis referred to Küssel's native

Austria, he oversaw the expansion of Kühnen's cadre network into Leipzig, Dresden, Cottbus, and other East German redoubts. Wherever Küssel surfaced, a racist outbreak was almost sure to follow. A convicted criminal who described Hitler as "the greatest man in German history," this blubbery, ultra-right-wing fanatic liked to sing songs about turning Jews into soap. If he had his way, Küssel proclaimed, he would put the entire German government in a concentration camp.[13]

Küssel was a frequent visitor at the skinhead squat in Lichtenberg. But Ingo Hasselbach didn't like being ordered about by Küssel, whose gruff, overbearing manner rankled some of the neo-Nazi locals. Several other leading Kühnenites also held court at Hasselbach's headquarters, but none carried as much weight, literally and figuratively, as Küssel. The beefy Austrian served as Kühnen's street army chief and was on the short list of candidates to succeed him as the de facto führer of the neo-Nazi underground. Infected with the HIV virus, Kühnen knew he did not have much time left. But he did not share his secret with any of his political associates.

One afternoon, Küssel dropped by the neo-Nazi crash pad in East Berlin with a dark-haired American friend, who wore a Hitler-style mustache and greeted everyone with a stiff-armed salute. His name was Gerhard Rex Lauck, and he ran a Nebraska-based outfit called the NSDAP-AO (National Socialist German Workers' Party — Foreign Section). The so-called Farm Belt Führer had worked closely with Kühnen since the mid-1970s. Most of the illegal neo-Nazi propaganda that circulated in Germany was supplied by this oafish American, who spoke English with a contrived German accent. ("I sink zat zeh Jews vehr treated a little too nicely in zeh concentration camps," Lauck hissed. "Personally, I'd say zat is a mistake ve should not make again.") By the early 1990s, Lauck was churning out massive quantities of hate literature in more than a dozen languages, including French, Dutch, Spanish, Portuguese, Danish, Swedish, Hungarian, Russian, and, of course, German and English. A pivotal figure in the international neo-Nazi underground, he also distributed computer diskettes that explained how to build bombs and wage a terrorist campaign. His other products included bumper stickers with swastikas and missives such as "We're back," which was certainly apropos.[14]

German neo-Nazis received other kinds of assistance from overseas. Küssel's deputy, Günter Reinthaler, traveled frequently to South America, where he collected donations from wealthy Nazi sympathizers. Some of the funds were used to purchase weapons from dwindling remnants of the once-powerful Soviet army, which was still posted in eastern Germany. Kalashnikov machine guns were sold openly for three hundred deutsche marks on the streets of Berlin, where demoralized Russian soldiers swapped grenades for a bottle of vodka. Neo-Nazis procured additional firepower and explosives by raiding Red Army installations. Stockpiled for future use, these munitions formed part of a deadly arsenal that included bazookas, dynamite, laser-controlled arms, and other sophisticated equipment. "Getting hold of weapons is not a problem. Never has been," Küssel boasted.[15]

Dressed in camouflage fatigues, Küssel's troops staged paramilitary drills in a forest near Vienna, where they learned various ways to kill. These practice sessions used straw dummies dressed as concentration camp inmates, with striped uniforms and yellow Jewish stars. Kühnen and his inner circle considered such maneuvers necessary preparation for Day X, when the inevitable armed confrontation would usher in the Fourth Reich.

But combat training was not for everyone who walked in the door. Most of the "babyskins," as the youngest of the lot were called, knew very little about Hitler or Nazism when they first got involved with the neofascist scene. Kühnen explicitly counseled his lieutenants against heavy-handed methods of indoctrination. Better to bring the newcomers along slowly by limiting political discussion in the early going to complaints about how the Allies continued to dominate Germany. To assuage their guilt and provoke their anger, teenage recruits were told that the Holocaust was a lie. At this stage, however, inculcating an ideology was less important than offering a sense of belonging and camaraderie to those in desperate need of a quick identity fix.

It was Kühnen's luck that many impressionable East German youth lost their bearings after the Wall collapsed. Confused and insecure, they were gradually introduced to the violent neo-Nazi subculture, a largely hidden world with its own language and mythology, its own heroes, and its own macabre rituals. The Brown brats played video games, which awarded points for killing foreigners and sending Jews to the gas chambers. They listened to music from skinhead bands that provided a way of bonding and attracting more people to the movement. About fifty hate-rock groups performed regularly in Germany; their songs, which were usually sold under the counter, celebrated violence and mayhem. A National Socialist orientation was evident in titles such as "New Storm Troopers," "Fetch the Rope," "Blood and Honor," "White Warrior," "Head Kicked In," "Rescue the Race," and "Adolf Hitler, I Love You."*

On November 9, 1990, Germany celebrated the first anniversary of the opening of the Berlin Wall amid a groundswell of right-wing extremist violence. Critics accused the authorities of burying history by neglecting to mention the other ninth of November — the Kristallnacht pogrom — in their public pronouncements. The following month, reunified Germany held its first nationwide parliamentary elections. Kohl and the Christian Democratic Union emerged victo-

* After they had shown sufficient enthusiasm for the cause, neo-Nazi enlistees were subjected to more intensive political education. Teaching aids included Third Reich propaganda films, such as *Der ewige Jude (The Eternal Jew),* which depicts Jews as rats and vermin. "Wherever rats turn up, they bring destruction with them. They destroy goods and foodstuffs and they spread disease. . . . Among animals, they represent an element of treacherous, subterranean destruction, just as Jews do among men," the narrator explains.

The hate-filled script had been written by Dr. Eberhard Taubert, one of Goebbels's assistants. Taubert was also a judge on the People's Tribunal, which handed down numerous death sentences during the Hitler era for "crimes" such as sleeping with a Jew. Like so many other Nazis, Taubert eluded punishment after the war. Instead, he found favor with the West German government and worked for the army's Division of Psychological Defense. He also served as a legal advisor to Fritz Ries, a wealthy industrialist who made a fortune from expropriating "Aryanized" Jewish property and from employing slave labor in factories near Auschwitz. Not only was Ries never condemned for his crimes but he went on to become the patron of several conservative West German politicians, including Helmut Kohl. As a token of his gratitude, Kohl gave Ries West Germany's highest civil decoration, the Bundesverdienstkreuz (Federal Cross of Merit). Another recipient of this award was Hermann Schlosser, chairman of Degussa, the company that invented and manufactured Zyklon B, the lethal nerve agent used in the gas chambers.

rious with 43.9 percent of the vote — by coincidence, the same percentage to the decimal point that Hitler and the Nazis polled on March 5, 1933, the last time an all-German vote was held. But no one likened Kohl to Hitler. The Hitler comparison was reserved for Iraqi dictator Saddam Hussein, whose army had recently invaded Kuwait.

As the United States rattled its saber and threatened Baghdad, Michael Kühnen contacted the Iraqi embassy in Bonn. His overtures culminated in a memorandum of agreement with Iraqi officials, which stipulated that Baghdad would finance and equip an anti-Zionist legion composed of neo-Nazi mercenaries from Germany and other countries. This so-called international Freedom Corps was supposed to assist Iraq if it came under attack by the United States. Kühnen, the designated commander of the volunteer brigade, praised Saddam Hussein as a freedom fighter: "We have common ideals — the creation of living spaces for different people and races in accordance with their own culture and tradition." Referring to Kuwait as "the Silesia of Iraq," Kühnen claimed that Arabs were not Marxists but nationalists "just like we are." Moreover, they had the same enemy — "the United States and its backers, the Zionist forces." But the martial prowess of the neo-Nazis, who pretentiously strutted around Baghdad in SS uniforms, left much to be desired. As soon as the bombs started to fall on the Iraqi capital, Kühnen's motley delegation scurried back to Europe.[16]

Kühnen and his clique were not the only fascists who supported Saddam during the 1991 Gulf War. The Republikaner Party dispatched a representative to Baghdad, where he was warmly received by Iraqi leaders. Jean-Marie Le Pen of the French Front National also got the red-carpet treatment when he met Saddam. And several British neo-Nazis ventured to Iraq shortly before the onset of the American-led blitzkrieg. South African white supremacists sent messages of support to Saddam as well. Not surprisingly, Kühnen was quick to applaud when Iraqi Scuds began hitting Israel. Even if Saddam Hussein used biological and chemical weapons, the German neo-Nazi chief maintained, he deserved respect for standing up to the United States.[17]

Kühnen's bluster on behalf of Iraq was curiously in synch with the covert policy that Bonn had been pursuing for nearly a decade.

With the full knowledge and cooperation of the federal government and its BND spy apparatus, dozens of German companies were instrumental in helping Saddam Hussein develop one of the world's most diversified unconventional-warfare arsenals. Several of West Germany's biggest firms supplied equipment and expertise to set up entire plants for the production of nuclear, chemical, and biological weaponry. Other countries, including the United States, cashed in on the macabre bonanza that created Iraq's high-tech death machine during the 1980s, but Bonn's role far outstripped the international competition. In addition to constructing Saddam's underground bunker and extending the range of the Scud missiles to be able to hit Israel, German engineers concocted new delivery systems for poison gas and dispensed advice on the most efficient way to enrich uranium into weapons-grade fuel for a nuclear bomb.[18]

West German corporations, including Siemens and other firms that had profited from slave labor in Nazi concentration camps, were also involved in the construction of a chemical-warfare factory in Rabta, Libya.* A key figure in this scheme was Volker Weissheimer, a shadowy Third Reich veteran whose wartime efforts in the area of "special weapons" development were personally praised by Hitler. Prior to formulating plans for the Libyan poison-gas plant, Weissheimer had worked with Otto Skorzeny on several business projects. (A brochure for the RMS–Volker Weissheimer Group once listed Skorzeny as its representative for Spain and North Africa.) After Hitler's favorite commando passed away, Weissheimer kept up the Nazi connection by attending annual meetings of a Skorzeny "old comrades" group at a Frankfurt hotel.[19]

Although West German officials were aware of BND intelligence reports regarding the nature of the Rabta facility, for several years Bonn took no action against the companies that supplied Libya with lethal technology. When the U.S. government demanded that

* While West German corporations lined up to facilitate Qaddafi's chemical-warfare schemes, the Libyan government maintained links with neofascist militants in several countries. In 1986, for example, a high-ranking Libyan embassy official in Madrid was expelled from Spain because of his role in aiding ultra-rightists in the Spanish military who were plotting to overthrow the government. During this period, Qaddafi was courted by neofascists from Great Britain, Italy, Switzerland, Argentina, Australia, Canada, and the United States.

a formal inquiry be undertaken, Chancellor Kohl accused Washington of launching a smear campaign against his country. After much stonewalling, Kohl finally admitted that German firms had created Qaddafi's chemical-weapons facility. "We always had flaps with the Germans about what they were peddling to Libya and other countries," recalled Douglas H. Jones, a U.S. foreign service officer. "They would sell chemicals for fertilizer, which were immediately reprocessed into something deadly. . . . Kohl would say that it wasn't something he had a lot of control over, but of course he did."[20]

More tensions between Washington and Bonn arose during the 1991 Gulf War. Disregarding the United Nations trade embargo, more than fifty German companies continued to provide Iraq with missile parts, chemical agents, and state-of-the-art engineering equipment right up until the United States attacked Baghdad. Once again, Chancellor Kohl ignored repeated requests by the U.S. government to probe these illicit business transactions. Later it would be disclosed that the BND had trained Iraqi and Libyan secret-police units.[21]

Germany's willingness to go its own way in the international arena would result in sharp arguments with its Western allies in the months ahead.

Groomed to Be Führer

On April 8, 1991, a hundred youths in ski masks converged upon Frankfurt an der Oder, a city in eastern Germany that straddles the Polish border. They had come to denounce the opening of the border to Polish tourists without visas. The demonstration had been flagged a few days earlier in a local flyer, which carried an advertisement about "Führer Kühnen" under the headline THE NEO-NAZIS ARE COMING TO ODER. Undeterred by the presence of police, a horde of *sieg-heiling* assailants threw rocks and beer bottles at cars and buses. Dozens of people were injured by flying glass as they tried to cross into Germany. Skinheads assaulted Polish travelers in several other German towns that month, prompting Polish officials to issue a formal protest to the German ambassador in Warsaw about the violence and the inaction of German law-enforcement personnel.

The Polish border flare-up was Michael Kühnen's last hurrah. Weakened by AIDS, the emaciated neo-Nazi leader realized the end was near. For a while, he claimed his weight loss was due to a strenuous exercise regimen. But his closest friend, Christian Worch, knew something was wrong. With fanatical determination, Kühnen continued his political work until he could barely walk on his own. Unable to conceal his illness any longer, he told Worch the truth.[22]

On April 25, 1991, Kühnen died at a hospital in Kassel. Agence France Presse described Kühnen postmortem as "the most prominent and eloquent supporter of Nazism since World War II." To his followers, he was a kind of neo-Nazi Moses who led them toward the promised land of National Socialism without getting there himself.[23]

Dozens of prominent figures in the ultra-right-wing scene attended Kühnen's graveside ceremony in Kassel. Included among those who came to pay their respects was a representative of Stille Hilfe, an organization founded forty years earlier to provide financial and material assistance for Third Reich veterans convicted of war crimes. An arm of the international postwar SS self-help network, Stille Hilfe was originally headed by Dr. Rudolf Aschenauer, the Nuremberg defense attorney and Socialist Reich Party booster. H. Keith Thompson served as the point man for Stille Hilfe in the United States. He was still contributing money to this group when Kühnen croaked. In a gesture that underscored the link between the old guard and the younger generation of neo-Nazi militants, Stille Hilfe laid a burial wreath that bore the SS motto: "Michael Kühnen — his honor is loyalty."[24]

The death of Kühnen created a leadership void just when the neo-Nazi movement was picking up steam. By then, brutal hate crimes had become a daily occurrence in reunified Germany, where racism was alive and — literally — kicking. A lot of random thuggery ensued, including a wave of head-cracking incidents that entailed booting someone's skull as though it were a soccer ball. Much of it was copycat violence triggered by organized neo-Nazi militants engaging in the sustained harassment of Gypsies and other ethnic minorities. Arson attacks against immigrant hostels, the proliferation of skinhead gangs, the desecration of concentration camp memorials and Red Army monuments — all were expressions of a neofascist resurgence that had gathered momentum since the Berlin Wall fell. But instead of focusing on the big picture, Kühnen's minions often argued over irrelevant questions, such as whether it was politically correct for a German nationalist to eat Italian pizza or Chinese food.

More important issues were at stake when 250 neo-Nazis met in Cottbus, an eastern city in Brandenburg, on May 1, a week after Kühnen passed away. The purpose of this gathering was to plot strategy and choose a new leader in light of Kühnen's departure. He had bequeathed a diffuse and mixed array of groups with different names in every region of the country; although they appeared to operate as distinct entities, they were linked by a secret, nationwide cell structure known informally as the Gesinnungsgemeinschaft der Neuen Front (Patriotic Community of the New Front). Gottfried Küssel, the corpulent Austrian brute, was named to succeed Kühnen as head of the New Front. But Küssel was arrested and placed in preventive detention by Austrian authorities before the fledgling führer could prove himself. He was later sentenced to a ten-year prison term.[25]

With Küssel behind bars, a neo-Nazi junta composed of a handful of individuals took control of the Kühnen network and its multiple cover groups. The real brains behind the scenes was Christian Worch, a moonfaced millionaire with deep-set eyes whose considerable organizational talents made up for his drab personality. As the executor of Kühnen's will and his most trusted longtime associate, Worch was widely respected within the ultra-right-wing scene. Having already spent four years in prison, he knew what advice to give his peers so that they could flaunt their virulent views without technically breaking the law. (One trick was to use the so-called Kühnen salute at demonstrations, which entailed raising a stiff arm Nazi-style, but with only three fingers extended.) Described by U.S. Army intelligence as "a violent neo-Nazi," Worch lived in an upscale Hamburg apartment protected by a vaultlike steel door. There he held sway as the thirty-four-year-old boss of a local extremist troupe called the National List. His personal hero was Joseph Goebbels, the Nazi propaganda chief, "because he was a kind of artist," Worch explained. "He made politics like other people make art."[26]

Unlike many of his comrades, Worch knew his own limitations. For the most part, he was content to pull strings in the background while several would-be führers vied for the spotlight. Although just in his mid-twenties, Frank Hübner seemed to have all the makings of a prime contender for the neo-Nazi throne. A former East German hoodlum with the magnetic presence of a film star, Hübner was the up-and-coming leader of the Deutsche Alternative (German Alternative), created by Kühnen shortly before he died. Clad in a jacket and tie, Hübner presided over weekly beer hall sessions in Cottbus, where the denizens of Deutsche Alternative congregated. These ultranationalist zealots denounced race mixing as "ethnic murder" and called for nothing less than a return to the German borders of 1410, when the Holy Roman Empire was at its peak! Hübner's main drawback was his lack of experience — he had been involved with the Kühnen network only since 1989.[27]

This handicap did not apply to Bela Ewald Althans, another young, neo-Nazi leader who exuded charisma. Althans had already chalked up a decade of training as a hard-core militant, including several years in which he studied at the feet of his erstwhile master, Major General Otto Ernst Remer. Althans later formed his own group, the German Youth Education Enterprise, which attracted a bevy of leather-jacketed followers. Fluent in English and French and capable of conversing in a sophisticated manner, he was definitely a rising star among right-wing extremists in Germany.

After the Berlin Wall fell, the twenty-three-year-old Althans emerged as a kind of self-styled press secretary for the neo-Nazi movement. From a well-equipped office in Munich, he ran his own public-relations firm, selling racialist literature, buttons, and stickers to support his political habit. Situated in a ritzy neighborhood preferred by attorneys and accountants, Althans's neo-Nazi headquarters was easy to spot thanks to a large picture of Adolf Hitler easily visible through a street-level window. "This is open National Socialism," he proclaimed in a 1992 interview. "I like to provoke people."[28]

An imposing presence at six foot four with short blond hair and blue eyes, Althans oozed confidence as he spoke freely about his hatred of Jews and foreigners, his determination to take back the so-called eastern territories, his steadfast devotion to Hitler's legacy ("I am living proof that Hitler can happen again!"), and his overall excitement about the burgeoning neo-Nazi movement. "I could use my intelligence to get a job in this system, make a lot of money, and have fun," he asserted. "But I don't want it. Because I'm thinking of the future. I'm thinking about power. I'm thinking that the system is dying, and when the system is dying, people will look for heroes."

Sprinkling his discourse with quotes from Nietzsche and other writers, Althans personified the suave new face of German extremism — the Yuppie neo-Nazi with a taste for vintage champagne, whose polished manners and smooth intellect seemed worlds apart from the rabble of swastika-tattooed skinheads that were wreaking havoc throughout Germany. Quick to condescend, Althans referred derisively to violent neo-Nazi lumpen as lowbrow types "with little understanding of Hitler." But he acknowledged their utility as cannon fodder for the cause. "If the boys didn't kick up a row, nobody would bother listening to me," Althans quipped.[29]

By his own account, Althans was born into "a typical middle-class family" in Hanover, West Germany. His father and stepmother had raised him to reject Nazism and respect the government, but Althans rebelled at an early age. When he was thirteen, he fell under the influence of a group of Third Reich veterans who recognized his leadership potential and groomed him to fulfill their dream of resurrecting National Socialism. Althans was tutored in Nazi philosophy, oratory style, and secret party lore. "I became fascinated by the Führer's genius. He created a classless society and prepared the way for a supercivilization," said Althans, who studied old films of Hitler, memorized parts of his speeches, and learned to mimic his gestures.

Teaming up with Michael Kühnen in the early 1980s, Althans directed the Hanover branch of the Action Front of National Socialists before it was banned by the government. When Kühnen went to prison, Althans searched for a new mentor. Expelled from high school and disowned by his parents, the teenage militant went to live with Ernst Remer, who had recently moved to Bad Kissingen, a small town in the Bavarian mountains. "Remer is a political father figure to me. He's a living part of history," Althans acknowledged. "I became part of his family. He helped me get my feet on the ground. He provided me with a home when I had nowhere else to go."

Remer influenced an entire generation of neo-Nazi juveniles, but none more so than Althans, who became his prime pupil. The old Nazi took Althans under his wing, showed him how to set up a political cell, and introduced him to key figures in the international fascist underground. Ewald (he preferred his middle name because it sounded more Teutonic) emerged as the leader of the youth section of the Freedom Movement, the group Remer established in the mid-1980s to push for a new Rapallo agreement between Germany and the Soviet Union. "The most important thing Remer taught me was the idea that Germany needs Russia," Althans explained. "This was also Bismarck's thinking."

Remer counseled his protégé on various matters and introduced him to books that Althans, a voracious reader, had never heard of. One of the texts that Remer touted was by a little-known author named Ulick Varange. He gave Althans a copy of Yockey's *Imperium* and told him to read it carefully. "It's important," Remer insisted.

The political education Althans received from Remer convinced him that his country had been hoodwinked by corrupt historians, journalists, and government officials who were bent on making Germans feel shame and guilt for what transpired during the Nazi era. It was all part of a master plot, according to Remer, to justify reparation payments to Israel and postwar domination by the United States. "Germany has been colonized by America, and people are sick of it," said Althans. "We must eradicate everything that is alien, non-German, from our culture."

In September 1988, while still working with Remer, Althans made the first of several trips to the United States. He lived for a month in the Howard Beach section of Brooklyn, the site of a highly publicized racist attack that resulted in the death of a black teenager. Then he bought a '57 Chevrolet and drove across country to southern California, where he stayed with Tom Metzger, a former Ku Klux Klan Grand Dragon who had become the guru of America's neo-Nazi bonehead scene. Although he praised skinheads as "frontline warriors," Metzger always wore a toupee. Aptly described as a "pied piper of hate," he headed a group called the White Aryan Resistance (WAR), which staged several "Reich 'n' roll" concerts, including a sparsely attended "Aryan Woodstock." Vowing to "take the game away from the Left," WAR promoted environmental politics, working-class unionism, and racial solidarity between white people in the United States and Russia.

Although Metzger claimed to be a follower of Nazi heretic Gregor Strasser, he was a cordial host to Ewald, the young Hitlerite. Althans appeared on Metzger's weekly cable-access television program, *Race and Reason,* which aired in several American cities. Shortly after Althans visited Metzger, an Ethiopian man was beaten to death by skinheads in Portland, Oregon. Metzger was subsequently convicted of inciting this fatal assault, which WAR's telephone hotline had praised as a "civic duty."[30]

Metzger and Althans both admired Black Muslim minister Louis Farrakhan, whose anti-Semitism and message of racial separation appealed to many neo-Nazis. "He's someone I really like," said Althans, who agreed with Farrakhan's assessment that Jews were a deleterious influence in the United States. The Jews, Althans insisted, controlled everything from the White House to Wall Street and the news media. The Jews ran Hollywood. They even ran the movie industry in Germany. "We want a Germany for the Germans, not for the Jews," he whined.[31]

At one point, Althans interrupted his predictable anti-Semitic tirade and conceded that there was something he respected about Jewish people: "They can laugh at themselves. Germans absolutely cannot laugh at themselves."

"Ewald, you seem to have a good sense of humor. Maybe you have some Jewish blood in you," I suggested.

"No, I don't think so," he shot back with an intense glare. "I've investigated it. I'm sure this is not the case."

"Well, I guess you proved your point about Germans being serious, since I was only joking."

Althans looked deadpan for a moment, then burst out laughing.

Cadre Building

Eight hundred guests were carousing inside Munich's smoke-filled Löwnbräukeller, one of the biggest and most famous beer halls in Bavaria. Shafts of afternoon sunlight beamed through huge windows at the front of the building as a phalanx of young men in bomber jackets stood near the speaker's platform, hoisting imperial war flags and signs that proclaimed *"Warhheit macht frei!"* ("The truth will make you free!") The slogan was a variation on the concentration camp maxim *"Arbeit macht frei"* ("Work will make you free"). Suddenly several people wearing donkey outfits entered the hall and scampered between the tables. To the delight of the assembled clan, the masked marauders had come to mock the Nazi holocaust. Those who accept the fact that 6 million Jews perished during World War II were depicted as donkeys who will believe anything.

Held on April 20, 1990, the negationist conclave in Munich was organized by Bela Ewald Althans, who chose that date because it was Hitler's birthday. A rogues' gallery of Nazi apologists responded to Althans's invitation, including Otto Ernst Remer, who had slowed down considerably in recent months after suffering a stroke. One of the last surviving links to the Hitler era, Remer was greeted respectfully by his younger colleagues at the Löwnbräukeller. Although many of the attendees had argued bitterly among themselves in the past, they put aside their differences on this occasion to emphasize a common theme, as summed up by the ever quotable Althans: "The [H]olocaust is a fabrication, the pictures of the dead, of gas chambers, of mass murder are filmed by Hollywood, narrated by Trevor Roper, and directed by Hitchcock."[32]

The negationist convention in Munich was a blatant violation of German law, which forbids outright Holocaust denial.* But the proprietors of the Löwnbräukeller made arrangements with the po-

* In 1985, after years of legal wrangling, the Bundestag passed a Holocaust-denial bill, which — in keeping with the tendency among mainstream politicians to relativize Auschwitz — equated the postwar expulsion of Germans from Eastern Europe with the Nazi Holocaust.

lice not to intervene, and the keynote speaker, British author David Irving, pooh-poohed Nazi atrocities in a joke-filled address that drew a standing ovation from the audience. Some of Irving's historical analysis may have also rung true to Chancellor Helmut Kohl, who gave one of his speechwriters a book by the British negationist as a Christmas gift.[33]

Among Irving's closest allies in Germany was a squat, balding rabble-rouser named Karl Philipp, who looked like Friar Tuck in lederhosen. At fifty years of age, Philipp was a major muckety-muck in the revisionist scene. His political résumé included contributions to *CODE*, an ultra-right-wing monthly edited by Ekkehard Franke-Gricksch. (Ekkehard's father, Alfred Franke-Gricksch, was the pro-Russian leader of the Bruderschaft who mysteriously disappeared while on an undercover mission in East Berlin in the early 1950s.) Franke-Gricksch junior attended the negationist conclave in Munich along with Karl Philipp, who helped Althans organize the event.[34]

After Remer suffered a stroke, Philipp emerged as his part-time minder. He was usually present at Remer's side when the Nazi octagenarian entertained queries from journalists at his home in Bad Kissingen. Fortified by several rounds of schnapps, Remer held court in his living room, where a bust of Bismarck, a large photograph of Hitler, and a medallion from the Socialist Reich Party were prominently on display. With little prompting, he told me of his eternal affection for the Führer and his fanatical hatred of the Jews: "They are our deadly enemies. They have no business being here. They all must be killed!"[35]

"Now, now," said Philipp, gently admonishing his elder. "We really don't want to kill anyone, do we?"

Remer proceeded to recount various episodes of his postwar career. He talked about the time he spent in Egypt as an advisor to Nasser and the smuggling operations he conducted on behalf of the Algerian rebels. He also spoke highly of his good friend Otto Skorzeny.

Remer was quick to offer his opinion of various leaders in the Middle East. When the United States bombed Tripoli, allegedly in retaliation for a terrorist attack in West Berlin, he denounced Reagan's "gangster tactics."

"What about Qaddafi?"

"He's a good man, a little crazy perhaps, but he knows what he wants."

"And the Ayatollah Khomeini?"

"Anyone who makes trouble for the United States is very welcome."

Inevitably, the conversation turned toward Russia, which Remer still saw as the great white hope. "The survival of the white race is at stake," he insisted. "Russians are white people. They are a hundred times closer to us than the fucking Americans, who are mixed."

After two hours, Remer retired to his den to watch the news on television. Shaking his head, he exclaimed after one report, "We need another Hitler to set things straight." A few minutes later, the Führer's bodyguard dozed off.

While he snored away, several elderly women downstairs in the basement were stuffing envelopes with books, videotapes, pamphlets, and copies of the general's own newsletter, *Remer Despeche* (*Remer Dispatch*), which harped on the "myth" of the Holocaust. "There were no gas chambers. There was no genocide against the Jews," the *Dispatch* droned. When Iraqi Scud missiles enhanced by German technicians began to hit Israel during the 1991 Gulf War, Remer claimed that the attacks were fabricated by Jews to extract more money from Bonn. In an open letter to German president Richard von Weizsäcker, he ranted: "For year after year, you have eaten crow for these very special Jewish liars, which has made many upstanding Germans vomit. . . ."[36]

Remer's pro-Nazi and anti-Semitic declarations triggered a long-running legal battle with the Federal Republic. In 1985, he was convicted of defaming the dead by distributing material that claimed the Holocaust was a ruse. Angered by this verdict, Remer referred to the governing Christian Democrats as "toads." Ordered on procedural grounds, a retrial was postponed because of Remer's poor health. A regional court later sentenced him to a twenty-two-month prison term for inciting and spreading racial hatred. But Remer continued to publish his *Dispatch* while free pending appeal.

When Remer awoke from his early-afternoon snooze, lunch was served and more conversation followed in the living room. "I see very big opportunities for us," he said during an April 1992 interview in response to a question about the neo-Nazi revival in Germany. But he admitted that he had mixed feelings about the skinhead scene: "I don't like the image they produce, but a political fight starts with all kinds of people, everyone who is available." As for the former German Democratic Republic: "There are a lot of young people, especially from East Germany, who are interested in political activism. Many of them have a healthier way of thinking and are not as corrupted by money as people are in the west."

"What is the biggest problem for the neo-Nazis?" I asked.

"We have no strong leader," he replied.

Remer had once hoped Bela Ewald Althans would grow into such a role, but his disciple had let him down. "Althans lived in this house. My wife and I tried to raise him the right way. He is smart and he could have become someone," Remer lamented, shaking his head as his voice trailed off.

Clearly, he felt betrayed by Althans, who left the Freedom Movement after Hitler's former bodyguard had suffered a stroke. Remer's influence in the neo-Nazi scene diminished on account of his deteriorating condition. But he was too stubborn to admit that he lacked the stamina to engage in protracted political struggle. "He still could give a rousing speech for fifteen minutes," said Althans. "His role could have been that of an elder statesman, but he was not interested in this. He always wanted to be the general. A person like Remer cannot accept that a younger person with less experience has taken over his part."

Since the fall of the Wall, Althans functioned as a roving ambassador for the neo-Nazi cause. In this capacity, he conferred regularly with right-wing extremists in Europe, North and South America, and South Africa. His contacts in France included Ivan Blot, a close aide to Front National chief Jean-Marie Le Pen — even though Le Pen insisted that his party had nothing to do with neo-Nazis. Althans also befriended the leaders of CEDADE, the Spanish neo-Nazi group that Otto Skorzeny had helped establish. Every November, CEDADE held a public rally in honor of General Francisco Franco that attracted a large crowd of fascists from many countries. Althans and other Germans participated in this annual pilgrimage, which provided an opportunity to develop new connections and deepen old ones.[37]

Several of Althans's international associates began traveling to Germany each year to commemorate the death of Rudolf Hess, Hitler's deputy, who ended decades of incarceration in 1987 by hanging himself with an electric cord at age ninety-three. The Hess memorial soon became an important touchstone and international networking opportunity for neofascists. In August 1991, two thousand ultrarightists flocked to Bayreuth to participate in a Hess demonstration, which had been organized by Christian Worch and publicized beforehand by Althans. Prior to German unification, it was unthinkable that such a large number of neo-Nazi militants could parade in public with swastikas and banners. But times had changed quickly, much to the delight of Althans and his comrades.

Althans belonged to an elite coterie of young neo-Nazi leaders who were pumping fresh blood into the far Right in Germany. According to Germany's internal spy service, the Verfassungsschutz, the number of organized right-wing extremists shot up from thirty-two thousand in 1990 to forty thousand in 1991 (and this figure did not include the twenty-eight thousand members of the Republikaner Party, which was not officially listed as an extremist organization). About five thousand hard-core neo-Nazis constituted the knife's edge of the radical Right spectrum, which encompassed as many as seventy-six different organizations.

Never far from a car phone or fax, Althans dashed around the country in his BMW, weaving a web of contacts in an effort to unify a myriad of extremist groups and forge them into a trenchant political force capable of challenging the German government. He even collaborated with far Right political parties that eschewed the neo-Nazi label while playing the parliamentary game. This tactical compromise did not bother Althans, who described his main task as "cadre building." "We are doing cadre work," he explained. "That means inside of any nationalist group in Germany I have two or three people and through them I can take my influence. That makes me dangerous politically because I have people in place everywhere."

Althans and Worch also mended fences with neo-Nazis who had opposed Kühnen because of his homosexuality. Kühnen's death made it easier for hitherto antagonistic factions to reconcile. "There are distinctions between nationalist groups," Worch acknowledged. "Everybody has their own ideas about National Socialism and what it means. But the differences between us are very small, while the differences between us and our enemies are great."[38]

Neo-Nazi strategists saw a chance to advance their cause, as East Germany made the whiplash transition from Communism to capitalism. By mid-1992, unemployment in the former GDR hovered at 40 percent.* The euphoria of their newfound freedom quickly faded as the standard of living among easterners plummeted. Hundreds of thousands of civil servants — which in East Germany included everyone from schoolteachers to janitors and government bureaucrats — were purged from the workforce, as Bonn embarked upon a frenetic campaign to exorcise Communists from positions of influence. This effort was a marked contrast to West Germany's reluctance to denazify after World War II.

When the better times promised by Chancellor Kohl showed no signs of arriving, many easterners became disillusioned with democracy and nostalgic for the bad old days of the GDR, with its guaranteed work and social services. The number of marriages dropped, birthrates fell, crime soared, and health care centers were inundated by people unable to cope with the angst of an uncertain future. Compounding the trauma were property claims by West Germans, who sought to repossess 5 million homes in the east. The ensuing legal wrangles exacerbated a nasty postunity hangover, which put the east-west relationship under considerable strain. Easterners felt like second-class citizens, and their western cousins resented having to pay higher taxes to help rebuild the former GDR's shattered

* With a mandate from Bonn to administer former state properties in the ex-GDR and prepare them for privatization, a government office known as the Treuhand proceeded to ravage an already frail eastern economy. The Treuhand shut down numerous firms, even profitable ones, without seeing if they could be salvaged, leaving millions of people jobless and demoralized. Hundreds of other enterprises were sold to big West German corporations at ridiculously low prices. The grand theft of East German assets continued despite protests and hunger strikes. Instead of reaping profits that were supposed to be distributed to residents of the former GDR, the Treuhand ran up a large debt and helped turn the region into an industrial wasteland.

economy. "Why are the Chinese happier than Germans?" the joke went. "Because they still have their wall."[39]

Among the hardest hit by all the changes were young eastern Germans. The state-supported cinemas and youth clubs they once frequented were shut down after the collapse of the GDR. Bored and frustrated, they became easy prey for clever neo-Nazi manipulators like Ewald Althans, whose antidemocratic diatribes were often tinged with violent overtones. "Everywhere in the world they are trying to install democracy without success," said Althans. "But the people in the east are no more free than they were before. They have changed their old, rusted chains for new, golden ones. In Germany we say, 'Russia stole the liberty, but America steals the soul.' For us, National Socialism is the only way out." He predicted that with the demise of Communism, "capitalism is going to collapse faster now."

The vulgar anticapitalism espoused by Althans touched a raw nerve in the bleak east, where neo-Nazi agitators found a mass constituency receptive to their pitch. Althans's message appealed to many down-and-out youth, in part because it offered an aggressive national identity to replace that of a vanished country. His attempts to blame their plight on guest workers and asylum seekers seemed all the more reasonable given that Helmut Kohl and other mainstream politicians had begun to scapegoat the same targets.

The Deutsche Mob

In an effort to divert attention from his government's broken promises and its mismanagement of the unification process, Chancellor Kohl pointed a politically expedient finger at foreigners. He and other CDU leaders understood the popular potential of racially tinged nationalism, and they could not resist the temptation to snatch votes by promoting misconceptions, half-truths, and outright lies about refugees, who were portrayed as competitors in the fight for scarce resources at a time when so many Germans were needy. Approximately 6 million foreigners, including nearly 2 million Turkish guest workers, lived in Germany, which had a total population of 77 million.

"Germany is no immigration country," Kohl declared time and time again while neglecting to point out that guest workers, who were welcomed en masse during the economic boom of the late 1950s and early 1960s, contributed much more in taxes, social security, and pension payments than they received from the state. Although asylum seekers were legally forbidden the right to work in Germany, they were accused of stealing jobs. Mouthing neofascist catchphrases, prominent Christian Democrats linked foreigners to drug-pushing, welfare fraud, and violent crime.[40]

Privately, however, key members of Kohl's inner circle acknowledged that immigration was a bogus issue. Wolfgang Schäuble, the hard-line CDU leader who headed negotiations between the two Germanys that led to unification, candidly told a high-ranking U.S. official that Germany had the economic means to successfully absorb large numbers of refugees (438,000 arrived in 1992 alone). It was an astonishing confession by Schäuble, who had been confined to a wheelchair as a result of an assassination attempt. In effect, he had acknowledged that the government's antiforeigner campaign was driven primarily by political concerns. Officials in Bonn seized upon the "problem" of asylum seekers as a smokescreen to hide their own policy failures.[41]

Seeking to save his own political neck and outflank his far Right rivals, Kohl exploited the presence of foreigners for all it was worth. Top CDU officials claimed the only way to prevent a flood of immigrants from deluging the country was to repeal the constitutional provision that guaranteed the right of asylum for all political refugees — a law that had been adopted in atonement for the crimes of the Third Reich.

Incessant talk within the German government and news media about "fake asylum seekers" was music to the ears of Bela Ewald Althans. For years, neo-Nazi militants had railed against immigration, and now Kohl and his ilk were singing the same tune. By adopting the rhetoric of the far Right, mainstream politicians incited an atmosphere of racial hatred. "The neo-Nazis took this as a signal," said Graeme Atkinson, a special investigator for the European Parliament's Commission of Inquiry on Racism and Xenophobia. "It legitimized their views and gave them the green light to step up their attacks."[42]

Eager to instrumentalize the asylum question, the government of Helmut Kohl was deeply implicated in the neofascist resurgence that occurred in Germany after the Wall fell. Günter Grass went so far as to liken members of Kohl's cabinet to "white collar skinheads" who were even more dangerous than the ultra-right-wing street gangs. "They are nicely dressed with beautiful hair. They speak well. But they think in the same way as the young kids who shave their heads and carry swastikas and demonstrate," said Grass. "They encourage these ideas and these brutal actions."[43]

On September 19, 1991, violence erupted in Hoyerswerda, a desolate eastern German factory city of seventy thousand. The trouble began when a gang of unemployed skinheads pelted a hostel for Asian and African guest workers with rocks, beer bottles, and Molotov cocktails. As news of the assault spread throughout the region, the Deutsche Alternative and other ultra-right-wing groups quickly mobilized their troops. More than a hundred neo-Nazis from out of town joined the rabble in Hoyerswerda as a crowd of local residents stood nearby and applauded. The mood was both jovial and mean-spirited as right-wing extremists marched arm in arm, waving Third Reich flags and shouting *"Auslander raus!"* ("Foreigners out!") — a chant redolent of the Third Reich refrain *"Juden raus!"* ("Jews out!") They surrounded a dormitory where political refugees were housed, letting loose a torrent of projectiles. When some of the asylum seekers tried to escape, they were beaten mercilessly by the mob.

Not until four days after the pogrom began did the police arrive to evacuate the asylum seekers. Townsfolk jeered insults and threw stones at the buses as they departed. Hoyerswerda was now foreigner-free. Instead of fighting the neo-Nazis with the full power of the state, the German authorities had bowed to their demands.

Having tasted blood, the Deutsche mob was not easily sated. Neo-Nazis went ballistic, stabbing immigrants on street corners, burning children to death in their homes, and beating up "non-Germans" in dozens of cities and towns. It was as if an ugly, prurient glee had been unleashed throughout the country. Attacks on dark-skinned foreigners were particularly brutal, resulting in several fatalities. According to official sources, there were 1,483 violent racist incidents in 1991 — a tenfold increase over the combined figure for the two Germanys during the previous year.[44]

But Chancellor Kohl maintained that there was no cause for alarm. His government continually downplayed the dangers of right-wing extremism and censored those who dissented from the party line, which went as follows: racist attacks were unorganized, spontaneous outbursts by bored and aimless individuals or small groups of drunken youth who lacked a political motivation. Bernd Wagner, the head of a police unit that monitored ultra-right-wing activity in the five eastern states, was dismissed from his job at the end of 1991 after he explicitly linked the wave of brutal assaults to neo-Nazi organizations. Kohl, it seemed, had other fish to fry. In a classic case of blaming the victim, the chancellor continued to insist that the violence was caused by the presence of too many foreigners in Germany. In the spring of 1992, he stunned everyone by declaring that Germany was on the verge of a "national state of emergency" because of the refugee invasion, which had replaced the Red Army as the immediate threat from the East.

While Kohl pushed forward with the CDU crusade to alter the German constitution, neo-Nazis who mauled foreigners were treated as misbehaving children rather than as political terrorists. The response to the Hoyerswerda pogrom typified the lassitude of German law-enforcement personnel, who frequently failed to respond to pleas for help when immigrants came under attack. The government claimed that police in eastern Germany were understaffed, poorly trained, and therefore unprepared to handle large-scale riots. Another unspoken factor was that many police sympathized with the neofascists. Eighty-nine officers in a sample study of two hundred auxiliary police in Berlin had either a criminal or a fascist background, and many participated in paramilitary exercises sponsored by right-wing extremists. Other surveys disclosed that 60 percent of the police in Hesse and 50 percent in Bavaria (two western states) supported the aims of the extreme Right Republikaner Party.[45]

Racist law-enforcement officers often watched passively as neo-Nazis brutalized immigrants. In some cases, the police actually joined the fray and assaulted the same targets after skinheads left the scene. Amnesty International and other human rights organizations condemned what they saw as a pattern of police brutality in unified Germany. "At a time when foreign nationals and ethnic minorities in Germany need to feel the police are there to protect them, many have felt instead a police officer's fist, boot or baton," Amnesty concluded.[46]

Manfred Kanther, Germany's Christian Democratic interior minister, summarily rejected the Amnesty probe. But Jürgen Bulga of the National Working Group of Critical Police Officers, attested to the existence of "a thoroughly aggressive climate" against foreigners within German law enforcement and maintained that Amnesty's findings represented just "the tip of the iceberg." The Nigerian government went a step further, lodging a formal protest with the United Nations and the German government over the deaths of thirty-one Nigerian citizens in German police custody, most of whom died of brain hemorrhages. Hanoi also protested to Bonn about the lack of protection for Vietnamese citizens, who had been repeatedly attacked since the Wall fell.[47]

When police arrested neo-Nazis for engaging in criminal violence, the assailants were usually released after a few hours. Back on the street, many quickly resumed their racist attacks. Those who stood trial tended to get off lightly, as evidenced by countless examples: Karl Polacek, a neo-Nazi chieftan in Lower Saxony, received an eight-month suspended sentence for bloodying a female antifascist with an axe; ten members of the Hamburg-based National List, led by Christian Worch, got suspended sentences for the savage beating of a pregnant Vietnamese woman; ten other rightists were given suspended sentences after they burned down a hostel for asylum seekers in August 1991. Even murderers could count on scandalously lenient treatment, as long as they claimed that they were drunk at the time (which is what their gang leaders instructed them to say). A group of neo-Nazis were sentenced to two-to-four years in youth detention for beating to death an Angolan guest worker in Eberwald. One of the defendants testified that the police stood by and did nothing while the African man was pummeled senseless. Asserting that there was no political dimension to the case, the judge described their actions as a "typical youthful misdemeanor."[48]

Occasionally harsher sentences were meted out, as when two

skinheads killed a German sea captain because he made a negative comment about Adolf Hitler. For the most part, however, neo-Nazi youth were pampered by the courts, leading to complaints by legal experts that the German criminal-justice system was "blind in the right eye." "Punishment for violent crimes has become progressively less severe. When there is a political motive, a rightist defendant is usually treated more gently than one who comes from the Left," remarked Herman Blei, a law professor at the Free University in Berlin. He added, "We are seeing the results of trends that have existed here for decades."[49]

The coddling of ultra-right-wing offenders dated back to the early years of the Bonn Republic, which stacked its courts with hanging judges who were responsible for dispensing Hitler's justice. Virtually the entire West German judiciary had served the Nazi state, but these arbiters of racial hatred hardly got a spanking after the war, even though they had ordered the execution of forty-five thousand people for dubious reasons. Reinstated in West German courtrooms, they polluted the climate of German jurisprudence throughout the Cold War and later.[50]

The actions — or lack thereof — by the police and the courts, which generally followed the agenda set by politicians in Bonn, only served to encourage additional fits of neo-Nazi depravity. A group of radical rightists, led by the local Republikaner chief in Zittau, stormed a hostel that housed Ukrainian children suffering from radiation sickness due to the Chernobyl nuclear disaster. Even gorier, a neo-Nazi gang grabbed a Polish tourist in Berlin's Tiergarten district and sliced out a third of his tongue with a pair of flower-cutting shears. Adding insult to injury, the partially tongueless Pole received an expensive bill from the hospital after undergoing an emergency operation.[51]

"One speaks of European civilization, but all I see here is barbarism," said an African antiracist activist in Germany. The situation had deteriorated to the point where for the first time since World War II, immigrants began to flee Germany to hoped-for safe havens in other countries. A high court in Great Britain, a country not known for its liberal immigration policies, made headlines with its decision to grant asylum to a Sudanese refugee who feared assault if sent back to Germany. The Netherlands also opened its doors to foreigners driven from Germany. Asylum seekers who remained in the Fatherland were subjected to dubious procedures that recalled the racialist practices of the Third Reich. New rules implemented by the German Interior Ministry required non-EC (European Community) and non-U.S. citizens applying for residency to have their skull and nose size measured. Official immigration questionnaires specifically asked what type of nose a person had. A German nose was identified as a "normal" nose, and the "abnormal" nose shapes of various non-Germans were coded accordingly.[52]

As the attacks on foreigners escalated, so did the frequency of anti-Semitic offenses. Neo-Nazi vandals firebombed the "Jewish barracks" at the Sachsenhausen concentration camp in 1992, one of eighty anti-Semitic desecrations that year. The surge of anti-Jewish hate crimes occurred against a backdrop of latent anti-Semitism that had persisted in German society. After World War II, it was not kosher for respectable Germans to openly express such sentiments, so other minorities served as scapegoats. But this taboo also fell when the Berlin Wall toppled. A poll taken by *Der Spiegel* in 1991 indicated that 62 percent of Germans felt that it was better to "draw a line under the past" and not "talk so much about the persecution of the Jews." Another survey the following year indicated that 36 percent of Germans agreed that "Jews have too much influence in the world."[53]

As Jewish refugees from the Soviet Union began arriving in the Federal Republic, Bavarian interior minister Edmund Stoiber recommended that only those who had family members living in Germany should be allowed to remain in the country. An editorial in the *Frankfurter Rundschau* called Stoiber's recommendation "a nasty satire" in light of the fact that most German Jews had been systematically exterminated by the Nazis.* Those who survived the war and

* The presence of forty thousand Jewish residents in the Federal Republic apparently did not please some influential Germans. Hans Klein, Helmut Kohl's official spokesperson, blamed "international Jewry" for a change in the chancellor's itinerary during a visit to Poland. (Klein had also praised the Waffen SS for defending the Fatherland.) Additional complaints came from Father Heinrich Basilius Streithofen, Kohl's personal chaplain, who stated, "The Jews and the Poles are the biggest exploiters of the German people." Blatant anti-Semitism was also evident in Christian Democratic Union campaign ads in

Colonel Otto "Scarface" Skorzeny played a pivotal role in Nazi escape routes after the war.

Adolf Hitler with his favorite commando, Otto Skorzeny.

Major General Otto Ernst Remer thwarted the July 20, 1944, anti-Hitler plot.

Remer mentored a new generation of neo-Nazi youth after German reunification.

General Reinhard Gehlen, Hitler's top anti-Soviet spy, protected Nazi criminals while working for the CIA during the Cold War.

H. Keith Thompson, U.S. point man for the postwar ODESSA network. German intelligence had this photo ID of Thompson in its files, which were seized by Interpol in May 1945.

German flying ace Hans-Ulrich Rudel, the most celebrated figure in Latin America's large Nazi expatriate scene.

Argentina's first couple, Juan and Evita Perón, arriving in Spain, where their close friends Otto and Ilse Skorzeny lived in the early 1950s.

Leaders of the Socialist Reich Party, including Otto Ernst Remer (seated, center), with the inscription "to our friend H. Keith Thompson," who lobbied for the SRP in the early 1950s before it was banned by Bonn as a successor to the Nazi Party.

Francis Parker Yockey, a shadowy intellectual fascist, under arrest in San Francisco in June 1960, shortly before he committed suicide.

A rare photo of Liberty Lobby wire-puller Willis A. Carto, who promoted Yockey's writings posthumously.

Jean Thiriart, neofascist-turned-"National Communist," called for a pan-European alliance with the USSR.

French New Right philosopher Alain de Benoist's ideas about "ethnopluralism" and "the right to difference" helped to facilitate a resurgence of Eurofascism.

Eduard Limonov, leader of the National Bolshevik Front in Russia.

A Red-Brown demonstration in post-Soviet Moscow.

Otto Ernst Remer's protégé, Bela Ewald Althans, addressing a German revanchist meeting in Polish Silesia, 1992.

German neo-Nazi leader Michael Kühnen (left) and his principal U.S. collaborator, Gary Lauck (right), in Berlin, July 1990.

Neo-Nazis demonstrating in Dresden, October 1990 (front row, from left to right: Christian Worch, Michael Kühnen, and Gottfried Küssel).

German neo-Nazis commandeering a Red Army jeep at the site of the Sachsenhausen concentration camp.

Third Reich holders of the Knight's Cross officially honored at a German army base, 1993.

Hooded neo-Nazis give the Hitler salute in front of a burning immigrant hostel in Rostock, August 1992.

Attorney Kirk Lyons speaking before the Council of Conservative Citizens, a white supremacist organization praised by Senate Majority Leader Trent Lott. An advisor to U.S. militia groups, Lyons has close ties to neo-Nazis at home and abroad.

Militia of Montana chief John Trochman, obsessively spinning antigovernment conspiracy yarns.

Lyons's best man, Aryan Nations ambassador Louis Beam, formulated a "leaderless resistance" strategy for the white racialist underground.

NATIONAL POPULISTS WITH A NEOFASCIST EDGE

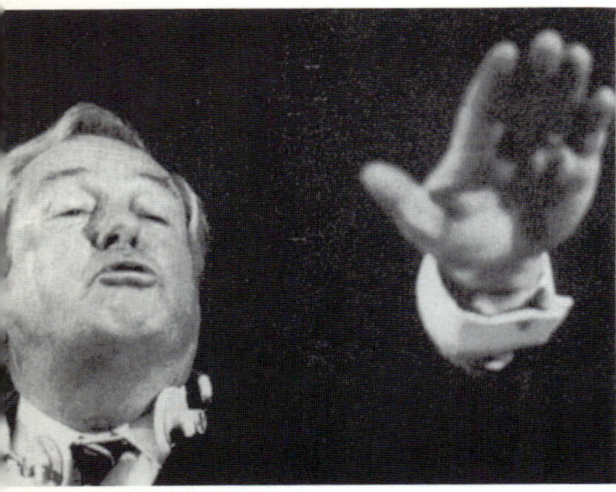

French Front National chief Jean-Marie Le Pen.

Gianfranco Fini, head of Italy's National Alliance.

Austrian Freedom Party führer Jörg Haider (right) greeting Waffen SS veterans.

Patrick Buchanan on the campaign trail speaking at a Christian Coalition meeting, 1996.

stayed in Germany were typically viewed as Jewish, not German. This perception had a legal basis, dating back to the Third Reich. Under German law — which defines citizenship by blood ties and ethnicity rather than residency or birth on German soil — German blood and Jewish blood are different. The obsession with German *Blut* came to the fore once again when aides to Chancellor Kohl, including his minister of health, demanded an end to the use of "foreign blood" in German hospitals.[54]

The chancellor himself was not above catering to anti-Jewish prejudice when crucial votes were at stake. In March 1992, Kohl met with outgoing Austrian president Kurt Waldheim in Germany. It was the first time the former U.N. secretary-general had been welcomed in a Western country since the revelations six years earlier about his wartime involvement in Nazi acts of persecution in the Balkans. When several Jewish groups registered their dismay, Kohl lashed out at them, saying, "I don't need any advice."[55]

More calculated than heartfelt, such gestures were geared to attract conservative support for the Christian Democratic Union at a time when far Right parties were making strides at the ballot box after a brief postunification slump. In April 1992, the Republikaner scored 11 percent of the vote in elections in Baden-Württemberg, causing the CDU to lose its twenty-year hold over the state. And the Republikaner's far Right competitor, the Deutsche Volksunion (DVU), broke the 5 percent barrier and elected candidates to state governments in Schleswig-Holstein and Bremen. Pegged as "a neo-Nazi political party" by U.S. Army intelligence, Gerhard Frey's DVU was only a shade more extreme than Schönhuber's party. But a bitter personal rivalry prevented the two ultra-right-wing leaders from forming a united front.

The growing strength of the extreme Right forced the Christian Democrats to make additional adjustments to stop the hemorrhaging of their electoral base. It got to the point where the policies of

---

Frankfurt, which emphasized the Jewish background of Greens candidate Daniel Cohn-Bendit: "Should Cohn-Bendit determine our homeland?" In February 1993, the town hall in Bad Hersfeld and the Social Democrat mayor's home were daubed with anti-Semitic slogans after the local branch of the CDU distributed an anti-Semitic leaflet.

the CDU and the Republikaner were "similar enough to mistake them," according to a journalist at the *Franfurter Allgemeine Zeitung.* Even Republikaner chief Franz Schönhuber acknowledged that Kohl's stance on key issues had become "precisely what our program called for." Every rightward nudge from Kohl, in turn, lent additional credibility to hard-core neofascists and made their scapegoat arguments more acceptable. This insidious dynamic accentuated a climate of bigotry that was conducive to the schemes of demagogues and violent neo-Nazi agitators. More pogroms were inevitable.[56]

Capitulation

There had been thousands of right-wing extremist attacks throughout Germany since reunification, but one incident was particularly symbolic. In October 1991, neo-Nazis vandalized the cemetery in the village of Rhoendorf, near Bonn. Dozens of tombstones were defaced with swastikas, including the burial site of Konrad Adenauer, West Germany's first chancellor. The desecration of Adenauer's grave dramatized the perpetrators' abiding hatred of the democratic system and their desire to abolish it.

Most neo-Nazi leaders were not foolish enough to believe that seizing power was a realistic possibility at that point. Although Christian Worch could summon two thousand to three thousand militants to a demonstration, he knew this in and of itself did not constitute a serious threat to the state. But to assert that the neo-Nazis played no role in German politics, as Chancellor Kohl claimed, was a serious misrepresentation, for they had already succeeded in poisoning the mainstream political process by acting out their ethnic hatreds. Not without justification, Worch and his colleagues beat their breasts and took credit when Kohl zeroed in on foreigners after the Berlin Wall came down.

The neo-Nazis saw themselves as the driving force behind the German government's rapid goose step to the Right. Their efforts to influence the mainstream political agenda were facilitated by German officials who continued to deny that organized groups of right-wing extremists were behind much of the racist violence. While Kohl and his cohorts kept ascribing the attacks to "aimless individuals" and apolitical street gangs, neo-Nazis forged tighter links among themselves through computer technology. The Thule network, which consisted of more than a dozen electronic bulletin boards, provided information on upcoming political rallies, directions on how to put out a newspaper, and even recipes for bomb-making. Books banned in Germany, such as those that disputed the Holocaust, could easily be accessed through e-mail. The extraordinary growth of electronic fascism was an important aspect of the internationalization of the far Right.[57]

At times, German neo-Nazi leaders were able to beat the authorities in a game of cat and mouse by using computers, walkie-talkies, portable phones, and answering machines. New methods of communication enabled the neo-Nazis to avoid police roadblocks and deliver commands to convoys of ultrarightists as they made their way to political demonstrations. Such high-tech gimmickry was employed in late August 1992, when Ewald Althans and hundreds of his cohorts slipped into the Baltic seaport of Rostock in eastern Germany under the cover of darkness. Some had come all the way from Austria and Scandinavia to participate in a frenzied outburst of ethnic cleansing.

In a scene starkly reminiscent of the 1930s, thousands of local residents roared approvingly as a throng of neo-Nazis attacked a refugee center for Romanian Gypsies. As the immigrant shelter went up in flames, an ecstatic crowd sang "Tannenbaum" (a Christmas hymn) and "Deutschland über Alles." A local law-enforcement official, Jürgen Deckert, later acknowledged that "the police had an arrangement with the rowdies not to intervene."[58]

While the police stood idly by, the neo-Nazis regrouped and attacked another guest hostel with a barrage of Molotov cocktails. More than a hundred Vietnamese guest workers and their families were trapped inside the burning building, along with a German television crew. The reporters telephoned Rostock's fire and police departments in a futile attempt to summon help. Nearly suffocating from smoke, the terrorized inhabitants moved from floor to floor until they reached the top level of the twelve-story apartment complex. Down below, the angry mob screamed, "Lynch them!" and

"Blood justice!" With only minutes to spare before the entire structure turned into a deadly inferno, they pried open a locked door with iron bars, crawled onto the roof, and narrowly escaped by leaping to the top of another building. Miraculously, no one was killed.[59]

Government authorities in the German state of Mecklenberg–West Pommerania subsequently disclosed that they had learned of neo-Nazi plans to "clean up" Rostock before the violence erupted, yet no preventive measures were ordered. Interior Minister Rudolf Seiters refused to call out the Bundesgrenzschutzpolizei (Germany's national military police) to defend the Rostock refugee center, allegedly because of a shortage of manpower. But plenty of heavily armed law-enforcement personnel were available when more than a thousand antifascists turned up in town to show solidarity with the beleaguered foreigners. Suddenly keen to assert their authority, the police arrested ninety people, two-thirds of whom had come to protest against the neo-Nazi violence. By tuning into police banter on citizens-band radio and jamming official signals, the neo-Nazis had a distinct advantage over their antifascist foes during street clashes that turned Rostock into a virtual combat zone. "It was terrible, like a civil war," said a stunned Rostock resident. "We switched off all our lights and were afraid to look out the window."[60]

Alarm bells started to ring in foreign embassies and boardrooms, as photos of neo-Nazi youth hurling Molotov cocktails at immigrant hostels flashed around the world. Suddenly people were asking questions that until then had seemed unthinkable: Could it happen again? Had the German demons returned? "This is how something began that ended at Auschwitz," said Manfred Stolpe, premier of the German state of Brandenburg. "These riots are the worst thing that has happened in Germany since 1945." President Richard von Weizsäcker spoke of "a serious and evil sign for the future, a warning of fascism."[61]

The week-long pogrom tapered off after the German government caved in to the neo-Nazi mob by ordering all refugees out of Rostock. Henceforth, this economically depressed city of 250,000 would be foreigner-free, just like Hoyerswerda and several other ethnically cleansed redoubts in the Fatherland. Next came an official announcement that close to one hundred thousand Gypsies would soon be deported to Romania and other parts of Eastern Europe. Human rights organizations strongly criticized Bonn's decision on the grounds that many Roma and Sinti, as the Gypsies call themselves, suffered physical attacks and other forms of persecution in these countries.[62]

Rather than defusing tensions, the government's response to Rostock sparked a wave of terror unlike anything Germany had witnessed since Hitler was in power. Within a two-week period, right-wing extremists attacked foreigners and other targets in more than a hundred cities and towns. ROSTOCK IS EVERYWHERE! declared one newspaper headline. *Stern,* Germany's largest newsmagazine, minced no words about how serious the situation had become: "Germany faces a political catastrophe. . . . The rule of law has capitulated before the terror. . . . Events in Rostock have shown that the German security forces have neither the capacity nor the will to protect innocent people from the terror troops of the radical right."[63]

The violence continued at a fever pitch during the autumn of 1992, as blazing refugee centers lit up the sky. That year, according to German officials, more than forty-five hundred racist assaults killed seventeen people and injured hundreds. Firebombings and explosives attacks jumped 33 percent from 1991. And these figures did not reflect the full extent of the violence.[64]

"The trail of death from rightists has just begun," warned Ernst Uhrlau, head of the Office for the Protection of the Constitution in Hamburg. Neo-Nazi violence had taken on "terrorist dimensions," according to Uhrlau, who disclosed that ultrarightists schooled in guerrilla tactics were firing live ammunition at immigrants. Uhrlau also indicated that the number of organized right-wing extremists in Germany had increased to sixty-five thousand by the end of 1992, 10 percent of whom were deemed to be hard-core neo-Nazi militants. Predicting that far Right extremism, aggressive nationalism, and the hatred of foreigners would continue to intensify, he issued a blunt warning: "This is the tip of a social protest movement. There is a whole new character to the neo-Nazi scene. They are emboldened by success and very ready to demonstrate and act. . . ."[65]

An alarming sense of déjà vu sent shivers up the spine of Germany's vestigial Jewish community. "When we watch houses burning and people running, it is connected to our history," said Irene Runge of the Berlin-based Jewish Cultural Federation. "It is as if fifty years of history have gone missing, then this generation started again where the previous one left off. It seems they forget everything in between." In an open letter to Chancellor Kohl, Jewish Holocaust survivor Ralph Giordano called upon German Jews to "arm themselves" and expressed wonder that other victims of the neo-Nazis had not already done so. "We have lost our belief and hope that you and your government can offer effective protection against right-wing extremism and its anti-Semitic criminals," Giordano asserted.[66]*

There were even a few dissenting voices within Kohl's own party, such as Heiner Geissler, the former general-secretary of the CDU, who cut to the chase when he warned that the real issue was not asylum for refugees but the assault on democracy by the forces of fascism. "Throwing firebombs into an occupied building is attempted murder," said Geissler. "The real cause of these crimes lies in the radical right's acceptance into the mainstream."[67]

Neo-Nazi leaders were jubilant over the course of events. By meeting their demands, the German government had allowed a violent minority to decisively shape the national political agenda. "At first, people said we were mad. Then they said we were dangerous," Christian Worch remarked. "Now they say we are trendy. And I think we will be trendy for a long time."[68]

In the wake of Rostock, Worch felt that much of the public was on his side. Polls indicated that 51 percent of Germans agreed with the neo-Nazi slogan "Germany for the Germans," and 37 percent felt that the influx of foreigners should be stopped by any means whatsoever. Growing sympathy for the neo-Nazi cause appeared to coincide with a strong tendency among German youth to minimize

* With Jews queuing up to leave Germany, veteran Nazi-hunters Beate and Serge Klarsfeld led a protest delegation from France to Rostock in October 1992. When they tried to unfurl a plaque in memory of the millions of Jews and Gypsies killed by the Nazis, the Klarsfelds and fifty other antifascists were roughed up and arrested by police. Some of the French Jews remained in jail for more than a week, while violent neo-Nazi youth, per usual, were released after a few hours in detention.

or deny the horrors of the Third Reich. According to a survey conducted by *Der Speigel,* a quarter of German schoolchildren believed that descriptions of the Holocaust were "greatly exaggerated," and one out of five supported the neo-Nazi admonition "Jews out!"[69]

Some neo-Nazi leaders started to believe that they had entered a prerevolutionary phase in Germany comparable to the Weimar years. All the essential elements appeared to be in place — the fascist shock troops, a lax police force, and a mass base of potential supporters. The fin de siècle atmosphere on the street inflated the pretensions of Ewald Althans. "There is no ideology fighting against us," he declared. "There is nobody else trying to give an alternative. Today there is none except the neo-Nazis who are saying, 'We want the country. We want the power. We want the world.' "

While mustering only a lukewarm condemnation of neo-Nazi violence, Helmut Kohl steadfastly maintained that "asylum abuse," not racism, was the source of the problem. The chancellor and his aides expressed far less concern about the harm inflicted upon immigrants than the negative impact neo-Nazi attacks had on Germany's image and its international business prospects. Various damage-control strategies were set in motion, including a deceptive attempt to depict the violence as an "eastern problem," as if it were merely a poisonous holdover from the Communist regime. In fact, more than two-thirds of the racist attacks in 1992 occurred in western Germany. Several polls indicated that xenophobic attitudes were actually less prevalent in the eastern part of the country, where the worst episodes of violence had resulted from an alliance of local youth and western neo-Nazi leaders.[70]

The degree to which neo-Nazi violence was concentrated in the west did not escape the attention of U.S. Army intelligence, which warned in a lengthy post-Rostock report that skinheads posed a "threat to the personal security of U.S. soldiers in Germany," particularly those of "racial and ethnic minority groups." Army analysts readily acknowledged what the German government still disputed: "Neo-Nazis plan attacks and coordinate movements of large numbers of right-wing demonstrators and assailants." Noting the widespread passivity among German citizens, the army report commented that it was "not uncommon" for foreigners "to be attacked in clear view of German passersby and to receive no assistance whatsoever. . . . U.S. Army personnel cannot assume that they will be aided by German passersby should they be harassed by skinheads."[71]

The plethora of neo-Nazi attacks in prosperous western Germany, where U.S. soldiers were based, called into question reductive sociological interpretations that attributed the rising tide of xenophobic violence to the ills of modernization or economics gone sour. Nor could it simply be sloughed off as a case of racist hormones run wild among overexcited youth, a momentary spasm that would pass when unified Germany adjusted to its new role as a Continental superpower. The causes of the neo-Nazi revival were far more complex. Rooted in the traumas of the past and nurtured by decades of denial, something awful was laid bare by the fall of the Berlin Wall. The fascist beast had reawakened and was on the prowl again.

True to form, conservatives in Kohl's coalition preferred to fret about the alleged danger posed by left-wing radicals. Typical in this regard was Germany's chief prosecutor, Alexander von Stahl, who characterized animal rights activists as "terrorists" but refrained from such blunt descriptions when referring to perpetrators of racist violence. Several of Kohl's allies maintained that the biggest threat to German democracy came not from the extreme Right but from the Greens and the former East German Communists, who had been reconstituted as the Party of Democratic Socialism (PDS). Invoking the specter of the dreaded Stasi, German officials disseminated false reports suggesting that ex-GDR spies were responsible for fomenting racial strife in Rostock and other eastern cities.[72]

Although a large number of East Germans had collaborated with the Communist secret police, this issue served as a convenient brickbat for professional Red-baiters who were eager to stymie their domestic critics at a time when so much had gone sour with unification. To suit their current needs, certain heavyweights in Kohl's government revised history and trivialized the Holocaust by claiming, in the words of CDU "legal affairs" expert Norbert Geis, that East Germany "was every bit as criminal a regime as the Nazi regime."[73]

Chastising the ghost of the GDR, however, was not a viable response to the horrific firebombing that occurred in the western

German city of Mölln on November 23, 1992. Three Turks — two children and a grandmother — burned to death after neo-Nazis torched their home. The arsonists signed off a telephone call to the police by saying, "Heil Hitler!" This had "special meaning," according to Chief Prosecutor von Stahl, because it showed that the culprits (two of whom would later receive lengthy prison terms) were intent on reestablishing "a national socialist dictatorship in Germany."[74]

It was as if von Stahl had suddenly woken up to the fact that a neo-Nazi problem existed in his country. After pretending for so long that the epidemic of racist violence lacked a political dimension, top German officials abruptly did an about-face and called for what was tantamount to police-state legislation to fight the recently discovered neo-Nazi scourge. But they failed to explain why new laws were necessary when a far-reaching 1972 decree had proved effective in combating left-wing terrorists.

A few weeks after the Mölln conflagration, German police launched more than a hundred raids against neo-Nazi gangs across Germany. Despite all the commotion, the dragnet resulted in only eight arrests, fueling speculation that official sources may have alerted right-wing extremist leaders to the impending crackdown. By the end of 1992, four neo-Nazi organizations were outlawed after they had been publicly forewarned of the government's intentions, allowing them to destroy incriminating material. Nevertheless, Chief Prosecutor von Stahl considered the crackdown a major success. In February 1993, he proclaimed that the neo-Nazis were under control and that the government could again turn its attention to the more serious threat from the Left. A few months later, a friendly, full-page interview with von Stahl was published in Otto Ernst Remer's neo-Nazi broadsheet, *Remer Despeche.*[75]

"The bannings only had a small impact," Christian Worch explained in June 1993, "because the outlawed organizations could easily continue their activities under a new name." That's exactly what Kühnen had in mind when he set up an elaborate web of front groups — every time one got the boot, its members were able to rebound with much of their structure intact. Deutsche Alternative chief Frank Hübner, for example, continued to preside over weekly meetings at the same bar in Cottbus. And those who called his office got the same message on the answering machine: "Speak after the machine-gun burst."[76]

Hassled but largely unscathed by the government's law-and-order posturing, the neo-Nazi movement would suffer a bigger blow when one of its young stars defected. Shaken by pangs of conscience in the wake of the Mölln massacre, Ingo Hasselbach quit the neo-Nazi scene. He wrote a book about his experiences as a neo-Nazi gang leader in East Berlin, the Kühnen network's expansion into East Germany, and the steady infusion of funds that ultra-right-wing militants received from German doctors, lawyers, and other middle-class professionals. Hasselbach also confirmed that crucial assistance was provided by neo-Nazis in the United States and other countries.[77]

Hasselbach was not the only person disturbed by what happened in Mölln. Huge candlelight demonstrations took place in the bitter cold as Germans from all walks of life condemned the avalanche of racist attacks. But Chancellor Kohl, anxious not to alienate right-wing voters, again showed little sympathy for the victims. By then, however, it was clear that something needed to be done to restore Germany's reputation, which had been sullied by the violence. The public-relations factor undoubtedly figured in Bonn's decision to proscribe a handful of neo-Nazi groups. But why did the German government wait so long before it chose to implement such measures? And why were dozens of other neo-Nazi organizations still legally permitted to function?

For more than two years, Kohl had vilified asylum seekers while neo-Nazi violence scarred the political landscape. Had he become a prisoner of the right-wing extremists? Or were neo-Nazis functioning as a de facto fifth wheel of state policy, forcing foreigners to leave the Fatherland under a hail of bullets, bombs, and baseball bats? Hajo Funke, a professor of political science in Berlin, was among those who argued that Kohl's government tolerated the wave of racist assaults in order to pressure its main opponent, the Social Democrats, into amending Article 16 of the German constitution, which guaranteed the right to asylum. Without support of the Social Democrats, the conservative ruling coalition could not have mustered the required two-thirds majority to alter the constitution. But how easy would it be to turn off the neo-Nazi spigot when the ultra-right-wing mob had served its purpose and was no longer politically useful?

Chancellor Kohl finally got what he wanted in the fall of 1992 when the Social Democrats buckled under and agreed to slam the door shut on political refugees. This, of course, had been a long-standing neo-Nazi demand. Despite harsh condemnation from human rights organizations, the Bundestag passed a greatly restricted asylum law on May 27, 1993. Henceforth, asylum seekers who entered the Federal Republic would have to come directly from the country where they were persecuted; no one would be allowed entry from a so-called safe country that he or she passed through en route to Germany. The United Nations High Commission for Refugees warned in July 1993 that the new German asylum law set the stage for the "agonizing suffering and needless death" of "tens of thousands of persons fleeing persecution."[78]

Neo-Nazi leaders celebrated the parliament's decision as a victory for their movement. "It is enough for us to have forced these changes on the government," said Worch, who welcomed the Interior Ministry's decision to build an electronic wall along Germany's eastern border to keep out unwanted foreigners. A "Brown Curtain" was erected, which utilized night-vision and infrared spotting devices to discern the shapes of illegal border-crossers. Less impressive than the sophisticated surveillance equipment was the quality of some of the new personnel hired by the Bundesgrenzschutzpolizei (military police), which enlisted skinheads and neofascists to serve in border patrol units.[79]

Instead of guarding against the potential threat of the Red Army, an expanded force of soldier-cops would try to turn back the tide of desperate refugees. But the Brown Curtain did not keep the Germans from moving into Eastern Europe, where various neo-Nazi groups quickly set up shop after the fall of the Wall. They were joined by an army of businessmen, diplomats, and spies, who assiduously looked after German national interests throughout the region. Once again, Germany was gazing eastward at a vast swath of territory that until recently had been dominated by Soviet Russia.

CHAPTER EIGHT

SHADOW OVER THE EAST

"Prussia Lives!"

At the stroke of midnight on August 17, 1991, a casket containing the bones of Frederick the Great was lowered into its original resting place at the Sans Souci Palace near Potsdam. The royal homecoming extravaganza, complete with black, horse-drawn carriages, imperial flags, and a military honor guard, was broadcast live on German television. Chancellor Helmut Kohl and eighty thousand others had come to pay their respects to the legendary Prussian monarch, who ruled an enlarged kingdom from 1740 to 1786. Several onlookers nodded approvingly at a sign in the crowd that read "Prussia lives!" An ornate and lavish ceremony marked the end of a long odyssey for the body of "Old Fritz," whose remains had been spirited to western Germany in the waning days of World War II to keep them from being seized by Soviet occupation forces. The collapse of Communist rule in the German Democratic Republic paved the way for Frederick's return to his former dynastic retreat.

The exhumation and reburial of this fierce Prussian warrior raised eyebrows among those who worried about revanchist tendencies in the new Germany. Some felt that this official display of necrolatry would send the wrong message to neo-Nazis and other right-wing extremists. Within these circles, Frederick was venerated as a cult figure because of his martial accomplishments. He often invaded foreign lands and boasted of gobbling up Silesia "like an artichoke." Hailing Frederick the Great as a supreme example of Teutonic willpower, Adolf Hitler went to his original grave in Potsdam in 1933 to declare the beginning of the Third Reich.

By honoring Frederick the Great less than a year after reunification, Chancellor Kohl's government reignited the debate about Germany's ignoble past. Kohl was quick to emphasize that the Prussian king had bequeathed a dual legacy that epitomized the best and worst of German traditions. In addition to waging expansionist wars, Frederick protected Jews and other religious minorities, abolished torture, encouraged the arts, composed musical symphonies, and befriended Goethe and Voltaire (with whom Frederick was said to have had sexual relations). Instead of demonizing him, Kohl insisted that the German people should acknowledge both sides of this controversial figure—the aesthete as well as the combatant—in order to understand their difficult history. But skeptics wondered whether it was possible to do this in a responsible way without glorifying violence and militarism. "Many Germans no longer see a connection between today and yesterday, and that indifference can be dangerous," said historian Heinz Knobloch.[1]

By symbolic coincidence, two days after Old Fritz had been tucked away (presumably for the last time), Soviet hardliners launched an abortive putsch against Mikhail Gorbachev and his government. Although the coup attempt proved to be a fiasco, it served notice that the Soviet Union was terminally ill. By the end of the year, Russian president Boris Yeltsin shoved Gorbachev aside and declared the once-mighty USSR dead and gone. The precipitous implosion of the Soviet Union into fifteen separate countries left a huge power vacuum on the Continent—a vacuum that a reunified Germany, by virtue of its pivotal location and economic might, was poised to fill. No longer confined to the perimeter of the Atlantic system, Germany would once again become the arbiter of *Mitteleuropa*, a geopolitical construct that lay dormant while the Federal Republic bode its time as a frontline state during the Cold War. German hegemony throughout the region, whether consciously pursued or otherwise, appeared to be a fait accompli. "Central Europe is going to have a strong Germanic flavor again," said retired State Department officer Douglas H. Jones. "Even if it's not intentional, Germany could lurch into a destabilizing role."[2]

Some U.S. intelligence experts felt that Germany was inherently expansionist-minded, that its destiny was rooted in its geography. Reflecting this school of thought, a CIA analyst predicted that by the end of the century Germany would not be able to resist the temptation to break free of its Western moorings and embark upon another round of Bismarckian adventures. In the past, Germany's *Drang nach Osten* (drive to the east) entailed armed conquest. But the prevailing sentiment among German nationalists early in the post-Soviet era was that the deutsche mark would accomplish what the Wehrmacht had failed to achieve. Because of the high cost of reunification, Germany invested strategically, rather than profusely, in Eastern Europe, focusing on crucial areas such as energy supplies, transportation, telecommunications, and mass media. German economic gains translated into greater political clout. A bossier manner was evident as Bonn demanded a United Nations Security Council seat and insisted that German be elevated to the status of an official language within the European Community.[3]

Germany's new assertiveness spilled over into the military arena as well. Responding ostensibly to the war in former Yugoslavia, Germany's Constitutional Court ruled in July 1994 that German forces could take part in military operations beyond NATO's jurisdiction. "This decision gives Germany freedom of action in foreign policy. The brake that was holding us back is gone," exulted Foreign Minister Klaus Kinkel, who had previously served as head of the West German BND intelligence agency. Although German officials publicly gave assurances that they would not pursue an interventionist or militarized foreign policy, Defense Minister Volker Rühe asserted in a 1994 white paper that the German army would henceforth function as "an instrument of foreign policy."[4]

By this time, Germany had emerged as the world's second-leading arms exporter, behind only the United States. After it absorbed the East German military, the Federal Republic reduced its overall troop strength to 350,000—the largest standing army in Europe. Germany had regained its status as the continent's premier military power thanks to NATO and U.S. policy-makers who sought Bonn's help in defending Western Europe against the USSR during the Cold War. Although NATO was supposed to contain Germany as well as Russia, it proved to be the vehicle through which German military power was restored. And now that the superpower face-off had ended, German leaders indicated that they were ready to develop new security structures outside of NATO, including a European military force composed initially of 35,000 French and German soldiers. Such plans disturbed U.S. officials, who sought to prevent the renationalization of German defense policy. Another area of concern to Washington was Germany's nuclear weapons research program. Echoing sentiment expressed by German military think tanks, *Der Spiegel* publisher Rudolf Augstein asserted that there were situations in which Germany would have to obtain its own nuclear weapons "in spite of existing treaties."[5]

General Klaus Naumann, the first military chief of reunified Germany, sought to transform his army into an independent military power imbued "with a victor mentality." Described by *Die Zeit* as someone who "has the stuff of fanaticism," Naumann was the driving force behind the Bundeswehr's revamped offensive strategy that entailed being "strategically alert rather than reactively averting war." Former German Fleet Admiral Elmar Schmälling publicly accused Naumman of preparing an army of aggression modeled after its Prussian predecessors.[6]

The shift to an offensive military posture coincided with officially sanctioned efforts to reevaluate military performance during the Nazi period. Naumann insisted on modifying an old West German army decree that said a "linkage of the tradition of the Bundeswehr to [Hitler's] Wehrmacht as an institution is impossible." Under Naumann's command, such a linkage was not only possible but desirable. The change in attitude was noted in *Europäische Sicherheit* (*European Security*), a periodical closely associated with the German army, which spoke of "finding common ground, fairly, with our fathers' and grandfathers' generations, which in other nations is taken for granted." Henceforth, the Bundeswehr would not "separate itself from the roots which our founders from the Wehrmacht so painstakingly and with exemplary personal commitment sank in the earth, because these are roots which reach deep into the German past and German military history."[7]

As part of its renewed emphasis on "tradition building," the Bundeswehr announced that the inclusion of all ranks (SS officers not excepted) on German military gravestones was an absolute necessity. This decision extended to war cemeteries in central and Eastern Europe as well, according to General Naumann, who put it country simple: "Those East European states which have objected will have to have the thumbscrews put on them because they depend on us for large-scale economic assistance."[8]

Of course, there had never really been a clean break from the Nazi past, given that the original leadership of the West German Bundeswehr was recruited directly from the upper echelons of Hitler's army. (Only three out of 217 Bundeswehr generals in 1976 were not Third Reich veterans, and 37 military bases in the Bonn Republic were named after soldiers who made their reputations during the Hitler years.) Under Naumann's watch, the Bundeswehr gave its seal of approval to a rally hosted by the Ordensgemeinschaft der Ritterkreuzträger (Association of Holders of the Knights' Cross of the Iron Cross). Held at a castle in Celle on October 16, 1993, this confab attracted more than one hundred of the surviving eight hundred Nazis who had been personally chosen by the Fuehrer to receive the Wehrmacht's highest award for valor. Several hard-line veterans greeted one another with the customary "Heil Hitler!" as they assembled to honor their departed peers. They were joined by an army marching band and delegation from the Bundeswehr's 334th Panzer Division, which presented a memorial wreath to those who fought for the Third Reich.[9]

By way of explaining why the Bundeswehr had patronized such an affair, a spokesman said that the Knight's Cross society embodied "the traditional soldierly qualities of loyalty, comradeship, courage and discipline . . . qualities useful for us." But this cantankerous veterans association also fostered right-wing extremism and revanchism. Its membership bulletin ranted about how FDR and Churchill were responsible for starting World War II. It also blamed the Allies for causing Germany to lose its eastern territories, which German Nazis, young and old, continued to covet.

Official attempts to instill a sense of patriotism among soldiers may also have contributed to the growth of extremist tendencies in the German armed services, whose members suffer from glaring deficiencies in historical and political knowledge—especially of the World War II period. This is not surprising given that the army has employed members of the far right Republikaner Party to teach history and political education to Bundeswehr recruits. "Germany's only crime was to lose two world wars," proclaimed Republikaner chief Franz Schönhuber, who boasted of his close ties to high-ranking Bundeswehr officers.[10]

Christian Krause, whose father served in Chancellor Helmut Kohl's cabinet in the early 1990s, claims he witnessed numerous neo-Nazi outbursts during his ten months as an army conscript. "At parties there were always toasts made to the Fuehrer," said Krause, "and after drinking alcohol, many officers would give each other the Hitler salute and scream 'Sieg Heil!'" Several reports indicated that the German army harbored a thriving black market in SS songbooks, Hitler's *Mein Kampf*, skinhead music, swastika-adorned flags, and other outlawed Nazi paraphernalia. This type of material circulated at the Franz-Josef-Strauss barracks in Bavaria, where soldiers celebrated Hitler's birthday by chanting Nazi hymns and viewing Third Reich propaganda films. "It was clear to me that some of our superiors wanted to instill in us young soldiers the traditions of the Wehrmacht," an ex-trainee told *Stern*.

In 1992, active-duty military personnel were implicated in at least sixty-eight neo-Nazi incidents, which resulted in three deaths; on more than a dozen occasions, German soldiers used government firearms and munitions to attack foreigners. That year, a survey by the Bundeswehr's own social sciences research institute revealed that the army "was becoming increasingly popular among young men with little or no interest in democratic principles or values." This was partly due to loopholes in German law, which permitted a third of the population to opt for community service instead of military duty; consequently, the army attracted a more conservative constituency than society in general. Another factor was that fascist groups urged their members to enlist in order to learn military skills. The tone of training sessions had become noticeably harsher since the end of the Cold War, as evidenced by a German drill instructor who barked, "What makes grass grow?" while his unit shouted back: "Blood, blood, blood!"[11]

Upon learning that some of his men had joined neo-Nazi gangs, General Naumann pointedly denounced racist violence and anti-Semitism. He also visited the Yad Vashem memorial in Jerusalem to pay respect to victims of the Holocaust. On other occasions, however, Naumann projected a different demeanor. After German reunification, he enthusiastically told members of his general staff that they had come to the end of a historical era that began not in 1945 but "in the French Revolution of 1789." His eagerness to bid good riddance to the democratic promise of "liberty, equality, and fraternity" unintentionally conjured up memories of Joseph Goebbels's famous comment that the task of National Socialism was "to erase the year 1789 from German history."[12]

Naumann's antipathy toward 1789 was shared by New Right theoreticians who were spearheading the ideological backlash against liberalism in post–Cold War Germany. Having emerged during the dog days of the neofascist scene, the German New Right remained for the most part a marginal phenomenon until the Berlin Wall fell, when its rejuvenated proponents strove to capture the intellectual high ground. Their principal mouthpiece, *Junge Freiheit* (*Young Freedom*), was a slick, well-funded weekly.

Founded in 1986 by nineteen-year-old Dieter Stein, *Junge Freiheit* ran several articles by and interviews with GRECE leader Alain de Benoist. But the German New Right disagreed with some of de Benoist's latest ideas, particularly his contention that the classical nation-state did not have much of a future. An emphasis on redemptive ultranationalism was crucial to *Junge Freiheit,* which sought to rehabilitate the discredited thinkers of the Conservative Revolution of the 1920s. It overflowed with tributes to Ernst Jünger, Carl Schmitt, Oswald Spengler, and other antidemocratic cogitators who extolled the pagan sources of German culture and helped set the stage for Hitler's rise to power.[13]

For Stein and other New Right intellectuals, the ultimate enemy was always American-style consumer society rather than Communism. With the collapse of the Soviet bloc, the United States became the lone foe to rally against—a situation tailored for *Junge Freiheit* as it struggled to win over the hearts and minds of the masses. Like its fascist conservative revolutionary forebears, it rejected parliamentary democracy as an alien form of government and stressed the need for Germans to rediscover their authentic identity by celebrating past glories and slackening ties to the West.

Stein's editorials in favor of an independent German military policy were appreciated by leaders of the post–Cold War Bundeswehr.

On several occasions, articles by *Junge Freiheit* authors graced the pages of German army publications. *Junge Freiheit* also featured the work of Ernst Nolte, the far Right historian who depicted Hitler's crimes as a defensive reaction to Soviet Communism.[14]

Junge Freiheit's presence was most strongly felt at German and Austrian universities, where far Right student fraternities, known as Burschenschaften, were experiencing a revival. Notorious for their virulent nationalism, these all-male drinking societies promoted saber dueling without face guards, which left permanent scars on many who indulged in this macho sport. (This is how Otto Skorzeny's face got disfigured.) According to Bremen sociologist Gerhard Schäfer, "a substantial minority of Burschenschaft members can be regarded as part of the neofascist scene." *Junge Freiheit* received financial support from several of these dueling fraternities. Students who joined the Burschenschaften often espoused the same pan-Germanic beliefs as *Junge Freiheit,* which was advertised in Vienna as the "paper for Austria and the rest of Germany."[15]

Stein, however, disavowed any connection with skinheads and neo-Nazis, even though some *Junge Freiheit* editors had matriculated from cadre organizations linked to Michael Kühnen. Despite daily assaults against foreigners in Germany, Stein maintained that the threat of neo-Nazi violence was exaggerated by the media. "Germans have shown a lot of restraint in not attacking foreigners," he asserted.[16]

Stein tried to distance himself from the neo-Nazi underground so as not to undermine *Junge Freiheit*'s efforts to build bridges to nationalist-minded individuals in the political and business establishment. But Herbert Schnoor, the interior minister of North Rhine–Westphalia, saw through the ruse. "I consider the 'New Right' more dangerous than the right extremists of old," he declared. Schnoor warned that reactionary intellectuals were trying to create an authoritarian climate on German campuses. "They proceed so adroitly that one does not notice immediately that one is being taken in," Schnoor stated. "They could succeed in shifting the democratic parties further to the right."[17]

Nonplussed, Stein kept calling for a return to Germany's 1937 borders. "Germany is like a waking Gulliver whose ropes have all been cut away," he asserted. "It just doesn't realize it yet."[18]

Territorial Imperative

When asked about Germany's official 1993 calendar, an embarrassed government spokesperson called it a hastily put together mistake. Published and distributed by the federal Interior Ministry, this big-format calendar included a dozen photographs of "German" cities, one for each month of the year. But two of the so-called German cities were actually situated in Poland, and a third was the capital of newly independent Estonia. Despite the brouhaha that erupted as a result of these photos, instructions filtered down from on high that the controversial calendar was not to be removed from thousands of schools and colleges throughout Germany.[19]

The calendar caper was hardly an anomaly in post–Cold War Germany, where calls for "border corrections" had become commonplace. "Whoever travels around the country and talks to the party grassroots feels very strongly the influence of the New Right," said Friedbert Pflüger, a Christian Democratic parliamentary member. Pflüger acknowledged that in many of his meetings, "Poland's western frontier is questioned and the return of Silesia and East Prussia is demanded." Top German officials routinely spoke of "Middle Germany" when describing what had previously been Communist East Germany. In a televised address to German student fraternities, Wolfgang Schäuble (Kohl's number two and heir apparent) referred to the area that was once "the east of Germany" as "really in the center of Germany." By promoting this dangerous notion, Schäuble and his colleagues gave credence to neo-Nazis who insisted that territories east of reunified Germany rightfully belonged to the Fatherland.[20]

Unlike the extraparliamentary neo-Nazis, German officials were in a position to back their revanchist rhetoric with significant financial resources. During the early 1990s, Germany's federal budget — which also refers specifically to *Mitteldeutschlands* (Middle Germany) when describing the ex-GDR — generously earmarked funds for the Bund der Vertriebenen (Association of Expellees), an umbrella group with dozens of subsidiaries that shared the neo-Nazi belief that Germany must reclaim its "true ethnic borders." They dreamed of a *Grossdeutschland* that encompassed not only a formi-

The "real Germany" as seen by neo-Nazis and militant expellee groups

dable swath of eastern turf but also Germanic enclaves in France, Belgium, Austria, and South Tyrol in northern Italy.[21]

After World War II, more than 11 million Germans were ejected from their homes in contested eastern zones where borders had fluctuated for centuries. With erstwhile German areas stranded in the Soviet bloc, embittered expellees emerged as natural allies of the CIA and the Gehlen Org, which recruited anti-Communist intelligence assets from displaced-persons networks. Several *Vertriebenen* organizations that sprang up in the early 1950s were founded and led by ex-SS officers. These militant exiles and their descendants formed a strong right-wing lobby in West Germany, where expellees accounted for more than 20 percent of the population. Over the years, they delivered a sizable portion of the vote to Chancellor Konrad Adenauer's — and later Helmut Kohl's — Christian Democratic Union, which lavished money and attention on *Vertriebenen* activists, even though many of them espoused pro-Nazi views. Some *Vertriebenen* leaders used their government-funded publications to argue that the Holocaust was merely anti-German propaganda.[22]

Vertriebenen pressure groups "were always leaning on Kohl," recalled Douglas Jones of the U.S. Foreign Service. Determined not to alienate a powerful, well-organized constituency, the chancellor and several of his cabinet members asserted on several occasions during the Cold War that Germany's 1937 borders were still legitimate. Kohl himself was given the Medal of Honor from the expellees' federation in 1984 after he declared that territorial issues were "open." Ever mindful of their concerns, after the Berlin Wall fell his government substantially increased subsidies for expellee associations even as support for domestic social services was being slashed (cutbacks deemed necessary to help foot the bill for reunification). Bowing to irredentist fanatics in such a manner "formed part of a political ritual which irresponsibly and stubbornly refused to recognize the origins or accept the consequences of a war begun and lost by the Germans," said Günter Grass.[23]

State Department officials understood Kohl's indulgence toward openly revanchist groups as a calculated attempt to keep in check extremist elements that wanted to extend Germany's borders yet again. But this rationalization did not mollify those who discerned a more ominous ring to pleas for boundary revisions now that the Cold War was over. Although it may not have been the government's intention, official backing for expellee associations also facilitated the designs of neo-Nazi leaders who traveled frequently to the eastern territories to prepare for their eventual incorporation into the Fatherland. At times, neo-Nazi agitators coordinated their activities with state-financed *Vertriebenen* organizations that were directed by high-ranking German government officials.

Such was the case with Eduard Lintner, who wore two hats in the early and mid-1990s. While serving as Germany's deputy interior minister, he was also a key figure in the government-funded Sudetendeutsche Landsmannschaft (SL), a Bund der Vertriebenen affiliate that advocated German expansion into neighboring Czechoslovakia. This group, in turn, had close connections to a pro-Nazi organization called the Sudeten German Witikobund. Ironically, one of Lintner's tasks as deputy interior minister was to investigate neo-Nazi activity.[24]

The SL's ties to neo-Nazis and their New Right cousins were in keeping with the organization's political origins. Founded by former

SS officers and other Third Reich veterans, the SL never stopped calling for the return of the Sudetenland, which Hitler had annexed in 1938. Brutal memories of the Nazi occupation made the Czechs all the more sensitive to bullyboy tactics by German expellee associations, which stepped up their efforts in the post–Cold War era.[25]

Czechoslovakia split into two countries at the end of 1992 — a rupture fostered in part by a German foundation closely linked to the Christian Social Union (the Bavarian sister party of Kohl's CDU), which channeled funds to Slovak separatists and supported the rise of Slovakian strongman Vladimir Meciar, who enjoyed cordial relations with Bonn. During this period, the Sudetendeutsche Landsmannschaft and its neo-Nazi allies stubbornly maintained that ethnic German expellees and their descendants should be allowed to resettle in the Sudetenland — which composed one-third of the Czech Republic — while retaining their German citizenship.

Pressed to compensate Hitler's Czech victims, Bonn raised the matter of financial compensation for property expropriated from 2.5 million Sudeten Germans after the collapse of the Third Reich. After Czech courts nixed the idea, German finance minister Theo Waigel delivered a political broadside in which he barely masked a threat to block Prague's entry into the European Union. Czech officials were furious, but they could ill afford to cross swords with Bonn. With German capital accounting for the lion's share of foreign investment in the Czech Republic, Bonn had considerable leverage over its weaker neighbor. "The status of the Czech Republic has gone from that of a Soviet satellite to that of a German protectorate," declared a commentator for the *Prague Post.*[26]

The Polish government had similar qualms about German maneuvers in Silesia, Pomerania, and what used to be East Prussia. Neo-Nazis from across the Oder–Neisse line sought to galvanize support for a German takeover of large chunks of Polish territory. As in the Sudetenland, neofascist agitation paralleled — and in some ways complemented — efforts by Bonn-backed *Vertriebenen* groups that supplied revanchist propaganda to ethnic German enclaves in Poland. Several neo-Nazi groups focused on Upper Silesia, an area rich in coal, iron, and other natural resources. Most notable was the role of the National Offensive, which had been formed in 1990 by erstwhile followers of Michael Kühnen. A year later, the National

Offensive purchased a house in the Polish village of Dziewkowice, which soon changed its name back to Fraünfeld. This served as the base of operations for National Offensive spear-carrier Günter Boschütz, who published a strident German-language journal, *Silesian Report*. In cahoots with Bonn-financed *Vertriebenen* groups such as Deutsche Freundeskreise (German Friends), the National Offensive posted bilingual road signs and launched a twenty-four-hour German radio station. In May 1992, Boschütz hosted a public meeting in Kadlub, which featured an ultranationalist pep talk by Bela Ewald Althans, who visited Silesia on numerous occasions.[27]

Günter Boschütz was declared an undesirable alien and thrown out of Silesia by Polish authorities in December 1992, the same month that German officials banned the National Offensive. This belated measure by Bonn underscored the German government's ambiguous relationship with militant neo-Nazis, whose activities were sometimes oppositional in nature and sometimes supportive of government policy. Although hard-core neo-Nazis and New Right intellectuals rejected parliamentary democracy as a matter of principle, their efforts dovetailed with official efforts to limit immigration and promote ethnic German concerns beyond the borders of the Federal Republic. Neo-Nazi groups usually staked out extreme positions, thereby enabling the German government to appear comparatively moderate while pursuing hegemonic goals.

To be sure, some of the cultural projects promoted by Bonn were innocuous — sewing courses for traditional Silesian dresses, for example. The more sensitive *Vertriebenen* representatives ensured that subsidies from the Fatherland benefited Poles as well as Germans. But many *Volkdeutsche* in Poland could be ham-handed about expressing their reawakened ethnic pride. Old-fashioned German chauvinism had not been been completely smothered by decades of Communist oppression. (Teaching German in Silesian schools was prohibited until 1990.) Pent-up nationalist sentiment made the German minority all the more susceptible to manipulation by far Right revanchists, whose constant tub-thumping for *Grossdeutschland* tried the patience of Polish officials. President Lech Walesa accused ethnic Germans in Silesia of participating in an illegal *Vertriebenen* campaign to build monuments for German soldiers who died in World War II.[28]

Officials in Warsaw had already voiced their concerns about neo-Nazi violence directed against Polish visitors in the Federal Republic. More sparks flew in February 1993, when a Polish governor criticized German diplomats for organizing "unofficial groups" and holding unauthorized meetings with German community leaders in Silesia. The following month, a Polish army officer of German descent was convicted and jailed on charges of spying for Bonn. These incidents attested to nervousness among Polish officials about German economic encroachment and the subversive influence of German expellees. Warsaw, however, had little choice but to knuckle under when Bonn insisted that special rights and privileges be given to the German minority in Poland. Thus, *Volkdeutsche* in Silesia and Pomerania were able to vote in German elections and travel with a German passport. But the German parliament refused to pass legislation to protect the rights of ethnic minorities in the Federal Republic. This blatant double standard reinforced the impression that Bonn was engaging in traditional power politics.[29]

Kaliningrad was another target of pan-German nationalist agitation. Formerly known as Königsberg, this old Prussian seaport was transformed into a major staging area for the Soviet navy after World War II. When the Soviet Union collapsed, Kaliningrad ended up a geographic oddity wedged between Poland and the Baltic states but cut off from the rest of Russia. As a first step toward re-Germanizing this city, Bonn offered financial incentives to encourage *Volkdeutsche* to settle there. It quickly became a magnet for right-wing extremists, including the ubiquitous Ewald Althans, who tried to ingratiate himself with the growing German population by calling for renewed German rule in Kaliningrad. Once again, neo-Nazi machinations appeared to be largely in synch with the agenda of mainstream German politicians.[30]

Soon the Deutsche Bank had opened a branch office in Kaliningrad and German entrepreneurs established shops and restaurants to cater to a flood of tourists from the Federal Republic. In some parts of the city, street signs changed from Russian to German. Short of an outright *Anschluss,* German business leaders envisioned a demilitarized Kaliningrad, which would be accorded special status as a free port and a free-trade zone. While they spoke enthusiastically about a future Hong Kong in the Baltics, another Bonn-supported revanchist group, the Verein fur das Deutschum im Ausland, or VDA (Association for Germans Abroad), quietly promoted a German landgrab in the Kaliningrad region.[31]

Farther up the Baltic coast, German ultrarightists were flexing their muscle in Latvia. Joachim Siegerist, a German national who became a Latvian citizen by virtue of his father's Latvian heritage, formed a political party (For Latvia) in his adopted country that won 15 percent of the vote in October 1995. With this tally, Siegerist emerged as a potential political power broker in Latvia, even though he had been sentenced to an eighteen-month prison term in Germany for violating a law against inflammatory racist speech. A veteran of the Free Rudolf Hess campaign, Siegerist benefited from his extensive connections to the far Right in Germany, which supported his foray into Latvian politics.[32]

Siegerist's success was indicative of a dramatic shift to the Right in post–Cold War Latvia, where Holocaust-denial and the whitewashing of war criminals were encouraged by the government. Latvian youth enlisted in a resurrected version of the Aizsargi, the fascist militia that collaborated with Nazi Germany and conducted anti-Jewish pogroms of its own during World War II. Dressed in the same type of uniform as before, these political extremists patrolled the streets of Riga, Latvia's capital, as if Hitler had prevailed. The Latvian government also formed a 15,000-member paramilitary organization called the Zemisargi (Home Guard), which included two honorary units composed of Waffen SS veterans. In April 1993, the Latvian parliament observed a minute of silence in commemoration of the fallen soldiers of the Latvian SS legion. That year, the German government announced it would pay a monthly pension to former SS members in Latvia. But Bonn would not agree to compensate Hitler's Latvian victims.[33]

The Balkan Furnace

High up in the mountains, a flag emblazoned with the swastika flew over a military camp in the village of Klek. The Serbian street signs were torn down, and the town plaza was given a new name: Rudolf

Hess Square. Several soldiers in black uniforms congregated there at dawn, guzzling gin and comparing weapons. They were part of an international brigade of neo-Nazis who had come to fight for Croatia, which had split off from Yugoslavia in 1991. Much of the fiercest combat took place in Bosnia, where the territorial aspirations of Croats, Serbs, and Muslims collided amid a bedlam of violence and mutual slaughter.

As many as two hundred neo-Nazis from Germany volunteered for an irregular tour of duty in this Balkan battle zone. They were joined by right-wing extremists from France, Great Britain, Austria, Spain, Portugal, and the United States. German neo-Nazi leader Christian Worch endorsed the mercenary mission in his Hamburg-based periodical, *Index:* "Even though the political warriors at home have enough urgent tasks to perform, we view the support of the valiantly fighting and suffering Croatian people as an important issue."[34]

Most of these imported belligerents operated in tandem with the Croatian Defense Association (HOS), a private militia credited with putting up a tougher fight than Croatia's official combat units. With fifteen thousand men under arms, the HOS sought to create not just a greater Croatia but a National Socialist state. Their high-collared uniforms and black berets were modeled after those worn by Ustaše forces during World War II, when a Nazi puppet government led by Ante Pavelić ruled Croatia. This demented, vampiric criminal presided over the massacre of hundreds of thousands of Serbs, Jews, and Gypsies. Even Croatia's Nazi sponsors were shocked by the severity of the Ustaše atrocities, which left a deep scar on the collective memory of the Serbs. Not surprisingly, Serbian civilians feared the stiff-armed-saluting HOS members who sported Ustaše symbols and buttons with the likeness of Pavelić. Ustaše insignia were also worn by many soldiers in Croatia's regular army units.

The murderous record of the Ustaše was praised by neo-Nazi publications, such as Gerhard Lauck's U.S.-based *New Order,* which appeared in a dozen languages. After the Cold War ended and Yugoslavia fractured into national particles, the *New Order* ran numerous appeals on behalf of Croatia and recruited mercenaries to battle the Serbs. Several neo-Nazis from Western Europe who fought for Croatia were veterans of Michael Kühnen's anti-Zionist "inter-

the NEW ORDER

National Socialists Fight in Croatia !

National Socialist volunteers from France, Germany, Austria, Belgium, Hungary, England, Australia and other countries are fighting in an openly National Socialist unit in Croatia.

continued on page 2

Gary Lauck's New Order *recruits neo-Nazi mercenaries to fight for Croatia*

national brigade," which traveled to Baghdad to show its support for Saddam Hussein during the 1991 Gulf War. While this was largely a propaganda ploy, neo-Nazi adventurers in Croatia were involved in bloody confrontations with the enemy. "In Serbia we are killing the last Communists and tomorrow we shall destroy the tyranny of democracy," explained Michel Faci, a French neo-Nazi with close ties to the Kühnen network.[35]

The HOS set up training camps for Faci and his colleagues to prepare them for sabotage, night attacks, and raids behind Serbian lines. They learned how to build and detonate bombs and mines. Some were given military awards for shooting Serbs. After serving in Croatia, they returned home with their newly acquired knowledge of weapons and tactics. Bonn took no action against these neo-Nazi hired guns, even though their battlefield antics in Croatia constituted a clear violation of German law.*

* German neo-Nazi mercenaries were also active in South Africa, where they helped train Afrikaner extremists who opposed the end of apartheid. There was extensive contact between German neo-Nazis who had fought in Croatia and

Whatever assistance Croatia may have gotten from foreign mercenaries was a pittance compared with the political and military support provided by the German government. Whereas the United States and the rest of the European Community tried to prevent the breakup of Yugoslavia, Bonn unilaterally recognized Croatia as an independent nation at the end of 1991 and twisted arms to get other countries to comply with its wishes. American officials subsequently charged that Bonn was responsible for provoking the crisis in Yugoslavia, which had existed as a single country since 1919, except for the gruesome interlude when Hitler created a Croatian client state.

Reunified Germany's preemptive diplomatic maneuver led to a major escalation of the civil war in the Balkans, which took hundreds of thousands of lives and displaced more than a million people. Bonn exacerbated the conflict by supplying Croatia with large quantities of weapons. Between 1992 and 1994, Germany exported $320 million of military hardware — including MiG fighter jets, surface-to-air missiles, and late-model tanks — to Croatia, despite a United Nations arms embargo forbidding such commerce. Convoys of up to fifteen hundred military vehicles from former East Germany were discovered en route to the Balkan farrago. Germany also trained Croatian pilots and provided intelligence reports in an effort to vanquish their mutual enemy. Heleno Sano, an expert on German defense issues, commented on the psychological underpinnings of this policy: "In their 'historic unconscious,' the Germans have resented the Serbs since World War II, because despite the fact that Hitler sent in thirty divisions, he was unable to defeat the antifascist guerrillas led by Tito."[36]

Under the auspices of NATO, German warplanes saw action for the first time since 1945, carrying out aerial patrols to prevent Serbian fighter jets from flying over Bosnian territory. And when the tide turned in Croatia's favor in the summer of 1995, Bonn agreed to contribute up to four thousand military personnel to enforce a tenuous peace accord. German intervention was widely depicted in

---

members of the Afrikaner Resistance Movement, a far Right terrorist organization that was funded by the German BND in the early 1990s. Members of the Afrikaner Resistance Movement were implicated in the murder of African National Congress leader Chris Hani in 1993.

humanitarian terms, but General Klaus Naumann had something else in mind when he lobbied behind the scenes for a wider military role. While some German officials expressed a genuine reluctance to interfere in a place that had been devastated by Hitler, Naumann saw a chance for his men to test their mettle in a combat setting.

Bonn's decision to commit troops had significant implications that extended far beyond the Balkan furnace. It marked a new phase in a gradual, step-by-step process orchestrated by German leaders to expand their influence across the Continent. Critics warned that the Bosnia assignment would open the door to future military intervention in other areas — a development that Germany had prepared for by creating a highly mobile, 50,000-strong strike force capable of rapid deployment in any part of the world.[37]

In the short term, the principal beneficiary of reunified Germany's new military policy was Croatia, a country ruled by an unscrupulous opportunist who invoked the rhetoric of self-determination in order to manipulate popular opinion. President Franjo Tudjman's moral record was as dubious as that of his Serbian counterpart, Slobodan Milošević. Both leaders were former Communist Party hacks who opted for strong-arm measures while promoting the ultranationalist fantasy of a pure ethnic identity that had to be defended at all costs. Although Croatia and Serbia massacred their enemies with equal ferocity, Tudjman received much less criticism from abroad. This was partly because of Croatia's status as the victim of Serbian aggression at the outset of the civil war and Tudjman's willingness to forge a belated alliance with the Bosnian Muslims. Tudjman also gained sympathy in the West by promoting the spurious notion that Croatia was a democratic state struggling against Communist tyranny in Serbia. On several occasions, NATO launched reprisal raids against the Serbs, but no punitive action was taken when Croatian planes deliberately attacked United Nations posts, killing several peacekeepers in the summer of 1995.[38]

Tudjman, meanwhile, was engaged in a makeover of Croatian history. His book *Wastelands of Historical Truth* minimized the role of the Croatian people in the genocidal campaign against the Serbs during World War II. Tudjman insisted that far fewer Serbs had been killed by the Ustaše than generally thought. He also claimed that the figure of 6 million murdered Jews was vastly overblown. His attempt to diminish the importance of the Holocaust (a word he put between quotations) was applauded by the California-based Institute for Historical Review. "While Holocaust Revisionism is suppressed in some countries, in Croatia it has the official support from the highest level," the IHR gloated.[39]

Instead of repudiating Croatia's pro-Nazi legacy, Tudjman emphasized the continuity between his government and the wartime Ustaše puppet state, which, in his words, "reflected the centuries-old aspirations of the Croatian people." At Tudjman's instigation, Croatia changed its currency to the *kuna,* the same national currency used during the Ustaše regime. In the Croatian capital of Zagreb, the Square of Victims of Fascism was renamed the Square of Croatian Rulers. Leading personalities of the Ustaše period were rehabilitated, including Roman Catholic churchman Alojzije Stepinac, who collaborated with the Nazis and helped Ante Pavelić and many of his henchman escape to safe havens after the war. Right-wing Croatian exiles — especially those in South America, the United States, and Canada — were instrumental in supporting Tudjman's rise to power, and he repaid them by appointing a handful of former Ustaše officials to government positions. In deference to his principal backer, Tudjman made sure that no films were shown on Croatian television that depicted Germany as the aggressor during World War II.[40]

Croatia was not the only country in Eastern Europe to distort the history of the war years so that those who fought on Germany's side would appear in a more favorable light. A campaign to rehabilitate Marshal Ion Antonescu, the brutal leader of Romania's Axis-allied Iron Guard dictatorship, enjoyed wide support among opposition forces as well as members of the post–Cold War government in Bucharest. In May 1991, the Romanian parliament rose for a minute of silence in Antonescu's honor. While Romanian president Ion Iliescu disapproved of this gesture, he proceeded to forge a ruling coalition with several ultranationalist parties that hailed Antonescu as a martyr.[41]*

* The positive reappraisal of Antonescu was accompanied by attempts to deny the Holocaust in *Romania Mare,* the country's largest weekly (with a circulation of more than 500,000), which emerged as a mainstay of racial nationalism

By 1992, the Iron Guard had reemerged in Romania. Its revival was facilitated by the Hans-Seidl Stiftung, a German foundation associated with the Bavarian Christian Social Union, Chancellor Helmut Kohl's conservative coalition partner. Adulation for Antonescu and the Iron Guard was much in evidence at a June 1995 symposium in Sighet (a city in northern Romania) that the Hans-Seidl Stiftung funded. A symposium exhibit featured positive portraits of several officials in Antonescu's Iron Guard dictatorship, along with the chief of the Romanian section of Hitler's Nazi Party.[42]

The Hans-Seidl Stiftung was the same German foundation that provided financial support to Slovakian separatists who embraced Father Josef Tiso's wartime Nazi puppet state as a role model for fulfilling their dreams of national independence and sovereignty. Attempts to rehabilitate Tiso and his German-trained Hlinka Guard, which played a major role in the deportation of an estimated seventy thousand Slovakian Jews to Auschwitz, became part of the political mainstream in post–Cold War Slovakia. The governing coalition, led by Vladimir Meciar, included members of the far Right Slovak National Party who openly praised Tiso. Stanislav Panis, the deputy of the Slovakian Federal Assembly, pooh-poohed the notion that 6 million Jews died during the war.[43]

"A nation that cannot repudiate a fascist past may condemn itself to a fascist future," wrote Michael Ignatieff. This adage pertains to much of Eastern Europe, where radical nationalist movements have returned with a vengeance since the demise of the USSR. As in East Germany, many people naively expected a quick transition to a prosperous "free market" economy. But instead of instant improvement, jettisoning the Communist system resulted in poverty, homelessness, malnutrition, rampant crime, and "a deterioration of

---

after Nicolai Ceauşescu's "National Communist" regime was overthrown in December 1989. ("Who is an anti-Semite?" asked *Romania Mare*. "Someone who hates Jews more than necessary.") This xenophobic screed ran articles that cited negationists from Western Europe and the United States — including Mark Weber, editor of the IHR's *Journal of Historical Review* — to "prove" that the Holocaust never happened. It also espoused conspiracy theories about world-controlling Freemasons and Zionists. In the early 1990s, Paul Everec, the author of a rabidly anti-Semitic, Holocaust-denying book, *Reactionarul (The Reactionary)*, served as the director of Romanian state television.

unparalleled proportions in human welfare throughout the region," a 1994 UNICEF study concluded.[44]

Economic and social distress have always been exploited by scapegoating demagogues. Post-Soviet Eastern Europe was certainly no exception. Rumors of dark and sinister forces were spread by national chauvinists who blamed their country's hardships on the usual hidden cabals. Once again, anti-Semitism became "the spoken and unspoken lingua franca of exclusionist and xenophobic politics," even though there were hardly any Jews left in most places. Whether it assumed the form of cemetery desecrations by neo-Nazi vandals or cynical pandering by mainstream vote-seekers, anti-Semitism functioned as an index of social and psychological distress in the former Communist states. But more proximate enemies — mainly Gypsies and ethnic minorities — bore the brunt of xenophobic violence by skinhead gangs, which plagued every country in the region.[45]

The post–Cold War resurgence of racism and neofascism in Eastern Europe was fueled by the obsessive notion of an ethnically determined nation-state, whose members were bound together by the primacy of blood, lineage, and language rather than by recognized international borders or a set of laws that afforded equal rights and protections to all citizens. The latest conflagration in the Balkans showed just how dangerous the fallacy of ethnic purity could be, but it was not enough to discredit those who espoused such a fairy tale. On the contrary, far Right populists in Eastern Europe were implicitly legitimized by Germany, the strongest country on the Continent, which based its legal system on a racist conception of citizenship.*

* In addition to homegrown agitators who dredged up anti-Semitic motifs that harkened back to the 1930s, some countries had to contend with groups that were led or supported by profascist exiles who repatriated from the West, where they had carried on as vocal anti-Communists during the Cold War, often with CIA support. The Free Congress Foundation, founded by American far Right strategist Paul Weyrich, became active in Eastern European politics after the Cold War. Figuring prominently in this effort was Weyrich's right-hand man, Laszlo Pasztor, a former leader of the pro-Nazi Arrow Cross organization in Hungary, which had collaborated with Hitler's Reich. After serving two years in prison for his Arrow Cross activities, Pasztor found his way to the United States, where he was instrumental in establishing the ethnic-outreach arm of the Republican National Committee.

The nationalist crescendo in Eastern Europe was not simply a reaction to years of Soviet domination, as if steam had suddenly blown the top off a pressure cooker. A more complex dynamic had left its mark on the region. Unable to fulfill the high expectations generated by their own propaganda, Communist rulers manipulated popular prejudice to shore up an unpopular system. Indigenous racist tendencies were encouraged by hard-core nationalist factions that existed inside every Communist party in Eastern Europe. Periodic waves of officially inspired anti-Semitism during and after Stalin were manifestations of this tendency.[46]

When the Cold War ended, numerous Communists dropped their Marxist trappings and became active members of burgeoning ultranationalist groups. Similar developments ensued in Russia and other parts of the former Soviet Union, where neo-Nazis from Germany were eager to establish ties.

Courting Mother Russia

For several months, Russian security forces had been monitoring the activities of the Werewolf Legion, a neo-Nazi terrorist cell based in Moscow. When they raided the group's headquarters in July 1994, counterintelligence officers seized a cache of explosives. They also found a glass jar with a pair of human ears preserved in alcohol.

The cut-off ears belonged to a Werewolf legionnaire who had tried to set fire to the Moscow Sports Center during a Jews for Jesus conference. The would-be arsonist was murdered by his comrades after he failed to accomplish his mission. His ears were kept in a jar as a warning to other members of this neo-Nazi clique, which included several hitmen and ex-convicts. A Werewolf leader subsequently admitted that he had planned to firebomb other targets, including Moscow cinemas that were showing *Schindler's List*, a movie about the Holocaust that depicted Jewish people in a sympathetic light.[47]

Favorable portrayals of Jews were rare in Russia, where anti-Semitism — masquerading as "anti-Zionism" — had been a hallmark of Soviet propaganda since the late 1960s. Some widely published Russian authors, such as Lev Korneev, even questioned whether millions of Jews had been killed by the Nazis. After asserting that "the true number must be at least half or one-third the commonly assumed estimate," Korneev revised his figure yet again, citing "hundreds of thousands of Jews" murdered during World War II. Korneev's books, which were printed by the state-run Pravda publishing house in the late 1970s and early 1980s, listed Holocaust-denial texts from the United States and Western Europe as bibliographic references.[48]

After saturating the public with Judophobia, the Kremlin brought its strident anti-Zionist campaign to a halt when Mikhail Gorbachev came to power. But this officially sponsored crusade had left a huge imprint on the population. One of the unintended consequences of glasnost was the explosive growth of a grassroots anti-Semitic movement, which picked up where the government hatemongers had left off but abandoned their strictly anti-Zionist pretensions.

The expression of anti-Jewish prejudice increased dramatically as social and economic conditions deteriorated during the post-Soviet period. Anti-Semitic texts — including *The Protocols of the Elders of Zion* and the works of Hitler and Goebbels — were sold openly on the streets of Moscow and St. Petersburg, along with more than 150 ultranationalist newspapers that popped up like mushrooms after the Communist reign. Some neofascist broadsheets featured swastika-like symbols on their mastheads. Caricatures of Jews with big noses were traded like baseball cards at kiosks next to swanky hotels, where prostitutes catered to Western businessmen. Russian law technically forbade racist publications, but the authorities did little to prevent the widespread circulation of bilious literature that blamed the "Yid-Masonic conspiracy" for all of the country's past and present ills.

Although Russia had a long and virulent tradition of anti-Semitism, there was still something incongruous about public displays of Nazism in a country that had suffered so much at the hands of Hitler. Aleksandr Barkashov, a prominent Russian neofascist, explained why he bore no grudge against the Third Reich. World War II, he said, was the result of a plot by Jews to divide two great Aryan peoples — the Russians and the Germans. "The Holocaust against the Jews was created artificially to conceal a Jewish-inspired genocide which killed one hundred million Russians," Barkashov asserted.[49]

A former lance corporal and karate instructor in the Soviet army, Barkashov established his extremist credentials by joining Pamyat, a motley group of anti-Semitic fanatics who staged noisy public demonstrations in the late 1980s. Pamyat members wore black outfits in mourning for their country and passed out handbills that read "Russia for the Russians!" and "Death to the Yids!" One of their chiefs, Valery Emelyanov, had spent a few years in a mental institution after he chopped his wife to pieces with a butcher's knife. Another Pamyat leader, Dmitri Vasiliev, claimed that "the Jew Eichmann" had misled the Nazis on racial matters, which accounted for Hitler's misplaced hatred of the Slavs. "It is not necessary to be Jewish to be a Jew. . . . Everybody in power is a Jew, or their wives are," said Vasiliev.[50]

In the tangled skein of Soviet politics that characterized the Gorbachev era, Pamyat was backed by hard-line elements who opposed perestroika and the reform process. This support is how Pamyat received permission to hold meetings in Communist Party buildings in several Russian cities. Assisted by powerful forces within the Kremlin, it became the focal point of right-wing extremism in Russia during the waning days of the USSR.[51]

But Barkashov eventually grew disenchanted with Pamyat, which was riven by factionalism and incapable, in his view, of launching serious action against the government. In 1991, he founded his own organization — a well-disciplined, heirarchically structured paramilitary cadre called Russian National Unity (RNU). Dedicated to the principle of racial purity, the RNU was the largest and most dangerous of several neo-Nazi groups that emerged in post-Soviet Russia. All RNU initiates swore an oath of absolute loyalty to Barkashov, who called for the eradication of "racially inferior peoples" and the "genetic healing" of Mother Russia. The RNU führer often expressed his admiration for "Adolf Aloizovich" Hitler. "Yes, I am a Nazi," Barkashov boasted. "What's so bad about that? 'Nazi' stands for two words — nationalism and socialism. The first means the exultation and revival of one's nation, and socialism means justice. . . ."[52]

Dressed in military camouflage with modified fantail swastikas on their sleeves, RNU members underwent special training in hand-to-hand combat, shooting, and political ideology. Some of these young, muscle-bound troopers would participate in the defense of the "White House" in Moscow after Boris Yeltsin outlawed the Russian parliament and ordered an armed assault against his opponents in October 1993.

As Barkashov saw it, Russia's post-Soviet leaders were merely hired hands. "Our main adversary is quite clear — world Zionism, with its merry puppets, the United States and other Western countries," the RNU chief ruminated. "They are trying to tear apart and destroy Russia [because] Russia is the only force standing in the way of Jewish world hegemony. They also want to turn Russia into a source of cheap raw materials for the West."[53]

Operating out of a well-financed office close to the Kremlin, the RNU cultivated sympathetic contacts inside the Russian power structure. Barkashov claimed to have significant support at high levels inside the army, the police, the Interior Ministry, and the former KGB. Russian Interior Ministry spokesman Aleksei Petrenko confirmed that several officials in his department looked favorably upon the RNU: "I'm sure there are officers who share the viewpoints of Barkashov, but they do not speak openly about it."[54]

Barkashov endorsed the abortive putsch mounted by confused and partially inebriated Soviet reactionaries in August 1991. This comic opera coup attempt set the stage for a more decisive power grab by Yeltsin and hastened the undoing of the USSR. By the end of the year, sovereign Russia would emerge from the ashes of the Soviet empire. Barkashov viewed the sudden changes as an opportunity. "I simply feel it in my bones . . . our time is approaching," he stated.[55]

The breakup of the Soviet Union was both a major calamity and a catalyst for right-wing extremists in Russia, who sought to capitalize on the disorientation, despair, and humiliation that gripped many of their countrymen. This traumatic event would shape the course of Russian politics for many years to come. When the USSR disintegrated at the end of 1991, more than 25 million Russians were left stranded in someone else's state. They would become the target of an increasingly assertive anti-Russian nationalism, which provided a volatile issue for Barkashov and other Russian chauvinists to rally around. At the same time, Russia itself was home to more than one hundred different nationalities. Like Germany's neo-Nazis, Russian fascists played upon the resentment of foreigners and ethnic minorities, who were subjected to sporadic attacks by ultra-right-wing gangs.[56]

In addition to causing a great deal of personal and political insecurity, the demise of the Soviet superpower exacerbated an ongoing Russian identity crisis that was partly rooted in geography. Again the comparison to Germany, with its often-shifting borders, is relevant. Whereas Germany is situated in the middle of a continent and has flip-flopped neurotically between East and West, Russia is sprawled over two continents. The Russians have had a hard time figuring out whether they belong first and foremost to Europe or to Asia — or whether they have a unique "Eurasian" destiny to fulfill. Intrinsic to Russia's national psyche is a vision of itself as "the Third Rome," a country entrusted with a historical and spiritual mission to redeem humankind.

Oscillating amid the double pull of Europe and Asia, Russian political culture was, in a broad sense, split into two opposing camps: Westernizers versus Slavophiles. The former was typified by Peter the Great, who derided Russian backwardness and emphasized the need to emulate the West, while the latter maintained that indigenous methods and institutions were better suited for Russia than a capitalist economic system and a democratic form of government. Ardent Slavophiles like Barkashov disparaged Western materialism and condemned the Enlightenment as a source of moral decay that eroded ancestral Russian values and contaminated the Russian soul.[57]

A preoccupation with the moral degeneracy of liberalism in general and American culture in particular was central to Russian nationalist thought. German neo-Nazis were similarly obsessed. Therein lay the basis of an ideological affinity between right-wing extremists in both countries. "I feel more sympathy for Russian patriots than for American cosmopolitans," said the Hamburg-based neo-Nazi leader Christian Worch, who condemned the United States as a purveyor of decadence. "America is on another continent and the people there are not a *Volk*, as we mean it in Germany. The

United States is a mixture of different races." But Worch was quick to emphasize that the Russians "are white people. They are much closer to us, racially and geographically."

Of course, this is what Major General Otto Ernst Remer had been saying all along, but the U.S.-Soviet face-off had foreclosed any possibility of a revived German-Russian alliance. "Remer had some interesting ideas, but he was ahead of his time," said Worch, who met the aging Nazi legend on several occasions. "Remer wanted to deal with the Communists in Russia to further German interests, not for ideological reasons. This was not realistic during the Cold War."[58]

After the USSR collapsed, the prospects for constructing a Berlin-Moscow axis as a hedge against the United States improved considerably. By this time, however, Remer was too old to assume an active role in such a project. But several of Remer's erstwhile associates, including Bela Ewald Althans, would attempt to make his dream come true.

In the early 1990s, German neo-Nazis fanned out across the ruins of the former Soviet Union. Some went to the Ukraine, where former members of the Waffen SS Galicia Division held a series of public reunions in Kiev and Lvov in August 1993. Several veterans of the Galicia Division, which was composed entirely of Ukrainian Nazi collaborators who fought against the Soviet Union, had carried on their anti-Communist crusade as CIA assets during the Cold War. After living as expatriates in the United States, Canada, and Great Britain, some of these die-hard fascists returned home to greet their SS comrades. A few stayed in the Ukraine and became advisors to the new government. "It's fantastic what's going on there," exulted Althans, who visited the Ukraine and conferred with local neo-Nazi groups that favored close relations with Germany.[59]*

Developments in the Ukraine may have pleased the likes of Althans, but the real prize was Mother Russia. Several neo-Nazi dele-

* Officials from the Ukrainian Defense Ministry attended the Waffen SS Galicia Division reunion in Kiev, where a neo-Nazi organization called the Society of Ernst Röhm's Friends had recently been founded. The event in Lvov — where 140,000 Jews had been exterminated by Ukrainian nationalists *before* the arrival of Hitler's soldiers — was endorsed by the city council. City officials in Lvov also renamed Peace Street after Stephan Bandera, a notoriously savage Ukrainian Nazi collaborator who worked for the CIA during the Cold War.

gations from Germany traveled to Moscow and St. Petersburg to meet their Russian counterparts. On two occasions — in 1992 and 1993 — Althans undertook fact-finding missions in Russia, where he held strategy sessions with leading National Socialists, including Aleksandr Barkashov. These excursions were financed by Ernst Zündel, a Toronto-based Holocaust-denier who became Althans's chief sponsor during the post–Cold War era. Zündel was enthusiastic about the prospects of a revitalized German-Russian linkup. "Our generation could pull this off if we really put our mind to it. If we are going to have a National Socialist government anywhere in the world, it will be in Russia," he predicted in 1995. "I foresee such a government coming to power within a decade."[60]

Althans journeyed to Russia again in August 1994 — this time accompanied by his German émigré boss from Canada. "I was fascinated to see copies of Russian newspapers with swastikas on them, illustrated with lurid Jewish stars dripping with blood," said Zündel, who bought a gold-embossed edition of *Mein Kampf* in downtown Moscow. During his visit, he hobnobbed with representatives of Barkashov's Russian National Unity and other prominent opponents of Boris Yeltsin. "Some of the former KGB and army officers I spoke to carried on as if they were having a conference with von Ribbentrop," Zündel mused. "They were all thinking in geopolitical terms."[61]

Zündel was particularly impressed by Aleksandr Stergilov, a tall, striking ex-KGB general in his late forties with blue eyes, wavy hair, and sharp Slavic features. Like the German neo-Nazis who wooed him, Stergilov hated democracy with a passion and blamed the Jews for nearly every problem under the sun. "We talked about pan-Slavism in a new white racialist form," Zündel recounted, "and how the Russians have become what the Germans used to be for the rest of Europe. The Russians are now the racial border guards on the eastern frontier. They have taken over the task of guarding against the influx of Muslims from the south and Chinese from the east."

In an effort to forge a broad-based, antigovernment alliance, Stergilov, the ex-KGB bigwig, teamed up with Barkashov, the unabashed neo-Nazi. Together they were instrumental in setting up a militant umbrella organization called the Russian National Assembly (RNA), which called for the reunification of all Slavs living in the former USSR. "The security organs were always composed of patriotically-minded people who fought against the destruction of our nation," Stergilov explained. "Many of my former colleagues are doing the same as I."[62]

That a large percentage of RNA members were active-duty intelligence officers enhanced Stergilov's standing among the bewildering array of antigovernment groups that took shape in post-Soviet Russia. The general was widely recognized as one of the key leaders of the fledgling "Red-Brown" opposition. Actually, the so-called Red-Brown alliance of neo-Communists and right-wing nationalists was somewhat of a misnomer, for this inchoate coalition also included a significant component of "Whites" who favored returning to a monarchy. While the Whites romanticized the czarist period, the Reds pined for the second coming of Stalin. Despite their differences, the anti-Yeltsin forces were united in the belief that a strong hand was necessary to rescue Russia from the depredations of the West. Intoxicated by the heady brew of great power chauvinism, they wanted to redraw their country's boundaries to reflect the better days of a bygone empire. This longing for an expanded territorial domain was well understood by Ewald Althans and other German neo-Nazi suitors who courted Mother Russia after the USSR split apart.

Here Come the National Bolsheviks

His Serbian hosts couldn't have been happier when Eduard Limonov, one of the most charismatic of the new wave of Russian nationalist leaders, donned battle dress and joined a sniper detail at a military outpost perched in the hills of Bosnia-Herzegovina. Television cameras recorded his gleeful expression as the handsome Russian impresario took aim and squeezed off a long burst of machine-gun fire in the direction of Sarajevo down below. Limonov loved to pose for photos with Serbian irregulars when he visited rump Yugoslavia shortly after the outbreak of the civil war. The

Russian press subsequently reported that the Bosnian government had put a $500,000 bounty on his head — a story that further enhanced Limonov's status as a cult hero back home.[63]

"Russians and Serbs are blood brothers," Limonov crooned. He was among the more than one thousand volunteers from Russia who flocked to Yugoslavia as if on a pilgrimage. Bound by ethnic ties, a shared Cyrillic alphabet, and the Christian Orthodox faith, high-profile Russian nationalist delegations regularly turned up in Belgrade, where they were welcomed by top Serbian officials. They all came to fight for Serbia, Russia's traditional military ally — a gesture that put them distinctly at odds with German neo-Nazi mercenaries who sided with Croatia. En route to joining a Chetnik regiment in a Serbian-held enclave in Bosnia, Limonov was feted by Serbian president Slobodan Milošević.[64]

Like their German counterparts, the Russian "mercs" who toured the Balkans saw it as an opportunity to sharpen their military skills in preparation for future confrontations closer to home. Limonov and his colleagues spoke of employing "Serbian tactics" (otherwise known as "ethnic cleansing") in an effort to regain areas of the former USSR where Russians were heavily concentrated. Russian fighters figured in numerous armed conflicts in neighboring ex-Soviet republics, including Georgia, Moldova, Tajikistan, Armenia, and Azerbaijan. Limonov bragged of smelling gunpowder in five different combat zones.

For Limonov, war was life at its peak. A novelist by profession, he saw no contradiction between his calling as an artist and his military kick. Aptly described as the "leather-clad bad lad" of Russian radical politics, Limonov had spent eighteen years abroad as a dissident writer — first in New York, then in Paris. He counted among his heroes the Russian anarchist Michael Bakunin ("our national pride") and Stalin ("the Bolshevik Caesar of our country in its best period"). Limonov also admired the Italian futurists who inspired Mussolini, and he recognized a kindred spirit in Yukio Mishima, the Japanese ultranationalist who committed hara-kire in 1970. "Mishima and I belong to the same political camp," Limonov explained. "He is a traditionalist like me."[65]

But Limonov's modus operandi was hardly traditional. It was as if he had fashioned his crop-haired, bare-armed, movie-star image after "Eddie-baby," the bisexual persona he embroidered in a series of fictionalized autobiographical adventures. With his charming hoodlum air, Limonov quickly developed a reputation as the Johnny Rotten of the Russian expatriate scene. At one point during a writer's conference, he reacted to an anti-Russian gibe by slamming a British author over the head with a champagne bottle. Limonov enjoyed giving the literary finger to more-staid Russian exiles who were vexed by his maverick writing style, which at times seemed like a cross between Ernst Jünger and Henry Miller. Aleksandr Solzhenitsyn despised young Eduard, calling him "a little insect who writes pornography." But Limonov was quite popular in Russia, where his novels became bestsellers when they were finally published in the early 1990s.

Limonov had a definite bone to pick with Soviet dissidents like Andrei Sakharov, who idealized the West without any firsthand experience of what it was like. After living in New York City for six years, Limonov concluded that American society was anything but a dream come true. He ridiculed the banality of American culture and dismissed democracy as little more than window dressing for unaccountable corporate powers that dominated Western politics. He believed that far from being a panacea for Russia's ills, this kind of "democracy" would only make matters worse. "We are a ruined country, a country that is dying," said Limonov. "Only a national revolution can save us."

Limonov ended his lengthy exile and returned to Russia, where he joined the growing Red-Brown opposition. On February 23, 1992, he attended a militant protest march in Moscow. "It was the first time I saw the red flags with the hammer and sickle flying together with the black, yellow, and white flags of old Russia," Limonov recounted. "It was absolutely gorgeous, a perfectly natural combination." But the demonstration turned violent, as Limonov and other extremists clashed with police. One person died and dozens were wounded in what proved to be a harbinger of much bloodier battles in the months ahead.

To rescue his troubled homeland, Limonov prescribed several remedies — reviving pre-Communist Russian culture, creating a true socialist economy, and widening Russia's borders to include areas in the nearby republics with predominantly Russian populations. "It's an absolutely sick situation," he asserted. "More than twenty-five million Russians living outside their country. At the very least, the new borders of Russia should correspond to the ethnic borders of the Russian people." Limonov also maintained that Russian foreign policy should emphasize contact with old allies, such as Iraq and Cuba. He even favored giving nuclear weapons to Serbia.

As for a possible German-Russian tryst in the future, Limonov felt this was "wishful thinking, unfortunately, because it would do a lot of good for both countries." He believed that German priorities would inevitably clash with Russian interests in the Balkans, Kaliningrad, the Ukraine, and other areas. In this respect, Limonov differed from Aleksandr Barkashov, who was more optimistic about a rapprochement with the Germans. Although they viewed themselves as comrades in the same struggle, Limonov felt that Barkashov's Nazi fetish was counterproductive. "The swastika has no chance in our country," said Limonov. "We lost so many people in the war with Germany that we are immune to it."[66]

In an effort to carve out a unique niche for himself on the Red-Brown landscape, Limonov created the National Bolshevik Front (NBF). The Front was an amalgam of half a dozen groups of mostly young people who shared Eddie-baby's intuition that overt neo-Nazi manifestations would not get very far in Russia. National Bolshevism was deemed more congenial to the masses. After two of its members were arrested for possessing hand grenades (Limonov claims they were planted), the NBF generated a publicity flash by calling for a boycott of Western goods. "We want the Americans out of Russia. They can take their McDonald's and Coca-Cola with them," Limonov declared. At political rallies, his organization chanted refrains such as "Ruble yes, dollar no!" and "Yankees go home!"[67]

Although the slogans lacked originality, Limonov insisted that National Bolshevism was the most avant-garde political movement in the world. Actually, it was by no means a new phenomenon. National Bolshevism had a long and complex history, dating back to the 1920s. Championed by writers such as Ernst Niekisch and Ernst Jünger, it was one of several non-Nazi fascisms that percolated in Germany's conservative revolutionary mix before Hitler seized power.* For the most part, the German version of National Bolshevism remained an intellectual curiosity — unlike in Russia, where it emerged as a significant political tendency within both the ruling elite and certain dissident circles.

The roots of National Bolshevism in the USSR can be traced to the tumultuous period following the October Revolution. In order to stabilize the new regime and win the civil war against the "Whites," Vladimir Lenin and other Communist leaders realized they had to make concessions to Russian ethnic sentiments. By casting "1917" in national terms and identifying themselves with Russian interests, they hoped to assuage some of the malcontents of the czarist empire, which was rapidly crumbling.[68]

Many of the Whites switched sides when they realized that the Bolsheviks offered the best hope for resurrecting Russia as a great power. This was a crucial reason why much of the czarist High Command joined the Red Army. Former czarists made up about half of the 130,000-member Red Army officer corps. The Bolsheviks also incorporated elements of the protofascist Black Hundreds (the Russian gangs that instigated anti-Jewish pogroms in the early 1900s) into their ranks.[69] The steady stream of defectors from the ultra-Right contributed to the rise of National Bolshevism in Mother Russia and laid the basis for the Red-Brown alliance of the future.†

* Whereas the eastern orientation of many conservative revolutionary intellectuals was largely a matter of foreign policy, Ernst Niekisch saw some advantages in Communism, as long as it assumed a national form. But Niekisch, Germany's leading proponent of National Bolshevism, was never a member of the German Communist Party. He was, however, enthusiastic about Bolshevik revolutionaries in Russia. A radical anticapitalist, Niekisch maintained that Soviet Russia was Germany's only effective counterforce to Versailles and "the decadent West." Waxing poetically, he mused: "Where Germanic blood mingles with the Slav, that is where a true state exists. . . . In the east, from Germanic-Slav stock, Prussia rose to greatness."

† During and immediately after the Bolshevik power grab, hundreds of thousands of Russians abandoned their homeland to escape the violence, chaos, and destitution of a country in the throes of revolution. Many of these embittered refugees joined fascist exile organizations, such as the National Toilers' Alliance, which sought to topple the Soviet state. But other right-wing nationalists took a different tack.

After the creation of the Soviet Union in 1922, the official ideology of the USSR developed into a kind of National Bolshevism as Stalin took up the banner of "socialism in one country." Stalin's famous dictum was tempered by geopolitical considerations: Communist Russia sought to reassure capitalist Germany that the spirit of Rapallo would take precedence over exporting world revolution.

In the wake of October 1917, some Russian anti-Communists came to view the Bolshevik takeover as a positive development. One of the more notable converts was Professor Nikolai Ustrialov, who changed his mind about the revolution after fleeing his native country. Ustrialov felt that the defeat of the Bolsheviks would be a great tragedy because they offered the best hope for "reestablishing Russia as a Great Power." As far as he was concerned, the internationalist verbiage spouted by Bolshevik leaders was merely camouflage, a useful tool for the restoration of Russia as a unified state and for its future expansion. "The Soviet regime will strive with all its power to reunite the borderlands with the center — in the name of world revolution," said Ustrialov. "Russian patriots will fight for this too — in the name of a great and united Russia. Even with the endless difference in ideology, the practical road is the same."

Although he rejected Communism as an alien import from Europe, Ustrialov insisted that the Bolshevik revolution was an authentic expression of the Russian spirit. Calling for an end to the civil war, he urged all Russian nationalists to collaborate with Lenin. This was the upshot of a collection of articles by Ustrialov and several other right-wing émigrés published in Prague under the title *Smena vekh (Change of Landmarks)* in 1921. The Smenavekhites thought of themselves as "National Bolsheviks," a term Ustrialov first discovered while reading German newspapers that reported on the political philosophy of Ernst Niekisch.

As Mikhail Agursky notes in *The Third Rome*, the Soviet government subsequently opted to subsidize the Smenavekhist review, which functioned as the principal National Bolshevik tribune in Russia during the early years of the USSR. Sanctioned by the Kremlin, the views of Ustrialov began to exert a subtle influence on the Soviet political system. He spoke for many right-wing extremists in Russia when he praised Stalin's strong hand. "One cannot help rejoicing in seeing how [the Communist Party] is now being led on a confident iron march by the great Russian Revolution to the national pantheon prepared for it by history," he declared. Although Ustrialov was later executed during one of Stalin's maniacal killing sprees, some of his Smenavekhite colleagues not only survived but went on to play important ideological roles in the Soviet Union. The Soviet historical encyclopedia indicates that several former Smenavekhites held leading positions in government and society.

When Hitler double-crossed his Soviet partner and invaded the USSR, Stalin roused the Russian folk with nationalist rhetoric about fighting "the Great Patriotic War." Of course, internationalism was still touted as a central Communist tenet by Stalin, whose Georgian roots enabled him to cloak his extreme Russian chauvinism.[70]

During the Cold War, Soviet officials sought to motivate the masses by whipping up Russian pride. At the same time, they continued to mouth the requisite Marxist-Leninist incantations. The result was an uneasy synthesis of Communism and Russian nationalism, which contradicted yet reinforced each other. Soviet leaders realized that playing the nationalist card was conducive to fortifying a patriotic mood. But there was always the danger that it would trigger a backlash among ethnic minorities in the USSR (which it did) and undermine the internationalist doctrine that was still a key source of legitimacy for the Kremlin. German scholar Klaus Mehnert aptly compared Soviet Russia to an airplane running on two ideological engines — one Marxist-Leninist, the other nationalist — that were never entirely in synch. Sooner or later, the two motors would cease to function as a viable pair. Under the circumstances, a crash landing was inevitable.[71]

The National Bolsheviks were well positioned to survive the wreckage. Unlike the dissidents who challenged the legitimacy of the Soviet Union and often ended up in labor camps, many National Bolsheviks had accommodated themselves to the system in the interests of maintaining a powerful state. Instead of rejecting Communism outright, they sought to minimize its significance by emphasizing "traditional Russian values." This resonated with a deeply entrenched nationalist faction within the Soviet ruling elite. The dissemination of National Bolshevik ideas by certain state-run media* was a clear indication that powerful forces — including im-

* The main National Bolshevik mouthpiece in the late 1960s was *Molodaya Gvardiya (Young Guard)*, the official journal of the Communist Youth League. In poems and essays devoted to the resurrection of the "national spirit" and "land and soil," this xenophobic magazine exalted the Soviet military and trumpeted Russian racial superiority. Instead of engaging in Marxist class analysis, *Molodaya Gvardiya* writers often juxtaposed Russian spirituality against crass American materialism. Dismissing modern Western civilization as "barbarism in a cellophane wrapper," the journal warned that Russian youth were in danger

portant sectors of the Communist Party apparatus (particularly its youth organization) and the Red Army — regarded such views as politically expedient and desirable.[72]

When the titanic crack-up finally came in December 1991, the nationalist serpent emerged from its Communist cocoon with a full set of teeth. It slithered into the hothouse of post-Soviet politics, where neo-Stalinists collaborated with monarchists, fascists, Orthodox Christians, pagans, conservative ecologists, and other strange bedfellows. They were all spinning in a weird ideological vortex that defied standard interpretation. "What's going on in Russia is a whole new kind of politics," Limonov asserted, "with new goals and new movements that cannot be categorized or classified according to the old vocabulary of Left versus Right. These definitions belong to the past. To apply them to [post-Soviet] Russia is wrong."[73]

This notion was shared by Alain de Benoist, who visited Russia in March 1992 and participated in several public meetings with prominent opposition figures. For a number of years, the leading French New Right philosopher had argued that it was important to move beyond the traditional Left/Right dichotomy. Since the end of the Cold War, this cleavage had become completely antiquated, according to de Benoist. Rather than Right against Left, he felt it made more sense to think in terms of the establishmentarian "cen-

---

of becoming "transistorized." Democracy was depicted as a product of social degeneration, and strong-arm governing methods were cheered. The Molodaya Gvardiya publishing house also printed immensely popular science fiction novels, a genre replete with thinly disguised racist and anti-Semitic themes. Its rabidly nationalist orientation notwithstanding, *Molodaya Gvardiya* was awarded the Order of the Red Banner of Labor by the Supreme Soviet on the fiftieth anniversary of the journal's founding.

During the Brezhnev years, National Bolshevik ideas were also featured in *Veche,* a dissident journal published in West Germany, which functioned as a sounding board for various strands of Russian nationalism. Gennadii Shimanov, an occasional contributor to *Veche,* hailed Russians as "God's chosen people" and described the Soviet Union as a "mystical organism," a "spiritual detonator" for all mankind. Another *Veche* author, Dr. Valeri Skurlatov, published a "Code of Morals," which advocated the preservation of racial purity and the sterilization of Russian women who have sexual intercourse with foreigners.

ter" versus all antisystem forces on the "periphery." The center versus the periphery was a concept that appealed to his Red-Brown hosts in Russia. They were also delighted to hear de Benoist's harsh criticism of "globalization" and his depiction of the United States as the supreme enemy.[74]

Eduard Limonov first encountered de Benoist in Paris, a city that bored the Russian exile because, as he put it, "there is no war there." Nevertheless, he frequently returned to the French capital, where he hobnobbed with various iconoclasts, including another ardent proponent of National Bolshevism, Jean-François Thiriart. The eccentric optician from Brussels had recently come out of political retirement, and he welcomed the chance to share his thoughts at a colloquium in Paris. At the time, Thiriart was working with the Belgian-based Parti Communautaire National-Européen (PCN), a small organization composed of former Maoists and neofascists who agitated against "American-Zionist imperialism" and "cosmopolitanism." Run by Luc Michel, a self-described "National Communist" with a long history of neo-Nazi associations, the PCN reprinted and distributed several books by Thiriart, who held forth as the group's ideological leader.[75]

In August 1992, Thiriart led a delegation of National Communists from Western Europe to Russia, where he discussed his views with leading members of the political opposition. Whereas Ewald Althans and his German cohorts always made a beeline to Aleksandr Barkashov's neo-Nazi lair, Thiriart met with a mostly different cast of Red-Brown characters. While in Moscow, the Belgian extremist carried on like a geopolitical know-it-all, dispensing advice to people such as Yegor Ligachev, the top conservative within the Soviet Politburo and the de facto deputy of the Communist Party until Gorbachev dumped him in 1990. During their conversation, Ligachev warmed to Thiriart's proposal for a continental partnership that would unite Europe and Russia as a counterweight to the United States. But Ligachev added the following proviso: "I think that an authentic unification with Europe can be possible only once we have reestablished the Soviet Union, perhaps under a new name." Thiriart nodded in assent.[76]

"Eurasia contra America" — this was the main point of convergence between Thiriart and his retinue of newfound Russian comrades, which included a dreamy-eyed, thirty-year-old journalist named Aleksandr Dugin. It was Dugin who first suggested to Eduard Limonov that they establish the National Bolshevik Front. An influential figure in Red-Brown circles, Dugin helped write the political program for the Communist Party of the Russian Federation, led by Gennadi Zyuganov, who also strategized with Thiriart. Zyuganov rarely referred to Marx or Lenin, preferring instead to elegize Russia as "the dreamer-nation" and the "mobilizer-nation." Dugin's influence was evident when Zyuganov declared, "We [Russians] are the last power on this planet that is capable of mounting a challenge to the New World Order — the global cosmopolitan dictatorship."[77]

A vociferous critic of "one-worldism," Dugin founded and edited a journal called *Elementy* that ran a lengthy and laudatory article about Thiriart in its inaugural issue. The young Russian shared the European New Right's fascination with the Conservative Revolution of the 1920s. Dugin tried to set up something like a New Right network in Moscow, but de Benoist was put off by his feverish nationalism. *Elementy* simultaneously glorified Russia's czarist and Stalinist past, while praising everyone from Arthur Moeller van den Bruck to Heinrich Himmler. Its readers were treated to the first Russian translations of Julius Evola, the Italian Nazi philosopher and "traditionalist" much admired by neofascists throughout Europe. But Dugin never bothered to disclose Evola's affiliation with the SS. "Dugin is a paradoxical man who can support ten points of view or more at the same time," Limonov said of his close friend and political collaborator.[78]

In addition to *Elementy,* which was geared toward an intellectual audience, Dugin had a hand in editing *Dyen (The Day),* a fiery, nationalist newsweekly with a huge circulation. Billed as the voice of "the spiritual opposition" in Russia, *Dyen* ran excerpts from *The Protocols of the Elders of Zion* and reported favorably on neo-Nazi movements in the West. Its political humor column was filled with vulgar anti-Jewish jokes. Each issue featured a section on "conspiratology" (a word coined by the editors), which included zany stories about how Yeltsin's brain had secretly been altered during a visit to the United States. *Dyen* claimed that those who rallied to Yeltsin's call during the abortive coup in August 1991 had been "zombified" by "psychotropic generators" housed in the U.S. embassy in Moscow.[79]

Wild conspiracy theories were a staple of Russian right-wing extremists. In this respect, they were no different than their neofascist counterparts in other countries. But *Dyen*'s "conspiratology" had the endorsement of several members of the Russian parliament, who sat on the paper's editorial board along with former KGB General Aleksandr Stergilov. Most significant, *Dyen* functioned as the unofficial mouthpiece for the National Salvation Front (NSF), Russia's leading Red-Brown umbrella organization. *Dyen*'s editor in chief, Aleksandr Prokhanov, was cochairman of the NSF, which encompassed the usual mish-mash of ideological tendencies, National Bolshevism not excepted.[80]

While he was in Moscow, Jean Thiriart attended several planning sessions with neo-Communists and right-wing nationalists that culminated in the formation of the National Salvation Front in September 1992. Eduard Limonov was involved in launching the NSF, and he also served on its steering committee. Headed by Limonov and Dugin, the National Bolshevik Front was one of more than forty militant opposition groups that joined the NSF and endorsed its call for the overthrow of the Russian government. In its initial manifesto — which *Dyen* dutifully published — the NSF assailed the "rapacious experiments" of the Yeltsin administration, including privatization, the lifting of price controls, and other shock-therapy techniques that resulted in enormous hardship throughout the country. Yeltsin countered by trying to ban the NSF. He also threatened to crack down on *Dyen* and several other ultranationalist newspapers, but Yeltsin's efforts were stymied by members of the Russian parliament, many of whom supported the Red-Brown opposition.

Thiriart kept abreast of this evolving power struggle after he returned to Brussels. He intended to visit Russia again, but the seventy-year-old Belgian died from a heart attack in his asleep on November 23, 1992. After his sudden passing, Thiriart was eulogized in several nationalist press outlets in Russia, including *Dyen*, which published some of his writings. One article implored his National Bolshevik colleagues to work toward the construction of the grand Continental power bloc that he had long envisioned. "It is imperative to build ideological, theoretical, and political bonds between clear thinking elites of the former USSR and Western Europe," said Thiriart. "This revolutionary elite must unite and prepare to expel the American invader from European soil."[81]

Thiriart's Western European disciples proceeded to set up a support group known as the European Liberation Front (ELF), which maintained regular contact with the leaders of the National Salvation Front in Russia. By coincidence, the European Liberation Front was the same name chosen by Francis Parker Yockey and his British cohorts in the late 1940s, when they tried to develop an underground neo-Nazi network that would work in cahoots with the Soviet Union against American occupation forces in Europe. The latter-day ELF consisted of "National Communist" grouplets in several European countries, including Belgium, France, Italy, Switzerland, and Hungary. Each of these small Red-Brown hybrids was comprised of neofascists and neo-Stalinists who embraced Thiriart's political credo.[82]

The ELF cheered when the leaders of the National Salvation Front announced that they had formed a shadow government in Russia and were preparing to take power. In September 1993, Yeltsin summarily disbanded the Russian parliament. This presidential decree set the stage for the bloody confrontation between Yeltsin loyalists and the so-called "patriotic forces" who gathered at the Russian White House, where the parliament normally functioned.

Sensing that the long-awaited civil war was about to begin, Limonov and his supporters flocked to the parliament building. They were joined by thousands of Red-Brown extremists, including Barkashov's black-shirted storm troopers who brought their weapons with them, expecting a fight. As tensions escalated, the European Liberation Front dispatched several people to Moscow to underscore their solidarity with the Russian opposition. Michel Schneider, a French neofascist representing the ELF (who had previously accompanied Thiriart on a trip to Moscow), was among those injured in the White House when Yeltsin finally convinced the army to send in the tanks in early October.[83]

Hundreds were killed during the assault and many more were wounded. Limonov and several opposition leaders were thrown in jail. But Barkashov and dozens of armed resisters escaped through a network of underground tunnels after putting up a fierce fight. A few weeks later, Barkashov was shot by an unknown assailant from a moving car. Security officials arrested Russia's top neo-Nazi as he lay recovering in a hospital bed. He, too, was headed for prison.

Yeltsin, meanwhile, moved quickly to muzzle his critics by outlawing *Dyen* and a dozen other antigovernment newspapers. Several political parties were also banned. As the year drew to a close, it appeared that the Russian president had gained the upper hand. Then something happened that he never expected.

Dreaming of a New Rapallo

"When I come to power, there will be a dictatorship. . . . I'll do it without tanks on the streets. Those who have to be arrested will be arrested quietly at night. I may have to shoot a hundred thousand people, but the other three hundred million will live peacefully."[84]

Thus spoke Vladimir Volfovich Zhirinovsky, the mercurial, reddish-haired ultranationalist who trounced his rivals in Russia's December 1993 parliamentary elections. A strong speaker with Hitler-style charisma, this would-be tyrant challenged his foes to duels and made shocking statements as a matter of course. Zhirinovsky seemed to enjoy playing the role of the *yurodivy*, the eccentric political clown whose unpredictable antics somehow managed to convey a dose of Russian folk wisdom. At a moment's notice, he could shift from holy fool to holy terror: "I am all-powerful! . . . I will follow in Hitler's footsteps."[85]

Zhirinovsky often bemoaned the dire racial threat facing "white civilization." His advice to Russia was simple: "We must deal with minorities as America did with the Indians and Germany did with the Jews."

Less than two months after the deadly shoot-out at the White House, Zhirinovsky's mistitled Liberal Democratic Party won 25 percent of the vote, far exceeding the rest of the electoral pack. Because he had stayed out of the bloody fray, Zhirinovsky was favorably positioned to reap a huge protest vote while most

Red-Brown leaders stewed in jail. Promising the moon and cheap vodka, his telegenic campaign tapped into the wounded pride and deep despair that gripped the population. Zhirinovsky's election posters resounded with the slogan "I will bring Russia off her knees."[86]

Zhirinovsky's victory sent shock waves around the world and stunned President Boris Yeltsin, who now had to tangle with a new parliament that was just as Red and even more Brown than the one he had recently crushed. Yeltsin's weakened status was evident in February 1994 when the Duma (the Russian parliament) granted an amnesty to his political enemies — the instigators of the August 1991 coup attempt and the participants in the October 1993 White House rebellion. Dozens of Red-Brown militants were released from prison and vitriolic opposition newspapers began to roll off the presses again. *Dyen* reappeared under a new name, *Zavtra (Tomorrow),* and immediately called for the execution without trial of Yeltsin's inner circle. Emboldened by the sudden turn of events, Aleksandr Barkashov's neo-Nazi followers paraded through the streets of Moscow on the anniversary of Hitler's birthday in April 1994, chanting antigovernment and anti-Semitic refrains. Eduard Limonov also returned to the limelight, speaking at political rallies and publishing his own newspaper, *Limonka (Little Lemon);* more than just a play on its founder's name, the title was Russian slang for *hand grenade.*

Limonov quickly recognized Zhirinovsky's remarkable talent as an orator and shared his penchant for exhibitionism. "I went to him in early 1992," the punk novelist recounted. "I picked Zhirinovsky out of the crowd of political figures because I thought he had the potential to be a real leader. He was an unusual sort of politician. He had real energy." At first, Limonov could discern only one drawback — Zhirinovsky's father was of Jewish extraction. "In our country, this is a big disadvantage," Limonov acknowledged.[87]

Although their egos would eventually clash, for a while Limonov was a gung-ho supporter of Zhirinovsky's crusade. When Mr. Z put together a shadow cabinet, he designated Limonov as his security minister and secret-police chief. Zhirinovsky's shadow cabinet also included a couple of neo-Nazi rock musicians, and his Liberal Democratic Party headquarters sold recordings by a heavy metal group called Vomit, the Russian equivalent of a skinhead band.[88]

In September 1992, Limonov showed Zhirinovsky around Paris and arranged for him to meet with Jean-Marie Le Pen, head of the far Right Front National. (Le Pen subsequently endorsed Zhirinovsky's bid for the Russian presidency.) The flamboyant Russian politician also visited Saddam Hussein in Baghdad. They spoke for four hours about the need to unite against "the American-Israeli plot" to dominate the world.[89]

The pace of Zhirinovsky's international travels picked up considerably after his party's sensational triumph in the December 1993 elections. During a trip to Austria, he stayed with Edwin Neuworth, a Waffen SS veteran who claimed that the Nazis never used gas chambers to kill Jews. In Strasbourg, France (the home of the European Parliament), Zhirinovsky threw dirt at Jewish picketers. Following this temper tantrum, he told the French press, "It's all over for you once you've become Americanized and Zionized."[90]

Zhirinovsky had many neo-Nazi admirers, particularly in Germany. During one of his sojourns to Moscow, Ewald Althans met the notorious Russian loudmouth. Althans's mentor, Ernst Zündel, also conferred with Zhirinovsky when he visited Russia, but the Toronto-based Holocaust-denier was not exactly bowled over by their encounter. "Zhirinovsky is an interesting man and a clever tactician," Zündel conceded. "He told me that if he didn't generate theatrics no one would take notice of him. . . . He's a natural-born headline-grabber, who would say whatever it takes to get power." But what did Zhirinovsky truly believe? For Zündel and Althans, anti-Semitism was a faith; for Zhirinovsky, it seemed to be a ploy, a cynical attempt to exploit a popular Russian prejudice. Zündel wondered whether Zhirinovsky was a bona fide fascist or a shyster.[91]

Gerhard Frey, chief of the Munich-based Deutsche Volksunion (DVU), had no such doubts. He was Zhirinovsky's principal German contact and his biggest booster in the Fatherland. Zhirinovsky spoke at two DVU conventions — in August 1992 and October 1993 — and Frey, a wealthy publisher, provided financial support for Zhirinovsky's political campaigns. The ultra-right-wing DVU later signed a friendship accord with Zhirinovsky's party.[92]*

To Frey and his DVU colleagues, Zhirinovsky was the best thing to come along since sliced bratwurst. The reason for their enthusiasm stemmed from Zhirinovsky's call for "a strategic union between Russia and Germany." In essence, Zhirinovsky endorsed a renewal of the Hitler-Stalin Pact of 1939, which he insisted was still legally valid. "Germany and Russia should again have a common border," he asserted. This would entail dividing up Poland between them and giving back East Prussia and Königsberg to Germany, which Zhirinovsky favored, as long as Russia regained the Baltics, the Ukraine, and other ex-Soviet republics. Germany, according to Zhirinovsky's plan, could also have Austria and the Czech Republic in exchange for helping Russia's southward expansion. If Germany and Russia worked together, Zhirinovsky insisted, no power could defy them.[93]

Although Zhirinovsky later spoke of destroying Germany with nuclear weapons if it got out of line, his close association with the DVU was beneficial to both parties. The Russian got much-needed cash, while Frey, a marginal figure in German politics, gained extensive media attention by rubbing shoulders with Zhirinovsky. This enhanced Frey's reputation among German neo-Nazi groups, which had quarreled with the DVU during the Cold War because of its support for NATO and the Atlantic alliance. Even before he formed

* Gerhard Frey was a shrewd German businessman and a tireless fund-raiser who invested large amounts of money in several hard-line publications that promoted his political views. Most notable among these was the Munich-based *Deutsche National-Zeitung,* which boasted a weekly circulation of close to one hundred thousand. Decorated with Iron Crosses, it whitewashed Hitler's crimes and offered Nazi memorabilia for sale. In addition to caustic attacks against Jews and leftists, the *National-Zeitung* emphasized the need to "win back our national identity" by ridding Germany of its guest workers and asylum seekers. Typical headlines read ARE A MILLION JEWS COMING? STOP THE GYPSY INVASION! GERMANY IN GRAVE DANGER, and PENANCE FOREVER FOR HITLER? Frey's newspaper also called the gas chambers "Zionist propaganda" and serialized American writers who claimed that the Holocaust never happened. Although the German government classified Holocaust-denial as forbidden speech, the *National-Zeitung* was available throughout the county.

the DVU in 1971 with the professed objective to "save Germany from Communism," Frey received behind-the-scenes support from General Reinhard Gehlen, Bonn's powerful spy chief. But after the superpower face-off ended, the DVU führer quickly shifted gears and demanded that Germany leave NATO. His newspapers began to run inflammatory articles that denounced the United States and praised Russia as a more suitable partner for post–Cold War Germany. Frey also joined the chorus of neo-Nazi agitators who expressed solidarity with Saddam Hussein and condemned the U.S.-led war against Iraq in 1991.[94]

Frey's about-face was symbolic of the skin-deep allegiance that many German nationalists felt toward "the West," which, after all, was largely an artificial construct based on the political division of Europe and enforced by American economic and military power. Germany and Russia, by contrast, were part of the same "Eurasian" land mass, and they shared a long and complex history. After the Berlin Wall fell, Germany emerged as Russia's biggest trading partner, and the two nations also forged closer military ties. These developments were carefully monitored by U.S. intelligence officials, who feared a revived Berlin-Moscow axis and took steps to nip it in the bud. Although never explicitly acknowledged, this was one of the reasons why Washington joined Germany in providing covert support for a Croatian weapons buildup, despite a U.N. arms embargo. At first, American diplomats had criticized German recognition of Croatia; by shifting gears and siding with Zagreb, U.S. policy makers appeased Bonn, angered Moscow, and exacerbated tensions between Germany and Russia, whose fluctuating power relationship continued to be plagued by spy scandals and other problems.[95]

Zhirinovsky's meteoric ascendance as Russia's most popular and hyperbolic politician posed a new set of challenges to American strategists. This fascistlike buffoon had to be reckoned with not only because he reflected widely held sentiments in his country but also because of his unmistakable influence on Yeltsin, who proceeded to adopt a more confrontational posture toward NATO and the United States. Soon Yeltsin and his top aides were mouthing some of the same anti-Western language spoken by Zhirinovsky and other Russian ultranationalists. American Army intelligence predicted that

Yeltsin's lurch to the Right would only serve to "legitimize some of Zhirinovsky's arguments and make the emergence of a liberal nationalism all that much more difficult to accomplish."[96]*

As social and economic conditions in Russia continued to deteriorate, Yeltsin played the race card to shore up his flagging support. Singling out non-Russians, he authorized massive raids against "unregistered persons" in Moscow and other cities. This ethnic dragnet targeted people from the Caucasus republics — Armenians, Azerbaijanis, Georgians, and Chechens — who were regarded as "darkies" by many Russians. Police units roughed up and expelled tens of thousands of swarthy street traders and their kin. Eduard Limonov could have been whispering into Yeltsin's ear when the former literary expatriate criticized the Russian capital for being "too complacent" and infested with "rotten people and profiteers." "Moscow isn't a Russian city anymore," Limonov quipped. "It ought to be shut down and sprayed with DDT for a long time." Zhirinovsky went a step further, calling for the deportation of all ethnic Chinese and Japanese in the Russian Far East.[97]

In 1994, Yeltsin unleashed the Russian military against Chechnya, a small, predominantly Muslim region near the Caspian Sea. Several extremist leaders supported this effort, including Zhirinovsky, who received accolades of appreciation from Yeltsin's defense minister for his "outstanding contribution to strengthening the Motherland's defense." Limonov also endorsed the Chechnya invasion, saying, "We don't like you, Mr. President, but we are with you. Long live war!" And Barkashov, Russia's top neo-Nazi, offered to place his storm troopers under government command to fight the Chechen separatists.[98]

But the bloodbath in Chechnya, which was repudiated by most of Yeltsin's former allies in the "democratic" camp, also threw the Red-Brown coalition into disarray. Key figures associated with the National Salvation Front criticized the incursion, putting them at odds with Limonov and Barkashov. Before long, the head of National Bolshevik Front declared he was severing all ties with the

* After the December 1993 elections, Mikhail Poltoranin, a close Yeltsin advisor, asserted in a televised interview that Jews dominated the Russian news media — a canard that echoed similar comments by Zhirinovsky.

politically treacherous NSF "moderates." By this time, Limonov had also denounced Zhirinovsky in no uncertain terms, accusing him of being "an opportunist" and "a charlatan with no real convictions." [99]

Zhirinovsky provoked special indignation among Reds and Browns who felt that his clownish escapades cheapened and ridiculed ideals they held sacred. "We would never work with him, not because he's a Jew, but because he's crazy," said Barkashov. Some of Zhirinovsky's detractors accused him of being a Zionist agent. His Jewish roots, which he tried to obfuscate, were emphasized in a scorching polemic entitled *Limonov vs. Zhirinovsky,* published in the summer of 1994. "A Jew masquerading as a Russian nationalist is a sickness, a pathology," Limonov said of his erstwhile friend. "We don't want power to fall into the hands [of] Eidelstein-Zhirinovsky." [100]

A pain in the neck to nearly everyone else, Limonov got along famously with Aleksandr Barkashov, the neo-Nazi, whom he described as "a politician of principle." But fascism, as Limonov recognized, was still a dirty word among Russians who had not forgotten the savagery of Hitler's armies. The legacy of World War II rendered National Socialist ideas and practices untenable in Russia, if they were readily identifiable as such; to make much headway, they would have to be introduced through the back door, so to speak, using a different vocabulary. Under the circumstances, a National Bolshevik movement had a greater chance of success than an outright neo-Nazi undertaking. Barkashov implicitly acknowledged this in 1995 when he recast himself as a "serious politician" who rejected the neo-Nazi label. After his ideological face-lift, the Russian National Unity chief continued to collaborate with Limonov and the National Bolshevik Front.[101]

Numerous commentators and historians have noted alarming resemblances between the Weimar Republic and post-Soviet Russia, where impoverished masses have endured high unemployment and inflation, falling birthrates and life expectancy, and rampant crime and official corruption. Humiliated but not completely crushed, nationalists in the Russian military have pushed for a return of lost land. As in Weimar Germany, the bleak political climate fostered stab-in-the-back legends about Jewish financiers, liberal intellectuals, and other traitors from within while a majority of Russians long for an iron hand to restore order. Well aware of these parallels, neo-Nazis in Europe and North America looked to post-Soviet Russia as the Great White Hope, a beacon of possibility. "In Russia, there are magnificent young men who think like us," Waffen SS General Léon Degrelle rhapsodized. "Russian families are a great biological reserve for Europe. Maybe a young Russian will lead the European revolution."[102]

After several years of painful economic restructuring that benefited few Russians other than organized criminals and the offspring of the Soviet *nomenklatura,* there was ample reason to fear that a financial meltdown or a social implosion could pave the way for an ultranationalist take-over in the Kremlin. President Yeltsin had already prepared a fabulous gift for his successors, whomever they might be—unlimited power enshrined in a new constitution. Talk of a Russian Bonaparte or a Pinochet-style military dictatorship was rife in Moscow. If Yeltsin's disastrous policies had proven anything, it was that democracy and "free market" reforms were incompatible in his country; the former had to be sacrificed to keep the latter going, much like in Chile during the 1970s. In keeping with the spirit of National Bolshevism, some kind of authoritarian solution seemed likely in Russia, where the vast majority had little to show for reforms except the freedom to complain openly about their wretched state.

CHAPTER NINE

FROM THE MARGINS TO THE MAINSTREAM

Playing with Fire

Thousands of flowers covered the pavement in front of a charred, roofless house in the western German city of Solingen. "Born Here, Burned Here" was written on a banner that marked the site of one of the worse racist attacks since reunification. Three Turkish girls and an eighteen-year-old mother perished in the blaze, while another Turkish woman leaped to her death from a window. Several neighbors heard someone shout, "Heil Hitler!" before dousing the front porch and door with gasoline and setting fire to the home of a Turkish family that had resided in Germany for twenty-three years.

The killings in Solingen, the birthplace of Adolf Eichmann, occurred on May 29, 1993, just three days after the German parliament yielded to pressure from the extreme Right and revoked the constitutional provision that guaranteed asylum for all political refugees. But the 1.8 million Turks who lived in Germany were not asylum seekers; they were part of a stable community of guest workers and their families who had contributed significantly to Germany's "economic miracle." Encouraged by Bonn to immigrate, Turkish laborers began arriving in large numbers three decades earlier to ease a perennial shortage of native workers. Over the years, they bore the brunt of widely held racist attitudes among West Germans, who routinely referred to Turks as *Kanaker* (a derogatory term tantamount to *nigger* in the United States). There were no civil rights laws that protected West Germany's Turkish inhabitants against discrimination.

The pent-up resentment harbored by the long-silent Turkish community finally exploded in the wake of the Solingen murders, which sparked a wave of national and international outrage. On four consecutive nights, furious young Turks took to the streets in several German cities. Screaming, "Nazis out!" they blocked highways, smashed storefront windows, and dodged baton-swinging police. Foreign Minister Klaus Kinkel urged all Turkish residents to show restraint. "We appeal to the Turks in Germany not to overreact but to use democratic ways to express their anger," he declared.[1]

Kinkel's suggestion that Turks "use democratic ways" to get their point across was yet another insult to a much-abused people. Because of Germany's racist naturalization laws, it was nearly impossible for tax-paying Turks to gain citizenship, which was defined strictly along bloodlines. This meant that second- and third-generation Turks who were born in Germany, spoke the language fluently, and attended German schools were not eligible to vote or exercise other democratic rights — whereas someone born and raised in Volga Russia, for example, who spoke no German but could prove German ancestry (a father's or grandfather's Nazi Party card would suffice) would be entitled to citizenship in the Bonn Republic.

President Richard von Weizsäcker addressed this gnawing issue when he spoke at a funeral service for the Turks who died in Solingen. A voice of conscience who held a largely ceremonial post in German politics, von Weizsäcker stood on a podium above a row of five coffins draped with Turkish flags. Two of the coffins — the ones that contained the bodies of nine-year-old Hulya Genc and her four-year-old sister, Saymie — were no wider than the length of a shoe box. Directing his comments not only to the audience of grieving Turks but to Germany as a whole, the white-haired president declared that the wave of terror attacks were "not unrelated or isolated atrocities, but the result of a climate created by the extreme right." "Would it not be more honest and more humane," he asked, "to say 'German citizens of Turkish heritage?' They live by German rules, but without the ability to influence that other citizens have. Should that remain so forever?"[2]

Rejecting calls to grant dual citizenship to longtime Turkish residents, Chancellor Kohl chose not to attend the Solingen funeral service. Instead, he issued a perfunctory statement through his office that deplored violence against foreigners and warned Turks and other non-Germans not to seek retribution through unlawful means. Depicting the Solingen attack as a police matter rather than a political issue, Kohl's aides quickly pinned the blame on a local firebug who supposedly did not have any connections to the organized neo-Nazi scene. A sixteen-year-old skinhead named Christian Riha had acted on his own, according to Chief Prosecutor Alexander von Stahl.

When three other right-wing extremists were arrested along with Riha, von Stahl continued to weave a web of lies and half-truths in an effort to cover up the suspects' ties to neo-Nazi groups. But parliamentary investigators soon confirmed that Riha and his accomplices had frequented a martial-arts school in Solingen run by Bernd "Karate" Schmitt. The Hak Pao sports club served as a meeting place and training center for about two hundred local neo-Nazi militants. Three of the youngsters charged in the Solingen burnings had "studied" at Schmitt's studio, where Nazi ideology was taught along with fighting techniques.[3]

Schmitt was a person of some consequence in unified Germany's neo-Nazi underground. Well-connected to several ultranationalist groups, he counted among his allies Bela Ewald Althans and other ultra-right-wing leaders. Schmitt's martial-arts school supplied "security personnel" to guard meetings when visitors such as Ernst Zündel, Althans's Toronto-based sugar daddy, lectured in Germany. Schmitt also maintained ties with a handful of Third Reich veterans, including Major General Otto Ernst Remer, who was registered as an "associate member" of the Hak Pao sports club.[4]

Fifty years old at the time of the Solingen bombing, Schmitt had chalked up seventeen criminal convictions (some for violent assaults) during a checkered neo-Nazi career that dated back to the late 1960s. In an effort to stay out of jail, Schmitt began supplying data on the neo-Nazi scene to the Verfassungsschutz, the German equivalent of the FBI. One of his many tasks was to keep his secret-service handlers abreast of what the Brown brats were doing in Solingen. Over the years he carried out intelligence chores for the neo-Nazis as well as for the secret service, which shared a common enemy — the radical Left. Schmitt filmed antifascist demonstrations and distributed photos of left-wing activists, which had been supplied by his secret-service contacts.

Confirmed at the Solingen murder trial, Schmitt's status as a paid undercover operative raised far more questions than it answered. Had he any forewarning that such an attack was imminent? To what extent was he responsible for inciting the murderous assault? (Witnesses indicated that Schmitt had told his students, "We have to tear the heads off the foreigners.") The revelation that Schmitt was a covert operative opened a can of worms, which German officials tried to shut by limiting his testimony during the Solingen trial. Thus, what he actually knew about the neo-Nazis who were charged with setting the fatal fire would remain a secret.[5]

The disclosure of Schmitt's role as a secret agent confirmed, if nothing else, that German intelligence had not only penetrated and monitored right-wing extremist groups but also helped to build, sustain, and guide some of them at a time when attacks against foreigners were surging. This, in turn, lent credence to speculation that certain German officials implicitly sanctioned the violence, believing that it could be kept at a politically advantageous level while they maneuvered to scuttle the asylum law.

Schmitt's shadowy tale is reminiscent of the complex and sordid relationship between U.S. intelligence agencies and the Ku Klux Klan, which served as a clandestine tool for tracking and attacking civil rights activists in the Deep South in the 1960s. Army intelligence utilized KKK initiates to spy on Dr. Martin Luther King, Jr.; FBI and police agents infiltrated and, in some cases, organized Klan associations that murdered civil rights activists and set fire to dozens of African-American homes and churches. (During this period, the FBI had nearly two thousand informants operating inside the Klan and other white hate groups in the United States, accounting for 20 percent of their total membership.) Gary Thomas Rowe, a violent Klansman who was on the FBI payroll, shot a black man to death but kept quiet about his role in the killing — at the Bureau's insistence — so as not to blow his cover. Speaking at a KKK rally, another FBI agent declared, "We will restore white rights if we have to kill every Negro to do it."[6]

By the early 1980s, the Ku Klux Klan had forged an alliance with neo-Nazis in the United States and abroad. Klan chapters sprang up in Great Britain, Sweden, Canada, and Australia. An American air force sergeant based in Bitburg served as a Klan recruiting officer in West Germany, even though KKK activities were forbidden by U.S. military authorities. The nazification of the Klan coincided with a drive by American white supremacists to raise funds for their German counterparts. Shortly before he died, Michael Kühnen urged ongoing cooperation between his network and U.S. Klansmen.[7]

In September 1991, Dennis Mahon, chief of the White Knights of the KKK in Tulsa, Oklahoma, embarked upon a nine-day, twenty-five-city tour of reunified Germany. As Mahon recounted in his Klan newsletter, *White Beret:* "I had no trouble getting through Customs even though my 85 pounds of luggage was choked [sic] full of National Socialist and Klan 'T' shirts, patches, stickers, jewelry and literature." Although it was illegal to make a stiff-armed salute in Deutschland, Mahon boasted that he "gave hundreds of them all across Germany."

In addition to attending a hate-rock concert that featured a skinhead band from England, Mahon met several Russian soldiers in Dresden, which left an enduring impression. "White Russian pride was evident," he stated. "They were all Aryan-looking men, well behaved, with fine military bearing. I believe our Negro-infested Army would be no match for these men with modern high-tech weaponry." At every stop, Mahon encouraged his German comrades to undertake violent attacks against foreigners, which he referred to as "patriotic actions." Of course, Mahon himself was a foreigner, but he felt right at home, particularly in Berlin, where he visited the Reichstag building. "It was very inspiring to walk up the same steps that Adolph Hitler walked up," Mahon effused.[8]

The crowning moment of Mahon's propaganda tour was a cross-burning ceremony in a dusky forest clearing near Berlin. Flanked by Nazi, Ku Klux Klan, and Confederate flags, sixty white-robed German youths attended this ritual. "Forward for the Aryan race!" a Klan supporter shouted to a cheering audience as a ten-foot cross burst into flames. Wearing a green silk gown and hood, Mahon punctuated a brief speech with a boisterous *"Sieg Heil!"* "We called up the spirits of the Waffen SS and the Teutonic Knights and released the power," he later explained. "That's what the fiery cross does."[9]

Mahon's main contact in Germany was the Nationalistische Front (Nationalist Front), a neo-Nazi group that sponsored the cross-burning ceremony outside Berlin. Bernd Schmitt, the fascist martial-arts instructor in Solingen who two-timed as a government spy, was an important member of the Nationalist Front. In addition to directing "battle games" at a Front conference in August 1992, he provided protection for visiting dignitaries who made the rounds of the German neo-Nazi circuit.[10]

Founded in 1985, the Nationalist Front quickly emerged as one of the most dangerous neo-Nazi organizations in Germany, with several hundred members. Harkening back to the Strasser brothers, the Front's "national revolutionary" rhetoric was stridently anticapitalist and nominally supportive of Third World "freedom movements." In order to achieve its goal of a pure people's state, the Front vowed to liquidate the parasitical ruling class, the landlords, and the Jewish financial sharks who were allegedly sucking the blood out of the German *Volk*. Front leaders had their sights set on a fully reconstituted Reich encompassing Austria and Switzerland along with parts of Italy, France, Belgium, Czechoslovakia, Poland, and Russia. Pagan fire rituals on new moons and the summer solstice were part of their campaign for "racial socialism."

In the autumn of 1991, shortly after it hosted the KKK cross-burning rite, the Nationalist Front created a network of mobile paramilitary units composed of highly dedicated comrades who were primed to carry out surprise attacks against foreigners, leftists, and the bourgeois order as a whole. The nationwide commando operation was the brainchild of Meinolf Schönborn, the wavy-haired chief of the Nationalist Front. A heavyset man in his mid-thirties who had previously served as press secretary for the Republikaner Party, Schönborn envisioned his street-fighting force as the heir to Ernst Röhm's SA storm troopers. For guidance and inspiration, Schönborn turned to his favorite old Nazi, Major General Otto Ernst Remer. The Front was also counseled by Herbert Schweiger, an Austrian SS veteran who fought under Otto Skorzeny's command during World War II.[11]

Organized into conspiratorial cells, members of the Nationalist

Front vowed to make life "as miserable as possible" for foreigners. Schönborn's followers instigated numerous attacks against refugee shelters. They also beat up a man they mistakenly thought was Jewish, drenched him with alcohol, set him on fire, and dumped his dead body on a road just over the Dutch border. Perhaps most disturbing of all, Nationalist Front skinheads were paid by affluent residents in the village of Dolgenbrodt (near Berlin) to burn down a home for asylum seekers that had been built at the end of their residential street. "Nobody was sad that the problem was solved that way," said Dolgenbrodt's mayor.[12]

In November 1992, the Nationalist Front became the first neo-Nazi group to be outlawed by the German government in the post-Wall era. Alerted beforehand, Schönborn went into hiding across the border in Silesia, where he ran a mail-order business that sold neo-Nazi paraphernalia. He later set up shop in Denmark. By then, his group had been reincarnated in various guises, including Direct Action Middle Germany, which provided fascist ideological training to fledgling terrorists. Before long, Direct Action Middle Germany and another Nationalist Front successor organization, the Social Revolutionary Workers Front, were also banned. But these proscriptions, combined with the decision to scrap Germany's liberal asylum law, did not result in the abatement of neo-Nazi violence. Contrary to predictions by officials in Bonn, racist attacks continued with numbing regularity.

Aryan Machinations

Underneath tall, swaying pine and maple trees, children were playing among themselves while men clad in blue uniforms and SS insignia stood guard with automatic rifles. Speaking in front of a large swastika banner, Reverend Richard G. Butler told a group of journalists about his service as a soldier in the U.S. Army during World War II. "I fought on the wrong side of the war because I fought against my own race," said the leathery-faced septuagenarian.[13]

On a remote, twenty-acre compound in Hayden Lake, Idaho,

Butler held sway as pastor of the Church of Jesus Christ Christian and head of its militant political arm, the Aryan Nations. To enter the church itself, which Butler immodestly described as the "international headquarters of the White race," one passed through an antechamber lined with northern European flags. The walls displayed pictures of young Nordic warriors plunging spears into a serpent and a dragon, which were identified by the six-pointed Star of David and the Communist hammer and sickle. Dredging up the old canard about a worldwide Jewish-Bolshevik conspiracy, Butler likened the collapse of the Soviet Union to a "branch office" closing down.[14]

For Butler, no anti-Semitic or anti-African smear was too corny or hackneyed to invoke. In accordance with the racialist gospel known as Christian Identity, he preached that Aryans were God's chosen people and that Jews were Satan's offspring and nonwhites were subhuman "mud" creatures. As the dominant religious orientation of the white supremacist movement, Christian Identity provided a theological bond that united different Klan and neo-Nazi factions across the United States. Although one did not have to fixate on the Third Reich to be a Christian Identity believer, Butler's sect openly worshipped the swastika as the "revolving resurrection cross." Nazi symbols were evident throughout his church, which featured an idealized portrait of Adolf Hitler, with high cheekbones, a noble

Aryan Nations insignia

forehead, and intense, gleaming eyes. Next to the altar lay a memorial wreath to Rudolf Hess.

With Butler at the helm, the Aryan Nations gained prominence as a strategic hub for various elements of the white racialist scene. It became the home away from home for people like Dennis Mahon, the vitriolic KKK leader who toured reunified Germany, and his close friend Tom Metzger, leader of the California-based White Aryan Resistance. Buoyed by the reappearance of the Iron Guard in Romania and the fascist resurgence in other parts of Europe and the former Soviet Union, Metzger maintained contact with numerous "white warriors" abroad. A good place to meet like-minded militants from other countries was the World Congress of Aryan Nations that Butler sponsored each year at his Idaho outpost. Three shouts of "Hail Victory!" (English for *"Sieg Heil!"*) accompanied a cross-burning at the end of these annual summer gatherings, which attracted representatives from a loose-knit network of Christian Identity churches and other hate groups that mixed revolutionary millenarianism, wacky conspiracy theories, and violent anti-Semitism.

The dreaded ZOG — shorthand for the Zionist Occupation Government — was the Aryan Nations' bête noire. Rejecting any hope of repairing a system they saw as hopelessly corrupt, Butler and his acolytes felt their only recourse was to establish an independent "White American Bastion" in five Pacific Northwest states, which would eventually secede from the rest of the "Jew-nited States of America." The goal of a separate, all-white homeland was often discussed during religious services conducted by Butler. He also performed marriage ceremonies at his heavily armed fortress.

Kirk Lyons, an attorney from Texas who defended a rogues' gallery of neo-Nazis and white supremacists, tied the knot at the Aryan Nations encampment in September 1990. It was actually a Scottish-style double wedding, with kilts and bagpipes. Lyons and his friend Neil Payne married two sisters, Brenna and Beth Tate, respectively. Their brother, David Tate, was then in prison for murdering a Missouri state highway patrolman. David had been a member of "the Order," a terrorist offshoot of the Aryan Nations that embarked upon a spree of bank heists and killings in the United States during the early 1980s. Tate had participated in several commando raids against armored cars before the police caught up with him.[15]

Otherwise known as die Brüder Schweigen (German for "the Silent Brotherhood"), the Order was led by a young, neo-Nazi zealot named Robert Jay Mathews, who recruited followers when he frequented the Aryans Nations headquarters. Mathews fancied himself a latter-day Robin Hood who robbed from the Jews and gave to the Aryans. Using stolen money and counterfeit bills, he waged a campaign of terror modeled after *The Turner Diaries,* a novel that described a successful paramilitary insurgency by white supremacists in the United States. The author of *The Turner Diaries,* William Pierce, was a featured speaker at the Hayden Lake compound. He had cut his racialist teeth with the American Nazi Party. After George Lincoln Rockwell was assassinated, Pierce set up a West Virginia–based group called the National Alliance.[16]

Pierce's vision of "the Day of the Rope," when race traitors throughout the United States would meet their maker, inspired Mathews, Tate, and a dozen other members of the Order. Together, they plotted to sabotage dams, water supplies, public utilities, and communication lines with the intention of sparking a full-scale race war. But before they could bring ZOG to its knees, Mathews was cornered by an FBI manhunt that ended on Whidbey Island in Washington State. Refusing to surrender, he died in a fiery shoot-out with FBI agents, who donned baseball caps with the letters ZOG on them for the grand finale — a stroke of gallows humor rare for G-men but hauntingly visible to Mathews as he bit the dust in December 1983.

"Mathews believed the only way they could achieve their goal of a separate domain was by so terrorizing the government that Uncle Sam would be happy to see us go," explained Aryan Nations ideologue Robert Miles. An avuncular backslapper and former Ku Klux Klan Grand Dragon from Michigan, Miles functioned as an elder statesman for America's racialist underground. Much like his third-position counterparts in Europe, he viewed the U.S. and Soviet governments as the "twin satans." "Communism and capitalism to us are almost one and the same thing," he explained prior to the demise of the USSR. Miles professed support for Third World revolutionary movements, and he favored collaboration between right-wing and left-wing extremists. He also advocated multiple-partner marriages as the best way to ensure the survival of the white race.[17]

In 1988, thirteen white supremacists, including Miles and Reverend Butler, were prosecuted for conspiring to overthrow the U.S. government. Federal authorities argued that the defendants had hatched their sinister plans while meeting at the Aryan Nations headquarters five years earlier. Miles, Butler, and a third defendant, Louis Beam, Jr., were pegged as the subversive ringleaders, the hardest of the hard-core, who secretly directed the Silent Brotherhood. Following their command, members of the Order murdered several people and stole more than $4 million, according to U.S. officials, who suspected that most of the missing cash ended up in the coffers of American neo-Nazi groups.

Kirk Lyons, then in his early thirties, represented fellow Texan Louis Beam at the sedition trial, which was held in Fort Smith, Arkansas. A former helicopter gunner in Vietnam, Beam became the Ku Klux Klan Grand Dragon of the Lone Star State. To avoid arrest on charges related to the Order, he fled to Mexico with his wife. A fugitive on the FBI's "Ten Most Wanted" list, Beam was captured after a gunfight in Guadalajara and returned to the United States. He later served as an ambassador-at-large for the Aryan Nations. But the federal government failed in its attempt to convict Beam and the other defendants of seditious conspiracy. Lyons and his client celebrated the verdict at a Confederate memorial opposite the courthouse, where Beam proclaimed victory over the enemy: "I think ZOG has suffered a terrible defeat here today. I think everyone saw through the charade and saw that I was simply being punished for being a vociferous and outspoken opponent of ZOG."[18]

The Fort Smith sedition trial marked Lyons's debut as a lawyer for the white supremacist movement. He became something of a celebrity among ultrarightists for his successful defense of Beam, who, by all accounts, was one of the key players in America's neo-Nazi underground. In addition to his role as the movement's premier military strategist, a techno-savvy Beam created the first computer bulletin boards for the Aryan Nations and several other Christian Identity groups. Kirk Lyons would remain one of his closest collaborators. When Lyons got married at Hayden Lake, Beam was his best man.[19]

An activist attorney who sympathized with the views of his clients, Lyons defended several Aryan Nations members charged with felonies ranging from weapons violations to murder. He also coordinated the legal appeal of White Aryan Resistance leader Tom Metzger after he was found liable for the skinhead killing of an Ethiopian immigrant in Portland.[20]

Another beneficiary of Lyons's legal counsel was Fred Leuchter, a Boston-based supplier and installer of electric chairs, lethal injection devices, and other execution equipment. Dubbed "Dr. Death" by ABC News, Leuchter ran afoul of the law by practicing engineering without a license. Still, he managed to make a name for himself when he traveled to Auschwitz as a self-proclaimed engineering expert, took a few soil samples, and concluded that the gas chambers were a myth. The so-called Leuchter Report was the product of a $37,000 "study" funded by German-Canadian Ernst Zündel.

The Institute for Historical Review quickly embraced Leuchter's "scientific findings," which were also hailed by Major General Otto Ernst Remer and other die-hard Holocaust-deniers. Leuchter and Lyons attended an IHR conference in southern California in October 1992 at which they met some of the leading lights of the negationist circuit, including Bela Ewald Althans. "I enjoyed the IHR conference," Lyons recounted. "It was mainly a lot of old men with interesting views on World War Two. I support all forms of revisionism. . . . When the World War Two veterans are gone, I think revisionism will come into its own."[21]

Althans subsequently arranged a fund-raising tour for Lyons and Leuchter in Germany. Security was provided by one of Bernd Schmitt's martial-arts-trained, strong-arm squads. Schmitt was both a neo-Nazi and a secret police snitch, but he did not arouse the suspicion of Lyons during the ten-city sojourn. Instead, Lyons came to harbor serious doubts about Althans. Lyons got angry when he discovered that his young German host was pocketing most of the cash that should have gone to Leuchter's defense team.[22]

During a previous trip to the Fatherland, Lyons had befriended a man who was in many ways his German counterpart, Jürgen Rieger. Described by *Die Zeit* as "a neo-Nazi in lawyer's robes," Rieger headed a group called the Society for Biological Anthropology, Eugenics, and Behavioral Research, which was based in Hamburg. In this capacity, Rieger edited *Neue Anthropologie,* a pseudo-scientific journal for intellectual racists who believed in Aryan supremacy. At the same time, Rieger served as defense counsel for Michael Kühnen, Christian Worch, Ernst Zündel, and several other key neo-Nazis. Widely respected within the neo-Nazi scene, Rieger had connections to all factions of the extreme Right in Germany.[23]

Lyons maintained ongoing ties to the German neo-Nazi movement through CAUSE, a group he set up in Black Mountain, North Carolina. An acronym for "Canada, Australia, United States, South Africa and Europe" (places where the democratic rights of white people were in jeopardy, according to Lyons), CAUSE functioned as an information clearinghouse and gossip-mill for right-wing extremists at home and abroad. Jürgen Rieger was one of a handful of CAUSE-affiliated attorneys in Germany.[24]

Another key link to the German neo-Nazi underground was Gerhard Lauck, the Nebraska-based Hitlerite who spoke English with a phony German accent. Churning out an enormous quantity of hate literature, Lauck had worked closely with the Kühnen network since its inception in the late 1970s. Like Lyons and Klan leader Dennis Mahon, he was connected to the Aryan Nations, which distributed copies of Lauck's broadsheet, *New Order.* In 1994, one of Lauck's lieutenants spoke at the annual, whites-only confab at Hayden Lake. When Lauck was arrested the following year in Denmark, the Aryan Nations urged its supporters to contact the Danish government and demand that he not be deported to Germany, where Lauck was wanted for supplying neo-Nazi propaganda.[25]

The Aryan Nations also hosted youth gatherings — usually coinciding with Hitler's birthday — that featured music by hate-rock bands, such as Bound for Glory, the top bonehead act in North America. Bound for Glory claimed to be inspired by "the soldiers of the Reich that battled the odds against the Red tides for the love of their Fatherland." The band's heroes included Waffen SS General Léon Degrelle, Nazi flying ace Hans-Ulrich Rudel, and the illustrious Otto Skorzeny.[26]

Referring to the United States as "a Zionist fornicator of other nations," Bound for Glory spread its racialist message while performing in reunified Germany, where Ku Klux Klan imagery and Confederate flag insignia had become stylish among neo-Nazi youth. English phrases like "White Power" and "White Aryan Resistance" were adopted by German skinheads. This shared vocabulary was emblematic of the cross-pollination between American neo-Nazis and their German comrades, who conferred by fax, e-mail, telephone, and face-to-face strategy sessions. Neofascist leaders from several countries, including Germany, attended the annual Aryan Nations powwow in Idaho. Commenting on these cross-border links, WAR chief Tom Metzger stated, "There is only one movement. Our goals are similar." Kirk Lyons agreed. "We are in a common fight against a common enemy," he stated in a German skinhead magazine.[27]

There were notable parallels between the German neo-Nazi scene and its interlocking North American counterpart. White Power advocates on both sides of the Atlantic believed they had reached a historic juncture with the passing of the Cold War, which gave them a unique window of opportunity. Some felt that their agenda, if presented in the right manner, had the potential to resonate with the masses. "Although their numbers are relatively small, these groups network intensively and exchange intelligence," warned former CIA analyst Stanley Beddlington. "They are very dangerous. We ignore them at our own peril."[28]

During mid-1990s, the Aryan Nations underwent a growth spurt, attracting new adherents and opening offices in several countries. It was the most significant of the thirty different neo-Nazi clusters that dotted the political landscape in the United States, where the militant white racialist scene consisted of about 25,000 hard-core activists and some 150,000 sympathizers. Membership in this semiclandestine milieu was always in flux, with recruits circulating in and out of various sects. But a cohesive inner circle of influential leaders provided continuity and coordinated strategy for a loose confederation of ultra-right-wing organizations. Kirk Lyons and his best man, Louis Beam, were part of this elite leadership cadre. In addition to cultivating ties to German neo-Nazis, they played a pivotal, behind-the-scenes role in the fast-growing American militia movement.

The Road to Oklahoma City

For most Americans, the bombing that killed 169 people and injured more than 500 at the federal building in Oklahoma City came like a bolt from the blue. After years of mass media fixation on Arab, Islamic, and Third World terrorists, it was unexpected news, to say the least, that an extensive, homegrown, antigovernment militia network existed in the United States. Yet, those with an ear to the ground did not have to read tea leaves to discern that something ominous was brewing in the so-called heartland. What happened in Oklahoma City on April 19, 1995, differed in scope, but not in kind, from a persistent drumbeat of far Right violence that had been building across the country for some time.[29]

With an estimated forty thousand to one hundred thousand members by the mid-1990s, militia groups were distributed unevenly in pockets throughout the United States, despite laws in many states that barred or regulated paramilitary activity. Various tributaries fed into the raging river of the militia movement, which attracted gun-control opponents, anti-abortion zealots, tax protesters, family-values fundamentalists, Vietnam vets dreaming of Rambo vengeance, "wise use" anti-environmentalists, and off-the-grid "freemen" who recognized only the first ten amendments to the Constitution and eschewed driver's licenses and Social Security ID.

A complex and multifaceted phenomenon, the militia movement also included an important component of white supremacists and neo-Nazis. At least 25 percent of an estimated 225 far Right paramilitary formations in the United States had explicit ties to white hate groups. While these elements were often entrenched in leadership roles, it would be a distortion to characterize the militias in toto as consciously racialist or anti-Semitic.

To be sure, no small amount of bilious claptrap flushed through the militia mix. The *Militia News*, for example, was given to carping about "Judeo-Bolsheviks." Published by the Christian Civil Liberties Association in Afton, Tennessee, it asserted that Hiroshima and Nagasaki were chosen as A-bomb targets because these two Japanese cities had sizable Christian populations. Although this type of material was typically available at militia meetings, blatant anti-

Semitism did not characterize the scene as a whole. Racialist fixations generally took a backseat to other rank-and-file issues — most notably, gun control — which white supremacists addressed by disguising old hatreds with new rhetoric. Seeking to "mainstream" their message in an effort to win new converts and widen their base, militia leaders vilified the U.S. government rather than ethnic minorities.[30]

Although hard-core *racialists* — that is to say, *those who consciously embrace racism as an ideology* — remained a numerical minority, they were the motor that propelled and guided the militia movement since its inception. Wolfgang Dröge, a German neo-Nazi based in Toronto, admitted that his U.S. colleagues utilized stealth tactics in an effort to steer the militias in a desired direction. "If they were to be identified as white supremacists, they would lose credibility. As a result, some important people in the militias shy away from this label. But I'm certain that they are still secretly committed to the White Power struggle," said Dröge, who met with American militia strategists when they visited Canada.[31]

One of the pioneers and key spokespersons of the post–Cold War militia movement was John Trochmann, who got the ball rolling when he launched the Militia of Montana (MOM) in February 1994. Dubbed "the mother of all militias," MOM served as a prototype for numerous paramilitary groups that quickly formed across the United States. Like many of the militias, MOM traced its origins to neo-Nazis and professional white supremacists.

MOM leader John Trochmann was a familiar figure at the Aryan Nations encampment in northern Idaho. With his long, scraggly beard, he carried on like a biblical prophet when addressing the Aryan Nations Congress at Hayden Lake in 1990. Trochmann seized the occasion to argue that they should drop the swastika and the hood in favor of Jesus Christ and the Bible. This was what he did when he set out to create the Militia of Montana. By downplaying overt neo-Nazi themes and disguising his racialist beliefs, Trochmann hoped to influence a broad audience of disgruntled Americans, who would doubtless have recoiled if they were blitzed with Hitlerian raves.[32]

Trochmann's tactical approach made sense to Kirk Lyons and Louis Beam. They were all friends and supporters of Randy Weaver, a ZOG-obsessed Vietnam veteran who visited Hayden Lake on several occasions. Weaver became a cause célèbre of the far Right after he was injured and his wife and only son were killed in a shoot-out with U.S. government agents in August 1992. A federal marshal also died during the siege at Weaver's secluded cabin in the backwoods of Ruby Ridge, Idaho, where he and his family held out for eighteen months before the FBI and the ATF barged in. Several Aryan Nations colleagues, including Trochmann, brought food and other supplies to the Weavers while they were barricaded in the wilderness. Trochmann and Beam later formed Citizens United for Justice, a Randy Weaver support group, and Lyons offered to file a lawsuit against the U.S. government for violating Weaver's civil rights.[33]

Lyons and Beam kept stirring the pot in other ways as well. Like a pair of vultures hovering over the scent of death, they reappeared during the fifty-one-day standoff between the federal government and David Koresh's Branch Davidian sect in Waco, Texas. Beam and several other white supremacists gathered outside the Branch Davidian enclave to show their support for the besieged religious cult. Lyons, meanwhile, announced that he was representing Koresh's mother. In this capacity, he tried to get a temporary restraining order placed on federal law-enforcement personnel, but a judge denied it. As many as eighty-five people subsequently died in a fiery inferno triggered by an ill-conceived federal raid. After the massacre, Lyons filed a $520 million lawsuit on behalf of relatives of some of the Waco victims. "The U.S. government is the greatest force for evil, the greatest threat to civil liberties in the world today," said Lyons, who would later serve as a legal advisor for numerous militia groups.[34]

"No more Wacos, no more Weavers!" became the rallying cry for a slew of angry right-wing extremists who shared Lyon's antipathy toward the U.S. government. While these two tragedies served as lightning rods for the growth of the militias, the actual nuts-and-bolts strategy for building up a nationwide paramilitary network was forged at a closed-door meeting in Estes Park, Colorado, on October 23, 1992. Lyons and Beam were among 150 ultra-right-wing leaders who attended this session, which was hosted by Christian Identity pastor Pete Peters. A tub-thumping white supremacist who claimed that the Bible justified killing homosexuals, Peters had encouraged members of the Order to embark upon their deadly crusade a decade earlier. Like Trochmann, Peters had since come to realize that neo-Nazi sloganeering was counterproductive. "Peters packaged his message for the 1990s," explained former Aryan Nations member Floyd Cochran. "He doesn't espouse Hitler. He doesn't use the swastika or Klan robes. Instead, he uses the Bible and the American flag. Peters talks in a language we're used to hearing. His hatred is masked in God."[35]

During the Rocky Mountain assembly, several speakers endorsed the idea of a grassroots militia movement that would serve both as a focal point of mass opposition to gun control and as a pool from which terrorist cells could be recruited. Aryan Nations ambassador Beam emerged as a key player at this parley. He laid out his plan for "leaderless resistance," which entailed the creation of small autonomous units composed of five or six dedicated individuals who were bound together by a shared ideology rather than a central commander. "All members of phantom cells or individuals will tend to react to objective events in the same way through the usual tactics of resistance," Beam explained. "Organs of information distribution such as newspapers, leaflets, computers, etc., which are widely available to all, keep each person informed of events, allowing for a planned response that will take many variations. No need to issue an order to anyone. Those idealists truly committed to the cause of freedom will act when they feel the time is ripe, or will take their cue from others who precede them."

One advantage of Beam's guerrilla-warfare scenario was that it reduced the risk of infiltration or detection. By virtue of its secretive structure, the cell system would immunize leading tacticians, like himself, while affording underground components an unrestricted operational range. As Beam noted, "[T]he *last* thing federal snoops want, if they had any choice in the matter, is a thousand different small phantom cells opposing them."[36]

Beam's proposal would soon be adopted by much of the militia movement as part of a sophisticated two-tiered strategy that enabled White Power advocates to bury their leaderless resistance cadres inside a sprawling network of aboveground, hierarchically structured paramilitary organizations. This is how Trochmann's Militia of Montana operated. It quickly established itself as a nerve center for the entire militia milieu, distributing guerrilla training manuals to hundreds of fledgling groups. The MOM manual opens with a biblical justification for "patriots" to prepare for war against the U.S. government and other enemies. This terrorist guidebook provides detailed instructions for different types of actions — bombing, raiding armories, attacking vulnerable federal buildings, kidnapping important people, destroying the property of non-Americans, sabotaging food supplies, and executing undesirables.[37]

MOM and other militia groups utilized shortwave radio, fax trees, video training films, computer bulletin boards, Internet user groups, and the World Wide Web to beam inflammatory messages through the patriotic grapevine. "It was probably the first grassroots social movement anywhere to rely mainly on non-traditional electronic media to communicate with its constituents," noted Chip Berlet of Political Research Associates, an independent watchdog organization of the far Right. MOM boasted that it could get the word out to half a million supporters in less than an hour through the Patriotic Fax Network. Under the circumstances, it was predictable, if not inevitable, that some twisted individuals would bite the bait and act out their violent fantasies in accordance with the leaderless resistance plan that neo-Nazi strategists had developed.[38]

MOM augmented its paramilitary pointers with kooky conspiratorial literature about international banking elites and United Nations troops that were bent on imposing martial law and one-world government. In this regard, it shared much in common with the Liberty Lobby's weekly tabloid, the *Spotlight,* which formed a publicly acknowledged alliance with MOM. "Thank God for the *Spotlight,*" Trochmann declared at a Liberty Lobby conference in Washington, D.C., a few months after the Oklahoma City bombing.[39]

MOM spokesmen were frequently interviewed in the *Spotlight,* which was widely read among white supremacists, neo-Nazis, and other militia members. Playing up tales of nefarious black helicopters and other alleged new world order emanations, stories in the *Spotlight* were often based on "scoops" and photographic "evidence" provided by Trochmann and his associates. MOM also advertised its materials in the *Spotlight,* including a videotape that purported to expose how the U.S. government had enlisted inner-city street gangs to confiscate the weapons of God-fearing Americans. Accounts of this sort, no matter how ludicrous, were the militia movement's bread and butter.[40]

Perhaps even more disturbing than the large arsenals stockpiled by the militias was the extent to which their "don't tread on me" phobias dovetailed with mainstream hunches and anxieties. Offering scapegoats rather than solutions, the militias tended to attract deeply disenchanted individuals with real, down-home gripes. Shunted aside while multinational corporations got leaner and meaner, many of these people were treading water economically and aching for someone to blame. They concluded, not without some justification, that the political process was stacked in favor of a powerful few, who acted against the interests of ordinary folks. Although this belief had a rational basis, militia members mistakenly attributed their plight to far-fetched, all-encompassing conspiracies. A more plausible analysis saw tacit collusion among elements of a self-serving, ruling elite that had presided over a steady decline in real earnings for the vast majority.[41]

With so many Americans taking the paramilitary oath, wacky ideas began trickling down to millions of malcontents much faster than crumbs were falling from the tables of the wealthy. The militia milieu was rife with wild rumors about government mind-control plots, Midwest tornadoes caused by CIA weather modification, and secret markings encoded on the backs of road signs to assist an imminent U.N. invasion. It was the American Dream in blacklight: everything pointed to "a conspiracy so immense," as Senator Joseph McCarthy once said, a cabal so sinister, a future so bleak, that armed rebellion seemed the only sensible response.

Enter Timothy McVeigh and his presumed partner in crime Terry Nichols, who were charged with bombing the federal building in Oklahoma City on April 19, 1995. Having served together in the same infantry unit at Fort Riley, Kansas, both were habitués of that volatile zone where the militia movement overlaps with the crazed racialist fringe. Toward the end of his military career, McVeigh got involved with an off-post, right-wing group with strong antigovernment views. Convinced that army doctors had implanted a microchip in his buttocks, he became a paranoid drifter with a scowling face. Obsessed with guns, he never went anywhere unarmed.

McVeigh's hatred of the government was fanned by the calamitous federal raid of the Branch Davidian compound in Waco, Texas. He made a pilgrimage to Waco and visited Randy Weaver's abandoned Ruby Ridge cabin to inspect the scene of the gunfight that loomed large in the militia's frontier folklore. During the fall of 1994, McVeigh roamed in and out of Kingman, Arizona, where he befriended several Aryan Nations members. He also attended the annual *Soldier of Fortune* convention in Las Vegas, where Kirk Lyons gave a keynote speech about his Waco-related lawsuit.[42]

McVeigh followed Nichols, his Army buddy, to Michigan, where they attended militia meetings. Closely linked to Trochmann's organization in Montana, the Michigan Militia was one of the strongest and most influential paramilitary formations in the United States. Like MOM, it had ties to white supremacists. McVeigh also reportedly turned up at a militia gathering in Florida.[43]

Hooked into the seamier side of the militia movement, McVeigh and Nichols immersed themselves in ultra-right-wing newspapers and videotapes. They were avid readers of the *Spotlight*. When McVeigh decided to sell an antitank launcher and 37mm firing flares, he took out an advertisement in the Liberty Lobby's newspaper. Perusing this publication, he kept abreast of Aryan Nations events that were announced in the datebook section of the *Spotlight*, which also ran classified ads for Christian Identity literature and other white racialist propaganda. McVeigh also read, sold, and gave away copies of *The Turner Diaries*, the novel that had galvanized members of the Order to undertake their looting and killing spree.[44]

Using a long-distance calling card that he got from the *Spotlight*, McVeigh telephoned Elohim City, a four-hundred-acre Christian Identity encampment on the Arkansas-Oklahoma border, two weeks before the Oklahoma City bombing. According to Robert Millar, head of Elohim City, McVeigh asked to speak with Andreas Strassmeir, a former German army lieutenant in his mid-thirties who handled security duties and led paramilitary training at the white supremacist enclave. As for why he chose to live in Elohim City since 1991, where churchgoers spoke in tongues and participated in quasi-religious hate rituals, Strassmeir would say only, "I was attracted to the alternative lifestyle."

For his part, Strassmeir maintains that he has no recollection of McVeigh's mysterious phone call. But the German paramilitary expert admitted in a court affidavit that he had met McVeigh at a Tulsa gun show shortly after the Waco massacre. Strassmeir sold a combat knife to McVeigh and gave him his business card. That's as far as it went, according to Strassmeir, who insists he had no further dealings with McVeigh.

While in Tulsa, Strassmeir also visited the home of his beer-drinking buddy, Dennis Mahon, the Oklahoma-based Klansman who lit crosses in reunified Germany. And Mahon often spent weekends at Elohim City, boozing it up with Strassmeir. ("When you get drunk with a guy over a period of days, you get to know him," said Mahon, who became a leader of the White Aryan Resistance after his 1991 sojourn to Germany.) Mahon and Strassmeir both befriended an attractive young woman named Carol Howe, who served as a paid undercover informant for the Bureau of Alcohol, Tobacco and Firearms (ATF) while keeping tabs on the local neo-Nazi scene. Howe later testified under oath that she saw McVeigh in Strassmeir's company at Elohim City. She also told her ATF handlers that she heard Strassmeir and Mahon making plans to blow up federal buildings in Oklahoma several months prior to the April 1995 bombing. But Howe's allegations have never been corroborated, and she has weakened her credibility by changing crucial aspects of her story on various occasions.[45]

Strassmeir denies any involvement in the Oklahoma City attack. There is no doubt, however, that he had extensive links to America's violent racialist underground. Strassmeir's roommate at Elohim City was Michael Brescia, who subsequently confessed to his own role as a member of the Aryan Republican Army (ARA), a fanatical white supremacist sect that sought to overthrow the U.S. government, purge the country of blacks and Jews, and install a new legal system based entirely on their own weird interpretation of the Bible. (Four of the six known ARA members lived at Elohim City or often visited there.) To raise money for the cause, the ARA robbed twenty-two banks in eight Midwestern states during the mid-1990s. These armed assaults were carried out by ARA extremists who had been trained in weapons and guerrilla tactics by Strassmeir. Not without a sense of humor, the ARA bandits wore whimsical disguises, such as Count Dracula and Ronald Reagan masks, during the bank heists. Peter ("Commander Pedro") Langan, the acknowledged leader of the group, was a cross-dressing, preoperative transsexual who shaved his genitals and painted his toenails pink. Langan is now serving a lengthy prison sentence, and the other ARA zealots are either dead or behind bars.[46]

The ARA's German paramilitary instructor managed to elude the long arm of the law, even though the Oklahoma State Patrol had issued a BOLO ("Be on the look-out") alert for Andreas Strassmeir, which indicated that he was an armed and potentially dangerous "illegal alien." Although several U.S. government agencies were aware of Strassmeir's presence at Elohim City, immigration authorities never tried to deport him. The most plausible explanation for this hands-off treatment lay in Strassmeir's high-powered family connections back in Germany. Andreas's father, Günter Strassmeir, served at one time as Chancellor Helmut Kohl's de facto chief of staff. A top Christian Democratic official in Berlin, Günter was a close friend and advisor to Kohl. When the Berlin Wall opened in November 1989, they celebrated together in the streets. Günter is known to have pulled diplomatic strings when his wayward son got into trouble.

In 1991, Andreas Strassmeir's American attorney, the ubiquitous Kirk Lyons, visited his client's parents at their plush residence in Berlin. Lyons assured them that Andreas was happy living in Oklahoma. It was Lyons who had arranged for Andreas to come to America in the first place. Lyons has also introduced his young German friend to the folks at Elohim City.

On April 18, 1995, the day before the Oklahoma City blast, Kirk Lyon's North Carolina law office received a 15-minute phone call from Timothy McVeigh, who was using an alias. McVeigh had already cased the federal building in Oklahoma City. The "patriot" movement went on high alert as the Militia of Montana issued a call to arms to mark the second anniversary of the Waco raid. That's when McVeigh—with help from Terry Nichols and "others unknown," according the original federal indictment—chose to attack. Apprehended shortly thereafter, McVeigh would be tried and sentenced to death for the bombing. Nichols was later convicted in a separate trial and sentenced to life in prison.*

It appears that McVeigh was a part of a small terrorist cell, which functioned in accordance with the leaderless resistance strategy promoted by Aryan Nations tactician Louis Beam. The goal of this strategy was to engender antigovernment violence while providing semipublic militia organizations with a built-in means of plausible deniability that would obscure any direct tie to breakaway extremist cadres.

The immediate reaction in ultra-right-wing circles to the Oklahoma City blast was one of unrestrained glee. Dennis Mahon, among others, could not hide his excitement. "The bombing was a fine thing. I hate the federal government with a perfect hatred. . . . I'm surprised that this hasn't happened all over the country," Mahon mused.[47]

H. Keith Thompson, the aging American Hitlerite, initially shared Mahon's enthusiasm. "Frankly, news of the Oklahoma City bombing delighted me. Violence is the only thing these people understand," he remarked. But Thompson said his opinion changed when he "realized" that the U.S. government had instigated the attack to discredit the far Right. "The bombing could not have been put together by a couple of hayseeds," he concluded.[48]

This soon became the party line promoted by Thompson's friends at the *Spotlight* and the militia movement as a whole. The federal government, they claimed, was behind the fatal explosion; McVeigh was merely a patsy. They contended that U.S. officials would use the bombing as an excuse to quash the militias, which were now indelibly linked to mass murder in the public mind. Along with everything else, the carnage in Oklahoma City fit neatly into the Big Conspiracy.

* Terry Nichols's defense team presented strong evidence that other as yet unidentified men were involved in the bomb plot with McVeigh. Nichols's attorneys raised serious doubts about the prosecution's contention that the fertilizer bomb was mixed only by McVeigh and Nichols; such a task was too much for two people to complete in a few hours. Most compelling was the eyewitness testimony of Charles Farley, who saw five men at Geary State Lake in what was apparently the bomb-making scene on the morning before the Oklahoma City massacre. An Oklahoma grand jury later concluded there was no credible evidence that the federal government had prior knowledge of the bomb plot but left open the possibility that other people may have played a role in the attack.

THE SPOTLIGHT.

Ex-Agent Claims Feds Employed 'Dupes' to Bomb Murrah Building

FBI Set Jewell Up

If you ruin a person's life, isn't an apology in order? Not if you're the FBI.

The Inside Story:

The *Spotlight*, November 11, 1996

Onward Christian Patriots

At the time of the Oklahoma City bombing, the Liberty Lobby was still the U.S. racialist movement's leading umbrella group. It continued to serve as a bridge between various sectors of the extreme Right at home and abroad, hyping the militias and their heroes to no end. After Randy Weaver won his lawsuit against the government, the *Spotlight* announced that he was one of several "outstanding speakers" slated to appear at a Christian Identity shindig in Lake Tahoe, Nevada. Aryan Nations strategist Louis Beam and Liberty Lobby founder Willis Carto were also listed as speakers for this event.[49]

The Liberty Lobby also played the electoral game in various countries overseas by promoting candidates who were deemed to be suitably "populist"—a code word for individuals and groups more accurately described as "neo-Nazi" or "neofascist." Populists touted by the *Spotlight* included Russia's Vladimir Zhirinovsky, who warned during a visit to the United States that white Americans were in danger of turning "their country" over to blacks and Hispanics. (The Republican Party embodied his views on race, Zhirinovsky added.) The *Spotlight* lauded Zhirinovsky for "talking sense," even though he had recently threatened to attack several countries with nuclear weapons. The Liberty Lobby also sang the praises of French Front National leader Jean-Marie Le Pen, the neo-Nazi Deutsche Volksunion in Germany, and Filipino billionairess Imelda Marcos.[50]

On the home front, the Liberty Lobby was instrumental in launching the political career of former Klansman David Duke. Once a swastika-wearing member of an American Nazi Party splinter group, Duke was featured in the *Spotlight* ("smart as a tack") while he was Imperial Wizard of the Louisiana Knights of the Ku Klux Klan in the mid-1970s. During that period, he recruited and mentored several Klansmen, including Louis Beam and Tom Metzger, who would later become important figures in America's violent racialist underground. For several years, Duke sold books through a mail-order catalog that offered neo-Nazi classics, such as *Imperium* by Francis Parker Yockey.[51]

After leaving the Klan, Duke formed the National Association for the Advancement of White People (NAAWP), which he claimed was a civil rights organization designed to protect the identity and interests of Caucasian Americans. The NAAWP advocated partitioning the United States into separate racial areas. To avoid the negative connotation of "white supremacist," Duke and many other neo-Nazis adopted the more innocuous-sounding "white separatist" label.

Like his Liberty Lobby advisors, Duke was an ardent Holocaust-denier, calling it "a myth perpetrated on Christians by Jews." In 1986, the NAAWP chief attended a negationist conference in southern California hosted by the Institute for Historical Review. During this gathering, a conversation between Duke and a neo-Nazi colleague was recorded on audiotape. "I hate to be Machiavellian, but I would suggest that you don't really talk much about [National Socialism] . . . publicly," said Duke. When asked why, he explained, "I'm trying to bring new people in, like a drummer. The difference is, they can call you a Nazi and make it stick — tough, really hard. . . . It's going to hurt your ability to communicate with them.

It's unfortunate it's like that. . . . It might take decades to bring this government down."

Whereupon Duke's colleague chimed in, "It doesn't take that many people, though, to start something rolling. Hitler started with several men. . . ."

"Right!" Duke gushed. "And don't you think it can happen right now, if we put the right package together?"[52]

Putting the right package together was exactly what Duke had in mind when he followed the "tripartisan" electoral strategy recommended by the *Spotlight,* which entailed working inside both major parties as well as supporting an independent third party — whatever seemed most opportune. Beginning as a Democrat in the Southern primaries, Duke ran for president in 1988. Quickly shifting gears, he became the presidential candidate for the far Right Populist Party, another Cartoid creation. Next, Duke campaigned as a Republican in a special election for a seat in the Louisiana state legislature. To raise funds for this bid, he drew upon a national network of donors culled from the Liberty Lobby's extensive mailing list, which Duke rented; his direct-mail pitch was crafted by Liberty Lobby staffers, who also provided advice on how to file campaign-finance reports. After winning by a slim margin in February 1989, Duke hired Trisha Katson, a Liberty Lobby crony and a regular contributor to the *Spotlight,* as his legislative aide.[53]

Duke, age thirty-nine, insisted that he had cleaned up his racialist act and was now a true-blue Republican. But he still sold Holocaust-denial tracts and other books published by Liberty Lobby's Noontide Press from his legislative office. And he also spoke admiringly of Josef Mengele, the Nazi doctor who performed ghastly experiments on inmates at Auschwitz. "He was a genius," Duke told a Republican state committee member from New Orleans in August 1989. "His genetic research on twins was incredible."[54]

In 1991, Duke ran a heated campaign for governor of Louisiana. His bid was supported by the Liberty Lobby's Populist Action Committee, which raised money through appeals to subscribers of the *Spotlight.* With his blow-dried hair and surgically enhanced smile, Duke was careful to avoid crude, racialist formulations. Instead of white superiority or black inferiority, he emphasized cultural differences. "In Duke's hands, racism takes on a people-loving, positive spin," observed *Village Voice* correspondent Leslie Savan. She put her finger on the crux of the matter by noting that Duke had managed "to redefine his prejudice as pluralistic pride." When he appeared on national television, Duke sounded tolerant and reasonable. "There's nothing wrong with black people being proud of their heritage and their race," he insisted. "There's nothing wrong with white people being proud of theirs."[55]

Duke's smooth-talking campaign was confusing to many people who could recognize extremism when garbed in Nazi or Klan regalia but not when it hid behind the slippery rhetoric that mainstream Republicans were using to attack welfare, undocumented immigration, minority set-asides, and affirmative action. Although he emphasized identical themes and employed the same calculated vocabulary that had served the GOP so well in recent years, Duke was roundly condemned by President George Bush and other Republican leaders. Still, Duke managed to win a majority of the white vote in a losing gubernatorial effort. His strength at the polls demonstrated that the views of white supremacists, if packaged correctly, could have mainstream appeal.[56]

One of the least-noticed aspects of Duke's campaign for governor was the endorsement of Reverend Billy McCormick, the head of the Louisiana chapter of the Christian Coalition. Led by televangelist Pat Robertson, the Christian Coalition had emerged as the most powerful grassroots force within the Republican Party. In alliance with Duke's organization, the Christian Coalition proceeded to gain control of the GOP state organization in Louisiana. This was part of a precinct-by-precinct, state-by-state drive to take over the Republican Party across the country. Toward this end, Robertson's foot soldiers were initially told to soft-pedal their religious message and, if necessary, conceal their affiliation with the Christian Coalition, which supposedly operated as a nonpartisan, tax-exempt group.[57]

By 1995, the Christian Coalition claimed to have more than a million and a half members. Its collaboration with Duke in Louisiana was surprising at first glance, given the former Klansman's ongoing antipathy toward Israel and Jews in general, which put him at loggerheads with pro-Zionist evangelicals like Robertson. But

Robertson's support for Israel had little to do with a sincere affection for Jews, whom he viewed as "spiritually deaf" and "spiritually blind"; rather, it was predicated on end-of-the-world New Testament prophesy, which stipulated that all Jews must gather in the State of Israel before the Second Coming, whereupon they would be converted en masse to Christianity or killed in the battle of Armageddon.[58]

The Christian Coalition's sympathy for David Duke is more understandable upon closer examination of Pat Robertson's paranoid ideology. His bestselling 1992 book, *The New World Order,* purports to reveal an elaborate, centuries-old conspiracy dominated by a satanically spawned clique of Freemasons, occultists, and European bankers who just happen to have Jewish names. Refurbishing the old canard about a handful of rich Jews who backed both godless Communism and monopoly capitalism as part of a sinister, long-range plan, the Christian Coalition commander claimed this ongoing superconspiracy was behind everything from the French and Russian Revolutions to the assassination of President Abraham Lincoln.[59]

Robertson's musings resembled not only anti-Jewish motifs of the past — he listed several notorious anti-Semites in his bibliography* — but militia fables of the present. In his books and on his ubiquitous cable network, he railed against one-world government and the United Nations. Robertson's nightly TV show, *The 700 Club,* also promoted the militia line on Waco and gun control.

* When challenged by the *New York Times* (March 4, 1995), Robertson did not repudiate any of his anti-Semitic sources. Instead, he insisted that his book was "carefully researched [with] seven single-spaced pages" of references. One of the so-called authorities Robertson cited was Eustace Mullins, an advisory board member of the Liberty Lobby's Populist Action Committee, who depicted the Federal Reserve as a front for a handful of sinister Jews. Described by the *Spotlight* as "the dean of America's populist authors," Mullins was a frequent speaker at Liberty Lobby events over the years. While a member of the neo-Nazi National Renaissance Party in the early 1950s, Mullins penned an article entitled "Adolf Hitler: An Appreciation," which he never repudiated. Yet, it did not hurt Robertson's standing as a GOP power broker to be associated with this raving Jew-baiter, who recently praised the militias as "the only organized threat to the Zionists' absolute control of the U.S."

Spokesmen for the Militia of Montana appeared on this program as experts, commenting upon photos of black helicopters and other misinterpreted phenomena that were allegedly threatening American citizens. *New York Times* columnist Frank Rich summed it up best when he accused Pat Robertson of throwing "gasoline on the psychic fires of the untethered militias running across this country."[60]

Although they were both nourished by the odiferous compost of conspiracy theory and hate that has long moldered on the American margins, the Christian Coalition and the militia movement parted ways in their approach to politics. Robertson's Christian soldiers went the mainstream electoral route, seeking to take over the system from within, while the militias picked up their guns and declared war against the "Republicrats" who ran the country at the behest of sinister, hidden forces. Like Robertson, some militia stalwarts fretted about Freemasons and the eighteenth-century Illuminati; others obsessed over an international Jewish cabal. Whether explicitly racialist or not, these conspiratorial motifs reflected the same anti-Semitic archetype — although this was not readily apparent to most militia initiates. Such widespread ignorance shows the profound potential for hatred that lurked on the far Right fringe, where yesterday's secret societies could easily shape-shift into ZOG.

Cross-fertilization between American white supremacists and their somewhat less extreme (and far more numerous) religious Right cousins is emblematic of the profound political changes that had been catalyzed by the end of the Cold War. Prior to the collapse of the USSR, anti-Communism served as the ideological glue that bound together disparate right-wing factions in the United States. It provided a convenient cover for segregationists who attacked the civil-rights movement by accusing Martin Luther King, Jr., of being a Communist (charges that were repeated in the *Spotlight*). When the Soviet Union unraveled, the cry of anti-Communism became archaic rather than cohesive, and racially charged themes reemerged with a vengeance to fill the void. The Cold War meltdown fostered not only the resurgence of the far Right, both nationally and internationally, but a realignment of forces that blurred the line between conservatives and hitherto marginalized sectors of the racialist Right.

While U.S. neo-Nazis and the religious Right differed in crucial respects, they saw eye-to-eye in their opposition to gun control, abortion, homosexuality, nonwhite immigration, and other shared concerns. These issues figured prominently in Patrick Buchanan's quest for the Republican presidential nomination.* "Our culture is superior to other cultures, superior because our religion is Christianity," he declared. Reeking of Christian patriot rhetoric, his antiforeigner stump speech scapegoated undocumented "aliens" ("Listen, José, you're not coming in this time!") and called for protectionist trade measures. During the 1996 GOP primaries, Buchanan was endorsed by several prominent religious Right leaders and by the Liberty Lobby. "Buchanan's campaign platform reads like nothing less than a statement of the Liberty Lobby's positions on the issues," the *Spotlight* noted.†[61]

* The cochairman of Pat Buchanan's 1996 presidential campaign was Larry Pratt, a key figure in militia leadership circles. As head of Gun Owners of America, Pratt attended the October 1992 militia planning meeting in Colorado hosted by Christian Identity pastor Pete Peters. A featured speaker at Liberty Lobby conferences, Pratt also appeared at rallies with prominent white supremacists such as Eustace Mullins, Aryan Nations chief Richard Butler, and former KKK leader Louis Beam. In addition, Pratt was a financial supporter of CAUSE, the ultra-right-wing legal foundation run by Kirk Lyons. After Pratt's association with the neo-Nazi fringe was disclosed by the news media, he was forced to resign from the Buchanan campaign, which officially employed several other white supremacists.

† Although it disparaged the Christian Coalition's close ties to the GOP leadership, the Liberty Lobby began to collaborate with other influential religious Right organizations, including James Dobson's Focus on the Family, which has more than 3 million members. An article by Dobson attacking women's rights ran in the *Spotlight*, which also praised the American Family Association, led by Rev. Donald Wildmon, for its tough stand against homosexuality. In addition, Wildmon's strident views were featured on LogoPlex, the Liberty Lobby's racialist computer bulletin board service. The Institute for First Amendment Studies described LogoPlex as an "electronic meeting place of Christian Identity, Aryan Nations, White Supremacists, gun owners, and Christian Patriots." Through this computer bulletin board, one could download an entire copy of *The Protocols of the Elders of Zion*, along with Wildmon's latest publications and information about how to join his group. Another popular figure on the Liberty Lobby's LogoPlex was Pete Peters, the Colorado-based Christian Identity pastor who hosted the militia planning meeting that Aryan Nations ambassador Louis Beam and attorney Kirk Lyons attended in October 1992. Despite

Even the discredited science of eugenics made a comeback after the Cold War with the publication of *The Bell Curve* by Charles Murray and Richard J. Herrnstein. This controversial 1994 best-seller argued that intelligence is a genetically linked characteristic of race, and precious resources should not be squandered on futile efforts to improve the lot of the permanently poor — and mainly black and brown — underclass consisting of genetically inferior people. The authors based their conclusions on "evidence" derived from tainted sources. *The Bell Curve*'s bibliography is littered with references to pseudoscholarly journals, such as Roger Pearson's *Mankind Quarterly,* which once ran an article alleging that Jews, in their quest for world domination, supported black civil rights to weaken the white gene pool through miscegenation.* Several of Pearson's ruminations on the Aryan advantage were published by the Liberty Lobby's Noontide Press.[62]

Pearson's crackpot ideas were endowed with legitimacy by the authors of *The Bell Curve.* The *Wall Street Journal* gave the book its unequivocal endorsement, and *Newsweek,* in a sympathetic review, described *The Bell Curve*'s scholarship as "overwhelmingly mainstream." It wasn't often that the *Spotlight* and establishment press outlets clamored over the same treatise, but such was the case with *The Bell Curve,* which relied heavily on pseudoscholars with neo-Nazi ties.[63]

Many of the "experts" cited in *The Bell Curve,* including Roger Pearson and other contributors to *Mankind Quarterly,* were bankrolled by grants from the Pioneer Fund, which the London *Sunday*

---

his links to unabashed neo-Nazis, Peters enjoyed increasing acceptance among conservative evangelicals thanks to the Keystone Inspiration Network, a self-described "family TV" channel available in 120 American cities. The Keystone network aired Peters's bigoted sermons along with Pat Robertson's *The 700 Club* and other religious Right programming.

* *Mankind Quarterly* had a sister journal in West Germany, *Neue Anthropologie,* which was edited by neo-Nazi attorney Jürgen Rieger. In addition to carrying advertisements for each other, these kindred periodicals featured many of the same writers and had interlocking editorial advisory boards. While editing *Neue Anthropologie* and collaborating with Pearson, Rieger defended German neo-Nazi leader Michael Kühnen. Rieger later worked with American militia advisor Kirk Lyons.

Telegraph described as a "neo-Nazi organization closely integrated with the far right in American politics." Founded in 1937 by American admirers of Hitler's eugenics program, the Pioneer Fund was dedicated to "race betterment" through selective breeding. Although eugenics fell into disrepute after World War II because of the Third Reich's horrible crimes, the Pioneer Fund continued to keep scientific racism alive within North American academic circles by doling out millions each year to support research on the relationship between race, heredity, and IQ. It underwrote numerous studies that tried to prove the intellectual inferiority of black people.[64]

But the authors of *The Bell Curve* did not require neo-Nazi financial support. Instead, Murray and Hernnstein were underwritten by the American Enterprise Institute, a quintessentially mainstream Washington think tank that supplied a brigade of pro-corporate pundits for TV talk shows. Endowed by numerous Fortune 500 companies, the American Enterprise Institute also gave its imprimatur to Dinesh D'Souza's *The End of Racism,* which defended slavery and depicted segregation as an attempt to protect blacks. Like *The Bell Curve,* D'Souza's book revived demeaning racial stereotypes; but rather than making genetic claims, he attributed African-American shortcomings to a distinct and inferior black culture.[65]

That both of these high-profile books were funded by the American Enterprise Institute highlights how ultra-right-wing ideas once shunned by the Washington establishment have moved from the sidelines to center stage. It also reveals the willingness of some U.S. corporate powers to support racialist propaganda in an effort to direct the economically driven anger of middle-class whites toward people of color and the poor. American politicians who argued for drastic cuts in welfare and other social programs could rest their case on the once taboo (but now respectable) notion that the intended beneficiaries cannot be helped because of innate cognitive or cultural deficiencies. David Duke and his fellow Klansmen had been saying as much for years. "That Contract with America of Gingrich's — that's mine. That's the exact platform I ran on," said Duke, who was quite pleased by how the political situation was evolving. "Imitation is the sincerest form of flattery," he added.[66]

Pity the Poor Immigrant

"Say America is number one!" the guards shouted as they shoved an undocumented alien's face into a toilet in New Jersey's Union County jail. Strip-searched, punched, and kicked, another illegal refugee suffered a broken collarbone while held in the same institution in 1995. Three Union County corrections officers were later convicted and sentenced to prison terms for beating and torturing immigrants.

Citing Union County as an example, attorney Peter Schey claimed that mainstream politicians had deliberately fostered an anti-immigrant mood that encouraged the psychological and physical abuse of inmates in U.S. detention centers. "It comes from desperate politicians who are running for re-election and are looking for someone to blame for fiscal policies, for unemployment, for underemployment, someone to blame for the unhappiness of voters," said Schey, the executive director of the Center for Human Rights and Constitutional Law in Los Angeles.[67]

Like their counterparts in Germany, American neo-Nazis were at the forefront of antiforeigner brutality in the 1970s and 1980s. During their respective heydays with the Klan, David Duke, Tom Metzger, and Louis Beam were all involved in violent anti-immigrant activities. But it was not until after the Cold War that immigration became a hot-button issue and U.S. officials frantically jumped on the antirefugee bandwagon.* Writing in 1993, Ruth Conniff commented on the political sea change: "[W]hat were once considered right-wing views on immigration—that the United States is being

* The deliberate efforts of white supremacists were instrumental in mobilizing public opinion against immigration. Especially pernicious was the role of the ultra-Right tax-exempt Pioneer Fund, which financed pseudoscientific studies on race and intelligence and was a major source of cash for the Federation for American Immigration Reform, the group that spearheaded the post–Cold War crusade to severely limit immigration to the United States. Another Pioneer Fund beneficiary, the Center for Individual Rights, launched a national campaign to roll back affirmative action legislation. "In the early 1970s, hard-core opposition to affirmative action really was limited to the purview of the Ku Klux Klan," explained human rights activist Daniel Levitas. "It was not commonly held that affirmative action was an affront to white people. Now that idea has broad appeal."

'invaded' by the Third World, that immigrants pose a threat to the American economy and way of life, and that the borders need military fortification—have become part of the accepted wisdom."[68]

During the Clinton administration, the Immigration and Naturalization Service began a $300 million technological overhaul in an effort to create an "electronic wall" along the entire Mexican border to keep undocumented foreigners from entering the United States. "Operation Gatekeeper," the U.S. Border Patrol's program to reduce illegal crossings into California, forced many would-be immigrants to seek entry under life-threatening conditions, which resulted in over 300 deaths during a four-year period starting in 1994. Amnesty International condemned abuses by the U.S. Border Patrol, charging that detainees were beaten, raped, and denied food, water, warmth, and medical attention for long periods.

Immigrants were targeted by politicians not only in the United States and Germany but throughout Western Europe, where a racial assault occurred once every three minutes in the mid-1990s, according to the European Parliament. The alarming frequency of xenophobic violence on the Continent coincided with the rise of several radical, right-wing populist parties that successfully tapped into widespread uncertainties precipitated by the end of the Cold War. The collapse of Communism triggered a mass migration from Eastern Europe toward the more prosperous West, which also attracted refugees from the Third World. Although Western governments had previously condemned the pharaohs of the Soviet bloc for refusing to let their people go, now that they could travel, the welcome mat was removed. *"Auslander raus!"* was no longer just the frenzied slogan of German neo-Nazis on the margins; it reflected the attitude of a sizable portion of the Western European public.

The presence of 20 million immigrants in Western Europe was perhaps the most visible sign of the chaotic structural transformation that accompanied the emergence of a global economy with its interdependent markets, unfettered capital mobility, and novel information technologies. All these factors had a dramatic impact on the Western European workforce as it grappled with high unemployment and stagnating wages. As in the United States, most people had to struggle harder to get less. Those who could not adapt to the rapid changes found themselves in increasingly precarious circumstances, a situation that mainstream politicians often failed to appreciate. In addition to mobilizing anti-immigrant sentiment, far Right populists scored well by assuming the mantle of the opposition and attacking the corrupt bipartisan status quo. At least, they claimed to be different — which is what mattered most to voters disillusioned with politics as usual, an ever widening constituency that, if given the chance, might otherwise have pulled the lever for "none of the above."

Extreme Right demagogues touched a raw nerve by linking jobless statistics to the number of guest workers or immigrants who resided their country. This ploy was utilized in a dishonest and destructive way by the leaders of Vlaams Blok (Flemish Bloc), the most blatantly xenophobic, if not overtly racist, of the major right-wing populist parties in Western Europe. Calling for an independent Flemish state cleansed of foreigners, Vlaams Blok gained more than 25 percent of the vote in Antwerp in 1991 to become that city's biggest political party. Four years later, Vlaams Blok garnered 13 percent of the total Flemish vote. Among its top strategists were several ex-members of the neo-Nazi Vlaamse Militanten Orde (VMO), which had been banned by the Belgian government as a terrorist organization.* Led by these erstwhile inhabitants of the lunatic fringe, the Vlaams Blok had a profound impact on all of Belgium. Under pressure from the far Right, the Belgian government restricted

* Xavier Buisseret, the propaganda chief of Vlaams Blok, had previously been the chief of the VMO, which collaborated with an array of white supremacist groups, including the neo-Nazi Kühnen network in West Germany and the Ku Klux Klan in the United States. Before it was outlawed by the Belgian government, the terrorist VMO played a key role in the annual Dixmude festival that drew neofascists and white supremacists from around the world. Buisseret also edited *Haro,* a monthly publication that denied the Holocaust. But Buisseret severed his ties with this negationist journal when he joined Vlaams Blok in 1979, a year after it was founded. Buisseret often used scare tactics to convey his party's antipathy to non-Europeans. This was expressed in propaganda leaflets, which showed a helpless white woman being attacked by immigrants. Another flyer featured a blond maiden carrying a grocery basket at an outdoor market; as she passes several women dressed in Islamic garb, the blond female is portrayed as thinking, "A person can't feel at home anymore in her own country."

immigration and the commissioner-general of refugees gave his lawyers bonus points for every asylum request they rejected.[70]

An analogous process transpired in France, where mainstream leaders kowtowed to Jean-Marie Le Pen's insurgent Front National. Thanks to Le Pen, it became politically correct for French officials to speak disparagingly of foul-smelling alien invaders. In 1994, the French National Assembly, hoping to take the wind out of Le Pen's sails, reversed a law that granted citizenship to anyone born on French soil; henceforth, the privilege of bloodline would supersede other factors in determining whether someone was a French national. The following year, the Front National scored 15 percent in presidential elections that swept into power a conservative government that proceeded to implement many of Le Pen's policies. Immigrants were subjected to random, and often brutal, police checks throughout the country, prompting an investigation by Amnesty International, which condemned French law enforcement for a pattern of abuse that included the unprovoked shooting and killing of several Muslim youths. Taking a cue from their German counterparts, French officials deported tens of thousands of foreigners. It was no secret that these measures were a direct response to Le Pen.[71]

Who was this sinister figure that cast such a long shadow over France? A former rugby player who dyed his hair blond to accent his Aryan origins, Le Pen had lost his left eye in a youthful political brawl. Known for his complimentary references to Nazism, which he called a "purely popular and democratic mass movement," Le Pen formed the Front National in 1972. To raise money for the cause, he sold recordings of Hitler's speeches and Third Reich war songs. The founding committee of the Front National included Vichy apologists, Waffen SS veterans, Catholic integralists, and ex-members of a white supremacist terrorist sect that tried to kill President Charles de Gaulle.[72]

With his sights set on breaking into the political mainstream, Le Pen claimed that his movement had nothing to do with fascism, which he dismissed as an antiquated Italian doctrine. But this did not stop him from forming an alliance with the Movimento Sociale Italiano, the oldest neofascist party in Western Europe, after the Front National elected a handful of representatives to the European

Parliament in 1984. A year earlier, at a public meeting guarded by skinheads, Le Pen showed his true colors when he proposed to "bring together the *fasces* of our national forces so that the voice of France is heard once more, strong and free." Anti-Semitism lurked just below the surface of his strident political rhetoric. At one point, Le Pen belittled the Holocaust as a historical "detail." He later filed charges against a journalist who had called him "the spiritual son of Hitler," but an appeals court ruled in favor of the reporter. Nazi diehard General Léon Degrelle described Le Pen as "a close friend." Front National representatives occasionally met with Degrelle at his sumptuous seaside suite in Spain.[73]

A convergence of auspicious circumstances boosted the fortunes of the Front National, whose electoral breakthrough in the mid-1980s served as a model for a host of right-wing extremist parties in Western Europe. Invariably, the key issue was immigration, which Le Pen blamed for unemployment, street crime, drugs, and the AIDS epidemic. Worst of all, according to the Front National, the influx of non-Europeans posed a deadly threat to French identity. Emphasizing the urgent need for national rebirth, Le Pen's party frequently won 30 to 35 percent of the vote in local elections and controlled city hall in four towns during the mid-1990s.

Although xenophobic appeals elicited wide support from a jittery populace, one person who didn't fall for Le Pen's sucker show was Alain de Benoist. "To say that the core of the problems which our society today confronts is caused by the presence of immigrants on our national soil is simply grotesque," he asserted. "If there were not a single immigrant in France, we would have exactly the same problems." In unequivocal terms, de Benoist rejected the notion that French identity was endangered by immigrants. After all, he argued, they had not imposed "an ideology based on commodities." Nor could immigrants be held responsible for "colonizing France when the French watch only American films on TV." If France was unable to cope with immigration, de Benoist asserted, it was because the French were already seriously confused about their own identity.

The cogency of de Benoist's critique was all the more ironic given that his ethnopluralist formulations enabled Le Pen and the Front National to sidestep charges of racism by claiming that they did not hate foreigners but were merely trying to defend their own identity.

Acknowledging that his ideas had been misused for xenophobic purposes, de Benoist urged solidarity with refugees and asylum seekers. Having fled their native lands, these people were most in danger of losing their identity and traditions, de Benoist pointed out. Moreover, immigration was triggered by capitalist expansion and forced uprooting associated with rapid structural changes in the developing world. "Those who remain silent about capitalism should not complain about immigration," de Benoist stated.[74]

This last remark was a swipe at Le Pen, who emerged as a gung-ho proponent of "free market" economics, while trying to be the Ronald Reagan of France in the 1980s.* During the East-West face-off, the Front National also espoused a pro-NATO line and called for strengthening the Atlantic alliance. But after the collapse of the Soviet bloc and the reunification of Germany, anti-Communism lost its raison d'être and Le Pen's party revised its policies accordingly. As in the United States, so too in Western Europe: the end of the Cold War catalyzed a resurgence and a realignment of far Right forces.

With the USSR out of the picture, anti-Americanism became more pronounced among right-wing radicals. Atlantic-oriented extremists such as Le Pen gravitated closer to those who previously espoused pan-European, third-position views.† At the same time, Le Pen began

* The liberal ideology of the marketplace was then sacrosanct for Le Pen, who sought to pass himself off as a Reagan clone. At one point, Le Pen posed for a picture with the American president — a photo opportunity arranged by the head of CAUSA, the political arm of Rev. Sun Myung Moon's Unification Church, despite heated objections from image-conscious State Department officials. CAUSA provided financial backing to Le Pen's party and facilitated U.S. covert operations against Sandinista-led Nicaragua.

† Indicative of this post–Cold War shift was the decision by Jean-Gilles Malliarkis, leader of a hard-core, extraparliamentary neofascist group Troisième Voie (Third Way), to join the Front National in 1991. A self-described "orthodox pagan," Jean-Gilles Malliarkis ran a neofascist bookstore in Paris (La Librairie Francaise) that peddled works by French negationists such as Robert Faurisson, who denied the existence of the gas chambers. Usually associated with neo-Nazi circles, this genre was also promoted by an ultra-left-wing clique in Paris called La Vieille Taupe (the Old Mole). Malliarkis's bookstore even sold a comic book that claimed the Holocaust never happened. There were

to distance himself from Washington. This shift became evident when the Front National leader praised Saddam Hussein as a great "Arab patriot" and condemned the American-led war against Iraq.[75]

In another significant post–Cold War departure, the Front National abandoned its "free market" fundamentalism in favor of a national populist approach that called for more state intervention, including protectionist measures to defend France against the vagaries of the global economy. The main fight was now between economic nationalists and internationalists, according to Le Pen, rather than capitalists versus Communists. This was also the position of Gulf War opponent Patrick Buchanan, who changed his "free market" tune after serving in the Reagan administration. "I read Patrick Buchanan's program, and it's practically the same as ours," a Front National official noted.[76]

A similar shift in economic strategy — away from laissez-faire platitudes to a national populist program — was adopted by the Austrian Freedom Party in the early 1990s. Trading on xenophobic rhetoric and a telegenic presence, Freedom Party chief Jorg Haider has emerged as the most successful far Right politician in Western Europe. In October 1996, his party won 27.6 percent of the vote in Austria's European parliamentary elections, only a shade behind the two mainstream governing parties, which tried to steal the clothes off Haider by passing racist immigration laws. Instead of weakening him, this imitative response endowed the Freedom Party führer with greater legitimacy. Like Le Pen, he was able to frame the political debate in his country and pull the centrist parties further to the Right. By coupling its anti-immigrant message with harsh denunciations of the 1991 Maastricht Treaty and its provisions for European economic and political unity, the Freedom Party gained more seats in a national parliament than any other right-wing extremist party on the Continent.

---

other items for children as well, including Third Way stickers with fascist cartoon characters and slogans. One showed an angry sewer rat pointing a knife at the gizzard of a terrified Mickey Mouse. Another featured a variation on the "I Love New York" theme — with a picture of bomb instead of a heart (see page 205). "It's kind of a joke," explained Malliarkis. "We have nothing against the American people . . . only the American government."

Although Haider steered clear of overt anti-Semitism, the Porsche-driving populist expressed admiration for Waffen SS veterans. He also praised Hitler's employment policies without mentioning slave labor in concentration camps, which he referred to as "punishment camps," as if inmates somehow deserved to be confined there. When Italy released Austrian war criminal Walter Reder, who had been serving a life sentence for his role in the massacre of eighteen hundred Italian civilians in 1944, Haider said he was simply "a soldier who had done his duty."[77]

Haider's attempts to downplay Nazi crimes was in keeping with the Freedom Party's origins in the mid-1950s as a catch basin for former SS members and other Nazis, many of whom preferred to see Austria as a German province rather than as a separate nation. An overwhelming majority of the population had hailed the 1938 *Anschluss* with Hitler's Germany, and a disproportionately high number of Austrians had joined the SS and administered the extermination apparatus. Much as in Germany, however, postwar denazification was largely superficial, and many erstwhile Hitlerites attained key positions in Austrian society. The Allies facilitated Austria's unwillingness to own up to its wartime role by characterizing that country as Hitler's first victim rather than as his first collaborator. High levels of postwar anti-Semitism paralleled routine omissions in Austrian schoolbooks, resulting in a distorted view of World War II. This pattern of denial had a direct bearing on the ultra-right-wing revival after the Cold War. "The resurgence of the neo-Nazis is a symptom of not coming to terms with the past," said Willi Lasek of the Center for Contemporary History in Vienna. "There are, of course, other factors such as unemployment . . . but the past cannot be separated from it."[78]

An estimated five hundred extraparliamentary militants in Austria were closely tied to the neo-Nazi underground in Germany. Despite his mainstream veneer, Haider was much admired by members of VAPO, the Austrian wing of the Kühnen network. Some VAPO fanatics were implicated in a series of letter-bomb attacks that injured a dozen people during the mid-1990s, including the former mayor of Vienna. A neo-Nazi booby trap also killed several Gypsies. These bloody outrages escalated during election campaigns, prompting the head of the Austrian Greens Party to accuse

Haider, an inveterate immigrant-basher, of being "the foster-father of right-wing terrorism." Haider promptly sued for defamation, but the Austrian supreme court ruled against him.[79]

As Haider edged closer to the citadels of power, he moderated his tone. In 1995, he expelled a Freedom Party official who refused to acknowledge that the Holocaust had occurred. By this time, Haider's odes to pan-Germania had tapered off, while he refashioned himself as an Austrian patriot. But detractors charged that this makeover was merely part of a strategy to get more votes.[80]

Gianfranco Fini, the young, charismatic leader of the neofascist Movimento Sociale Italiano (MSI), also found that modulating his image enhanced his vote-getting potential. Looking like a paragon of respectability in his expensively tailored business suits and gold-framed spectacles, Fini was determined to lead the MSI out of the political wilderness in which it had wallowed since 1946, when the party was founded for the expressed purpose of preserving the Fascist heritage. For forty-five years, the MSI's electoral strength oscillated in the single digits, with never more than a handful of deputies in the parliament. But the end of the U.S.-Soviet confrontation precipitated major changes in Italy, which worked to Fini's advantage.

An astute strategist, Fini realized that his party was well positioned to make headway in the post–Cold War era, given that the Italian political establishment had been thoroughly discredited by revelations of widespread government corruption.* In 1993, he ran for mayor of Rome and nearly prevailed with 47 percent in a runoff vote. A year later, several public-opinion polls showed that Fini had

* In an effort to keep the Italian Communist Party from taking power during the Cold War, the United States propped up a political system that was riddled with corruption. The country endured one scandal after another — coup attempts, neofascist bombings, the CIA's Gladio army, the assassination of Prime Minister Aldo Moro, influence-peddling by the Mafia and the P-2 Masonic lodge, the mysterious deaths of Vatican bankers Michele Sindona and Roberto Calvi — that were never fully explained, because the truth would have probably destroyed the anti-Communist coalition that ruled Italy for several decades. When the USSR disappeared, so did the Communist threat, and the entire political edifice in Italy crumbled almost overnight. Italian journalist Lucia Annunziata described it as "the symbolic equivalent of the fall of the Berlin Wall."

become Italy's most popular politician. The MSI had another rising star within its ranks: Mussolini's granddaughter, Alessandra, won a seat in the parliament by campaigning on an anti-immigrant, law-and-order platform. Dressed in her trademark miniskirt and silk blouse, the young Mussolini said she admired her grandfather's policies and intended to carry on his legacy.

The sudden resurgence of the MSI, which Alessandra Mussolini said was "like a dream," coincided with a dramatic increase in anti-immigrant assaults. Much of the racist violence, according to Italian interior minister Nicola Mancino, was inspired by the vicious wave of antiforeigner attacks in reunified Germany. Italian "Nazi-skins" committed anti-Semitic desecrations in Rome and other cities, but xenophobic behavior was not restricted to these latter-day jackboots. Rebuking the Italian government's anti-immigrant policies, the Vatican defended immigration as a basic human right and condemned those who used the issue for "political blackmail." "In some quarters — and even in some that consider themselves Catholic — immigrants are not forgiven the mere fact of their existence," noted *L'Osservatore Romano,* the Vatican's semi-official newspaper.[81]

Fini's big break came when he forged an alliance with Silvio Berlusconi, a billionaire media and real estate tycoon, who was elected prime minister of Italy in March 1994. For the first time in postwar history, an avowedly fascist party joined the governing coalition of a major Western European country. Fini's party was given five ministerial posts and several other key assignments.

Shortly thereafter, Fini began calling himself a "post-fascist," as he sought to recast the MSI as a conservative party along the lines of the British Tories or the French Gaullists. He sent a delegation to lay a wreath at Auschwitz and denounced Mussolini's belated racial laws that discriminated against Jews. But he also called Mussolini the twentieth century's "greatest statesman" and stated that the Allied troop landings in 1944 "marked the loss of Europe's cultural identity." The ghost of Mussolini continued to stir, as MSI officials made noises about expanding Italy's borders. (Referring to parts of former Yugoslavia, the MSI official foreign-policy program stated: "Italy must be reunited just as Germany has been reunited.") And a MSI candidate for the European Parliament caused a row by stating that homosexuals should be put in concentration camps.[82]

In January 1995, MSI stalwarts gathered for their final convention. Declaring that it was time to turn the page of history, a forty-two-year-old Fini told a tearful audience that he was pulling the plug on the party. Henceforth, they would operate as the National Alliance. Most of the MSI faithful who gave fascist salutes at the beginning of the convention joined the new organization.

Although Berlusconi's government was short-lived, the participation of the MSI had huge implications, not only for Italy but for all of Europe. It broke a long-standing, antifascist taboo and established a precedent for conservative politicians, who had previously shunned alliances with the ultra-Right. A momentous political threshold had been crossed, which made governing coalitions with neofascists disguised as right-wing populists more acceptable, and more likely, in the future.

Fifty Years After

Franz Schönhuber, the autocratic, seventy-year-old leader of the Republikaner, was delighted when the election results came in for the German state of Hesse in March 1993. His extreme-right-wing party gained more than 8 percent of the total vote (up from less than 1 percent four years earlier), and nearly 10 percent in the city of Frankfurt. The conservative government in Bonn, led by Chancellor Helmut Kohl's Christian Democratic Union, responded immediately to the Republikaner's success in Hesse by announcing a nationwide "Germans first" employment policy that discriminated against foreigners.[83]

That year, a public opinion survey found that only 54 percent of western Germans and 41 percent of eastern Germans said they were satisfied with the democratic system. This was yet another sign of what Germans referred to as *Politikverdrossenheit* (disaffection with politics). Like its radical right-wing counterparts in Western Europe, the Republikaner benefited from foraging on a political terrain where the ideological distance between the two major parties had shrunk. In keeping with the nationalist momentum, Germany's erstwhile left-of-center Social Democrats had scurried rightward to the point where they were hardly an opposition party anymore. Basing their positions on tracking polls rather than principles, both the CDU and the Social Democrats seemed to be out of fresh ideas — creating a vacuum that was conducive to the growth of the extreme Right.[84]

After conferring with his street-active comrades, neo-Nazi leader Christian Worch declared publicly that they would rally behind the Republikaner for the national elections in October 1994. "We want to see our people in parliament, if only for the shock to the rest of the political system," he explained. Worch's reference to "our people" was a candid acknowledgment of how German neo-Nazis viewed Schönhuber's organization, even though the Republikaner usually toned down their rhetoric for the sake of democratic appearances. But the encoded vocabulary of post–Cold War neofascism — with its references to self-determination, identity, ecology, and its rejection of a multiracial society — was easily understood by Worch.[85]

Contrary to neo-Nazi expectations, the Republikaner fared poorly in 1994, gaining only 3.9 percent of the vote for the European Parliament in June (about half of what they tallied in 1989 and less than the minimum needed for representation). And in October, they failed to get enough votes to enter the Bundestag. Campaigning on a tough law-and-order platform in a bid to win back Republikaner sympathizers, the CDU squeaked by in a razor-thin victory. Kohl's successful bid for a historic fourth consecutive term as chancellor was aided by an estimated fifty thousand ethnic Germans living in Poland, whose "special rights" allowed them to cast their ballots by mail.

Several factors contributed to the anemic performance of the Republikaner, which lost its principal campaign issue when the Bundestag scrapped Germany's liberal asylum law. Schönhuber, a lackluster leader, attracted little support in eastern Germany, where most of the protest vote went to the left-wing Party of Democratic Socialism (PDS). While the Republikaner bickered with other far Right parties, the PDS secured a foothold in the new parliament and emerged as the strongest political force in former East Berlin and much of the former GDR, where bitter feelings about reunified Germany were widespread. This was part of a pattern in the ex-

Soviet bloc, as reformed Communists mounted successful comebacks in Hungary, Poland, and Lithuania.[86]

Closing the door to political refugees may have temporarily weakened the Republikaner, but it did not put an end to neo-Nazi brutality in Germany. According to the federal Office for the Protection of the Constitution, the incidence of right-wing extremist crimes stood at 7,952 in 1994 — down from 10,561 in 1993, but higher than the previous year. Violent assaults against foreigners dropped in 1994 compared with 1993, but the number of anti-Semitic abuses doubled. Several more concentration camp sites were desecrated, and anti-Semitic vandals set fire to the synagogue in Luebeck. It was the first arson attack on a Jewish temple in Germany since the Third Reich. Skinheads also beat up an African-American bobsledder and a fellow U.S. athlete. On another occasion, a neo-Nazi gang accosted a wheelchair-bound teenager and carved a swastika on her cheek when she refused to chant nasty slogans about foreigners and disabled people. These attacks were cited by critics who charged that German officials still had not done enough to curb neo-Nazi violence.[87]

For several years, neo-Nazi aggression had facilitated official efforts to change the asylum law. Once this change was accomplished, skinhead attacks became redundant and counterproductive to image-conscious German officials who, after much delay, finally decided to crack down hard against neo-Nazi agitators. Secret-service informants led police to hidden arms caches, the homes of ultra-right-wing militants were raided, dozens were placed in preventive detention, and several more neo-Nazi groups were outlawed. In addition, Interior Minister Manfred Kanther placed the Republikaner Party under national surveillance after Schönhuber tried to form an alliance with his longtime rival, Gerhard Frey, head of the more overtly extreme Deutsche Volksunion, which was already on the government's subversive watch list. Kanther had previously stated that the CDU "must have policies for which Republikaner supporters can vote."[88]

The government's dragnet extended to key figures in the neo-Nazi scene, including Christian Worch, who was sentenced to two years in prison for violating the ban on National Socialist organizing — something he had been doing openly for a long time without incurring the wrath of the state. Several other prominent neo-Nazis, including Meinolf Schönborn of the outlawed Nationalist Front, ended up behind bars. That's where Major General Otto Ernst Remer also appeared to be heading after a federal high court upheld his conviction for denying the Holocaust. But the eighty-one-year-old Nazi failed to show up at the Bayreuth prison on March 14, 1994, the day he was supposed to begin serving a twenty-two-month sentence. After police failed to locate him at his home in Bad Kissingen, a state prosecutor issued a nationwide order for Remer's arrest. As defiant as ever, Hitler's former bodyguard had no intention of spending his last days in prison. Instead he fled to Spain, where local neo-Nazi leaders sheltered him.[89]

Remer's protege, Ewald Althans, was also feeling the legal pinch. In December 1994, a Munich court sentenced him to eighteen months in prison for distributing videos that denied the Holocaust. He also faced charges related to his role in a documentary film, *Profession: Neo-Nazi.* Althans, the star of the film, was shown on a visit to Auschwitz, which he described as having been a resort center with swimming pools, rather than a Nazi concentration camp. "What's happening here is a giant farce!" Althans shouted at several visitors.

But half a year in prison had already taken its toll on Althans, who appeared to crack under the pressure of confinement. When he stood trial in Berlin in the summer of 1995, he insisted that he was no longer a neo-Nazi, but his story was fraught with contradictions. Some of his friends from Munich's gay community testified for the defense, confirming rumors that Althans was bisexual. Althans also claimed he had been working for the Verfassungsschutz since 1991. A Bavarian security official acknowledged that Althans had offered to sell five thousand addresses of neo-Nazis in Germany and abroad, but his proposal was rejected when he demanded a quarter of a million dollars. Former undercover agents who infiltrated the neo-Nazi movement have suggested that as many as 10 percent of its members were government informants. It seems unlikely, however, that Althans had functioned in this capacity. The story he told about spying for the state was part of his failed legal strategy to avoid additional prison time.[90]

Calling Althans a "mental arsonist" whose rhetoric had contributed to a wave of violence against foreigners, a Berlin judge imposed a three-and-a-half year sentence in addition to the term he was already serving. It was quite a downfall for the twenty-nine-year-old Hitler poster boy who had been groomed to be the next führer. His pathetic display in court disgusted his former comrades, who denounced Althans as a prostitute and a traitor.

Things had also gone awry for Gerhard Lauck, the obnoxious American neo-Nazi. Deported to Hamburg to stand trial for smuggling massive amounts of neo-Nazi propaganda into Germany, he was convicted and given a four-year sentence. By this time, however, new computer technology and the Internet had supplanted Lauck's traditional methods of pamphleteering. Getting on the Web and upgrading their means of communication was one of the ways that neo-Nazis responded to pressure by the German government. Some sectors of the neo-Nazi movement went further underground, forming clandestine terror cells based on the leaderless resistance model that American militia strategists had developed. Others hid their neo-Nazi affiliation while seeking alliances with student dueling fraternities, government-funded *Vetriebenen* groups, New Right intellectuals, and conservative political parties.[91]

Although the government had succeeded in locking up much of the hard-core neo-Nazi leadership, these long overdue steps deflected attention from other disconcerting developments. There were stark indications that powerful German officials had not yet rid themselves of their propensity to nationalist excess.

In January 1995, Manfred Roeder, a convicted neo-Nazi terrorist and notorious Holocaust-denier, delivered a well-received lecture at Germany's most prestigious military academy in Hamburg. Although the German government keeps detailed lists of political extremists, academy officials subsequently claimed they were unaware that Roeder, a headline-grabbing fanatic, served eight years behind bars for his role in a fire bomb attack that killed two Vietnamese immigrants. Prior to this incident, Roeder had visited the United States on several occasions, functioning as a roving neo-Nazi ambassador to the Aryan Nations in Idaho, the Liberty Lobby in Washington, DC, and other North American racialist groups.

Upon his release from prison in 1990, Roeder became vice-president of the German-Russian Aid Society, a revanchist sect that called for the German recolonization of Kaliningrad. This was the subject of Roeder's speech at the elite Hamburg military academy, after which he was the guest of honor at a banquet. An internal Defense Ministry investigation would later refer to the Roeder episode as "a striking mistake," but it failed to explain how his neo-Nazi–led organization was able to secure material assistance from the German army. With the approval of the German Foreign Office, the Bundeswehr supplied money and surplus vehicles in 1993 for Roeder's politically sensitive project, which sought to repopulate the area previously known as East Prussia with ethnic Germans from Russia and the ex-Soviet republics.

During the same period, the Foreign Office repeatedly turned down applications from the Twenty-Third Psalm Association, an Aachen-based Christian charity, for emergency material aid to impoverished children in St. Petersburg. The Foreign Office rejected these requests on the grounds that there was "no pressing national interest" at stake. By contrast, German officials viewed Roeder's efforts as furthering Germany's national interests.[92]

Manfred Roeder surfaced once again during street demonstrations against a controversial museum exhibit on "Crimes of the Wehrmacht," which traveled around Germany in the mid- and late 1990s. This exhibit included graphic photographs that showed ordinary German soldiers, rather than SS members, committing horrendous crimes against civilians on the Eastern Front. The exhibition was vociferously denounced by members of the ruling coalition in Bonn, who falsely—and repeatedly—claimed that only the SS, not the German army, was responsible for wartime atrocities. When the exposition came to Dresden, Roeder and a horde of neo-Nazis clashed with antifascist counter-demonstrators. In another protest, neo-Nazi skinheads marched shoulder-to-shoulder with active-duty German soldiers and the mayor of Munich.

For several years, significant changes had been unfolding in Germany that were potentially far more dangerous than ongoing thuggery by teenage skinheads. The conservative *Wende,* or shift in political culture, which began when Kohl became chancellor in the early 1980s, accelerated after the Berlin Wall fell. Suddenly a broad spectrum of thinkers and public officials were keen to espouse a more conspicuous nationalist line, one that stressed German power and identity and was antagonistic toward foreigners, in general, and U.S. influence, in particular. Proclaiming the need for discipline, authority, and "internal renewal," these born-again nationalists painted a harrowing picture of their country on the verge of multicultural chaos. They disparaged the comparatively liberal consensus of former West Germany, which, in their view, was not truly German because of the stultifying dominance of low-brow American culture.

Manfred Krock, council chairman of Germany's large Protestant church, warned that a growing intellectually based radicalism was stirring up xenophobic violence in his country. Krock and many other Germans feared that this conservative nationalist groundswell—which harkened back to an imperial tradition that predated Hitler—served to facilitate the aims of violent neo-Nazis who were driving foreigners out of town.

Those at the forefront of the post–Cold War German nationalist resurgence did not rely on old Nazi symbols and slogans. Instead they drew heavily from the ideological arsenal of the Conservative Revolution that preceded the Nazi takeover. Held aloft by New Right intelligentsia as an authentic expression of German conservatism, the cultural pessimists of the Weimar era were becoming chic again. By invoking the Conservative Revolution, right-wing extremists were able to pursue their dream of ultranationalist regeneration without having to defend Hitler's excesses. The fact that a growing number of academics, military officers, politicians, and other opinion-leaders longed for such a dispensation attests to the durability and influence of Germany's conservative ideological tradition.

The nationalist revival in Germany was accompanied by widespread yearnings for the imperial glories of yesteryear. This tendency has been "gaining strength," according to social critic Jürgen Habermas, who detected an urge to renew Bismarck's great power project. "If you look at the German elites," Habermas observed in 1994, "it is possible to discern a powerful desire to turn Germany into an independent great power in the center of Europe, with its gaze fixed on the East."[93]

As the German government made preparations to move the capital from Bonn to Berlin by the end of the decade, it seemed inevitable that the center of gravity of Europe's economic powerhouse would shift eastward as well. Would the return to Berlin, roughly halfway between Moscow and the Atlantic, facilitate a new continental equilibrium by serving as a bridge to the fragile young democracies in Eastern Europe? Or would it presage a dramatic transformation of Europe with reunified Germany flexing its Teutonic muscles and wielding more political clout in a manner that made other countries nervous?

Concerns about a too-powerful Germany figured in Washington's decision to support NATO's eastward expansion. "By enveloping Germany in a wider Euro-Atlantic framework," explained ex-presidential advisor Zbigniew Brzezinski, "NATO enlargement resolves Europe's central security problem of the twentieth century, which has been how to cope effectively with the reality of German power."[94]

The extent to which Germany deals honestly with its history will undoubtedly have a significant impact on what unfolds in the future. For several decades after World War II, there was a tendency to sterilize the past and minimize the role of "ordinary" Germans in the Holocaust. It wasn't until a generation had passed that Germans began to speak much about the Nazi period. Once the silence was broken, heated debate ensued between those who accepted a national responsibility for the Holocaust and those who tried to exonerate a majority of Germans from any culpability for the crimes of the Nazi era.

With the passing of the Cold War, a rising nationalist chorus opined that the German people should view their past in a less guilt-ridden way. Of course, official condemnations of Hitler did not cease, even as German memories of the Third Reich underwent a revision. One month before the fiftieth anniversary of the end of World War II, a controversial manifesto appeared in the *Frankfurter Allgemeine Zeitung*, a conservative German newspaper. Signed by 280 right-wing intellectuals and politicians, this declaration challenged the view that May 8, 1945—the day the Nazis surrendered—was a day of liberation. The war's end, the document maintained, ushered in a bleak period of expulsions, national dismemberment, and foreign tyranny. While emphasizing that German suffering should be remembered, this revisionist appeal made no mention of the horror that Germany inflicted upon other people or the responsibility that Germans bore for supporting Hitler. Nor did it recall the fact that Germany had started the conflict by invading its neighbors.[95]

Cynically entitled "Against Forgetting," the manifesto triggered an uproar. Just as disturbing as the message it conveyed was the group of Germans who affixed their names to it. Outright fascists and New Right intellectuals were listed as endorsers along with active-duty and retired military officers, bank directors, police chiefs, and leaders of the Christian Democratic Union and its coalition partners. The peevish tone of the document epitomized the gray zone of German politics, where ultrarightists commingled with conservatives. It showed the extent to which extremist thinking had penetrated into the mainstream, metastasizing like a cancerous growth in German ruling circles.

Persistent efforts to relativize the Holocaust by equating it with other twentieth century atrocities had influenced a large portion of the German population. According to a poll by Der Spiegel, 36 percent of Germans believed that "exiling the Germans in the East was as great a crime against humanity as was the Holocaust against the Jews." This skewed perception of history was encouraged by Chancellor Kohl, who sought to portray Germany as partly a victim rather than solely a perpetrator of World War II. Although Kohl did not sign the manifesto, he expressed sympathy for those who did, including his close political ally, Alfred Dregger, then the honorary chairman of the CDU faction in parliament. A few weeks before the manifesto appeared, Dregger went on record stating that May 8 "was no liberation." He also praised the "decency" of Hitler's army and claimed that "most Germans knew nothing about the murder of the Jews." His assessment typified revisionist mythology, which implied that two separate struggles had been waged during World War II, one for Germany and one for National Socialism. Similarly, Kohl referred to atrocities committed "in the name of Germany," as if some extraterrestrial force took over while the German populace stood on the sidelines.[96]

For many years, the remembrance of World War II had been consciously maintained in Berlin, with its overgrown bomb rubble, scarred edifices, and walled partition of east and west. But much of this imagery was swept away by construction workers and renovators, as the German government prepared to move, with hardly a peep of criticism, into buildings associated with the most gruesome machinations of the Third Reich. Reunified Germany's financial experts would settle comfortably into Göring's Air Ministry; defense specialists would devise their strategies in the same offices where Hitler's generals plotted the invasion of the east; the Labor Ministry would be in Goebbels's offices; the Foreign Ministry would formulate its policies under the spacious ceilings of the Reichsbank, the Nazi central bank where stolen gold and other ill-gotten assets were stored; and the German parliament would once again take up residence in the infamous Reichstag.

Farther afield, Bavarian officials were planning to turn the ruins of Hitler's alpine retreat, the so-called Eagle's Nest, into a luxurious holiday resort. And in Poland, the Wolf's Lair (Hitler's eastern front headquarters) was slated for conversion into a private theme park, where staffers dressed in replica Wehrmacht and Luftwaffe uniforms would preside over nightly dancing at "Hitler's Bunker Disco."[97]

Slowly but surely, in ways that were sometimes subtle and sometimes heavy-handed, Germany's past was being transformed, glossed over, touched up and played down, normalized, commercialized, repackaged, and forgotten—as if history was some kind of trick that the living played on the dead. A new national war memorial opened in east Berlin where an East German monument to the victims of fascism and militarism once stood. But the words fascism and militarism were omitted from the replacement memorial, which "utterly fails to distinguish between victims and perpetrators," according to Berlin's Jewish community leader Jerzy Kanal. Not far away, state-funded artists had re-created the facade of the Hohenzollern palace in the center of the city so that Berliners could proudly gaze upon an old imperial glory.

On the eve of the fiftieth anniversary of the defeat of the Third Reich, vandals torched a Jewish synagogue in Luebeck for the second time in fourteen months. The next day in Dresden, a memorial plaque to a Mozambican guest worker who died after being attacked by skinheads was daubed with swastikas. Erected in honor of twenty-eight-year-old Jorge Gomandai, the first fatal victim of neo-Nazi violence in reunified Germany, the plaque was damaged only hours after ceremonies across Europe marked the end of World War II. Seventy others had been killed by German right-wing extremists since Gomandi passed away. Each loss of life was a vivid reminder that Germany's past continued to roil in the depths of the present.

CONCLUSION

Otto Ernst Remer sat in a large, comfortable chair, sipping schnapps in a villa overlooking the Mediterranean on Spain's Costa del Sol. Having suffered two strokes in recent years, the Nazi octogenarian was not in good health. But at least he wasn't in jail.

Accompanied by his wife, Anneliese, Remer made his way to Marbella after fleeing Germany. Settling into a new routine, he contacted several Nazi fugitives who lived in Spain, including Waffen SS General Léon Degrelle. The Belgian war criminal passed away on March 31, 1994, a few days after meeting with Remer. At Degrelle's funeral, Remer vowed to carry on the fight in his usual way—by denying the Holocaust. During a lengthy interview on Spanish national television, Remer reiterated his contention that there were no wartime gas-chamber killings of Jews.[1]

Shortly after this TV appearance, Remer was apprehended by police at the Málaga airport. He was en route to Madrid for an appointment with the Spanish Interior Ministry to argue his case for political asylum. The German government had requested his extradition, but Remer's lawyers argued that Holocaust-denial was not illegal in Spain and, therefore, he should not be deported. (Under Spanish law, extradition could only be carried out if a crime was recognized by both countries.) Instead of sending Remer back to Germany, a judge placed him under house arrest. But no policemen were posted outside his residence in Marbella to enforce the ruling, and Remer was often seen in a wheelchair pushed by friends in the city center.

Even in his frail condition, Remer kept abreast of events in the Fatherland. On June 18, 1994, the German army held a Prussian-style torchlight parade in front of Berlin's Brandenburg Gate to celebrate the departure of British, French, and American troops. Conspicuously absent were the Russians, who had not been invited to participate in this farewell ceremony.[2] Not everyone, however, was happy to see the soldiers go, as U.S. State Department officer Douglas Jones noted: "The withdrawal of Allied forces from Berlin filled ethnic community leaders with dread, because they had come to regard the Allies as protecting powers not from the Russians, but from the Germans."[3]

Hardly a week went by without the observance of another war-related anniversary. On July 20, 1994, German officials commemorated the anti-Hitler plot that nearly killed the Führer half a century earlier. Much to Remer's disgust, Chancellor Kohl praised the heroism of those who lost their lives when the conspiracy failed. Ignored amid all the solemn and hypocritical pronouncements were several important facts: the German government had yet to rehabilitate those who were punished for refusing to serve in Hitler's army and the thirty thousand soldiers who deserted; most resisters were still legally considered traitors; and German courts continued to recognize as valid most expropriations of Jewish businesses that occurred during the Third Reich as part of Nazi efforts to "Aryanize" the economy.[4]

It was somehow fitting that Remer should have been in Spain on the fiftieth anniversary of the anti-Hitler coup attempt, for this was where his Twentieth of July comrade, Otto Skorzeny, had resided after the war. Remer's affairs during his Spanish exile were managed by the leaders of CEDADE, a neo-Nazi group that Skorzeny was instrumental in founding in the mid-1960s.

When H. Keith Thompson, the faithful Nazi bloodhound, heard that his old friend had fled to Spain, he once again offered his assistance. After Thompson sent some money to Remer and his wife, they wrote and thanked him for his enduring loyalty and "extraordinary endeavors." The years had also taken their toll on

Thompson, who in his late seventies was not in the best of health. But his dedication to the Nazi cause had never wavered. Contemplating the demise of the Soviet Union, he felt that events had proven Francis Parker Yockey's thesis was correct — the United States was more dangerous to Europe than Russia was. "In many ways it's too bad that there is no USSR left, but merely another satellite of US/Israel, economically dependent on the U.S. taxpayer, run by a drunk surrounded by paper-shredders," Thompson griped. "Zhirinovsky seems a good man to me in many ways, certainly better than Yeltsin."[5]

Thompson watched with dismay as a bitter legal fight erupted between Liberty Lobby founder Willis Carto and the staff of the Institute for Historical Review. As his negationist colleagues bickered among themselves, Thompson followed the same strategy that several leading figures of the racialist Right were pursuing — he cultivated ties to the Republican Party. Financially well-off, Thompson gave generously to several Republican candidates, including Senator Jesse Helms, would-be Senator Oliver North, David Duke, and Pat Buchanan. Thompson's largesse earned him official membership in the GOP's Presidential Legion of Merit, as well as numerous thank-you letters from the Republican National Committee and its sundry permutations.[6]

But Nazi Germany remained Thompson's true passion. "I've always given my life to the Third Reich," he stated proudly. After serving covertly as a German officer during World War II, he functioned as the principal contact in North America for surviving SS veterans and Nazis worldwide. Working in tandem with Ernst Remer, Otto Skorzeny, and other well-placed ODESSA operatives, Thompson assisted a host of Hitler diehards during the difficult years after the Third Reich collapsed. Often more by instinct than conspiracy, they performed an agile dance between the superpowers, playing one off the other in the early phases of the Cold War. Utilizing the seesaw strategy, many fascists were able to hang on and eventually recoup some of their severe losses.

As the years went by, however, it became increasingly apparent that collaborating with various intelligence agencies may have afforded immunity for many disreputable characters, but this, in and of itself, did not advance a neo-Nazi agenda on a mass scale. At the outset a saving grace, the Cold War hardened into a no-exit quagmire for frustrated fascists. For several decades, they languished on the margins, dreaming of the day when they would return to power. Idiosyncratic schemes were tested in an effort to overcome their political isolation. But the hegemony of the Western capitalist order seemed insurmountable. Ernesto Mila Rodriguez, a leading Spanish neofascist, summed up their predicament. "Western society is like a diamond," he explained, "very hard and nearly impossible to break. But if you put enough pressure on exactly the right point, it will crack."[7]

The jackals of the extreme Right believed they found the crucial pressure point when they seized upon immigration as the main issue to rally around. While a network of ultra-right-wing cadres continued to function as the violent vanguard of xenophobia, some shock troops from Europe's neofascist underground split off to form mass-based political parties. One of the advantages of this dual-pronged effort was that it provided an electoral front for hard-core militants, who underwent an ideological face-lift and watered down their pronouncements to conform to electoral requirements.

By the mid-1980s, a flock of radical right-wing parties had found a nesting place on the democratic landscape. The initial success of the Front National in France and its emulators elsewhere showed that large segments of Western European society were vulnerable to appeals from national populists and the totalitarian temptation they embodied. These forces had already started to gain momentum when the Berlin Wall parted and the Soviet Union disintegrated. Some Western analysts quickly sounded the trumpets and proclaimed "the end of history," as if liberal democracy had notched an unequivocal victory. But instead of ushering in a new world order of clanging cash registers and busy voting booths, the vertigo brought on by the sudden changes had an unsettling impact in the East as well as in the West. Deprived of the bipolar certainties of the previous era, many felt their moorings slip. The epiphany of freedom was followed by social chaos, political instability, rabid nationalism, and morbid outbursts of ethnic hatred.

Rather than eliminating a major cause of right-wing extremism, the collapse of Communism triggered its resurgence throughout the Northern Hemisphere. Not since the Third Reich had such a virulent and enraged Right made its presence felt in so many countries. Tracing the rise of Hitler, George Mosse observed that "one of the Nazis' principle victories before seizing power" was that they forced centrists and leftists "to argue on terrain occupied by the racist right." European and American neofascists posing as right-wing populists could claim a similar victory half a century after World War II. Even when they lost elections and were not formally part of the government, far Right politicians had a significant influence on public policy. To a great extent, their scapegoating rhetoric framed key debates and shaped the post–Cold War political agenda.[8]

Fascism is on the march again. No simple formula, however, can predict how strong contemporary fascist movements (or their functional equivalents) will become. A vibrant democratic culture is not conducive to the growth of fascism. But unchecked corporate power has, to a significant degree, stultified the democratic process, and fascist groups in Europe and the United States feed upon this malaise. British scholar Roger Griffin likened fascism to "a supervirus which constantly evolves to accommodate changes in its habitat, producing a wide variety of new strains resistant to traditional prophylactics."[9]

Although there are definite parallels to the interwar years, today's neofascist movements have emerged under a unique set of circumstances. Ironically, their success hinged to a great extent on their ability to distance themselves from the historical image of fascism. While neo-Nazi nostalgics fixated on the swastika, the more astute theoreticians of the European New Right understood that efforts to justify Hitler and the fascist dictatorships of the past were futile and ill-conceived. Much of the New Right's revamped ideology was scooped up by camouflaged neofascist organizations as they embarked upon their quest for power. By campaigning, first and foremost, as protectors of Western Europe's cultural identity and economic prosperity, right-wing extremists were able to elbow their way into the mainstream.

"It is only a matter of time," historian Paul Johnson predicted, "before the fascism of the 1990's, under new names, of course, and 'responsible' leaders, becomes respectable." But these latter-day fascists would not be so easy to recognize. Some would even assume an antifascist guise. In Moscow, for example, a group of prominent ultranationalists announced that they were forming an Anti-Fascist Patriotic Center in May 1995. One of the principal figures behind this initiative was Boris Mironov, who had recently been fired from his post as Yeltsin's press minister after he stated, "If Russian nationalism is fascism, then I'm a fascist." Mironov sued the *Moscow News* for libel after they called him a fascist, but he lost the case; apparently, the courts felt that this label was appropriate.[10]

Similarly, American militia groups affected an antifascist stance by claiming that Hitler was a gun-control proponent. A few militia units even welcomed Jews and people of color into their ranks. But this only served to underscore that overtly white supremacist and neo-Nazi attitudes were not an adequate litmus test to determine whether the militias represented a serious menace. A paranoid style had long been part of the American political scene, along with right-wing paramilitary groups such as the Ku Klux Klan, the Minutemen, and the Posse Comitatus. What distinguished the post–Cold War militia movement was how it reinvented fascism in a uniquely American way by combining muddled arguments for anti–big government constitutionalism with traditional isolationist appeals, reactionary conspiracy theories, and frontier myths (à la Randy Weaver) that promised national regeneration through violence.[11]

Despite their proven penchant for bloodshed, the militias had several champions within the Republican Party and on Capitol Hill. Several GOP officeholders spoke at local militia events, and a bevy of presidential contenders vied for the blessings of Pat Robertson, whose conspiratorial worldview was just a nuance away from the kind of anti-Semitism that many neo-Nazis espoused. After the Oklahoma City bombing, House Speaker Newt Gingrich stymied a much-needed congressional probe into right-wing paramilitary activity in the United States. Instead, the Republican-controlled Congress held extensive hearings on government misconduct at Waco, Texas, and Ruby Ridge, Idaho.[12]

In the midst of these hearings, Americans were treated to a new book coauthored by Gingrich. Titled *1945,* this fantasy novel featured none other than Otto Skorzeny as the supervillain of a hackneyed "what if Nazi Germany had won?" plot. After the Germans conquered Europe and the Soviet Union, according to Gingrich's yarn, they raced against the Americans to make the first atomic bomb. Dispatched by Hitler, Skorzeny set out to destroy a top-secret atomic research facility in Tennessee, but his efforts were foiled by a passel of local sheriffs, war veterans, and civilian militias with their trusty rifles.[13]

In real life, Skorzeny was recruited by U.S. intelligence after the war, along with thousands of other Nazis and fascists. Ironically, some of these espionage assets, Skorzeny among them, would later work with ultra-right-wing organizations that flaunted their antipathy toward the U.S. government. These neofascist groups, in turn, were symptomatic of a much wider authoritarian malaise, according to Theodore Adorno, whose midcentury diagnosis retains its relevance in the fin de siècle 1990s. Adorno viewed "the continued existence of National Socialism *within* democracy [as] more threatening than the continued existence of fascist tendencies *against* democracy." His studies suggest that the potential for fascism was embedded in the fabric of mass consumer culture, which typically engenders weak personalities with high dependency needs that could easily be manipulated by commercial advertisers and political demagogues. Seen from this perspective, fascism has persisted as a permanent possibility in advanced industrial societies, including post–Cold War Germany.[14]

Fifty years after World War II, however, the risk of another Nazi-like dictatorship in Germany seemed very remote. With many of its leaders behind bars, the German neo-Nazi movement appeared to be in retreat. Chancellor Kohl was able to defang his far Right competitors by adopting much of their program. But this calculated attempt to stay in power, while successful in the short term, also perpetuated long-range problems that make the reappearance of a more virulent strain of nationalism likely in the future.

Restricting immigration did not alleviate the deep-rooted xenophobia in German society that fostered racist violence. Skinhead attacks did not stop, nor did the brutal beatings of asylum seekers by German police. Xenophobia as a habit of the heart, a taste on the tongue, was unrelenting. Douglas Jones, principal officer of the U.S. embassy in Berlin, spoke about this phenomenon shortly before he retired in June 1994. "I don't know of a single foreigner, including myself," said Jones, "who has not had on at least one occasion the impression, through an incident or a comment from a German, that he is unwelcome, that he does not belong here, or that his 'differentness' did not attract unpleasant attention."[15]

Those unsure of who they are often define themselves in terms of who they are not. This was the real basis of xenophobia among Germans and other Europeans, which had more to do with indigenous confusion and insecurity than with the presence of foreigners per se. Fewer political refugees was not the key to resolving Germany's festering identity crisis that expressed itself both as abhorrence of the other and feelings of German exceptionalism. (A post–Cold War survey found that a majority of Germans considered themselves "cleaner and more intelligent" than non-Germans.)

While the troubled 1990s in Germany were much different from the 1930s, something seemed to be going wrong. "I observe, in our country, a sense of yearning for authoritarian solutions," commented psychologist Horst-Eberhard Richter. "A lot of people think that the increasingly difficult problems can be managed only with authoritarian means, as if an open society can't manage capitalism, and only a hard hand and an iron broom will work."[16]

Vexed by a stagnant economy, vanishing jobs, acrimonious relations between eastern and western residents, a charged politics of ethnicity, and the unfulfilled quest for a "normal" identity, Germany still needed to invoke the enemy within to have faith in itself. Instead of telling the truth about immigration, German political leaders persisted in playing hide-and-seek with reality. Seven million foreigners resided in Germany (mainly in the west), comprising 9 percent of the population. Yet top officials kept insisting that their country must not become "a country of immigration"—which it already was. Lacking civic courage to speak honesty about Germany's problems and eager to deflect attention from their own policy failures, influential politicians continued to stir up xenophobic fears and hatred.

But as long as huge disparities existed between prosperous Western Europe and the feeble economies of Eastern Europe and the Third World, Germany would remain an immigration zone. Changing the constitution and stepping up border patrols posed additional obstacles for refugees, but they continued to come. They made their way in small groups, scrambling through the underbrush or fording the marshy River Oder that separates Poland from Germany. Several dozen asylum seekers drowned while trying to swim across the border at night. But no one in Germany wanted to take responsibility for burying them because the cost was too high. So their bloated bodies were left to drift downstream with the current.

NOTES

INTRODUCTION

1. Among those executed was Count Claus von Stauffenberg, principal leader of Valkyrie, the code name for the assassination plot. Other victims of the post–July 20 purge included twenty-one generals, thirty-three colonels, two ambassadors, seven senior diplomats, one minister of state, and three secretaries of state. For Skorzeny's account of the events on July 20, 1944, see Otto Skorzeny, *Skorzeny's Secret Missions*, pp. 162–67.

2. Kai Bird, *The Chairman*, p. 332.

3. Allen Dulles, *Germany's Underground*, p. xii.

4. Arthur Schlesinger, "Lessons from the Cold War," in Michael J. Hogan, ed., *End of the Cold War*, pp. 60–61.

5. In *Roads to Dominion* (p. 9), Sara Diamond provides this useful definition: "To be right-wing means to support the state in its capacity as *enforcer* of order and to oppose the state as *distributor* of wealth and power more equitably in society."

6. Scholars continue to mull over the relationship between fascism and Nazism. For the purposes of this book, I treat Nazism as the most extreme variant of fascism. According to this interpretation, all Nazis are fascists, but not all fascists are Nazis. Similarly, all fascists are right-wing extremists, but not all right-wing extremists are fascists. In keeping with the accepted practice of historians, I refer to fascism generically with a lowercase *f*, reserving the uppercase *F* specifically for the Italian variety.

7. Umberto Eco, "Ur-Fascism," *New York Review of Books*, June 22, 1995. Others maintain that fascism has an essential, if

somewhat elusive, theoretical core. Fascism, writes Walter Laqueur, "resembles pornography in that it is difficult — perhaps impossible — to define in an operational, legally valid way, but those with experience know it when they see it." In an effort to arrive at a clear-cut definition of a slippery political phenomenon, certain scholars have focused on compiling a list of innate qualities that all fascist movements presumably possess; Stanley Payne, for example, emphasizes extreme nationalism, the redemptive power of violence, the cult of the leader, and several other key features. This scholarly methodology has been criticized by Robert O. Paxton, who argues that "the study of fascist movements must concentrate at least as much on their surrounding circumstances and accomplices as the movements themselves" in order to account for their success or failure. (See, in general, Stanley Payne, *A History of Fascism;* Walter Laqueur, *Fascism: Past, Present, Future;* and Robert O. Paxton, "The Uses of Fascism," *New York Review of Books,* November 28, 1996.)

CHAPTER ONE: *Shifting Alliances*

1. "Otto SKORZENY, alias 'SOLAR,' " Office of the Assistant Chief of Staff, G-2 [U.S. Army intelligence], June 13, 1951. For background on Skorzeny, see Robert S. Wistrich, *Who's Who in Nazi Germany,* pp. 286–88; Louis L. Snyder, *Hitler's Elite,* pp. 299–316; Philip Rees, *Extreme Right Since 1890,* p. 362; and, in general, Glenn B. Infield, *Skorzeny.*

2. Gerald Reitlinger, *The SS: Alibi of a Nation,* p. 161.

3. Paul Meskil, *Hitler's Heirs,* p. 87.

4. Snyder, *Hitler's Elite,* p. 299.

5. William Tuohy, "SS Officer Wrongly Credited with Deed, Historian Says," *Los Angeles Times,* December 26, 1987; Charles Foley, *Commando Extraordinary,* p. 139.

6. While posted in Switzerland, Dulles fielded overtures from a multitude of corporate and diplomatic sources that he had cultivated

over the years as a partner for Sullivan and Cromwell. This elite New York law firm catered to a high-powered clientele on both sides of the Atlantic, including a number of prominent German firms that backed Hitler's rise to power. Dulles functioned as legal counsel for the Anglo-German Schröder banking empire, which included the wealthy Cologne-based Stein Bank, whose chairman, Kurt von Schröder, was Himmler's financial angel. When Hitler was contemplating a power grab in the early 1930s, Schröder rallied other major industrialists to his side. This did not dissuade Allen Dulles from serving as a director of one of Schröder's American subsidiaries. Schröder Banking Corporation and Schröder Trust served as conduits for CIA monies during the 1950s when Allen was CIA director. His older brother and the future secretary of state, John Foster Dulles, was also a partner at Sullivan and Cromwell. In addition to representing the Bank of Spain shortly after Franco took over, he personally lawyered for the likes of IG Farben, the huge chemical cartel that formed the backbone of the Nazi war machine. Several major U.S. firms — including blue-chip clients of Sullivan and Cromwell — secretly continued to collaborate with their German business associates while American soldiers fought against the Nazis during World War II.

7. Hohenlohe's version of the meeting was recorded in German documents that U.S. forces retrieved after the war. Declaring that he was "fed up with listening all the time to outdated politicians, émigrés and prejudiced Jews," Dulles purportedly told Hohenlohe that he liked the idea of a separate peace agreement, the sooner the better, with the proviso that Hitler be ousted from power. The OSS wire-puller spoke of establishing a cordon sanitaire in Eastern Europe to keep the Bolsheviks at bay. And he offered a bit of friendly advice, suggesting that the SS "act more skillfully on the Jewish Question" to avoid "causing a big stir." (Christopher Simpson, *Splendid Blonde Beast,* pp. 122–23, 347; Heinz Höhne, *Order of the Death's Head,* p. 521.)

8. Walter Schellenberg, *The Labyrinth,* pp. 300–01.

9. Simpson, *Splendid Blonde Beast,* p. 124.

10. T. H. Tetens, *Germany Plots with the Kremlin,* pp. 234–35.

11. The State Department announced on March 30, 1945, that the Allies had copies of German plans for the exfiltration of German capital, technicians, and agents for postwar propaganda and other purposes. State officials based much of their evidence on a November 27, 1944, report circulated by SHAEF (Supreme Headquarters, Allied Expeditionary Forces, Europe) regarding Nazi postdefeat plans delineated in Strasbourg some months earlier. (See Foreign Economic Administration, Department of State bulletin, April 1, 1945, "Discovery of Nazi post-war plans," 537-38, exhibits file, box 991, record group 169, Washington Travel Records Center, Suitland, Maryland.)

12. The Reichsbank theft was listed in the 1957 edition of the *Guinness Book of Records* under the heading "Robbery, Biggest Unsolved." Subsequently, U.S. Army Counterintelligence Corps agents unearthed an estimated twelve tons of gold bars and coins from various sites in Bavaria and western Austria, including a treasure trove concealed in a barn near Salzburg believed to be Himmler's personal fortune. Another $500,000 worth of gold hidden in Austria was retrieved by the OSS, which also assisted the State Department in its Safehaven program. As the name implies, Safehaven sought to investigate foreign currency manipulations and counterfeit scams by the Nazis and to trace the movement of stolen funds and other assets through an international network of money-laundering conduits that had been activated after the Strasbourg conference. (Glenn B. Infield, *Secrets of the SS,* p. 222; Ian Sayer and Douglas Botting, *Nazi Gold,* pp. 42–45; Sayer and Botting, *America's Secret Army,* p. 228; Charles Higham, *American Swastika,* pp. 247–48; Anthony Cave Brown, ed., *Secret War Report of the OSS,* pp. 562–63; see also, in general, Marc Jean Masurovsky, *Safehaven Program,* doctoral thesis, American University, 1990.)

13. Tom Bower, *Pledge Betrayed,* p. 75; *Kölnische Rundschau,* September 30, 1962; Sayer and Botting, *Nazi Gold,* p. 176. After he was captured at war's end, Walter Schellenberg disclosed that by 1944, $600 million in stolen gold had poured into Switzerland alone.

14. The best sources on Gehlen are Heinz Höhne and Hermann Zolling, *The General Was a Spy;* Christopher Simpson, *Blowback;* and Mary Ellen Reese, *General Reinhard Gehlen and the CIA.*

15. Burton Hersh, *Old Boys,* p. 162.

16. Sayer and Botting, *America's Secret Army,* p. 202. Two months before the end of the war, U.S. State Department officials revealed that they knew of a Nazi scheme to undermine the military victory of the Allies and eventually win the peace for Germany. This was spelled out in the *New York Herald Tribune* on March 31, 1945: "The Department of State announced today that reliable information collected by Allied governments clearly indicates that the Nazi regime in Germany has developed well-arranged postwar plans for the perpetuation of Nazi doctrines and domination. Some of these plans have already been put into operation and others are ready to be launched on a widespread scale immediately upon termination of hostilities in Europe." On April 7, 1945, Assistant Secretary of State Julius C. Holmes whetted the public's appetite with additional information: "We Americans are too ready to believe things like this don't really happen. But they *do.* There *are* villains in the plot. They'll search for every possible loophole in the Allied military plans for controlling Germany. One of the most interesting angles of the German plan is to place technicians where they can be most useful to the Nazi underground. . . . Certain Nazis are assigned to pose as Communists, Socialists, and members of trade union organizations. The Nazi strategists intend to use these people to penetrate into anti-Nazi circles, in Germany and outside."

17. Sayer and Botting, *America's Secret Army,* p. 208; "Memorandum on Nazi Resistance Plans, OSS German Section, No. 2-290, USAISC," cited in Infield, *Skorzeny,* p. 111.

18. Henrik Kruger, *Over the Green Border* (unpublished manuscript).

19. Hersh, *Old Boys,* p. 112. According to Höttl, Dulles's "wireless messages to Washington . . . were picked up and for the most part deciphered and passed to the Germans by the Hungarian moni-

tor service," allowing "the German Secret Service . . . to obtain accurate knowledge of his views." (William Höttl, *Secret Front,* p. 285.)

20. It appears that for some U.S. intelligence officials, the Cold War started before World War II had actually ended. The OSS had been spying on Italian Communists at least since 1944, even though they were ostensibly fighting against a common fascist foe. Ditto for OSS operatives in France and the Balkans, where Communists also played a major role in the antifascist resistance. As Thomas Powers has written: "The history of the OSS, which is indistinguishable from the secret political history of the war, is marked by a preoccupation with Communism almost as intense as its commitment to victory against Germany." (Roger Faligot and Pascal Krop, *La Piscine,* p. 26; Hersh, *Old Boys,* p. 196; Thomas Powers, *Man Who Kept the Secrets,* p. 25.)

21. Hersh, *Old Boys,* p. 131.

22. Bradley F. Smith and Elena Agarossi, *Operation Sunrise,* p. 191.

23. Höhne and Zolling, *The General Was a Spy,* p. 61; Charles Allen, *Heusinger,* p. 16. See also "Generalplan 1945," initialed by Admiral Karl Doenitz and Field Marshall Wilhelm Keitel, dated April 5, 1945, which stated: "The two great peoples, the Russians and the Germans, have extraordinary possibilities for development without collision of their interests." The document went on to recommend the formation of "an alliance between the young Socialist forces against the old rotten entrenched powers of the West." (Tetens, *Germany Plots with the Kremlin,* pp. 239–42.)

24. Timothy Garton Ash, *In Europe's Name,* p. 406.

25. Bower, *Pledge Betrayed,* pp. 96–97; Simpson, *Blowback,* p. 26; Sayer and Botting, *America's Secret Army,* pp. 77–78. For more on the postwar recruitment of Nazi scientists, see Linda Hunt, *Secret Agenda,* and Clarence Lasby, *Project Paperclip.* See also "Soviet Recruitment of German Scientists," National Archives record group 319, box 31, file no. ZE152328, NND844013.

26. This became clear to American medical inspectors in July 1945, two months after the fighting stopped, during a routine inspection of a lunatic asylum in Kaufbeuren, Bavaria. Much to their horror, they found that this institution continued to function as an extermination center, where mentally impaired adults and children were slowly starved to death or murdered by lethal injection. Subsequent inquiries disclosed that the local population felt no sense of contrition, even though they knew the asylum pursued "experiments on improvements in the race." (Bower, *Pledge Betrayed,* p. 143.)

27. President Franklin Delano Roosevelt was in a vengeful mood when he suggested that "we either have to castrate the German people or you have got to treat them in such a manner so they can't just go on reproducing people who want to continue the way they have in the past." He shared the position advocated by his feisty treasury secretary Henry Morgenthau, who drew up a harsh blueprint for postwar Germany that called for a mostly agrarian society with all but light industry dismantled; the highly industrialized Ruhr Valley ("the cauldron of wars") was slated to become an international commercial zone off-limits to German trade. To make sure that Germany would not overpower its neighbors once again, FDR explicitly forbid U.S. military authorities from taking action that would strengthen the German economy. However, these plans were scrapped after FDR died.

28. "SKORZENY, Otto," May 19, 1945, CIC document signed by Special Agents George A. Pepper and Peter Regis. About 650 pages of U.S. Army documentation on Skorzeny, some of it sanitized, is available through the Freedom of Information Act: U.S. Army INSCOM dossier no. XE00 0417, and National Archives record group 165, box 739, entry 179, enemy POW interrogation file MIS-Y 1943–1945.

29. *New York Times* and *Christian Science Monitor* cited in Infield, *Skorzeny,* p. 126; *Daily News* cited in Foley, *Commando Extraordinary,* p. 154.

30. "The German Sabotage Service," July 23, 1945, Consolidated Interrogation Report (CIR) No. 4, Headquarters, U.S. Forces European Theater Interrogation Center, APO 655; "Personalities of

AMT VI S of RSHA," April 6, 1945; "Vienna; RIG-554," February 11, 1945; "Interrogation Report on DE PAOLIS, Alvaro," Appendix A, September 18, 1944.

31. Simpson, *Splendid Blonde Beast,* p. 251.

32. Bower, *Pledge Betrayed,* p. 323. American judges and prosecutors tried the cases of 177 German functionaries, army officers, judges, medical doctors, industrialists, and SS leaders. Of the twenty-five defendants who were sentenced to death, thirteen were eventually executed; the last prisoners were released by 1958.

33. Bower, *Pledge Betrayed,* p. 322; Hersh, *Old Boys,* p. 486n.

34. This part of the Gehlen story has been told by several sources, including Höhne and Zolling, *The General Was a Spy,* p. 70.

35. Simpson, *Blowback,* p. 44; Höhne and Zolling, *The General Was a Spy,* pp. x, 38–39.

36. Carl Oglesby, "The Secret Treaty of Fort Hunt," *Covert Action Information Bulletin* 35 (fall 1990).

37. Typical of those who found gainful employment in the Gehlen Org were men like the Willi Krichbaum, a fanatic Gestapo foe of the July 20 plotters; SS Sturmbannführer Hans Sommer, best known for torching synagogues in Paris; Heinz Jost, who had directed Gestapo activities outside of Germany; and a slew of fascist collaborators from Romania, Croatia, the Ukraine, White Russia, Hungary, Poland, and the Baltics. (Reese, *General Reinhard Gehlen and the CIA*, pp. 83, 104, 136; Höhne and Zolling, *The General Was a Spy,* pp. 199, 282.)

38. Author's interview with Nikolaus Ryschkowsky, June 30, 1993.

39. Sayer and Botting, *America's Secret Army,* p. 319. Washington's abrupt end to denazification left approximately 640,000 "highly incriminated persons" unprosecuted.

40. Simpson, *Blowback,* p. 73; Sayer and Botting, *America's Secret Army,* pp. 224–29.

41. Höhne and Zolling, *The General Was a Spy,* p. 107; Jean Edward Smith, *Lucius D. Clay,* p. 466; Simpson, *Blowback,* pp. 54–55, 140–41.

42. Simpson, *Blowback,* p. 65.

43. Höhne and Zolling, *The General Was a Spy,* p. xi.

44. A top-secret National Security Council directive adopted in August 1948 authorized the CIA to undertake "propaganda, economic warfare; preventive direct action, including sabotage and anti-sabotage . . . subversion against hostile states, including assistance to underground resistance movements, guerrillas and refugee liberation groups, and support of indigenous anticommunist elements." (U.S. Senate, *Final Report of the Select Committee to Study Governmental Operations with Respect to Intelligence Activities,* book IV, April 23, 1976, p. 31.)

45. E. H. Cookridge, *Spy of the Century,* p. 158; Bird, *The Chairman,* p. 304; Simpson, *Blowback,* p. 53.

46. Stewart Steven, *Operation Splinter Factor,* pp. 29, 63, 223; Simpson, *Blowback,* p. 159.

47. Hersh, *Old Boys,* p. 268; Reese, *General Reinhard Gehlen and the CIA,* pp. 134–35.

48. Reese, *General Reinhard Gehlen and the CIA,* pp. 93, 119; Hersh, *Old Boys,* p. 277; Höhne and Zolling, *The General Was a Spy,* p. xv. It turns out that Dulles did bring Gehlen to not one but several of the CIA director's clubs, including the posh F Street and Chevy Chase watering holes. But Dulles was far less cordial to American officers such as Major General Arthur Trudeau, who expressed grave misgivings about the Org only to find himself demoted at Dulles's insistence.

49. Reese, *General Gehlen and the CIA,* pp. 110, 120.

50. Höttl, *Secret Front,* p. 319.

51. Dale M. Garvey, "Alleged Soviet-Sponsored Organization to Recruit Former SS Personnel," October 5, 1946; Ignacio Carranza, Special Agent, CIC, "Alleged Soviet-Sponsored Organization to

Recruit Former SS Personnel," October 17, 1946; Joseph Radford, Jr., Special Agent, CIC, "Recruiting of Former Military Personnel in the Soviet Zone," June 19, 1947; Bill Grubert, Special Agent, CIC, "THEO, Pro-Soviet SS Group," March 29, 1948. See National Archives record group 319, box 39, "Alleged Soviet-Sponsored Organizations to Recruit Former SS Personnel," August 1945–March 1948, vol. 1, file no. XE131926.

52. "Report of Interrogation of OTTO SKORZENY," Headquarters, 7707 European Command Intelligence Center, APO 757, U.S. Army, February 19, 1948.

53. "ODESSA," CIC dossier 41878; and "Organization, 'ODESSA,' " 970th CIC Detachment, APO 139, U.S. Army, July 15, 1947. See National Archives record group 319, box 64, file no. ZF015116, "Odessa Organization."

54. Untitled CIC document, September 7, 1946.

55. "Operation BRANDY," CIC Region IV, APO 205, January 15, 1947; "Operation BRANDY, RE: Organization ODESSA," 970th CIC Detachment, January 20, 1947.

56. Vincent La Vista, "Illegal Emigration Movement in and through Italy," U.S. State Department report, May 15, 1947.

57. Kruger, *Over the Green Border.* See also, "Werewolf Activities in Denmark," Strategic Services Units, War Department, Mission to Germany, U.S. Forces, European Theater, APO 757, April 24, 1946.

58. Infield, *Skorzeny,* p. 151. Ilse Skorzeny repeated her husband's claim of American assistance in his escape.

59. Author's interview with Ilse Skorzeny, June 3, 1993. All quotations from Ilse Skorzeny derive from this interview unless otherwise indicated.

60. "Request for Intelligence Information," September 15, 1948; "SKORZENY Movement," Headquarters, U.S. Constabulary, G-2, December 10, 1948; "German Nationalist Underground (Communist Penetration)," CIC document, December 8, 1948.

61. "SUBJECT," BARNES, Sidney U., Major USAR, 0-116600 (S), October 18, 1955.

62. Another former SS officer who recruited new members for the Gehlen Org was Dr. Emil Augsburg, formerly of the Wannsee Institute, where the Nazi hierarchy planned the annihilation of the Jews.

63. Corson quoted in Oglesby, "The Secret Treaty of Fort Hunt."

CHAPTER TWO: *The Seesaw Strategy*

1. "REMER, Otto-Ernst (Biographical Request)," August 11, 1952, U.S. Army document in National Archives record group 319, box 371, file no. XE062963, NND 931149.

2. Author's interview with Otto Ernst Remer, April 16, 1992. All quotations from Remer are from this interview unless otherwise indicated.

3. "Watch List of German Generals in the British and U.S. Zones of Germany and in the U.K.," April 3, 1946, in National Archives record group 319, box 37, file no. XE049474, "German General Watch List."

4. *Der Spiegel,* December 5, 1949.

5. Thomas Alan Schwartz, *America's Germany,* p. 47.

6. Kurt Tauber, *Beyond Eagle and Swastika,* p. 22.

7. As of October 1948, 57 percent of Germans still believed that National Socialism was "a good idea that was badly put into practice." In another survey that year, only 20 percent thought that Germany was responsible for starting World War II, and the same percentage supported Hitler's anti-Jewish policies, while a further 19 percent were generally in favor but felt that he had gone too far. (Bower, *Pledge Betrayed,* p. 139; Charles Rand Lewis, *Right-wing Extremism,* p. 80; Otto Dov Kulka, "History and Historical Progno-

ses," in Yehuda Bauer, ed., *Danger of Antisemitism;* see also Anna J. and Richard L. Merritt, *Public Opinion in Occupied Germany.*)

8. Ernest Leiser, "The Blackshirts March Again," *Saturday Evening Post,* May 31, 1952; Tauber, *Eagle and Swastika,* p. 94; Roger Dow, "Report on the SRP (Sozialistische Reichspartei)," December 1, 1950, U.S. State Department document 762A.00/12-150 in National Archives civil records division.

9. Tauber, *Eagle and Swastika,* p. 88.

10. Remer cited in "SRP Literature," *Wiener Library Bulletin,* May–August 1952.

11. "Allegation of SRP Infiltration into British Labor Service Units," U.S. Foreign Service Dispatch 5843, June 4, 1951, U.S. State Department document 762A.00/6-451 in National Archives civil records division.

12. Dow, "Report on the SRP (Sozialistische Reichspartei)"; "Weekly Political Report for Hamburg, Schleswig-Holstein and Lower Saxony," February 22, 1952, U.S. State Department document 762A.00/2-2952 in National Archives civil records division.

13. Schwartz, *America's Germany,* p. 216; Leon Fuller, "Major Political Trends in the German Federal Republic," June 30, 1951, U.S. State Department document 762A.00/6-3051 in National Archives civil records division.

14. Schwartz, *America's Germany,* p. 49.

15. Schwartz, *America's Germany,* p. 83; Jerome K. Holloway, Jr., "Forwarding Research Study on SRP," May 16, 1951, U.S. State Department document 762A.00/5-1651 in National Archives civil records division.

16. *U.S. High Commissioner Report,* cited in Tetens, *Germany Plots with the Kremlin,* p. 105.

17. T. H. Tetens, *New Germany and the Old Nazis,* p. 63.

18. Angelo Del Boca and Mario Giovana, *Fascism Today,* p. 110; Tetens, *New Germany and the Old Nazis,* pp. 50–51.

19. *Die Welt* cited in Tetens, *New Germany and the Old Nazis,* p. 40.

20. Wistrich, *Who's Who in Nazi Germany,* pp. 93–94; Tetens, *New Germany and the Old Nazis,* pp. 37–40; Bower, *Pledge Betrayed,* p. 356.

21. Adenauer acknowledged that among the 383 officials and employees of his Foreign Office, 134 were former Nazi Party members and 138 had served under von Ribbentrop. Walter von Cube, director of the Bavarian Radio Network, reported subsequently that 85 percent of the leading officials in the Bonn Foreign Ministry had been Nazi Party members. (Tetens, *New Germany and the Old Nazis,* pp. 46–47; Michael Heinz-Mansfield, "You Have Returned, You Ghostly Creatures," *Frankfurter Rundschau,* September 1–6, 1951; Tauber, *Eagle and Swastika,* p. 950.)

22. Reinhard Gehlen, *The Service,* p. 151.

23. "German Saboteurs Betray U.S. Trust," *New York Times,* October 10, 1952; Tauber, *Eagle and Swastika,* pp. 369–70, 1076, 1171; Simpson, *Blowback,* pp. 146–48; Jonathan Kwitny, "The CIA's Secret Armies in Europe," *The Nation,* April 6, 1992.

24. Norris B. Chapman, "Bundestag Debate on BDJ Affair," October 24, 1952, U.S. State Department document 762A.00/10-2452 in National Archives civil records division; "Government Confirms Gladio Existence, Activities," Hamburg Deutsche Press Agency, November 14, 1990, cited in Foreign Broadcast Information Service (Western Europe), November 16, 1990; Gehlen, *The Service,* p. 187; Höhne and Zolling, *The General Was a Spy,* pp. xxix, xxxv, 189–91, 323.

25. Henry Ashby Turner, Jr., *Partition to Reunification,* p. 8.

26. Del Boca and Giovana, *Fascism Today,* p. 122.

27. Brewster H. Morris, "Ultra-Nationalist Organizations in Western Germany," December 28, 1950, U.S. State Department document 762A.00/12-2850; Ernest E. Ramsaur, Jr., "SRP Electoral Campaign Activities in Bremen," September 14, 1951, U.S. State

Department document 762A.00/9-2151, both in National Archives civil records division.

28. Ramsaur, "SRP Electoral Campaign Activities in Bremen"; Tauber, *Eagle and Swastika,* p. 713.

29. The American-educated Schacht eventually grew disenchanted with Hitler. He was briefly imprisoned after the failed coup attempt of July 1944. This incarceration was a feather in his cap when Schacht faced charges as a major war-crimes offender at Nuremberg. He also had another ace up his sleeve — he knew a lot about deals between German industrialists and their American and British counterparts during the Third Reich. Sensitive to such arrangements, legal advisors in the U.S. State Department quietly assisted Schacht's defense. Unlike most of his Nazi codefendants, Schacht was acquitted — despite pleas by Nuremberg prosecutor Robert H. Jackson, who argued: "Few businessmen had such close relations with the regime or held offices which imply close knowledge of the political plans and aggressive intentions behind rearmament, as did Schacht." (Simpson, *Splendid Blonde Beast,* pp. 64–65, 228; Bower, *Pledge Betrayed,* p. 320.)

30. Harold Denny, "Germans Pour Agents into Spain in Last Stand Against Shift to Allies," *New York Times,* January 17, 1944. Peter Nadsen, "Spanish Activity, Re: Restaurant HORCHER, MADRID, Spain," April 18, 1948, Army CIC document in National Archives, record group 319, box 34, "Illegal Emigration to Spain, June 1946–November 1948," NND 853108.

31. Peter R. Renno, "Escape Organization to Spain, Re: Operation BRANDY," February 13, 1947, Army CIC document in National Archives, record group 319, box 34, "Illegal Emigration to Spain, June 1946–November 1948;" NND 853108; *Newsweek,* January 15, 1945.

32. Masurovsky, *Safehaven Program,* American University doctoral thesis, p. 40; Del Boca and Giovana, *Fascism Today,* p. 78.

33. Ivan B. White, "Speech of Dr. Hjalmar SCHACHT in Madrid, May 8, 1952," June 10, 1952, U.S. State Department document 762A.00/12-150 in National Archives civil records division.

34. According to State Department analyst Roger Dow, Remer "had been launched onto the political scene" in 1949 "in the shadow of Hjalmar Schacht and other bigshot Nazis." See Dow, "Report on the SRP (Sozialistische Reichspartei)," and Ernest E. Ramsaur, Jr., "The SRP," July 19, 1951, U.S. State Department document 762A.00/7-1951 in National Archives civil records division; Carl R. Hebbe, "Meetings in Rodenkirchen and Jaderberg," January 12, 1950, U.S. Army CIC document in National Archives, record group 319, box 371, file no. XE062963, NND 931149; Erna Paris, *Unhealed Wounds,* p. 144.

35. Del Boca and Giovana, *Fascism Today,* p. 476n.

36. Author's interview with Léon Degrelle, May 23, 1993. All quotations from Degrelle are from this interview unless otherwise indicated.

37. "SS Colonel Otto SKORZENY, Alias Rolf Steinbauer," U.S. Air Force intelligence information report, June 28, 1951.

38. "To: Director, FBI; From: LA, Madrid, Spain; Re: COLONEL OTTO SKORZENY, Internal Security — GE," October 17, 1951.

39. Omer Anderson, "Noted Adventurer Power Behind the Throne," *Montreal Star,* March 3, 1960. Ilse Skorzeny traveled frequently on business to the United States, West Germany, and other countries where her husband was officially not welcome. She arranged profitable transactions with American military contractors, such as Honeywell. A frequent guest at her sister's apartment in New York City, Mrs. Skorzeny befriended prominent American businessmen and entertainers, including TV personality Art Linkletter. Her connections were such that she became an honorary member of the New York Women's Republican Club. During one visit in the mid-1950s, she tried unsuccessfully to secure a visa so that Otto could join her in the United States.

40. "OTTO SKORZENY, wa. Rolf Steinbauer," FBI document dated July 18, 1951; "To: Director, FBI; From: LA, Madrid, Spain; Re: COLONEL OTTO SKORZENY, Internal Security — GE," October 17, 1951.

41. "To: Director Central Intelligence; From John Edgar Hoover, Director Federal Bureau of Investigation; COLONEL OTTO SKORZENY, Internal Security — GE," December 6, 1951; "To: Director, FBI; From: LA, Madrid, Spain; Re: COLONEL OTTO SKORZENY, Internal Security — GE," October 17, 1951; McCloy to Secretary of State, incoming telegram dated August 17, 1950, U.S. State Department document 762A.00/10-3152 in National Archives civil division.

42. "To: Director, FBI; From: LA, Madrid, Spain; Re: COLONEL OTTO SKORZENY, Internal Security — GE," October 17, 1951.

43. Dennis Eisenberg, *Re-Emergence of Fascism,* p. 207; Lawrence van Gelder, "Otto Skorzeny, Nazi Commando, Dead, Rescued Mussolini from Italian Peak," *New York Times,* July 8, 1975. State Department officials were concerned that some of the profits from the sale of Skorzeny's memoirs were being used to support neo-Nazi activity in Germany. (See outgoing telegram from Frankfurt, August 7, 1950, U.S. State Department document 762A.52/8-750 in National Archives civil division.)

44. David Clay Large, "Reckoning without the Past: The HIAG of the Waffen-SS and the Politics of Rehabilitation in the Bonn Republic, 1950–1961," *Journal of Modern History* 59 (March 1987); "Nationalist Journals," *Wiener Library Bulletin,* September–December 1953; Tetens, *New Germany and the Old Nazis,* p. 102.

45. Dow, "Report on the SRP (Sozialistische Reichspartei)."

46. Tetens, *New Germany and the Old Nazis,* p. 78; "Weekly Political Report," June 22, 1951, U.S. State Department document 762A.00/6-2251 in National Archives civil records division.

47. Charles Whiton, *Adenauer,* p. 89; Del Boca and Giovana, *Fascism Today,* p. 103; Large, "Reckoning without the Past"; Tauber, *Eagle and Swastika,* pp. 300–01.

48. Far from being an anti-Hitler bastion, as some U.S. officials claimed, the German army was umbilically linked to the SS. According to scholar Omer Bartov: "The Army was neither simply

forced to obey the regime by terror and intimidation, nor was maneuvered into collaboration by the machinations of a minority of Nazi and opportunist officers, nor, finally, supported the regime due to some misunderstanding of what National Socialism really meant and stood for. . . . The Wehrmacht was the army of the people, and the willing tool of the regime, more than any of its military predecessors."

49. Cookridge, *Spy of the Century,* p. 351.

50. Several other high-ranking West German military officers rose to top positions in the NATO hierarchy, including General Hans Speidel, who became commander of all NATO forces in Western Europe. By the early 1960s, according to Charles Allen, more than two hundred West German military officers, including at least eighteen former Wehrmacht generals, occupied important NATO posts. (Höhne and Zolling, *The General Was a Spy,* p. 87; Cookridge, *Spy of the Century,* p. 351; Allen, *Heusinger,* pp. 9, 19, 208–09.)

51. "Madrid Circular Letter," cited in Tetens, *Germany Plots with the Kremlin,* pp. 209–32.

52. Omer Anderson, "Noted Adventurer Power Behind the Throne," *Montreal Star,* March 3, 1960.

53. Bird, *The Chairman,* p. 320.

54. Infield, *Secrets of the SS,* p. 9.

55. "Personality Report — IV-10515 — ASCHENAUER, Rudolf," September 2, 1949, U.S. Army CIC document; "Malmédy Case (U.S. Senate Subcommittee Investigation)," September 15, 1949, U.S. Army CIC document, both in National Archives military division, record group 319, boxes 8A and 8B, file no. XE260416. McCarthy apologists in the United States suggest that the senator had been duped by Aschenauer, whom they wrongly describe as a Communist agent. See also Richard Halwort Rovere, *Senator Joe McCarthy,* pp. 110–17; Thomas C. Reeves, *Life and Times of Joe McCarthy,* pp. 183–85; Fred J. Cook, *Nightmare Decade,* pp. 136–38.

56. Bower, *Pledge Betrayed,* p. 354; Simpson, *Blowback,* pp. 46–49; Bird, *The Chairman,* p. 369; also see generally Ingo Müller, *Hitler's Justice.* Among those prematurely pardoned was Dr. Herta Oberheuser, who faced twenty years in prison for her role in medical experiments that resulted in the death of more than a thousand women prisoners at the Ravensbrück concentration camp. She had a fetish for surgically removing limbs and vital organs, and rubbing ground glass or sawdust into the open wounds during the postoperative period. Freed a year after McCloy reduced her sentence, Oberheuser resumed working as a family doctor in Schleswig-Holstein, an SRP stronghold. The West German government even pitched in with a cash grant to help rebuild Oberheuser's medical practice.

57. Bower, *Pledge Betrayed,* p. 316; Wistrich, *Who's Who in Nazi Germany,* pp. 179–81; author's interview with Ilse Skorzeny, June 3, 1993.

58. Schwartz, *America's Germany,* p. 262.

59. "Neutralism in Berlin," May 19, 1952, U.S. State Department document 762A.00/5-852 in National Archives civil records division; Schwartz, *America's Germany,* p. 264.

60. "Outline of factors bearing on the Western reply to the Soviet note on Germany," March 14, 1952, U.S. State Department document 762A.00/3-1452; "Neutralism in Berlin," both in National Archives civil records division. See also, in general, Carolyn Eisenberg, *Drawing the Line.*

61. Edmund Taylor, "Germany: Where Fascism and Communism Meet," *Reporter,* April 13, 1954; Drew Pearson, "Reds, Nazis Renew Act," *Denver Post,* March 31, 1954; *New York Times,* March 20, 1950; "Weekly Political Report No. 61," March 27, 1952, U.S. State Department document 762A.00/3-2752 in National Archives civil records division.

62. Taylor, "Germany: Where Fascism and Communism Meet."

63. Paul Hockenos, *Free to Hate,* pp. 94–95; Tauber, *Eagle and Swastika,* pp. 191–92; Walter Laqueur, *Russia and Germany,*

p. 292; Charles Ashman and Robert J. Wagman, *The Nazi Hunters,* p. 17; Bower *Pledge Betrayed,* p. 361. By 1950, West Germany (consisting of the former British, French, and U.S. zones of occupation) had punished about 6,500 Nazis, while the much smaller German Democratic Republic, as East Germany was called, had punished about twice as many. An estimated 25,000 war criminals were convicted by Yugoslavia, Russia, and East Germany— whereas 1,814 war criminals (mostly Germans) were convicted by the United States at Dachau and Nuremberg; 1,085 were convicted by Britain; 2,107 by France; 197 by the Netherlands; 92 by Norway; and 5,452 by Poland.

64. "Legislation to end and partially undo 'Denazification' in the Soviet Zone," November 16, 1949, U.S. State Department document 862.00/11-1649 in National Archives civil records division; Höhne and Zolling, *The General Was a Spy,* p. 243; Höttl, *Secret Front,* p. 303; Simpson, *Blowback,* p. 79n. Examples of Third Reich veterans who worked in East Germany's police and intelligence apparatus: Abwehr Lieutenant General Rudolf Balmer, who became head of a department at state security headquarters in East Berlin; SS Captain Louis Hagemeister, who was tapped to run a police interrogation unit in Schwerin; and Gestapo graduate Johann Sanitzer, who served in another branch of the East German police.

65. Author's interview with Otto Ernst Remer, April 16, 1992; author's interview with Bela Ewald Althans, April 21, 1992.

66. Dow, "Report on the SRP (Sozialistische Reichspartei)"; Brewster H. Morris, "Recent Activities of the Sozialistische Reichspartei," May 11, 1951, U.S. State Department document 762A.00/5-1051; "Report on the SRP," April 12, 1951, U.S. State Department document 762A.00/1-25; LaVerne Baldwin, "The Split in the SRP in North Rhine-Westphalia," June 15, 1951, U.S. State Department document 762A.00/6-1451; Cecil B. Lyon, "SRP in Berlin," January 2, 1952, U.S. State Department document 762A.00/1-252, all in National Archives civil records division. Eberhadt Stern, an SRP organizer in Berlin, defected from the group when he discovered "that it took help from the West German Communist Party." And Heinrich Keseberg, the regional SRP chief in North Rhine–

Westphalia, renounced his membership, claiming he had abundant evidence that both Ernst Remer and Fritz Dorls were collaborating with the East.

67. Tauber, *Eagle and Swastika,* pp. 198, 888.

68. *Ibid.,* p. 151.

69. Ibid., p. 122; "Weekly Political Report," September 14, 1951, U.S. State Department document 762A.00/9-1451; "Quarterly Political Review," October 5, 1951, U.S. State Department document 762A.00/10-551; LaVerne Baldwin, "History and aims of the Bruderschaft, with brief notes on 'Chancellor' Franke-Gricksch," November 3, 1950, U.S. State Department document 762A.00/11-350, all three in National Archives civil records division.

70. Tauber, *Eagle and Swastika,* pp. 260–73; Roger Dow, "The Bruderschaft and the BHE," September 22, 1950, U.S. State Department document 762A.00/9-2250; Baldwin, "History and aims of the Bruderschaft," both in National Archives civil records division; "Die Spinne," August 30, 1951, U.S. Army CIC document.

71. Robert T. Cowan, "Interview with Beck-Broichsitter and Dr. Achenbach of the Brotherhood (Bruderschaft)," October 12, 1950; U.S. State Department document 762A.00/10-1250; Robert T. Cowan, "Bruderschaft Activities: Conversation with Helmut Beck-Broichsitter, Bruderschaft leader," November 20, 1950, U.S. State Department document 762A.00/11-2050, both in National Archives civil records division; Tauber, *Eagle and Swastika,* pp. 260–73.

72. Tauber, *Eagle and Swastika,* pp. 260–73; Cowan, "Bruderschaft Activities: Conversation with Helmut Beck-Broichsitter"; Robert T. Cowan, "Resignation of Helmut Beck-Broichsitter from the Bruderschaft," March 2, 1951, U.S. State Department document 762A.00/3-251, both in National Archives civil records division.

73. Tauber, *Eagle and Swastika,* p. 1055.

74. Mikhail Agursky, *The Third Rome,* pp. 300–03; D. H. Lawrence quoted in "The Lure of the East," *Wiener Library Bulletin,* April 1962.

75. Fritz Stern, *Politics of Cultural Despair,* p. 22. See also Rees, *Extreme Right Since 1890,* pp. 265–66; Roger Woods, "The Radical Right: The 'Conservative Revolutionaries' in Germany," in Roger Eatwell and Noel O'Sullivan, eds., *Nature of the Right,* pp. 124–45.

76. Peter Fritzsche, *Rehearsals for Fascism,* p. 227; Rees, *Extreme Right Since 1890,* pp. 200–02; "Nationalists Against Hitler," *Wiener Library Bulletin,* vol. XIII, nos. 1–2 (1959); Laqueur, *Russia and Germany,* p. 163; Sebastian Haffner, *The Ailing Empire,* p. 176. For a while in 1932, the Nazis emphasized their pseudo-left-wing populist side, joining forces with the Communists in the Berlin transport workers' strike. A photograph taken during this period shows Goebbels and German Communist Party leader Walter Ulbricht sharing a platform. The following year, Hitler declared May Day a national holiday.

77. Whiton, *Adenauer,* p. 153.

78. Del Boca and Giovana, *Fascism Today,* p. 104.

79. Walter Russell Mead, "The Once and Future Reich," *World Policy Journal,* fall 1990, p. 616; Joyce and Gabriel Kolko cited in Hersh, *Old Boys,* p. 370.

80. Ladislas Farago, *Aftermath,* p. 261.

81. Jerome K. Holloway, Jr., "Remer Sentence: Bremen Reaction Is Against It," June 1, 1951, U.S. State Department document 762A.00/6-151 in National Archives civil records division.

82. "Weekly Political Report," June 15, 1951, U.S. State Department document 762A.00/6-1551; Sam E. Woods, "Remer Conducts Two Week Organizational Campaign in Bavaria," August 31, 1951, U.S. State Department document 762A.00/8-3151; Halleck L. Rose, "Weekly Report for Hamburg, Schleswig-Holstein and Lower Saxony," November 30, 1951, U.S. State Department document 762A.00/11-3051, all in National Archives civil records divi-

sion. See also "Motion of the Federal Government, represented by the Federal Minister of the Interior, versus Brigadier General Otto Ernst Remer ret.," p. 24, June 17, 1952, U.S. Army document in National Archives, record group 319, box 371, file no. XE062963, NND 931149.

83. Much to the delight of his admirers, Remer often spoke about the events of the Twentieth of July. Maintaining steadfastly that Germany lost the war because of treason, he called the coup attempt a "stain on the shield of honor of the German officers' corps." Polls showed West Germans were split over the anti-Hitler plot: 30 percent of the population agreed with Remer's condemnation of the conspirators; 40 percent disagreed. One's attitude toward Remer and the abortive putsch became a crucial yardstick by which a person's political orientation was measured in the Federal Republic. (Wistrich, *Who's Who in Nazi Germany,* pp. 244–45; Tauber, *Eagle and Swastika,* p. 1127n.)

84. "Motion of the Federal Government . . . versus Brigadier General Otto Ernst Remer ret.," p. 23.

85. Tauber, *Eagle and Swastika,* p. 714; "Weekly Political Report for Hamburg, Schleswig-Holstein and Niedersachsen," September 19, 1952, U.S. State Department document 762A.00/9-1952 in National Archives civil records division.

86. "Motion of the Federal Government . . . versus Brigadier General Otto Ernst Remer ret.," pp. 25, 28.

CHAPTER THREE: *Neo-Nazi Diaspora*

1. H. Keith Thompson, letter to the author, December 4, 1995.

2. O. John Rogge, *Official German Report,* pp. 14–15, 117; Susan Canedy, *America's Nazis,* pp. 129, 213; author's interview with H. Keith Thompson, November 10, 1993. All quotations from Thompson are from this interview unless otherwise indicated.

3. Author's interview with H. Keith Thompson; H. Keith Thompson, letter to the author, December 4, 1995. According to Thompson, half a dozen ODESSA bank accounts were managed by "dedicated men" in different countries.

4. Letter to Dean Acheson from H. Keith Thompson, June 24, 1952, and letters from H. Keith Thompson to Adenauer, May 19, 1952, and September 17, 1952, in the H. Keith Thompson section of the Hoover Institute Special Collections Library; Norris B. Chapman, "Committee for the Freedom of Major General Remer," June 25, 1952, U.S. State Department document 762.00/6-2552 in National Archives civil records division.

5. Letter from H. Keith Thompson to Dr. Gerhard Krüger, September 13, 1952, and letter from Otto Ernst Remer to H. Keith Thompson, October 23, 1952, in the H. Keith Thompson section of the Hoover Institute Special Collections Library.

6. Author's interview with H. Keith Thompson; see also H. Keith Thompson's memo for Keith Stimely, April 10, 1986, in the H. Keith Thompson section of the Hoover Institute Special Collections Library.

7. "Neo-Nazis Still Alive, Agent Active in U.S.," *New York Post,* October 13, 1952.

8. Charles Thayer, *Farther Shores of Politics,* p. 59.

9. *National Renaissance Bulletin,* May 1953.

10. John George and Laird Wilcox, *Nazis, Communists, Klansmen and Others,* p. 352.

11. Committee on Un-American Activities, U.S. House of Representatives, *Preliminary Report on Neo-Fascist and Hate Groups,* December 17, 1954, p. 8.

12. *Prevent World War III,* summer 1957.

13. *National Renaissance Bulletin,* October 1952, cited in the HUAC's *Preliminary Report on Neo-Fascist and Hate Groups.*

14. Author's interview with H. Keith Thompson; see also H. Keith Thompson interview by Keith Stimely, March 13, 1986, in H. Keith Thompson section of the Hoover Institute Special Collections Library.

15. Untitled FBI memo, Baltimore field office, May 20, 1954; "Francis Parker Yockey, was.," FBI, Chicago field office, February 20, 1956.

16. "Francis Parker Yockey, was., Francis Dowey, Franz, Frank Healy . . . ," FBI, Chicago field office, July 8, 1954; "Francis P. Yockey alias Ulick (also Ulik) Varange," FBI director John Edgar Hoover to Director, Central Intelligence Agency, January 5, 1952; "Francis Parker Yockey, was.," FBI, Chicago field office, February 20, 1956. The Legion of American Silver Shirts was founded by William Dudley Pelley on January 31, 1933, the day after Hitler seized power. Pelley's 15,000 followers dressed in silver shirts, blue corduroy knickers, and gold stockings. One of Pelley's men declared at a German-American Bund meeting in Los Angeles that the time would come when a Jew would be hanged from every lamppost and tree in the country. Pelley was jailed for sedition in 1942.

17. "Yockey, Francis Parker; Jockey, Francis," U.S. Army intelligence document, October 4, 1951; "Francis Parker Yockey, was., Registration Act 1950, Passport and Visa Matters," FBI, WFO field office, December 16, 1954.

18. "Francis Parker Yockey, was., . . . ," FBI, Chicago field office, July 8, 1954; "Francis Parker Yockey, Egidio Boschi, Security Matter," FBI, St. Louis field office, December 28, 1951; "Francis Parker Yockey," FBI, Chicago field office, July 3, 1952.

19. "Yockey, Francis Parker," CIA document, February 8, 1950; "Francis P. Yockey alias Ulick (also Ulik) Varange," January 5, 1952; H. Keith Thompson, draft for *Expose,* in the H. Keith Thompson section of the Hoover Institute Special Collections Library.

20. John C. Obert, "Yockey: Profile of an American Hitler," *The Investigator,* September 1981; "Yockey, Francis Parker, aka Jockey, Francis, Jockey, Franz, with alias Varange, Ulick," U.S. Army intelligence document, January 16, 1950.

21. Ulick Varange, *Imperium,* p. 618.

22. Ibid., p. xivii.

23. Ibid., p. 437.

24. Ibid., pp. 222–23, 228; Obert, "Yockey: Profile of an American Hitler"; see also Richard Thurow, "Destiny and Doom: Spengler, Hitler and 'British' Fascism," *Patterns of Prejudice* 15, no. 4 (1981).

25. *Imperium,* pp. 391, 497.

26. Ibid., pp. 533, 608, 617. Wehland G. Steenken, S/A, "Yockey, Francis Parker; Jockey, Francis," 66th CIC Detachment, October 4, 1951; Charles W. Lutman, S/A,"Yockey, Francis Parker," 66th CIC Detachment, February 25, 1952; "Francis Parker Yockey, was.," FBI, Detroit field office, March 2, 1953.

27. For an analysis of Yockey's *Imperium,* see Frank P. Mintz, *The Liberty Lobby,* pp. 24–31.

28. *Imperium,* p. 595.

29. Mosley quoted in Del Boca and Giovana, *Fascism Today,* p. 261.

30. For more on Yockey's relationship with Mosley, see Richard Thurow, *Fascism in Britain,* and Robert Skidelsky, *Oswald Mosley.*

31. Anthony Gannon, "Francis Parker Yockey, 1917–1960: A Remembrance of the author of *Imperium* (Ulick Varange)," in the H. Keith Thompson section of the Hoover Institute Special Collections Library. All quotations of Gannon are from this source.

32. Peter J. Huxley-Blythe, letter to the Federal Bureau of Investigation, October 2, 1961.

33. Untitled FBI report, Baltimore field office, November 4, 1952; Francis Parker Yockey, *Enemy of Europe,* p. 42; author's interview with Otto Ernst Remer, April 16, 1992.

34. "Changed," FBI, Baltimore Field office, September 26, 1952; Gannon, "Francis Parker Yockey, 1917–1960," in the H. Keith

Thompson section of the Hoover Institute Special Collections Library.

35. Jeffrey Bale, "Right-wing Terrorists and the Extraparliamentary Left in Post-World-War 2 Europe: Collusion or Manipulation?" *Berkeley Journal of Sociology,* vol. 32 (1987).

36. Letter to Dean Acheson from H. Keith Thompson of the Committee for the Freedom of Major General Remer, October 15, 1952, U.S. State Department document 762.00/10-1552 in National Archives civil records division. James Madole, leader of the National Renaissance Party, was on the board of directors of the American Committee for the Survival of Western Culture; the committee's American Advisory Staff included Frederick C. F. Weiss, head of LeBlanc Publications; the Honorary Advisory Staff included well-known international fascists such as South Africa's Oswald Pirow and Erwin Schönborn, editor of the German neo-Nazi publication *Nation Europa.*

37. Drew Pearson, "Reds, Nazis Renew Act," *Washington Post,* March 31, 1954. Pearson's column summarized an exposé by Edmund Taylor, "Germany: Where Fascism and Communism Meet," in the *Reporter,* April 13, 1954.

38. Vierick waved the propaganda banner for Germany through two world wars. Touting Hitler as a "genius" who should command admiration regardless of his ideology, Vierick contributed articles to several racialist publications in the United States. In Father Coughlin's dubiously titled *Social Justice,* Vierick portrayed fascism as a necessary antidote to Communism in Europe. When German troops mowed over Czechoslovakia, Vierick was quick to defend the invasion as rectifying "some of the injustices of Versailles." "No man worked more effectively in this country for the Nazi cause than Vierick," asserted Assistant Attorney General O. John Rogge, who was involved in prosecuting Vierick during the Great Sedition Trial of 1944, which also targeted leading figures in America's profascist isolationist movement. (Niel M. Johnson, *George Sylvester Viereck,* pp. 169, 194, 204, 215, 236, 255; G. S. Vierick, "Mussolini Knew . . . Twelve Years Ago," *Social Justice,* May 9, 1938; G. S. Vierick,

"The 'Messiah' in the Sealed Car," *Social Justice,* June 6, 1938; Rogge, *Official German Report,* p. 159.)

39. Author's interview with H. Keith Thompson.

40. "Changed: Francis Parkey Yockey, was. Frank Yockey; Egidio Boschi," FBI, Baltimore field office, March 2, 1953.

41. Louis Rapoport, *Stalin's War,* pp. 140–41.

42. "Changed: Francis Parker Yockey, was.," FBI Chicago field office, November 24, 1953.

43. "What is Behind the Hanging of the Eleven Jews in Prague?" *National Renaissance Bulletin,* December 1952.

44. Author's interview with H. Keith Thompson.

45. "What is Behind the Hanging of the Eleven Jews in Prague?"

46. William Goring, "The National Renaissance Party," 1970 (mimeographed manuscript).

47. Arnold Forster and Benjamin R. Epstein, *Cross-Currents,* p. 208.

48. See, for example, *Common Sense,* Condé J. McGinley's New Jersey–based racialist periodical, which congratulated the Kremlin for striking at the Jewish menace: "A Stalinist represents primordial Russian Nationalism. A Trotskyite represents the Jewish interests of New York City."

49. "Francis Parker Yockey," FBI, Chicago field office, February 7, 1955; "Francis Parker Yockey," FBI, Chicago field office, June 24, 1958.

50. Author's interview with Ilse Skorzeny, June 3, 1993.

51. Gerald L. Posner and John Ware, *Mengele,* pp. 104–07; Gabriel Escobar, "Documents Show Evidence Argentina Aided Escaped Nazis," *Washington Post,* December 8, 1996; Bronwen Maddox, "US documents show Nazis hid £1 bn hoard in Argentina," *The Times* (London), December 4, 1996.

52. "Perón and the Dissident Communists," July 31, 1952, U.S. State Department document 735.00/7-3152. "Mussolini was the greatest man of our century," Perón declared, "but he committed certain disastrous errors. I, who have the advantage of a precedent before me, shall follow in his footsteps but also avoid his errors."

53. "Hans Ulrich Rudel, World War II Ace Decorated by Nazis," *New York Times,* December 21, 1982. For background on Rudel, see Wistrich, *Who's Who in Nazi Germany,* pp. 259–60, and Rees, *Extreme Right Since 1890,* p. 334.

54. Kruger, *Over the Green Border;* author's interview with Ilse Skorzeny.

55. Rudel quoted in Simpson, *Blowback,* p. 179.

56. Kruger, *Over the Green Border;* see also Richard Plant, *The Pink Triangle.*

57. Ralph Blumenthal, "Papers Indicate Mengele May Have Been Held and Freed After War," *New York Times,* January 23, 1985; "3 Nations Joining to Hunt Mengele," *New York Times,* May 11, 1985; Posner and Ware, *Mengele,* pp. 137, 169, 211.

58. Notimex News Service, March 2, 1992. Josef Schwammberger, known as the "mass murderer of Poland" for labor-camp atrocities he committed as an SS captain, was among those who lived comfortably in Argentina for several decades. (See Aaron Freiwald, *The Last Nazi.*)

59. Hersh, *Old Boys,* p. 182; Simpson, *Blowback,* p. 180; see also Vladimir Dedijer, *Yugoslav Auschwitz and the Vatican.* According to a U.S. Army document dated September 12, 1947, "Pavelić's contacts are so high and his present position is so compromising to the Vatican that any extradition of Subject would deal a staggering blow to the Roman Catholic Church."

60. Joseph Page, *Perón,* pp. 90, 347.

61. "German Nazis Rally in South America," *Wiener Library Bulletin,* January 1950; George de Monteverde, "German-language

Magazine *Der Weg,*" May 24, 1950, U.S. State Department document 762.5235/5-2450 in National Archives civil records division.

62. Meskil, *Hitler's Heirs,* p. 90.

63. Author's interview with H. Keith Thompson; *Der Weg,* February 1955; see also Rudel's correspondence with H. Keith Thompson in the H. Keith Thompson section of the Hoover Institute Special Collections Library.

64. *Der Weg,* February 1953; "Activities of ex-Luftwaffe Ace Oberst Rudel in Argentina," December 4, 1950, U.S. State Department document 762A.52/12-450 in National Archives civil records division; *Prevent World War III,* summer 1957; Anthony Gannon, "Francis Parker Yockey, 1917–1960," in the H. Keith Thompson section of the Hoover Institute Special Collections Library.

65. See Rudel file in National Archives military division, record group 319, file no. 308 XE153440.

66. Ernest E. Ramsaur, Jr., "Rudel, the Freikorps and the SRP," June 6, 1952, U.S. State Department document 762A.00/6-652 in National Archives civil records division.

67. Andrew G. Lynch, "Rudel Launches DRP Campaign in Oldenburg," March 15, 1955, U.S. State Department document 762A.00/3-1555 in National Archives civil records division; Meskil, *Hitler's Heirs,* p. 179.

68. "Prison Break Plot Revealed," *New York Times,* March 21, 1953. H. Keith Thompson said that at his request Francis Parker Yockey hand-carried papers, which contained a feasibility study for a surprise assault on Spandau prison, to one of Rudel's contacts in West Germany.

69. Tauber, *Eagle and Swastika,* p. 471.

70. Ibid., pp. 160, 200, 201, 770, 837, 1129, 1328; Ernest E. Ramsaur, Jr., "Right Radicalism: Periodical *Die Nation,*" September 23, 1954, U.S. State Department document 762A.00/9-2354 in National Archives civil records division.

71. "French Right-wing's 'Crisis of Identity,' " *Wiener Library Bulletin,* March–April 1978; Skidelsky, *Oswald Mosley,* p. 492.

CHAPTER FOUR: *The Swastika and the Crescent*

1. Tauber, *Eagle and Swastika,* p. 1111; Rees, *Extreme Right Since 1890,* p. 362; Cookridge, *Spy of the Century,* p. 353; author's interview with Ilse Skorzeny, June 3, 1993.

2. Robert S. Wistrich, *Hitler's Apocalypse,* pp. 172, 282n; Janet and John Wallach, *Arafat,* p. 67; John Roy Carlson, *Cairo to Damascus,* p. 112.

3. Philip Mattar, *Mufti of Jerusalem,* p. 100; William Stadiem, *Too Rich,* pp. 8, 195–96, 208; John Weitz, *Hitler's Diplomat,* p. 228; Del Boca and Giovana, *Fascism Today,* p. 395.

4. H. M. Nahmad, "The Third Reich and the Arab East," *Wiener Library Bulletin,* spring 1967; Paris, *Unhealed Wounds,* p. 168.

5. Mattar, *Mufti of Jerusalem,* pp. 104–05; Robert S. Wistrich, *Antisemitism,* p. 245; Carlson, *Cairo to Damascus,* p. 420; Wallach, *Arafat,* p. 62. After the war, some Zionist propagandists were so eager to prove the Mufti guilty of war crimes that they exaggerated his contribution to the fascist cause. The British Foreign Office, however, concluded that the Mufti was "not responsible for acts of atrocity" against the Jews. While there is no getting around the fact that he had worked closely with the most heinous regime in modern times, the basis for his collaboration with Nazi Germany was rooted less in a shared political ideology than in an antipathy toward mutual enemies. In this respect, the Mufti's rationale was not much different from what motivated members of Menachem Begin's Irgun Zvai Leumi and Yitzhak Shamir's Stern Gang — two Zionist terrorist groups that engaged in anti-British agitation in Palestine — which put out feelers to the Axis during the war. Said a Stern Gang representative years later, "Our obligation was to fight the enemy. We were justified in taking aid from the Nazi oppressor, who was in this case the enemy of our enemy — the British." Stern Gang

representatives expressed sympathy for the Nazis' goal of a Jew-free Europe as they lobbied Hitler's emissaries to support the establishment of a totalitarian Jewish state that would be bound by treaty with the German Reich. Misunderstanding the categorical nature of Nazi anti-Semitism, the Stern Gang sought to convince Hitler's men that it was "closely related to the totalitarian movements of Europe in its ideology and structure." Menachem Begin subsequently disclosed that the World Zionist Organization had sent Hitler a cable of condolence on the death of German president Hindenburg. Both Begin and former Stern Gang member Yitzhak Shamir would later become prime ministers of the State of Israel.

6. Tauber, *Eagle and Swastika,* pp. 1114–15. Among the first batch of Germans in postwar Egypt were several with good reason to disappear — people like SS General Oskar von Dirlewanger and Willi Berner, who had been instrumental in organizing the Mauthausen concentration camp. They were later joined by SS officer Heinrich Willermann, formerly the medical director at Dachau.

7. James Sheldon, "Middle East Caldron," *Prevent World War III,* no. 47 (1955); "German Advisors with Egyptian Armed Forces," Foreign Service dispatch from Cairo, no. 1211, December, 20, 1952, in State Department records at the Suitland, Maryland, branch of the National Archives; "The German Influence Behind the Egyptian Revolt," *Newsweek,* August 25, 1952.

8. Del Boca and Giovana, *Fascism Today,* p. 398.

9. Miles Copeland, *Game of Nations,* p. 103; Cookridge, *Spy of the Century,* p. 352.

10. Copeland, *Game of Nations,* p. 104.

11. Cookridge, *Spy of the Century,* p. 353; Copeland, *Game of Nations,* p. 104.

12. Gehlen, *The Service,* p. 260; Cookridge, *Spy of the Century,* p. 353; Simpson, *Blowback,* p. 251; Copeland, *Game of Nations,* p. 96.

13. Gehlen, *The Service,* p. 203; "Germans in Egypt," *Wiener Library Bulletin,* May–August 1953.

14. Francis Parker Yockey, *The Destiny of America* (Reedy, West Va.: Liberty Bell Publications, 1981), p. 16; "Francis Yockey, aka . . . ," State Department document dated August 7, 1953; "Francis Parker Yockey, with aliases," FBI document dated October 7, 1953, from J. Edgar Hoover to Assistant Chief of Staff, G-2.

15. Author's interview with Otto Ernst Remer, April 16, 1992.

16. See U.S. Army intelligence documents on Remer in National Archives record group 319, box 371, file no. XE062963, NND 931149; Tauber, *Eagle and Swastika,* pp. 1114–16.

17. Otto Ernst Remer, "Deutschland und die Arabische Welt," *Der Weg,* June 1953.

18. Author's interview with Otto Ernst Remer; George L. West, Jr., "Evidence of German Desire for US Support in Egypt," April 24, 1953, U.S. State Department document 762.5200/4-2453 in National Archives civil records division; U.S. Army intelligence documents on Remer in National Archives record group 319, box 371, file no. XE062963, NND 931149.

19. Wallach, *Arafat,* pp. 70–71; author's interview with Otto Ernst Remer.

20. Author's interview with H. Keith Thompson; Tauber, *Eagle and Swastika,* p. 1110.

21. Wistrich, *Who's Who in Nazi Germany,* p. 187; *Wiener Library Bulletin,* vol. xiv, no. 2 (1960); Tauber, *Eagle and Swastika,* p. 1112; Andrew and Leslie Cockburn, *Dangerous Liaison,* p. 52. While working in Goebbels's Propaganda Ministry, Johann von Leers authored dozens of vile anti-Semitic books that called for the physical extermination of all Jews. His titles include such works as *The Criminality of Jews, History on a Racial Basis, Blood and Race in Legislation* and *The Jews Are Watching You.* After the war, he spent eighteen months in an American internment camp. After his release, he met with Otto Ernst Remer and then departed via the northern ratline through Scandinavia to Buenos Aires, where he became one of the editors of *Der Weg.* A few years later, the Grand Mufti publicly welcomed von Leers when he arrived in Cairo. Con-

vinced that Christianity was nothing more than a corrupt outgrowth of Judaism, von Leers vented his rage in several letters to H. Keith Thompson, his principal contact in New York. "If there is any hope to free the world from Jewish tyranny," von Leers fumed, "it is with the Moslems, who stand steadfastly against Zionism, Colonialism and Imperialism." Thompson and von Leers maintained a lively correspondence until the latter's death in March 1965. At one point, von Leers tried to convince his American friend to be his literary agent, but Thompson didn't think his hyperbolic style would go over well with a U.S. audience. Von Leers was given to quirky rhetorical flourishes, referring, for example, to "the brutal tyranny of the swine Adenauer, who Allah may strike blind!" and "the devilish Bonn clique, which Allah may burn in the coming atomic conflagration."

22. "Nazis in Cairo," *Patterns of Prejudice,* May–June 1967; Wistrich, *Antisemitism,* p. 254. Another edition of the *Protocols* was published in 1966 by Shauki Abdel Nasser, the Egyptian president's brother.

23. Gil Carl Alroy, "The Arab Myth of Zionism," *Patterns of Prejudice,* November–December, 1970; *Manchester Guardian,* February 5, 1957, cited in "Germans in Egypt," *Wiener Library Bulletin,* vol. xi, nos. 1–2 (1957).

24. *The Times* (London), May 30, 1953, and *Frankfurter Allgemeine Zeitung,* June 16, 1953, cited in *Wiener Library Bulletin,* May–August 1953.

25. Wallach, *Arafat,* p. 85; author's interview with Ilse Skorzeny. See also Infield, *Skorzeny,* p. 237.

26. "Nazis in Cairo"; Tauber, *Eagle and Swastika,* p. 1114.

27. Ian Black and Benny Morris, *Israel's Secret Wars,* pp. 118–19; Joel Beinin, *Was the Red Flag Flying There?,* p. 11.

28. Irving Sedar and Harold Greenberg, *Behind the Egyptian Sphinx,* p. 60; Infield, *Skorzeny,* p. 210.

29. Nasser quoted in Mohamed Heikal, *Sphinx and the Commissar,* p. 55.

30. Beinin, *Was the Red Flag Flying There?*, p. 153; Hashim S. H. Behbehani, *The Soviet Union and Arab Nationalism*, p. 133.

31. Roger Faligot and Remi Kauffer, *Le Croissant et la Croix Gammée*, p. 182. The choice of Czechoslovakia as a weapons conduit was rather ironic given that country's role in supplying crucial armament to the State of Israel shortly after it was formed in 1948. With the approval of the Soviet Union, which quickly recognized the Jewish state, several hundred Israelis received training at Czech military installations as Arab armies were clashing with Jewish forces. Early Soviet support for Israel was part of the Kremlin's anticolonial strategy that sought to undermine British authority in the region. Within a few years, however, British influence had waned and the Russians began tilting decisively toward the Arabs in their conflict with Israel. (Cockburn, *Dangerous Liaison*, p. 21; Black and Morris, *Israel's Secret Wars*, p. 77; Heikal, *Sphinx and the Commissar*, p. 52.)

32. Simpson, *Blowback*, pp. 78–79; Sedar and Greenberg, *Behind the Egyptian Sphinx*, pp. 70–74. One of Grobba's colleagues in von Ribbentrop's Foreign Office, Werner-Otto von Hentig, served as Bonn's official minister to Sukarno's Indonesia and later accompanied the Saudi Arabian delegation to the nonaligned conference in Bandung in 1955. *Der Spiegel* subsequently reported that von Hentig had been in regular contact with Moscow, furthering German-Soviet collaboration in the Middle East.

33. *Der Spiegel*, October 26, 1955, cited in James Sheldon, "Middle East Caldron," *Prevent World War III*, no. 47, 1955; "German Advisors with Egyptian Armed Forces," Foreign Service dispatch from Cairo, no. 1211, December, 20, 1952, in State Department records at the Suitland, Maryland, branch of the National Archives.

34. Jefferson Caffery, "German Ambassador re: Dr. Wilhelm Voss and International Nazi-Communist Organization," April 10, 1953, U.S. State Department document 762.5200/4-1053 in National Archives civil records division.

35. Tauber, *Eagle and the Swastika*, pp. 1114–16.

36. J. Roland Jacobs, "Alleged clandestine group engaged in returning former Waffen SS officers to Germany, and planning an anti-American riot in Tehran," March 2, 1953, U.S. State Department document 762.5200/3-253 in National Archives civil records division.

37. The ringleader of the plot was Dr. Werner Naumann, a former Brownshirt officer who served as undersecretary of state in Germany's wartime Propaganda Ministry. Naumann was named in Hitler's will as Goebbels's successor. Although he dropped out of sight for a number of years after the war, Naumann maintained clandestine contact with a select group of comrades until the time was right for him to resurface. That moment came in 1950, when the West German government declared a general amnesty for Nazis. Shortly thereafter, Naumann began to consult with key Third Reich veterans — including Hans-Ulrich Rudel, Otto Skorzeny, and Hjalmar Schacht — regarding plans for a future Nazi power grab. Naumann's underground leadership cadre coordinated efforts to place Nazis in positions of influence in West German political parties, the press, youth organizations, veterans and refugee groups, and other significant institutions. Top priority was given to penetrating the three right-wing parties that formed Chancellor Konrad Adenauer's governing coalition: the Christian Democratic Union, the Free Democratic Party, and the German Party. Recognizing that the tentacles of the Naumann organization extended to both sides of the Cold War divide, a U.S. State Department document concluded: "Ideologically these former Nazis are rabid nationalists although they do not publicly endorse the anti-Semitic policies of national socialism. Politically, they maintain a neutralist position, playing both ends against the middle and intimating that failure to attain favors from the West could land Germany quickly and easily in the Eastern camp." Less than six months after they were arrested, Naumann and associates were released without bail by the West German Supreme Court, pending further investigation; the charges were later dropped for "lack of evidence." (LaVerne Baldwin, "Minister of Interior's Appraisal of the Werner Naumann Affair," March 26, 1953, U.S. State Department document 762A.00/3-2653, and "H. S. Lucht Company, Düsseldorf, Germany," July 23, 1954, U.S.

State Department document 460.529/7-2354 in National Archives civil records division. See also Edmund Taylor, "Where Fascism and Communism Meet," *The Reporter,* April 13, 1954; Infield, *Secrets of the SS,* pp. 174–75; Infield, *Skorzeny,* p. 210; Henry J. Kellermann, "Background on Nazi Arrests in the British Zone," January 16, 1953, U.S. State Department document 762A.00/1-1653 in National Archives civil records division; Tauber, *Eagle and Swastika,* pp. 134–135, 241.)

38. Faligot and Kauffer, *Le Croissant et la Croix Gammée,* p. 182.

39. Copeland, *Game of Nations,* p. 105.

40. *Maariv* cited in Tom Segev, *The Seventh Million,* p. 297.

41. Copeland, *Game of Nations,* p. 202

42. Martin A. Lee and Bruce Shlain, *Acid Dreams,* p. 35; Powers, *Man Who Kept Secrets,* p. 431.

43. Kermit Roosevelt cited in Hersh, *Old Boys,* p. 332.

44. Gehlen, *The Service,* p. 260; author's interview with Isser Harel, March 23, 1993.

45. Author's interview with Isser Harel.

46. Sedar and Greenberg, *Behind the Egyptian Sphinx,* pp. 67, 75.

47. Simpson, *Blowback,* p. 249; Cookridge, *Spy of the Century,* p. 354; *Chicago Sun Times,* November 1, 1987.

48. Tauber, *Eagle and Swastika,* p. 242; "The German Influence Behind the Egyptian Revolt"; Hunt, *Secret Agenda,* p. 191.

49. Robert Fisk, "Non-existent Nazi is alive and well protected in Syria," *Independent,* January 15, 1990.

50. Alistair Horne, *A Savage War of Peace,* pp. 62, 63, 110; Muhammed Saahir Lone, letter to the *New York Times,* August 22, 1992.

51. Robert Merle, *Ahmed Ben Bella,* p. 67; Horne, *A Savage War of Peace,* p. 74.

52. Remer's principal partner in the weapons trade was Ernst-Wilhelm Springer, who had helped the Grand Mufti organize the Muslim SS division during the war. By the mid-1950s, Springer was running a successful import-export business from his office in Hanover. Occasionally he shipped Eastern European munitions — including brand-new weapons from Skoda Works, the Czech arms factory — to Damascus, where Springer and Remer had set up the Orient Trading Company. This firm provided a cover for illicit arms deals and other business ventures.

53. Author's interview with Otto Ernst Remer; Joachim Joesten, *The Red Hand,* pp. 93–96; Faligot and Kauffer, *Le Croissant et la Croix Gammée,* pp. 196, 216.

54. Joesten, *The Red Hand,* pp. 140–43; Faligot and Kauffer, *Le Croissant et la Croix Gammée,* pp. 207–08; "Skorzeny, Otto," U.S. Army intelligence document dated July 12, 1956.

55. Joesten, *The Red Hand,* p. 143.

56. Tauber, *Eagle and Swastika,* p. 1110; author's interview with Ilse Skorzeny. Whenever Skorzeny traveled to South Africa on business, he was a guest of Senator Louis Theodore Weichardt, an outspoken Nazi and Jew-baiter who had founded the paramilitary Greyshirts organization. Skorzeny also collaborated with Oswald Pirow, the former South African defense minister and leader of the neo-Nazi New Order movement. Several German expatriates were employed by South Africa's police and security forces. Lieutenant General Friedrich Wilhelm von Mellenthin, ex-chief of staff of Germany's Fourth Panzer Army, for example, became a director of Trek Airways, which undertook special charter operations for police agencies involved in disciplining the native black population.

57. "Right-wing Activity," *Wiener Library Bulletin,* vol. xiv, no. 2 (1960); "Arabs and the German Right-Wing," *Wiener Library Bulletin,* vol. xx, no. 1 (1966).

58. Tauber, *Eagle and Swastika,* pp. 237–38.

59. *Wiener Library Bulletin,* vol. x, nos. 5–6 (1956), and vol. xi, nos. 5–6 (1957); Tauber, *Eagle and Swastika,* p. 238.

60. Edward H. Quales, "Algerian Terrorist Attacks in France," U.S. Army CIC report, October 28, 1958, in National Archives record group 319, box 54, file no. ZF010201; see also Faligot and Kauffer, *Le Croissant et la Croix Gammée,* pp. 215–16.

61. Faligot and Krop, *La Piscine,* p. 166. Hamburg-based arms dealers Otto Schülter and George Puchert were also murdered by the Red Hand.

62. Horne, *A Savage War of Peace,* p. 129; Richard Deacon, *The French Secret Service,* p. 191; Joesten, *The Red Hand,* pp. 94–95; Faligot and Krop, *La Piscine,* p. 105.

63. Alistair Horne, *The French Army and Politics,* pp. 84–85.

64. Joesten, *The Red Hand,* p. 64; Horne, *A Savage War of Peace,* p. 526; see also Pierre Demarest and Christian Plume, *Target De Gaulle.* These efforts to assassinate President de Gaulle inspired the thriller *The Day of the Jackal.*

65. Tauber, *Eagle and Swastika,* p. 1095; Horne, *A Savage War of Peace,* pp. 252–53, 350, 485.

66. Among the executed was Roger Degueldre, leader of the OAS "Delta commandos," who had once served with the SS Walloon Division led by General Léon Degrelle during World War II.

67. René L. Maurice and Ken Follet, *Under the Streets of Nice,* pp. 34–39; Horne, *A Savage War of Peace,* p. 550.

68. The capture of Eichmann sparked an international controversy when Dr. Mario Amadeo, the Argentine United Nations delegate, appealed to the U.N. Security Council to censure Israel for violating his country's sovereignty. A short time later, it was revealed that Amadeo had himself been classified by the U.S. State Department as a onetime "trusted collaborator" of Hitler's SS.

69. Hannah Arendt, *Eichmann in Jerusalem,* pp. 10–13; Simpson, *Blowback,* p. 245.

70. Tauber, *Eagle and Swastika,* pp. 41, 1097; Eisenberg, *Re-Emergence of Fascism,* p. 11; see also Leni Yayil, *"Memoirs" of Adolf Eichmann,* Yad Vashem Studies, vol. xviii (1987).

71. Interpol, the global police agency, refused to help track Nazi war criminals on the grounds that they had committed "political" offenses, which were allegedly outside Interpol's purview. As it turns out, the Interpol hierarchy had a history of close connections to Nazis and fascists. Interpol shared its headquarters with the Gestapo during World War II. In 1963, Interpol's president was Jean Nepote, who collaborated with the French Vichy government. Paul Dickopf, a former SS officer, served as Interpol's president from 1968 to 1972.

72. Robert Fisk, "Non-existent Nazi is alive and well protected in Syria," *Independent,* January 15, 1990.

73. John Bierman, "War criminal Alois Brunner Reported Dead," *The Guardian,* January 9, 1993.

74. Michael Bar-Zohar, *The Hunt for German Scientists,* p. 187; Stewart Steven, *Spymasters of Israel,* p. 160; Sedar and Greenberg, *Behind the Egyptian Sphinx,* p. 67.

75. Robert St. John, *The Boss,* p. 304; Steven, *Spymasters of Israel,* p. 161; "Appeals to Rampant Nationalism," *Wiener Library Bulletin,* October 1964.

76. Gerd Wilcke, "500 From Europe Aid Cairo on Arms," *New York Times,* April 5, 1963; Kenneth R. Timmerman, *The Death Lobby,* pp. 402–03.

77. Wolfgang Lotz, *The Champaign Spy,* pp. 50–51, 59, 67; Dan Raviv and Yossi Melman, *Every Prince a Spy,* p. 147.

78. Author's interview with Otto Ernst Remer; Hunt, *Secret Agenda,* p. 191.

79. Bar-Zohar, *Hunt for German Scientists,* p. 201; Gerd Wilcke, "Bonn Urged to Curb Scientists Aiding Cairo Missile Work," *New York Times,* April 3, 1963; author's interview with Isser Harel.

80. Steven, *Spymasters of Israel,* p. 161; Posner and Ware, *Mengele,* p. 201. In the early 1960s, Skorzeny's business associate, Willi Messerschmitt, was contracted by the Egyptian government to build an aircraft plant. While blueprints for jet aircraft and guided missiles were drawn up, Dr. Ferdinand Brandner, an Austrian engineer, oversaw the day-to-day operations at Messerschmitt's factory near Cairo. A former SA captain who was captured by the Soviets at the end of the war, Brandner worked for five years in Russia as a jet-engine designer before coming to Egypt. Dr. Hans Eisele, a drug addict who was wanted for committing medical atrocities at the Buchenwald concentration camp, served as the chief medical officer of Messerschmitt's plant. Eisele eventually died of an overdose of morphine — a far more pleasant death, no doubt, than the dreadful treatment he inflicted upon thousands of his wartime victims.

81. *Matara,* September 1989, cited in "Ex-SS Man Worked for the Mossad against Egyptian Rocket Project," *Jerusalem Post,* September 20, 1989; Raviv and Melman, *Every Prince a Spy,* p. 122; Black and Morris, *Israel's Secret Wars,* p. 198; Heikal, *Sphinx and the Commissar,* p. 151.

82. Simpson, *Blowback,* p. 261; Reese, *General Reinhard Gehlen and the CIA,* pp. 143–71, especially p. 167.

83. "Former Top Soviet Spy Savouring Life as a KGB Pensioner," Reuters, March 15, 1986.

84. Reese, *General Reinhard Gehlen and the CIA,* p. 134; Copeland cited in David Horowitz, "Game-Player," *Jerusalem Post,* July 21, 1989.

CHAPTER FIVE: *Nostalgics and Revisionists*

1. "Francis Parker Yockey, aka Richard Allen," FBI, San Francisco field office, June 20, 1960.

2. "Francis Parker Yockey, aka . . . ," FBI, San Francisco field office, July 1, 1960.

3. "3 Passports Jail Mystery Visitor Here," *San Francisco Examiner,* June 9, 1960; "Both Sides Favor Yockey Mind Test," *San Francisco Examiner,* June 14, 1960.

4. "Francis Parker Yockey," FBI report by Special Agent Wayne K. Welch, July 7, 1960.

5. H. Keith Thompson, "A Survey of the Right-Wing," *Independent,* August 1962. In 1961, H. Keith Thompson and Frederick Weiss paid tribute to Yockey by publishing his last essay, "A World in Flames: An Estimate of the World Situation," in which he spoke favorably of "the Arab revolt" led by Nasser, as well as of the emergence of nonaligned "nationalist, neutralist regimes" in Yugoslavia, Indonesia, and other Third World countries. In this article, Yockey also restated his belief that the Soviet Union, as opposed to the United States, was no longer under Jewish control.

6. *Right,* July 1960.

7. William Turner, *Power on the Right,* pp. 150–51; Mintz, *The Liberty Lobby,* p. 71; C. H. Simmons, "The Strange Story of Willis Carto," *National Review,* September 10, 1971; *Los Angeles Times,* January 16, 1992, p. B6.

8. W. A. Carto, introduction to *Imperium,* pp. ix, xxiii, xli. Carto's introduction to *Imperium* was based largely on an essay by Revilo P. Oliver, an eccentric classics professor who taught at the University of Illinois. One of Carto's former associates, Keith Stimely, claimed that Oliver had written 90 percent of the introduction, with Carto merely adding the anecdotal material pertaining to his meeting with Yockey. Oliver, at one time an editor at Buckley's *National Review,* was also listed as an associate editor of *American Opinion,* the mouthpiece of the John Birch Society. But Oliver was forced to leave the Birchers after he referred indiscreetly at a public forum to "vaporizing" the Jews as a "beatific vision." (Turner, *Power on the Right,* p. 26.)

9. Memo from Willis Carto to F. C. F. Weiss, Russell Maguire, Condé McGinley, Womens Voice, Re: Francis Parker Yockey, June 10, 1960, in the H. Keith Thompson section of the Hoover Institute Special Collections Library; C. H. Simmons, "The Strange Story of Willis Carto."

10. H. Keith Thompson cited without attribution by George and Wilcox, *Nazis, Communists, Klansmen and Others,* p. 235.

11. Drew Pearson and Jack Anderson, "Eastland Linked to Liberty Lobby," *Washington Post,* October 21, 1966; Richard Cohen, "Does It Really Matter If He Didn't Believe It?" *Washington Post,* April 28, 1981; Turner, *Power on the Right,* p. 159; Drew Pearson and Jack Anderson, "Retired Brass Turns to Liberty Lobby," *Washington Post,* October 29, 1966.

12. Turner, *Power on the Right,* p. 146; Mintz, *The Liberty Lobby,* pp. 5–6; Joseph Trento and Joseph Spear, "How Nazi Manpower Has Invaded Capitol Hill," *True,* November 1969.

13. Drew Pearson and Jack Anderson, "Liberty Lobby Links Right-Wing Drive," *Washington Post,* October 26, 1966.

14. Drew Pearson and Jack Anderson, "Neo-Nazi Movement Lobbying on Hill," *Washington Post,* April 17, 1969; Pearson and Anderson, "Liberty Lobby Adopts Wallace Unit," *Washington Post,* April 21, 1969; Paul W. Valentine, "Far-Right Youth Group Reports Rapid Growth," *Los Angeles Times,* December 25, 1969; Jason Berry, *Gambit,* September 3, 1991. See also Mintz, *The Liberty Lobby,* p. 129.

15. Author's interview with Roy Frankhauser, October 14, 1994. All quotations from Frankhauser are from this interview unless otherwise indicated.

16. Thayer, *Farther Shores of Politics,* p. 16.

17. *Searchlight,* September 1987.

18. Thayer, *Farther Shores of Politics,* p. 30; A. M. Rosenthal and Arthur Gelb, *One More Victim,* p. 160; Warren Commission Hearings, vol. 16, p. 56. There is some evidence to suggest that Lee

Harvey Oswald, officially alleged to be a leftist, was actually an FBI informant, which may shed light on why he was interested in the American Nazi Party. After the JFK assassination, H. Keith Thompson contacted Oswald's mother, Marguerite, and became her business representative, arranging press interviews and negotiating the sale of rights and documents. "We developed a personal relationship, we had a minor affair," said Thompson. Be that as it may, Thompson's friends at the Liberty Lobby eventually jumped on the Kennedy assassination conspiracy bandwagon and promoted the dubious theory that the CIA was behind JFK's death. Attorney Mark Lane, whose first book, *Rush to Judgment,* raised legitimate questions about the Warren Commission's findings (that Oswald was the lone assassin), later teamed up with Willis Carto and represented the Liberty Lobby and its spin-off, the Institute for Historical Review (which claimed the Holocaust never happened) in several controversial legal cases. Lane's 1992 bestseller *Plausible Denial* was vigorously promoted by the Liberty Lobby's weekly, the *Spotlight*—an ironic development given that Carto had once denounced the Kennedy administration as a "communist takeover" when JFK was in office. Another so-called expert on the JFK murder, former U.S. Air Force officer L. Fletcher Prouty, served on the board of the Liberty Lobby's Populist Action Committee, which raised money for white supremacist and ultra-right-wing political candidates in the early 1990s. While publicly affiliated with the Liberty Lobby, Prouty also served as an advisor to Oliver Stone's film on the JFK assassination.

19. Rosenthal and Gelb, *One More Victim,* pp. 161–63; author's interview with Roy Frankhauser.

20. Ibid., pp. 223–26; Thayer, *Farther Shores,* pp. 30–31.

21. Author's conversation with Jim Hougan, October 1994.

22. CBS *Evening News,* July 28, 1975.

23. George and Wilcox, *Nazis, Communists, Klansmen, and Others,* p. 289; Frank Donner, *The Age of Surveillance,* p. 346; author's interview with Robert Miles, November 25, 1986.

24. Stephen G. Thompkins, "Army feared King, secretly watched him," *Commercial Appeal,* March 21, 1993. FBI director J. Edgar Hoover, meanwhile, was waging a full-scale vendetta against Dr. King in an effort to "neutralize" his political work and disrupt his personal life. At one point, the FBI tried to break up King's marriage by anonymously sending him a tape of an extramarital affair along with a blackmail note threatening to expose his "filthy fraudulent self" unless he committed suicide. When word of King's assassination on April 4, 1968, reached the Bureau's field office in Atlanta, an FBI supervisor began jumping up and down, gleefully shouting, "They finally got the son of a bitch." Despite Hoover's well-known animosity toward King, the FBI was entrusted with the task of investigating his death. Ignoring key leads, Hoover's men insisted that James Earl Ray was solely responsible for killing the nation's most gifted civil rights leader. In 1977, however, the House Select Committee on Assassinations found that the FBI's inquiry was riddled with holes. One of the most glaring weaknesses was the Bureau's refusal to investigate the claim of Ray's brother, Jerry, who said he knew of a $100,000 bounty for the murder. During the year that King was killed, Jerry Ray served as the bodyguard of J. B. Stoner, head of the violently racist National States' Rights Party. The congressional probe concluded that there was "a serious likelihood of conspiracy" in the King case and pointed toward an ultra-right-wing plot hatched in St. Louis, involving Ray and his brothers. Congressman Louis Stokes blamed the FBI for helping to create a climate in which King's murder "was not only thinkable, but could be thought of as justifiable."

25. Regarding Koehl's alleged homosexuality, see *NSV Report* (October–December 1993), a quarterly newsletter published by the National Socialist Vanguard. Dismissed by Koehl in 1970, Frank Collins went on to form the National Socialist Party of America, a group best known for staging a march in the predominantly Jewish town of Skokie, Illinois, later in the decade. Collins was subsequently arrested for molesting adolescent boys; one of the followers of this sect, John Hinckley, shot and nearly killed President Ronald Reagan in 1981.

26. Author's interview with Povl Riis-Knudsen, April 7, 1993.

27. Povl Riis-Knudsen, *National Socialism: A Left-Wing Movement* (Aalborg, Denmark: World Union of National Socialists, 1984).

28. Ibid.

29. "Neo-Nazi glee at Soviet antisemitism," *Patterns of Prejudice,* March–June 1979; "Neo-Nazis' hopes of Russia," *Patterns of Prejudice,* July 1981; Walter Laqueur, *Black Hundred,* p. 110.

30. Idiotic they may have been, but Soviet officials utilized anti-Semitism for domestic social control as well as a hedge against liberal currents percolating in Eastern Europe. When Alexander Dubček attempted to chart a course back to the progressive and humanist roots of Communism during the Prague Spring of 1968, Soviet journals warned that a sinister "Zionist hand" was pulling the strings of the Czech government. Reverberations of the Soviet anti-Zionist campaign were felt among Communist authorities in Warsaw, who blamed student unrest at Polish universities on that country's tiny Jewish community. Moscow raised the specter of Zionism once again when it was having trouble with the Kadar regime in Hungary in the early 1970s. And after armed clashes on the Sino-Soviet border, the Kremlin began warning of a Maoist-Zionist plot! (Alfred D. Low, *Soviet Jewry and Soviet Policy,* pp. 141, 149–50, 177, 227n; *Jews and Jewish Topics,* summer 1987; William Korey, *The Soviet Cage,* p. 306.)

31. Korey, *The Soviet Cage,* p. 18; Howard Spier, " 'Zionists and Freemasons' in Soviet propaganda," *Patterns of Prejudice,* January–February 1979; John Dunlop, *The New Russian Nationalism,* p. 90; Laqueur, *Black Hundred,* pp. 112–114; Arthur Lyons, "Russian Nationalists and Anti-Semitism," *Midstream,* February 1987; *Jews and Jewish Topics,* summer 1987; M. Kaganskaya, "*The Book of Vles:* The Saga of a Forgery," *Jews and Jewish Topics,* winter 1986–87.

32. Thiriart spoke of his relationship with Skorzeny when interviewed by journalist Kevin Coogan in November 1986. When asked whether Skorzeny worked for the CIA, Thiriart responded with a sly grin: "Yes, but not all the time." As for General Gehlen, Thiriart

quipped, "Half his staff worked for the Americans, and the others worked for the Soviets."

33. "Jean Thiriart repond aux questions de Bernardo Gil Mugarza," *Voulour,* January–March 1993.

34. Yannick Sauveur, *Jean Thiriart et le National Communautarisme Europeen,* p. 20; Del Boca and Giovana, *Fascism Today,* p. 228.

35. Tauber, *Eagle and Swastika,* p. 221.

36. Jean Thiriart, *Europe* (English language manuscript, translated by W. G. Eaton, 1964), pp. iii, 33, 38, 50, 62, 64, 65.

37. Thiriart, *Europe,* pp. 39, 58–59, 75.

38. Thiriart, *Europe,* pp. 20–21; Thiriart, *The Great Nation,* theses 15–17.

39. Sauveur, *Jean Thiriart,* p. 40; "Jean Thiriart repond aux questions de Bernardo Gil Mugarza."

40. Thiriart, *Europe,* pp. 4, 66–67, 71, 75; Thiriart, *The Great Nation,* theses 6, 14.

41. Luc Michel, "Questions for Mr. Jean Thiriart"; Thiriart, *Europe,* p. 5; Thiriart, *The Great Nation,* thesis 28; *La Nation Européenne,* no. 16, cited in Sauveur, *Jean Thiriart,* p. 114.

42. Thiriart, *Europe,* pp. 2, 97.

43. "De 'Jeune Europe' aux 'Brigades Rouges,' " *Conscience Européenne,* March 1985.

44. Stephen Fischer-Galati, "Romanian Nationalism," in Peter F. Sugar and Ivo J. Lederer, eds., *Nationalism in Eastern Europe,* p. 394; Simpson, *Blowback,* p. 78; Hockenos, *Free to Hate,* pp. 70–71; Stanley Payne, *History of Fascism,* p. 396.

45. "De 'Jeune Europe' aux 'Brigades Rouges' "; author's interview with Luc Michel, June 20, 1993.

46. *Nation Europa,* April 1967, cited in "Right-wing view on foreign affairs," *Patterns of Prejudice,* May–June 1967. Gerhard

Frey's *Deutsche National-Zeitung,* another ultranationalist publication, concurred: "All European powers hope that a weakening of Russia's position in the Far East will reduce her pressure in Europe."

47. Gehlen, *The Service,* p. 235.

48. For an in-depth discussion of the German National Democratic Party, see John David Nagle, *National Democratic Party.*

49. Rees, *Extreme Right Since 1890,* p. 387; *Deutsche National-Zeitung,* April 11, 1969, cited in C. C. Aronsfeld, "Right-wing flirtation with a Chinese alliance," *Patterns of Prejudice,* July–August 1969; "Right-wing over the East," *Patterns of Prejudice,* September–October 1968.

50. See, for example, *La Nation Européenne,* February 1969; author's interview with Luc Michel.

51. "Peron's 'third world' dreams," *Patterns of Prejudice,* May–June 1969; *La Nation Européenne,* May 1967, June 1967, December 1967, January 1968.

52. Page, *Perón,* p. 405.

53. Donald C. Hodges, *Argentina,* pp. 136–37; Page, *Perón,* pp. 405, 422; Tauber, *Eagle and Swastika,* p. 1097.

54. Martin Edwin Anderson, *Dossier Secreto,* pp. 45, 72, 143; Eisenberg, *Re-Emergence of Fascism,* p. 293.

55. Donald C. Hodges, ed., *Urban Guerrilla,* pp. 9–10.

56. Hodges, ed., *Urban Guerrilla,* pp. 9–10; Ellwood M. Rabenold, Jr., "Government Moves to Suppress Terrorist Group," U.S. State Department airgram from the American embassy in Buenos Aires, July 3, 1965; "Pro-Fascist Cuban Organizations in Miami, Florida," FBI airtel from Legat, Buenos Aires (105-242) (RUC) to Director, FBI, August 1, 1965.

57. John Simpson and Jana Bennett, *The Disappeared and the Mothers,* pp. 56–58.

58. Donald C. Hodges, *Argentina's "Dirty War,"* pp. 117–19; Page, *Perón,* p. 480.

59. *La Nation Européenne,* January 1967, July 1967, October 1967; author's interview with Luc Michel.

60. *La Nation Européenne,* July 1967, cited in "Jean Thiriart's anti-U.S. crusade," *Patterns of Prejudice,* July–August 1967.

61. *Baghdad Observer,* September 8, 1968; author's interview with Luc Michel.

62. Author's interview with Luc Michel.

63. Author's interview with Otto Ernst Remer, April 16, 1992; transcript of the British TV documentary, "The Other Face of Terror."

64. Martin A. Lee and Kevin Coogan, "Killers on the Right," *Mother Jones,* May 1987; see also Sauveur, *Jean Thiriart.*

65. *Conscience Européenne,* March 1985; author's interview with Luc Michel; author's interview with Claudio Mutti, June 2, 1993; Lee and Coogan, "Killers on the Right."

66. State Department memorandum of conversation, April 14, 1967, obtained by the author through the Freedom of Information Act, case control no. 9402953; George Thayer, *The War Business,* pp. 116–18, 203, 305; Stuart Christie, *Stefano delle Chiaie,* p. 161.

67. Sayer and Botting, *America's Secret Army,* pp. 322–33; "He guarded the Nazi 'Butcher'," *San Francisco Sunday Examiner & Chronicle,* February 13, 1983; "Ex-U.S. Agents Tell of Efforts to Help Barbie," *New York Times,* July 6, 1983; "Vatican Is Reported to Have Furnished Aid to Fleeing Nazis," *New York Times,* January 26, 1984; Magnus Linklater, et al., *The Nazi Legacy,* pp. 237–39. According to *The Nazi Legacy,* Barbie and his principal business partner, Fritz Schwend, "acted as agents, negotiating purchases not only on behalf of the Bolivian and Peruvian governments but, through their friendship with the Nazi Hans Rudel, sales to Paraguay and Chile, and through Otto Skorzeny in Spain, further deals in Madrid." The authors cite Schwend's correspondence with Merex, in which he and Barbie proposed buying M14 tanks "for Herr Skorzeny" and several other pieces of military hardware for additional clients in 1966. Merex responded: "We are cabling the

prices of 'birds' being inquired about, sending specifications. What do you mean by 'exceptional things'? . . . Find a secure way to tell us, perhaps via courier through Peruvian embassy in Bonn. Our common friend Colonel R[udel], who also works for us, will be coming out soon; he could take a message. We must be paid in cash for official German and American equipment." During the mid-1980s, Lt. Col. Oliver North arranged for the Merex corporation to deliver 3 million rounds of ammunition to the Nicaraguan Contras while a ban on U.S. military aid was in effect. (Michael Wines and William C. Rempel, "CIA's Purchase of Smuggled Arms from North Aides Probed by Panels," *Los Angeles Times,* March 31, 1987.)

68. Linklater, *The Nazi Legacy,* p. 275; Kai Hermann, "Klaus Barbie: A Killer's Career," *Covert Action Information Bulletin,* winter 1986, originally published in *Der Spiegel;* Xavier Vinader, "Me Trabajado en Bolivia con Barbie y delle Chiaie," *Interviu,* June 17, 1987.

69. Ralph Blumenthal, "Canadian Says Barbie Boasted of Visiting the U.S.," *New York Times,* February 28, 1983; "Barbie Entered U.S. in 1969, '70," *Denver Post,* March 16, 1983; William Stevenson, *The Borman Brotherhood,* p. 154.

70. Christie, *Stefano delle Chiaie,* p. 72.

71. TASS, "TV Programme on Nazi Criminals," May 14, 1987; Anthony Herbert, *Soldier,* pp. 85–86.

72. Faligot and Kauffer, *Le Croissant et la Croix Gammee,* pp. 230–31, 270; *Le Nouvel Observateur,* September 23, 1974, cited in Henrik Kruger, *Great Heroin Coup,* p. 210. Colonel George Papadopoulos, the leader of the Greek military junta, had previously served in a pro-Nazi security battalion whose main task was to hunt down Greek resistance fighters during World War II. Once a believer in Hitler's "New Order," he subsequently became the principal liaison between the CIA and the Holy Bond of Greek Officers, an ultra-right-wing sect made up primarily of Nazi collaborators. Backed by U.S. intelligence, this heavily militarized secret-service network was involved in a murderous counterinsurgency campaign against left-wing antifascists during the Greek civil war in the late

1940s. Various threads linking the official security apparatus with underground "parastate" formations coalesced in Red Sheepskin, the Greek version of the Gladio program (see footnote on p. 44). Several members of the Greek "stay behind" unit — which was supposed to respond to Soviet aggression — participated in the 1967 putsch that ousted a democratically elected, non-Communist government. It is not clear whether the CIA gave the green light to Papadopoulos before the coup, but U.S. intelligence certainly assisted afterward when the junta imposed martial law, abolished press freedom, tortured and murdered thousands of political opponents, deported others to remote islands, banned rock music and books (including Greek classics by Sophocles and Aristophanes), and issued moralistic decrees condemning miniskirts and long hair.

73. See, for example, Skorzeny's front page piece in the *Deutsche Wochen-Zeitung,* March 3, 1967.

74. "Rightist Group Sends Telegram of Condolence on Death of George Lincoln Rockwell," Department of State airgram, September 14, 1967.

75. "Guide noir," *The Economist,* November 1, 1975; author's interview with Eduardo Arrojo and Christian Ruiz, May 22, 1993; author's interview with Ernesto Mila Rodriguez, May 28–29, 1993; author's interview with Pedro Varella, May 29, 1993; "Spanish 'Friends of Europe,' " *Patterns of Prejudice,* July–August 1978, and January 1982, pp. 41–43; Sheelagh Ellwood, "The Extreme Right in Spain: A Dying Species?" in Luciano Cheles, et al. *Neo-fascism in Europe,* p. 156.

76. Author's interview with Ilse Skorzeny, June 3, 1993; author's interview with Léon Degrelle, May 23, 1993.

77. Skorzeny, *Skorzeny's Secret Missions,* p. 123; author's interview with Ilse Skorzeny.

78. Peter Thompkins quoted in *Gladio* (BBC series); Rees, *Extreme Right Since 1890,* p. 41; author's interview with Ilse Skorzeny.

79. Linklater, *The Nazi Legacy,* p. 204.

80. Richard Drake, *Revolutionary Mystique,* pp. 130–33; Philip Willan, *Puppet Masters,* p. 44; Rees, *Extreme Right Since 1890,* p. 86; Linklater, *The Nazi Legacy,* p. 205; Christie, *Stefano delle Chiaie,* p. 23. During the early 1960s, delle Chiaie's thugs were given police truncheons to break up left-wing street demonstrations. A scandal erupted when word leaked out that a secret police unit, the Rome "Special Squad," had connived with neofascists; as a result, the Special Squad was disbanded and its director was reassigned to a provincial constabulary. Ever since this disclosure, rumors of ongoing collusion with the Italian secret service continued to dog Avanguardia Nazionale. Several of delle Chiaie's former colleagues acknowledged his close relations with the Interior Ministry, giving rise to the moniker "Avanguardia Ministeria." When the Italian government belatedly initiated legal proceedings against delle Chiaie's men in the mid-1970s, the group threatened to "call to the witness stand ministers, politicians, party secretaries, secret services, and all those who, in one way or another, first sought the 'friendship' of Avanguardia Nazionale."

81. Author's interview with Stefano delle Chiaie, June 8 and 11, 1993.

82. Linklater, *The Nazi Legacy,* pp. 212–13; author's interview with Stefano delle Chiaie. The specter of anti-Semitism within Argentina's security forces has persisted over the years. Three police officials and a former detective in Buenos Aires were charged as accomplices in the 1994 bombing of a Jewish community center in the Argentine capital, which killed eighty-seven people.

83. Unclassified CIA Directorate of Intelligence report, "Right-Wing Terrorism in Europe: A Research Paper," April 1983; for more on WACL, see Scott and John Lee Anderson, *Inside the League.*

84. Linklater, *The Nazi Legacy,* pp. 266–84. According to former DEA agent Michael Levine, "The Bolivian military leaders began to export cocaine and cocaine base as though it were a legal product, without any pretense of narcotics control. At the same time there was a tremendous upswing in demand from the United States. The Bolivian dictatorship quickly became the primary source of supply for the Colombian cartels, which formed during this period.

And the cartels, in turn, became the main distributors of cocaine throughout the United States. It was truly the beginning of the cocaine explosion of the 1980s."

85. "Otto Skorzeny, Nazi Commando, Dead, Rescued Mussolini from Italian Peak," *New York Times,* July 8, 1975.

CHAPTER SIX: *A Gathering Storm*

1. The scene at Dixmude has also been described in several press accounts; see, for example, Mark J. Kurlansky, "Neo-Nazis, Fascist Groups Flock to Peace Demonstration in Belgium," *International Herald Tribune,* July 5, 1983.

2. Ray Hill, interviewed by the author and Kevin Coogan, October 15, 1986.

3. European Parliament Committee of Inquiry on Racism and Xenophobia, *Report of the Findings of the Inquiry* (1991), pp. 19–21; Ciarán Ó Maoláin, *The Radical Right,* p. 31.

4. *Searchlight,* September 1984.

5. Remer quoted in Paris, *Unhealed Wounds,* p. 183.

6. Author's interview with Otto Ernst Remer, April 16, 1992.

7. *Der Bismarck-Deutsche,* "Manifest 1983 der Deutschen Freiheitsbewegung für eine Deutsch-Russische Allianz Rapallo 1983/90."

8. "Right-Wing Extremism," U.S. Army intelligence information report, May 17, 1985; Ralph Boulton, "International News," Reuters, June 27, 1984.

9. "Activities of the Right-Wing Extremist Michael Kühnen," U.S. Army intelligence information report, August 2, 1982; author's interview with Otto Ernst Remer.

10. Michael Schmidt, *The New Reich,* p. 5; "Action Front of National Socialists/National Activists (ANS/NA)," U.S. Army intel-

ligence information report, October 28, 1983; Paul Hainsworth, ed., *Extreme Right in Europe and the USA*, p. 18; Lewis, *Right-wing Extremism*, pp. 162–63, 283.

11. "Translation of selected news items dated 11 May 1983," U.S. Army intelligence information report no. 2 212 1256-83.

12. Charles William Maynes, "Facing the Dark Side of Nationalism," *Los Angeles Times*, April 21, 1985; Eva Kolinsky, "A Future for Right Extremism in Germany?" in Hainsworth, *Extreme Right in Europe and the USA*, p. 74.

13. "Seeds of a Fourth Reich," *Daily Express*, April 21, 1978.

14. "Unconstitutional Right Extremist Organizations — Propaganda and Logos," U.S. Army intelligence information report, March 2, 1989.

15. Peter H. Merkl, ed., *Political Violence and Terror*, p. 241. Originally a spin-off from the Socialist Reich Party in the early 1950s, the Viking Youth was first led by Walter Matthei, an ex-SS captain and SRP member who later moved to Spain amid allegations that he fancied preteen boys. Upon his return to West Germany after many years abroad, Matthei emerged as one of Kühnen's elder deputies.

16. "Local Agitational Groups: Radical Right Activities," U.S. Air Force intelligence report, May 2, 1978; "West German Neo-Nazi Organizer May Be Hiding in Belgium," U.S. Army intelligence information report, August 2, 1984; Lewis, *Right-Wing Extemism*, pp. 226–27.

17. Bruce Hoffman, "Right-Wing Terrorism in Europe," Rand Corporation report prepared for the U.S. Air Force, March 1982; "Right-Wing Terrorism in Europe: A Research Paper," unclassified CIA Directorate of Intelligence report, April 1983; Lewis, *Right-Wing Extemism*, p. 171; Martin A. Lee and Kevin Coogan, "Killers on the Right," *Mother Jones*, May 1987.

18. "Nazi sympathizers at funeral of German ace," United Press International, December 22, 1982; Mike Cass, "Nazi incidents yesterday and today," *Canadian Jewish Times*, June 1983.

19. "Action Front of National Socialists/National Activists (ANS/NA)," U.S. Army intelligence information report, October 28, 1983; *Searchlight,* December 1990; Fanta Voogd, "Nazis in dienst van het koninkrijk," *Forum,* February 21, 1991.

20. John Vincour, "Foreign Workers in West Germany Live Under the Shadow of Prejudice," *New York Times,* February 22, 1982.

21. Ralph Boulton, "International News"; Peter Bruce, "Neo-Nazis Exploit Refugee Fears," *Financial Times,* July 30, 1986.

22. Christa Ritter, *Tempo,* February 1989, cited in Christopher T. Husbands, "Militant Neo-Nazism in the Federal Republic of Germany in the 1980s," in Cheles, *Neo-Fascism in Europe,* p. 118n.

23. Friedhelm Busse, the chief of the anti-Kühnen wing of the Free German Worker's Party, was a convicted felon and a longtime ultra-right-wing activist. Busse began his neo-Nazi career in the early 1950s when he joined the *Bund Deutscher Jugend,* a paramilitary youth group that composed part of the CIA's multinational "stay behind" program. Ironically, he later led a neo-Nazi organization that pegged the United States as enemy number one.

24. Maoláin, *The Radical Right,* p. 92; Bruce Hoffman, "Right-Wing Terrorism in Europe"; "Euro-Nazis: Fearsome, fanatic and few," *The Economist,* October 11, 1980.

25. Zeev Sternhell, "Fascist Ideology," in Walter Laqueur, ed., *Fascism: A Reader's Guide,* p. 344.

26. European Parliament Committee of Inquiry on Racism and Xenophobia, *Report of the Findings of the Inquiry* (1991), p. 27; author's interview with Christian Worch, June 29, 1993.

27. Author's interview with Ray Hill.

28. Author's interview with Ray Hill; Andrew Bell, *Against Racism and Fascism in Europe.* Hill's undercover adventure is described in his book, *The Other Face of Terror.*

29. *Liberation,* April 16, 1985 and July 1, 1985; *Searchlight,* December 1985; Lee and Coogan, "Killers on the Right." Shortly after Hepp was arrested in Paris, a U.S. State Department dispatch indicated that the West German neo-Nazi had "an eclectic set of ties to anti-Zionist groups, including extreme left and Palestinian terrorist organizations."

30. *Searchlight,* February 1986, August 1988, and June 1988.

31. *Searchlight,* March 1984 and July 1986.

32. Simon Frith cited in Jack B. Moore, *Shaved for Action,* pp. 35, 173; Bill Buford, *Among the Thugs,* pp. 219, 265.

33. "Translations of selected news items on right-wing extremism, 30 Sep 83 to 27 Oct 83," U.S. Army intelligence information report No. 2 212 1601-83, prepared by Elke Ogrissek; Anna Tomforde, "Neo-Nazis terrorise the terraces," *Manchester Guardian,* October 19, 1983.

34. "Echoes of Dreyfus and Vichy," *Patterns of Prejudice,* March–April 1968; Rees, *Extreme Right Since 1890,* pp. 29–30.

35. "Three Interviews with Alain de Benoist," *Telos,* winter 1993–spring 1994, p. 189.

36. Armin Mohler quoted in Tomislav Sunic, *The European New Right and the Crisis of Modern Polity* (doctoral thesis, University of California, Santa Barbara), p. 64.

37. Editions Copernic, GRECE's publishing house, printed French translations of Julius Evola's writings. Evola helped compose Italy's belated racialist laws toward the end of Fascist rule. He also wrote the preface to the Italian version of *The Protocols of the Elders of Zion.*

38. Alain de Benoist quoted in Robert Cottrell, "Paris shrugs off Mickey Mouse's cultural imperialism," *Independent,* February 12, 1991.

39. Sunic, *The European New Right,* p. 40.

40. Those who depicted Alain de Benoist as a clever cryptofascist pointed to his ongoing association with certain less-than-savory New Right emulators in Western European countries, where journals akin to *Nouvelle Ecole* and *Elements* (two GRECE publications) sprang up in the mid-1980s. Michael Walker, for example, had been a chief organizer for the British National Front in London until he launched the *Scorpion,* which ran English-language translations of de Benoist and other European New Rightists. More a dandy than a soccer hooligan, Walker complained about his former comrades in the Front. "I don't like gratuitous cruelty. . . . There's a rough element there," he admitted. Such refined sentiments, however, did not prevent Walker from safehousing Roberto Fiore, the young Italian terrorist who fled to London after the 1980 Bologna bombing. The *Scorpion* and its companion newsletter, the *Sting,* evinced an unmistakable sympathy for neo-Nazi Holocaust-deniers. By contrast, Marco Tarchi, the preeminent Italian New Rightist, has adamantly asserted the reality of the Nazi genocide. Nor was the whiff of anti-Semitism particularly obvious in the latest incarnation of Alain de Benoist, who projected an aura of tolerance as he welcomed debate with all political takers.

41. Pierre-André Taguieff, "The New Right's View of European Identity," *Telos,* winter 1993–spring 1994, p. 108.

42. "Three Interviews with Alain de Benoist," p. 173; Alain de Benoist, letter to the author, July 27, 1996.

43. Alain de Benoist, "The Idea of Empire," *Telos,* winter 1993–spring 1994, p. 97. De Benoist was hardly the only person grappling with this question. The San Francisco–based Planet Drum Foundation, for example, proposed a bioregional schema as a decentralist, ecologically oriented option preferable to outdated and dysfunctional nation-states.

44. Taguieff, "The New Right's View of European Identity," p. 124.

45. Ibid., p. 124.

46. C. C. Aronsfeld, "The German Far Right Press and the 40th Anniversary of VE Day," Institute of Jewish Affairs Research

Report, May 1985; "Three Interviews with Alain de Benoist," pp. 183–84.

47. In 1927, Mussolini ridiculed Nazi racial theories, asserting that the Germans did not constitute a homogenous race or nation at all, but were a blend of at least a half dozen different peoples.

48. William Pfaff, *Minneapolis Star Tribune,* September 8, 1992.

49. *Nation Europa,* July 1989, quoted in Roger Griffin, ed., *Fascism,* p. 364.

50. Hans-Georg Betz, "Deutschlandpolitik on the Margins: On the Evolution of Contemporary New Right Nationalism in the Federal Republic," *New German Critique,* spring/summer 1988. An ideology akin to that of GRECE emanated from the Thule Seminar, whose name derived from a quasi-Masonic lodge founded in Munich in 1917, which used the swastika as its emblem and included among its members several of Hitler's future inner circle. The latter-day incarnation of the German Thule Society was launched in 1980, when its chief, Pierre Krebs, assembled an array of "determined Europeans" who were concerned about the future of the Continent. Functioning for a while as the West German chapter of the New Right, Thule Society initiates dreamed of a cultural revival in Europe that would challenge both superpowers, of which the United States was clearly, in their eyes, the more onerous. Krebs made this point explicit in diatribes spiced with the phraseology of the French New Right. "America is a nation completely conquered by money and business. America is the home of the *homo dollaricus uniformis,*" he complained. Although it lacks "a superior spiritual principle," the United States "wants in spite of everything to be the model for the rest of the world." Ridiculing American "TV democracy," Thule partisans sought to inculcate a "personal and social identity" based on the ideas of "*volkish* pluralism" and the "doctrine of differentiation," so that Europe could avoid "being ground into the dust of a soulless uni-world," as Krebs put it. (Sunic, *The European New Right,* p. 277; "GRECE in German," *Patterns of Prejudice,* October 1981.)

51. Hans-Georg Betz, "On the German Question: Left, Right, and the Politics of National Identity," *Radical America,* 20, no. 1 (1986); *Searchlight,* November 1995. A blurring of ideological distinctions was likewise evident in groups such as *Linke Deutschland Diskussion* (Left German Discussion), which called for an "emancipation movement" to free Germany from American and Soviet hegemony. Listed among its supporters was Pierre Krebs of the Thule Seminar, who also conducted "leadership seminars" for neo-Nazi groups.

52. Tauber, *Eagle and Swastika,* pp. 122, 126, 720–21, 781–82; Betz, "Deutschlandpolitik on the Margins."

53. Betz, "On the German Question"; Andrei S. Markovits, "Coping with the Past," in Peter Baldwin, *Reworking the Past,* pp. 272, 275n; "Greens Accuse Berlin Chapter of Neo-Nazi Ties," U.S. State Department telegram, January 11, 1985. The Greens demonstrated their antipathy to Nazism once again in 1983, when it became the only political party in West German history to dismiss one of its Bundestag representatives because he had previously been a member of Hitler's NSDAP.

54. Janet Biehl, " 'Ecology' and the Modernization of Fascism in the German Ultra-right," *Society and Nature,* spring 1994; Betz, "On the German Question."

55. Biehl, " 'Ecology' and the Modernization of Fascism"; Betz, "On the German Question"; *Searchlight,* January 1992. Neo-Nazi groups in other countries were more candid about their motivations, as epitomized by this slogan of the British National Front: "Racial preservation is green!"

56. Biehl, " 'Ecology' and the Modernization of Fascism."

57. Betz, "On the German Question."

58. Betz, "Deutschlandpolitik on the Margins"; Aronsfeld, "The German Far Right Press"; author's interview with Otto Ernst Remer. Falin claims that he does not remember talking with Remer. "I attended many diplomatic functions and met with many people," he stated in a June 1993 interview with the author.

59. Jonathan Steele, "A strain on the axis that is now beginning to tell," *Guardian,* February 7, 1983; Betz, "Deutschlandpolitik on the Margins."

60. William Bole, "Bitburg: The American Scene," in Geoffrey M. Hartman, ed., *Bitburg in Moral and Political Perspective,* p. 68; see also p. xv. Despite incontrovertible evidence that Bitburg contains the graves of SS troops who had massacred civilians, prominent American conservatives defended Reagan's decision to go to Bitburg as a study in presidential courage. "Reagan did the right thing," William F. Buckley declared in a widely syndicated column.

61. John Tagliabue, "Summit in Europe: Bitburg Graves Cast a Pall; SS Veterans Feel 'Rehabilitated' by Reagan Visit," *New York Times,* May 3, 1985; James M. Markham, "As Bitburg Visit Nears, Kohl, Under Fire, Says It Will Go On," *New York Times,* April 30, 1985.

62. Timothy Garton Ash, "Germany After Bitburg," in Hartman, *Bitburg in Moral and Political Perspective,* pp. 202–03.

63. Mary Nolan, "The *Historikerstreit* and Social History," in Baldwin, *Reworking the Past,* p. 231.

64. For a detailed discussion of the Historians' Dispute see Richard J. Evans, *In Hitler's Shadow,* and Baldwin, *Reworking the Past.*

65. Nolte maintains that Germany's invasion of the Soviet Union was essentially a preventive attack undertaken in defense of Western civilization. According to this scenario, Hitler's lurch toward the East was driven by his fear of the Russian Revolution, the Gulags, and Stalin's brutal methods. Invoking racist terminology that recalled Goebbels's harangues in which Communism was depicted as the creed of slit-eyed barbarians, Nolte queries: "Did the Nazis, did Hitler only commit an 'Asiatic' deed, perhaps, because they thought that they and those like them were potential or real victims of an 'Asiatic' deed themselves?" Nazi race war was preceded by Bolshevik class war, which in some nebulous way caused Hitler to undertake the Final Solution, Nolte opines. Although he fails to account for Nazi actions such the wholesale annihilation of Gypsies, homosexuals, beggars, vagrants, and the physically and mentally handi-

capped, as well as the Jews, several mainstream press outlets have supported Nolte's theories. The way the debate played out in the West German mass media affirms the extent to which that country's political spectrum had shifted to the Right since Bitburg. Ideas previously associated with the neofascist fringe were being entertained by respected journalists. "Whether the anti-Hitler allies committed fewer crimes than Hitler is not at all certain," wrote Rudolf Augstein, publisher of *Der Spiegel.* "The one who initiated such crimes against humanity was, in any case, Stalin, in 1928." Nolte's staunchest supporters included Joachim Fest, editor-in-chief of the leading conservative newspaper. *Frankfurter Allgemeine Zeitung.*

66. Otto Dov Kulka, "Singularity and Its Relativization: Changing Views in German Historiography on National Socialism and the 'Final Solution,' " in Baldwin, *Reworking the Past,* p. 152; Evans, *In Hitler's Shadow,* p. 83; Deborah Lipstadt, *Denying the Holocaust,* p. 214. Nolte has even suggested that the 1942 Wannsee Conference, at which a group of prominent Nazis worked out plans for the Final Solution, may not have occurred — despite the fact that detailed minutes of the meeting survive and several participants have subsequently corroborated what had been discussed.

67. "The Institute for Historical Review: 'Revisionists' Who Whitewash Nazism," Institute for Jewish Affairs research report, May 1982. Several professors from around the world joined the IHR's advisory committee, including Wilhelm Staglich, a retired West German judge, and Arthur Butz, an electrical engineer from Northwestern University, who wrote *The Hoax of the Twentieth Century.*

68. In his autobiography Rudolf Hoess wrote: "I must admit that the gassing process had a calming effect upon me. I always had a horror of the shootings, thinking of the number of people, the women and children. I was relieved that we were all to be spared these blood-baths."

69. Robert Eringer, "The Force of Willis Carto," *Mother Jones,* April 1981; *Spotlight,* January 6 and 13, 1986.

70. P. Samuel Foner, "General Survives Finger Pointing," *Spotlight,* September 13, 1993; George Lardner, Jr., "Quayle Drew on Energy, Affability in Political Rise," *Washington Post,* October 2, 1988; Lipstadt, *Denying the Holocaust,* pp. 144–45.

71. See, for example, H. Keith Thompson, "Phony Photo Used to 'Prove' Hatred," *Spotlight,* June 16, 1986, and H. Keith Thompson, "Grand Admiral Karl Doenitz: Last President of a United Germany," *Journal of Historical Review,* fall 1983; letter from H. Keith Thompson to Lois Peterson, secretary, board of policy, Liberty Lobby, February 20, 1985, in the H. Keith Thompson section of the Hoover Institute Special Collections Library.

72. David Lowe, "Revisionists gather steam," *Washington Jewish Week,* February 3, 1994; letter from Bradley Smith to H. Keith Thompson, December 18, 1986, in the H. Keith Thompson section of the Hoover Institute Special Collections Library.

73. Ray Hill, *The Other Face of Terror,* p. 233; George and Wilcox, *Nazis, Communists, Klansmen and Others,* p. 262; *Searchlight,* December 1990; see also more than one hundred issues of the *David McCalden Revisionist Newsletter* that ceased publication when McCalden died in 1990.

74. See, in general, Russ Bellant, *Old Nazis, the New Right and the Republican Party;* David Lee Preston, "Fired Bush backer one of several with possible Nazi links," *Philadelphia Enquirer,* September 10, 1988. In February 1986, another GOP ethnic leader, Dr. Alexander Ronnet of the Romanian American National Congress, was a featured speaker at an IHR meeting, where he waxed effusively over the *Volk*-ish mysticism of the fascist Iron Guard.

75. Because of these disclosures, eight GOP ethnic leaders were forced to resign from the Republican Party's ethnic-outreach division in September 1988. These news accounts were based primarily on a report by Russ Bellant (see previous footnote), who cited numerous examples of fascist collaborators who were involved with the Republican Party, including Laszlo Pasztor, the founding chairman of the Republican Heritage Groups Council, who previously belonged to the Hungarian Iron Cross, a pro-Nazi group; Radi

Slavoff, the GOP Heritage Council's executive director, who had been a member of a Bulgarian fascist group; ex-Waffen SS officer Nicholas Nazarenko, who led a Cossack GOP ethnic unit; Iron Guard recruiter Floridian Galdau, who directed the GOP's outreach efforts among Romanian émigrés; Slovak GOP mover and shaker Method Balco, who organized annual memorials for the Nazi puppet regime led by Josef Tiso; Walter Melianovich, head of the GOP's Byelorussian unit, who worked closely with various fascist collaborators; and the Croatian GOP unit, which defended the Ustaše's World War II alliance with Hitler. For additional examples, see Russ Bellant, *Old Nazis, the New Right and the Republican Party.*

76. Simpson, *Blowback,* p. 216; Bellant, *Old Nazis, the New Right and the Republican Party;* David Lee Preston, "Nazi-affiliated emigres and the Republican Party," *Philadelphia Enquirer,* September 18, 1988.

77. Jeff Cohen and Norman Solomon, *Adventures in Medialand,* pp. 172–74; Jacob Weisberg, "The Heresies of Pat Buchanan," *New Republic,* October 22, 1990. By April 1987, the OSI had succeeded in bringing legal proceedings against fifty-three suspected Nazi criminals, obtaining twenty-one denaturalization orders and twelve deportation orders and actually deporting five suspects. More were in the offing.

78. Richard Bernstein, "The Roots of a Populist Who Would Be President," *New York Times,* March 24, 1996; John M. Broder, "Rabbi Campaigns for Buchanan, the 'Equal Opportunity Insulter,' " *San Francisco Chronicle,* March 24, 1996; Collette, *Public Eye,* September 1994. Christina Jeffrey, the political scientist at Kennesaw State College in Marietta, Georgia, who gave the proposed Holocaust curriculum a negative evaluation, was later appointed the official historian for the House of Representatives by Speaker Newt Gingrich. But Gingrich, who had known of Jeffrey's role in rejecting the Holocaust history program when he named her the House historian, withdrew the appointment in the wake of embarrassing press disclosures regarding her background.

79. Mermelstein's legal wrangles with the Holocaust-deniers highlighted the role of IHR attorney Mark Lane as a propagandist

for the pro-Nazi Liberty Lobby. Lane, whose main claim to fame was his criticism of the Warren Commission's investigation of the Kennedy assassination, later wrote a book suggesting that the CIA was behind JFK's death. This book, *Plausible Denial,* was heavily promoted by the conspiracy-oriented Liberty Lobby. A former leftist and a Jew, Lane returned the favor by signing a direct-mail fund-raising appeal for the Foundation to Defend the First Amendment, a Liberty Lobby front. Lane has also written several self-serving articles about the Kennedy assassination and other topics for the *Spotlight.*

80. Author's interview with H. Keith Thompson, November 10, 1993; "The World," *Los Angeles Times,* July 10, 1986; Robert Tilley, "The SS veterans who still march to Hitler's tune," *Sunday Telegraph,* November 15, 1992.

81. *Spotlight,* October 26, 1987; Otto Ernst Remer, "My Role in Berlin on July 20, 1944," *Journal of Historical Review,* spring 1988.

82. U.S. Army intelligence information report, July 15, 1988.

83. European Parliament Committee of Inquiry on Racism and Xenophobia, *Report on the Findings of the Inquiry* (1991), p. 27; author's interview with Christian Worch; *Der Spiegel,* March 27, 1989.

84. Kühnen quoted in Ferdinand Protzman, "West German Neo-Nazi Speaks of a Revival," *New York Times,* March 12, 1989.

85. "The Republikaner: Where Are They Coming From, How Far Can They Go, and What Do They Mean For German Politics?" U.S. State Department document, March 10, 1989; *Searchlight,* March 1989 and October 1989; John D. Ely, "The 'Black-Brown Hazelnut' in a Bigger Germany," in Michael G. Huelshoff et al., eds., *From Bundesrepublik to Deutschland,* p. 240.

86. "The Radical Right in Bavaria After the Elections," U.S. State Department document, April 15, 1992; Schmidt, *The New Reich,* pp. 9, 12, 225. Kühnen subsequently identified Harald Neubauer, second-in-command of the Republikaner who had been

elected on the party ticket to the European Parliament, as a member of his clandestine neo-Nazi network.

87. Gordon A. Craig, "The Rising Star of the German Right," *New York Review of Books,* June 15, 1989; Hans-Georg Betz, *Radical Right-Wing Populism in Western Europe,* pp. 134–35.

88. Betz, *Radical Right-Wing Populism,* p. 135; Schönhuber quoted in Huelshoff, *From Bundesrepublik to Deutschland,* p. 240.

89. European Parliament Committee of Inquiry on Racism and Xenophobia, *Report on the Findings of the Inquiry* (1991), p. 25; *Searchlight,* May 1989. Several members of the CDU youth group, Junge Union, had already split off to form the Berlin chapter of the Republikaner. In an effort to prevent additional defections, the Junge Union swung sharply to the Right; overtly racist literature began to circulate at chapter meetings. At the same time, leaders of the Christian Democratic Union and its Bavarian counterpart, the Christian Social Union, openly entertained the possibility of forming an alliance with the Republikaner, which viewed a coalition with Kohl's party as highly desirable.

90. European Parliament Committee of Inquiry on Racism and Xenophobia, *Report on the Findings of the Inquiry* (1991), pp. 24, 27.

91. Remer interviewed in the Swedish TV documentary by Michael Schmidt, *Wahrheit Macht Frei.*

CHAPTER SEVEN: *Germany Reunited*

1. Author's interview with Jaye Müller, April 1992; Jeff Cohen, "The Writing on the Wall," *In These Times,* February 20–26, 1985.

2. "Neo-Nazi Organizations in Federal Republic of Germany," U.S. Army intelligence information report, July 31, 1992.

3. Schmidt, *The New Reich,* pp. 67–69.

4. James Ridgeway, "Wie Deutsch Ist Es?" *Village Voice,* December 3, 1991; Hockenos, *Free to Hate,* pp. 53–54; *Searchlight,* September 1990.

5. Ingo Hasselbach, "Extremism: A Global Network," *New York Times,* April 20, 1995; Ridgeway, "Wie Deutsch Ist Es?"

6. Ridgeway, "Wie Deutsch Ist Es?"; Schmidt, *The New Reich,* p. 57; Hockenos, *Free to Hate,* pp. 78–85; "The East German Neo-Nazi Phenomenon," U.S. State Department document, December 1, 1987. This maneuver by the East German secret police was preceded by an analogous ploy in West Berlin during the mid-1980s, when Heinrich Lummer, a leading Christian Democratic politician, transferred money from his party's funds to far Right groups in order to discourage them from participating in forthcoming elections. The goal was to increase the vote for the CDU, which also recruited neo-Nazis to tear down election posters of the Social Democrats, the leading opposition party, and disrupt their meetings. (*Searchlight,* June 1986.)

7. "Skinheads in the GDR: A Thorn in the Side of Anti-Fascism," U.S. State Department document, July 27, 1988; also see generally Hans Joachim Maaz, *Behind the Wall.* Throughout the Cold War, the East German government denied its share of responsibility for the crimes of the Third Reich and refused to pay reparations to Jews and other victims of Nazi atrocities. It wasn't until April 1990 that the GDR parliament passed a resolution, one of the last in its history, expressing contrition for the Holocaust. East German officials belatedly acknowledged their "co-responsibility for the humiliation, expulsion and murder of Jewish women, men and children." Such a frank confession went considerably further than anything that had been expressed over the years by the West German government, which had evasively apologized for crimes committed "in the name of the German people," as if the Germans hadn't committed these crimes themselves.

8. Hockenos, *Free to Hate,* p. 42; Hasselbach, "Extremism: A Global Network"; "Violent Crimes Committed by Right-Wing Extremists on the Increase in GM," Department of Defense intelligence information report, June 12, 1991.

9. Hockenos, *Free to Hate,* p. 84; Schmidt, *The New Reich,* pp. 57–58; "Summary of the Berlin Press," U.S. State Department document, June 28, 1988; Christopher T. Husbands, "Neo-Nazis in East Germany: The New Danger?" *Patterns of Prejudice* 25, no. 1, 1991.

10. Günter Grass, *Two States — One Nation?,* p. 52.

11. Grass, *Two States — One Nation?,* p. 66; Hockenos, *Free to Hate,* p. 56.

12. Schmidt, *The New Reich,* pp. 64–66.

13. *Searchlight,* February 1992 and November 1993.

14. "Extreme Right Groups in the New Länder: An Introduction," U.S. State Department document, December 13, 1990; Schmidt, *The New Reich,* pp. 222–25. Lauck's broadsheet sold various neo-Nazi books, including *Imperium* by Francis Parker Yockey.

15. Author's interview with Graeme Atkinson, February 1992; *Searchlight,* April 1993; Stephen Kinzer, "A Neo-Nazi Whose Ardor Was Cooled by Killings," *New York Times,* February 2, 1994; "Danger on the Right," *Vancouver Sun,* October 26, 1991; Foreign Broadcast Information Service (Western Europe), January 17, 1992; Ridgeway, "Wie Deutsch Ist Es?"; Schmidt, *The New Reich,* p. 100.

16. *Searchlight,* September 1991; "German Neo-Nazis Volunteer for Iraqi Army, Extremist Says," Reuters, January 21, 1991; "Germany Embarrassed by Neo-Nazis Wanting to Fight for Iraq," Reuters, February 6, 1991.

17. *Searchlight,* March 1991; *Wiener,* March 1991, cited in "Right-Extremist Activities in Germany, Lower Saxony, Situation Report for February 1991," U.S. State Department document, April 8, 1991; Michael Novick, *White Lies, White Power,* p. 307.

18. See, generally, Timmerman, *The Death Lobby;* "U.N. Says a German Promoted Iraq A-Arms," *New York Times,* January 26, 1996. Participating in these efforts were a handful of German technicians who had worked on Egyptian rocket projects nearly three decades earlier.

19. David Buchan, *Financial Times,* January 13, 1989; Robert McCartney, "Bonn Says Probe Fails to Back U.S. Charges on Libyan Plant," *Washington Post,* January 6, 1989; "Gas, guns . . . and gardening," *Searchlight,* September 1992.

20. Author's interview with Douglas Jones, July 19, 1995; "Libya's Use of Foreign Labor and Foreign Material," Department of Defense intelligence information report, November 8, 1988.

21. Timmerman, *The Death Lobby,* p. 491; "German minister trained Iraqi murder squads," *Searchlight,* August 1993; "German military taught Libyan troops," Reuters, January 4, 1995; Bjorn Edlund, "Kohl connived in 'business of death,' German opposition says," Reuters, January 18, 1989; David Goodhart, "Bonn Knew of Libya Supplies," *Financial Times,* January 19, 1989; "Bonn Again Revises Line on Libyan Chemical Plant," Facts on File, January 27, 1989.

22. Author's interview with Christian Worch, June 29, 1993.

23. "Neo-Nazi chief's ashes are stolen," Agence France Presse, April 8, 1992.

24. *Searchlight,* April 1994; H. Keith Thompson, letter to the author, June 1, 1995. Although firmly rooted in the neo-Nazi fringe, Stille Hilfe developed amicable relations with conservative West German politicians, such as CDU Bundestag parliamentary leader Alfred Dregger, who praised the efforts of Stille Hilfe only two years before it honored Kühnen. A scandal erupted in January 1994, when Siegfried Vergin, a Social Democrat Bundestag deputy, demanded an inquiry after it was disclosed that Stille Hilfe had obtained tax breaks for SS veterans.

25. *Searchlight,* June 1991 and March 1992. A 1992 police search of Küssel's home in Vienna turned up several computer discs with information about his neo-Nazi contacts in neighboring Hungary. Shortly thereafter, several Hungarian neo-Nazis were arrested and sent to prison.

26. Author's interview with Christian Worch; "Neo-Nazi trial in Frankfurt/Main [Germany] on 8 April 1992," U.S. Army intelli-

gence information report, April 13, 1992; Andrew Phillips, "Skinheads, Jackboots — Hatred is also a part of the new Germany," *Maclean's,* November 23, 1992.

27. "The Far Right in Berlin and the New Länder: The 'Old Right' Parties and the 'New Right' Neo-Nazis," U.S. Army intelligence information report, December 18, 1991.

28. All quotations from Bela Ewald Althans are from the author's interview with him, April 21, 1992, unless otherwise indicated.

29. Ian Murray, "Becker love match inflames Nazi desire for master race," *The Times* (London), March 4, 1992.

30. See generally, Morris Dees and Steve Fiffer, *Hate on Trial.*

31. After he attended a Farrakhan meeting in Los Angeles in 1985, Metzger donated $100 to the Nation of Islam as "a gesture of understanding." Said Metzger, "They want their own government and their own territory and that's exactly what we want for them and for ourselves. . . . They speak out against the Jews and the oppressors in Washington." (*Searchlight,* December 1985.)

32. Robin Gedye, *Daily Telegraph,* March 2, 1992.

33. Adrian Bridge, "Irving's dangerous liaison with Germany," *Independent,* May 10, 1992; "Ein Reich, Ein Irving," *Independent on Sunday,* March 3, 1991.

34. Schmidt, *The New Reich,* pp. 107, 211–12. Former CIA agent Victor Marchetti, a featured speaker at meetings of the negationist Institute of Historical Review, was listed as *CODE*'s Middle East editor.

35. All quotations from Otto Ernst Remer are from the author's interview with him, April 16, 1992, unless otherwise indicated.

36. *Remer Depeche,* February 1991, March 1991, June 1992.

37. Author's interview with Bela Ewald Althans.

38. Author's interview with Christian Worch.

39. An April 1992 public-opinion poll indicated that only 32 percent of eastern Germans viewed democracy as the best form of government.

40. After the Berlin Wall crumbled, the Federal Republic became a magnet for several hundred thousand asylum seekers annually, but only a small percentage of refugees were granted their wish. Most were eventually repatriated, while some disappeared beyond the reach of the authorities. Manfred Ritter, a top official in the Christian Social Union, Kohl's coalition partner, likened refugees to "a plague of locusts who leave a desert in their wake." (Graeme Atkinson, "Germany: Nationalism, Nazism and Violence," in Tore Bjorgo and Rob Witte, eds., *Racist Violence in Europe,* p. 160.)

41. Author's interview with Douglas H. Jones.

42. Author's interview with Graeme Atkinson.

43. Searchlight, *Reunited Germany: The New Danger,* p. 5.

44. Verfassungsschutz figures cited in Bjorgo and Witte, *Racist Violence in Europe,* p. 4.

45. *Searchlight,* April 1993; Atkinson, "Germany: Nationalism, Nazism and Violence," p. 157.

46. "Federal Republic of Germany — Failed by the System: Police Ill-Treatment of Foreigners," Amnesty International, May 1995; " 'Foreigners Out' — Xenophobia and Right-wing Violence in Germany," Helsinki Watch, October 1992.

47. *Searchlight,* October 1994.

48. Stephen Kinzer, "German Judge Frees 3 in an Attack on Foreigners," *New York Times,* March 1, 1992; Reuters, October 2, 1992; *Searchlight,* October 1991 and May 1993; Agence France Presse, September 14, 1992.

49. Stephen Kinzer, "Germany's Justice System Said to Favor Rightists," *New York Times,* November 7, 1993.

50. "The West German legal system always regarded the foundations on which sentences were based during the Third Reich as 'valid

law at the time,' " wrote Ingo Müller, who points out that racial laws enacted under Hitler were never declared null and void. This was underscored in 1985 by the West German parliament, which opted not to overturn a single judicial decision of the Nazi era. This was in keeping with a series of official decisions that favored ex-Nazi judges. Dr. Hans Puvogel, author of a Third Reich dissertation that argues for the "removal of inferior beings through killing," was appointed minister of justice in Lower Saxony in 1976. When another judge publicly criticized this appointment, disciplinary proceedings were initiated against the objecting judge rather than against Puvogel. In 1978, Baden-Württemberg premier Hans-Karl Filbinger was exposed as having been a murderous judge in Hitler's navy, but Helmut Kohl, then chairman of the CDU, remained his staunch defender. The right-wing bias of the German justice system reared its head after the Cold War when Otto Jürgens, a retired, eighty-eight-year-old East German judge, was charged with "perverting justice" for allegedly meting out excessive punishment to Nazi war criminals; yet an SS guard at the Ravensbrück concentration camp received financial compensation for time she had spent in a GDR jail for her wartime crimes. The leniency the courts displayed toward Nazi murderers contrasted sharply with the life sentence given to sixty-eight-year-old Gerhard Bögelein in 1992 for killing Erich Kallmerten, a Nazi military judge in a Soviet POW camp forty-five years earlier. While he sat on the bench during the Third Reich, Kallmerten had sent at least 175 antifascists to the gallows. (Ingo Müller, *Hitler's Justice,* pp. 213–14, 288–89, 297; Merhav, "Honouring Evil," in Hartman, *Bitburg in Moral and Political Perspective,* p. 197.)

51. *Searchlight,* December 1991 and March 1992; Peter H. Merkl, "A New Lease on Life for the Radical Right?" in Merkl and Weinberg, *Encounters with the Radical Right,* p. 210.

52. Igal Avidan, "African candidate seeks to make history," Interpress, October 13, 1994; Martin A. Lee, "Germany Moves to the Right," *Christian Science Monitor,* October 1, 1992; Marc Fisher, "Britain Moves to Grant African Asylum from Germany," *International Herald Tribune,* March 5, 1992; Marc Fisher, *After the Wall,* p. 213.

53. Cited in Fisher, *After the Wall,* p. 217. *Der Spiegel* publisher Rudolf Augstein made an astonishing statement in his magazine on July 2, 1990: "Prussia-Germany was no more anti-Semitic than France or Poland, even during the years 1933 to 1945." What's more, his assertion did not elicit a single rebuke from officials in Bonn — a sure sign that the politics of denial had become eminently mainstream.

54. *Searchlight,* February, 1991; Fisher, *After the Wall,* p. 217; *Germany Alert,* October 18, 1993.

55. John Tagliabue, "Waldheim Is Given Welcome by Kohl," *New York Times,* March 28, 1992.

56. Fisher, *After the Wall,* p. 97; Lee, "Germany Moves to the Right"; John D. Ely, "The 'Black-Brown Hazelnut' in a Bigger Germany," in Huelshoff, *From Bundesrepublik to Deutschland,* p. 246.

57. Elizabeth Neuffer, "Neo-Nazis spreading hate with high-tech," *Boston Globe,* June 12, 1994.

58. Author's interview with Bela Ewald Althans, September 1992; Agence France Presse, August 25, 1992; Schmidt, *The New Reich,* p. 164.

59. Leon Mangasarian, "Pols trade accusations after right-wing violence," UPI, August 25, 1992.

60. Anna Tomforde, "Neo-Nazis on the attack," *Manchester Weekly Guardian,* August 30, 1992; "The Meaning of Rostock," *Searchlight,* October 1992; Volker Warkentin, "Neo-Nazi trend endangers democracy says SPD leader," Reuters, August 26, 1992.

61. Stephen Kinzer, "A Mayor in Germany Acts to Prevent Attacks on Foreigners in Eastern City," *New York Times,* September 6, 1992; Steve Vogel, "Germany's Rightist Violence Sparks Concerns," *Washington Post,* September 5, 1992; *Searchlight,* December 1992.

62. See, for example, " 'Foreigners Out' — Xenophobia and Right-wing Violence in Germany," Helsinki Watch, October 1992. The Nazis murdered half a million Gypsies during the Third Reich,

but a West German court ruled that those who survived had no legal claim to reparations.

63. Hockenos, *Free to Hate,* p. 30; *Stern,* September 3, 1992.

64. "Another night of racist violence in Germany," Reuters, September 4, 1992; *Searchlight,* December 1992 and January 1993. The official tally did not reflect that many racist attacks went unreported by refugees who feared police reprisals, and some blatantly racist attacks were not specifically recorded as such by the German authorities.

65. George Boehmer, "Official Predicts Rise in Rightist Violence," Associated Press, September 12, 1992; Marc Fisher, "Bonn Parties Move to Stem Refugee Tide," *Washington Post,* October 16, 1992; *Searchlight,* December 1992.

66. Adam Lebor, "Anti-fascist veterans fight resurgent enemy," *The Times* (of London), September 14, 1992; Jewish Telegraph Agency, November 24, 1992.

67. *Searchlight,* October 1992; Schmidt, *The New Reich,* p. 148.

68. Author's interview with Christian Worch. The removal of asylum seekers from Rostock and other cities "cannot be judged favorably enough for the militant extreme rightists," a U.S. Army intelligence report concluded. "The fanatics are overjoyed that their violent actions did something. They accomplished their goal. The foreigners were gone. That inspired similar actions." ("German Right-Extremism in Respect to the Riots in Rostock and other German Cities," U.S. Army intelligence information report, November 23, 1992.)

69. *Searchlight,* October 1992.

70. Atkinson, "Germany: Nationalism, Nazism and Violence," pp. 162–63; Nomi Morris, "Refugees: Stasi East German Link to Rostock Attacks, Says Paper," InterPress Service, September 3, 1992; Victoria J. Barnett, "Fear of Foreigners Haunts German Politics," *Christian Century,* June 3–10, 1992.

71. "Right-Wing Extremist Violence: A Threat to the U.S. Army?" U.S. Army intelligence and threat analysis brief, September 1992. Nine months before this report was issued, an American GI was badly beaten by skinheads outside a disco in Augsburg.

72. Anna Tomforde, "Bonn line on race violence attacked," *Guardian,* October 15, 1991; *Searchlight,* January 1992 and April 1993; Nancy Nusser, "Neo-Nazis or just hoodlums?" *Atlanta Journal and Constitution,* September 4, 1992; George Boehmer, "Official Warned Months Ago of Tensions Against Refugees," Associated Press, September 2, 1992; Stephen Kinzer, "In Retreat, Europe's Neo-Nazis May Be More Perilous," *New York Times,* December 12, 1993. In October 1992, a U.S. State Department analyst noted that the regional Office for the Protection of the Constitution in Bavaria had issued a quarterly report that "warned of the dangers of left extremism . . . but was silent on the subject of violence against asylum-seekers and foreigners."

73. *Der Spiegel,* January 15, 1990; *Searchlight,* May 1994. Right-wing politicians and journalists used smear tactics to undermine the PDS, whose local offices had been firebombed by neo-Nazis and raided on several occasions by German law-enforcement units. They hounded PDS chairman Gregor Gysi, an eastern German human rights attorney with the gift of gab. Gysi was also one of the few politicians of Jewish descent in Germany, and an undertone of anti-Semitism lurked behind the slander campaign. *Der Spiegel* described him as a "hooknosed operator," a "wire-puller," and a Stasi agent. Embroidered and repeated endlessly in the press, Gysi's Stasi affiliations were never proved.

74. Stephen Kinzer, "Germans Hold Suspect in Firebombing That Killed 3 Turks," *New York Times,* November 27, 1992.

75. "Germany Turns Attention to Threat from Leftists," *International Herald Tribune,* February 17, 1993; *Searchlight,* January 1995. In September 1993, Alexander von Stahl was fired from his post as Germany's chief prosecutor in the wake of allegations that he covered up the point-blank-range execution of a captured Red Army Faction member by a government antiterrorism squad.

76. Author's interview with Christian Worch; see also "Counter-intelligence Daily Summary CIDS 202-92/ Counterintelligence Assessment . . . ," U.S. Army document, December 11, 1992: "The move by the German government against the . . . neo-Nazi groups is long overdue even though the banning of one neo-Nazi group usually results in the formation of a newly named group."

77. Ingo Hasselbach, *Fuehrer-Ex.*

78. Stephen Kinzer, "Rights Groups Attack German Plan on Refugees," *New York Times,* February 7, 1993.

79. Author's interview with Christian Worch; *Searchlight,* February 1993.

CHAPTER EIGHT: *Shadow Over the East*

1. Kirsten Galagher, "German Again Put King to Rest," *Orlando Sentinel Tribune,* August 17, 1991.

2. Author's interview with Douglas H. Jones, July 19, 1995.

3. Marc Fisher, *After the Wall,* p. 283.

4. Rick Atkinson, "Court Rules German Constitution Allows Sending Troops Abroad," *Washington Post,* July 14, 1994; "Reunited Germany: The New Danger," *Searchlight,* p. 31.

5. Thalif Deen, "U.S. and Germany Top U.N. Arms Register," Interpress, October 25, 1994; W. R. Smyzer, *Germany and America,* p. 102; Ramesh Jaura, "Bonn said to be keeping nuclear option open," *Interpress Service,* April 14, 1995; "Germans Reject Demand to Alter Nuclear Plant," *New York Times,* January 21, 1996; Augstein cited in Schmidt, *The New Reich,* p. 142. A Pentagon official cited in a *New York Times* editorial (March 10, 1992) stated: "We must seek to prevent the emergence of European-only security arrangements which would undermine NATO."

6. *Reunited Germany: The New Danger,* pp. 18, 25.

7. "German Media Reaction Report," U.S. State Department document, April 6, 1992; *Europäische Sicherheit,* February 1992, cited in *Reunited Germany: The New Danger,* p. 22.

8. *Searchlight,* May 1994.

9. *Reunited Germany: The New Danger,* pp. 15–16; *Searchlight,* December 1993.

10. Francine S. Kiefer, "German Violence Puts Heat on Police," *Christian Science Monitor; Searchlight,* December 1992 and April 1994.

11. Ian Traynor, "Nazi spectre haunts 'citizen army'," *The Independent* (London), December 17, 1997; "Would-be officers make a right turn," *The Times* (London), October 30, 1997; Roger Boyles, "Germany budgetary cuts sap army's morale and supplies," *The Times,* March 12, 1997; Martin A. Lee, "Germany Goosesteps to the Right," *Moment,* June 1998.

12. Matthias Küntzel, *Konkret,* cited in *Searchlight,* December 1993; Ingo Mueller, *Hitler's Justice,* p. 70.

13. For an analysis of the post–Cold War rehabilitation of the Conservative Revolution, see Elliot Neaman, "Fascism and postmodernism," *Tikkun,* November 1993.

14. For example, Alfred Schickel, a regular contributor to *Junge Freiheit,* has written for the Bundeswehr's *Periodical for Inner Leadership.*

15. Robin Gedye, "Student societies raise spectre of Right-wing revivial," *Daily Telegraph,* October 15, 1992; Graham Lees, "Right-wing students rattle German sabre," *The Times* (London), October 18, 1992; Roger Boyles, "Fascist thrust scars student duelling clubs," *The Times* (London), January 16, 1996.

16. *Searchlight,* August 1989. As late as the summer of 1994, some *Junge Freiheit* editors traveled to Dixmuide, Belgium, to participate in the annual neofascist festival.

17. Author's interview with Herbert Schnoor, January 23, 1996; "Schnoor warnt vor 'Neuer Rechten' und 'Feierabend-Terroristen'," Deutsche Press Agentur, April 4, 1995.

18. Associated Press, September 9, 1994.

19. *Reunited Germany: The New Danger,* p. 40.

20. *Frankfurter Rundschau,* April 19, 1994, cited in *Reunited Germany: The New Danger,* p. 58; Schmidt, *The New Reich,* p. 136. Revanchist sentiment is widespread in reunified Germany. A 1991 survey by the *Los Angeles Times* (September 17, 1991) disclosed that 39 percent of Germans — 43 percent of western Germans and 25 percent of eastern Germans — believed that parts of neighboring countries rightly belonged to Germany.

21. Martin A. Lee, "Germany Moves to the Right," *Christian Science Monitor,* October 1, 1992; *Searchlight,* July 1993. In 1992 alone, *Vertriebenen* organizations received an estimated 1.8 billion deutsche marks ($1.2 billion) from the federal government to pursue various projects, including the formation of special schools and "cultural centers" in European countries with large German minority communities. German government documents described Silesia, Pomerania, East Prussia, and other lost provinces as "at the moment under foreign administration."

22. "The Fourth Reich," *Argonaut* (new series no. 2), p. 79; *Searchlight,* September 1989; *Reunited Germany: The New Danger,* p. 39. Typical in this regard were the ruminations of the officially sponsored League of Middle Germans, which asserted in its state-financed newspaper that Hitler's invasion of Russia "was a preemptive strike to prevent a surprise attack by the Soviet Union."

23. Author's interview with Douglas H. Jones, July 31, 1995; Grass, *Two States — One Nation?,* p. 33; Schmidt, *The New Reich,* p. 127; Konrad Jarausch, *Rush to German Unity,* p. 29. More than fifty years after the end of World War II, German officials were still stroking various *Vertriebenen* groups. In June 1996, for example, Chancellor Helmut Kohl addressed a meeting of the Deutschland Stiftung (Germany Foundation), even though it had been branded by the state court in Munich as an organization "which works together with right-wing extremists and which in its journal, *Deutschland Magazin,* promotes anti-liberal, anti-democratic, historical revisionist and xenophobic positions."

24. *Searchlight,* July 1993 and September 1994; *Reunited Germany: The New Danger,* pp. 46–49.

25. Del Boca and Giovana, *Fascism Today,* p. 458n; *Reunited Germany: The New Danger,* pp. 41, 45–46.

26. France S. Kiefer, "German Presence in Czechoslovakia Sparks Concern over Dominance," *Christian Science Monitor,* February 26, 1992; James L. Greenfield, "Here Come the Westerners," *New York Times,* September 7, 1993; Roger Boyles, "Sudeten Germans threaten Kohl over pact with Prague," *The Times* (London), December 5, 1996. Bonn and Prague eventually signed a pact on wartime abuses wherein Germany apologized for Hitler's invasion and the Czech government expressed regret for the postwar expulsion of the Sudeten Germans. This pact angered Sudeten German expellees, who continue to demand compensation for lost property.

27. Schmidt, *The New Reich,* pp. 191–92; *Reunited Germany: The New Danger,* p. 42; author's interview with Bela Ewald Althans.

28. Anne Olson, "Walesa criticizes German minority activities," Interpress Service, December 10, 1992.

29. *Reunited Germany: The New Danger,* p. 42; *Zycie Warszawy* cited in *Germany Alert,* February 3, 1992.

30. *Reunited Germany: The New Danger,* pp. 37–39. Professor Michael Sturmer, a prominent German historian and an advisor to Chancellor Kohl, spoke for many of his colleagues in Bonn when he suggested that Russia should relinquish control of "Königsberg."

31. The VDA had a long and checkered history of pan-German activity. Under Hitler, it functioned as an arm of the German Foreign Office. This Nazi front was outlawed by Allied authorities after the war, but Bonn permitted Third Reich veterans to resurrect the VDA in 1955. Since then, it enjoyed close relations with right-wing extremists and German government officials. The VDA had a broader mandate than other expellee organizations, serving as an intermediary between Bonn and German minority communities wherever they existed, not just in the "lost territories."

32. Stephen Kinzer, "Fretful Latvians Turn to German with a Racist Past," *New York Times,* October 17, 1995.

33. John Goetz, "Something Nazi Stirs," *Guardian* (London), February 12, 1993; Edward Barnes, "Soon They Will Come for Us," *Life,* December 1992; *Searchlight,* May 1993.

34. Graeme Atkinson, "Germany: Nationalism, Nazism and Violence," in Bjorgo and Witte, *Racist Violence in Europe,* p. 92.

35. See, for example, *New Order,* January–February 1993; *Searchlight,* September 1992.

36. *Jane's Defense Weekly* cited in *Reunited Germany: The New Danger,* p. 27; Anna Tomforde, "Germany: Government Officials Deny Croatia Is Using Their Tanks," *Guardian* (London), August 5, 1992; Christopher Bellamy, "Croatia Built Web of Contacts to Evade Weapons Embargo," *Independent,* October 10, 1992; Stephen Kinzer, "Croatia Reportedly Buying MIG's, Defying U.N.," *New York Times,* September 23, 1993; Carlos Bendana, "Experts warn of Germany's growing militarisation," Interpress Service, April 7, 1994.

37. "Bonn denies military influences policy," UPI, December 15, 1994; *Reunited Germany: The New Danger,* p. 27.

38. Misha Glenny, "And the Winner Is . . . Croatia," *New York Times,* September 26, 1995.

39. "Croatia's President Rejects 'Six Million' Story," *Journal of Historical Review,* July–August 1995. Tudjman subsequently apologized to an American Jewish organization for the views expressed in his book.

40. Slavenka Drakulic, "Nazis Among Us," *New York Review of Books,* May 27, 1993; "Violent passions stirred by a long-dead turbulent priest," *Independent on Sunday* (London), February 9, 1992; Stephen Kinzer, "Pro-Nazi Legacy Lingers for Croatia," *New York Times,* October 31, 1993.

41. Radu Ioanid, "Treatment of the Holocaust in Romania," in Randolph L. Braham, ed., *Anti-Semitism and the Treatment of the Holocaust in Postcommunist Eastern Europe,* p. 168.

42. Radio Free Europe/Radio Liberty Daily Report, September 23, 1992; John Goetz, "Wiedergaenger in Transsivanien," *Konkret,* November 1995.

43. *Reunited Germany: The New Danger,* pp. 41, 45–46; Fred Hahn, "Treatment of the Holocaust in the Czech Republic," in Braham, *Anti-Semitism and the Treatment of the Holocaust,* p. 71; Jewish Telegraph Agency, March 17, 1992.

44. Michael Ignatieff, *Blood and Belonging,* p. 34; Barbara Crossette, "U.N. Study Finds a Free Eastern Europe Poorer and Less Healthy," *New York Times,* October 7, 1994.

45. *Antisemitism World Report 1994,* pp. xxiii. In July 1995, for example, thirty skinheads set a Gypsy youth on fire in a village near the Slovakian capital of Bratislava. This murder by immolation provoked a perfunctory expression of regret by Slovakian president Vladimir Meciar, who had previously referred to Gypsies as "social and mentally ill citizens."

46. In 1980, for example, "National Communists" within the Polish government coalesced around the Patriotic Grunwald Association, which utilized anti-Semitism to weaken the Solidarity trade-union movement led by Lech Walesa. Ironically, Walesa also invoked anti-Jewish stereotypes while campaigning for the Polish presidency a decade later.

47. *Moskovsky Komsomolets,* cited in *Soviet Press Digest,* July 7, 1994.

48. L. Dymerskaya-Tsigelman, "L. Korneev as a Phenomenon of Soviet Anti-Semitism in the 1970s–1980s," *Jews and Jewish Topics,* June 1986.

49. "The rise of the new right," *Economist,* January 28, 1995.

50. Kevin Coogan, "Russia for the 'Russians'?" *Guardian,* June 13, 1990; "The rise of the new right," *Economist,* January 28, 1995.

51. "Glasnost and the Jews," U.S. State Department telegram, January 28, 1990; Vladimir Nosenko, "Antisemitism in the Soviet Union: The Years of Perestroika," in *The Danger of Antisemitism in Central and Eastern Europe in the Wake of 1989–1990,* p. 91; "The Protocols of Pamyat," *Hadassah Magazine,* February 1991; "Where the flag of racism flies free," *Manchester Guardian Weekly,* August 9, 1992; *Searchlight,* December 1990. Arab embassies in Moscow provided additional support to Pamyat, which distributed Qaddafi's *Green Book* and carried on endlessly about "Tel Avivision" and Jewish control of the Soviet news media.

52. Radio Free Europe/Radio Liberty Daily Report, January 4, 1994; Yelena Lebedeva, "Russia Outlaws Extremist Associations," *Moscow News,* June 2, 1995; "Is a Mystical, Patriotic Russia in the Offing?" *Argumenty i fakti,* no. 16, April 1994, p. 3, cited in *Current Digest of the Soviet Press,* May 25, 1994.

53. A. Zhukov, L. Terentyeva, A. Milkus, " 'Czar Wolves' Come to The Call of Blood," *Komsomolskaya Pravda,* Russian Press Digest, February 26, 1993; Walter Ruby, "New extremist, antisemitic group said to threaten Soviet reforms," *Jerusalem Post,* December 1, 1991.

54. Pyotr Yudin, "Extremist Group Conducts Military Training," *Moscow Times,* December 30, 1994. Judging from the contents of *Voenno-istorichesky zhurnal,* the monthly history journal published by the Red Army, it would appear that Barkashov was not exaggerating when he said that he enjoyed the backing of key figures in the military. In 1990, this journal ran excerpts from Hitler's *Mein Kampf* without any negative commentary and announced plans to serialize *The Protocols of the Elders of Zion.* The editors said they found the essence of *The Protocols* — the idea of a Jewish world conspiracy — to be valid, even though it was a well-known forgery concocted a century earlier by elements of the czar's secret police.

55. Ruby, "New extremist, antisemitic group said to threaten Soviet Reforms."

56. Howard Witt, "Russia extremists feed on nation's pain," *Chicago Tribune,* October 11, 1992.

57. The anti-Western perspective was epitomized by Igor Shafarevitch's book, *Russophobia,* which became the bible for much of the political opposition in post-Soviet Russia. A famous Russian mathematician who had been an anti-Communist dissident during the Cold War, Shafarevitch argued that the Jews were at the forefront of the Western drive to belittle and destroy Mother Russia. The Jews, in his view, had brought Communism to Russia and were responsible for its litany of failures. Published in 1989, *Russophobia* was praised in the *Spotlight,* the weekly newspaper of the Liberty Lobby (see, for example, *Spotlight,* February 6, 1995). Shafarevitch's book was also excerpted in the *Barnes Review,* the negationist successor to the *Journal for Historical Review.*

58. Author's interview with Christian Worch, June 29, 1993.

59. "The Ugly Face of Freedom," *60 Minutes* (CBS) October 23, 1994; Institute of Jewish Affairs, *Antisemitism World Report 1994,* pp. 153–55; *Searchlight,* October 1993 and March 1994.

60. Author's interview with Ernst Zündel, November 5, 1995. In Toronto, Zündel ran the Samisdat Publishing Company, one of the world's largest suppliers of anti-Semitic propaganda. An ardent admirer of Francis Parker Yockey, Zündel devoured *Imperium* after Liberty Lobby founder Willis Carto had sent him a copy in 1961. "I loved it!" Zündel exclaimed. "Much of my thinking was shaped by Yockey's concepts. For me, it's repeat reading. I consider Yockey a Post–National Socialist thinker who took the vision much further. I consider him a refiner and improver of National Socialism." Zündel kept a fake concentration camp uniform that he wore in court when charged with distributing Holocaust-denial tracts. Although he was convicted of fomenting racial hatred, his sentence was later overturned, whereupon Zündel resumed sending negationist material to European countries where it was banned.

61. Ernst Zündel, "My Impressions of the New Russia," *Journal of Historical Review,* September/October 1995; author's interview with Ernst Zündel.

62. Stephen Handelman, *Comrade Criminal,* p. 297; Radio Free Europe/Radio Liberty Daily Report, August 3, 1994. When asked about his role in this project, Barkashov remarked, "Apart from the KGB Fifth Directorate, I was one of the founders of the RNA." It was a curious comment, given that the RNA was launched in April 1992, several months after the KGB and its notorious "Fifth Directorate" (the unit responsible for persecuting dissidents) had been abolished. General Stergilov, for his part, insisted that his essential political concerns had not changed, even though he was no longer a Communist.

63. Unless otherwise indicated, all quotations from Eduard Limonov are from the author's interview with him, July 11, 1993; Vanora Bennett, "Russia's leather-clad bad lad is at war," Reuters, September 5, 1994.

64. Dusan Stojanovic, "The Russians Are Coming — Or Are they Already Here?" Associated Press, January 13, 1993; author's interview with Eduard Limonov.

65. Author's interview with Eduard Limonov; "Emigre writer Eduard Limonov on life and politics," *Moscow News,* November 4, 1992.

66. Author's interview with Eduard Limonov; Helen Womack, "Eddie's right-wing chapter shocks Russian readers," *Independent,* January 24, 1993.

67. Author's interview with Eduard Limonov; Lucy Jones, "Peaceful Patriotic Day Demonstration," *Moscow News,* May 12, 1993.

68. A patriotic leitmotiv emerged in statements by prominent Bolsheviks such as Leon Trotsky, who described the October Revolution as "profoundly national," and Lenin, who praised "Russia's national awakening" in 1917. Nationalist buttons were pushed once again when Poland attacked Russia in 1920, and Lenin called upon

the Red Army to defend "the socialist fatherland" against foreign invaders. (Agursky, *The Third Rome,* p. 209; Roman Szporluk, *Communism and Nationalism,* p. 229; Frederick C. Barghoorn, "Russian Nationalism and Soviet Politics: Official and Unofficial Perspectives," in Robert Conquest, ed., *The Last Empire,* p. 35.)

69. Lenin implicitly acknowledged this when he stated: "In Germany, too, we have seen a similar unnatural bloc between the Black Hundreds and the Bolsheviks. There has appeared a strange type of Black-Hundred revolutionary." (Agursky, *The Third Rome,* pp. 155, 195–96; see also Darrell P. Hammer, "Russian Nationalism and Soviet Politics," in Joseph L. Nogee, ed., *Soviet Politics,* pp. 128–29, 138.)

70. As Mikhail Agursky has noted: "Many nationalist movements have been led by people who did not belong to the national group they identified with. For example, the leader of Romanian fascism was a half-Pole, Corneliu Codreanu, and the leader of Hungarian fascists was an Armenian, Ferenz Szalasi. Assimilated aliens often identify themselves with local nationalism in their search for some universalism that will make up for their minority status." (Agursky, *The Third Rome,* p. 211.)

71. Klaus Mehnert cited by Barghoorn in "Russian Nationalism and Soviet Politics," p. 35.

72. Alexander Yanov, *Russian New Right,* pp. xii, 48; Barghoorn in *The Last Empire,* pp. 40–42; M. Kaganskaya, "*The Book of Vles:* The Saga of a Forgery," *Jews and Jewish Topics,* winter 1986–87.

73. State Department analysts agreed with Limonov on this point. "In the current political climate," a March 1992 State Department report noted, "political markers such as 'left' and 'center' have little meaning — hard-line communist groups, for example, are currently referred to as 'extreme right' and 'extreme left' with roughly equal frequency." ("A Roadmap to Major Russian Political Parties and Reform Movements," U.S. State Department confidential report, March 18, 1992.)

74. Shortly after he returned from Russia, Alain de Benoist spoke at a conference in Paris sponsored by the Institute of Marxist Research, an affiliate of the French Communist Party. During this period, he was editing a new periodical, *Krisis,* which featured nonconformist intellectuals irrespective of their leftist or rightist bent. The prolific New Right gadfly wrote for a wide range of publications, including an ultra-left-wing monthly called *L'Idiot International.* This quirky Parisian journal also showcased a regular column by Eduard Limonov, who was a member of its editorial board. *L'Idiot International* was founded by Jean-Paul Sartre and Jean-Edern Hallier in the aftermath of the 1968 student-worker uprising in France. It died in 1973 but was revived by Hallier, a self-indulgent left-wing dandy, in the late 1980s. "I'm a historic leader of the Left, yet the Right, too, finds me fascinating," said Hallier, who opened the pages of his journal to an eclectic assortment of contributors, including Woody Allen and Jacques Verges. Verges, a flamboyant ultra-left-wing attorney, defended former Gestapo captain Klaus Barbie when he stood trial in 1987 for crimes against humanity. As for Limonov and the Red-Brown alliance in Russia, Hallier would only say, "We publish him because he's a good writer."

75. Author's interview with Eduard Limonov; author's interview with Luc Michel, June 20, 1993.

76. *In Memoriam JEAN THIRIART* (Bruxelles: Edition Machiavel, 1993), pp. 8–10, 99–106.

77. Author's interview with Eduard Limonov; author's interview with Marco Battara, October 17, 1992; Zyuganov quoted in *Spotlight,* May 20, 1996.

78. Author's interview with Luc Michel; author's interview with Eduard Limonov; *Elementy,* August 1992.

79. *Dyen,* no. 18, p. 5. cited in *Russian Press Digest,* May 1, 1992; Andrei Ostalsky, "Back to the bad old days of going West," *Sunday Telegraph* (London), September 26, 1993; Daniel Snieder, "Confronting the Resurgence of Anti-Semitism," *Christian Science Monitor,* April 1, 1992.

80. Helen Womack, "Russia: Hardline Communists take road to fascism," *Independent* (London), December 1, 1992. Prokhanov was also a close advisor to Gennadi Zyuganov, chairman of the Communist Party of the Russian Federation. Prokhanov's intimate ties to the Russian military earned him the nickname "the Nightingale of the General Staff."

81. *Dyen,* August 23–29, 1992. Another publication closely associated with the NSF was *Sovetskaya Rossiya* (formerly the newspaper of the Red Army), which ran a front-page photo purporting to show Boris Yeltsin in Masonic regalia.

82. European Liberation Front components included the Parti Communautaire National-Européen (PCN) in Belgium; Nouvelle Resistance in France; and the Orion group in Italy. Each of these small "national revolutionary" parties bore the imprint of Thiriart's political cosmology, which advocated an alliance of political extremes. Luc Michel, Thiriart's personal secretary since the early 1980s and the director of the PCN, made overtures to imprisoned members of Direct Action, the ultra-left-wing terrorist cadre in France. Nouvelle Resistance also developed contacts with Direct Action. Led by Christian Bouchet and Michel Schneider, Nouvelle Resistance published a propaganda organ called *Lutte de Peuple (Struggle of the People),* which advertised T-shirts with effigies of the group's heroes, including Nietzsche, Mishima, National Bolshevik ideologue Ernst Niekisch, and Che Guevara. *Lutte de Peuple*'s correspondent in Russia was Aleksandr Dugin. *Lutte de Peuple* is the French translation of "Lotta di Popolo," the name of a Thiriart-inspired organization that sprang up in Italy in the early 1970s. Lotta di Popolo was cofounded by Thiriart's leading Italian disciple, Claudio Mutti, who visited Russia twice in the early 1990s. The contacts Mutti made with Dugin during his initial visit paved the way for Thiriart's trip to Russia in August 1992. A convert to Islam, Mutti published Italian books on a variety of subjects, including the Conservative Revolution, Indo-European shamanism, Russian nationalism, and the Romanian Iron Guard, along with a book of quotations by the Ayatollah Khomeini and several Holocaust-denial tracts. ("The submission of Europe is based on the culpability of Germany," Mutti explained. "If revisionism can demonstrate that

Germany is no more culpable than other nations that waged World War II, then the basis for the subjugation of Europe is demolished.") Since the end of the Cold War, Mutti has worked closely with Marco Battara, a neofascist-turned–National Communist who accompanied Thiriart on his Russian expedition. Battara edited a Milan-based journal, *Orion,* which ran glowing tributes to Stalin and the Red-Brown opposition in Russia. *Orion* also endorsed candidates of the Communist Refoundation (CR), a radical left-wing group that split off from the Italian Communist Party after the latter changed into the Democratic Party of the Left. "They were the only candidates who seriously opposed U.S. imperialism," explained Battara. "We have the same position as the Communist Refoundation on many issues, including the defense of Cuba. . . . Some of them want to have a dialogue with us, but others are unwilling to overlook our prior fascist associations." *Orion* (April 1992) defended Cuban premier Fidel Castro for holding out against the U.S.-dominated New World Order.

83. Luc Michel, letter to the author, November 16, 1993.

84. Lee Hockstader, "How Zhirinovsky Rose," *Washington Post,* December 18, 1993; Radio Free Europe/Radio Liberty Daily Report, April 5, 1994.

85. Vladimir Solovyov and Elena Klepikova, *Zhirinovsky,* p. 161.

86. *Time,* December 27, 1993, cited in Graham Frazer and George Lancelle, *Absolute Zhirinovsky,* p. 138. Zhirinovsky's gift for rabble-rousing first came to the attention of his countrymen when he placed third in Russia's 1991 presidential elections, with 7.8 percent of the vote. But his outrageous campaign style — replete with bigotry, bullying, and ridiculous pledges ("The whole nation will feel orgasm next year!") — seemed like a parody of politics, and most people did not take him seriously in the early going.

87. James P. Gallagher, "He Says He Wants a Revolution," *Chicago Tribune,* July 4, 1994; author's interview with Eduard Limonov.

88. Author's interview with Eduard Limonov; Solovyov and Klepikova, *Zhirinovsky,* p. 100; *Economist,* January 28, 1995.

89. Solovyov and Klepikova, *Zhirinovsky,* pp. 120–21; "Russia-Iraq: Liberal Democratic Party Support," Defense Intelligence Agency Commonwealth Report, January 24, 1993; Vladimir Kartsev, *!Zhirinovsky!,* p. 157–58; *La Stampa,* December 12, 1993, cited in Frazer and Lancelle, *Absolute Zhirinovsky,* p. 81.

90. "Uproar Over Zhirinovsky in Germany," *San Francisco Chronicle,* December 24, 1993; Angeline Oyog, "Activists Call for Zhirinovsky's Expulsion," Interpress Service, April 12, 1994; Michael Specter, "Here Comes the Clown," *New York Times,* November 6, 1994.

91. Author's interview with Ernst Zündel.

92. "Zhirinovsky Meets German Soul Mate at Munich Airport," U.S. State Department document, December 22, 1993; James Meek, "Zhirinovsky Finds an Ally in Germany," *Guardian,* August 9, 1994; "Zhirinovsky's party and German People's Union sign friendship accord," BBC Summary of World Broadcasts, August 10, 1994.

93. Frazer and Lancelle, *Absolute Zhirinovsky,* pp. 36–39, 77–79.

94. "The Role of Dr. Gerhard Frey and the Deutsche Volksunion in Right Radicalism in Germany," U.S. State Department document, October 30, 1991; *Searchlight,* May 1991 and December 1993; "Small Fish in a Big Pond: The Deutsche Volksunion," U.S. State Department telegram, October 1, 1987; "IIR 2 212 3046 90/Activites by Right-Wing Extremists Living in Ge[rmany] — Lower Saxony," September 13, 1990; "IIR 0 212 2568 92/Pro-Iraqi Position by German Right-Wing Extremist Political Party," U.S. Army intelligence information report, June 11, 1992. After Gehlen died, Frey published portions of a letter from him in the *National-Zeitung* (June 22, 1979), which indicated Gehlen's support for Frey's political efforts.

95. "U.S. allows breach of Bosnia embargo — British TV," Reuters, October 27, 1995; Roger Cohen, "U.S. Cooling Ties to Croatia

After Winking at Its Build-Up," *New York Times,* October 28, 1995; "Germany says Russia is worrying the West," Reuters, April 29, 1995; David Hoffman, "Attack on Bosnia Shows Russia's Drift From West," *Washington Post,* September 16, 1995; "Moscow aide accuses Bonn of staging plutonium sale," Reuters, April 19, 1995; Alan Cowell, "Possible German Role in Russian Plutonium Deal Is Investigated," *New York Times,* May 18, 1995.

96. "Zhirinovsky's Electoral Success: Implications for Russia's National Security Policy," Defense Intelligence Agency report, PC-20-94, April 23, 1994.

97. *American Spectator,* September 1993; *OMRI Daily Digest,* February 17, 1995.

98. Fred Weir, "Boris's Big Bash," *Nation,* May 22, 1995; Boris Slavin, "Myth About 'Red And Brown' Ones Dispelled, *Pravda* in *Russian Press Digest,* December 24, 1994; Rajiv Tiwari, "Russia: Fringe Parties Take Advantage of Upheavals," Interpress, January 26, 1995.

99. Lyudmila Alexandrova, "Radical Opposition Wants to Sever Ties with Moderates," TASS, June 11, 1994; Gallagher, "He Says He Wants a Revolution"; Howard Witt and James P. Gallagher, "Russia Could Be Ripe for Fascism's Rise," *Chicago Tribune,* December 19, 1993.

100. *Economist,* January 28, 1995; Kartsev, *!Zhirinovsky!,* p. 27; Solovyov and Klepikova, *Zhirinovsky,* p. xxi.

101. Dmitry Pushkar, "Alexander Barkashov Revises his Methods," *Moscow News,* June 30, 1995; Vanora Bennett, "Russia's leather-clad bad lad is at war," Reuters, September 5, 1994. " 'Fascist' . . . we are demonized by that term," said Aleksandr Prokhanov, cochair of the National Salvation Front and chief editor of *Zavtra,* a National Bolshevik press organ. Barkashov agreed: "No one talks about positive fascism — about Argentina, for example."

102. Author's interview with Léon Degrelle, May 19, 1993.

CHAPTER NINE: *From the Margins to the Mainstream*

1. Marc Fisher, "Turks Riot in Germany to Avenge 5 in House Fire," *International Herald Tribune,* June 1, 1993.

2. "The Solingen Tragedy," *International Herald Tribune,* June 5–6, 1993.

3. In October 1995, a German court sentenced Riha and three others to prison terms of ten to fifteen years. One of the convicted firebombers flashed the three-fingered Kühnen salute as he was taken away by police after the trial. Another was identified in press accounts as having been a member of Gerhard Frey's Deutsche Volksunion, the ultra-right-wing political party that forged a close alliance with Vladimir Zhirinovsky.

4. "Das waere eine Bombe," *Der Spiegel,* May 30, 1994; *Searchlight,* July 1994 and October 1994.

5. "Das waere eine Bombe"; *Searchlight,* October 1994.

6. "Informant of FBI Says He Killed Black," *New York Times,* July 11, 1978; Novick, *White Lies, White Power,* pp. 65–66. Police in Greensboro, North Carolina, collaborated with the Klan in a 1979 attack that killed five members and sympathizers of the Communist Workers Party.

7. Paul Wilkinson, *The New Fascists,* pp. 106–07; "KKK recruiting in Germany," Agence France Presse, October 12, 1991. There were also close links between the Ku Klux Klan and the Flemish VMO, which organized the annual neofascist gathering at Dixmude.

8. "Victory in Germany," *White Beret,* December 1991–February 1992.

9. Roy Gutman, "Klansman Woos Skinheads in Germany," *Newsday,* November 8, 1991.

10. "The Far Right in Berlin and the New Länder: The 'Old Right' Parties and the 'New Right' Neo-Nazis," U.S. State Department document, December 18, 1991; "Das waere eine Bombe," *Der Spiegel,* May 30, 1994.

11. Author's interview with Otto Ernst Remer, April 16, 1992; "The Far Right in Berlin and the New Länder: The 'Old Right' Parties and the 'New Right' Neo-Nazis"; Stephen Kinzer, "Germany Outlaws A Neo-Nazi Group," *New York Times,* November 28, 1992; *Searchlight,* October 1995; *Antifascistiches Info-Blatt,* no. 27, June–July 1994.

12. Hockenos, *Free to Hate,* p. 54; *Searchlight,* December 1992 and October 1993; Stephen Kinzer, "Did a Town in Germany Pay Firebug for Attack?" *New York Times,* August 25, 1993.

13. Michael Janofsky, "True Believers Gather to Honor White Race," *New York Times,* July 23, 1995.

14. Raphael S. Ezekial, *The Racist Mind,* pp. 40–41, 68.

15. Author's interview with Floyd Cochran, August 30, 1995.

16. For a journalistic account of "the Order," see Kevin Flynn and Gary Gerhard, *The Silent Brotherhood.*

17. Author's interview with Robert Miles, November 25, 1986.

18. "13 Supremacists Are Not Guilty of Conspiracies," *New York Times,* April 8, 1988.

19. Author's interview with Floyd Cochran.

20. Kirk Lyon's other clients included Stephen Nelson, one of three Aryan Nations members convicted of plotting to blow up gay bars in Seattle, and Tim Hall, a Klansman who lost his job as a security officer at Carswell Air Force Base in Texas when his KKK connections were exposed. ("Klan members to fight discharge," UPI, February 18, 1990.)

21. "Waco lawyer exposed," *Ethnic NewsWatch,* January 26, 1995; Andra Varin, "Dr. Death barred from practicing engineering," UPI, June 11, 1991; Center for Democratic Renewal, *Weekly Up-*

date, November 16, 1992; author's interview with Kirk Lyons, August 24, 1995.

22. Author's interview with Kirk Lyons.

23. Michael Billig, "Psychology, Racism & Fascism," (a Searchlight Booklet [1979]); " 'New anthropology', *Patterns of Prejudice,* January 1982; "Jürgen Rieger and his pseudo-science," *Patterns of Prejudice,* April 1983; "Claim Letter for the Arson Attack on a Hotel and the Car of a Right-Extremist Attorney," U.S. Army intelligence information report, September 17, 1987; author's interview with Ernst Uhrlau, January 24, 1996.

24. Author's interview with Kirk Lyons. "If I was going to call someone in Germany for advice, it would be Jürgen Rieger," Lyons confided.

25. Author's interview with Aryan Nations spokesperson Gerald Gruidl, August 17, 1995; *Searchlight,* April 1995; *Klanwatch Intelligence Report,* March 1995.

26. *Searchlight,* May 1993 and April 1995.

27. *Searchlight,* May and December 1993; Joe R. Feagin and Hernan Vera, *White Racism,* p. 77. A German neo-Nazi group, the Weissenseer Arischer Widerstand was modeled after Tom Metzger's White Aryan Resistance (WAR). It distributed hate propaganda supplied by WAR and Gary Lauck's NSDAP-AO. A Swedish neo-Nazi group, *Vitt Ariskt Motst nd,* also took its name from Metzger's WAR.

28. Author's interview with Stanley Beddlington, August 17, 1995.

29. In October 1994, for example, Francisco Duran pulled an assault rifle from under his coat and fired away at the White House. President Clinton's would-be assassin had left a pickup truck parked nearby with bumper stickers about Waco and gun control. He was known to have attended meetings of the Colorado-based Save America Militia, where racialist tracts were sold in book stalls. Two months later, John Salvi sprayed gunfire into a Planned Parenthood clinic near Boston, killing two employees and wounding five others.

A believer in Masonic conspiracy theories and shadow government plots, Salvi said he had trained with a militia unit in the Florida Everglades. "Legalized abortion" was cited in a 100-page militia field manual, which circulated in several states, as one of the main reasons why "Christian patriots" should arm themselves and prepare for battle against the federal government. Salvi later committed suicide in prison.

When police raided Salvi's apartment, they found inflammatory posters and brochures published by Human Life International (HLI), one of the world's largest and most extreme anti-abortion groups. Father Paul Marx, the HLI's U.S.-based founder and chairman, emphasized the role of Jewish doctors in leading "the greatest holocaust of all time, the war on unborn babies." In his writings and speeches, Marx promoted an updated version of the anti-Semitic blood libel that blamed Jews for the murder of Christian babies. Fearing that "the white Western world is committing suicide" by using contraception and terminating pregnancies, he warned of fast-breeding Muslims taking over France and of Turkish doctors aborting German women en masse. His racist tirades struck a responsive chord among neofascist groups in Europe, where the HLI had many chapters.

In 1991, Marx presented the HLI's highest award to Dr. Siegfried Ernst, a leading figure in Germany's anti-abortion movement. Ernst was listed as one of the HLI's international advisors, even though several German court rulings had determined that "neofascist" was not an inappropriate label for this ultra-right-wing fanatic "because . . . the things he says are so racially discriminating that any impartial observer can see parallels to the ideology of the Third Reich." Ernst and Wolfgang Borowsky, another prominent German neo-Nazi, cofounded a militant anti-abortion group called European Doctors Action. Formerly a member of the Freedom for Rudolf Hess Committee, Borowsky often quoted from *The Protocols of the Elders of Zion* to back up his claim that "Communism is mainly a creation of Jews."

Reverend Matthew Trewhella, a militia proponent who led a Milwaukee group called Missionaries to the Pre-Born, urged his followers to form assault teams to protect the unborn. "We should do what thousands of people across this nation are doing," said

Trewhella. "We should be forming militias. Churches can [sponsor] militia days and teach their men how to fight." (Chip Berlet, "Armed Militias, Right Wing Populism, and Scapegoating," Political Research Associates, June 30, 1995; Free Militia, *Field Manual Section 1: Principles Justifying the Arming and Organizing of a Militia,* 1994; *Front Lines Research,* June and August 1994, May 1995.)

30. *Militia News,* edition 94.

31. Author's interview with Wolfgang Dröge, August 18, 1995. A confidant of the Aryan Nations and an erstwhile collaborator with the Order, Dröge also had close ties to Ewald Althans and other German neo-Nazi leaders. Dröge was the leader of the Heritage Front, Canada's largest and best organized neo-Nazi group, which was formed in 1989 at the instigation of a Canadian government provocateur named Grant Bristow. Bristow befriended Dröge during a neo-Nazi junket to Libya, underwritten by the Qaddafi government, in September 1989. During this trip, Bristow convinced Dröge to establish the Heritage Front. While working for the Canadian Security Service, Bristow supplied money and directives to help build the organization. "Without Grant Bristow, there probably wouldn't have been a Heritage Front, and, if there was, I don't believe it would have been as effective," a Heritage Front member told *The Fifth Estate* (the Canadian Broadcasting Company's premier investigative news show). A national scandal erupted in 1994 when Bristow's link to the secret service was exposed, prompting speculation that Canadian intelligence launched the Heritage Front to justify a large post-Communist spy budget.

32. Marc Cooper, "Montana's Mother of all Militias," *The Nation,* May 22, 1995; author's interview with Floyd Cochran.

33. Jess Walters, *Every Knee Shall Bow,* pp. 63, 240; Kenneth S. Stern, *A Force Upon the Plain,* pp. 25–26; author's interview with Kirk Lyons. A 1989 family portrait of Weaver shows him wearing a T-shirt that reads "Just Say 'No' to ZOG."

34. Author's interview with Lyons. A message posted at the David Koresh Foundation Internet site says that the Waco raid was initiated by "Janet Reno, a Jew" to "silence a prominent critic of the

Jewish plan for One World Government, and the Jewish plan for human Enslavement."

35. James Ridgeway and Leonard Zeskind, "Revolution U.S.A.," *Village Voice,* May 2, 1995; author's interview with Floyd Cochran.

36. Scott McLemee, "Public Enemy," *In These Times,* May 15, 1995; Ridgeway and Zeskind, "Revolution U.S.A."

37. Keith Schneider, "Manual for Terrorist Extols 'Greatest Cold-bloodedness,' " *New York Times,* April 29, 1995; *Klanwatch Intelligence Report,* June 1995; Stern, *A Force Upon the Plain,* pp. 41, 75–78.

38. Chip Berlet, "Armed Militias, Right Wing Populism, and Scapegoating," Political Research Associates, June 30, 1995. "Militias must avoid allowing any persons to become indispensable leaders, so that the militia movement could be suppressed by attacking its leaders," instructed the Patriot Archives site on the Internet prior to the Oklahoma City massacre. "The Militia must be, to the extent possible, 'leaderless' and spontaneous."

39. John Trochmann, speech at the Liberty Lobby's fortieth annual board of policy conference, September 4, 1995.

40. "Many of the photos used by *The Spotlight* of foreign military equipment in this country were supplied by the Militia of Montana [which] has helped thousands of Americans to form militias in every state," reported J. B. Campbell in the *Spotlight,* January 9, 1995; see also "Militia of Montana Member Talks of Crisis, Preparedness," *Spotlight,* June 12, 1995, and *Spotlight*'s special September 1994 issue.

41. Since 1973, real family income has fallen for 60 percent of all Americans, even as the income of the wealthiest 5 percent increased by nearly one-third, and income for the top 1 percent almost doubled. Widespread disillusionment nourished mistrust of the officialdom, as evidenced by a Gallup Poll conducted shortly after the April 1995 Oklahoma bombing, which found that 40 percent of

Americans believed their government "poses an immediate threat to the rights and freedoms of ordinary citizens."

42. Alex Heard, *New Republic,* May 15, 1995.

43. Michigan Militia co-commander Ray Southwell met with the coordinator of the Tennessee Aryan Nations chapter, Bobby Norton.

44. David Johnstone, "Friend Ties McVeigh to Oklahoma City Bombing," *New York Times,* May 20, 1995; Stern, *A Force Upon the Plain,* p. 192; see also *Spotlight,* December 12, 1994.

45. Michael Whiteley, "McVeigh tried to call colony aide," *Arkansas Democrat,* January 26, 1996; *Germanu Alert,* January 26, 1996; James Ridgeway and Leonard Zeskind, *Village Voice,* April 9 and November 26, 1996; J. D. Cash, "Informant Who Warned of Bombing Now Fears for Her Life," *McCurtain Daily Gazette,* February 11, 1997; Kevin Flynn, "Tracking the Truth," *Rocky Mountain News,* July 20, 1997; *Searchlight,* February 1998.

46. *Klanwatch Intelligence Report,* August 1996; Judy Pasternak, "A Bank-Robbing Army of the Right is Left in Tatters," *Los Angeles Times,* January 15, 1997; Richard Leiby, "The Saga of Pretty Boy Pedro," *Washington Post,* February 13, 1997.

47. *Klanwatch Intelligence Report,* June 1995.

48. H. Keith Thompson, letter to the author, June 1, 1995.

49. The Lake Tahoe gathering was previewed in the *Spotlight* (February 19, 1996) under the headline: "Populists are preparing to meet in Nevada. Their message: 'We want this country back.'"

50. See, for example, *Spotlight,* December 7, 1987; February 28, 1988; March 23, 1992. In his book *Profiles in Populism,* Liberty Lobby founder Willis Carto defined capitalism as "the symbiotic partner and bedmate of communism."

51. Elinor Langer, "The American Neo-Nazi Movement Today," *The Nation,* July 16/23, 1990.

52. Jason Berry, "Duke's Disguise," *New York Times,* October 16, 1991.

53. Jason Berry, *Gambit,* September 3, 1991; Linda P. Campbell, "Liberty Lobby in the spotlight with Duke, Buchanan in race," *Chicago Tribune,* January 12, 1992; Jason Berry, "The Hazards of Duke," *Washington Post,* May 14, 1989. Trisha Katson considered Duke's victory nothing less than a "turning point in American history."

54. David Maraniss, "Duke's Obsession: White Supremacy with a Plan," *Washington Post,* November 10, 1991.

55. Leslie Savan, "Duke," *Village Voice,* November 26, 1991.

56. Encouraged by Duke's success, Ku Klux Klan leader Thom Robb announced his intention to train "one thousand David Dukes." Toward this end, Robb opened a camp in Arkansas to groom white supremacists to infiltrate the political mainstream. According to Robb, potential leaders "will be taught to avoid statements that sound hateful and 'turn people off.' Their dress and speech will be honed." Lacking Duke's baggage, these Republican "sleepers," as Robb called them, would not be readily identifiable as neo-Nazis. Robb, a Christian Identity pastor, had previously praised Hitler as "the great German leader and statesman who was ordained by God to lift Germany from the Jewish depravity."

57. Joe Conason, "The Religious Right's Quiet Revival," *Nation,* April 27, 1992; Diamond, *Roads to Dominion,* p. 292.

58. "Anti-Semitism: Its Prevalence Within the Christian Right," *Freedom Writer,* May 1994.

59. Michael Lind, "Rev. Robertson's Grand International Conspiracy Theory," *New York Review of Books,* February 2, 1995; Pat Robertson, *New World Order.*

60. Frank Rich, "Shotgun Hearings," *New York Times,* July 19, 1995.

61. James Bennet, "Buchanan, Beset by Many Critics, Still Unbowed," *New York Times,* February 17, 1996; Gustav Niebur, "Full

GOP Menu Splits the Religious Right," *New York Times,* January 19, 1996; *Spotlight,* February 26, 1996.

62. For example, *Eugenics and Race* (1966) and *Early Civilizations of the Nordic Peoples* by Roger Pearson. Pearson served as chairman of the World Anti-Communist League (WACL) in the late 1970s, when that ultra-right-wing umbrella organization was most riddled with neo-Nazis, Waffen SS veterans, Eastern European collaborators, Latin American death-squad chiefs, and other hard-core anti-Semites. He was relieved of his WACL duties in 1980 because of a partial housecleaning by General John Singlaub, who proceeded to turn the league into an instrument of Reagan-era covert operations in Central America and Southwest Asia.

63. *Newsweek,* October 24, 1994, p. 56, cited in Charles Lane, "The Tainted Sources of 'The Bell Curve'," *New York Review of Books,* December 1, 1994. According to Lane, five articles from the *Mankind Quarterly* were referenced in *The Bell Curve's* bibliography (pp. 775, 807, 828), and seventeen researchers cited in the bibliography had contributed to Roger Pearson's racialist journal; of these, ten were current or former editors or members of its editorial advisory board. Murray and Herrnstein also cited no fewer than thirteen "scholars" who got money from the neo-Nazi Pioneer Fund during the past two decades — grants totaling more than $4 million.

64. *Sunday Telegraph,* March 12, 1989.

65. Dinesh D'Souza, *The End of Racism.*

66. John Nichols, "Righter Than Thou," *Progressive,* June 1995; *Spotlight,* January 30, 1995.

67. Ravi Nessman, "Immigrant Abuse," Associated Press, October 15, 1995.

68. Ruth Conniff, "The War on Aliens," *Progressive,* October 1993.

69. European Parliament session news press release, April 25, 1995. The best source on the rise of mass-based, extreme Right political parties on the Continent is Betz, *Radical Right-wing Populism.*

70. *De Morgen,* December 17, 1994.

71. Adrian Dascalu, "Expelled Romanians charge ill-treatment by France," Interpress Service, July 10, 1995; Amnesty International, *France: Shootings, killings, and alleged ill-treatment by law enforcement affairs,* October 12, 1994; *Searchlight,* October 1993.

72. "France's Extreme Right: The Le Pen Phenomenon," telegram from U.S. embassy in France to secretary of state, Washington, D.C., June 21, 1984; Maoláin, *The Radical Right,* pp. 93–96.

73. Edwyn Plenel and Alain Rollat, "The Revival of the Far Right in France," *Patterns of Prejudice,* April 1984; author's interview with Léon Degrelle, May 19, 1993.

74. Alain de Benoist, letter to the author, March 8, 1996; "The French New Right," *Telos,* winter 1993–spring 1994, pp. 28, 173–75, 185–86; Franklin Hugh Adler, "Racism, *difference* and the Right in France," in *Modern and Contemporary France* (1995).

75. Jean-Yves Camus, "Political Cultures within the Front National," *Patterns of Prejudice* 26, nos. 1 and 2, (1992); author's interview with Jean-Gilles Malliarkis, November 1986; "The Ultimate Odd Couple — Saddam Hussein and Jean-Marie Le Pen," U.S. State Department document, November 23, 1990.

76. Betz, *Radical Right-wing Populism,* p. 128; Mark Hunter, "Europe's Reborn Right," *New York Times Magazine,* April 21, 1996.

77. John Bunzl, "National Populism in Austria," Patterns of *Prejudice* 2, nos. 1 and 2 (1992); James M. Markham, "Chancellor Ends Austrian Coalition," *New York Times,* September 16, 1986; Betz, *Radical Right-wing Populism,* p. 123.

78. Steve Pagani, "War anniversary confronts Austria with Nazi past," Reuters, March 7, 1995. A survey of Austrian history books for ten-year-olds revealed that National Socialism was never even mentioned in ten of twenty-five sample texts; the Holocaust was discussed in only six of twenty-five; and only one book indicated that Austrians had participated in Hitler's regime.

79. A number of Nazi sympathizers found a home in the Austrian Freedom Party, including one of Haider's top "ideological" advisors, Werner Konigshofer, who had previously edited *Sieg,* a Holocaust-denial publication banned by the Austrian government. Another Freedom Party member, Dr. Erhard Hartung, had been sentenced in absentia by an Italian court to life imprisonment in 1967 for carrying out a neo-Nazi terrorist attack that killed four people in Italy's South Tyrol region. But Austria refused to extradite Hartung to Italy. Despite his well-known history as a convicted terrorist and murderer, Hartung was chosen by Chancellor Helmut Kohl to represent Germany at an international medical symposium in China in May 1994. Kohl specifically designated Hartung to deliver the chancellor's personal greetings to the assembly. (See generally Wolfgang Purtscheller, *Aufbruch der Volkischen.*

80. Betz, *Radical Right-wing Populism,* p. 124; "Haider dumps MP who doubts Holocaust," Reuters World Report, October 18, 1995.

81. "Italian hotel bars alleged Nazi group," Reuters, September 10, 1992; Celestine Bohlen, "Italy Rebuked by Vatican over Migrants," *New York Times,* November 20, 1995.

82. Adrian Lyttleton, "Italy: The Triumph of TV," *New York Review of Books,* April 11, 1994.

83. *Searchlight,* April 1993; Marc Fisher, "Right-Wing Party Gains in 1 German State," *Washington Post,* March 8, 1993.

84. Betz, *Radical Right-wing Populism,* p. 56.

85. *Searchlight,* April 1994; Thom Shanker, "The New Fascists of Europe," *Chicago Tribune,* December 15, 1993.

86. After Schönhuber resigned as the leader of the Republikaner, the party rebounded in 1996 state elections, winning 9 percent of the vote in Baden-Württemberg.

87. Kevin Liffey, "Right-wing extremism declines in Germany," Reuters, July 6, 1995; Terrence Petty, Associated Press, July 6, 1995. Serbian tennis star Monica Seles was stabbed by a crazed German nationalist; her assailant received a two-year suspended sentence

after he explained that he wanted a German woman to be the number-one tennis player in the world. A *New York Times* editorial described the lenient sentence, which was upheld by a German court, as "shocking." A German skinhead gang also stabbed a Japanese figure skater.

88. "German neo-Nazi leads police to arms cache," Reuters, August 17, 1995.

89. Remer's escape from Germany was aided by Günter Deckert, a neo-Nazi leader who had recently been convicted of inciting racial hatred in the Fatherland. The charges stemmed from Deckert's participation in a November 1991 meeting that featured a speech by American gas chamber "expert" Fred Leuchter. Adding a few words of his own, Deckert told the audience that the Holocaust was a myth perpetrated by "a parasitical people who were using a historical lie to muzzle and exploit Germany." When Deckert appealed the verdict, a sympathetic judicial panel gave him a one-year suspended sentence; one of the judges described him as an "intelligent man of character for whom the claim was a matter of the heart," while another declared that Deckert had "expressed legitimate interests" in questioning the financial and political demands that Jews continued to impose on Germany fifty years after World War II. The de facto acquittal of Deckert attested to the ingrained anti-Semitism and right-wing extremism that persisted within the German judicial system. After an international outcry, the two judges who had ruled in his favor were suspended (only to be reinstated a few months later), and Deckert was given a two-year prison term.

90. "Nebeneruf V-Mann," *Der Spiegel,* July 19, 1995; "Neonazi Althans soll nie V-Mann gewesen sein," *Frankfurter Rundschau,* August 2, 1995; "Neonazi Althans soll nicht fur den Verfassungsschutz spioniert haben," *Die Tageszeitung,* August 2, 1995; *Searchlight,* August 1995.

91. *Searchlight,* November 1995.

92. Imre Karac, "German Officer in Neo-Nazi Scandal," *Independent,* December 9, 1997; Imre Karac, "Defense Ministry Aided Neo-Nazi 'Aryan Project'," *Independent,* December 12, 1997; Geoff

Kitney, "Germany: Inquiry Into Nazi Links to Armed Forces," *Sydney Morning Herald,* December 12, 1997; *Searchlight,* January 1998.

93. " 'More Humility, Fewer Illusions'—A Talk Between Adam Michnik and Jürgen Habermas," *New York Review of Books,* March 24, 1994.

94. "Brzezinski Backs NATO Expansion," AP Online, December 7, 1997.

95. "Gegen Das Vergessen," *Frankfurter Allgemeine Zeitung,* April 7, 1995. Among the signatories of this manifesto were outspoken neofascists such as Dr. Siegfried Ernst, a leader of Germany's anti-abortion movement; Peter Froehlich, a veteran of Kühnen's Action Front of National Socialists; *Junge Freiheit* editor Dieter Stein; former chief federal prosecutor Alexander von Stahl; German finance minister Theo Waigel; and various CDU Bundestag members and youth leaders.

96. *Searchlight,* May 1995; Reuters, May 1 and May 4, 1995.

97. *Searchlight,* December 1993; Elliot Neaman, "Fascism and postmodernism," *Tikkun,* November 1993; Gary Krist, "Tragedyland," *New York Times,* November 27, 1993.

CONCLUSION

1. Phil Davidson, "Nazi who saved Hitler is in Spain," *Independent,* July 20, 1994.

2. *Time* magazine (June 6, 1994) engaged in its own form of revisionism when it ran a cover photo of General Dwight D. Eisenhower with the caption "The man who beat Hitler"—as if the 20 million Soviets who sacrificed their lives during World War II played only a minor role in defeating Nazi Germany.

3. Speech by Douglas H. Jones, principal officer, U.S. embassy office, Berlin, April 14, 1994.

4. Tom Heneghan, "Hamburg exhibition questions honour of Hitler's fighting men," Reuters, March 27, 1995; "Leading anti-Nazi pastor still not rehabilitated," Reuters, April 5, 1995; Simpson, *Splendid Blonde Beast,* p. 60.

5. H. Keith Thompson, letters to the author, June 6, 1994; April 5, 1995; May 15, 1995. Otto Ernst Remer died in Spain on October 4, 1997.

6. Author's interview with H. Keith Thompson, November 1, 1993; H. Keith Thompson, letter to David Duke, February 23, 1989, and several letters from the Republican National Committee to H. Keith Thompson in the H. Keith Thompson section of the Hoover Institute Special Collections Library.

7. For this anecdote, I am indebted to Petko Azmanov, a Bulgarian journalist who interviewed Mila Rodriguez in 1993.

8. George Mosse cited by Elinor Langer, "The American Neo-Nazi Movement Today," *Nation,* July 16/23, 1990.

9. Griffin, *Fascism,* p. 10.

10. Paul Johnson quoted in William Miller, "A New Europe," *Boston Globe,* January 5, 1992; *OMRI Daily Digest,* May 5, 1995.

11. Huey P. Long once said, "If fascism came to America, it would be on a program of Americanism."

12. For example, Representatives Helen Chenowith (R-Idaho), Steve Stockman (R-Texas), Jack Metcalf (R-Washington), David Funderburk (R-North Carolina), James Trafficant (D-Ohio), and Senator Jesse Helms (R-North Carolina).

13. Newt Gingrich and William R. Fortschen, *1945.*

14. Theodor W. Adorno, "What Does Coming to Terms with the Past Mean?" in Hartmann, *Bitburg in Moral and Political Perspective,* p. 120.

15. Speech by Douglas H. Jones, principal officer, U.S. embassy office, Berlin, April 14, 1994.

16. Horst-Eberhard Richter quoted in Mary Williams Walsh, "Qualified, Educated," *Los Angeles Times,* April 12, 1997.

BIBLIOGRAPHY

Abanes, Richard. *American Militias.* Downers Grove, Ill.: Inter Varsity Press, 1996.

Adorno, Theodor et al. *The Authoritarian Personality.* New York: Harper, 1950.

Adorno, Theodor W. *The Stars Come Down to Earth and Other Essays on the Irrational in Culture.* New York: Routledge, 1994.

Agursky, Mikhail. *The Third Rome.* Boulder, Colo.: Westview Press, 1987.

Aho, James A. *The Politics of Righteousness.* Seattle: University of Washington Press, 1990.

Allardyce, Gilbert, ed. *The Place of Fascism in European History.* Englewood Cliffs, N.J.: Prentice-Hall, 1971.

Allen, Charles, R., Jr. *Heusinger of the Fourth Reich.* New York: Marzani & Munsell, 1963.

Allen, William Sheridan. *The Nazi Seizure of Power.* New York: Franklin Watts, 1984.

Allworth, Edward, ed. *Ethnic Russia in the USSR.* New York: Pergamon Press, 1980.

Anderson, Scott and Jon Lee Anderson. *Inside the League.* New York: Dodd, Mead, 1986.

Anderson, Martin Edwin. *Dossier Secreto.* Boulder, Colo.: Westview Press, 1993.

Andreyev, Catherine. *Vlasov and the Russian Liberation Movement*. London: Cambridge University Press, 1987.

Antifaschistische Infoblatt. *Drahtzieher im Braunen Netz*. Berlin: Edition ID-Archiv, 1992.

Ardagh, John. *Germany and the Germans*. London: Hamish Hamilton, 1987.

Arendt, Hannah. *Eichmann in Jerusalem*. New York: Viking Penguin, 1994.

Ash, Timothy Garton. *In Europe's Name*. New York: Random House, 1993.

Ashman, Chuck and Robert J. Wagman. *The Nazi Hunters*. New York: Pharos Books, 1988.

Aycoberry, Pierre. *The Nazi Question*. New York: Pantheon, 1981.

Baldwin, Peter, ed. *Reworking the Past*. Boston: Beacon Press, 1990.

Bancroft, Mary. *Autobiography of a Spy*. New York: Morrow, 1983.

Bar-Zohar, Michel. *The Hunt for German Scientists*. London: Arthur Baker, 1967.

Barkun, Michael. *Religion and the Racist Right*. Chapel Hill: University of North Carolina Press, 1994.

Bartov, Omer. *Hitler's Army*. New York: Oxford University Press, 1992.

Bauer, Yehuda, ed. *The Danger of Antisemitism in Central and Eastern Europe in the Wake of 1989–1990*. Jerusalem: Institute of Contemporary Jewry, 1991.

Bauman, Zygmunt. *Modernity and the Holocaust*. Ithaca, N.Y.: Cornell University Press, 1989.

Behbehani, Hashim S. H. *China's Foreign Policy in the Arab World, 1955–1971*. London: KPI, 1981.

———. *The Soviet Union and Arab Nationalism 1917–1966.* London: KPI, 1986.

Beinin, Joel. *Was the Red Flag Flying There?* Berkeley: University of California Press, 1990.

Bell, Andrew. *Against Racism and Fascism in Europe.* Brussels: Socialist Group, European Parliament, 1986.

Bellant, Russ. *Old Nazis, the New Right and the Republican Party.* Boston: South End Press, 1991.

———. *The Coors Connection.* Boston: South End Press, 1991.

Bennett, David H. *The Party of Fear.* Chapel Hill: University of North Carolina Press, 1988.

Benz, Wolfgang, ed. *Rechtsextreismus in der Bundesrepublik.* Frankfurt: Fischer Taschenbuch Verlag, 1989.

Bergner, Jeffrey T. *The New Superpowers.* New York: St. Martin's Press, 1991.

Berlet, Chip and Mathew Lyon. *Too Close For Comfort.* Boston: South End Press, 1997.

Berman, Marshall. *All That Is Solid Melts Into Air.* New York: Simon & Schuster, 1982.

Betz, Hans-Georg. *Radical Right-Wing Populism in Western Europe.* New York: St. Martin's Press, 1994.

Billig, Michael. *Psychology, Racism & Fascism.* London: Searchlight, 1979.

Bird, Kai. *The Chairman.* New York: Simon & Schuster, 1992.

Bjorgo, Tore and Rob Witte, eds. *Racist Violence in Europe.* New York: St. Martin's Press, 1993.

Black, Ian and Benny Morris. *Israel's Secret Wars.* New York: Grove Weidenfeld, 1991.

Blinkhorn, Martin, ed. *Fascists and Conservatives.* London: Unwin Hyman, 1990.

Blum, Howard. *Wanted! The Search for Nazis in America.* Greenwich, Conn: Fawcett, 1977.

Blum, William. *The CIA: A Forgotten History.* London: Zed Books, 1986.

Blundy, David and Andrew Lycett. *Qaddafi and the Libyan Revolution.* Boston: Little, Brown, 1987.

Borkin, Joseph. *The Crime and Punishment of I. G. Farben.* New York: Free Press, 1978.

Bower, Tom. *The Pledge Betrayed.* New York: Doubleday, 1982.

Branch, Taylor and Eugene M. Propper. *Labyrinth.* New York: Viking, 1982.

Brissaud, André. *The Nazi Secret Service.* New York: Norton, 1974.

Braham, Randolph L., ed. *Anti-Semitism and the Treatment of the Holocaust in Postcommunist Eastern Europe.* New York: Columbia University Press: 1994.

Brogan, Patrick and Albert Zarca. *Deadly Business.* New York: Norton, 1988.

Brown, Anthony Cave, ed. *The Secret War Report of the OSS.* New York: Berkeley Medallion, 1976.

Buford, Bill. *Among the Thugs.* London: Mandarin, 1992.

Bullock, Alan. *Hitler and Stalin.* New York: Knopf, 1992.

Burstein, Daniel. *Euroquake.* New York: Simon & Schuster, 1991.

Byron, John and Robert Pack. *The Claws of the Dragon.* New York: Simon & Schuster, 1992.

Camus, Jean-Yves and Rene Monzat. *Les Droites Nationales et Radicales en France.* Lyon: Presses Universitaires de Lyon, 1992.

Canedy, Susan. *America's Nazis.* Menlo Park, Calif.: Markgraf Publications, 1990.

Cannistraro, Philip V. *Historical Dictionary of Fascist Italy.* Westport, Conn.: Greenwood Press, 1982.

Carlson, John Roy. *Cairo to Damascus.* New York: Knopf, 1951.

———. *Under Cover.* New York: Dutton, 1943.

Carr, Edward Hallett. *German-Soviet Relations Between the Two World Wars, 1919–1939.* Baltimore: Johns Hopkins University Press: 1951.

Carsten, F. L. *The Rise of Fascism.* Berkeley: University of California Press, 1967.

Carto, Willis, ed., *Profiles in Populism.* Old Greenwich, Com.: Flag Press, 1982.

Casillo, Robert. *The Genealogy of Demons.* Evanston, Ill.: Northwestern University Press, 1988.

Cheles, Luciano et al., ed. *Neo-fascism in Europe.* London: Longman, 1991.

Christie, Stuart. *Stefano delle Chiaie.* London: Anarchy Magazine/ Refract, 1984.

Clark, Alan. *Barbarossa.* New York: Qill, 1985.

Coates, James. *Armed and Dangerous.* New York: Noonday, 1987.

Cockburn, Andrew and Leslie. *Dangerous Liaison.* New York: HarperCollins, 1991.

Codrescu, Andrei. *The Hole in the Flag.* New York: Avon, 1991.

Cohen, Jeff and Norman Solomon. *Adventures in Medialand.* Monroe, Maine: Common Courage Press, 1993.

Cohn, Norman. *Warrant for Genocide.* Chico, Calif.: Scholar's Press, 1981.

Conot, Robert E. *Justice at Nuremberg.* New York: Harper & Row, 1983.

Conquest, Robert. *The Last Empire*. Stanford, Calif.: Hoover Institution Press, 1986.

Cook, Fred J. *The Nightmare Decade*. New York: Random House, 1971.

Cookridge, E. H. *Gehlen*. New York: Random House, 1971.

Copeland, Miles. *The Game of Nations*. New York: Simon & Schuster, 1969.

———. *Without Cloak or Dagger*. New York: Simon & Schuster, 1974.

Corcoran, James. *Bitter Harvest:* New York: Viking, Penguin 1990

Corson, William R. *The Armies of Ignorance*. New York: Dial, 1977.

Corson, William R. and Robert T. Crowley. *The New KGB*. New York: Morrow, 1985.

Crawford, James. *Hold Your Tongue*. Reading, Mass.: Addison-Wesley, 1992.

Crenshaw, Martha, ed. *Terrorism, Legitimacy, and Power*. Middletown, Conn.: Wesleyan University Press, 1983.

Crowe, David M. *A History of the Gypsies of Eastern Europe and Russia*. New York: St. Martin's Press, 1994.

Dabringhaus, Erhard. *Klaus Barbie*. Washington, D.C.: Acropolis Books, 1984.

Dagan, Avigdor. *Moscow and Jerusalem*. London: Abelard-Schuman, 1970.

Deacon, Richard. *The French Secret Service*. London: Grafton, 1990.

Dedijer, Vladimir. *The Yugoslav Auschwitz and the Vatican*. Buffalo, N.Y.: Prometheus Books, 1992.

Dees, Morris. *Hate on Trial*. New York: Villard, 1993.

Dees, Morris with James Corcoran. *Gathering Storm.* New York: HarperCollins, 1996.

Degrelle, Léon. *Campaign in Russia.* Costa Mesa, Calif.: Institute for Historical Review, 1985.

Del Boca, Angelo and Mario Giovana. *Fascism Today: A World Survey.* New York: Pantheon, 1969.

Demarest, Pierre and Christian Plume. *Target De Gaulle.* New York: Dial, 1975.

Denitch, Bogdan. *After the Flood.* Hanover: Wesleyan University Press, 1992.

Diamond, Sara. *Roads to Dominion.* New York: Guilford Press, 1995.

———. *Spiritual Warfare.* Boston: South End Press, 1989.

Diehl, James M. *The Thanks of the Fatherland.* Chapel Hill, N.C.: University of North Carolina Press, 1993.

Diggins, John P. *Mussolini and Fascism.* Princeton, N.J.: Princeton University Press, 1972.

Dinges, John and Saul Landau. *Assassination on Embassy Row.* New York: Pantheon, 1980.

Domenico, Roy Palmer. *Italian Fascists on Trial 1943–1948.* Chapel Hill, N.C.: University of North Carolina Press, 1991.

Donner, Frank. *The Age of Surveillance.* New York: Vintage, 1981.

Drake, Richard. *The Revolutionary Mystique and Terrorism in Contemporary Italy.* Bloomington: University of Indiana Press, 1989.

D'Souza, Dinesh. *The End of Racism.* New York: Free Press, 1995.

Duffy, James P. and Vincent L. Ricci. *Target Hitler.* Westport, Conn.: Praeger Publications, 1992.

Duggan, Christopher. *Fascism and the Mafia.* New Haven, Conn.: Yale University Press, 1989.

Dulles, Allen. *The Secret Surrender.* New York: Harper & Row, 1966.

———. *Germany's Underground.* New York: Macmillan, 1947.

Dunlop, John. *The New Russian Nationalism.* New York: Praeger Publications, 1985.

Duranton-Crabol, Anne-Marie. *L'Europe de L'Extreme Droite.* Brussels: Editions Complexe, 1991.

Dyakov, Yuri and Tatyana Bushuyeva. *The Red Army and the Wehrmacht.* Amherst, N.Y.: Prometheus Books, 1994.

Eatwell, Roger. *Fascism: A History.* New York: Allen Lane, 1996.

Eatwell, Roger, and Noel O'Sullivan, eds. *The Nature of the Right.* London: Pinter, 1989.

Eisenberg, Carolyn. *Drawing the Line.* New York: Cambridge University Press, 1996.

Eisenberg, Dennis. *The Re-Emergence of Fascism.* London: MacGibbon & Kee, 1967.

Ellwood, Sheelagh M. *Spanish Fascism in the Franco Era.* London: Macmillan, 1987.

Enzensberger, Hans Magnus. *Civil Wars.* New York: New Press, 1993.

European Parliament, Committee of Inquiry into the Rise of Fascism and Racism in Europe. Report on the findings of the inquiry (1985).

European Parliament, Committee of Inquiry on Racism and Xenophobia. Report on the findings of the inquiry (1991).

Evans, Richard J. *In Hitler's Shadow.* New York: Pantheon, 1989.

Evola, Julius. *Imperialismo Pagano.* Padua: Edizioni di Ar, 1978.

———. *The Metaphysics of Sex.* New York: Inner Traditions International, 1983.

———. *Nei Documenti Segreti del Terzo Reich.* Rome: Europa, 1986.

Ezekial, Raphael S. *The Racist Mind.* New York: Viking, 1995.

Faligot, Roger and Remi Kauffer. *The Chinese Secret Service.* London: Headline, 1987.

———. *Le Croissant et la Croix Gammée.* Paris: Albin Michel, 1990.

Faligot, Roger and Pascal Krop. *La Piscine.* London: Blackwell, 1989.

Falk, Richard. *Revolutionaries and Functionaries.* New York: Dutton, 1988.

Faller, Kurt and Heinz Siegbold, eds. *NeoFaschismus.* Frankfurt: Roederberg-Verlag, 1986.

Farago, Ladislas. *Aftermath.* New York: Avon, 1974.

Farrell, Stephen Lawrence. *Jean-Marie Le Pen and the National Front.* American University doctoral dissertation, 1991.

Feagin, Joe R. and Hernan Vera. *White Racism.* New York: Routledge, 1995.

Feffer, John. *Shock Waves.* Boston: South End Press, 1992.

Fisher, Marc. *After the Wall.* New York: Simon & Schuster, 1995.

Flynn, Kevin and Gary Gerhardt. *The Silent Brotherhood.* New York: Free Press, 1989.

Foley, Charles. *Commando Extraordinary.* Costa Mesa, Calif.: Noontide Press, 1988.

Forster, Arnold and Benjamin R. Epstein. *Cross-Currents.* New York: Doubleday, 1956.

———. *Danger on the Right.* New York: Random House, 1964.

———. *The New Anti-Semitism.* New York: McGraw-Hill, 1974.

Fraser, Steven, ed. *The Bell Curve Wars.* New York: Basic Books, 1995.

Frazer, Graham and George Lancelle. *Absolute Zhirinovsky.* New York: Viking Penguin, 1994.

Freedland, Richard M. *The Truman Doctrine and the Origins of McCarthyism.* New York: New York University Press, 1985.

Freedman, Theodore, ed. *Anti-Semitism in the Soviet Union.* New York: Freedom Library, 1984.

Freiwald, Aaron and Martin Mendelsohn. *The Last Nazi.* New York: Norton, 1994.

Fritzsche, Peter. *Rehearsals for Fascism.* New York: Oxford University Press, 1990.

Garten, Jeffrey E. *A Cold Peace.* New York: Times Books, 1992.

Gedmin, Jeffrey. *The Hidden Hand.* Washington, D.C.: AEI Press, 1992.

Gehlen, Reinhard. *The Service.* New York: World Publishing, 1972.

George, John and Laird Wilcox. *Nazis, Communists, Klansmen and Others on the Fringe.* Buffalo, N.Y.: Prometheus Books, 1992.

Gerber, David A., ed. *Anti-Semitism in American History.* Champaign, Ill.: University of Illinois Press, 1987.

Germani, Gino. *Authoritarianism, Fascism, and National Populism.* New Brunswick, N.J.: Transaction Publications, 1978.

Gibson, William James. *Warrior Dreams.* New York: Hill and Wang, 1994.

Gingrich, Newt and William R. Fortschen. *1945.* Riverside, N.Y.: Baen Books, 1995.

Ginsberg, Benjamin. *The Fatal Embrace.* Chicago: University of Chicago Press, 1993.

Ginsborg, Paul. *A History of Contemporary Italy.* New York: Viking Pengiun, 1990.

von Goldendach, Walter and Hans-Rüdiger Minow. *"Deutschtum Erwache!"* Berlin: Dietz Verlag GmbH, 1995.

Goldhagen, Daniel Jonah. *Hitler's Willing Executioners.* New York: Vintage, 1997.

Goodrick-Clarke, Nicholas. *The Occult Roots of Nazism.* Wellingborough (England): Aquarian, 1985.

Gould, Stephen Jay. *The Mismeasure of Man.* New York: Norton, 1983.

Grass, Günter. *Tin Drum.* New York: Vintage, 1964.

———. *Two States — One Nation?* San Diego: Harcourt Brace Jovanovich, 1990.

Gregor, James A. *The Ideology of Fascism.* New York: Free Press, 1969.

———. *The Fascist Persuasion in Radical Politics.* Princeton, N.J.: Princeton University Press, 1974.

Gregory, Steven and Roger Sanjek, eds. *Race.* New Brunswick, N.J.: Rutgers University Press, 1994.

Griffin, Roger, ed. *Fascism.* New York: Oxford University Press, 1995.

Griffiths, Stephen Iwan. *Nationalism and Ethnic Conflict.* New York: Oxford University Press, 1993.

Guenon, Rene. *The Reign of Quantity.* New York: Penguin, 1972.

Haaf, Karel ten. *. . . en morgen de hele wereld?* Amsterdam: FOP\K, 1992.

Haffner, Sebastian. *The Ailing Empire.* New York: Fromm International, 1989.

Hagen, Louis. *The Secret War for Europe.* New York: Stein and Day, 1969.

Hainsworth, Paul, ed. *The Extreme Right in Europe and North America.* London: Pinter, 1992.

Hamalainen, Pekka Kalevi. *Uniting Germany.* Boulder, Colo.: Westview Press, 1994.

Hamilton, Alastair. *The Appeal of Fascism.* New York: Macmillan, 1971.

Handelman, Stephen. *Comrade Criminal.* New Haven, Conn.: Yale University Press, 1995.

Harper, John Lamberton. *America and the Reconstruction of Italy, 1945–1948.* London: Cambridge University Press, 1986.

Hartman, Geoffrey, ed. *Bitburg in Moral and Political Perspective.* Bloomington, Ind.: Indiana University Press, 1986.

Hasselbach, Ingo. *Führer-Ex.* New York: Random House, 1996.

Heikal, Mohamed. *The Sphinx and the Commissar.* New York: Harper & Row, 1978.

Heller, Mikhail and Aleksandr M. Nekrich. *Utopia and Power.* New York: Summit Books, 1986.

Herbert, Anthony. *Soldier.* New York: Holt Rinehart Winston, 1973.

Herman, Edward S. and Frank Brodhead. *The Rise and Fall of the Bulgarian Connection.* New York: Sheridan Square Press, 1986.

Hersh, Burton. *The Old Boys.* New York: Scribner, 1992.

Herz, John H., ed. *From Dictatorship to Democracy.* Westport Conn.: Greenwood Press, 1982.

Higham, Charles. *American Swastika.* New York: Doubleday, 1985.

———. *Trading with the Enemy.* New York: Dell, 1983.

Hilberg, Raul. *The Destruction of the European Jews.* New York: Holmes & Meier, 1985.

Hill, Ray with Andrew Bell. *The Other Face of Terror.* London: Grafton, 1988.

Hingley, Ronald. *The Russian Secret Police.* New York: Dorset, 1970.

Hirsch, Kurt. *Rechts von der Union.* Munich: Knesebeck & Schuler, 1989.

Hockenos, Paul. *Free to Hate.* New York: Routledge, 1993.

Hodges, Donald C. *Argentina, 1943–1987.* Albuquerque: University of New Mexico Press, 1988.

———. *Argentina's "Dirty War".* Austin: University of Texas Press, 1991.

———, ed. *Philosophy of the Urban Guerrilla.* New York: Morrow, 1973.

Hoffer, Eric. *The True Believer.* New York: Perennial Library, 1966.

Hogan, Michael J., ed. *The End of the Cold War.* New York: Cambridge University Press, 1992.

Höhne, Heinz. *Canaris.* New York: Doubleday, 1979.

———. *The Order of the Death's Head.* London: Secker & Warburg, 1980.

Höhne, Heinz and Hermann Zolling. *The General Was a Spy.* New York: Bantam, 1972.

Hoopes, Townsend. *The Devil and John Foster Dulles.* Boston: Atlantic Monthly, 1973.

Horne, Alistair. *The French Army and Politics, 1870–1970.* New York: Peter Bedrick, 1984.

———. *Return to Power.* New York: Praeger Publications, 1956.

———. *A Savage War of Peace.* New York: Viking, 1978.

Höttl, William. *The Secret Front.* New York: Praeger Publications, 1954.

Hougan, Jim. *Spooks.* New York: Morrow, 1978.

Huelshoff, Michael G., Andrei S. Markovits, and Simon Reich, eds. *From Bundesrepublik to Deutschland.* Ann Arbor: University of Michigan Press, 1993.

Hughes, H. Stuart. *The United States and Italy.* Cambridge: Harvard University Press, 1965.

Hunt, Linda. *Secret Agenda.* New York: St. Martin's Press, 1991.

Ignatieff, Michael. *Blood and Belonging.* New York: Farrar, Straus & Giroux, 1993.

Infield, Glenn B. *Skorzeny: Hitler's Commando.* New York: St. Martin's Press, 1981.

———. *Secrets of the SS.* New York: Military Heritage, 1981.

Institute of Jewish Affairs. *Antisemitism: World Report 1993.* London, 1993.

———. *Antisemitism: World Report, 1994.* London, 1994.

———. *Antisemitism: World Report, 1995.* London, 1995.

Jäckel, Eberhard. *Hitler in History.* Hanover, N.H.: Brandeis University Press, 1984.

Jarausch, Konrad. *The Rush to German Unity.* New York: Oxford University Press, 1994.

Joes, Anthony James. *Fascism in the Contemporary World.* Boulder, Colo.: Westview Press, 1978.

Johnson, Niel M. *George Sylvester Viereck.* Chicago: University of Illinois Press, 1972.

Josephs, Jeremy. *Swastika Over Paris.* New York: Arcade, 1989.

Jösten, Joachim. *The Red Hand*. London: Abelard Schuman, 1962.

Jukes, Geoffrey. *Hitler's Stalingrad Decisions*. Berkeley: University of California Press, 1985.

Kaplan, Morton P., ed. *The Many Faces of Communism*. New York: Free Press, 1978.

Kartsev, Vladimir. *!Zhirinovsky!* New York: Columbia University Press, 1995.

Kater, Michael H. *The Nazi Party*. Cambridge: Harvard University Press, 1983.

Kedward, H. R. *Fascism in Western Europe 1900–45*. New York: NYU Press, 1971.

Kiernan, V. G. *From Conquest to Collapse*. New York: Pantheon, 1982.

King, Dennis. *Lyndon LaRouche and the New American Fascism*. New York: Doubleday, 1989.

Kinsella, Warren. *Unholy Alliances*. Toronto: Lester, 1992.

Knight, Amy. *Beria*. Princeton, N.J.: Princeton University Press, 1993.

Korey, William. *The Soviet Cage*. New York: Viking, 1973.

Krosny, Herbert. *Deadly Business*. New York: Four Walls Eight Windows, 1994.

Kruger, Henrik. *The Great Heroin Coup*. Boston: South End Press, 1980.

———. *Over the Green Border* (unpublished manuscript).

Kühl, Stefan. *The Nazi Connection*. New York: Oxford University Press, 1994.

Lacouture, Jean. *De Gaulle*. New York: Norton, 1991.

von Lang, Jochen. *The Secretary*. Athens: Ohio University Press, 1979.

Laponce, J. A. *Left and Right.* Toronto: University of Toronto Press, 1981.

Laqueur, Walter. *Black Hundred.* New York: HarperCollins, 1993.

———. *Fascism: Past, Present and Future.* New York: Oxford University, Press, 1996.

———. *Fascism: A Reader's Guide.* Berkeley: University of California Press, 1976.

———. *The Long Road to Freedom.* New York: Collier, 1990.

———. *Russia and Germany.* New Brunswick, N.J.: Transaction Publications, 1990.

Laqueur, Walter and George L. Mosse, eds. *International Fascism, 1920–1945.* New York: Harper & Row, 1966.

Lasby, Clarence. *Project Paperclip.* New York: Atheneum, 1971.

Laurent, Frederic. *L'Orchestre Noir.* Paris: Stock, 1978.

Lederer, Laura J. and Richard Delgado, eds. *The Price We Pay.* New York: Hill and Wang, 1995.

Ledwidge, Bernard. *De Gaulle.* New York: St. Martin's Press, 1982.

Lee, Martin A. and Bruce Shlain. *Acid Dreams.* New York: Grove, 1986.

Lesher, Stephan. *George Wallace.* Reading, Mass.: Addison-Wesley, 1994.

Lerner, Michael. *The Socialism of Fools.* Oakland: Tikkun, 1992.

Levin, Jack and Jack McDevitt. *Hate Crimes.* New York: Plenum, 1993.

Levine, Michael. *The Big White Lie.* New York: Thunder's Mouth Press, 1993.

Levy, Alan. *Wanted.* New York: Berkeley Medallion, 1962.

Lewis, Charles Rand. *Right-wing Extremism in West Germany, 1945–1989.* University of Idaho doctoral dissertation, 1990.

Limonov, Edward. *His Butler's Story.* New York: Grove, 1987.

———. *It's Me, Eddie.* New York: Grove, 1987.

———. *Memoir of a Russian Punk.* New York: Grove, 1990.

Linklater, Magnus, et al. *The Nazi Legacy.* New York: Holt Rinehart Winston, 1984.

Lipstadt, Deborah. *Denying the Holocaust.* New York: Free Press, 1993.

Litvinoff, Barnet. *Anti-Semitism and World History.* New York: Dutton, 1988.

Loftus, John. *The Belarus Secret.* New York: Knopf, 1982.

Lotz, Wolfgang. *The Champagne Spy.* New York: St. Martin's Press, 1972.

Low, Alfred D. *Soviet Jewry and Soviet Policy.* New York: Columbia University Press, 1990.

Lucas, James. *Kommando.* New York: St. Martin's Press, 1985.

Lukas, John. *The End of the Twentieth Century and the End of the Modern Age.* New York: Ticknor & Fields, 1993.

———. *A New History of the Cold War.* New York: Anchor Press, 1966.

Lunn, Kenneth and Richard C. Thurlow, eds. *British Fascism.* New York: St. Martin's Press, 1980.

Maaz, Hans Joachim. *Behind the Wall.* New York: Norton, 1995.

Malkin, Peter Z. and Harry Stein. *Eichmann in My Hands.* New York: Warner Books, 1990.

Maoláin, Ciarán Ó. *The Radical Right: A World Directory.* London: ABC-Clio, 1987.

Marable, Manning. *The Crisis of Color and Democracy.* Monroe, Maine: Common Courage Press, 1992.

Martin, David C. *Wilderness of Mirrors.* New York: Harper & Row, 1980.

Martinez, Thomas. *Brotherhood of Murder.* New York: Pocket Books, 1988.

Masurovsky, Marc Jean. *The Safehaven Program.* Doctoral thesis, American University, 1990.

Mattar, Philip. *The Mufti of Jerusalem.* New York: Columbia University Press, 1988.

Maurice, Rene L. and Ken Follet. *Under the Streets of Nice.* Markham, Ontario: Paperbacks, 1989.

Mazcaj, Paul. *The Action Francaise & Revolutionary Syndicalism.* Chapel Hill: University of North Carolina Press, 1979.

McKale, Donald M. *Hitler: The Survival Myth.* New York: Stein and Day, 1981.

Medvedev, Roy. *Let History Judge.* New York: Columbia University Press, 1989.

Mee, Charles L. *The Marshall Plan.* New York: Simon & Schuster, 1984.

Merkl, Peter H., ed. *Political Violence and Terror.* Berkeley: University of California Press, 1986.

Merkl, Peter H. and Leonard Weinberg. *Encounters with the Radical Right.* Boulder, Colo.: Westview Press, 1993.

Merle, Robert. *Ahmed Ben Bella.* New York: Walker, 1967.

Merritt, Anna J. and Richard L., eds. *Public Opinion in Occupied Germany, the OMGUS Surveys, 1945–49.* Urbana: University of Illinois Press, 1970.

Meskil, Paul. *Hitler's Heirs.* New York: Pyramid, 1961.

Mintz, Frank P. *The Liberty Lobby and the American Right.* Westport, Conn.: Greenwood Press, 1985.

Moioli, Vittorio. *I Nuovi Razzismi.* Rome: Edizioni Associate, 1990.

Monzat, René. *Enquetes sur la Droite Extreme.* Paris: Le Monde-Editions, 1992.

Moore, Barrington. *Social Origins of Dictatorship and Democracy.* Boston: Beacon Press, 1993.

Moore, Jack B. *Skinheads.* Bolling Green, Ohio: Bolling Green State University Press, 1993.

Mosely, Leonard. *Dulles.* New York: Dial, 1978.

Mosse, George L. *Nazi Culture.* New York: Grosset & Dunlop, 1968.

———. *Toward the Final Solution.* Madison: University of Wisconsin Press, 1985.

Müller, Ingo. *Hitler's Justice.* London: I. B. Taurus, 1991.

Murray, Charles and Richard J. Herrnstein. *The Bell Curve.* New York: Free Press, 1994.

Nagle, John David. *The National Democratic Party.* Berkeley: University of California Press, 1970.

Nelson, Jack. *Terror in the Night.* New York: Simon & Schuster, 1993.

Nimni, Ephraim. *Marxism and Nationalism.* London: Pluto Press, 1991.

Nogee, Joseph L., ed. *Soviet Politics.* New York: Praeger Publications, 1985.

Nolte, Ernst. *Three Faces of Fascism.* New York: New American Library, 1969.

Novick, Michael. *White Lies, White Power.* Monroe, Maine: Common Courage Press, 1995.

Oberdorfer, Dan. *The Turn: How the Cold War Came to an End.* London: Jonathan Cape, 1992.

Page, Joseph. *Perón.* New York: Random House, 1983.

Paris, Erna. *Unhealed Wounds.* New York: Grove, 1985.

Payne, Robert. *The Life and Death of Trotsky.* New York: McGraw-Hill, 1977.

Payne, Stanley. *Falange.* Stanford, Calif.: Stanford University Press, 1961.

———. *A History of Fascism, 1914–1945.* Madison: University of Wisconsin Press, 1995.

Perrault, Gilles. *The Red Orchestra.* New York: Schocken, 1989.

Persico, Joseph E. *Piercing the Reich.* New York: Viking, 1979.

Pfaff, William. *The Wrath of Nations.* New York: Simon & Schuster, 1993.

Pisan, Sallie. *The CIA and the Marshall Plan.* Lawrence: University of Kansas Press, 1991.

Plant, Richard. *The Pink Triangle.* New York: Henry Holt, 1986.

Poliakov, Leon. *The Aryan Myth.* New York: Basic Books, 1971.

Pool, James and Suzanne. *Who Financed Hitler?* New York: Dial, 1978.

Posner, Gerald L. and John Ware. *Mengele.* New York: Dell, 1987.

Posner, Steve. *Israel Undercover.* Syracuse, N.Y.: Syracuse University Press, 1987.

Powers, Thomas. *The Man Who Kept the Secrets.* New York: Pocket Books, 1981.

Prados, John. *Keepers of the Keys.* New York: Morrow, 1991.

———. *Presidents' Secret Wars.* New York: Quill, 1986.

Purtscheller, Wolfgang. *Aufbruch der Völkischen.* Vienna: Picus, 1993.

Ranelagh, John. *The Agency.* New York: Touchstone, 1987.

Rapoport, Louis. *Stalin's War Against the Jews.* New York: Free Press, 1990.

Rapoport, Yakov. *The Doctors' Plot of 1953.* Cambridge: Harvard University Press, 1991.

Raspail, Jean. *The Camp of Saints.* Petoskey, Mich.: Social Contract, 1987.

Raviv, Dan and Yossi Melman. *Every Prince a Spy.* Boston: Houghton Mifflin, 1990.

Read, Anthony and David Fisher. *The Deadly Embrace.* New York: Norton, 1988.

Read, Piers Paul. *The Train Robbers.* Philadelphia: Lippincott, 1978.

Rees, Philip. *Biographical Dictionary of the Extreme Right Since 1890.* London: Harvester, 1990.

Reese, Mary Ellen. *General Reinhard Gehlen and the CIA.* Fairfax, Va.: George Mason University Press, 1990.

Reeves, Thomas C. *The Life and Times of Joe McCarthy.* New York: Stein and Day, 1982.

Reich, Walter, ed. *Origins of Terrorism.* Cambridge: Cambridge University Press, 1990.

Reich, Wilhelm. *The Mass Psychology of Fascism.* New York: Noonday Books, 1971.

Reid, Douglas. *The Prisoner of Ottawa.* London: Jonathan Cape, 1953.

Reitlinger, Gerald. *The SS: Alibi of a Nation.* New York: Da Capo Press, 1989.

Remick, David. *Lenin's Tomb.* New York: Random House, 1993.

Ridgeway, James. *Blood in the Face.* New York: Thunder's Mouth Press, 1990.

Ritter, Gerhard. *Frederick the Great*. Berkeley: University of California Press, 1974.

Roberts, David D. *The Syndicalist Tradition and Italian Fascism*. Chapel Hill: University of North Carolina Press, 1979.

Robertson, Pat. *The New World Order*. New York: World, 1992.

Rogge, O. John. *The Official German Report*. New York: Thomas Yoseloff, 1961.

Rogger, Hans and Eugen Weber, eds. *The European Right*. Berkeley: University of California Press, 1966.

Rosenbaum, Eli M. *Betrayal*. New York: St. Martin's Press, 1993.

Rosenberg, Tina. *The Haunted Land*. New York: Random House, 1995.

Rosenthal, A. M. and Arthur Gelb. *One More Victim*. New York: New American Library, 1966.

Rositzke, Harry. *The KGB*. New York: Doubleday, 1981.

Rousso, Henry. *The Vichy Syndrome*. Cambridge: Harvard University Press, 1991.

Rovere, Richard Halwort. *Senator Joe McCarthy*. New York: Harper & Row, 1973.

Rowe, Gary Thomas, Jr. *My Undercover Years with the Ku Klux Klan*. New York: Bantam, 1976.

Rubenstein, Richard E. *Alchemists of Revolution*. New York: Basic Books, 1987.

Rubenstein, Richard L. *The Cunning of History*. New York: Harper, 1987.

Rudel, Hans-Ulrich. *Stuka Pilot*. Costa Mesa, Calif.: Noontide Press, 1987.

St. John, Robert. *The Boss*. New York: McGraw-Hill, 1960.

Saloma, John S., III. *Ominous Politics*. New York: Hill and Wang, 1984.

Sargent, Lyman Tower, ed. *Extremism in America.* New York: New York University Press, 1995.

Sartre, Jean-Paul. *Anti-Semite and Jew.* New York: Schocken, 1948.

Sauver, Yannick. *Jean Thiriart et le National Communautarisme Européen.* Typewritten manuscript available at the Hoover Institute Library, 1978.

Sayer, Ian and Douglas Botting. *America's Secret Army.* New York: Franklin Watts, 1989.

———. *Nazi Gold.* New York: Grove, 1986.

Schellenberg, Walter. *The Labyrinth.* New York: Harper & Brothers, 1956.

Schick, Irvin Cemil and Ertugrul Ahmet Tonak, eds. *Turkey in Transition.* New York: Oxford University Press, 1987.

Schmidt, Michael. *The New Reich.* New York: Pantheon, 1993.

Schwartz, Thomas Alan. *America's Germany.* Cambridge: Harvard University Press, 1991.

Scott, Peter Dale and Jonathan Marshall. *Cocaine Politics.* Berkeley: University of California Press, 1991.

Scott-Stokes, Henry. *The Life and Death of Yukio Mishima.* New York: Farrar, Straus & Giroux, 1974.

Searchlight. *Reunited Germany: The New Danger.* London: Searchlight, 1995.

Sedar, Irving and Harold Greenberg. *Behind the Egyptian Sphinx.* Philadelphia: Chilton, 1960.

Segev, Tom. *The Seventh Million.* New York: Hill and Wang, 1993.

Seidel, Gill. *The Holocaust Denial.* London: Beyond the Pale Collective, 1986.

Seldes, George. *Facts and Fascism.* New York: In Fact, 1943.

———. *Witness to a Century*. New York: Ballantine, 1987.

Shirer, William L. *The Rise and Fall of the Third Reich*. New York: Fawcett Crest, 1962.

Siegler, Bernd. *Auferstanderaus Ruinen: Rechtsextremisus in der DDR*. Berlin: Tianot, 1992.

Silj, Alessandro. *Never Again Without a Rifle*. New York: Karz, 1979.

Simpson, Christopher. *Blowback*. New York: Weidenfeld & Nicolson, 1988.

———. *The Splendid Blonde Beast*. New York: Grove, 1993.

Simpson, John and Jana Bennett. *The Disappeared and the Mothers of the Plaza*. New York: St. Martin's Press, 1985.

Singer, Kurt. *Spies and Traitors of World War II*. New York: Prentice-Hall, 1945.

Skidelsky, Robert. *Oswald Mosley*. New York: Holt Rinehart Winston, 1975.

Skorzeny, Otto. *Skorzeny's Secret Missions*. New York: Dutton, 1950.

Smith, Bradley F. *The War's Long Shadow*. New York: Simon & Schuster, 1986.

Smith, Bradley F. and Elena Agarossi. *Operation Sunrise*. New York: Basic Books, 1979.

Smith, Dennis Mack. *Mussolini*. New York: Vintage, 1983.

Smith, Jean Edward. *Lucius D. Clay*. New York: Holt, 1990.

Smith, R. Harris. *OSS*. New York: Delta, 1972.

Smyser, W. R. *Germany and America*. Boulder, Colo.: Westview Press, 1993.

Snyder, Louis L. *Hitler's Elite*. London: David & Charles, 1989.

Sodaro, Michael J. *Moscow, Germany, and the West from Krushchev to Gorbachev.* Ithaca, N.Y.: Cornell University Press, 1990.

Solovyov, Vladimir and Elena Klepikova. *Zhirinovsky.* Reading, Mass.: Addison-Wesley, 1995.

Sorel, Georges. *Reflections on Violence.* New York: Collier, 1967.

Soucy, Robert. *Fascist Intellectual.* Berkeley: University of California Press, 1979.

———. *French Fascism.* New Haven, Conn.: Yale University Press, 1986.

Spengler, Oswald. *The Decline of the West.* New York: Oxford University Press, 1991.

Stachura, Peter D. *Gregor Strasser and the Rise of Nazism.* London: Allen & Unwin, 1983.

Stadiem, William. *Too Rich.* New York: Carroll & Graf, 1991.

Stanton, Bill. *Klanwatch.* New York: Grove Weidenfeld, 1991.

Stephan, John J. *The Russian Fascists.* New York: Harper & Row, 1978.

Stern, Fritz. *The Politics of Cultural Despair.* New York: Anchor Books, 1965.

Stern, Kenneth S. *A Force Upon the Plain.* New York: Simon & Schuster, 1996.

Sternhell, Zeev. *The Birth of Fascist Ideology.* Princeton, N.J.: Princeton University Press, 1994.

Steven, Stewart. *Operation Splinter Factor.* Philadelphia: Lippincott, 1974.

———. *Spymasters of Israel.* New York: Ballantine, 1980.

Stevenson, William. *The Bormann Brotherhood.* New York: Harcourt Brace Jovanovich, 1973.

Stille, Alexander. *Excellent Cadavers*. New York: Random House, 1995.

Stock, Catherine McNicol. *Rural Radicals*. Ithaca, N.Y.: Cornell University Press, 1996.

Strik-Strikfeldt, Wilfred. *Against Stalin & Hitler 1941–1945*. New York: John Day, 1973.

Sugar, Peter F., and Ivo J. Lederer, eds. *Nationalism in Eastern Europe*. Seattle: University of Washington Press, 1969.

Sunic, Tomislav. *The European New Right and the Crisis of Modern Polity*. University of California at Santa Barbara doctoral dissertation, 1988.

Szporluk, Roman. *Communism & Nationalism*. New York: Oxford University Press, 1988.

Tatu, Michael. *Power in the Kremlin from Krushchev to Kosygin*. New York: Viking, 1969.

Tauber, Kurt P. *Beyond Eagle and Swastika*. (2 vols.). Middletown, Conn.: Wesleyan University Press, 1967.

Telos. *The French New Right* (Winter 1993–Fall 1994).

Tetens, T. H. *Germany Plots with the Kremlin*. New York: Schuman, 1953.

———. *The New Germany and the Old Nazis*. New York: Marzani & Munsel, 1961.

Thayer, George. *The Farther Shores of Politics*. New York: Simon & Schuster, 1967.

———. *The War Business*. New York: Simon & Schuster, 1969.

Thewelt, Klaus. *Male Fantasies* (2 vols.). Minneapolis: University of Minnesota Press, 1987.

Thiriart, Jean. *Europe: An Empire of 400 Million Men*. Brussels: 1964.

———. *The Great Nation.* Typewritten manuscript available at the Hoover Institute Library, 1965.

Thompkins, Peter. A *Spy in Rome.* New York: Simon & Schuster, 1962.

Thorwald, Jürgen. *The Illusion.* New York: Harcourt Brace Jovanovich, 1974.

Thurow, Richard. *Fascism in Britain.* London: Basil Blackwell, 1987.

Timmerman, Kenneth R. *The Death Lobby.* London: Bantam, 1992.

Toramska, Teresa. *"Them": Stalin's Polish Puppets.* New York: Harper & Row, 1987.

Troper, Harold and Morton Weinfeld. *Old Wounds.* Markham, Ontario: Penguin, 1989.

Turner, Henry Ashby, Jr. *German Big Business & the Rise of Hitler.* New York: Oxford University Press, 1985.

———. *Germany from Partition to Reunification.* New Haven, Conn.: Yale University Press, 1992.

Turner, William W. *Power on the Right.* Berkeley, Calif.: Ramparts Press, 1971.

Udovicki, Jasminka and James Ridegway, eds. *Yugoslavia's Ethnic Nightmare.* New York: Lawrence Hill, 1995.

Varange, Ulick. *Imperium.* Costa Mesa, Calif.: Noontide Press, 1991.

Veen, Hans-Joachim, et al. *The Republikaner Party in Germany.* Westport, Conn.: Praeger Publications, 1993.

Verdery, Katherine. *National Ideology Under Socialism.* Berkeley: University of California Press, 1991.

Viereck, Peter. *Meta-politics.* New York: Capricorn, 1965.

Wallach, Janet and John. *Arafat.* New York: Lyle Stuart, 1990.

Wallraff, Günter. *The Undesirable Journalist.* Woodstock, N.Y.: Overlook Press, 1979.

Walter, Jess. *Every Knee Shall Bow.* New York: HarperCollins, 1995.

Walters, Vernon A. *Silent Missions.* New York: Doubleday, 1978.

Wank, Ulrich, ed. *The Resurgence of Right-Wing Radicalism in Germany.* Atlantic Highlands, N.J.: Humanities Press, 1996.

Weber, Eugen. *Action Francaise.* Stanford, Calif.: Stanford University Press, 1962.

Weinberg, Leonard and William Lee Eubank. *The Rise and Fall of Italian Terrorism.* Boulder, Colo.: Westview Press, 1987.

Weitz, John. *Hitler's Diplomat.* New York: Ticknor & Fields, 1992.

Weschler, Lawrence. *A Miracle, A Universe.* New York: Pantheon, 1990.

Whaley, Barton. *Codeword Barbarossa.* Cambridge: MIT Press, 1973.

Whiting, Charles. *Gehlen.* New York: Ballantine, 1972.

———. *Skorzeny.* New York: Ballantine, 1972.

———. *The Spymasters.* New York: Dutton, 1976.

Whiton, Charles. *Adenauer.* London: Cox & Wyman, 1963.

Wilhelm, Maria de Blasio. *The Other Italy.* New York: Norton, 1988.

Wilkinson, Paul. *The New Fascists.* London: Pan Books, 1981.

Willen, Philip. *Puppet Masters.* London: Constable, 1991.

Wilmsen, Edwin N. and Patrick McAllister, eds. *The Politics of Difference.* Chicago: University of Chicago Press, 1996.

Wistrich, Robert S. *Antisemitism: The Longest Hatred.* New York: Pantheon, 1991.

———, ed. *Anti-Zionism and Antisemitism in the Contemporary World.* New York: New York University Press, 1990.

———. *Hitler's Apocalypse.* London: Weidenfeld & Nicolson, 1985.

———, ed. *Left Against Zion.* London: Valentine, Mitchell, 1979.

———. *Who's Who in Nazi Germany.* New York, Bonanza, 1984.

Woodhouse, C. M. *The Rise and the Fall of the Greek Colonels.* New York: Franklin Watts, 1985.

Woods, Roger. *Ernst Jünger and the Nature of Political Commitment.* Stuttgart: Akademischer Verlag, 1982.

Woolf, S. J., ed. *European Fascism.* New York: Vintage, 1969.

Yanov, Alexander. *The Drama of the Soviet 1960s.* Berkeley, Calif.: Institute of International Studies, 1984.

———. *The Russian Challenge and the Year 2000.* London: Blackwell, 1987.

———. *The Russian New Right.* Berkeley, Calif.: Institute of International Studies, 1978.

Yockey, Francis Parker. *The Enemy of Europe.* Reedy, West Va.: Liberty Bell, 1981.

———. *The Proclamation of London of the European Liberation Front.* Reedy, West Va.: Liberty Bell, 1981.

Zatarain, Michael. *David Duke.* Gretna, L. A.: Pelican Publishing, 1990.

Zimmerman, Michael E. *Heidegger's Confrontation with Modernity.* Bloomington: Indiana University Press, 1990.

Zuccotti, Susan. *The Italians and the Holocaust.* New York: Basic Books, 1987.

Zwick, Peter. *National Communism.* Boulder, Colo.: Westview Press, 1983.

INDEX